Shore Ecology of the Gulf of Mexico

Shore Ecology
of the Gulf of Mexico

BY JOSEPH C. BRITTON AND BRIAN MORTON

 University of Texas Press, Austin

First Edition, 1989

Requests for permission to reproduce material from this work
should be sent to Permissions, University of Texas Press, Box
7819, Austin, Texas 78713-7819.

LIBRARY OF CONGRESS CATALOGING-IN-PUBLICATON DATA

Britton, Joseph C.
  Shore ecology of the Gulf of Mexico.
  Bibliography: p.
  Includes index.
  1. Seashore ecology—Mexico, Gulf of.   I. Morton,
Brian.   II. Title.
QH92.3.B75   1989   574.5′2638′0916364   88-28078
ISBN 0-292-77610-1
ISBN 0-292-77626-8 (pbk.)

Publication of this book was made possible in part by a grant
from the Sid Richardson Foundation.

For reasons of economy and speed, the authors provided
computer-generated disks for typesetting. The authors assume
full responsibility for the contents of this volume.

⊗ The paper used in this publication meets the minimum
requirements of American National Standard for Information
Sciences—Permanence of Paper for Printed Library Materials,
ANSI Z39.48-1984.

Contents

Preface

The origins of this book are long and tortuous. They begin with, of all things, a joint interest in a small freshwater clam, introduced into North America from Asia, which fouls waterways in its introduced range. Not the least of its attributes is an ability to clog the cooling systems of power stations, including nuclear ones, with all too obvious implications. We had both been working on this clam, *Corbicula*, for a number of years when Texas Christian University organized the First International *Corbicula* Symposium in 1977. The authors of this book met at that symposium for the first time. What resulted was quite unexpected. As a result of interactions at the *Corbicula* meeting, the two authors learned they held several common interests apart from that of the biology of this biofouling clam. In particular, they were both avid students of the sea shore.

Since 1973, JB has conducted field trips for TCU students to numerous Gulf and Caribbean localities. In 1980, BM was able to join him on one of these field trips, to Roatan, Honduras. Both authors are teachers of shore ecology in their respective universities and both recognized a need for a small, unpretentious guide to the shores of Roatan. The two collaborated in the field and prepared text and illustrations for a student guide. With this simple guide, the authors' interest in the cooperative writing of a book of wider scope was born. Brian Morton had just completed a manuscript with John Morton on *The Sea Shore Ecology of Hong Kong* (Hong Kong University Press), and was available to devote time and effort to a similar project for Atlantic shores. In 1981, BM was appointed to the Ida and Cecil Green Honors Chair at TCU for the autumn semester. This generous and timely appointment gave the authors the opportunity they had been awaiting—a chance for extended periods of field work on Gulf of Mexico shores, particularly in Texas and Mexico. Basic work on the book was completed then. Return visits by BM to TCU in 1981, 1985, 1986, and 1988, and visits by JB to the University of Hong Kong in 1983 and 1986, provided the opportunities to further develop the book's themes. Of particularly crucial importance to the final drafting was the visit to TCU by BM in 1985 and which was funded by the Addran College of Arts and Sciences and the Biology Department of TCU.

This then has been a joint venture by two scientists of widely differing backgrounds, but sharing a common fascination with practical shore ecology and its teaching to undergraduates. The book was born with a Caribbean focus, but has evolved to become exclusively concerned with the shores and subtidal habitats of the western Gulf of Mexico. Much is based around Texas shores but we quickly realized that the Gulf of Mexico, west of the Mississippi and including the eastern shores of Mexico to Cabo Catoche, Yucatan, constituted a sufficiently discrete entity to justify treatment as a whole. For Texas and the Gulf there is a considerable volume of literature, less so for Mexican coasts. We particularly wanted, however, to bring Mexican shores to the readers' attention, but for the reason stated above our treatment of them is more circumscribed than it is for the Texas shores. We wanted to make this a readable account, but we have, wherever possible, referred to key sources in a particular subject to enable the reader to seek out more information as desired. The discerning reader will find many omissions of detail, particularly the specialist in one of the many plant or animal groups we discuss. Our treatment of the plankton is scanty, but this can be justified in our preoccupation with shores and what the reader might see if he visited them. Similarly, we pay only minimal attention to the smaller near-microscopic and microscopic life of the shores. We would be the first to acknowledge the great significance of such creatures in shore communities, but again we wish to emphasize that which shore visitors will most obviously see and collect for study.

Many have contributed, directly or indirectly, to the production of this book. Field reconnaissance was greatly facilitated by the cooperation of Sam Brush, Larry Champagne, Larry Cooke, Allison Craig, Gary W. Ferguson, Lisa Fitzgerald, James Howard, Glenn Kroh and Clifford Murphy. Sam Brush assisted immeasurably in assembling and acquiring a vast bibliography, consisting of several times more than we have been able to acknowledge within these pages. Various authorities have advised on matters of detail and it is a pleasure to acknowledge these: J. Breyer (geology), T. J. Bright (offshore banks), S. W. Brush (avifauna), A. Ehlmann (geology), D. F. Felder (crustaceans), G. W. Ferguson (herpetology), R. W. Heard (crustaceans and general ecology), R. S. Houbrick (molluscs), K. Hoagland (algae), S. P. Kool (neogastropod taxonomy), R. F. McMahon (molluscs, physiology and general topics), L. W. Newland (environmental aspects), E. C. Phillips

(*Astrangia* taxonomy), D. Reid (Littorinidae), J. Tunnell (shores and reefs of central Mexico), and A. Zlotsky (terrestrial vegetation). Carrie Bravenec provided hours of reading to suggest terms for inclusion in the glossary. Both of us owe a debt of gratitude to Texas Christian University, JB for the support he has received from the University as a member of the faculty and BM for the faith they have shown in funding his visits to initiate and complete this book.

Finally our deepest debt, and with it our love and gratitude, is to our wives Becky and Janice and our children. They have, largely ungrumblingly and always understandingly tolerated first our extensive field visits and then the hours of drawing and writing when we could not be with them. For BM it has meant many months away from home, and for JB long hours at a word processor and drafting table. The love and understanding of our wives enriches us and it is because of this that we dedicate this book to them.

JOE BRITTON AND BRIAN MORTON
September, 1988

PART ONE   Introduction

1. The Western Gulf of Mexico: An Introduction to Shores and Life

The Gulf of Mexico is a partially landlocked body of water indenting the southeastern periphery of the North American continent. United States and Mexico shores form its arcuate margin, extending over 4000 km (2600 miles) from Florida Bay to Cabo Catoche in northeastern Yucatan. Its southeastern boundary extends from the easternmost tip of the Yucatan peninsula in Mexico to Key West at the southernmost tip of Florida. This is not a restrictive margin, for there is considerable interaction between the waters and biota of the Gulf and those of the Caribbean basin which lies to the south and southeast. Low, sandy banks or marshlands characterize northern temperate and subtropical Gulf shores, with extensive barrier beaches, dune fields, salt marshes and mangroves present according to local climate and conditions. Frost-free tropical shores fringe the Florida Keys and the southern margins of the Gulf basin from central Mexico to both sides of the Yucatan peninsula.

There is a relatively high degree of community homogeneity and a moderate to high species compatibility at corresponding latitudes between eastern and western margins of the Gulf of Mexico. Many of the coastal animals and plants which occur along western Florida are present in similar habitats and at corresponding latitudes along the Gulf shores of Texas and Mexico, or are represented by very closely related species. The same cannot be said for the habitats or biota at opposite ends of the Gulf's longitudinal boundaries. Homogeneity is drastically disrupted as one moves from northern shores of primarily terrigenously-derived sediments to southern shores dominated by biogenic carbonates. These changes occur largely because the Gulf of Mexico lies within a region of temperate to tropical climatic transition. The transition is more pronounced with respect to the shore biota than for offshore or continental shelf species. The latter are dominated by a tropical biota that ranges further northward in the offshore waters than do the coastal counterparts (Briggs, 1974; Rezak *et al.*, 1985).

Northern Gulf shores lie within a warm-temperate province, and are isolated by tropical Florida from similar shores along the eastern seaboard from Virginia to Georgia. This isolation has existed at least several thousand years, producing a relic northern Gulf community that has begun to develop a character of its own (Briggs, 1974). The degree of endemism, although noticeable, is not extensive. There remains a

fair degree of correspondence between the northern Gulf biota and that along shores northeast of tropical Florida. Colder water species, more typical of the eastern coast of North America, are not excluded from the Gulf. Some occur year round, others are seasonally present or abundant. With a ready supply of meroplanktonic and nektonic colonizers inhabiting offshore waters, tropical biota (especially algae, molluscs and fishes) increases in numbers during the summer and yields to more temperate elements in the winter. Northern Gulf shore communities undergo a distinctly seasonal pattern of change. The temporally diverse communities of the northern Gulf contrast nicely with the time-stable, increasingly diverse shores of tropical southern Mexico.

Several of the coastal biota of Texas, Louisiana or Mississippi also occur on the carbonate sandy beaches of Yucatan or the low limestone platforms of Campeche. But there are also many kinds of life on the beaches of Mexico that never occur in the northern Gulf. Some tropical species replace missing temperate forms, and other tropical species occupy niches lacking representatives in temperate climates. Despite the latitudinal and climatic transition from northern to southern shores, the southern Gulf promises, but does not quite deliver, a wholly tropical biota as displayed on Caribbean shores.

We will not attempt to treat the shore communities of the entire Gulf of Mexico in this book. The region is simply too large and diverse to adequately chronicle in a single volume. Thus, we restrict our coverage to the shores of the western Gulf of Mexico. We shall utilize an imposing barrier, the delta of the Mississippi River, as the northeastern terminus of our region of coverage. Actually, our northern boundary lies somewhat west of the delta, outside the primary and immediate sedimentary influence of this largest of North American rivers. Our region begins along the western Louisiana coast and traces a sweeping 180 degree arc which ends at Cabo Catoche, Yucatan, the natural southern terminus of the Gulf of Mexico basin (Fig. 1-1). It traverses about 2400 km (1500 miles) of shores directly facing the sea, but with perhaps ten times as much shoreline facing waters enclosed behind barrier islands or estuarine embayments. The biota of the northwestern Gulf consists of hardy species capable of surviving climatic extremes and often heavy sedimentation. As we move southwestward around the Texas coastal bend and into northern Mexico, climates moderate, river sediments diminish, and many Caribbean species become established as more appropriate conditions prevail. In one chapter, we will extend our coverage slightly into the Caribbean province, along the northeastern Yucatan coast, primarily in order to complete a logical development of hard shore habitats. Thus restricted, we minimize the east to west biotic diversity of the Gulf of Mexico and focus upon the temperate to tropical transition with its inherent succession of communities that is especially apparent along western Gulf shores.

The shores we will discuss are long, dramatic and diverse. Many of them are of sand, but we have discovered a richness of habitats which is probably unapproached elsewhere in North America and certainly hitherto unappreciated. A well-studied geology and extensively documented history enable us to appreciate present coastal conditions in the context of past geological and human perspectives. This region is not nor ever has been static. Its physical and biological aspects are ever changing, sometimes in units measured by centuries or millennia, but frequently within the scale of years or weeks or days. Tropical hurricanes, for example, swinging into the Gulf from the tropical Atlantic, wreak havoc measured from the personal perspective, but also confer upon these shores a dynamism essential for their periodic renewal. We are able to illustrate the effects of freshwater upon shore life because of the numerous rivers that drain into low salinity coastal embayments. Many of these bays open into larger estuarine systems which more closely approach normal marine salinities. Others, influenced by locally harsh climatic regimes, become hypersaline lagoons behind dune fields of enormous proportions. Here we can examine the effects of salt loading upon intertidal communities on a grand scale and not from just an examination of high-zoned pools on rocky shores. The western Gulf of Mexico provides us with a diversity of dimensions. Variations in climate, geology, hydrography and even history permit us to approach the study of its shores from many perspectives. To begin our narrative some definitions and general descriptions are essential.

TAXONOMY: THE NAMES OF THINGS

Taxonomy and systematics, respectively the naming and classification of living things and the study of their interrelationships and evolution, are essential disciplines of biology. Their roots permeate the human quest for order and an insatiable desire to define and name all objects within our consciousness. Before the boundaries of the human experience achieved their present global dimensions, taxonomy was a provincial affair. Even today the common or vernacular names of a plant or animal frequently vary from place to place or from one language to another. Scientists devised the modern taxonomic method by which every kind of

life receives a unique name and a succinct verbal and visual definition. This is particularly important as we examine the life of the seashore, for it is home to probably the greatest diversity of life on this planet. The ultimate goal of taxonomy is to achieve a stable nomenclature for all life that can be uniformly employed throughout the world, regardless of locale or language. Unfortunately, for many groups of animals and plants, nomenclatorial stability has yet to be effectively achieved.

The biota of the western Gulf of Mexico has long been studied, but some species are just now becoming known. Scientific names applied for decades to animals and plants of Gulf shores have changed as new species or relationships are discovered. The stone crab of the western Gulf, once called *Menippe mercenaria*, is now *M. adina*. The tiny periwinkle snail of Texas jetties, once called *Littorina ziczac*, is now *Nodilittorina lineolata*, and the latter is, by no means, a certain epithet. The rock shell, known for decades as *Thais haemastoma*, is now considered in a separate genus, *Stramonita*. The fiddler crab *Uca pugilator* was once considered to range from Massachusetts to Mexico, but it has been split into several species. The original name, although frequently cited from Texas in the older literature, refers to a species ranging mostly outside the western Gulf region.

Since work on this book began over five years ago, several dozen species treated within these pages have received new generic or specific names as a result of taxonomic revision. Some of these changes, representing common species or involving previously widely published epithets, are summarized in Table 1-1. Taxonomic revision will likely continue with increasing intensity as interest in the western Gulf region grows and its flora and fauna are examined more critically. Taxonomic changes first appear in the specialized journals, and slowly become known to biologists, ecologists or laymen with primary interests other than synonymy or taxonomic revision. The nontaxonomist might perceive the increasing frequency of change as a renaissance of the provincialism which characterized the early history of taxonomy. In fact, the opposite has occurred. It is from a broadly regional or almost global perspective that local faunas such as those of the western Gulf are being actively redefined. This makes the work of the ecologist more difficult, for many familiar species acquire new names and are familiar no more.

Although we endeavor to use only presently accepted scientific names, some of our nomenclature inevitably will be rendered obsolete by taxonomic revision. Nomenclatorial changes, however, do not alter community structure. Most of the individuals now occupying the shores of Laguna Madre or the cobble beach at Campeche, Mexico were represented in these habitats long before humans came to study them. When the ecologist studies a species at a western Gulf locality, the findings are applicable to the species population at that locality, regardless of its name. It is only when two species are recognized from a popula-

1-1. The Gulf of Mexico.

tion formerly considered to be monospecific, or when characterizations are based on studies conducted far from the region of interest that problems of interpretation arise. Both cases are common pitfalls to ecological analysis, including some interpretations within these pages.

As we learn more about the species of the western Gulf region, we will likely discover some new features or behaviors that differentiate them from the taxa with which they were once confused. Many basic ecological relationships characterizing genera, subgenera or closely related species complexes will still remain valid. Thus, we will present ecological attributes as we now know them, highlight as best as possible studies done within the region without ignoring important works from other localities, and leave the correction of nomenclatorial errors and the attendant life history details to future editions of this or similar texts, when and if they are required.

This book is intended as a general introduction to the shore habitats and biota of the western Gulf of Mexico. We have selected numerous species as representative of the communities which occur here, but there remain many others within the region which we have not discussed. Appendix II presents a detailed classification of the biota of the western Gulf of Mexico described and illustrated within these pages. We summarize the more inclusive categories of this classification in Table 1-2, and associate common names with the technical names as a general source of reference. Each of these taxa is more fully defined in the glossary (Appendix I). Our illustrations and descriptions may assist the reader in identifying many of the species from the western Gulf region, but they are not intended to take the place of the primary taxonomic literature. Precise identifications of many species require attention to morphological detail beyond the scope of our general ecological perspective.

Table 1-1. Some Examples of the Recent Revisionary Taxonomy of Some
Common Western Gulf of Mexico Species and/or Genera

Former Designation	*Revised Designation and Authority*
Porifera:	
Haliclona longelyi	*Xestaspongia subtriangularis fide* Wiedenmayer 1977
Cnidaria:	
Astrangia astreiformis	* *Astrangia poculata fide* Peters *et al.* 1988
Crustacea:	
Alpheus heterochaelis	* *Alpheus estuariensis* Christoffersen 1984
Menippe mercenaria	* *Menippe adina* Williams and Felder 1986
Callianassa islagrande	*Callichirus islagrande fide* Manning and Felder 1986
Callianassa jamaicensis	* *Callianassa louisianensis fide* Manning 1987
Callianassa major	*Callichirus major fide* Manning and Felder 1986
Panopeus herbstii	* *Panopeus obesus fide* Williams 1983
Panopeus herbstii	* *Panopeus simpsoni fide* Williams 1983
Uca pugilator	* *Uca panacea* Novak and Salmon 1974
Uca pugnax	* *Uca longisignalis* Salmon and Atsaides 1968
Mollusca:	
Busycon spiratum	*Busycotypus spiratum fide* Edwards and Humphrey 1981
Diastoma varium	*Bittium varium fide* Houbrick 1981
Littoridinops sp. A (in Andrews 1977)	*Littoridinops monroensis fide* Heard 1982a
Planaxis lineatus	*Angiola lineata fide* Houbrick 1987
Planaxis nucleus	*Supplanaxis nucleus* Houbrick 1987
Purpura patula	*Plicopurpura patula fide* Kool 1988
Murex fluvescens	*Muricanthus fluvescens fide* Kool 1987
Thais haemastoma	*Stramonita haemastoma fide* Kool 1987
Thais rustica	*Stramonita rustica fide* Kool 1987
Vioscalba louisianae	*Probythinella louisianae fide* Heard 1979
Ervilia concentrica	*Ervilia nitens fide* de Rooij-Schuiling 1973
Flora:	
Euphorbia ammannioides	*Chamaesyce polygonifolia fide* Duncan & Duncan, 1987

* Revised designation pertains to populations in the northwestern Gulf; former designation may be valid in other geographic areas. The Littorinidae as a special case are dealt with on pp. 86–88.

COMMUNITY RELATIONSHIPS

Each shore or subtidal habitat is occupied by a community of organisms that helps to define its limits. As we describe the communities of the western Gulf in terms of commonly encountered conditions, we may give the impression that they exist in relatively stable equilibrium. In truth, dynamism rather than stability characterizes these communities. Environmental perturbations (sometimes called intermediate disturbances) trigger changes that alter community species compositions. Large scale perturbations, such as seasonal change or climatic excess, induce noticeable community adjustments, including the seasonal succession of algae on rocky shores or the change in species dominance on estuarine oyster reefs during times of drought. Interactions between community members, such as competition for settlement space, for freedom of movement, and especially for food, are more subtle perturbations, but they too can influence the species composition of the community. As a result

of intermediate disturbances, communities are not static, but exist in a dynamic equilibrium. Communities on a rocky shore or a sandy beach are not everywhere the same. They vary from place to place and time to time.

Access to appropriate nutrition is considered one of the major structuring forces at work in shore ecology and we give it considerable attention in this book. Differences in feeding modes and strategies are, of course, not the only ways that species interact to apportion the habitat and so create and maintain the community. Differences in reproductive style, timing and success are also important as are differences in physiological response to environmental extremes and patterns of behavior. Food, or its scarcity, is of fundamental importance on the shores, since rarely does it became so abundant that it ceases to be limiting to community structure.

A community can be defined in terms of its food or energy relationships as readily as it can be characterized by its species. Energy bound by producers moves through a simple food chain, pausing at each step or trophic level. Some energy is lost as it is transferred between each level, providing less support for each succeeding level. Producers support fewer primary consumers, primary consumers support fewer secondary consumers and these even fewer tertiary consumers. Thus, on a rocky beach we will find many barnacles, periwinkles and limpets, far fewer predatory gastropods feeding on them and even fewer secondary predators, such as stone crabs, feeding on them in turn. Such a "pyramid of numbers" allows us to see relationships clearer, but the simple food chain just described is, in fact, no more than a single strand in a web of food chains extending across and down the shore and with branches extending, ultimately, into every habitat on earth. The living world is, in fact, one gigantic food web and from which we can isolate but a few components.

The simplified food webs of a rocky shore and adjoining subtidal sand bed are united in Figure 1-2 to illustrate similarities, differences and the ways one environment or community can influence another. We know that rocky headlands are intimately linked to subtidal sands from a study of shore processes. Grains of rock erode from the hard shore and are deposited on the sandy bottom. It follows also that they are linked biologically. We replace species names in Figure 1-2 with feeding categories: algal grazer, suspension feeder, deposit feeder, scavenger, carnivore and top carnivore. Both communities are seen to be dependent upon sunlight and soluble nutrients for their sources of energy, although in both cases this may be endogenously produced on the beach by attached algae or of exogenous origin from the phytoplankton.

Exogeneous phytoplankton and endogenous attached algae (producers) are fed upon by rocky shore suspension feeders and algal grazers (primary consumers). These in turn are the food of carnivores and ultimately top carnivores. Scavengers consume dead plants and animals not washed away by the waves and tides. Wave scour insures that little detritus resides long on rocky shores. It is washed onto the adjoining sand and contributes to a nutrient pool of detritus arriving from other sources such as rivers and streams draining adjacent lands. Detritus is fed upon directly by detritivores (e.g., deposit feeders) and recycled by heterotrophic fungi and bacteria, and in the process, the decomposers also become available as food for detritivores.

Phytoplankton and attached algae provide relatively equal amounts of primary productivity on the rocky shore, but few algae can reside on the shallow unstable offshore sands. Here, primary production is provided mainly by the phytoplankton, with a second "primary" source of nutrition (although not primary production) being the rich soup of detritus and nutrient-adsorbed particles of silt on the sand surface. With few algae there are even fewer algal grazers. The primary consumers are dominated by infaunally buried suspension and deposit feeders. As on the rocky shores, carnivores and top carnivores are present, and the incidence of scavengers increases as the depositional environment tends toward the accumulation of finer particulates (i.e., the subtidal area becomes increasingly protected from the effects of currents, winds, and waves).

Despite the great physical differences that exist between the rocky shore and the subtidal sands, the communities are similar in character with respect to food relationships, if not in composition. Further, these communities are interlinked with one another, as well as with other communities which might occur nearby. The Gulf environments that we will describe, therefore, are parts of a physical and biological whole experiencing dynamic interactions on both a local and regional scale.

SHORE CATEGORIES AND GULF SHORE COMMUNITIES

Many of us consider the terms "shore" and "beach" approximately synonymous, but they are not. Geologists define a beach as one kind of shore, consisting of an accumulation of unconsolidated sediment along the coastal zone, extending from mean low water landward to some physiographic break such as the point where permanent vegetation becomes established. Geologists may also include within the beach province the subtidal nearshore and adjacent offshore regions which influence the beach proper. A majority of the western Gulf of Mexico coast is considered a beach according to this definition. But the region includes many additional kinds of shores, including hard rocky peninsulas, promontories and jetties; soft shores with a vegetated zone, where grasses of a salt marsh or trees known as mangroves take root in the sea; emergent bioherms which we call reefs, produced by oysters in bays of the northwestern Gulf or corals in normal marine waters of the southern region; and banks of unconsolidated gravel, cobble or small boulders, not quite a beach but not quite a rocky shore. Figure 1-3 is a hypothetical map, based around a simplified chart of the Gulf of Mexico, and showing some approximate locations and categories of shore habitats encountered here and which will be discussed in this book.

We will take our studies upwards into the maritime zone of coastal vegetation and dunes of these hard and soft shores and take particular cognizance of the peculiar habitats of marshlands and mangroves. We will look downwards to investigate the shallow sublittoral, including offshore sands, scoured banks, temperate oyster reefs, and tropical coral reefs. If we followed only the narrower definition of a beach, much would be lost. If we restricted our study to only the region between the tides, we would lose even more. Gulf shores have a theoretical mean vertical tidal expanse of but 0.7 meters. In reality, the influence of the tide, especially as modulated by winds and waves, spreads the shore realm more widely than this, and certainly

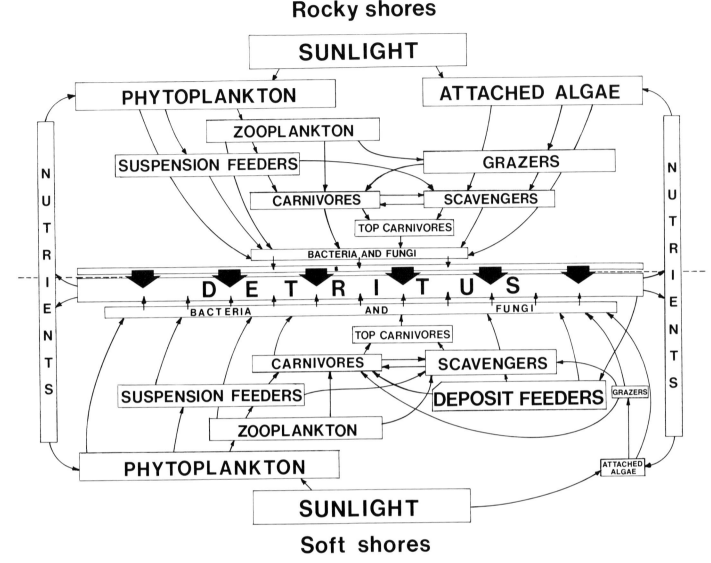

1-2. Trophic interactions in a rocky intertidal community (upper) and a sandy beach or shallow subtidal sand community (bottom).

beyond the physical tidal benchmarks.

This book is divided into a number of parts, most of which approximate major divisions of the shore environment, and each part consists of one or more chapters. In Part 1, we describe the general aspects of the shore and some of the principles which regulate its form. This section, consisting of Chapters 1 and 2, includes topics which transcend most or all of the habitats. The physical attributes of particular shores are left to the beginning of each chapter that addresses a specific habitat.

In Part 2, we discuss hard bottom environments from exposure to shelter and from Texas to Mexico. Natural EXPOSED ROCKY SHORES are absent from the northwestern Gulf, but, in Chapter 3, we find a man-made substitute with the jetties, groins and breakwaters of the Texas coast. In Chapter 4, we dis-

cuss the range of hard shore types along the coast of Mexico, including natural igneous rocky outcrops, man-made shores such as jetties and breakwaters, and the limestone hard shores of Yucatan. The limestone "ironshores" of eastern Yucatan, facing the broad fetch of the Caribbean Sea, are often high and rimmed by precipitous cliffs. A few SHELTERED and SEMI-SHELTERED ROCKY SHORES composed of limestone lie on the western side of the peninsula. Most are low, broad rocky platforms protected from direct oceanic fetch by the Yucatan peninsula. Water movement is sufficient to wash them clean of loose debris. Hard shores experiencing less exposure than the above are rare in the Gulf of Mexico but do occur within the bays. Most PROTECTED BOULDER AND COBBLE SHORES of this region are man-made, constructed to stabilize bay sediments around causeways and other

Table 1-2. A Summary of Higher Classification (based upon taxa in this book)

Classification	Common names or examples
KINGDOM MONERA	
Phylum Cyanophyta	Blue-green algae
KINGDOM PROTISTA	
Phylum Mastigophora	Flagellates
Order Dinoflagellida	Zooxanthellae
Phylum Sarcodina	Amoeboid protists
Order Foraminifera	Forams (*Gypsina*)
KINGDOM PLANTAE	
Phylum Chlorophyta	Green algae (sea lettuce, *Halimeda*)
Phylum Phaeophyta	Brown algae (*Sargassum, Padina*)
Phylum Rhodophyta	Red algae (*Gelidium, Digenia*)
Phylum Anthophyta (Spermatophyta)	Seed-bearing plants
Class Angiospermae	Flowering plants
Subclass Monocotyledonae	Grasses, sedges, palms, flowering plants
Subclass Dicotyledonae	Broadleaf plants, legumes, composites, plants
KINGDOM ANIMALIA	
Phylum Porifera	Sponges
Phylum Cnidaria	Cnidarians or coelenterates
Class Hydrozoa	Hydrozoans
Order Hydroida	Colonial and solitary hydroids, chondrophores
Order Siphonophora	Siphonophores (Portuguese Man-o-war)
Order Hydrocorallina	Fire corals
Class Scyphozoa	Jellyfishes
Class Anthozoa	Anthozoans
Subclass Octocorallia	Octocorals
Order Gorgonacea	Sea whips, sea fans
Order Pennatulacea	Sea pens, sea pansies
Order Zoantharia	Colonial anemones
Order Actiniaria	Solitary anemones
Order Scleractinia	Stony corals
Phylum Ctenophora	Comb-jellies
Phylum Platyhelminthes	Flatworms
Phylum Nemertina	Ribbon worms
Phylum Annelida	Segmented worms
Class Polychaeta	Marine segmented worms
Class Oligochaeta	Earthworms and kin
Phylum Echiura	Sausage worms
Phylum Sipuncula	Peanut worms
Phylum Mollusca	Molluscs
Class Polyplacophora	Chitons
Class Gastropoda	Snails, sea slugs, sea hares and kin
Class Scaphopoda	Tusk shells
Class Bivalvia	Clams, oysters, mussels, scallops
Class Cephalopoda	Squids and octopods
Phylum Arthropoda	Arthropods
Class Merostomata	Horseshoe crabs
Class Pycnogonida	Sea spiders
Class Crustacea	Crustaceans
Subclass Copepoda	Copepods
Subclass Cirripedia	Barnacles
Subclass Malacostraca	Crabs, shrimps and kin
Order Stomatopoda	Mantis shrimp
Order Cumacea	Cumaceans
Order Isopoda	Isopods, pill bugs
Order Amphipoda	Beach hoppers, skeleton shrimp, scuds
Order Decapoda	Shrimp, prawns, lobsters, crabs
Class Insecta	Insects
Phylum Bryozoa	Moss animals

Table 1-2, *continued*

Classification	Common names or examples
Phylum Echinodermata	Echinoderms
Class Crinoidea	Sea lilies
Class Asteroidea	Starfishes and kin
Class Ophiuroidea	Brittle stars
Class Echinoidea	Sea urchins, sand dollars, sea biscuits
Class Holothuroidea	Sea cucumbers
Phylum Tunicata	Sea squirts, salps
Phylum Chordata	Chordates
Subphylum Vertebrata	Backboned animals
Class Elasmobranchiomorphi	Cartilaginous fishes (sharks, rays and kin)
Class Osteichthyes	Bony fishes
Class Amphibia	Frogs, toads, salamanders, newts
Class Reptilia	Turtles, lizards, snakes, crocodiles
Class Aves	Birds
Class Mammalia	Mammals (e.g., rodents, rabbits, coyotes)

developments. Such shores are considered in Chapter 5 along with the peculiar environment of WHARF PILES. The primary bays of Texas shores also support a largely subtidal, semi-hard substratum community based around the oyster, *Crassostrea virginica*. Sometimes the upper portions of this community are widely exposed at low tide. Appropriately, therefore, OYSTER REEFS are also discussed in Chapter 5.

In Part 3, we consider the many different categories of soft shores and their communities: from open shores, to lagoons, bays, marshes and mangroves. The most prevalent exposed shores of the western Gulf of Mexico are the EXPOSED SANDY BEACHES, described in Chapter 6. These are fluid shores which can be moved by storms, hurricanes, currents, and waves, but are normally exposed to relatively gentle forces insufficient to carry away all the burden of sand. Sand beaches of vast extent and proportion dominate the shorelines of Texas and Mexico, steeply sloping in the face of moderate exposure and gently inclined when more sheltered from waves. Regularly swept by ocean surf, these beaches are dramatic locales. The stark barrenness of their Gulf faces contrasts sharply with the lofty majesty of their sea-oat-crowned dunes, and both of these fail to suggest the biotic diversity which appears on the vegetation-stabilized sands behind the dunes.

Texas and Mexico coasts are also characterized by large, broad or elongate PRIMARY BAYS, formed behind the sandy barrier islands and experiencing reduced exchange with the sea through narrow tidal channels. Where rainfall is moderate or high, as in Louisiana, the northeastern coast of Texas, or the southern coastal bend of Mexico, these bays usually have the salinities of typical estuaries. The shore biota and some aspects of the deeper water and pelagic life of the primary bays of the northwestern Gulf are discussed in Chapter 7.

1-3. Diagrammatic illustration of shore types and features of the western Gulf of Mexico. Localities serving as examples are cited in parentheses.

B	Barrier island (Padre Island, Texas)
C	Causeway (Port Isabel-South Padre Island, Texas)
Cp	Cape (Cabo Catoche, Quintana Roo, Mexico)
D1	Major river delta (Mississippi River delta)
D2	Minor river delta with numerous ox-bows (resacas) (Rio Grande, Texas and Mexico)
E	River mouth estuary (Sabine Lake, Louisiana and Texas)
En	Enclosed primary bay with restricted circulation (Matagorda Bay, Texas)
F	Hurricane washover fan (Padre Island, Texas)
G	Breakwater groins (Galveston Island, Texas)
Hb	Hypersaline bay (Baffin Bay, Texas)
Ht	Tropical hypersaline lagoon with mangroves (Progreso, Yucatan, Mexico)

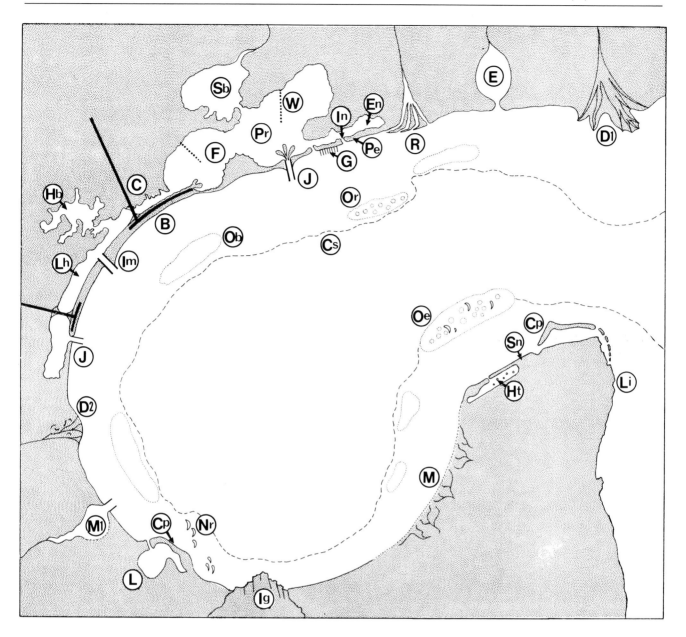

Ig	Igneous rocky headlands (Punta del Morro, Veracruz, Mexico)	Nr	Nearshore emergent bank reefs (Arrecife Lobos, Veracruz, Mexico)
In	Natural tidal inlet without jetties (Cavallo Pass, Texas)	Ob	Offshore submerged hardpan bank lacking large reef corals (Steston Bank)
Im	Excavated inlet protected by jetties (Port Mansfield Cut)	Oe	Offshore emergent bank reefs (Arrecife Alacran, Mexico)
J	Natural tidal inlet protected by jetties (Port Aransas, Texas)	Or	Offshore submerged bank coral reefs (Flower Garden Banks)
L	Tropical lagoon (Laguna de Tamiahua, Veracruz, Mexico)	Pe	Peninsula (Matagorda Peninsula, Texas)
Lh	Subtropical hypersaline lagoon with few mangroves (Laguna Madre, Texas)	Pr	Primary bay (Corpus Christi Bay, Texas)
		R	Rivermouth opening directly to the sea without significant delta development (Brazos River, Texas)
Li	Exposed limestone shores (Ironshores) (Cancun, Quintana Roo, Mexico)		
M	Mangrove-dominated outer shore (western Yucatan, Mexico)	Sb	Secondary (lower salinity) bay (Nueces Bay, Texas)
		Sn	Exposed mainland sandy shore (northern Yucatan, Mexico)
M1	Mangrove-dominated estuary (Tampico, Veracruz, Mexico)	W	Wharf pilings (throughout)

The dashed line indicates the 200 m depth contour.

Many of the primary bays adjoin smaller, shallower bodies of estuarine water toward the mainland and which we term SECONDARY or LOWER SALINITY BAYS. Again, the quantity of water which can be exchanged between the primary and secondary bays is usually limited by basin morphology, and this, in turn, influences the biota that occurs within the confines of both types of estuaries. The biota of the lower salinity bays grades slowly towards COASTAL FRESHWATER MARSHLANDS, and we make a special excursion to examine the latter as a natural conclusion to the normal estuarine environment. In decided contrast to the low salinity bays and marshlands are the HYPER-SALINE LAGOONS of southern Texas and northern Mexico. They are produced by a combination of low precipitation, lack of freshwater inflow and severely restricted communication with the open sea. The contrasting challenges of hyposalinity and hypersalinity are examined in Chapter 8.

The special case of tropical MANGROVE SHORES is discussed in Chapter 9. Of limited diversity on the mud flats of southern Texas, mangrove communities increase in size and biotic diversity south of the Rio Grande, reaching maximum development in appropriate localities from Veracruz to western Yucatan. In their optimum habitats, mangroves are not seasonally limited as are salt marsh plants of temperate climates. Yet, salt marshes and mangrove shores often occupy similar regimes of shelter, substratum and salinity. We take a few pages in Chapter 9 to compare these habitats and to account for some of the reasons why they have developed differently. Finally, we conclude the chapter with a description of the peculiar mangrove distributions in the hypersaline bays and associated salt pans of Yucatan.

The sequence of Chapters so described takes us in a real sense from exposure to shelter: from exposed rock faces to the deep shelter of mangroves. Each chapter also preserves another primary theme: that of the transition from warm-temperate North America to tropical Mexico. Sometimes, this is difficult to describe accurately; in other cases, it is much simpler. Wherever possible, we attempt to demonstrate that the shores of the Gulf are an ecological continuum.

In Part 4, we examine the subtidal world of the offshore sand and scoured hardpan banks, turning finally to the world of the coral reef. In Chapter 10, we focus upon the offshore world of SUBTIDAL SAND FLATS and SCOURED BANKS. So much of the life of these shallow offshore waters, or at least their skeletal remains, is deposited on exposed sand beaches that their existence is inescapable to the majority of shore goers. Such communities are largely inaccessible to most visitors to the seashore. We can justify the inclusion of these subtidal biota in this book on the basis that, because they contribute so greatly to the flotsam of sandy beaches, we should attempt to ascertain the nature of their habits and habitats while they live, rather than simply develop an appreciation of their body forms as they lie dead upon the strand. More impor-

tantly, the offshore sands and banks are part of a larger interactive ecosystem extending from the continental shelf to the barrier island dunes. Shore faunas are dependent in many ways upon offshore communities.

Chapter 11 describes the variety of communities associated with and including the tropical CORAL REEFS. Unpossessing of the greater diversity of reefs in the Caribbean, and being largely subtidal, they are close enough inshore, both at Texas and Mexico, to be influenced by the intertidal regime and thus fall within the scope of this book. A consideration of the reefs, we believe, returns us full circle to our starting point—the exposed rocky shores. Coral reefs are an organically derived hard substratum that contrasts nicely with and yet has many features in common with those surf-dominated rocky shores. In fact, the ironshores of Caribbean Yucatan were originally formed as coral reefs many millennia ago.

In Part 5 (Chapter 12), we consider the past history of Gulf shores to determine the extent of change and the impact of humans upon them. We briefly discuss those factors which are at work in the Gulf to destroy, modify and upset the balance of shore diversity described in the preceding chapters. We relate these processes to past and present development and the threat of pollution. We end on the optimistic note of conservation, because it is our belief that those who, like us, have gained immeasurable enjoyment from the study of the Gulf's rich pattern of intertidal life will want to preserve as much as possible of it for posterity.

CLIMATE

The climatology of the western Gulf region is complex, as perhaps should be expected along a temperate to tropical latitudinal gradient. Six major and distinctive climatic regions can be recognized as one proceeds southward from western Louisiana and eastern Texas. Coastal Louisiana and northern Texas lie within a warm-temperate to marginally subtropical region (Fig. 1-4 A). Ample rain falls here. Port Arthur receives over 140 cm (55 inches) annually, and Galveston records annual precipitation at about 109 cm (42 inches). This produces a humid climate which supports a diverse maritime flora, carpeting and stabilizing low, sandy, inactive dunes (chenier plains) along the mainland shore (there are no islands on the northern shore from Sabine Pass to Gilchrist). The vegetation is primarily deciduous, with periods of winter dormancy imposed by the dominantly temperate climate.

From the central Texas coast southward, the region is transitionally subtropical, presenting a varying face from north to south and east to west. Lush coastal forests in the north give way to arid thorn-scrub woodlands of southwestern Texas and northern Mexico. These even yield to sparsely vegetated mainland coastal flats or steppes along lagoon margins (Fig. 1-4 B). The climate here is subtropical, with hard winter freezes uncommon, but sufficiently frequent to exclude all but the most hardy tropical plants. Mean an-

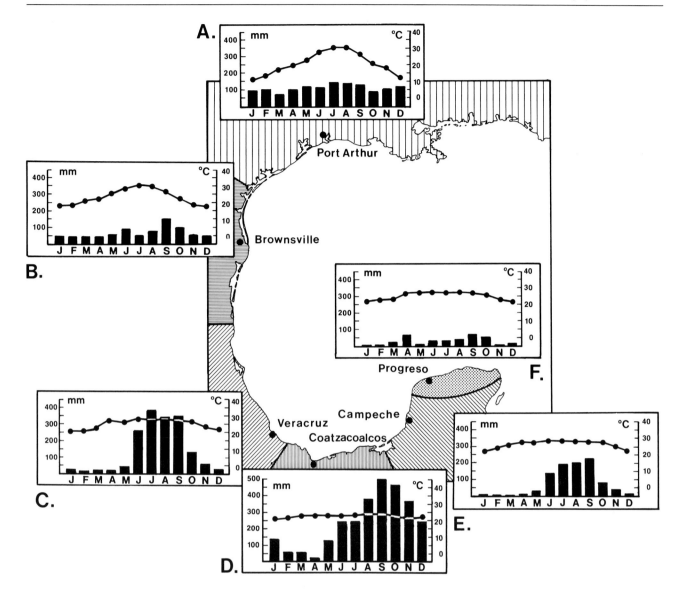

1-4. Climatic zones of the western Gulf of Mexico. Each climatic zone includes bar histograms of mean monthly precipitation in mm (left scale) and line plots of mean monthly temperature in °C (right scale).

A. Humid warm-temperate region. Characterized by Port Arthur, Texas. Rainfall is evenly distributed throughout the year; relative humidity is high throughout the year. Temperature demonstrates considerable seasonal variation with several nights of freezing temperatures in the winter.

B. Low latitude steppe. Characterized by Brownsville, Texas. Rainfall is sparse throughout the year; relative humidity is moderate to high most of the year. Temperature varies seasonally, but hard winter freezes are rare.

C. Tropical savanna. Characterized by Veracruz, Mexico. There is a distinct rainy season; relative humidity is high throughout the year. Yearly temperature fluctuations are slight; there are no winter freezes.

D. Tropical rainy forest. Characterized by Coatzacoalcos, Mexico. The distinctly seasonal rains preclude this region from being a true rain forest, but summer precipitation is exceptionally great; relative humidity is high throughout the year. Yearly temperature fluctuations are slight; there are no winter freezes.

E. Yucatan tropical savanna. Characterized by Campeche, Mexico. There is a distinct rainy season; relative humidity is high throughout the year. Yearly temperature fluctuations are slight; there are no winter freezes.

F. Tropical xeric scrub forest. Characterized by Progreso, Mexico. Rainfall is erratic and sparse; relative humidity is high throughout the year. Yearly temperature fluctuations are slight; there are no winter freezes.

nual rainfall is less than 75 cm (29 inches) throughout most of coastal southern Texas, and decreases to less than 52 cm (20 inches) along some portions of northern Mexico.

From near the southern termination of Laguna Madre de Tamaulipas in northern Mexico to the vicinity of Veracruz (and including Tampico and Cabo Rojo), the climate becomes decidedly tropical. The land is usually characterized as a tropical savannah (Fig. 1-4 C), with mean annual rainfall often in excess of 160 cm (64 inches). There is also a decided seasonality to the patterns of precipitation, with the rainy period occurring from June to October, and the dry season from November to May.

A tropical rainy climate characterizes the coastal bend of Mexico from just south of Veracruz to Isla de Carmen at the southwestern margin of the Yucatan peninsula (Fig. 1-4 D). Although total annual precipitation (> 290 cm or 115 inches) qualifies this region as a tropical rain forest, its seasonal nature causes climatologists to consider it as somewhat less. Nevertheless, vegetation is lush here and grows very close to the shore. The wet and dry seasons are similar to those of the tropical savannah to the north, but the winter is not as dry.

Western Yucatan is a transitional region where annual precipitation decreases from over 200 cm (80 inches) in the southwest near Isla Aguada to about 50 cm (20 inches) along the northwestern margin at Celestun (Fig. 1-4 E). The northern coast of Yucatan constitutes the final climatic region, described as semi-arid tropical and characterized by xeric vegetation (Fig. 1-4 F). The northwestern coast from Celestun to Progreso receives somewhat less than 50 cm (20 inches) of rainfall annually, and the annual precipitation gradually increases to about 100 cm (40 inches) near Cabo Catoche to the east. Here, as in the other portions of tropical Mexico, the pattern of rainfall is decidedly seasonal. The coastal vegetation of this region is dominated by grasses, sedges, and xerophytic shrubs and trees.

For much of its length, the waters of the Gulf of Mexico lie several kilometers away from the mainland, held at bay by shallow estuaries or hypersaline lagoons and long sandy, sinuous barrier islands. The maritime microclimate of the coast tempers the harsher, more extreme macroclimate of the mainland interior. Diurnal offshore and onshore breezes moderate thermal highs and lows and the proximity to the sea provides ample water, albeit of varying salinity, to create a lushness of vegetation that is more constant throughout the region than the broader sweep of the wholly terrestrial plants. Inland plant communities reflect the prevailing mainland climate, but the mediating effects of Gulf waters diffuse these patterns, and the maritime communities assume identities of their own. Gulf of Mexico shores, then, must be considered in the broader context of regional climate, but also according to their own merits within the physical variations they express.

A SURVEY OF THE COASTLINE

About 160 km (100 miles) of coastal Louisiana, all 587 km (367 miles) of Texas coastline, and perhaps 200 km of northern Mexico coastline constitute the warm-temperate northern margin of the western Gulf of Mexico. This is a predominantly alluvial shore, blending a complex mixture of sameness and difference, stability and change. The coastline arcs 90 degrees from the mouth of the Sabine River, Texas to the mouth of the Rio Grande and proceeds from here roughly southward into a tropical transition. Gulf beaches of western Louisiana and extreme eastern Texas face almost due south; whereas the Gulf of Mexico lies due east of the mouth of the Rio Grande, the arbitrary river boundary between nations. Along this coastal arc (primarily the Texas shore) and for a considerable distance south of the bend, land meets the sea with a very gentle slope, averaging about 1 m/km, and is mostly protected by offshore barrier islands.

Despite numerous embayments (Fig. 6-1), there are few good natural harbors along the northwestern Gulf. Early explorers of Texas and northern Mexico found the shifting spits, bars and tidal channels between barrier islands treacherous for navigation. Only a few of the natural tidal inlets communicating with the bays were suitable for ship passage during the early years of settlement. Today, the Texas coast has only nine major ports (Orange, Port Arthur, Beaumont, Galveston, Houston, Freeport, Corpus Christi, Port Isabel, and Brownsville), and all of these exist as the result of channel dredging and the construction of jetty breakwaters to protect tidal inlets. There are no natural harbors suitable for anchorage in western Louisiana or in Mexico north of Tampico. The latter coastal city, located upon the northern bank of the Rio Panuco, is one of Mexico's principal Gulf ports, lying near the southern terminus of the alluvial region. Like the Texas ports of the northern Gulf, the river anchorage at Tampico was made suitable for shipping only because of extensive dredging and the construction of offshore jetty breakwaters.

North and south of the Rio Grande, Gulf shores reflect the harsh climate. The marshlands of northern Gulf shores have almost disappeared, leaving many bayshores fringed by sparse vegetation and sands. Humidity is high along the coast, but belies the infrequency of precipitation. Barrier islands harbor vast, almost barren dune fields. Warm broad beaches beckon the beachcomber to search for shells, sand dollars or even gold doubloons which might have washed ashore from wrecked Spanish galleons of ages past. The resort community of South Padre Island with its vacation houses and high-rise condominiums attracts about equal numbers of holiday visitors from both the United States and Mexico. Similar accommodations can be found along the entire Texas coast, including those at Galveston, Surfside, Rockport, Fulton, Port Aransas, Corpus Christi, and Port Isabel, to name a few. South Padre Island, however, is the last major coastal community north of Tampico, Mexico.

The region between the Rio Grande and Tampico consists primarily of small fishing villages. The lands surrounding Laguna Madre de Tamaulipas seem even more harsh than those of southernmost Texas. The village of La Salinera derives its name from the vast nearby barren tidal flats, from which salt is commercially collected. El Mesquital is another village named for the hordes of mosquitoes which emerge from ephemeral pools following infrequent rainy periods. Much of the northern Laguna in Mexico has been dredged, channelized, impounded and otherwise exploited for the development of commercial fisheries. The effect has been highly destructive to the natural ecology of this unique region (Chapter 8).

Just north of Tampico, there is a distinctive climatic change, from the arid steppe of the Rio Grande basin to a tropical coastal savannah. Summer rainfall increases significantly, enabling the development of a moderately diverse tropical flora along the shore. The savannah extends from just south of La Pesca at the southern termination of Laguna Madre de Tamaulipas to Veracruz on the central Mexico coast. Cabo Rojo, the most conspicuous coastal feature of east central Mexico, arises south of Tampico and extends more than 100 km southward. It is another sandy barrier, but unlike the islands of Texas and northern Mexico, Cabo Rojo seems to be a tombolo, an offshore topographic high (probably a large reef) which has been buried by sand and joined to the mainland by a narrow sandy spit. It encloses a large embayment, Laguna de Tamiahua. The Gulf shore of Cabo Rojo is similar to the sandy barrier island beaches to the north, and the highest dunes of the western Gulf occur here. The lagoon shore is significantly different, consisting primarily of thick mangrove forests.

South of Cabo Rojo, the coastline of the state of Veracruz, Mexico, changes from a lowland depositional alluvium to one of orogenic influence with considerably more relief than that of the northwestern Gulf. Here, the mountains of central Mexico, or at least their foothills, reach the sea. In some places the shore rises steeply, with prominent rocky headlands extending tall fingers into the sea. Broadly lunate open sandy bays several kilometers in length separate the headlands. The few natural igneous rocky shores of the Gulf of Mexico occur in this region. The port of Veracruz nestles within an area of relatively low relief along the central portion of the orogenic coast. It is the premier Gulf port of Mexico. Much of the city faces the open Gulf, but the harbor lies within a small reef-fronted embayment reinforced by man-made breakwaters. The Veracruz region is further protected from the open Gulf by several banks or reefs lying a few to several kilometers offshore.

South of Veracruz, shore relief again increases to just north of Coatzacoalcos, another river port maintained by dredging and jetties. Here the land changes from soils of orogenic dominance to flat alluvial or deltaic deposits supporting lush stands of coastal man-grove. Another small port, Frontera, lies at the mouth of Rio Grijalva, near the center of the southern alluvial coast. The noncalcareous deltaic shore persists along the southernmost arc of the Gulf of Mexico to an area just north of Laguna de Terminos, where bedrock gradually changes to the limestones of Yucatan.

Yucatan Peninsula is mainly a low-relief karsted limestone platform, formed originally as a result of biological activity in a shallow tropical sea. The land is only a portion of the entire Yucatan platform, which extends far into the Gulf toward the north and west. The greatest reef development in the Gulf of Mexico occurs upon this presently submerged portion of the platform. Few streams and virtually no rivers drain the flat land, but the porous limestone absorbs rainfall and stores it in vast subterranean groundwater reserves. There are only a few flowing streams which reach the sea. Most of these lie along the western margin of the peninsula.

Laguna de Terminos is the largest embayment on the Yucatan Peninsula. It is a relatively well-protected and mangrove-fringed body of water comprising an area in excess of 1500 square kilometers. Isla del Carmen is the sandy barrier island protecting the Laguna from the open Gulf. Northward to the vicinity of Champoton, the low-relief coast persists as a narrow sandy veneer on limestone, with mangroves occasionally present. The beach at the southwestern end of Isla Aguada (which is now a peninsula lying northeast of Isla de Carmen) is relatively broad (20 m) and steep (rising about 4 m). Relief diminishes northeastward toward Champoton, and the width of the beach decreases to little more than 3 m. In some places limestone bedrock outcrops from underneath the sand. Between Champoton and the town of Campeche the shore rises upon a series of northwest to southeast trending ridges. Cobble and sand are common, and eventually the shore becomes a low, narrow limestone platform. Near Campeche, erosion has produced cliffs along the shore, a few rising to heights of 75 m, and forming the greatest coastal relief of Yucatan. Campeche is the important port on the west Yucatan coast.

The lowland trend resumes north of Campeche and continues almost to Progreso on northern Yucatan. Much of this region consists of impenetrable coastal mangrove forests directly facing the Gulf and which have hindered settlement and coastal development. Celestun and Sisal are the only two prominent settlements along this shore.

The northern Yucatan shore is, in some respects, similar to the barrier island beaches of Texas, except that the sandy beaches are much narrower and the lagoons behind the beach ridges are either absent or largely filled with sediment. These shallow basins frequently are dry salt pans during periods of drought, but hold shallow hypersaline waters during wetter times. They are especially prominent from Celestun to Progreso, where a unique mangrove community and a rich diversity of bird life have developed. East of Progreso, the coast consists of a series of linear sandy low-relief beach ridges, most of which have fused with the mainland. The outermost ridge presents a coarse, narrow sandy beach to the shallow aquamarine subtidal Yucatan platform. From the air the sandy beach appears as an unbroken white line separating the azure sea from the olive drab tropical scrub forest.

Northern Yucatan receives the least amount of precipitation of the entire peninsula. This, coupled with the fact that there is virtually no surface water flow reaching the sea along the northern coast, inhibits extensive mangrove development. But mangroves are not absent here, for where lagoons persist, as behind Punta Holohit and Cabo Catoche, mangrove development is extensive. The northeastern Yucatan shore, within the Caribbean province, lies outside of our primary area of concern. However, the hard limestone "ironshores" of this coast will receive some attention in Chapter 4.

Coastal features of the western Gulf of Mexico are molded by climate, winds, waves, tides, currents and organisms, including humans. All of these factors interact to produce the barrier islands, tidal channels, rivermouth estuaries, enclosed lagoons, mangrove shores, banks and reefs, and the man-made jetties, groins, dredge spoil banks, and landfill causeways of the region (Fig. 1-3). In the pages to follow we will examine each of the major features of the western Gulf coastline and discuss some of the factors which influence them.

2. The Tidal Shore: Principles and Processes

The shore, marking a transition between land and sea, is one of the most complex of all habitats. It skirts every land mass great or small, and is regularly, and usually predictably, covered and uncovered by the tides. It can be bound in ice or heated year round under a tropical sun. In estuaries it is washed by waters of variable salinity. Elsewhere it is inundated by normal seawater at high tide and exposed to air or doused with torrential rain at low tide. It may lie under the continual assault of huge breakers or be so sheltered from even small refreshing waves that its soils are black and anoxic. Some shores retreat under the erosive power of wind, waves and the sea. Elsewhere these same agents create an accreting shore. The place where land and sea meet is not static. At every instant physical forces acting upon it alter to create a habitat of great dynamism, diversity and capacity for life.

The shore that we see today is not the shore of the past. Even on the scale of a human lifetime, forces of erosion and accretion can visibly change topography. A seawall may crumble, undercut by longshore currents. Similar forces may accrete a sand spit to close a tidal inlet. On a broader human scale, new lands have emerged from the sea and others have descended into it. Much further back in geological time, seas such as the Tethys have come and gone as continents have rearranged themselves carried upon crustal plates. Each new climatological and geological event changes the shore perspective; every nuance of weather and sea adjusts its profile. The shore is first and foremost a place of great temporal, spatial and physical potential.

Early ecologists viewed and studied shores from the standpoint of physical regulation. We now appreciate, however, that shores are something more. They are also biological entities, as dynamic in this dimension as in the physical one. Biological vigor reflects physical diversity. Myriad plants and animals reside within definable shore boundaries. There is always a creature (or creatures) that can exploit some measure of sustenance available upon each shore, regardless of the seemingly life-defying pressures which beset it. Ephemeral intertidal colonizers exploit normally icebound polar shores briefly thawed under the summer sun. The heaviest surf or blackest muds harbor surprising biological abundance rarely encountered in other habitats. The incongruous sea shore is one of the more rigorous habitats on earth and simultaneously one of the richest. Yet, the density and distribution of animals and plants on the shore is temporally unstable, for every nuance of the physical environment is matched by variations in species abundance, patterns of recruitment, competition and mortality that will spread their effects to adjoining shore communities and into the sea itself.

Sea shores are formed of inanimate rock, sand, mud or clay, and, in exceptional cases, of living wood, grass or coral. Despite the composition of the shore, the sea is the principal medium upon which its life is ultimately dependent for nutrients or food and for the dispersal of progeny. The sea is the third dimension to the shore, and all shore studies should begin with the sea. In this chapter, we will consider some general aspects of tides, currents, winds, waves and weather. Each of these has the potential to build, transform and destroy. The tides immerse and expose the shore and define its primary limits. Wind-generated waves adjust this relationship, providing dynamism. Potential energy stored in waves at sea is kinetically transformed when they strike shore. Similarly, wind-generated currents mold the coastline and help mold its essential character. Potential energy stored in the tidal rise and fall becomes kinetic only in tidal flows— when the tide is channelled or funnelled into and out of narrow estuaries, bays or lagoons. The complex interactions of tides, waves and currents over distance and time mold horizontal and vertical variations in shore topography, the physical form and structure of the beach and ultimately the composition, diversity and abundance of its resident communities. Exactly how such forces mold specific shores is described in the first few pages of each subsequent chapter.

TIDES

Tides are harmonic vertical movements of water on earth caused by the gravitational attraction of celestial objects, primarily the moon and sun. All standing bodies of water on earth experience tides, but only the sea, with its immense volume, produces one sufficient to be noticed along the shore. Periodic tidal rhythms of immersion and emersion set boundaries for life on the sea shore. They also provide the water and nutrients essential for the survival of this life and help carry away its unwanted refuse.

The principal tide generating force is the moon. Although the sun is much bigger, it is also much further away (384,000 km vs 150 million km). Tide-generating effect is dampened by distance, leaving the sun with somewhat less tidal influence than that of the moon. Assume for a minute that the moon is solely responsible for the tide. As the earth rotates, two tidal bulges, one facing the moon, the other opposite it and resulting from a centrifugal counter force, remain relatively stationary relative to the moon. In essence, as the earth rotates, the two tidal bulges seem to sweep around the earth's surface from east to west, in the direction of the diurnal motion, creating a semidiurnal cycle of high tide, low tide, high tide, low tide within the period of a lunar day, i.e., every 24 hours, 50 minutes. A high tide can be expected at a specific locality approximately every 12 hours and 25 minutes. In this way the tidal timings advance each day. If high tide occurs at noon today, expect it at 12:50 tomorrow. The height and maximum effect of these lunar generated tides vary from day to day with changes in the angle of declination of the moon and its position in its elliptical orbit around the earth.

The sun exerts a modifying influence upon the basic earth-moon system. When the moon, earth and sun are in line (Fig. 2-1 A), i.e., when the moon is new or full as occurs twice each lunar month, or approximately every 14.5 days, then the combined gravitational effects of the moon (hatched tide) and sun (nonhatched tide) upon the earth's seas are greatest. High tides at this time are at their highest and low tides at their lowest, i.e., the tidal amplitude is maximal. Such tides are called "spring tides," the term referring to tidal amplitude, not season. Conversely, when the moon and sun are at right angles to each other with respect to the earth (Fig. 2-1 B), their gravitational attractions conflict to create tides in which high tide levels are lowest and low tide levels are highest, i.e., the tidal amplitude is minimal. Such tides are called "neap tides," and occur in the first or last lunar quarter.

The effect of the sun also varies with its angle of declination, being greatest at the equinoxes (spring and autumn) and least at the solstices (winter and summer). At these times spring tides have their maximum and minimum ranges respectively and neap tides their minimum and maximum ranges, again respectively (Fig. 2-1 G).

Other nearby celestial objects such as the planets Venus, Mars, Jupiter and Saturn also exert slight gravitational effects on the earth's waters. Because of their relatively small sizes in comparison to the sun and considerably greater distances from the earth in relation to the moon, their gravitational effects usually can be ignored except for the most precise tidal determinations.

Tides would be near perfect reflections of the astronomical relationships between sun, earth and moon if the oceans were of uniform depth and not interrupted by continents or islands. Land complicates the tidal picture. Because each of the major oceans is of a unique size and defined by unique land boundaries,

each basin produces its own, special harmonic tidal oscillations which can interact to produce other than semidiurnal tides. In the north central Atlantic, for example, most shores are subject to typical semidiurnal tides. New York harbor experiences two highs and two lows each day, and the range between succeeding highs and lows is approximately equal (Fig. 2-1 C and F). The Caribbean Sea and parts of the Gulf of Mexico experience mixed tides (Fig. 2-1 F). The harmonic oscillations of these semi-restricted basins impose diurnal inequality between the heights of the two daily tides. Sometimes they are "in phase" and seem to produce only a single high and single low tide each day. At other times, they are "out of phase" producing two unequal high and low tides each day. This is especially apparent in the Gulf of Mexico at Galveston and other Texas shores (Fig. 2-1 I), and along most of the western shore of North America, as at San Francisco, California (Fig. 2-1 D). Diurnal inequalities are so extreme along some Gulf of Mexico shores that there is but one high and one low tide each day. Such diurnal tides (Fig. 2-1 E and F) characterize the Gulf shores of Mexico as at Tampico (Fig. 2.1 H), and the northern Gulf coast from central Louisiana to northwestern Florida as at Pensacola (Fig. 2-1 E and F).

2-1. Tides.

    A. Spring tides occur when sun, moon and earth are aligned. Solar tides (indicated by hatch marks) add to lunar tides to produce maximal tidal range.

    B. Neap tides occur during the quarter moons when the sun and moon exert opposing gravitational attractions. Solar high tides (indicated by hatch marks) mediate lunar low tides and vice versa.

    C. A semi-diurnal tide. New York, N.Y., January 10–11, 1986.

    D. A mixed tide. San Francisco, California, January 10–11, 1986.

    E. A diurnal tide. Pensacola, Florida, January 10–11, 1986.

    F. Distribution of tide types along North American shores.

    ▨ Mixed tides   ▥ Diurnal tides   ▤ Semidiurnal tides

The numbers indicate tidal range in meters as reported for the year 1986.

    G. Mean monthly tide level (●) and mean monthly tidal range (□) for Galveston, Texas for 1985.

    H. Neap and spring tides for Tampico, Mexico, January 2–15, 1986.

    I. Neap and spring tides for Galveston, Texas, January 2–15, 1986. Notice the distinctive shift from diurnal to semidiurnal periodicity, which characterizes a mixed tide.

The data for C through I were obtained from tide tables published by the United States Department of Commerce.

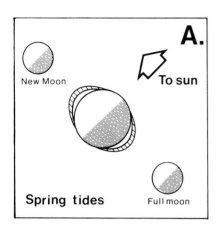

A.

New Moon

To sun

Full moon

Spring tides

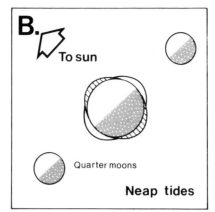

B.

To sun

Quarter moons

Neap tides

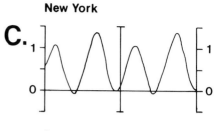

New York

C.

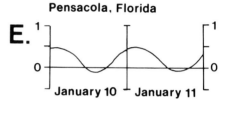

San Francisco

D.

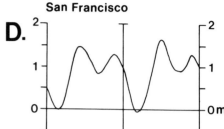

Pensacola, Florida

E.

January 10   January 11

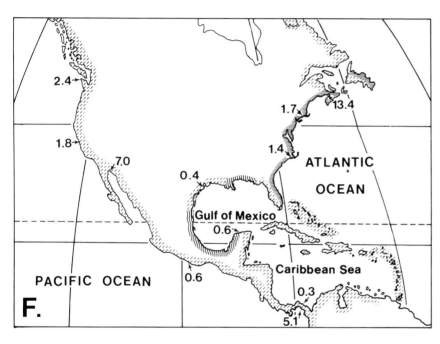

F.

2.4 →

1.8 →

7.0

0.4 →

Gulf of Mexico

0.6 →

0.6

PACIFIC OCEAN

1.7

13.4

1.4

ATLANTIC

OCEAN

Caribbean Sea

0.3

5.1

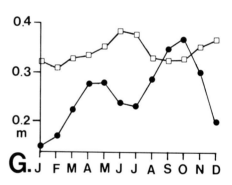

G. J F M A M J J A S O N D

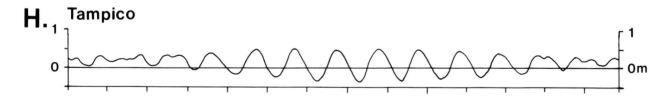

H. **Tampico**

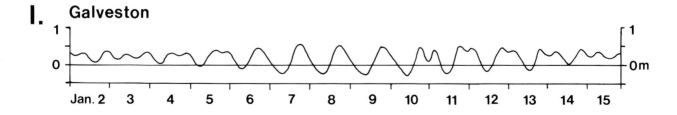

I. **Galveston**

Jan. 2   3   4   5   6   7   8   9   10   11   12   13   14   15

Atlantic tidal ranges are highly variable. In the Bay of Fundy it is as much as 15 m, whereas in the Gulf of Mexico, it varies between 0.4 to 0.7 m, and falls to as little as 0.3 m in parts of the Caribbean Sea. The mean tidal ranges for the year 1986 at several Atlantic and Pacific localities appear in Figure 2-1 F. Regardless of the tidal range, all shores influenced by tides can be characterized by definable tidal benchmarks.

There is a point on every shore above which normal tidal water does not rise (ignoring the complicating effects of surf and spray). It is called extreme high water spring tide (EHWST) (Fig. 2-2). There is another point below which the shore is never uncovered by normal tides. This location is called extreme low water spring tide (ELWST). The littoral or intertidal zone lies between these two points. Approximately midway between EHWST and ELWST lies mean sea level (MSL), the level at which the sea would be if it were uninfluenced by tides. Actual sea level rarely coincides with MSL as it is constantly either rising above or falling below this point within each tidal cycle. In the same manner, water rarely attains EHWST or ELWST as these points are the extraordinary limits of the tide. More frequently recognized points are mean high water spring tide (MHWST) and mean low water spring tide (MLWST). A similar set of points can be established for the neap tides, i.e., extreme high water neap tide (EHWNT), mean high water neap tide (MHWNT), mean low water neap tide (MLWNT) and extreme low water neap tide (ELWNT). These benchmarks are illustrated in Figure 2-2. Not shown on this figure is one additional benchmark, mean low water (MLW), which lies between MSL and ELWST and is the average of all low tides for a particular location. MLW is the "chart datum" for nautical charts of the United States. Sea level is shown on these charts as MLW and tidal predictions are calculated as deviations from MLW. The zero points on all graphs in Figure 2-1 represent MLW.

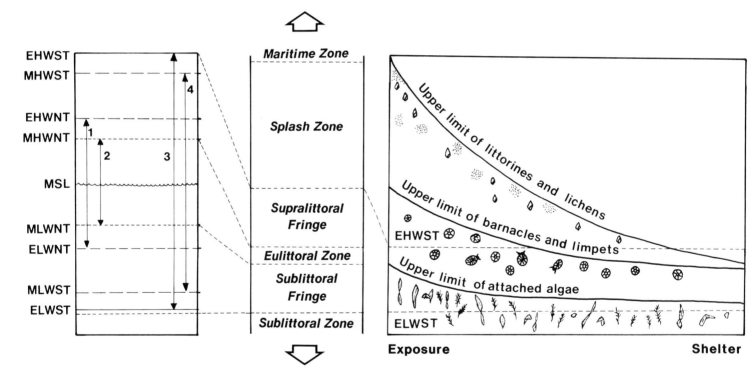

2-2. Tides and the shore.

Left panel. Tidal benchmarks. EHWST, extreme high water spring tides; MHWST mean high water spring tides; EHWNT, extreme high water neap tides; MHWNT, mean high water neap tides; MSL, mean sea level; MLWNT, mean low water neap tides; ELWNT, extreme low water neap tides; MLWST, mean low water spring tides; ELWST, extreme low water spring tides.

1. The range of neap tides; **2.** the mean range of neap tides which corresponds to the mid-littoral (eulittoral) zone; **3.** the total tidal range of this shore; **4.** the extent of the shore usually covered or exposed at least once during a tidal fortnight.

Center panel: Zonation on a hard shore, related to tidal benchmarks.

Right panel: Shelter and exposure on tidal shores. As exposure to wave activity increases, tidal benchmarks are displaced higher up the shore. Organisms restricted to intermediate tidal levels on sheltered shores likewise tend to move higher upon exposed shores. Barnacles, for example, characterize the eulittoral in shelter, but are able to live considerably higher than the tidal limit would impose when the shore is fully exposed to waves.

Other nations often employ different points for chart datum. For example, British charts recognize ELWST as chart datum.

Tidal benchmarks also are used to delimit regions of the shore. The supralittoral fringe extends above MHWNT, since this is the point above which average tides will not extend. Similarly, the sublittoral fringe extends downwards from MLWNT, since this is the point below which average tides will not fall. The sublittoral zone extends downwards from MLWST, the point below which the shore will not be uncovered by the average lowest tides. The great expanse of shore between the littoral fringe and the sublittoral fringe is called the mid-littoral (or eulittoral, or simply littoral) zone and comprises that region of the shore which over an average tidal cycle will be covered and uncovered regularly by 50 percent of all tides (Fig. 2-2).

WAVES

Most waves are surface water phenomena created by winds offshore. The wind disturbs the water surface and sets water molecules into circular motion. Although waves may move hundreds of miles across a sea, the water within the wave only describes a circular path corresponding to wave length and height (Fig. 2-3 A). The wave length is defined by the distance between succeeding wave crests. The wave height is the vertical distance between the crest and trough of the wave. Three major factors influence these basic wave dimensions: the strength of the wind and the time and distance over which it blows. Generally, storms of long duration create larger waves than squalls. Similarly, the greater the distance the storm is from the land, the more energy a wave generated by the storm will lose before reaching the shore (the energy lost by the wave is proportional to the distance it must travel). As illustrated in Figure 2-3 B, with a constant wind, wave height and length of effect are related to the distance (fetch) over which the wind blows.

Waves reaching the shore are rarely of uniform height. Offshore winds produced by a tropical depression far out to sea may create an ocean swell, whereas a nearshore squall may generate ripples. But the swell and the ripple may reach the shore about the same time, where they interact to produce a resultant wave. Most resultant waves breaking upon a shore consist of several dozen individual wave components. It is because of the interactive effects of the individual components that no two succeeding waves reaching a shore are of exactly the same dimensions. The wind also affects sea level, sometimes even overriding the effect of the tide. Onshore winds bank water upon the shore, whereas offshore winds act to lower water levels (Fig. 2-3 C).

EXPOSURE GRADIENTS

Shores are rarely of uniform frontage (except on man-made sea walls). Their form derives from the interaction of land-forming processes (geology and geomorphology), currents and waves. Generally, the world's shores display a complex pattern of variations in exposure to waves. Two contrasting examples will illustrate this point. On headlands facing the open sea, waves slap directly against rocky cliffs, their forward motion taking water high upon the shore. Leeward of prevailing winds, the power and influence of waves are markedly diminished. We can define such shores as respectively exposed and sheltered with a graded series of intermediate situations extending between.

On the shores more exposed to wave action, waves extend tidal benchmarks upwards. The position of mean sea level moves higher up the shore and the relative position of extreme high water spring tide may be a meter or more above that of a sheltered shore. Waves, therefore, regulate tidal heights according to the aspect of the shore along an exposure gradient. In high exposure, waves may be so high as to largely negate the effects of the tide and to all intents and purposes the tide stays in. Obversely, in shelter, the impact of waves is overshadowed by the tidal range. Rocky shores are either wave or tide dominated according to the degree of shelter. The former experience high energy, the latter experience low. For the ecologist, such an exposure gradient is of great significance, for it not only affects the species composition of the intertidal communities to be found on each exposure graded beach, but also determines the vertical height at which such communities and their elements, or zones, can exist (Fig. 2-2 right).

Exposure gradients exist for soft as well as rocky shores, but because on the latter the biota stands out upon the rock surface, such variations are more clearly definable. Conversely, much of the biota of a soft shore is infaunally buried and not readily apparent—its variations longitudinally and vertically hidden.

ZONATION

The concept of shore zones is a powerful tool for the study of shore communities. Each species upon the sea shore occupies a broadly definable level or position determined by a meld of physical and biotic pressures that are acting upon it and which it can individually circumscribe. This position usually persists within similar limits on most other shores the species occupies. Within only a few vertical meters of rocky shore, species sort themselves into several distinctly demarcated communities. This phenomenon is referred to as "zonation" and is a theme around which many intertidal studies are conducted.

Edward Forbes (1841) was perhaps the first to recognize ecological zonation of seashores. Ballantine (1961) established a biological scale of exposure for rocky intertidal organisms on the Dale Peninsula of Great Britain, but it is to the lifelong work and review of the subject by Stephenson and Stephenson (1972) that we turn for our broader definitions, particularly applicable to Atlantic hard shores. The major effect of tides, by their regular rise and fall, is to determine the broad distribution of the plants and animals. Three major zoning levels can be recognized and are encompassed within what the Stephensons established as a "Universal Tripartite Pattern of Zonation on Rocky Shores." A similar generalization is not readily apparent for soft shores, although they, too, are subtly (sand beaches) to distinctly (mangroves) zoned. On rocky shores the zones are:

(1) Lichen and littorine zone occupying the supralittoral fringe.
(2) Barnacle and limpet zone, occupying the midlittoral zone, and
(3) Brown and red algae zone occupying the sublittoral fringe.

This basic pattern, with characterizing organisms, is common to virtually all the rocky shores of the world, although component species vary greatly from place to place in accordance with their specific geographic distributions. We can compare the rocky shore communities to a dramatic play in which the diversity of interpretation and expression resides with the great variety of cast members that fill the same roles in the various theaters and languages of the world.

The basic theme is also modified in the vertical dimension by exposure to waves, for zones reach above normal tidal benchmarks (Fig. 2-2). Exposure gradients not only alter zoning heights, but have a horizontal impact. Species composition of the zones change as shores transgress from exposure to shelter and from hard to soft. It is from the study of such changes that the theme of our book will emerge, finding expression in the complex array of shores and their communities resident in the Gulf of Mexico.

THE MOLDING OF THE SHORELINE

Waves are sea surface phenomena (Fig. 2-3 A). As a wave approaches land, potential wave energy is transformed into forward kinetic energy and expressed when the wave literally smashes against the shore. Wave length shortens and wave height increases as the circular motions of water molecules "touch" the shoaling water. With further forward motion, the wave height increases to such an extent that the crest topples forward and surges up the shore in a sheet of water or swash. Gravity eventually overcomes forward momentum, and the wave returns as backwash before the succeeding wave arrives. Most of the backwash returns to the sea on the surface of impermeable rocky shores. On the surface of soft shores (e.g., sand), only part of the backwash returns on the surface. The remainder, depending upon particle size, returns more slowly within the sand. Stand on a beach and watch how the sand dries slowly downwards after the retreating wave.

Waves breaking upon shores can be divided into two general categories—destructive or constructive. The former are characterized by a short wave length and

tall wave height, the latter by a long wave length and short wave height. Obviously a range of conditions prevail, from awesome hurricane-driven waves on the one hand, to virtually dead calm seas on the other. We will consider the special case of hurricanes on Gulf shores at the end of this chapter, but here we examine more frequently encountered shore conditions.

Relatively few oceanic swells approach exactly parallel to a shore, but they usually break more-or-less directly upon it. Variably contoured shorelines refract waves, causing them to break almost parallel to the beach. The portion of a wave which touches bottom first is slowed down relative to that portion still in deeper water further out to sea. The latter has a chance to catch up with the former, and the swell seems to conform to shoaling contours and thereby break almost parallel to the shore. Wave refraction focuses energy upon headlands and dissipates it in lunate bays (Fig. 2-3 D).

The ways waves affect a shore depend in part upon the physical nature of that shore. Most Gulf of Mexico shores are composed of soft, loose sediments (sands, muds and clays), but the Gulf is not devoid of hard shores. We deal first with the simpler dynamics of the hard shores.

2-3. Waves and shores.

A. Winds generate waves offshore. Wave length (L) is measured from crest to crest; wave height is the vertical distance from the crest of a wave to the trough. Water molecules are moved in a circular motion by a passing wave, with the ability of the wave to move water molecules diminishing rapidly with water depth. As waves approach shore, the moving water molecules "touch bottom," causing wave length to shorten and height to increase until the wave breaks onto the shore. Breaking waves move onto shore as swash and move offshore as backwash. On sandy shores some of the backwash moves seaward within the sand.

B. Wave development under a constant wind (54 km/hr) and increasing duration and fetch. (After Sverdrup et al., 1942.)

C. Effects of winds upon water level on a shore. In addition to wave effects, onshore winds near the shore drive water upon the shore. In contrast, offshore winds dampen wave energy advancing toward the shore, reducing the shoreward movement of water. (After King, 1959.)

D. Wave refraction. Waves converge or focus on headlands and diverge within lunate bays. In both cases, wave direction is altered so as to cause the wave to break approximately perpendicular to the shore.

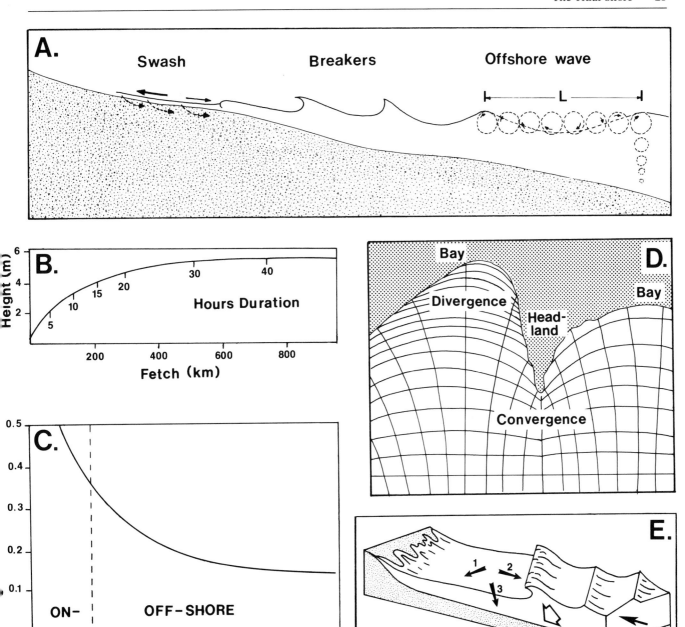

E. Longshore currents, waves and sand transport. In the presence of strong longshore currents, waves often break at a slight angle to the shore. On sandy beaches, sands are moved according to the relative strengths of the longshore current (open arrow) and the waves (unnumbered dark arrow). Sands move parallel to the shore (arrow 1) when longshore currents are strong in comparison to the incoming waves. Sands move seaward (arrow 2) or shoreward when longshore currents are slight in comparison to the incoming waves. When currents and wave motions exert approximately equal influence, sands tend to be moved obliquely offshore (arrow 3). (After Ingle, 1966.)

Waves on Rocky Shores—Erosion

The principal effect of waves or currents upon hard shores is erosion. Igneous headlands (e.g., granite or volcanic tuff) usually are more resistant to the erosive forces of aeolian and wave energy than are sedimentary shales, sandstones or limestones. In areas of mixed geology, granites are worn slower than sedimentary rocks and typically predominate upon exposed headlands, whereas softer rocks often characterize wave or river eroded embayments.

Destructive waves predominate upon hard shores. Erosion usually proceeds slowly on igneous rock. Winds and rain act above the shoreline, but the relentless movement of the sea is the more persistent erosive force. Waves suspend particles of sand and abrade them across rocky headlands like sandpaper, either polishing their surfaces to an almost mirror finish or progressively removing small particles from the fabric of the shore (Fig. 2-4 A).

Sedimentary hard shores are easier to erode. They are more easily shaped by aeolian forces and precipitation, as the microkarsted limestones of eastern Yucatan readily testify. Yet, waves still remain the primary agents of erosion. Layered bedding planes within sedimentary rock incorporate small fissures and crevices that, in turn, contain small pockets of air. Compression of the tiny air pockets by the force of the wave as it advances (Fig. 2-4 B1), and the release of pressure as it retreats (Fig. 2-4 B2), slowly splits the rock until it is eventually fragmented into pieces of variable size. With wave strike principally focussed between the tidal heights of MHWST and MLWST, a wave-cut notch can form in the sedimentary rock face (Fig. 2-4 C). Material eroded in this manner litters the beach platform as a beach veneer and progressively is further eroded into its constituent grains by continued abrasion. When the notch is unable to support the cliff above, it too falls down and contributes to the beach veneer. Retreat is rapid as measured in geologic time.

Waves on Soft Shores—Build-up and Erosion

Dynamic processes are more complex on soft shores, in part because they experience a greater variation of exposure and shelter than is usually encountered along rocky coastal margins. At one extreme, sandy beaches facing the open sea experience considerable wave exposure. At the other extreme, isolated inner

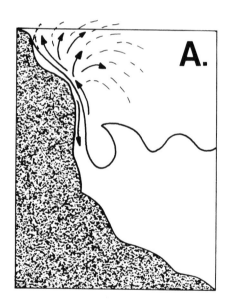
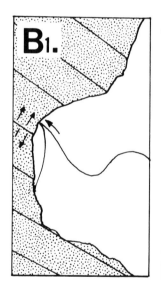
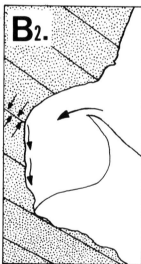
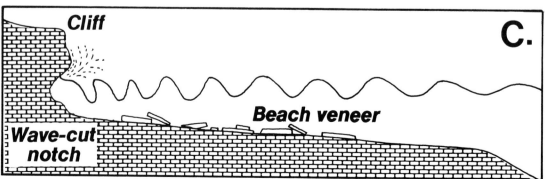

bays lie well protected from most winds and waves. Ephemeral, seasonal or longer variations in wind strength exert more profound effects upon soft shores, especially open sandy coasts, than they do upon rocky shores which are less susceptible to variations in wave height, direction and strength. Sand beaches respond almost immediately to any change in the direction or intensity of winds and the waves they produce. The results may be either constructive or destructive.

Soft shores are composed of almost infinite numbers of particles. The net transport of these particles is landward with constructive waves. As the swash sweeps in, its forward motion imparts greater energy than the backwash, especially since some of the water percolates into the sediment on the outward flow (Fig. 2-5 A). Particles moved landward by incoming waves are dried by air at low tide, picked up by winds, and lofted further landward. Eventually, particles originally in the sea may be moved high upon the shore where they become soil stabilized by vegetation. Successive layers of material accumulate until equilibrium with the topography is achieved. At this point, rates of input of material upon the shore are balanced by the rates of removal of material from it.

There is an energy threshold beyond which waves cease being constructive and become destructive on a soft shore. During storms, for example, sediment is removed from a beach and dumped offshore. The specific dynamics of each shore determine at what point the energy threshold is attained, so we cannot generalize as to a specific wind speed or wave force to define it. Destructive waves have relatively greater kinetic energy than constructive ones. Sand particles are held in suspension longer, allowing backwash to remove at least some of them downshore (Fig. 2-5 B).

2-4. Waves on hard shores. The principal effect of waves upon hard shores is erosion, but the effectiveness of waves varies according to the composition of the shore.

A. Igneous rocky shores tend to be relatively more resistant to wave attack than sedimentary rocky shores. Destructive waves gradually erode or polish the rocks.

B. Waves erode sedimentary rocky shores by attacking microcrevices along bedding planes. Incoming waves (B1) exert a force that tends to spread the rock along the plane, whereas receding waves (B2) release this pressure, permitting the weight of the rock to compress along the plane. Particles gradually loosen and fall away.

C. Sedimentary rocky shores frequently erode basally to form a wave-cut notch and an overhanging cliff. Fragments eroded from the notch may litter the subtidal nearshore as beach veneer.

The dynamics of an open sand beach are the forces acting to build it and those acting to destroy it. At Padre Island, Texas, constructive wave energy acts to build some parts of the island, but in other places destructive wave energy is acting rapidly to erode it. For most shores events are usually less dramatic. An equilibrium between seaward and shoreward sand transport is commonly developed, with only subtle changes in this equilibrium dictated by seasonal cycles of build up and erosion (Fig. 2-5 C). Material translocates between beach crest and subtidal bank in accordance with seasonally modified wave dynamics.

The slope of the beach is determined in part by the degree of wave exposure and in part by the amount of backwash water lost as percolation into the beach. High wave exposure favors deposition of coarse particles and removal of fine material from the beach face. Water and detritus seep more readily through well-sorted coarse sands or gravels than through fine sands, muds or poorly sorted mixtures. As backwash percolates into the beach, its ability to remove material from the forebeach by surface flow is markedly diminished. Gradually, additional coarse material accumulates on the forebeach, increasing its slope. As the beach slope increases, the median diameter of particles comprising it also increases (Fig. 2-5 D). Plants and animals find exposed sandy beaches difficult to colonize. These beaches, and especially the surf-swept sands, are almost universally depauperate of life. They are occupied by only a few hardy, highly specialized species.

In contrast, wave action is reduced on shores of embayments and lagoons. The slope of the shore is slight, particle sizes and interstitial spaces are smaller and the shore is usually accreting. Bayshore biota experiences different problems than that upon sandy beaches. In the absence of refreshing waves, sediments are poorly oxygenated to produce anoxic conditions just below the surface. In conditions of deep shelter, wave action may be so reduced that the effects of stream and riverine discharge outweigh those of the sea. The finest particles, the muds, silts, and associated organic nutrients, produce an anoxic layer right at the surface. The well sheltered shore is regulated not so much by water movement as by cycling of organic nutrients.

Sorting Coefficients and Exposure

The ultimate character of a soft shore, including its slope, stability and capacity as a habitat, is dependent upon the size and distribution of the particles that comprise it. On low energy mudflats, little sorting occurs. On high energy beaches under the influence of wave action, sorting capacity is greatly enhanced. Primary sorting occurs within the breaker zone, where the largest particles on the beach tend to accumulate (Fig. 2-5 E). Additional sorting is achieved by the swash and backwash. A breaking wave carries medium-sized and fine particles upshore in the swash. As the backwash retreats, the largest of these particles will be dropped first, and at higher levels than finer grains

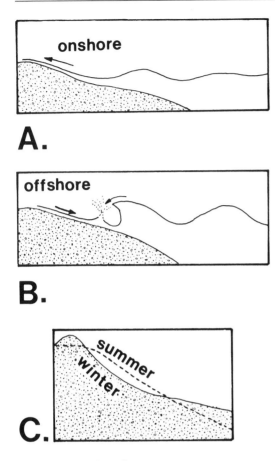

A. onshore

B. offshore

C. summer / winter

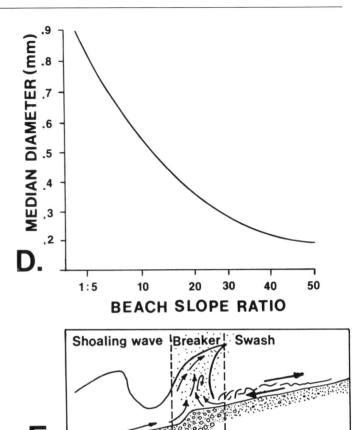

D.

MEDIAN DIAMETER (mm)

BEACH SLOPE RATIO

E. Shoaling wave | Breaker | Swash

fn   cr   fn

2-5. Waves and sand.

  A. A constructive wave transports sand onshore.

  B. A destructive wave transports sand offshore.

  C. Seasonal beach profiles. Solid line: a winter beach or a beach following a storm; dotted line: a summer beach resulting from constructive waves.

  D. The relationship between beach slope expressed as a ratio of vertical to horizontal dimension and median di-

ameter of sand particles on the forebeach. (After Bascom, 1951.)

  E. Breakers and sand. The coarsest particles on a beach accumulate just below the breaking waves, whereas the medium and fine particles are elevated by breakers and transported up or down the shore. fn, fine; cr, coarse. (After Miller & Ziegler, 1958.)

which are carried down the beach. On wave-sorted beaches, the coarsest grains occur at the top of the beach and the finest at the bottom typically below low water.

  To obtain a quantitative description of the particles which form a beach, a calculation of the median grain size is necessary. This is done by analysis of a beach sand sample, achieved by passing it through a series of Wentworth sieves logarithmically graded from pebbles to very fine sand. Particle sizes are today expressed as units on a ϕ (phi) scale which is a logarithmic scale of particle diameters, defined as a negative logarithm to base 2 of the particle size in mm. Values for different particle sizes are calculated as percentages of the total dry weight of the sample and are set out as a series of curves on a graph (Fig. 2-6). Such a family of curves,

2-6. Gulf Sands. Size distributions of sand grains from twelve Gulf of Mexico beaches are summarized in this figure. The relationship between grain size expressed in millimeters and as Phi values is summarized at the top of the diagram. Grain sizes expressed as Phi values appear along the abscissa of each histogram and percent frequencies are indicated along each ordinate. Localities: **A.** approximately 25 miles east of High Island, Texas; **B.** beach at High Island, Texas; **C.** beach at Galveston Island State Park, Texas; **D.** beach at San Luis Pass on Follets Island, Texas; **E.** beach at the mouth of the Brazos River, Texas; **F.** beach at the mouth of the Colorado River, Texas; **G.** beach at Mustang Island State Park, Texas; **H.** Little Shell beach, Padre Island, Texas; **I.** Big Shell beach, Padre Island, Texas; **J.** beach near southwestern margin of Isla Aguada, Campeche, Mexico; **K.** beach at Telchac Puerto, Yucatan, Mexico; **L.** beach at Las Coloradas National Park, Yucatan, Mexico. The histograms show sands on beaches at High Island and Galveston to be relatively well sorted, whereas those at Big Shell and Isla Aguada are relatively poorly sorted.

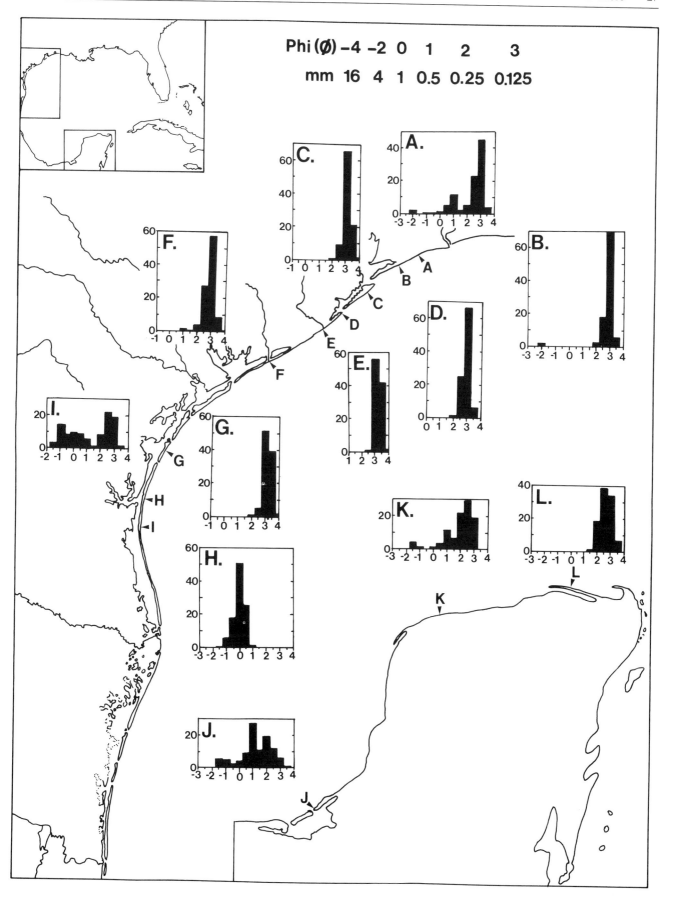

Phi (∅) −4 −2 0 1 2 3
mm 16 4 1 0.5 0.25 0.125

from successive stations down the beach, or the median grain sizes extracted from them, gives a quantitative description of the beach. From these data can also be obtained a sorting coefficient, which expresses the spread of the curve on either side of the most frequently occurring grain size. A small value for the sorting coefficient indicates a considerable degree of sorting, as would be obtained for the phi values in Figure 2-6 D or E. Higher values of the sorting coefficient, as would be obtained from the phi values in Figure 2-6 I, J, or K, characterize beaches with poorly sorted sediments.

Transport

We have now seen how waves act upon hard shores to erode them into constituent grains and how waves sort and grade such particles to create a wide variety of shore types, the most structurally complex of which in the Gulf of Mexico are the exposed barrier island beaches. The final element in this process is the transport of eroded sand. Hurricanes are the extreme examples of the influence of weather upon sediment transport in the Gulf and will be discussed later, but here we are concerned with more moderate effects of waves and currents.

Waves and currents can transport sediments onto, off or along a shore (Fig. 2-3 E). When transport velocities are high, the amount transported can be dramatic, as along portions of southern Padre Island. But even in moderation, currents and longshore drift (i.e., sediment transport by waves) are essential to the formation, maintenance, and sometimes the destruction of coastal peninsulas, spits and barrier islands (Fig. 2-7 A). Where shore features inhibit longshore transport (as do the jetties in Fig. 2-7 B), there is often an accumulation of particles on the side of the barrier facing the longshore current (Weise & White, 1980).

There are two types of sediment transport systems: (1), a cell circulation system created when waves strike nearly perpendicular to a shore (Fig. 2-8 A), and (2), longshore drift created when waves strike the shore obliquely (Fig. 2-8 B). When waves strike the shore perpendicularly, large quantities of water quickly accumulate on the beach. As wave energy dissipates, the water flows seaward seeking gravitational equilibrium, but a new series of onrushing breakers prevents it from having free access to the open sea. It is deflected laterally, where it flows in longshore currents along the beach. Eventually, the inshore mass of water overcomes the resistance of the incoming surf and breaks seaward, cutting a rip channel perpendicular to shore. The longshore currents turn seaward at the shoreward head of the rip channel, forming strong narrow rip currents flowing rapidly offshore. A series of rip channels, rip currents and associated longshore current cells develop on the beach. Midway between a pair of rip channels, divergent longshore currents form, flowing towards the rip channel heads. At their point of origin, the velocity of longshore currents is nearly zero, but increase in speed until they reach maximum velocity at the head of the rip channel. Due to the cyclic nature of this system, the net water transport in the nearshore current cell approaches zero. Beach sands are locally displaced, resulting in pronounced spurs and cusps along the shore.

Beach spurs (Fig. 2-8 C) are triangular accumulations of sand and other debris. Their pointed apices, and the shallow symmetrical concave cusps between them, usually lie regularly spaced, from about 1 m to as much as 100 m along the shore. The distance between spur apices increases as wave height increases. Spurs and cusps are produced by the cell circulation system, and, when present, indicate that waves are coming ashore exactly or nearly perpendicularly.

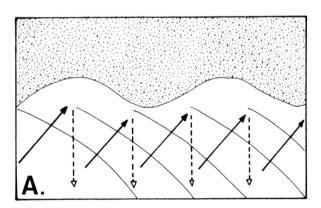

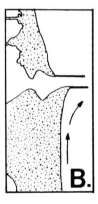

2-7. Components of longshore drift.

A. Waves approach a shore obliquely from the southwest. Particles lifted in suspension by breaking waves are carried obliquely toward the shore (solid arrows) in the swash, but are transported seaward perpendicular to the shore in the backwash (dotted arrows).

B. When barriers such as breakwaters or jetties impede longshore drift along sandy beaches, sand accumulates along the side of the barrier facing the direction of the drift, or, in this figure, along the southern jetty wall.

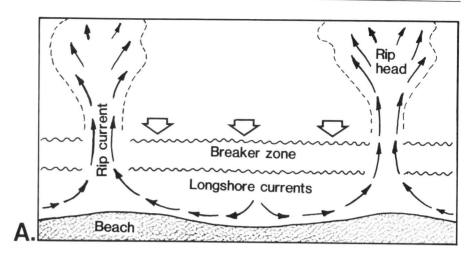

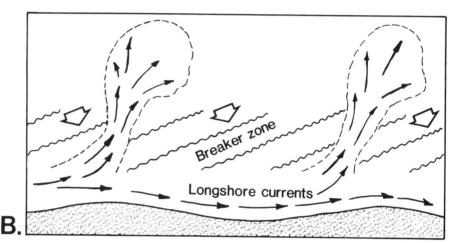

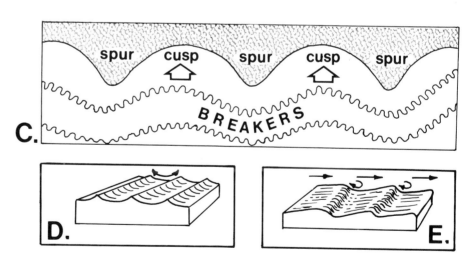

2-8. Beach dynamics.

    A. A longshore system when waves strike perpendicular to a coastline.

    B. A longshore system when waves strike obliquely to a coastline.

    C. Spurs and cusps.

    D. Oscillation ripple marks.

    E. Current ripple marks.

When waves strike the shore obliquely, the cell system is disrupted, and shore cusping diminishes or disappears. Particles picked up in suspension on the beach are carried at an angle up the shore, but come down perpendicularly in response to gravity. There will be, in effect, a net transport of material along the beach to the east. This process is longshore drift, and is augmented by currents flowing in the same direction just offshore. Longshore currents flow unidirectionally, with the direction imposed by the incoming wave train. The nearshore bars and troughs are cut occasionally by rip channels, which lie somewhat more obliquely to the shore. These uninterrupted longshore currents are the primary sediment movers of many sandy beaches throughout the world, and affect profoundly most of the sandy shores facing the Gulf of Mexico. Beaches rarely have just cell circulation or just unidirectional longshore flow. Both systems are usually present and interact to produce the specific circulation observed on a specific shore.

Ripple marks are the signatures of waves and currents on sandy beaches. They are usually minor features rarely more than a few centimeters tall and almost always less than a meter from crest to crest. (In contrast, some offshore ripple marks can be meters tall and dozens of meters across.) There are two types of ripple marks, both formed by water movements. Oscillation ripple marks are small-scale symmetrical troughs with pointed crests (Fig. 2-8 D). They form in response to the back and forth motion of the water on the shore and trend more or less parallel to the long axis of the beach. Current ripples (Fig. 2-8 E) are asymmetrical, their position indicating the direction of flow. The gently sloping side of a current ripple mark faces up-current, whereas the more abrupt scarp in front of the rounded crest faces down-current. Due to the prevalence of longshore currents along many sandy beaches, current ripple marks are usually much more commonly observed on the shore than oscillation ripples.

Regional Patterns of Nearshore Sediment Transport within the Gulf Basin

The pattern of sea surface circulation in the Gulf of Mexico is created as major incursions of water from the tropical Caribbean enter the Gulf via the Yucatan Channel, circulate, and exit via the Straits of Florida (Fig. 2-9 A). The circulation of surface waters varies seasonally, but roughly consists of two major elements: (1), a sweeping S-shaped element in the eastern Gulf, and (2), a complex double loop that focuses upon the south central Texas shore in the western Gulf. The latter has a profound effect upon several regional shores, such as central Padre Island, Texas, where currents strongly influence the composition of the barrier island beach, or western Yucatan where mangroves thrive in the lee of the primary current flow.

Longshore currents trend westerly along northern Yucatan, where they are an important sculptor of this shore. The effect is most obvious along the northeastern coast. Cabo Catoche is the elongate sandy spit created by the strong currents sweeping around the margin of Yucatan from the Caribbean basin. These currents transport sand along most of the northern Yucatan shore, depositing it layer upon layer. This effect is especially noticeable in high resolution satellite photography, where a series of beach ridges mark the prograding shore for several kilometers inland. Longshore currents gradually diminish toward northwestern Yucatan. Sandy beaches fed by the currents disappear, replaced by fine, organically rich deposits. Mexico's Gulf coastal bend is less influenced by longshore currents than by processes of local deposition and accretion.

South of Tampico, at Cabo Rojo, the importance of longshore processes again becomes evident. This cape is formed largely by longshore currents operating in conjunction with local topography and river deposition. From here northward to central Padre Island on the Texas coast, longshore currents move coastal sands northward within a nearshore bar and trough system. The barrier islands off Laguna Madre de Tamaulipas and southern Padre Island off Texas have formed from sands delivered by these currents.

About 80 km north of the mouth of the Rio Grande along central Padre Island the longshore bar and trough system fails to parallel the shore. Instead, a series of oblique open grooves, called "blind guts" by local fishermen, lie offshore. Maps identify the area as Big Shell, a name referring to the considerable accumulation of large, massive shell debris on the beach. Early oceanographers reported considerable agitation in the Gulf waters off Big Shell, and suggested that the area was the meeting place of opposing currents (Sweitzer, 1898). Mariners consider the waters treacherous. Numerous old and modern shipwrecks in the vicinity support the claim.

Big Shell approximately marks the location of the most acute flexure of the Texas coastal arc. It is also the approximate northern limit of beach sands derived from the Rio Grande. North of here beach sands have characteristics of sediments brought to the Gulf by central Texas rivers. The early oceanographers are apparently correct. Big Shell "blind guts" are most likely rip channels formed by strong currents produced by the convergence of two opposing longshore systems (Fig. 2-9 A). The distribution of beach sands suggests that north of Big Shell, longshore drift trends southwesterly, although this varies seasonally (see below). Rio Grande sediments can reach Big Shell only by a northerly drift (van Andel, 1960). Where the two currents meet at Big Shell, the effect upon the beach is striking. Large shells and shell debris are pushed ashore by wave energy undissipated by parallel offshore bars. The shoreward movement of shell material can be considerable, but more likely it occurs primarily during storms. At other times it probably is only slightly more than on other beaches. The apparent dominance of large shells on the beach may reflect the large scale transport of fine and medium sands off the

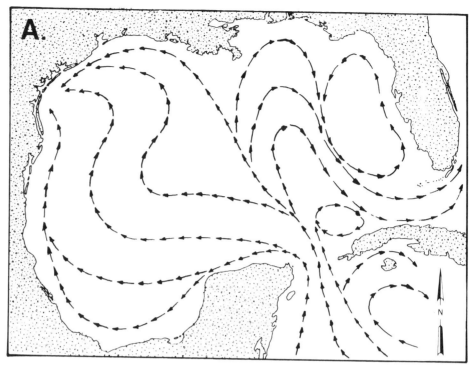

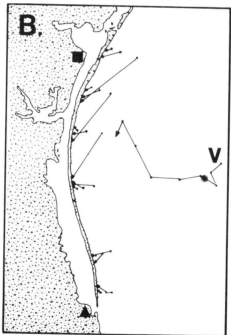

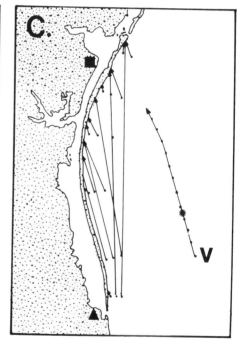

2-9. Surface currents.

A. Summer sea-surface circulation in the Gulf of Mexico. (After Leipper, 1954.)

B & C. Drift bottle patterns off the Texas coast in February (B) and July (C). Distance of release points offshore are exaggerated for clarity. Daily wind vectors (V) are shown for each season. The time of drift bottle release is indicated on the wind vector (⊶►) by the large circles; the lines between small circles indicate mean wind direction for successive days. (■) Corpus Christi; (▲) Port Isabel. (After Watson & Behrens, 1970.)

beach. Small particles sorted in the swash zone are removed from the heavier shell debris and washed to sea through the broad rip channels by receding waves that lack the energy needed to move larger shells. Some of the finer sands are also lofted off the beach by winds and deposited on backshore dune fields.

Longshore currents flow southwesterly along the upper Texas coast, moved by the same prevailing southeasterly winds that are responsible for the northeasterly longshore currents along the southern Texas and northern Mexico coasts (Fig. 2-9 A). The direction of longshore flow along the central Texas coast is mediated by local and seasonal factors.

Local current patterns are often moderated by the effects of prevailing, seasonal and local winds. Winter cold fronts or "northers" cause a temporary reversal of winds which often affect the entire Gulf coast. These arctic fronts displace the subtropical airflow with strong northerly or northeasterly winds. The northernmost longshore systems are affected modestly by the wind change, but as one moves southward along the coastal bend, the seasonal effects become more pronounced. Prevailing southeasterly winds at Mustang Island move longshore currents northeastward at a mean rate of 12 cm/sec (Fox & Davis, 1976), but with a winter "norther" these currents flow toward the southwest at an average rate of 24 cm/sec. This alternating flow, at least during the winter, is one of several stabilizing influences on the barrier island shore.

Offshore coastal currents also display longshore current components with sufficient energy to pick up and transport sand. Like their shallow water longshore counterparts, offshore currents are noticeably influenced by wind patterns (Smith, 1975)(Fig. 2-9 B & C). Off Port Aransas, in 14 m of water, winter currents flow west southwesterly at a mean rate of 21.5 cm/sec in response to northerly winds. These currents also have a slight tendency to move toward the shore. In the summer, currents alternately flow south southwesterly and north northwesterly in response to changes in wind direction. There is little net transport of sediment.

Tidal Inlets

We began this chapter with a consideration of tides. Now, we come full circle, to consider again tidally induced water movements through inlet channels lying between barrier islands. Gulf of Mexico bays communicate with offshore waters via tidal inlet channels. There is an intimate relationship between longshore drift, tidal currents and the number and location of tidal inlets between barrier islands. Other factors, including prevailing winds, river discharge, and periodic tropical storms and hurricanes also contribute to the water exchange and influence the location and condition of the channels. Where tidal amplitude is large, tidal currents readily cut and maintain numerous deep channels between offshore banks. Longshore drift still molds the shore, but primarily outside the influence of the strong tidal flows. When tidal fluctuations are

moderate or small, a longshore current system extends its influence to include the areas around tidal inlets. This has been particularly well illustrated on the Texas and northern Mexico coasts.

Several tidal inlets breach the barrier islands off Laguna Madre de Tamaulipas (Fig. 6-1), but little Gulf water enters the lagoons. Tidal channels are shallow here, in part due to the small tidal amplitude, and in part due to paucity of freshwater discharge from adjacent arid lands into the Laguna. Without sufficient water movement into or out of the channels, longshore currents deposit sand within them, occluding and fragmenting the inlets into numerous, small channels. Hurricanes flush the channels by redistributing the occluding sand onto large washover fans on either side of the lagoon side of the inlet (Yanez & Schlaepfer, 1968). The lack of tidal exchange, combined with an arid climate where evaporation far exceeds precipitation, has made Laguna Madre de Tamaulipas a shallow, shrinking, brine-filled hypersaline basin (Chapter 8).

Tidal currents are similarly weak along much of the Texas shore, but increasing freshwater discharge and favorable positions with respect to prevailing winds have made the relationship between longshore drift and tidal currents more complex. Most of the Texas bays are able to support at least one major, permanent tidal inlet (Brown *et al.*, 1980). Winter winds significantly influence the flow of waters through tidal inlets in the northern Gulf of Mexico. From Galveston to Corpus Christi, strong northerly winter gusts create waves in the bays which erode the inner shores of barrier islands. These winds also help move intracoastal waters out of the tidal inlets and into the Gulf. The combined flow of wind-generated currents and an ebbing tide scours the channel bottoms, flushing them free of any accumulated debris or sediment, especially that deposited by longshore drift. The winter winds, facilitated by river discharge in some basins (e.g., Galveston, San Antonio and Corpus Christi bays), help to keep tidal channels open in the face of limited tidal exchange.

It is no accident that several Texas tidal inlets are oriented in a roughly north-to-south direction. Price (1952) maintains that the stable orientation of a tidal inlet on the upper Texas coast is NNE/SSW. In that position, winter wind-generated currents can flow with the least resistance, provide the greatest scouring effect, and hence render the tidal inlet with the least chance of closure by longshore drift. Most of the passes between the northern barrier islands fail to achieve the ideal orientation exactly, for there are other factors which mediate a compromise position. Nevertheless, most of these inlets come close to it.

One might argue that the prevailing southeasterly winds, blowing for longer durations, should have greater influence on the tidal inlets of the northern Texas coast than the short duration winter "northers." If this were true, the passes should be oriented exactly opposite that observed. Apparently, periodic northerly winds creating strong southerly or southwesterly currents are necessary to overcome channel-closing longshore drift, the latter caused in part by the prevailing southeasterly winds. The virtually closed tidal inlets of Laguna Madre de Tamaulipas (Figs. 6-1 and 8-6) suggest that this is the case.

There is one other consequence of winter winds along northwestern Gulf shores. Southerly currents flowing from the intracoastal basins through the tidal channels remove sediments from within the basin, especially just north or northeast of the inner mouth of the channel. Some of this sediment is swept Gulfward, but much of it is deposited within the basin along the northeastern island shore (i.e., the southwestern side of the inner inlet mouth). Several of the barrier islands, including Galveston, Matagorda, and San Jose, are prograding into their respective bays along their northeastern margins. This is one reason why the northeastern ends of these barrier islands are wider than the southwestern portions. Northeastern barrier island bay shores are especially rich in nutrients, permitting development of a diverse tidal marsh community dominated by the cordgrass, *Spartina* (Chapter 7).

In south Texas and northern Mexico, waters move southward within the respective Laguna Madre systems without slamming waves against their barrier island bayshores (Fig. 8-5 C). This may be one reason why Laguna Madre of Texas is not cut by natural tidal passes and why the four inlets of the Laguna Madre de Tamaulipas system, remain essentially blocked by sand except following major storms. The lack of significant river discharge into both Laguna Madre estuaries also contributes to the uninterrupted courses of their respective barrier islands.

Since 1940, there have been several attempts to alter the natural balance of sand and sea by opening manmade channels across barrier islands. Some of these "cuts" have been successful and others have been disasters. All serve to illustrate the interaction between longshore transport and tidal currents.

The attempted construction of Yarborough Pass is a good example of how rapidly channels can be modified by longshore drift. It also represents the human persistence to attempt repeated alteration of a natural system in the face of certain failure. During the 1940s and early 1950s, a strong sportfisheries lobby persuaded governmental agencies to attempt the opening of a channel across Padre Island in the vicinity of Murdock's Landing (Gunter, 1945; Breuer, 1957). During a period of 32 months, from April 1941 to December 1944, the pass was opened four times by dredging. Each time it filled quickly with sand. The slight tidal amplitude, the weak tidal flow, and the lack of significant river discharge into Laguna Madre was insufficient to overcome accumulation of sand within the dredged channel, transported there by longshore currents and drift. The most rapid channel-filling occurred following a final attempt to open the pass in 1952. On February 14, a new 18.5 m wide channel breached Padre Island. Three weeks later it had shrunk

to a width of only 2 m, and by May it had closed again (Breuer, 1957). Today, Yarborough Pass is marked by only a weathering signpost among low dunes on Padre Island National Seashore. There is no trace of a channel.

Despite the failure of Yarborough Pass, several subsequent channels have been cut across Texas barrier islands. Two of these were successful, one marks limited success, and the last is an outright failure. The successful channels show us that closure of man-made inlets by longshore drift is not always assured along the Texas coast, but they also indicate that man-made channels on this coast are not enjoyed without at least some sand accumulation and the need for dredging maintenance.

Mansfield Cut, a jetty-reinforced channel many kilometers south of the location of Yarborough Pass, has breached Padre Island since 1962, permitting ships to reach Port Mansfield, a small anchorage on the mainland shore of Laguna Madre. The beach north of Mansfield Cut on the Padre Island Gulf shore is receding behind the north jetty, whereas the southern beach is accumulating a considerable amount of sand along the southern jetty wall. Similar processes occur along the Gulf margin of Matagorda Ship Channel across Matagorda Island. This channel was opened in 1963 near Pass Cavallo, a natural tidal inlet on the central Texas coast. Accretion and loss of Gulf beach are the reverse of that seen at Mansfield Cut, reflecting the northeast to southwest longshore drift of the northern coast.

Rollover Fish Pass is a narrow, short man-made channel across Bolivar Peninsula constructed on the northern Texas shore in 1955. Sand, which normally moves westward to the tip of Bolivar Peninsula, is shunted through this pass and deposited within Rollover Bay. The tidal flow is augmented by the strong longshore drift and the short channel to insure that the sand moves through the channel and is not deposited within it.

Fish Pass (sometimes called Corpus Christi Water Exchange Pass), located at the junction between Mustang and Padre Islands, and opening into Corpus Christi Bay, has not fared so well. Prior to the enlargement and deepening of Aransas Pass and the construction of the Corpus Christi ship channel, Mustang and Padre Islands were separated by Corpus Christi Pass (= Packery Pass), a natural tidal channel. The deeper man-made channels provided an easier path for flow of tidewater into Corpus Christi Bay than through the shallower Corpus Christi Pass. Thus, the latter filled with sand. Today, the junction between Mustang and Padre Islands is marked only by a group of hurricane surge channels which open following major storms, but fill with sands rapidly afterwards, creating low barren flats. Fish Pass was dredged across one of these flats in 1972. Each wall of the pass was reinforced by enormous granite blocks, which also extended a short distance into the sea on both sides of the channel. The granite jetties were to provide a firm margin where water could flow and retard the accumulation of sand.

Since it opened, Fish Pass has slowly but steadily filled with more sand than water. Today, one must crawl over the granite boulders to walk on the dry sand banks within the pass. Water trickles through, but it is an easy task to find a suitable spot to wade across the channel. One can only ponder what future generations will think about ours, spending much money and energy to place these granite boulders on barrier island shores, only for them cover with sand. The lesson, of course, is clear. Tidal flux alone, in the absence of assistance by winter winds, currents, river discharge, elongate jetties extending far into the Gulf, or deep channels reaching far into the bay, is, in some areas, insufficient to maintain open channels from the Gulf to intracoastal waters.

The tidewater which flows through inlets exerts minimal influence upon bayshores. It is neither that little water flows through the passes, nor does it move sluggishly. Indeed, water rushes into and out of the larger inlets at noticeably high velocities. In comparison to the volume of water in the estuaries, the amount which is exchanged on one tidal cycle is relatively small. Thus, the intracoastal tides (those which occur behind barrier islands, spits or peninsulas) are of considerably less amplitude than the oceanic tides of the Gulf of Mexico. They also peak or ebb at different times (Smith, 1974).

The Influence of Freshwater

When rain falls upon the sea surface its effects are minimal, usually causing little more than temporary surface dilution. Similarly, direct rainfall on most rocky shores (limestone shores excepted) has only short-term effects. Run-off is rapid and surface dilution is usually lost in the well-mixed waters of wave-dominated shores. It is on soft shores that the impact of freshwater is most keenly felt. This provides a perpetual challenge to the ecologist to discriminate between the complementary effects of shelter from wave action, sediment composition and reduced salinities as each acts upon resident intertidal communities.

Estuarine habitats are fundamentally different from those of the hard and soft shores of open coasts. Freshwater dilution, high turbidity, elevated nutrient loadings, reduced oxygen levels, and temperature fluctuations of greater amplitude than is typical at sea contribute to this difference. Soft shores of bays range from medium-sized, moderately sorted particles near tidal inlets to fine, poorly sorted silts near river mouths, the latter heavily loaded with nutrients and distinctly oxygen deficient. The smaller-grained, compacted sediments of estuaries seem more stable than those of exposed sandy beaches, but this is largely the result of the protection they receive from high waves or strong currents. Fluctuating extremes of water quality overshadow the relative stability of the substratum to become the primary constraint upon the biota living here.

Freshwater dilution at river mouths or tidal inlets has an obvious impact upon the sea. The degree of sa-linity reduction fluctuates as river discharge varies, often as a consequence of the season. The local biota must tolerate or adapt to these changes. Few stenohaline organisms, either truly marine or truly freshwater, occur in estuaries. The majority are euryhaline, adapted to survive a broad range of salinity. We will describe such habitats and their biota in Chapters 7, 8 and 9.

Tropical Storms and Hurricanes

Hurricanes are massive storms born in tropical seas. Their landfall brings changes to the coastal zone which persist months, years or decades. On the geological time scale, hurricanes are important, frequent events influencing the geologic history and development of the Gulf of Mexico coastline, and especially the barrier islands. So often we measure the catastrophic consequences of hurricanes, and rightly so, for they can be immensely destructive agents. But there are also constructive attributes of these storms. Without them, our coastline would be vastly different.

In other parts of the world, large tropical storms are variously known as cyclones, typhoons, or by other names. "Hurricane" is a word of the New World, originating with the original inhabitants of the Caribbean region. The Mayans spoke of Hunraken as their storm god. The Taino, an extinct Carib tribe of the Bahamas and Hispaniola, referred to the devastating storms that struck their shores from the sea as "huracan." Other Caribs, speaking in different dialects called these storms "aracan," "urican" and "huiranvucan" (Dunn & Miller, 1964). Early Spanish explorers, plagued by these storms during their voyages in the New World, quickly adopted the Carib term. Columbus experienced at least three hurricanes during his four voyages: in August, 1494, during the fall of 1495, and early July, 1502. Numerous shipwrecks now at the bottom of Gulf and Caribbean waters testify to the frequency of the storms at least during the last 500 years.

In an average year the tropical western Atlantic will spawn five hurricanes plus another half dozen tropical storms. From 1900 to 1980, a total of 31 hurricanes and about two dozen tropical storms have struck the Texas coast, and an additional 40 hurricanes and about 50 tropical storms have come ashore along the Gulf coast of Mexico. The region can expect an average of one hurricane every three years, or an annual frequency of between 0.3 and 0.4 (Fig. 2-10 A) and a mean frequency for all tropical disturbances of a little more than one every two years (0.67/yr).

The tropical cyclonic disturbances, of which hurricanes are the most destructive type, are likely to affect the Gulf coast any time from June through November. They are most common in September, with the month of August running a close second. Occasionally, two or more major storms strike the coast in a single year, and several times storms have crossed Gulf shores in consecutive years. Following Hurricane Fern in 1971, the Texas coast was without a major storm until 1980, when two hurricanes, Allen and Danielle, came

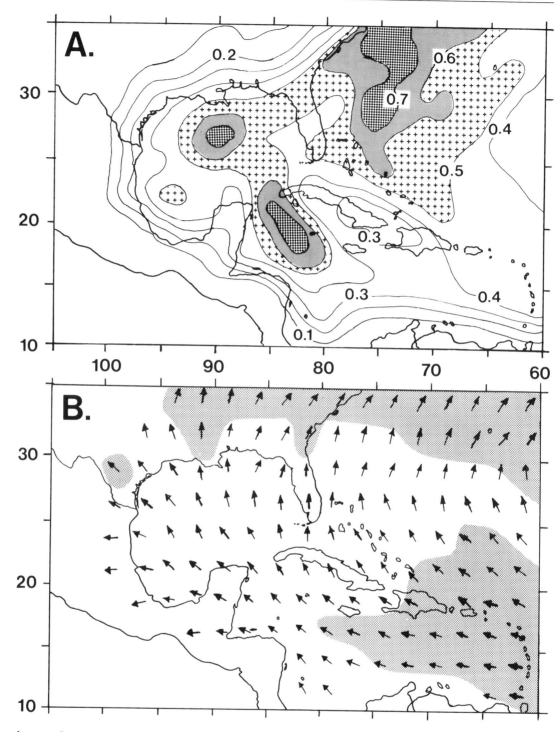

2-10. Hurricanes and tropical storms.

A. The annual frequency of tropical storms and hurricanes (sustained winds > 34 knots) in the northwestern Atlantic. Isometric lines represent the mean annual frequency of tropical storms in 0.1 year intervals. Areas crossed most frequently by storms are indicated by shading as follows:

┼┼┼┼┼   0.5 to 0.59 storms per year

▒▒▒▒   0.6 to 0.69 storms per year

▓▓▓▓   0.7 to 0.79 storms per year

Note the distinctive "hurricane alley" between Cuba and Central America.

B. Mean direction vectors of tropical storms and hurricanes in the northwestern Atlantic. Vectors are averaged over 2 1/2 degree latitude-longitude grids. Shaded areas indicate regions where the storms move with a mean speed of 10 knots/hr or greater; in the unshaded areas, storms move with a mean speed of between 5 to 10 knots/hr. (Both figures modified from Neumann & Pryslak, 1981.)

ashore. This was the longest period that the Texas coast was without a hurricane since records began in 1871. Yet, Mexico experienced 4 hurricanes during this period and Texas was landfall for 5 tropical storms, indicating the region retained the potential to develop and/or receive damaging storms. Storms and hurricanes tend to move from east to west across the western Gulf and Caribbean region (Fig. 2-10 B), but the paths of individual systems can be very erratic.

The Yucatan Peninsula is more susceptible to tropical storms and hurricanes than any other land mass within the region. Tropical storms spawned in the central Caribbean often come ashore over Yucatan before they generate hurricane-force winds. Many retain sufficient energy while crossing Yucatan to develop into hurricanes after they emerge in the Gulf of Mexico. Some kind of tropical disturbance crosses the Yucatan Peninsula almost every year (the seven years from 1957 to 1963 was the longest period within recent history that Yucatan was not affected by a tropical storm or hurricane).

Any specific point on the Gulf coast has a relatively low probability of being the landfall for the eye of the storm. Since 1900, four hurricanes have made landfall in the Freeport/Port O'Connor area, and three each near Port Arthur, Galveston, Corpus Christi, and Brownsville. The remaining storms of this century reaching Texas have come ashore at various points between. In addition to Yucatan, the Veracruz region of Mexico also seems to receive a disproportionately high number of hurricanes. Yet, hurricanes are large storms which cover hundreds of square miles. It is not unusual for all of the Texas coast or much of the Mexican coast to be affected in some way by a hurricane coming ashore. Hayes (1967) claims that as many as half of the major storms striking Texas severely affect the entire coastline.

Northern hemisphere hurricanes arise from steady, gentle easterly tradewinds blowing across a warm tropical sea, usually between latitudes 5 and 15°. Several essential steps must occur in sequence before a hurricane can form. The process begins with a warm sea. Solar radiation heats the lower levels of the atmosphere, which, in turn, transfers heat to the surface of the sea. At the lower latitudes, late summer sea surface temperatures usually exceed 27°C (80°F). There is sufficient energy not only to warm the sea, but also to evaporate massive quantities of water into the atmosphere. Since heated air rises, the warm air near sea level lofts vast quantities of water vapor upwards into higher levels of the atmosphere. As it rises, the air cools. Cool air has less capacity to hold water vapor than warm air, so excess moisture is squeezed out as the air mass climbs higher and higher. The water first appears in the atmosphere as clouds, and, with continued cooling, sufficient moisture is released to produce rain. Warm air masses near sea level push intermediate air masses even higher, squeezing even more water from the now cool air. Eventually, all water that can be removed from the air mass condenses as clouds or

raindrops. By now, the air is cold, dense and heavy. It begins to sink, but is pushed away from the warm air convection pump, to settle somewhere along the sides of the upward-moving system. This process of rising warm air masses producing precipitation is a normal, essential element of the earth's hydrologic cycle. Alone, it is insufficient to produce a hurricane, but is an essential initial ingredient.

In the tropics, warm water-laden air masses form cell-like pockets called convergences. A convergence is associated with ascending air, cloudiness, and precipitation. Adjacent convergences are separated by a divergence, or region of high pressure and clear weather. A divergence is produced in part by the displaced cold dense air moving away from the upper layers of a convergence. In the tropical Atlantic and Caribbean, convergences and divergences sweep east to west in alternating bands or waves, driven by the constant tradewinds. As long as they blow undisturbed across the sea, little but local thundershowers or minor squalls will develop, separated by periods of clear sunny weather. The movement of convergences in tropical seas is another climatic feature needed for the creation of a hurricane, but it is still not enough to start the motor of the cyclonic storm. Another ingredient is still required.

A convergence will produce a lowered air pressure at the earth's surface. This is caused by the movement of air masses up and out of the area by convection. Air surrounding the convergence will be drawn inwards to replace the air moving up and out at its center. Inrushing air does not move directly toward the center, but moves in an arc, imparting a rotational effect upon the system. The rotating movement is caused by the Coriolis effect (the influence of the rotating earth upon objects such as air masses which have low frictional contact with Terra Firma) and pressure differences between different air masses. Winds blow counterclockwise around northern hemisphere convergences. With this rotational motion, most of the ingredients are now present to form a hurricane. One final step is necessary, however, to rev the atmospheric engine.

If more air enters the lower levels of the convergence than can exit at higher altitudes, the system will simply die. In this situation, the convection flow is interrupted by high pressure at the earth's surface. On the other hand, if air at the upper levels can be transported rapidly away from the convergence, it will intensify. This is precisely what must occur for a hurricane to develop. A low-level easterly convergence must arrive at the same place and time as an upper level disturbance that will rapidly dissipate the upper level air mass. Once this occurs, and as long as the temperature of the lower level air mass within the convergence remains higher than that of the air surrounding it, the convection flow will continue and even accelerate. A hurricane is born when surface winds, rotating about a convergence center, exceed 117 km/hr (74 mph).

A fully developed hurricane is a massive storm

many kilometers wide with counterclockwise winds blowing about a center or eye. The eye, varying from 20 to 80 km across, is an area of relative calm. It is surrounded by walls of rotating clouds and intensive rainfall which rise to an altitude of almost 13,000 m. Atlantic hurricanes formed in the tradewind belt tend to move northwesterly, pushed initially by the prevailing winds (Fig. 2-10 B). Eventually, they move out of the direct tradewind influence and take a more northerly direction. Hurricanes are notorious for their erratic movements. Newly formed hurricanes usually move across the sea at speeds of 15 to 20 km/hr, but as intensity increases, they may progress with a forward motion of as much as 80 to 90 km/hr.

The average life of an Atlantic hurricane is nine days. A hurricane can exist only so long as there is sufficient energy to drive its atmospheric engine, derived primarily from latent heat of vaporization stored when water is converted to vapor at the air-sea interface. When the storm passes over land or reaches a latitude over the sea where water temperatures reduce sufficient levels of vaporization, it loses energy and eventually dies.

The destruction of life and property by hurricanes crossing shores is well known (Tannehill, 1956; Dunn & Miller, 1964; Bomer, 1983). We are most concerned here, however, with the ecological effects of hurricanes upon Gulf shores, and in this respect, there are three phenomena associated with these storms which significantly influence shores and the biota which live upon them. They are storm surges, waves, and currents.

The storm surge, or what is sometimes called the storm tide, is often responsible for the greatest loss of life and property when a hurricane strikes a shore. Strictly speaking, it is not a tide. It is generated by and precedes the arrival of the eye of the hurricane on shore. A storm surge is a rapid rise in water level produced by onshore hurricane winds and depressed barometric pressures. Wind velocities of hurricane force can pile considerable quantities of water against a shore. The low barometric pressure near the center of the storm enhances the effect, literally causing a rise in water level (Dunn & Miller, 1964). These forces interact with several other factors, including shoreline configuration, the shape and slope of the adjacent continental shelf, the length of the shoreline (insular or continental), and the angle of approach, to determine the resultant storm surge. One of the greatest ever recorded occurred at the mouth of the Hooghly River near Calcutta, India in 1737. An estimated 300,000 people lost their lives as water rose over 12 m above sea level. The 1900 Galveston hurricane, notable as the storm responsible for the greatest loss of life in the United States, was accompanied by a storm surge estimated at 4.5 m above sea level. Hurricane Camille, which struck the Mississippi and Louisiana coasts in 1969 with 320 km/hr (200 mph) winds, was accompanied by a surge which reached a little more than 6 m above sea level. The average storm surge for 30 hurri-

canes crossing Gulf of Mexico shores from 1893 to 1950 was 2.6 m above mean sea level (Connor *et al.*, 1957).

Just as hurricane-force winds can pile water against a shore, the rotating system can also move it offshore, especially if the shore lies to the right of the approaching eye of the storm. A hurricane reaching shore between Mobile, Alabama and Pensacola, Florida in 1926 caused sea level to drop almost 3 m in Mobile Bay while it rose about 2 m against the shore near Pensacola (Dunn & Miller, 1964). Hurricane Gloria was reported to blow water out of several shallow bays in the Carolinas as it grazed the eastern seaboard in 1985.

The winds that produce the storm surge also produce enormous waves which contribute to the destruction of a shore. There is no more dramatic example of the transformation of potential to kinetic energy than hurricane-generated waves exploding upon a shore. One 4 m breaker thrusts several tons of water into the air, to be driven shoreward with winds in excess of 117 km/hr. In only a few hours, this kind of pounding can undermine buildings and bridges, flatten 12 m high dunes, and displace sandy foreshores dozens of meters inland. The storm surge can transport damaging breakers far inland, exposing even more land area to erosion. On the other hand, shores faced by reefs, offshore bars, or even a gently sloping subtidal topography receive some protection from wave damage. The shallow offshore waters cause waves to break before they can reach shore. In this instance, subtidal offshore habitats experience extensive damage.

The effects of hurricane-produced currents on a shore are poorly known, due to the extreme difficulty of taking measurements, but one remarkable record exists (Murray, 1970). One week before hurricane Camille came ashore along the central Gulf coast, an instrument measuring current direction and speed was placed 360 m offshore in 6.3 m of water near the Florida/Alabama border. This site was about 160 km east of the landfall of the hurricane eye, but even here there were sustained winds of 60 km/hr, and occasional gusts up to 114 km/hr. The current direction meter operated 36 hours during the storm, and the current speed meter operated 29 hours before jamming. Despite only a partial record, the data obtained proved interesting. Before the arrival of the storm, longshore currents made an unexpected offshore extension, although they continued to flow westerly parallel to the shore. During the storm, bottom currents rotated from alongshore parallel to the wind to a southerly seaward direction moving against the wind (which had also shifted direction). Current speeds during this time ranged up to 160 cm/sec.

There is also some indirect evidence of the influence of currents during hurricanes. Currents created during a 1915 hurricane on the Texas coast carried a 15 ton buoy almost 16 km westward of its originally anchored position. Timbers and pilings from a fishing pier on northern Padre Island were moved many miles southward along the beach during hurricane Carla in 1961.

Carla was the largest and one of the most destructive storms to strike the Gulf coast of the United States. It made landfall near Port O'Connor on September 11, with sustained winds in excess of 230 km/hr. Hurricane-force winds extended from near the mouth of the Rio Grande to the Louisiana border and beyond. Carla was responsible for the greatest storm surge measured on the Texas coast, when water rose about 6 m above sea level at Port Lavaca. Hayes (1967) presents a comprehensive analysis of the geological and biological changes that this and a subsequent smaller storm, hurricane Cindy in 1963, produced on the central Texas barrier islands. Most of the following information is from this report.

The passage of a large storm across a barrier island modifies the typical shore morphology and creates what has been called a hurricane beach. Actually, the shore is differentiated into three zones: (1), a back beach, where foredunes are eroded away by storm waves, (2), the hurricane beach, which was the swash zone during the passage of the hurricane, and (3), a forebeach, where normal beach deposits accumulate following the storm (Fig. 2-11 A).

The back beach is formed during the storm by removal of 50 to 100 m of pre-hurricane foredune ridges (Fig. 2-11 B). The landward margin of the back beach is marked by dune remnants which face the shore with 3 to 5 m high cliffs. The back beach formed after Carla's passage averaged about 35 m in width, but was considerably wider in the vicinity of washovers (see below).

Sometimes the foredunes are completely washed away by the storm and flood waters deposit a bar on top of the foredune field (Fig. 2-11 C). After the storm the exposed bar becomes a hurricane beach, which is

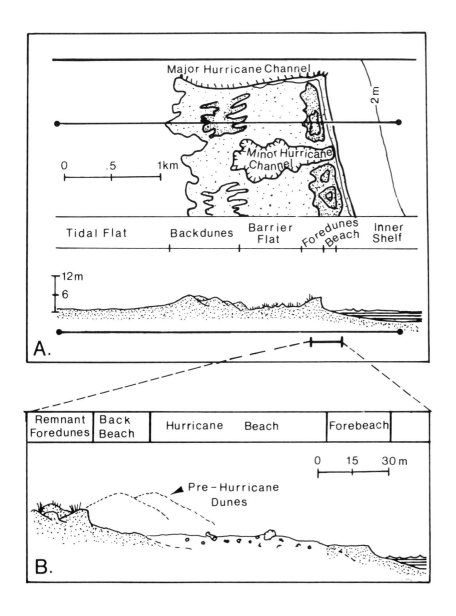

a low, rounded mound, the only topographic high on this portion of the island. Inland of the beach ridge and within the pre-hurricane barrier flat, a hurricane washover runway may form during the storm, presumably as a trough in front of the beach ridge bar (Fig. 2-11 C). Hurricane washover runways are found only in association with a hurricane beach ridge.

If the dunes are not completely removed but only breached during the storm, a hurricane channel is formed. A major hurricane channel crosses the island below mean sea level, permitting water exchange between open Gulf and bay or lagoon waters for several weeks following the storm. Major hurricane channels eventually close, but leave a persistent depression through the foredune ridge which can be reopened easily during a subsequent storm. Minor hurricane channels are narrow breaches of the dunes not cut below sea level, easily filled by wind-blown sand and

thus short-lived. Both major and minor hurricane channels terminate on the bay side of the barrier island in small water-filled embayments or hurricane notches flanked by washover fans (see below). A notch may extend through backdunes to the barrier flat, persisting for several years before being filled by sediments. Shortly after formation of the notch, a subtidal sill may form at the junction with the lagoon or bay, restricting water exchange. During the summer, water temperatures in the notch rise well above those of the adjacent lagoon or bay, and salinity rises markedly.

The hurricane beach is a broad flat plain lying seaward of the eroded foredunes and averaging about 60 m in width (Fig. 2-11 B). It is covered with a distinctive pavement of coarse particles, including large shells and shell fragments, sandstone fragments, caliche blocks, Pleistocene fossils, and a variety of invertebrate remains. Most of this material is from offshore deposits

2-11. Barrier islands and tropical storms (after Hayes, 1967).

A. Storm-imposed features of a barrier island. The lower profile is taken from the transect line indicated on the upper portion of the figure.

B. The hurricane beach.

C. Additional features of hurricane effects on a barrier island.

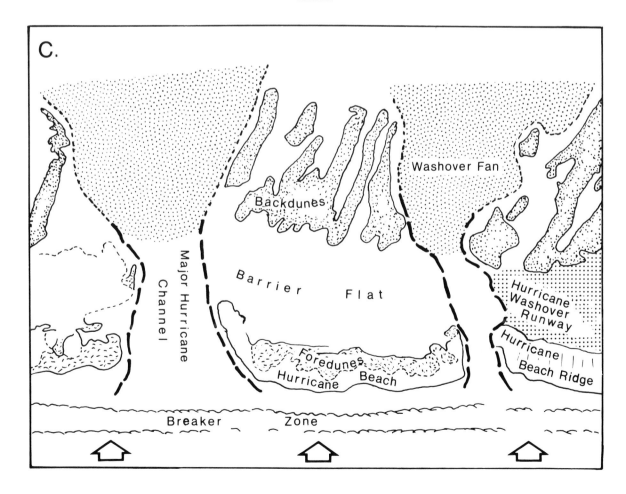

moved shoreward on the storm-surge flood, suggesting that shallow offshore banks are subjected to significant erosion during the storm. Members of several ecological communities come to rest upon the hurricane beach. For example, foreshore species (*Donax*), offshore sand species (*Dinocardium, Mercenaria, Dosina,* and *Spisula*), calcareous bank species (*Arca transversa, Echinochama*), and intermediate shelf species (*Muricanthus fulvescens, Strombus alatus*) may be found together in the drift of the hurricane beach. None are alive, of course, but this modern storm-sorted assemblage suggests that similar mixing also must have occurred in fossil storm deposits.

Large fragments of shell and other debris litter the hurricane beach for some time following the storm. Their presence is emphasized as finer sand particles are removed by wind and deposited in the dune fields. Hayes (1967) observed new active foredunes forming on the lee side of the hurricane beach within 8 months of the passage of the storm.

The forebeach is a post-hurricane feature which begins to form immediately following the passage of the storm. It reflects the return to normalcy with respect to wave activity and longshore transport. Hayes (1967) described the forebeach as consisting of "normal beach sediments" which accumulate from longshore deposition, providing the sand which will restore the remainder of the beach to its former morphology. The forebeach averages about 25 m in width.

The bay or lagoon-facing shore of the barrier island can also be distinctly modified with the passage of a hurricane, and here, perhaps more than any other part of the island, the long term effects of successive hurricanes are most evident. Under normal conditions the interior shore is well protected from winds, waves, and strong currents. A broad tidal flat typically develops, especially on the southern barrier islands. The flat is submerged only on the highest tides, but with each tidal episode thin layers of fine-grained detrital silts accumulate. These are bound in a laminated mat by a variety of blue-green algae (see Chapter 7). With the passage of a hurricane, the tidal flat may receive several centimeters of sand atop the typical algal mat. In areas of major hurricane channels, sediment accumulation is even more dramatic, with the creation of large hurricane washover fans hundreds of meters in diameter. Sediment deposited in washover fans is not easily dissipated. In fact, washover fans significantly contribute to the total sediment filling bays and lagoons behind the Gulf barrier islands. They are, for example, among the primary sediment sources of the Laguna Madres of Texas and Mexico. If the fan lies adjacent to a permanent channel between barrier islands, tidal currents assist in additional deposition long after the storm, as is the case along Boca de Sandoval and Boca de Jesus Maria, entering Laguna Madre de Tamaulipas. Both of these inlets were greatly enlarged in 1962 during the passage of hurricane Carla. By the following year, longshore currents had all but closed the inlets again, but not until tidal currents had passed huge quantities of sand onto the washover fans along the lagoon side of the inlets (Yanez & Schlaepfer, 1968). Similarly, Andrews (1970) describes such a system on San Jose (St. Joseph) Island, Texas, which has been accumulating sand for at least 1700 years.

TOWARD GULF SHORES

We have just considered several of the more important physical attributes that act upon coastlines to create a wealth of shore types and biological habitats. The interacting forces of geology, tides, weather, wave strength and direction, current speed and direction, and freshwater dilution all contribute to produce a specific environment. Other factors such as beach aspect, insolation, light, sand mineralogy or rates of terrigenous input also contribute to this environment, as do the multifarious ways that the biota can itself influence the shore. We will consider many of these biotic influences as we encounter the communities or organisms where they become important.

No two shores are ever exactly the same. They vary as the myriad factors that interact to form them vary. Two sides of a jetty will be ecologically distinct as will be two stretches of superficially similar sand. In fact, the physical factors acting upon shores but meters apart could affect each of them in significantly different ways, thereby altering the communities resident upon them. Faced with a potential for incredible variation, how is it possible to even contemplate a description of the shores of an area the size of the Gulf of Mexico, when a volume of equal proportions could be devoted to only one of its habitats? In order to appreciate the detail, we must first contemplate larger dimensions to gain the necessary perspective.

In the pages to follow, we arrange Gulf shores into a number of broad categories. There is the obvious distinction between hard and soft shores, the environments respectively dominated by erosion and deposition. Each of these, in turn, can be subdivided into exposed or protected categories, and then further characterized with respect to local geology or ecology. As we delve deeper into the attributes of these shores and their biota, it will lead us back to a broader appreciation of the total system, and we will have come full circle in the process of understanding.

Creeping railroad vines, *Ipomoea pes-caprae*, traverse seaward dune flanks near South Padre Island, Texas, and sea oats, *Uniola paniculata*, cap the dune crests.

Sea grapes, *Coccoloba uvifera*, with distinctive large oval leaves and green grape-like fruits, are trees which often fringe the landward margins of tropical sandy Gulf shores.

The ghost crab, *Ocypode quadrata,* is a ubiquitous denizen of sandy beaches throughout western Atlantic shores.

Shell deposits from the beach at Big Shell, central Padre Island.

Left: Sea oats, *Uniola paniculata,* characterize barrier island dunes from Virginia to Mexico. The inflorescence of spike-lets rises above leafy blades in mid-summer and persists conspicuously throughout the fall.

Spartina marshlands from the observation tower at Aransas
National Wildlife Refuge, Texas.

Young black mangroves (*Avicennia germinans*) rise above
the floor of the hypersaline lagoon near Cicxulub, Yucatan,
Mexico, surrounded by aerial roots or pneumatophores. Mangrove hummocks in the background present surprising diversity amid apparent hypersaline desolation.

The glasswort, *Salicornia bigelovii*, from the shore of
Laguna Madre, Texas, in late summer.

The mud banks at Sargent Beach, Texas.

Intertidal fauna clinging to a red granite boulder from the Port Aransas, Texas, jetty, including the periwinkle snail, *Nodilittorina lineolata,* the barnacle *Chthamalus fragilis,* and the false limpet *Siphonaria pectinata.*

Right: The Brazos-Santiago jetty at South Padre Island, Texas, in early spring.

Three basic stages of reef digenesis: bioherm formation by
the living coral (left center), death of the reef-formers (lower
right), and recolonization of the reef limestone by other species (the golden sponge in the center), some of which markedly alter the original reef fabric.

PART TWO Hard Shores

3. Hard Shores of the Northwestern Gulf

INTRODUCTION

Until inlet-protecting jetties and breakwater groins were constructed about 100 years ago, a hard shore biota was effectively absent along the northwestern Gulf of Mexico, for there are very few natural hard shores in this region. Most bedrock lies buried deeply under thick blankets of muds or sands. The bays provide modest clumps of intertidal oysters which harbor a small group of plants and animals adapted for life among shells. The oyster reef, however, is mostly a subtidal community of the estuarine bayfloor (Chapter 6). Its biota differs considerably from that found on exposed rocky headlands facing an open sea. The latter was and is absent along more than 1000 km of Gulf of Mexico shoreline from the Mississippi River delta to south of Tampico.

Barrier islands separate most mainland shores of the northwestern Gulf of Mexico from the open sea. Harbors for immigration or commerce were established, of necessity, on mainland sites behind the barrier islands or along river channels probing the heartland. Early seafarers, their cargo and passengers faced substantial risk with each passage through treacherous tidal inlets between barrier islands. Rapidly changing currents and shifting sand bars within each inlet claimed many ships and lives during the nineteenth century. Modern marine commerce demanded that the unpredictable passages be deepened and stabilized. About 100 years ago, the major inlets were dredged to safely navigable depths and flanked by rock jetties, protecting the new channels from sedimentation. Today, the jetties are still in place, extending a kilometer or more seaward of the natural mouth of each inlet. They serve as breakwaters or barriers against longshore sedimentation within the dredged channels.

Several tidal inlets between Texas barrier islands are protected by jetties, including those at Sabine, Bolivar, Aransas, and Brazos Santiago Passes. The Freeport Ship Channel, Matagorda Ship Channel, the Velasco Channel at the mouth of the Brazos River and Mansfield Cut are also protected by jetties. Smaller rock jetties such as at Fish Pass between Padre and Mustang Islands or breakwater groins on Galveston and other islands also provide an artificial hard substratum along the outer Gulf shore. At least as many jetties occur along the Mexico Gulf shore. From La Pesca along the northern coast to Progreso in Yucatan, most of the shipping and fishing ports have some form of jetty or rock breakwater protecting channels leading to protected harbors. The man-made jetties, groins and breakwaters provide an extensive and hitherto unavailable habitat for a characteristic assemblage of intertidal plants and animals.

Whitten *et al.* (1950) described physical features common to the Texas jetties. This information, with modifications for local conditions (e.g., Texas jetties consist mainly of granite rock whereas Yucatan jetties consist of massive limestone boulders), serves as an example for all man-made hard shores within the region. Each protected tidal inlet between Texas barrier islands is flanked by two parallel rock jetties lying on either side of a dredged tidal channel and usually extending up to 2 km into the Gulf of Mexico. The channels vary in width from 800 m to almost 2 km.

A Texas jetty is roughly triangular in cross section, having a base width of about 50 m and a crest width of about 4 m. Small granite rocks weighing 15 to 200 pounds form the base of the jetty. Core blocks weighing up to 3 tons cover this base. Huge granite boulders cut from central Texas quarries and weighing from 6 to 10 tons comprise most of the jetty crest. Massive blocks of limestone and/or sandstone also have been used as secondary fill on some jetties. The largest blocks on the jetty crest fit loosely together. Gaping crevices between them provide refuge for a variety of intertidal life. Several years ago the caps of several of the jetties were covered with concrete or asphalt pavement to facilitate public access, but time and storm waves have taken their tolls. The pavement has suffered severe erosion on most of the jetties, leaving large gaps between granite blocks.

BIOTIC ZONATION ON THE TEXAS JETTIES

That a rocky shore community occurs at all on the Texas jetties and groins is testimony to the effectiveness of larval dispersal by oceanic currents, the adaptability of some oyster reef biota to occupy a more exposed, higher salinity environment and the propensity of some tropical species to occupy artificial substrata. Perhaps because the jetties and groins are recently colonized, perhaps because of the limited tidal range in the Gulf of Mexico, perhaps because the region is transitional between temperate and tropical

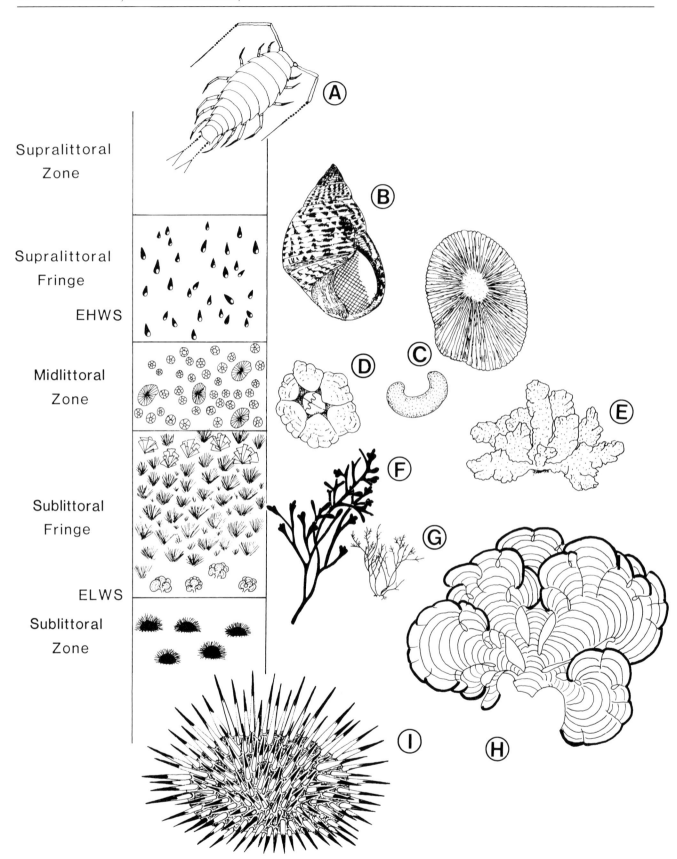

Supralittoral
Zone

Supralittoral
Fringe

EHWS

Midlittoral
Zone

Sublittoral
Fringe

ELWS

Sublittoral
Zone

realms, and perhaps because of all these and several other reasons, the hard shore community of the Texas jetties is one of the simplest anywhere in the world. It is an ideal community to commence studies of the shore environment.

Biotic zonation on Texas jetties and groins approximates the Stephensonian tripartite pattern (Fig. 3-1). Under ideal conditions three primary units can be distinguished: (1) a supralittoral fringe characterized by littorines (or, more accurately for the Texas coast, a single littorine species), (2) a midlittoral barnacle zone, and (3) a sublittoral fringe and zone characterized by several species of macroscopic and epiphytic algae. On several Texas jetties, the littorine and barnacle zones sometimes merge (see below). In addition to the primary zoning species, a number of others (subordinate biota) occur on the rocks, including errant and attached forms and a number of pelagic species which sometimes wash ashore (Fig. 3-2). This community gradually changes in species composition from the northern to the southern jetties, largely because of the temperate to tropical transition, culminating in a wholly tropical biota on the jetties of Mexico. A striking seasonal succession of jetty flora occurs on the northern Gulf jetties, with temperate forms dominating in the winter and tropical species prevalent in the summer. Each of these aspects of the Texas jetty biota will be described more fully below. First, however, we note some environmental gradients which affect these shores and distinctly influence the distribution of the life upon them.

ENVIRONMENTAL GRADIENTS AND TEXAS JETTIES

Wave exposure is an important factor influencing the distribution of intertidal biota on a hard shore (Lewis, 1964; Newell, 1979). Patterns of intertidal zonation are more obscure when wave exposure is reduced or absent. When there is also a limited tidal range, as in the Gulf basin, zones merge and indicator species intermingle. Conversely, biotic zonation becomes more apparent on shores frequently washed by waves, even in the face of limited tidal flux. Wave effects are always most apparent near the seaward end of a jetty. Here, deeper waters permit larger breakers to strike the rocks. Rather than inhibiting colonization, the waves further expand the wetted perimeter, thereby increasing the height of intertidal biotic zones.

Two shores lying only meters apart comprise the central portion of each jetty. One faces a narrow, restricted tidal inlet that promises protection from offshore waves. The other faces the open sea. If this face is leeward of the prevailing wind, it also may provide wave shelter; but if it faces the prevailing winds, it may receive almost as much wave exposure as the end of the jetty. This unusual juxtaposition provides us a rare opportunity to assess the ecological consequences of waves.

Currents and sand scour also influence the distribution of jetty life. Breakwaters extending at right angles to the direction of longshore drift along sandy beaches interrupt normal longshore flow. They also offer surfaces upon which sand can accumulate or abrade. The effects of sand scour are particularly noticeable where the jetty walls meet sandy beaches. Sessile organisms are inhibited from attachment in the nearshore scour zone. Scour is also an important inhibiting factor for subtidal life near the base of the outer portions of a jetty.

Temperature differences usually exist between the Gulf and inlet sides of the jetties, with the temperature variations of the Gulf waters being somewhat less than that experienced in the tidal inlets. Similar temperature variations occur from landward to seaward ends of the jetties, with temperature extremes tending to occur in the shallower waters (Whitten, *et al.*, 1950). On the northern jetties, salinities are consistently higher on Gulf-facing than on inlet-facing sides. Salinity may undergo annual variations by as much as 20 ppt in the inlets of the northern jetties, and may fluctuate quickly during the wet seasons. These fluctuations may be responsible for decreased biotic diversity on the northern jetties. There is less salinity variation between inlet and Gulf waters on the more southerly jetties.

3-2. Jetty biota at Port Aransas, Texas. Southern (left) and northern channel-facing (right) sides of the southern jetty at Port Aransas (map inset) illustrate differential zonation resulting from different degrees of wave exposure. Mean monthly wind vectors are shown at upper left. **A.** Sooty tern, *Sterna fuscata*; **B.** Royal tern, *Sterna maxima*; **C.** Forster's tern, *Sterna forsteri*; **D.** Caspian tern, *Sterna caspia*; **E.** Herring gull, *Larus argentatus*; **F.** Laughing gull, *Larus atricilla*; **G.** Stone crab, *Menippe adina*; **H.** Porcelain crab, *Petrolisthes armatus*; **I.** Hermit crab, *Clibanarius vittatus*; **J.** Tree oyster, *Isognomon bicolor*; **K.** Fragile barnacle, *Chthamalus fragilis*; **L.** Lined periwinkle, *Nodilittorina lineolata*; **M.** Sergeant major, *Abudefduf saxatilis*; **N.** Common octopus, *Octopus vulgaris*; **O.** False limpet, *Siphonaria pectinata*; **P.** Rock snail, *Stramonita haemastoma*; **Q.** Oyster, *Ostrea equestris*; **R.** Striped barnacle, *Balanus amphitrite*; **S.** Ivory barnacle, *Balanus eburneus*; and the anemones, **T.** *Bunodosoma cavernata*; **U.** *Anthopleura krebsi*; **V.** *Aiptasiomorpha texaensis*.

3-1. The basic pattern of zonation on Texas jetties. **A.** Sea roach, *Ligia exotica*; **B.** Lined periwinkle, *Nodilittorina lineolata*; **C.** False limpet, *Siphonaria pectinata* and spawn; **D.** Fragile barnacle, *Chthamalus fragilis*; **E.** Sea lettuce, *Ulva fasciata*; **F.** *Gelidium crinale* (enlarged); **G.** *Gelidium crinale*; **H.** *Padina vickersiae*; **I.** Red sea urchin, *Arbacia punctulata*.

MEAN MONTHLY WIND DIRECTIONS

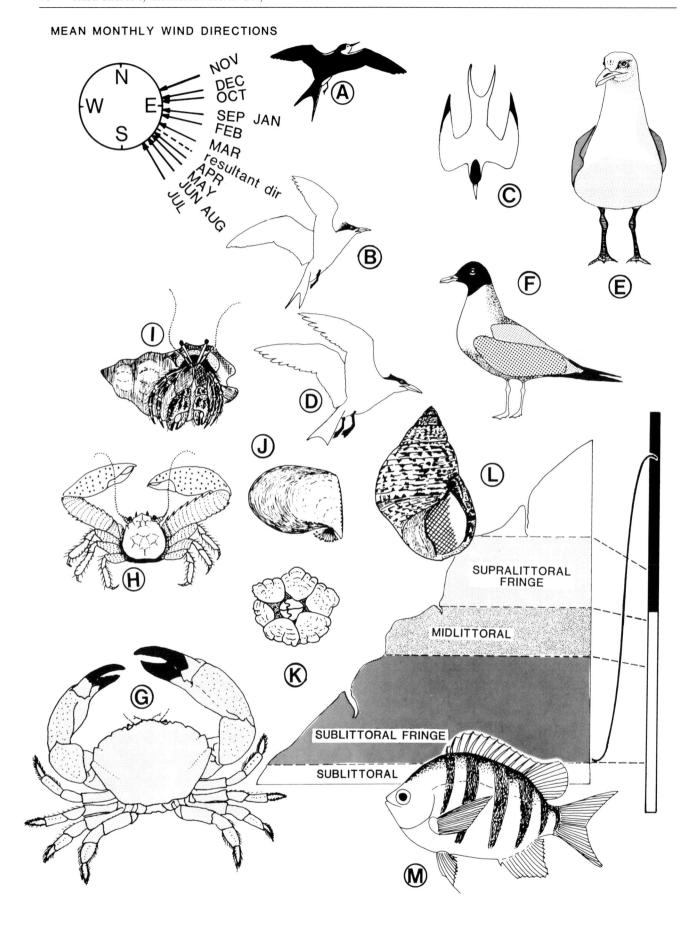

SUPRALITTORAL FRINGE

MIDLITTORAL

SUBLITTORAL FRINGE

SUBLITTORAL

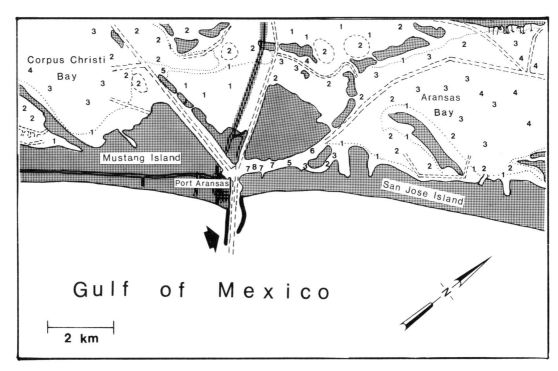

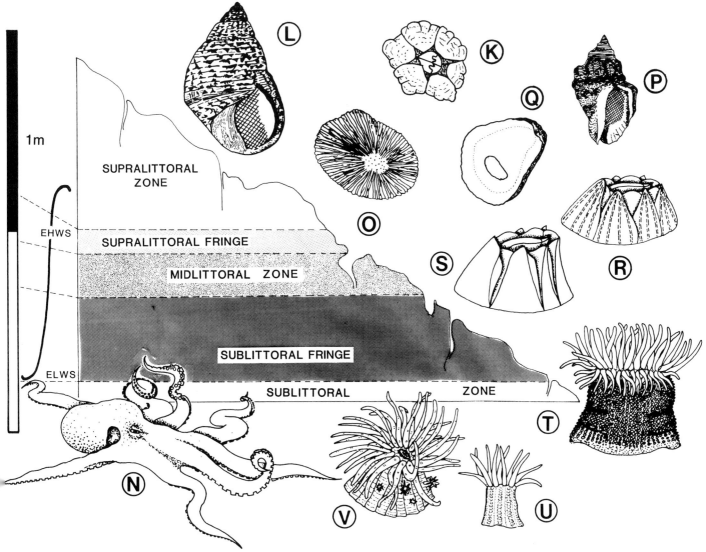

We have selected the Port Aransas jetty to represent many of the physical and biotic features of the artificial outer hard shore (Fig. 3-2). North of this location, jetty biota is either very similar to that at Port Aransas, or diversity decreases. South of Port Aransas we encounter increasingly tropical conditions and a biota in transition (Chapter 4). Also, the windward faces of Texas jetties south of Port Aransas are either more difficult to reach (Port Mansfield) or experience dangerous currents making study hazardous (Brazos-Santiago Pass). Accordingly, they have received less study. The northern Brazos-Santiago jetty at South Padre Island, with its relatively protected inlet-facing shore, is readily accessible. We will rely upon this locality to illustrate some tropical biotic components on southern Texas jetties. Thus, the discussions which follow will not be exclusively restricted to the Port Aransas jetty and its biota, but it will be our primary model.

Construction of the present pair of jetties now flanking Aransas Pass was completed about 1910. The southern jetty extends almost a kilometer offshore from the northern end of Mustang Island. It is easily accessible and a favorite spot for fishermen, who reach it by driving their cars and campers to a parking area on the beach at its shoreward end. Where the jetty joins the sandy beach, biotic zonation patterns are obscured by abrasive surf-driven sand. One must walk at least 200 m beyond the turbid surf zone to best appreciate zonation and the potentially differential effects of shelter and exposure.

From the central Texas coast southward, the southern outer jetty shores face prevailing winds (Fig. 3-2, upper left) and experience the greatest exposure to offshore waves. The supralittoral fringe and midlittoral zone usually extend higher on the exposed (left side of Fig. 3-2) than on the inlet-facing northern side of the jetty (right side of Fig. 3-2). Winter seasonal wind-shifts, heavy boat traffic along the channel, seasonal juvenile recruitment at higher levels, differential insolation and perhaps many other factors will alter the shelter-exposure relationships and thereby the zonation patterns that prevail along the southern Texas jetties. Depending upon the specific blend of these several factors, zonation patterns on the two sides of the Texas jetties may vary from essentially little or no difference to that illustrated in Fig. 3-2. At the end of the Port Aransas jetty, as on virtually all of them, intertidal biotic zones are distinctly heightened, reflecting the increasing influence of waves.

THE SUPRALITTORAL FRINGE
Littorinidae

A single littorine, which we shall identify (but see below) as *Nodilittorina lineolata* (Figs. 3-1 B, 3-2 L and 3-4 A) is the sole characterizing periwinkle of the Texas hard shore supralittoral fringe. It occurs wherever rocks emerge from the sea, including all jetties, groins, minor breakwaters, pilings and piers, and other rocky outcrops washed by waves and tides.

The taxonomic position of the Texas jetty littorine, and indeed many of the hard shore littorines of the Gulf and Caribbean, is problematical. For many years biologists called the Texas littorine *Littorina ziczac*. In fact, several species of zebra-striped littorines occupy similar habitats on tropical and subtropical Atlantic shores, including *Nodilittorina ziczac* (= "*Littorina ziczac*"), *N. lineolata* (= *L. lineolata* and possibly *Nodilittorina interrupta*), and *N. angustior* (= *L. angustior* and *L. lineata* of some authors). Many shore ecologists and malacologists including T.A. & A. Stephenson (1950), Lewis (1960), Whitten *et al.* (1950), Abbott (1954), Warmke & Abbott, (1961) and others failed to recognize that there was more than one species of striped littorine on the rocky shores of the tropical western Atlantic. They lumped all striped Littorinidae together under the collective title of "*L. ziczac.*" Abbott (1964) subsequently recognized two species, and Borkowski & Borkowski (1969) demonstrated that "*Littorina ziczac*" included three difficult-to-differentiate sibling species.

Today, the striped western Atlantic Littorinidae are thought to comprise seven species (Bandel and Kadolsky, 1982). A complete listing of them is given near the end of the next chapter. Most recent workers recognize *Nodilittorina lineolata* (often cited as *Littorina lineolata*) as the characteristic littorine of the Texas jetties, occurring from Sabine Pass southwards. However, Bandel and Kadolsky (1982) maintain that *Nodilittorina lineolata* is a periwinkle of the southern Atlantic and does not occur in either the Gulf of Mexico or Caribbean Sea. Unfortunately, these authors failed to examine any specimens from the northwestern Gulf of Mexico and they provide us little guidance for the identification of striped littorines in this region. Clearly the taxonomic positions of the zebra-striped littorines of western Atlantic hard shores require additional clarification. Until then, we will resort to the name *Nodilittorina lineolata* as the designation for this diminutive Texas species.

Texas specimens of *N. lineolata* rarely exceed 10 mm in height, although some specimens on Corpus Christi bay breakwaters often attain 18 mm. They cling to jetty boulders above or among the upper zone of barnacles. *Nodilittorina lineolata*, like other rock-dwelling littorines, is a grazing snail, using a file-like radula to scrape algae from the rocks. The radula is such an efficient scraper that, in softer rocks such as limestones and sandstones, the snail can erode small pits and crevices while foraging. Later the snails occupy some of these depressions for shelter. A few of the inlet-facing boulders at the Port Aransas jetty are massive blocks of limestone or sandstone. Numerous pits or grooves on these rocks usually harbor sizable aggregations of *N. lineolata*. Granite boulders are more common and considerably more resistant to the bioerosive activities of *N. lineolata*. On these rocks the snails seek refuge in natural crevices and depressions, between living barnacles or within empty barnacle tests.

There is little published information on the biology of *N. lineolata* from Texas shores. Borkowski (1971, 1974) studied reproduction and population biology of what he identified as this species in southern Florida. According to Bandel and Kadolsky (1982), this is *N. riisei*. The attributes of the Florida species are likely similar to those of the Texas populations. They reach sexual maturity at a shell height of between 3.0 to 3.5 mm., but the mean size of reproducing individuals is 9.0 mm. As in other littorines, sperm are transferred to the female during copulation, and held in seminal receptacles with the aid of nurse cells until eggs are ready to be fertilized. Mature eggs receive fertilizing sperm as they pass the receptacle, then are surrounded by fluid and a membrane in an albumen gland, and finally encapsulated by a separate gland prior to release from the female body. Borkowski's (1971) *Littorina lineolata* was the only Florida species observed with some specimens having ripe gametes all year, although fewer than 40 percent of the males and 60 percent of the females produced gametes from January to mid-March. The first spawn occurs in early April in Florida, and continues through early May. Females produce planktonic bell-shaped egg capsules from which free-swimming veliger larvae eventually emerge. Borkowski's data, covering only a single year of observations, suggest that this species goes through a period of spawning inactivity from mid-May to mid-August, then resumes releasing egg capsules into the sea until early November. The time of capsule release by Florida snails roughly corresponds to the lunar or tidal cycle, and always when tidal levels rise above MHWST. Borkowski estimates the fecundity of 9.0 mm females to be about 12,500 egg capsules per year based upon only seasonal spawning.

Juvenile snails appear throughout the summer on Florida rocky shores and the Texas jetties, with the heaviest recruitment in the early fall. Growth of Florida populations slows during the winter months, but on Texas shores there may be relatively heavy winter mortality due to colder temperatures. Florida populations experience about 50 percent mortality per year. Growth accelerates during the warmer months, with the mean size of 1 year old snails in Florida being about 10 mm, and the average life span being about two years (Borkowski, 1974). In Texas, either growth rates are slower, life expectancy is shorter, or the snail is a different species, for specimens larger than 10 mm are uncommon on the northern Texas jetties and only occasionally encountered on the southern jetties. Mean size of *N. lineolata* does increase slightly with decreasing latitude along the Texas coast. For example, a sample of 50 specimens collected from the Galveston jetties in August had a mean shell height of 4.6 mm, whereas a similar sample taken from the Brazos-Santiago jetties in late July had a mean shell height of 5.2 mm.

If the Texas striped littorine is conspecific with one of the Florida or central Caribbean species, it is not known why the former are so much smaller than the latter. Any number of factors might be responsible, including climatic stress, food availability, predation pressure and intraspecific or interspecific competition. It even may be a different species.

Population densities of *N. lineolata* within suitable refugia on the Texas jetties usually number several hundred specimens per m^2. This might suggest that intraspecific or interspecific competition for available resources has a role in keeping the mean size of the population in check. Another possibility may be related to the substratum upon which the snails are found. In Texas the granite boulders of the jetties are hard, and thus resistant to boring organisms, including the several species of endolithic algae upon which many of the Caribbean rock-dwelling littorines often feed. In other localities such as southern Florida, the typical natural shore consists of softer limestone, easily bored by endolithic algae and grazed by the littorines. Perhaps the littorines have greater difficulty obtaining sufficient food from the more resistant granite rocks, especially in the supralittoral fringe, where other superficial macrophytes tend to be sparse. The few limestone boulders on the Port Aransas jetties support a population of *N. lineolata* which average 2 to 3 mm larger than specimens on granite.

Ligia

The remaining animals of the supralittoral fringe are active species, moving into and out of the region at will. Of these, perhaps the most obvious is the semi-terrestrial isopod, *Ligia exotica*, variously known as the sea slater, sea louse, wharf louse, rock louse or sea, boat and rock roach (Fig. 3-1 A). Various species of *Ligia* characteristically occupy rocky beaches throughout the world (Schultz, 1969). *L. exotica* is an Old World, warm-water species which has been introduced onto Gulf and Caribbean shores, probably by wooden ships. *Ligia* does not characterize any particular intertidal zone, for it is capable of scurrying through all of them. It is mostly nocturnal, but frequently can be observed darting across jetty rocks on cloudy days and near dusk when temperatures are moderate and light levels subdued. It feeds primarily upon epiphytic algae, but will also take a variety of other foods including carrion.

Like many intertidal organisms, *Ligia exotica* has an interesting blend of aquatic and terrestrial adaptations. It respires primarily by gill-like abdominal pleopods, which it must keep moist by periodic immersions in the sea. *Ligia* also is capable of limited gaseous exchange directly with the atmosphere across thin membranes located on some parts of the abdomen and abdominal appendages. On very humid days, as much as 50 percent of the oxygen needed for respiration may be obtained directly from the atmosphere (Kaestner, 1970). The thin membranes also permit the loss of considerable body fluid to the atmosphere by evaporation, especially during periods of high temperature or low humidity. Thus, *Ligia* is bound to the intertidal region where it can readily access the sea to replace lost body fluids. It does this by drinking sea-water, either by mouth, or by a unique method of anal uptake. As *Ligia* moistens abdominal gills in the sea, it also dilates the rectum, allowing water to enter the digestive tract by an antiperistaltic process.

Ligia minimizes water loss by seeking shelter during the hot parts of the day. Many semi-terrestrial isopod species including *Ligia* have very sensitive humidity receptors and are capable of discrimination between subtle changes in external humidity. In laboratory tests, *Ligia* always sought areas of higher humidity when given a choice, and one European species, *Ligia italica*, is capable of discriminating between 97 and 100 percent relative humidity (Kaestner, 1970).

Ligia can modify its body color to blend with its surroundings. It does this by clumping or extending pigments in star-shaped subepidermal cells called chromatophores. The isopod has neither the variety of chromatophore pigments nor the ability to rapidly change them as, for example, an octopus or squid. It relies primarily upon one dark pigment, melanin, which can be selectively displayed in the chromatophores, rendering *Ligia* approximately the same shade as the substratum upon which it lives. When on dark rocks, *Ligia* expands the chromatophores during the day, approximating the same dark shading. At night the chromatophores contract, and the sea roach becomes pale gray.

Ligia, like other free-living isopods, does not rely upon planktonic larvae for dispersal, as is often characteristic for many shore invertebrates. Instead, females brood eggs, developmental stages, and juveniles in pouches located between the legs on the ventral surface of the body. A female may carry up to 120 juveniles in the brood pouch. Even without planktonic larvae, the genus is widely dispersed, for few rocky shores anywhere in the world are devoid of sea roaches. *Ligia* has fared well in the presence of humans, relying upon wooden ships for transport to distant shores, and, once there, thriving upon some of the debris humanity casts to the sea. Although *Ligia* is never hard to find on any Texas jetty, it is always common among the unsightly human discards which litter the rocks: the odoriferous unwanted carcasses of rough fish caught by jetty fishermen, the fish bait these same anglers leave behind to spoil under a Texas summer sun, or the beached organics from jettisoned garbage discarded by irresponsible crew members of vessels traversing the jettied inlets. These refuse piles may provide humans an uncomfortable visual or olfactory experience, but in isopod terms, the accumulated organic debris can provide forage for several score sea roaches. A few species, it seems, will never be endangered by humans. *Ligia* is probably one.

THE MID-LITTORAL ZONE
Barnacles

Sessile barnacles characterize the mid-littoral rocky shore. Despite the unarthropod-like appearance of adults, barnacles are crustaceans belonging to the subclass Cirripedia, which also includes other equally unarthropod-like and some unbarnacle-like members. Acorn barnacles are the most familiar cirripedians. Like all members of the subclass, they have lost the head and abdomen typical of most arthropods. Their outer cuticular body layer forms a sac-like membranous mantle which usually secretes a series of shelly skeletal plates surrounding the sides of the body. The bottom of the mantle sac is always closed, but a shelly plate may or may not form below it. The top bears closable membranous or shelly opercular valves. They can be opened to permit extension of jointed chitinous feeding limbs called cirri. The name of the subclass, Cirripedia, is derived from these characteristic appendages.

Adult acorn barnacles are filter feeders that live permanently attached to rocks, pilings, boats, or other organisms. Their main activity consists of moving cirri through the water, trapping particulate food on feather-like branches. Most species employ three or four pairs of posterior cirri as the primary filters. They resemble a funnel-shaped sieve surrounding the mouth. Feeding begins as opercular valves move aside, permitting the posterior cirri to elevate into the water outside the mantle cavity. The fully extended cirri sweep quickly forward toward the mouth, forcing water to move through the spaces between cirri limbs. Small particles of food impale on a mesh of hairlike setae which extend from the cirri. A single sweep may occur in the blink of an eye, and several may accompany each opercular opening. After each series of sweeps the barnacle withdraws the posterior cirri inside the shell. Smaller comb-like anterior cirri remove trapped food particles from the larger posterior cirri and move them to the mouth. The process is then repeated, continuing for the time of tidal immersion. Food usually consists of plankton, detritus, or a combination of the two. Food particles range in diameter from 2 m to 1 mm.

Most of the common stony barnacles are hermaphroditic. Despite this, reproduction is usually by copulation. The male gonads terminate in an elongate penis which can extend considerably beyond the shell margin. A barnacle will use the penis to search for adjacent members of its species. Upon finding one, it inserts the penis into the dorsal aperture of the neighbor. Sperm are deposited in the mantle cavity of the recipient, inducing oviposition. A barnacle often receives sperm from several neighbors and in turn provides sperm to them.

Gamete production, at least in some barnacles, is closely correlated with the availability of an adequate food supply (Patel & Crisp, 1960). Eggs are fertilized in the mantle cavity and remain there until a larval stage emerges. This brood stage can be long, often over winter. Eventually, planktonic larvae are released. Barnacles usually pass through two larval stages, nauplius and cypris, both of which reveal the true arthropod affinities of the cirripedians. The nauplius larva has a shield-shaped chitinous carapace and numerous jointed appendages which aid it in swimming. The later cypris larva resembles an ostracod crustacean, having a body with six pairs of thoracic appendages enclosed by a bivalved carapace. Nauplius larvae may remain in the plankton for as long as two or three weeks. The non-feeding cypris larva is the settling stage, and rarely persists for more than two or three days. Upon finding a suitable substratum, the cypris attaches and undergoes metamorphosis to the adult.

Barnacle larvae face enormous mortalities. Many succumb to predation in the plankton. The number unable to locate a suitable substratum in the vastness of the sea must also be very high. In order to overcome this massive larval mortality, the fecundity of adult barnacles is correspondingly high. A single specimen may release 12,000 to 13,000 larvae each year in two or three spatfalls (Moore & Frue, 1959). Recently settled barnacles can grow rapidly, increasing 10 to 20 mm in diameter in 30 days (McDougall, 1943; Smith et al., 1950). Some species grow so rapidly that they can contribute gametes for reproduction 60 to 90 days after settlement (Grave, 1933; Bousfield, 1954; Moore & Frue, 1959). With successful attachment and metamorphosis, the adult barnacle may survive several years.

The common intertidal barnacles on warm temperate and subtropical shores of the southeastern United States demonstrate distinctive patterns of both vertical zonation and environmental partitioning. *Chthamalus* species (*C. fragilis* and, the more tropical *C. proteus* and *C. angustitergum*) occupy the highest portions of the mid-littoral zone. *Balanus improvisus, B. amphitrite, B. venustus, Megabalanus antillensis* and *Tetraclita stalactifera* are the more typically mid-littoral species. *Balanus improvisus* and *B. eburneus* also occur in the lower mid-littoral and subtidally. All of these species have broad geographic ranges (Spivey, 1981), with several found outside the western Atlantic region (Table 3-1).

Local environmental conditions, including salinity, turbidity, climate, tidal range and wave exposure, also influence the distribution of a particular species. For example, *Chthamalus proteus* and *Tetraclita stalactifera* are adapted for warm tropical or subtropical shores. They fare poorly or are absent in more temperate climates, replaced there by *C. fragilis* (Dando & Southward, 1980) and several *Balanus* species.

Salinity fluctuates seasonally and geographically along the jetty-lined tidal inlets. Salinities off northern Gulf jetties (Sabine, Galveston, Brazos) range from about 19 to 30 ppt, with lower values common in winter and spring. From Port Aransas southward, the salinity of waters washing the jetties more closely approximates that of the open Gulf. Port Aransas salini-

ties fluctuate from moderate winter levels of 29 to 32 ppt and summer extremes of up to 36 ppt (Collier & Hedgpeth, 1950; and Fig. 7-2). At the Port Mansfield and Brazos-Santiago jetties, salinities are rarely less than those of the open Gulf waters. All *Chthamalus* species, *Tetraclita stalactifera* and *Balanus amphitrite* prefer waters of near-normal salinities. *Balanus eburneus* and *B. improvisus* tolerate the lower salinities of estuaries and are usually more commonly found there (Gordon, 1969; Moore & Frue, 1959). They also attach to offshore oil drilling platforms in the Gulf of Mexico (George & Thomas, 1979). An additional barnacle, *B. subalbidus*, has the lowest salinity tolerance of all the common Atlantic species. It survives salinity fluctuations between 0 to 16 ppt (Porrier & Partridge, 1979), and is found on upper bayshores and along river banks near the sea (Gittings et al., 1986).

A few normally intertidal barnacles are absent on northern Gulf jetties and groins apparently because they poorly tolerate the relatively turbid waters of this region. *Balanus reticulatus* is a recent immigrant to the Gulf of Mexico from Indo-Pacific shores. Since the mid-1970s, it has attained a position of dominance in the clear-water biofouling communities attached to offshore drilling platforms from central Louisiana to eastern Texas (George & Thomas, 1979). Within its natural range, *B. reticulatus* is an intertidal species on natural rocky shores, but it has apparently encountered difficulty in becoming established on the unnatural rock substrata along northern Gulf shores. Similarly, *Megabalanus antillensis* is an intertidal tropical Caribbean species. It is sometimes taken from outer shore jetties and rock breakwaters from Port Aransas southward, and is relatively common on offshore platforms along the northern Gulf. It is rare or absent on shore rocks from western Florida to central Texas.

Chthamalus fragilis (Figs. 3-1 D; 3-2 K) is the dominant mid-littoral barnacle on all Texas jetties and always the highest zoned species. It is sometimes the only barnacle present, especially on the outer (seaward) sections of the northern jetties and on all sections of the southern jetties. A very similar species, *C. proteus*, may also occur in Texas (Dando & Southward, 1980), but there is little evidence to date to support this claim (Gittings et al., 1986). The dominant chthamalid of the eastern Caribbean and Bermuda, *Chthamalus angustitergum*, apparently does not occur within the Gulf of Mexico.

Chthamalus fragilis is small, usually less than 8 mm in diameter, and about half its diameter in height. Its vertical range on the Texas coast is considerably narrower than that on shores with greater tidal range, such as at Beaufort, North Carolina or Charleston, South Carolina. On Texas jetties, *Chthamalus fragilis* occupies a band of about 30 to 40 cm in width, extending from 15 to 30 cm above EHWST to near the upper edge of dense macrophyte cover in the sublittoral fringe. The *Chthamalus* zone may be narrower than

Table 3-1. Common Rocky Shore Barnacles of the Western Gulf of Mexico

Species	Climatic Range	Geographic Range	Vertical Range	Salinity Range
Family Balanidae				
Balanus amphitrite	Mid-temperate to tropical	Circumtemperate & circumtropical	Middle to lower mid-littoral	Marine
Balanus eburneus	Mid-temperate to tropical	W. Atlantic (Massachusetts to Caribbean); E. Atlantic (France & Spain); Mediterranean, Black & Caspian Seas; Pacific (Hawaii)	Lower mid-littoral to sublittoral	Estuarine
Balanus improvisus	Cool temperate to tropical	W. Atlantic (Canada to Patagonia); E. Atlantic (Baltic to Spain); Mediterranean, Black, Caspian & Red Seas; E. Pacific (California to Colombia)	Middle to lower mid-littoral	Marine to low estuarine
Balanus reticulatus	Mid-temperate to tropical	Circumtemperate & circumtropical (first Western Atlantic record in 1962)	Lower mid-littoral to sublittoral and offshore drilling platforms	Marine
Balanus subalbidus	Mid-temperate to tropical	Massachusetts to Trinidad	Mid-littoral to sublittoral	Low estuarine to almost freshwater
Megabalanus antillensis (= Balanus tintinnabulum antillensis)	Warm temperate to tropical	Gulf of Mexico and Caribbean	Mid-littoral to sublittoral in clear waters and offshore drilling platforms	Marine
Family Chthamalidae				
Chthamalus fragilis	Mid-temperate to subtropical	Massachusetts to Gulf of Mexico	Upper mid-littoral	Marine
Chthamalus proteus	Subtropical to tropical	Eastern Florida, Caribbean, southern Gulf of Mexico (?) and southern Brazil	Upper mid-littoral	Marine
Family Tetraclitidae				
Tetraclita stalactifera	Subtropical to tropical	W. Atlantic (S. Carolina to southern Brazil); E. Pacific (Gulf of California to Acapulco, Mexico)	Middle mid-littoral to shallow sublittoral	Marine

40 cm on vertical rock faces and considerably wider on gently sloping boulders. Its vertical range widens in the more exposed portions of all jetties, where wave splash delivers water considerably above EHWST. Densities of *C. fragilis* commonly exceed 1000/m² on jetty boulders. This barnacle compensates for crowding in high density situations by growing 2 to 4 times the diameter in height. *Chthamalus fragilis* differs from *Balanus* species by being smaller, lacking a basal calcareous plate, and having lateral plates which overlap both end plates.

All *Balanus* species are sparsely distributed on the Texas jetties, but the most common is usually *B. amphitrite* (Fig. 3-2 R). Look for it attached to seaward jetty rocks in the lower mid-littoral, below the lower limit of most *Chthamalus*. *Balanus eburneus* (Fig. 3-2 S) and *B. improvisus* are much less common on outer Texas shores. When present, they usually attach to shoreward jetty rocks from the lower mid-littoral to sublittoral. Both *B. eburneus* and *B. improvisus* are rare or absent on the seaward ends of all jetties north of Padre Island, and generally absent from all portions of the jetties south of Port Aransas. Their numbers and distribution on the jetties tend to increase during years of high precipitation and correspondingly lower salinities. In contrast to the paucity of these species on jetty shores, *B. eburneus* and *B. improvisus* are the most common barnacles found attached to pilings, wharves, and other hard bottoms in the Texas bays (Chapter 5).

Where *Chthamalus* and *Balanus* coexist, interspecific competition and/or predation may influence their patterns of distribution on the shore (Connell, 1961a,b). For example, *B. balanoides* successfully eliminates *C. stellatus* from the mid-littoral Scottish coast by overgrowing most newly settled members of the latter species. As usual, *Chthamalus* fares best in the upper mid-littoral where it is free from competition. This does not permit *B. balanoides* to dominate the lower mid-littoral, for its populations are regulated by predation from the snail *Thais lapillus* (Connell, 1961b). When the mid-littoral is artificially maintained free of *Balanus balanoides*, *Chthamalus* quickly and successfully becomes established, extending its vertical range from the lower supralittoral fringe to the mean tide level (Connell, 1961a). Interestingly, predation of *Chthamalus* by *T. lapillus* in the mid-littoral is insignificant, even in the absence of *B. balanoides*. The results of these and similar studies led Connell to conclude that the lower limits of distribution of intertidal organisms are determined more by interaction of biotic factors such as competition for space or predation, whereas upper limits are more often determined by physical factors. The picture does not seem to be as clear on the Texas jetties.

First, interspecific competition between *Balanus* and *Chthamalus* does not seem to be as keen on the outer Texas coast as it is in Scotland, largely because *Balanus* is not nearly as common here. The paucity of *Balanus* on Texas jetties, in comparison to their abundance at other western Atlantic localities (McDougall, 1943; Stephenson & Stephenson, 1952), is not easily explained by biotic interactions. The biotic composition of the jetties is sufficiently simple that if *Balanus* were being excluded by competition for living space, the competitor should be easy to identify. *Balanus* has no obvious competitors for space here. Furthermore, the Texas jetty fauna largely resembles that from other southeastern United States shores where *Balanus* fares well. It is unlikely that species coexisting on several different shores would compete in one locality but not in others. For similar reasons, predation probably does not account for the paucity of *Balanus*. Intertidal predators of the Texas coast are essentially the same as those of the Carolinas. *Stramonita haemastoma* (Fig. 3-2 P) feeds on *Balanus* throughout warm temperate Atlantic shores, but it is difficult to understand how it or any other predator common throughout the region could exploit *Balanus* more efficiently on only Texas shores. If biotic interactions do not explain the fewer *Balanus* individuals on Texas jetties, then their paucity might be the result of one or several physical conditions approaching or exceeding the limits of tolerance for a particular species. Temperature is a possible suspect, as *Balanus* species tend to be rare or absent on exposed tropical Caribbean shores. Higher salinity will exclude the more estuarine-adapted species.

In the absence of *Balanus*, *Chthamalus* does not (or cannot) always take advantage of the unoccupied middle ground. On all Texas jetties beyond the effects of near-shore abrasion by wave-suspended sand, *Chthamalus fragilis* sometimes remains exclusively high-zoned, leaving a distinctly depauperate narrow band just above the upper limits of most macrophytes (the

"sparse zone" of Hedgpeth, 1953). According to Connell's hypothesis, the absence of *Chthamalus* here is most likely explained by a biotic factor such as competition or predation. As with the distribution of *Balanus* on the jetty, however, and in light of its poor showing, a competitor capable of excluding *Chthamalus* from the middle shore is not readily apparent. Furthermore, when the depauperate zone is present, it is devoid of dense concentrations of all species (not just barnacles), eliminating the likelihood that physical crowding by any intertidal organism is a limiting factor.

Predation may be a more likely cause for the absence of *Chthamalus* in the lower mid-littoral (assuming that it otherwise could survive there). A specific keystone predator for *Chthamalus* on Texas jetties has not been identified, but several have the potential to keep low ranging *Chthamalus* in check. For example, heavy indiscriminate grazing by the mid-littoral false limpet *Siphonaria pectinata* (Fig. 3-1 C; 3-2 O) may destroy newly settled *Chthamalus* spat in the depauperate zone. The predatory snails *Stramonita haemastoma* and *Cantharus cancellarius* may also take *Chthamalus*. On some Gulf shores, the flatworm *Eustylochus meridianalis* preys upon barnacles occupying the lower mid-littoral (Pearse & Wharton, 1938). The sea urchin, *Arbacia punctulata* (Figs. 3-1 I; 3-4 E), also grazes indiscriminately in the lower mid-littoral at night, and can denude an area of barnacles (Huntsman, 1918).

Despite these possibilities, there is no clear evidence that biotic interactions exclude *Chthamalus* from the lower mid-littoral zone of the Texas jetties, nor force them to live higher upon the shore. They do, nevertheless, concentrate their populations in the upper mid-littoral of the Texas jetties, as they do on other shores. By occupying this habitat, *Chthamalus fragilis* encounters considerably greater physical stress than if it lived lower on the shore. For example, high zoned *Chthamalus* may experience annual temperature extremes from -8 to 41°C on Texas jetties, while the temperature range for lower zoned species is effectively mediated by the sea. *Chthamalus* may pass hours under a hot drying sun or receive the maximum fury of storm waves crashing upon the shore. It can feed only in the instant of a receding wave, and then can ingest only what is carried to it. With these constraints, there is little wonder that *Chthamalus* is usually smaller than the lower zoned *Balanus* species.

We have emphasized the sparseness of *Balanus* on the outer Texas coasts and the propensity for *Chthamalus* to concentrate its numbers higher on the shore. In fact, abundance is relative. The numbers of barnacles on the Texas jetties (save *Chthamalus*) usually compare poorly with the numbers of similar species on other temperate western Atlantic shores. In comparison with many other western Gulf and Caribbean localities, however, intertidal barnacles on Texas shores seem to display greater abundance and diversity. As temperate becomes subtropical, several biotic and physical conditions seem to approach or exceed the limits of tolerance for many species of intertidal barnacles, regardless of their vertical position on shore. From north to south along the Texas coast there is increasing and progressively constant thermal stress, increasingly intense solar illumination and radiation, a less variable climate, and a relatively constant and limited tidal range. The shore is also undergoing a biological transition, with new tropical species replacing temperate ones. Even the water is changing, with the rich plankton pastures of temperate seas yielding to the more impoverished waters of the sub-tropical Gulf of Mexico. All of these factors have the potential to affect the distribution of barnacles, and in the face of these conditions it is little wonder that some species almost disappear.

Acorn barnacles are important constituents of the Texas jetties and hard bayshores, but farther south in similar environments along the northern Yucatan coast, they are sometimes only incidental faunal components (Chapter 4). Still farther south in the western Caribbean, intertidal rock suitable for barnacle attachment increases considerably. One might expect that an increase in barnacle density, diversity, or both would accompany the increase in habitable substrata. In fact, both the density and diversity of barnacles decline on many western Caribbean shores. Barnacles common in the Gulf of Mexico are usually uncommon in the western Caribbean, but rarely are they absent. A careful search of sheltered or shaded intertidal rocks usually reveals a few specimens of at least one or two warm-temperate species. The tropical barnacles *Chthamalus angustitergum*, *C. proteus* and *Tetraclita stalactifera*, may be locally abundant on some western Caribbean shores, but usually in numbers insufficient to suggest any more than moderate interspecific competition with each other or the temperate species for living space. In many localities throughout the region, even these barnacles are rare or absent (Chapter 4). Apparently the physical conditions on tropical shores may exceed tolerance limits for not only the warm-temperate barnacles, but also the species usually restricted to tropical waters. The importance of biologic interactions determining the lower distributional limits of intertidal organisms may require modification as species approach their limits of physical tolerance. Inevitably, all species must yield to the constraints imposed by the physical world.

Mid-littoral Molluscan Herbivores

Several species of gastropod herbivores occupy the mid-littoral zone on most rocky shores. As with the littorines and barnacles, however, Texas jetties have a considerably reduced diversity of mid-littoral herbivorous snails. *Siphonaria pectinata* (Figs. 3-1 C, 3-2 O, 3-4 B) is the only common species. It is easily recognized by its flattened, seemingly uncoiled limpet-like shell which may reach two or three cm in diameter. A large oval muscular foot covers most of the area beneath the shell, providing firm attachment to the sub-stratum. The low conical shell and strong muscular grasp enable *S. pectinata* to thrive on exposed rocky wave-swept shores, for crashing surf slips easily over the snail without dislodging it from the shore.

On shores where *Siphonaria* and true marine limpets coexist, the two types of snails sometimes may be confused. True limpets are rare on the Texas jetties, but in Chapter 4 we will describe some shores occupied by both. *Siphonaria* usually bears a characteristic bulge on the right side of the shell. It marks the opening to a highly vascularized mantle lung, a structure which identifies *Siphonaria* as a pulmonate gastropod, distinct from the true marine prosobranch limpets. Pulmonates are air-breathing terrestrial or freshwater gastropods and include a variety of common garden snails and slugs. They were originally derived from ancient marine stocks, but today only a few groups of pulmonates can tolerate marine conditions. *Siphonaria* is one of them. It seems closely related to the ancient gastropod line which originally left the sea to live on land.

There are several reasons why *Siphonaria* is regarded as a relatively primitive pulmonate. A mantle lung occurs in no other gastropods except pulmonates, establishing the affinity of *Siphonaria* to this group. But unlike most other pulmonates, *Siphonaria* also possesses an accessory true gill. Furthermore, it is one of the few pulmonates which produce veliger larvae (the Ellobiidae do also, Chapter 9), a feature generally associated with marine gastropods. Finally, *Siphonaria* lives in a habitat conducive to terrestrial adaptation and similar to that presumed to be the cradle of all pulmonate stocks, although mud flats occupied by many of the Ellobiidae may also bear this distinction (McMahon & Russell-Hunter, 1981).

Siphonaria pectinata lives in the mid-littoral zone decidedly lower than *Nodilittorina lineolata*, and usually below the greatest concentrations of *Chthamalus fragilis*. Like other mid-littoral species, its position on shore can be modified by exposure (zoning higher with increasing exposure), or by the presence of other organisms, especially closely crowded barnacle colonies (Voss, 1959). On natural rocky shores it is most common on wave-washed intertidal limestone platforms with a slight to moderate seaward slope. *Siphonaria pectinata* also occurs on vertical pilings, rugged limestone cliffs, cement sea walls, and isolated submerged rocks well below sea level (Voss, 1959). It prefers areas of sparse macrophyte cover where microscopic superficial and endolithic algae are the predominant plants (Voss, 1959; Craig *et al.*, 1969). There seems to be a positive correlation between the size and well-being of *S. pectinata* populations and the presence of the macrophytes *Ulva* and *Enteromorpha*, despite the fact that the pulmonate is rarely found foraging among these green algae. The presence of *Ulva* and *Enteromorpha* also indicates that the shore is washed by nutrient enriched waters. Voss (1959) suggests that the *Siphonaria/Ulva/Enteromorpha* connection may be indicative only of another relationship, the presence of an enriched microphyte population from which *Siphonaria* derives the majority of its sustenance.

Siphonaria pectinata is a significant factor in beachrock erosion on limestone shores, removing surface rock layers preweakened by the boring activities of endolithic plants (Craig *et al.*, 1969). It makes less impact upon the erosion of the granitic boulders on Texas jetties, indicated by the lack of pits, depressions and crevices which are clearly evident on limestone shores. The numbers and density of endolithic algal species living within the boulders are also restricted by the hardness of the rock (Hedgpeth, 1953), suggesting a potentially reduced food supply for the snail. The number and size of *S. pectinata* on the Texas jetties and groins are about equal to those from natural limestone shores, lending support to the hypothesis that it probably relies largely upon microscopic surface algae for food. Being a mid-zoned snail, *S. pectinata* likely finds a more abundant supply of all types of algae than that available to the higher zoned and presumably more specialized *N. lineolata*, suggesting a possible reason why only *N. lineolata*, and not *S. pectinata* has a smaller mean adult size on Texas shores.

Siphonaria pectinata tends toward protandric hermaphroditism, spawning primarily during the winter months (Voss, 1959; Zischke, 1974). Sperm is transferred to the female reproductive system by copulation, which is possibly reciprocal (Hyman, 1967). The spawn consists of yellow-green to light yellow oval crescents varying from 3 to 4 cm in length and 2 to 3 mm in diameter (Voss, 1959). Each crescent (Fig. 3-1 C) is filled with numerous egg capsules embedded in a gelatinous matrix. Zischke (1974) estimates there are about 200 egg capsules per mm of ribbon. The crescent is surrounded by a thick, tough, membranous wall. Each egg capsule within the ribbon measures about 0.19 mm in length and 0.15 mm in width. Crescents are deposited upon intertidal rocks and apparently are capable of tolerating periodic immersion without damage to the developing embryos. Lighter colored ribbons usually contain more developed embryos. Veliger larvae emerge from egg capsules 15 to 20 days after spawning (Dieuzeide, 1935; Voss, 1959), and enter the plankton for a period of about 11 days, swimming continuously without feeding (Zischke, 1974).

At the time of settling, the *S. pectinata* shell is about 0.3 mm in length. The veliger and juvenile snails display characteristically coiled nuclear whorls at the shell apex, but these disappear as the shells increase in size. Zischke (1974) reports that *S. pectinata* grows about 1.5 mm per month to a length of just under 9 mm. Thereafter the growth rate gradually decreases, with specimens over 10 mm in length increasing in size by about 0.6 mm per month. Specimens with a mean length of 5.5 mm have a formed gonad containing some spermatozoa. The first eggs appear in the gonad at about 7.0 mm shell length, and specimens over 20 mm in length are essentially female with little or no testicular tissue (Zischke, 1974).

Siphonaria pectinata is the dominant mid-littoral mollusc of the Texas jetties, but other gastropods and bivalves sometimes occur here, especially from Port Aransas south. These molluscs are largely tropical species, and find the Texas jetties a marginal habitat. *Nerita fulgurans* (Figs. 4-1 P; 4-2 K; 4-3 N) is common on Mexico jetties and certain Caribbean shores, usually preferring shoreward sheltered boulder habitats. It is occasionally found at Port Aransas, and increases in abundance toward the Mexico border. Moderate populations of *N. fulgurans* occur along the channel side of the northern Brazos-Santiago jetty, where the inlet traverses the southern termination of Padre Island. Another tropical species, *Supplanaxis nucleus* (Fig. 4-2 L), has been observed infrequently along this portion of the Brazos-Santiago jetty. *Nerita versicolor* (Fig. 4-1 Q) prefers a somewhat more exposed shore, and may occasionally be seen on the seaward portions of the southern jetties. The keyhole limpets *Diodora cayenensis* and *Lucapiella limatula* are rarely found under rocks in similar localities.

Several sessile bivalves often attach to jetty rocks in the mid-littoral zone, sometimes in sufficient numbers as to dominate local areas. *Isognomon bicolor* (Fig. 3-2 J) and *I. alatus* are tropical bivalves which occur on the southern Texas jetties. *Ischadium recurvum* (Fig. 5-2 O) and *Brachidontes exustus* (Fig. 5-2 M) are more widely distributed, but their presence on jetty rocks is always patchy. Both are more common on bay oyster reefs (see Chapter 5). *Ischadium recurvum* tolerates considerably lower salinities than *Brachidontes exustus*.

Predators of the Mid-littoral

Many of the animals which are commonly seen scurrying across rocks of the subtidal and sublittoral fringe are normally residents of other habitats, but for a variety of reasons have been able to adapt successfully to the jetty environs. For example, the stone crab, *Menippe adina* (Figs. 3-2 G, 3-4 F), and the rock shell or drill, *Stramonita haemastoma* (Fig. 3-2 P) are typically inhabitants of bay oyster reefs. Regional literature usually records these species by other names. The rock shell was formerly known as *Thais (Stramonita) haemastoma*, but the subgenus was recently elevated to generic status. Stone crabs of the northwestern Gulf of Mexico were included with *Menippe mercenaria*, a species ranging from the Carolinas to the Caribbean. Williams & Felder (1986) have shown them to be distinct from eastern populations of *M. mercenaria*.

Menippe adina constructs burrows on the muddy floor of the oyster reef and hides among the jumble of oyster shells. Similarly, the crab constructs burrows in sand-filled cracks and hides within secluded crevices on the jetty. *Stramonita haemastoma* crawls on the intertidal and subtidal rocks of the jetty, just as it does upon the oyster reef. It usually is the most conspicuous gastropod predator in both localities, with some specimens reaching 11 cm in length. The crab and the gastropod seek a similar, although not altogether identical, range of foods. They both prey upon oysters in the bays, but since oysters are uncommon upon the jetties, they seek alternative foods here. The stone crab has a massive cheliped adapted for crushing a variety of shelled animals, especially oysters, but it is equally effective upon balanoid barnacles, other sessile bivalves, and even *S. haemastoma. Menippe adina* feeds upon a variety of soft-bodied animals including several worms and flatworms (Powell & Gunter, 1968). It even scavenges for food, especially on the jetties where it is readily provisioned by a variety of carrion washed ashore or left by fishermen. In fact, a substantial part of the diet of the jetty-dwelling stone crabs may be from their scavenging activities.

Menippe adina and *S. haemastoma* make an interesting pair of reciprocal predators. Large stone crabs readily feed upon living *S. haemastoma* in the laboratory, using the large chela to chip away the snail's shell until the flesh is exposed. Conversely, *S. haemastoma* is also known to feed upon juvenile *M. adina*, using its radula to pierce the crab's chitinous shell (Powell & Gunter, 1968). Large *M. adina* rely upon *S. haemastoma* as a common food source on Texas jetties, and the latter reciprocates by feeding upon juvenile *Menippe*.

Stramonita haemastoma is probably the most important oyster pest in the Texas bays, although it poorly tolerates moderate to low estuarine conditions. It prefers mussels to oysters when they can be located (Burkenroad, 1931; Butler, 1953; Gunter, 1979a; Garton & Sickle, 1980), but as oysters are consistently more common in Texas bays, they are its usual food source there. Like *M. adina, S. haemastoma* finds a paucity of oysters on the jetties and must shift to alternate foods. These include balanoid barnacles, other sessile bivalves, occasional gastropods such as *Siphonaria pectinata*, and small crabs such as young *M. adina*. The snail cannot crush shells, but it has perfected another way to penetrate them. It uses its radula as a drill, and, aided by chemical secretions, bores a hole into the shell of its prey. The boring mechanism of *S. haemastoma* is similar to that described for *Urosalpinx*, a related muricid genus found on more temperate Atlantic shores (Carriker, 1955; 1958; 1959; 1961).

Upon encountering suitable prey, the snail explores the victim's shell with a proboscis as if searching for an appropriate place to begin active boring. When it locates a spot, it steadily rasps the site with the radula for several minutes, and then withdraws the radula and proboscis. An eversible glandular portion of the snail's foot, the accessory boring organ, is placed upon the site, providing secretions which soften and loosen the crystalline shell matrix. The secretions appear to be essential in the boring process, for snails with surgically removed accessory boring organs are rarely capable of completing a drill hole. The gland remains firmly applied to the drill site for periods ranging from a few minutes to upwards of an hour. Eventually it is withdrawn and the radula is called upon to remove loosened shell particles. *Stramonita haemastoma*

rasps with the radula for only a few minutes, and then repositions the boring gland on the site for another extended period. The total time required to penetrate a shell varies from several hours to several days, depending upon the thickness of the victim's shell. It is not uncommon for boring snails to abandon a drill site before perforating a shell. If a successful breach is made, the snail inserts the proboscis through the hole, shreds the soft flesh inside the shell with the radula and ingests it.

Stramonita haemastoma is not exclusively predatory. It is also a scavenger, feeding on dead or decaying crabs, shrimp, or fish, and is known to eat detritus. Butler (1953) compares the latter activity to that of a vacuum cleaner, with *S. haemastoma* "eating a great deal of diatomaceous ooze which collects on objects." When other foods are unavailable, this snail is known to cannibalize its young (Butler, 1953). All forms of feeding are influenced by temperature. *Stramonita haemastoma* will not feed at temperatures below 12°C, and, as temperatures approach 6 to 8°C, the snails tend to enter a state of hibernation.

Gamete production and subsequent reproductive activity in *S. haemastoma* is also influenced by temperature (Butler, 1953). Gonad activity is initiated when water temperatures reach about 20°C, with spawning following a few weeks later. Normally, the snail breeds in April and May in the northern Gulf (Burkenroad, 1931), but the reproductive season extends from February to November in southern Florida (D'Asaro, 1966). There is a similar lengthening of the reproductive season from northern to southern localities along the Texas and Mexico shores. Reproduction may occur earlier when winters are warm. For example, *S. haemastoma* spawned in mid-February at Pensacola, Florida during the warm winter of 1950 (Butler, 1953).

As in most prosobranch gastropods, sexes are separate and sperm are transferred to females by copulation. At the time of spawning the snails become markedly gregarious, congregating in large numbers (Burkenroad 1931). Any single female initiating spawning will set off a chain reaction. Nearby females are attracted to the first female and are induced also to spawn. *Stramonita haemastoma* spawning in southern Florida also attracts another species, *S. rustica*, with the result that a communal spawn consisting of egg masses of at least these two muricids has been observed (D'Asaro, 1966).

Stramonita haemastoma deposits egg capsules subtidally on a firm substratum just below ELWST, but elevated above any surrounding sand or mud. Rocks of the Texas jetties serve very well, as do *Rhizophora* (mangrove) prop roots, oyster reefs, sea walls, and subtidal limestones on other shores. The nature and location of the substratum upon which the spawn is deposited insure that the egg masses will be bathed by oxygen-rich waters with little danger of smothering by siltation.

Eggs are embedded in a gelatinous matrix which, in

turn, is enclosed by a horny transparent capsule. Each 6 mm capsule encloses about 600 eggs, and a female may produce as many as 100 capsules (D'Asaro, 1966). The size of the capsules is not uniform. Larger capsules will contain greater numbers of eggs (Burkenroad, 1931). A female can deposit from 1 to 17 capsules per hour with 6 to 8 being typical. In the laboratory up to 10 snails at a time were observed depositing egg capsules on a communal spawn (D'Asaro, 1966), but the number may be considerably higher in natural populations (Burkenroad, 1931). A spawn mass may consist of several thousand capsules (Galtsoff, 1964). The capsules are white when first deposited, but gradually change to light purple and finally to dull gray as development proceeds. Hatching commences about 25 days following production of the capsule. Veliger larvae emerge from the capsule and enter the sea as meroplankton.

Emerging veligers display a strong negative geotropism and a positive phototropism which helps to keep them near the water surface away from bottom sediments (Butler, 1953). They are capable of feeding upon a variety of phytoplankton immediately upon emerging from the capsule (D'Asaro, 1966). It is not known how long *S. haemastoma* veligers can remain in the plankton before metamorphosis into the adult, but D'Asaro traces organogenesis of the veliger for at least two weeks following emergence from the egg capsule.

Reproduction in stone crabs is also initiated by copulation, but the process and subsequent development of larvae is distinctly different. As with many marine crabs, the male must await a molt by the female before mating is possible. *Menippe mercenaria* mate during the summer (Savage, 1971), and the mating behavior and life history of the closely related *M. adina* is likely very similar. Mating is initiated when a male *M. mercenaria* encounters a female about to molt. The male and female remain constant companions within or near the entrance to a burrow until the female sheds the old exoskeleton whereupon copulation commences immediately. The mating pair may remain together for several hours, with the male usually in a protective position atop the female. Without the hardened exoskeleton, the female is defenseless, so the process of mating also provides her protection during an otherwise vulnerable period. Following copulation, the male maintains a vigil at the mouth of the burrow, presumably until the new exoskeleton of the female becomes sufficiently hardened that she is able to defend herself (Savage, 1971). The altruistic behavior of a male *M. mercenaria* to the recently molted female is even more interesting in light of this species' known propensity towards cannibalism, especially in crowded situations.

One copulation is sufficient to produce as many as six million eggs, although the female *M. mercenaria* (and likely *M. adina*) does not release all of them in a single spawn. She will produce 4 to 6 spawns during the summer, with each resulting egg mass containing between 500,000 to 1,000,000 eggs (Binford, 1912; Porter, 1960). Pre-zoeal hatchlings molt to the first zoea stage within a few hours. There are five or six zoeal stages, each lasting from 3 to 6 days (Porter, 1960). *Menippe mercenaria* spends a maximum of 36 days in the meroplankton, although the average duration is probably considerably shorter. Laboratory experiments suggest that the optimum temperature for larval development is between 23 to 25°C. Larvae do not survive in salinities less than 27 ppt, despite the fact that adults are frequently found in salinities considerably lower than this (Porter, 1960).

Menippe mercenaria and *M. adina* have only recently been differentiated, so many of the ways their ecology or life history differ are still to be determined. The former seems to prefer grass beds and salinities nearer that of the open sea, whereas the latter is more common on oyster reefs and jetties and occupies estuarine waters ranging from 35 to 10 ppt (Williams & Felder, 1986).

Stramonita and *Menippe* are not the only predators of the jetties. The snail *Cantharus cancellarius* (Fig. 10-1 V) frequents the lower mid-littoral jetty rocks in large numbers, especially during the late summer. During the last few years, this snail has almost replaced *S. haemastoma* on the Port Aransas jetty. Some of the smaller xanthid crabs described from other Texas shores occur among jetty crevices and feed upon some of the intertidal biota. Many of the shore birds described throughout the pages of this book, including various egrets, herons, willets, sandpipers, dowitchers, turnstones and gulls, are frequent visitors to the jetty. Most busy themselves searching for morsels within tide pools or as waves sweep across the rocks. We have often encountered feral cats, various rodents, and even an opossum living among jetty rocks and feeding upon the sessile mid-littoral jetty fauna.

THE SUBLITTORAL FRINGE AND SUBLITTORAL ZONE
The Texas Jetty Flora

The lower portions of rocky shores throughout the world are dominated by macroscopic marine algae and associated epiphytes. Until jetties were constructed, Texas outer shores were mostly devoid of macroscopic algae for they lacked the firm substratum required for algal attachment. We have no records of the marine algae of the western Gulf of Mexico prior to the construction of jetties, and few reports during the first half of this century (Taylor, 1954a,b), but there must have been considerably fewer species. Within recent time, humans have contributed a new habitat to the Gulf of Mexico coastal zone, and in so doing, increased the algal diversity of the region considerably. These, in turn, provide new nutrient resources which support new warm-temperate and a few hardy tropical herbivores.

Red algae are the most diverse group on all Texas jetties, but certain species of green algae may grow so prolifically as to be seasonally dominant. Algae on the northern jetties include many temperate species found commonly in other parts of the northern Gulf and temperate Atlantic and eurythermal species which range from Canada to the tropical Caribbean. The number of algal species increases toward southern Texas shores and the flora changes in composition, reflecting the temperate to subtropical transition. Temperate species disappear and are replaced by algae with tropical affinities.

About 200 species of multicellular algae (macrophytes) have been described from Texas shores or the adjacent Gulf states of Louisiana, Mississippi (Humm & Caylor, 1957; Humm & Darnell, 1959) and Alabama. Of these, about 90 have been reported from shore localities along the northern Gulf from Galveston to Mobile bays. An even more diverse assemblage is represented in the deeper, clearer waters offshore (Bert & Humm, 1979). Algal sporelings apparently abound in the Gulf waters. They opportunistically occupy habitats whenever and wherever suitable conditions are encountered, as evidenced by their rapid colonization of offshore oil platforms. Original algal colonization of the Texas jetties probably occurred in a similar manner and relied heavily on floating algal sporelings. Even today, the jetties likely draw at least part of their populations from the floating inoculate pool. Accordingly, community composition varies from place to place and season to season. For example, Lowe & Cox (1978) list only 28 species from Galveston Island, and suggest that only a few of these are common. Furthermore, they point out that the algal species at Galveston Island differ significantly from those described by Kapraun (1974) from Louisiana shores. The number of jetty algae increases to about 115 species in the vicinity of Brazos-Santiago Pass near Port Isabel.

About 52 species of algae can be expected to occur regularly on all Texas shores, provided a suitable substratum or habitat is locally available. (The exact number is difficult to determine because of insufficient habitat data or collections at some localities. For example, the literature records only 9 species of algae from the jetty at Freeport, an obviously incomplete census.) Of the remaining 134 species recorded from or likely to occur on the Texas coast, 25 are restricted to the northern Gulf. These are found no farther south than the Galveston area (Table 3-2). In contrast, 84 species are distributed from Aransas Pass southward, with 43 species reported only from the southernmost localities (and many of these extend farther southward into Mexico and the Caribbean). The Texas coast is a zone of transition for the algae, with jetty flora recruited from the diversity of algal sporelings floating offshore.

Algal Zonation and Succession: Physical Factors

There are a number of physical factors, including salinity, turbidity, light intensity, day length, tidal fluctuation, wave exposure, temperature and tolerance to desiccation, which may affect the distribution and abundance of intertidal and shallow subtidal algae. Salinity and turbidity are more important factors influencing the distribution of flora in the sublittoral bay waters (Chapter 7), but play only a minor role in determining the distribution of algae on the jetties. Some jetty algae, such as members of the green ulvacean genus *Enteromorpha*, may display polymorphic branching patterns in different salinities. Specific branching patterns are induced at different salinities among separate sexes of the same species (Kapraun, 1970), making species identifications in an already difficult group even more challenging.

Few algae can tolerate the dry, harsh supralittoral fringe, but *Bangia* (Fig. 3-3 K) and *Enteromorpha* (Fig. 3-3 A and B) are two genera which occur here. Most species succumb quickly to prolonged emersion as a result of desiccation. They are restricted to the midlittoral or lower, where effects of exposure and desiccation are less severe.

Temperature remains an important factor for sublittoral species, particularly in warm-temperate latitudes. Unlike the tropics where water temperatures remain almost constant, or high-latitude shores where seasonal fluctuations are usually moderate and tend toward the lower ranges, warm-temperate shores experience broad seasonal variations in water temperature (Fig. 3-4). Summer temperatures may approximate those of tropical waters, whereas winter temperatures may be 20°C colder. This variation induces a striking seasonal succession of the intertidal and shallow subtidal algae, particularly evident on the northern and central Texas jetties. During the winter months, these shores are dominated by cool-temperate species such as *Bangia fuscopurpurea* (Fig. 3-3 K), *Porphyra leucosticta* (Fig. 3-3 N), and *Petalonia fascia* (Fig. 3-3 H), but these give way to warm-temperate and subtropical forms in the summer, including *Ceramium fastigiatum* (Fig. 3-3 X), *Bryocladia cuspidata* (Fig. 3-3 C1), and *Padina vickersiae* (Figs. 3-1 H and 3-3 I). A third group of eurythermal species, including *Gelidium crinale* (Figs. 3-1 F & G and 3-3 B1), *Pterocladia capillacea* (Fig. 3-3 R), *Hypnea musciformis* (Fig. 3-3 W), and *Gracilaria foliifera* (Fig. 3-3 T), may persist throughout the year and constitute a significant percentage of the intertidal and shallow sublittoral flora (Edwards & Kapraun, 1973). Conover (1964) emphasized the importance of solar incidence to the development of the summer jetty flora, but Edwards (1969), conducting laboratory experiments with a number of common species, demonstrated that temperature and day length are more important influences on the seasonal alteration of the flora than seasonal variations in light intensity.

Algal species composition and diversity vary with latitude along the Texas coast, as do aspects of algal zonation and succession. We will examine the rocky intertidal flora on three jetties, Galveston, Port Aransas and South Padre Island, to see the changes that occur with latitude.

Table 3-2. Distribution of Algal Species on the Texas Gulf Shores

	Green		Brown		Red		Totals	
	#	%	#	%	#	%	#	%
All localities	11	17.7	9	28.1	32	34.7	52	27.9
North only	6	9.7	10	31.3	9	9.8	25	13.4
North and central	6	9.7	1	3.1	3	3.4	10	5.4
Central only	10	16.1	1	3.1	4	4.4	15	8.1
Central and south	11	17.7	5	15.6	25	27.1	41	22.1
South only	18	29.1	6	18.8	19	20.6	43	23.1
Totals:	62	100.0	32	100.0	92	100.0	186	100.0

Compiled from Taylor (1936, 1941a, 1941b, 1954a), Breuer (1962), Humm and Hildebrand (1962), Conover (1964), Kapraun (1974), Edwards (1976), Lowe and Cox (1978), Baca *et al.* (1979), Kapraun (1979, 1980). North = Sabine R. to Freeport; Central = Freeport to Mustang Island; South = Padre Island to Rio Grande.

The pattern of succession on the Galveston jetties, breakwaters and groins is relatively simple, involving only a few species (Lowe & Cox, 1978). In early summer the green algae *Enteromorpha clathrata* (Fig.3-3 A) and *Cladophora* sp., e.g., *C. albida* (Fig. 3-3 E), and the red *Bryocladia cuspidata* (Fig. 3-3 C1), and *Ceramium strictum* dominate. By mid-summer the green algae, which occupy a high position in the upper mid-littoral and lower supralittoral fringe, begin to decline. The red algae increase as the season progresses, thriving in the warm waters of the lower mid-littoral and sublittoral fringe. *Ceramium strictum* is especially characteristic of protected mid-littoral rock faces of the Galveston jetties. It and *Bryocladia* persist until the winter northers sweep the coast in November or December. As the water becomes colder, both species experience a population crash. They are quickly replaced by several new species including *Gelidium crinale* (Figs. 3-1 F and G, 3-3 B1), *Bangia fuscopurpurea* (Fig. 3-3 K), *Petalonia fascia* (Fig. 3-3 H), and resurgent *Enteromorpha* spp. To a lesser degree, *Ulva lactuca* (Fig. 3-3 C), *Ulva fasciata* (Fig. 3-1 E) and *Polysiphonia subtilissima* are also characteristic winter flora on the jetty rocks. By mid-February it is not unusual for the upper mid-littoral and lower supralittoral fringe to be covered with a thick green *Enteromorpha* carpet. Cooler temperatures and winter storm waves permit this luxuriant growth. It will largely disappear the next summer and the cycle will begin again.

As an example of the changing algal composition along the northwestern Gulf, three of the dominant Galveston jetty rhodophytes, *Ceramium, Bryocladia,* and *Gelidium* (*fide* Lowe & Cox, 1978), were not found in similar habitats on the Louisiana coast (Kapraun, 1974). *Bangia* and *Polysiphonia* were common at both localities.

The algal flora of the Port Aransas jetties has received more intensive study than any other locality on the Texas coast (Conover, 1964; Edwards, 1969, 1976; Edwards & Kapraun, 1973; Kapraun, 1970, 1979, 1980).

There is greater diversity here than at Galveston, with about 90 species. The distribution of the common species varies seasonally, vertically, and horizontally, influenced by factors such as temperature, day length, light intensity, and wave exposure (Edwards, 1969; Edwards & Kapraun, 1973).

As at Galveston, three groups of algae occur on the Port Aransas jetties (Fig. 3-4) with respect to seasonal variation: (1), species which appear in the cooler parts of the year (indicated by W on Fig. 3-4), (2), species which appear in the warmer parts of the year (indicated by S on Fig. 3-4), and (3), species which are generally present throughout the year (indicated by A on Fig. 3-4). The first group contains a number of species commonly associated with cool temperate North Atlantic shores, including *Bangia fuscopurpurea* (Fig. 3-3 K), *Petalonia fascia* (Fig. 3-3 H) and *Cladophora albida* (Fig. 3-3 E), whereas the last two groups include either eurythermal species such as *Acrochaetium flexuosum, Gelidium crinale* (Figs. 3-1 F & G and 3-3 B1), and *Grateloupia filicina* (Fig. 3-3 O) or those with definite tropical affinities, including *Padina vickersiae* (Figs. 3-1 H and 3-3 I), *Bryocladia cuspidata* (Fig. 3-3 C1), *Dictyota dichotoma* (Fig. 3-3 G) and *Ceramium fastigiatum* (Fig. 3-3 X). Edwards and Kapraun (1973) found species with tropical affinities in the majority (55.1 percent). Cool temperate north Atlantic species represented about 11.5 percent of the flora, and species restricted to warm-temperate shores were few (2.6 percent). A significant number of algae (30.8 percent) of uncertain latitudinal affinity mask the pattern of seasonal succession by other groups. Seasonal changes in dominance do occur, and sometimes strikingly so.

Vertical zonation of the algae is evident on the Port Aransas jetties, varying according to season and exposure. The orientation of the Port Aransas jetty (122°) exposes its outer southern face to the greatest waves driven by the prevailing southeasterly winds. The effect becomes increasingly pronounced toward the seaward end of the jetty. Algae (and the intertidal biota in general) tend to occur higher upon the southern shore of the jetty than on the northern shore in the face of this greater wave exposure. Furthermore there are some algal species which require greater exposure and are absent on the more sheltered face, and *vice versa* (Kapraun, 1980). Species which occur on both sides of the jetty may display conspicuously greater abundance on one side. For example, *Polysiphonia denudata*, *Rhodymenia pseudopalmata* (Fig. 3-3 Z), *Corallina cubensis* (Fig. 3-3 V), *Corallina subulata* (Fig. 3-3 A1), *Callithamnion byssoides* (Fig. 3-3 Q), *Callithamnion cordatum* and *Dictyota dichotoma* (Fig. 3-3 G) are most abundant in shelter, whereas *Giffordia rallsiae*, *Cladophora dalmatica*, *Pterocladia capillacea* (Fig. 3-3 R), and *Gracilaria foliifera* (Fig. 3-3 T) attain greatest densities on the exposed shore (Kapraun, 1980).

The vertical range of summer vegetation along the exposed seaward southwestern shore of the jetty is about 3 m with algae extending 1 m above and 2 m below mean sea level (Edwards & Kapraun, 1973). *Enteromorpha clathrata* (Fig. 3-3 A), *Chaetomorpha linum* (Fig. 3-3 D), *Cladophora dalmatica*, *Grateloupia filicina* (Fig. 3-3 O), and *Ceramium fastigiatum* (Fig. 3-3 X) dominate the upper shore, with the first two species sometimes extending into the supralittoral fringe. Dominant mid-littoral species include *Ulva fasciata* (Fig. 3-1 E), *Gelidium crinale* (Fig. 3-1 F & G), *Centroceras clavulatum* (Fig. 3-3 Y), *Bryocladia cuspidata* (Fig. 3-3 C1), *Padina vickersiae* (Fig. 3-3 I), and *Cladophora vagabunda*. *Giffordia mitchellae* (Fig. 3-3 F), *Erythrocladia subintegra* (Fig. 3-3 L), and *Goniotrichum alsidii* (Fig. 3-3 M) are common epiphytes. The summer flora of the exposed sublittoral includes *Solieria tenera* (Fig. 3-3 P), *Pterocladia capillacea* (Fig. 3-3 R) and *Rhodymenia pseudopalmata* (Fig. 3-3 Z). Tufts of *Bryopsis hypnoides* (Fig. 3-3 U) provide the lower shore a splash of dark green among the typically dominant red algae of summer. The relative densities of these species may vary from year to year as indicated by the differences between algal dominants reported by Edwards & Kapraun (1973) and Kapraun (1980).

The species composition is different and the vertical range of summer vegetation is diminished considerably on the protected inner jetty shore (Kapraun, 1980). Here, the common upper mid-littoral species are *Ceramium strictum*, *Chaetomorpha linum* (Fig. 3-3 D), *Grateloupia filicina* (Fig. 3-3 O), and *Bryocladia cuspidata* (Fig. 3-3 C1). The middle zone algae include *Cladophora vagabunda*, *Bryocladia thyrsigera*, and *Dictyota dichotoma* (Fig. 3-3 G), while the sublittoral dominants are *Enteromorpha lingulata* (Fig. 3-3 B), *Rhodymenia pseudopalmata* (Fig. 3-3 Z), *Solieria tenera* (Fig. 3-3 P), and *Padina vickersiae* (Fig. 3-3 I). The sheltered side of the jetty has a greater relative abundance and diversity of algae in the upper mid-littoral and sublittoral zones than on the exposed face (Kapraun, 1980).

During the winter months at Port Aransas, the diversity and vertical range of the jetty flora diminish significantly. The lower-zone species seem to be most affected. At the onset of winter, sublittoral algae with tropical affinities disappear, not to be replaced. The lower shore winter flora appears depauperate (Fig. 3-4). As at Galveston, *Bangia fuscopurpurea* (Fig. 3-3 K) emerges as a cold weather upper shore dominant. *Petalonia fascia* (Fig. 3-3 H) and *Porphyra leucosticta* (Fig. 3-3 N) also become more abundant in the mid-littoral. Green algae become prominent, largely at the expense of the reds which prefer warmer waters. By early spring, the jetties are usually surrounded by a bright green belt at mid-tide level, which gradually changes to a mixture of reds, browns, and greens as summer approaches. To date there have been no detailed studies of the differential distribution of winter algae on the exposed and sheltered faces of the jetty.

The flora of southernmost Texas has received less attention than other areas, although several floral surveys have appeared (Humm & Hildebrand, 1962; Baca *et al.*, 1979; Sorensen, 1979). The surveys indicate an increasing tropical component in the flora and a decreasing number of cool-temperate species. For example, Baca *et al.* (1977) cite the jetties at South Padre Island (Brazos-Santiago Pass) as the northernmost occurrence in the western Gulf of Mexico of three species, *Dasya rigidula*, *Spatoglossum schroederi*, and *Caulerpa mexicana*. To date, most floral surveys of the Brazos-Santiago jetties have been restricted to the inner shore of the northern jetty. It is a relatively protected location where wave exposure and the vertical range of macrophytes are minimal. The southwestern jetty shore receives the greatest exposure (and hence has the broadest band of macrophytes). It has received less study in part because of its remoteness but also because dangerous currents make field work here extremely hazardous. If an intensive survey of the southwest shore could be conducted safely, it would likely increase the number of species with exclusively tropical affinities occurring at the northernmost limit of their range. As on other Texas jetties, cool-temperate species flourish only during the cool seasons at the Brazos-Santiago jetties.

3-3. Algae and some algal associates of the Texas jetties. **A.** *Enteromorpha clathrata;* **B.** *Enteromorpha lingulata;* **C.** Sea lettuce, *Ulva lactuca;* **D.** *Chaetomorpha linum;* **E.** *Cladophora albida;* **F.** *Giffordia mitchellae;* **G.** *Dictyota dichotoma;* **H.** *Petalonia fascia;* **I.** *Padina vickersiae;* **J.** *Anachis semiplicata;* **K.** *Bangia fuscopurpurea;* **L.** *Erythrocladia subintegra;* **M.** *Goniotrichum alsidii;* **N.** *Porphyra leucosticta;* **O.** *Grateloupia filicina;* **P.** *Solieria tenera;* **Q.** *Callithamnion byssoides;* **R.** *Pterocladia capillacea;* **S.** Skeleton shrimp, *Caprella equilibra;* **T.** *Gracilaria foliifera;* **U.** *Bryopsis hypnoides;* **V.** *Corallina cubensis;* **W.** *Hypnea musciformis;* **X.** *Ceramium fastigiatum;* **Y.** *Centroceras clavulatum;* **Z.** *Rhodymenia pseudopalmata;* **A1.** *Corallina subulata;* **B1.** *Gelidium crinale;* **C1.** *Bryocladia cuspidata;* **D1.** Beach hopper, *Hyale frequens.*

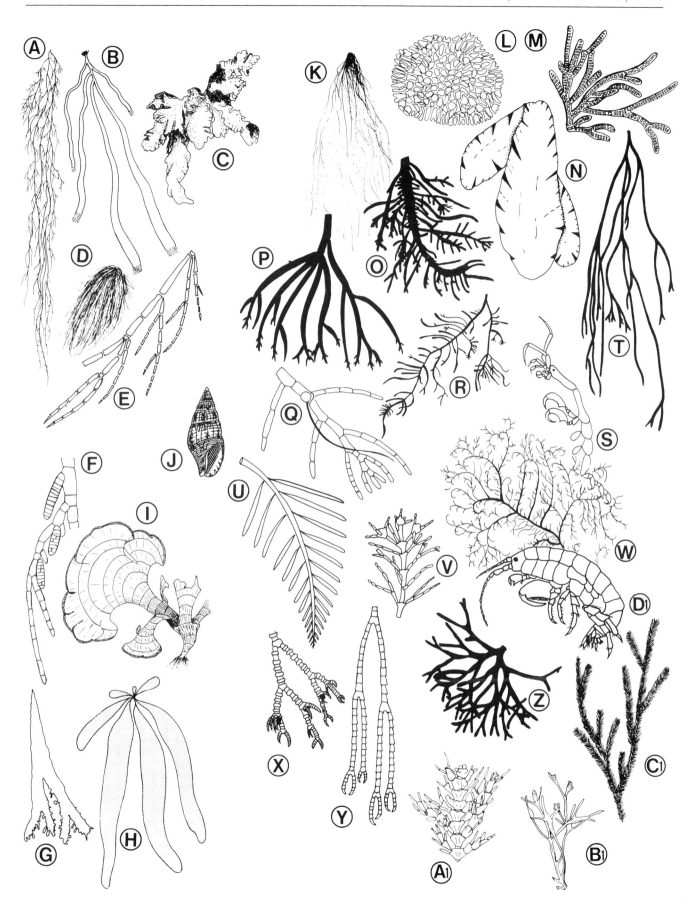

In addition to the eukaryotic macrophytes, another group of important microscopic plants is usually common on the Texas jetties, the primitive blue-green algae or Cyanophyta. They are frequently overlooked or dismissed as an organic scum covering thinly the flat, wave-washed upper surfaces of jetties. *Lyngbya* is a common genus consisting of cells aligned in microscopic filaments. Like other blue-green algae, it secretes a slippery gelatinous sheath around each filament. When *Lyngbya* carpets the upper splash pools and swash-influenced walkways on the surface of the jetties, it creates a hazard to unwary pedestrians. Seemingly solid granite boulders are transformed into dangerously slippery surfaces under a *Lyngbya* mat. Blue-green algae can live high upon the shore, in part protected from desiccation by the gelatinous sheath (Davis, 1972), and in part by the ability to form resistant spores in the face of adverse environmental conditions.

Algal Herbivores and the Effects of Herbivory

In addition to the physical factors which influence the distribution of jetty flora, the intertidal and shallow subtidal algae, like other producers throughout the world, are subjected to grazing by herbivores. In the sea, just as on land, herbivory can influence significantly the distribution and diversity of the flora (Ebert, 1977; Irvine, 1973; Vadas, 1977; Underwood & Jernakoff, 1981). Until recently, intertidal algae and their herbivores were studied independently, with little concern for interactions between the producers and consumers, or the combined impact of this interaction on the total community (Lubchenco & Gaines, 1981). Many papers on herbivore foraging and its impact on individual algal species have appeared, as have studies on anti-herbivore defenses of algae (see Lubchenco & Gaines, 1981, for an extensive bibliography). However, the importance of herbivores and their ultimate influence on community structure of a rocky shore has only relatively recently begun to be appreciated (e.g., May *et al.*, 1970; Dayton, 1971; John & Pople, 1973; Luckens, 1974; Lubchenco & Menge, 1978; Sousa, 1979; Duggins, 1981; Dayton, 1984; Jernakoff, 1985; Sebens, 1985; and Sousa, 1985).

A few generalizations have emerged. For example, intense herbivory tends to reduce macrophyte cover on hard substrata, leaving it open for settlement by other kinds of attached organisms such as barnacles, mussels, and limpets (Luckens, 1974; Underwood & Jernakoff, 1981). In the absence of herbivores, macrophytes increase through successional stages, eventually displacing other sessile biota (May *et al.*, 1970; Dayton, 1971; Sousa, 1979; Sousa *et al.*, 1981). Shores are rarely dominated by a single group of biota, but usually consist of a patchwork of several different groups. Dense macrophyte gardens may be separated by areas with sparse algae but dense aggregations of filter feeding mussels, barnacles, and microphytic grazers. The size of vegetated and nonvegetated patches fluctuates with time, controlled by the in-

crease or decrease in herbivory, or by a variety of environmental factors primarily related to biotic or abiotic disturbance (Lubchenco & Gaines, 1981). Unfortunately, none of these generalizations have emerged as a result of ecological investigations on Gulf of Mexico jetties. In the absence of specific regional studies, we can only speculate about herbivore impact on Texas jetty community structure.

Intertidal herbivores vary according to body size and the size of particle they are capable of ingesting, the method of browsing (scraping, grazing, or biting), means of access to the shore (crawling, swimming, etc.), and physiological adaptations for life on the shore (e.g., echinoids have poor resistance to desiccation whereas some pulmonate herbivores can drown with prolonged immersion). Upper shore herbivores tend to be small, well adapted for desiccation resistance, and usually scrape the shore for relatively small particles. *Nodilittorina lineolata* and *Siphonaria pectinata* are both good examples of upper shore herbivores. Mid- and lower shore herbivores may be considerably more varied with respect to size, diet, and forage pattern, but frequently less tolerant of environmental extremes.

There are few conspicuous mid- to lower shore macrophyte herbivores on the Texas jetties, again reflecting the general paucity of biota here. The most common include the false limpet, *Siphonaria pectinata* (which we have discussed above), the sea hare, *Aplysia brasiliana*, the sea urchin, *Arbacia punctulata*, and several fishes described in the paragraphs below.

Several species of sea hares occur on the Texas coast, the most common being *Aplysia brasiliana* (Fig. 3-4 D). The spotted sea hare, *A. dactylomela* is sometimes found along the south Texas jetties, and three additional species are rarely found here. Sea hares are large opisthobranch molluscs with a single

3-4. Algal zonation and seasonal succession on the Texas jetties, and some common jetty fauna. Characteristic algae for each of the major shore zones are listed in the left boxes. R, Rhodophyta; G, Chlorophyta; B, Phaeophyta; W, predominantly a winter species on Texas jetties; S, predominantly a summer species on Texas jetty; A, approximately equal abundance all year. The dark bars in the right boxes indicate relative seasonal abundance for each species of algae, with increasing thickness of the bars indicating increased abundance. The seasonal scale is at the top beginning with October (O). Mean monthly precipitation, sea and air temperatures, salinity, and wind duration from the north (open circles) and south (closed circles) are also indicated. Fauna include the herbivores: **A.** Lined periwinkle, *Nodilittorina lineolata*; **B.** False limpet, *Siphonaria pectinata*; **C.** Sergeant major, *Abudefduf saxatilis*; **D.** Spotted sea hare, *Aplysia brasiliana*; **E.** Red sea urchin, *Arbacia punctulata*; **F.** the predatory stone crab, *Menippe adina*.

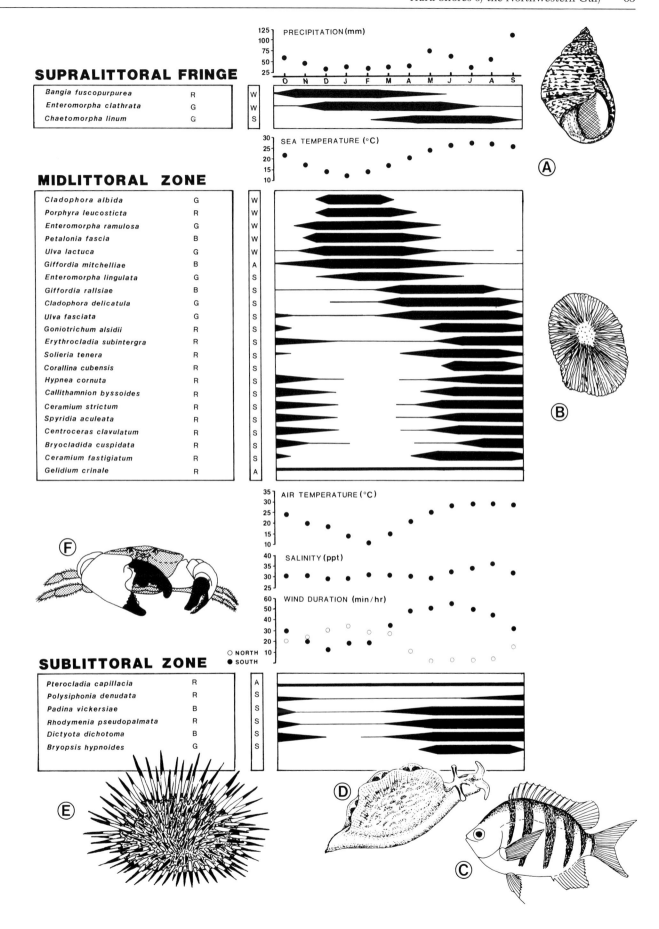

SUPRALITTORAL FRINGE

Bangia fuscopurpurea	R
Enteromorpha clathrata	G
Chaetomorpha linum	G

PRECIPITATION (mm)

SEA TEMPERATURE (°C)

MIDLITTORAL ZONE

Cladophora albida	G
Porphyra leucosticta	R
Enteromorpha ramulosa	G
Petalonia fascia	B
Ulva lactuca	G
Giffordia mitchelliae	B
Enteromorpha lingulata	G
Giffordia rallsiae	B
Cladophora delicatula	G
Ulva fasciata	G
Goniotrichum alsidii	R
Erythrocladia subintergra	R
Solieria tenera	R
Corallina cubensis	R
Hypnea cornuta	R
Callithamnion byssoides	R
Ceramium strictum	R
Spyridia aculeata	R
Centroceras clavulatum	R
Bryocladida cuspidata	R
Ceramium fastigiatum	R
Gelidium crinale	R

AIR TEMPERATURE (°C)

SALINITY (ppt)

WIND DURATION (min/hr)

○ NORTH
● SOUTH

SUBLITTORAL ZONE

Pterocladia capillacia	R
Polysiphonia denudata	R
Padina vickersiae	B
Rhodymenia pseudopalmata	R
Dictyota dichotoma	B
Bryopsis hypnoides	G

ctenidium located on the right side of the body, a very reduced shell hidden inside the mantle cavity, conspicuous dorso-lateral folds called parapodia derived from lateral foot tissue, and elongate sensory tentacles on the head which resemble lagomorph ears and hence provide the animal its common name. Because of the food preference of *Aplysia* species for intertidal or subtidal algae, sea hares are legitimately regarded as shore animals. *Aplysia brasiliana* is largely restricted to subtidal jetty habitats along the Texas coast, except during the reproductive season when it may move into the shallow bays for spawning (Hamilton *et al.*, 1982). In the Caribbean, *A. brasiliana*, *A. dactylomela* and related species may occur intertidally.

As *Aplysia brasiliana* may reach 15 to 20 cm in length, it is conspicuous as it swims just off the jetty or glides among the low-zoned macroscopic algae attached to jetty rocks. It is one of only a few species of sea hares capable of prolonged swimming, using the parapodia for propulsion. Parapodia pulsate in peristaltic-like waves, collecting water along the anterio-dorsal surface and funnelling it along the back, creating a slow but effective water jet which pushes the animal forward (Neu, 1932). *Aplysia brasiliana* is most commonly seen swimming along the jetty in late afternoon or early morning. Like all sea hares, it also has a broad, muscular and typically molluscan foot covering most of the ventral surface of the body. When the animal is swimming the foot is folded closed against the body, but becomes the primary organ of locomotion when the sea hare settles to the bottom to forage among the lush algal garden.

Sea hares are important subtidal and mid-littoral herbivores, grazing heavily upon macrophytic algae. They commonly browse jetty pastures at night, so you may need a flashlight and patience to see them feeding. Divers sometimes observe sea hares grazing on subtidal jetty boulders during daylight hours.

Aplysia has distinct food preferences and will flatly reject certain kinds of algae. Green algae are generally preferred, especially species of *Enteromorpha*, *Ulva*, and *Cladophora* (Kandel, 1979). These algae may be especially heavily grazed by sea hares along the Texas jetties, facilitating seasonal succession of lower shore macrophytes. *Aplysia* generally avoids many species of red algae, but will take species of *Centroceras*. Large (1 to 2 cm) pieces are taken into the buccal cavity and held by jaws while the radula rasps small bits to be ingested (Howells, 1942).

Aplysia has an oval structure, the mantle shelf, located on the dorsal surface of the body between the parapodia. It consists of mantle tissue surrounding a degenerate shell, and enclosing a small mantle cavity. It also bears two unique glands near the junction with the visceral mass. One of the glands, Blochmann's gland, named after its discoverer, produces a purple inky fluid. The second or opaline gland produces a thick, white, mucous-like substance. Either or both of these substances may be released by *Aplysia* when it is stimulated aggressively. Usually the purple ink is

discharged first. The exact function of the ink is uncertain. In a restricted tide-pool environment, it may produce sufficient camouflage to permit escape from a would-be predator. In the open sea, however, it is quickly diluted by currents, and affords little or no protection by concealment. Indeed, Carew & Kupfermann (1974) have shown that sea hares inhabiting calm waters or protected tide pools ink more readily than those in turbulent waters or in the open sea. The ink may be more than a simple concealment device, as it may provide a confusing or irritating chemical signal to the potential predator, inhibiting further attack. The inking behavior is definitely a defensive response, but its precise function or mode of action is still not entirely understood (Kandel, 1979).

The opaline substance is another defensive secretion with a more clearly defined mode of action. It is not as readily released as the purple ink, and seems to be withheld for only life-threatening situations. The opaline substance of some species of *Aplysia* has a nauseating odor to humans (Hyman, 1967). When injected into a variety of potential *Aplysia* predators including jellyfish, echinoderms, other molluscs, crabs, and fish, it produces convulsions and paralysis (Flury, 1915). It also has been shown to inhibit the feeding behavior of crabs (Kandel, 1979). Opaline substance is an effective chemical defense for this otherwise soft-bodied and apparently defenseless mollusc.

Aplysia is hermaphroditic but does not self-fertilize, nor is reciprocal fertilization (where sperm is transferred from one individual to another and *vice versa*) the rule. Individuals will act as either male or female to a second individual, but not both. The situation is complicated by the tendency to form mating chains when as many as a dozen individuals link together. The first individual of the chain will serve as a female to the second, and the last will serve as a male to the penultimate individual. In this way, a specimen may serve as both male and female, but not to the same individual. Occasionally, long chains close to form a circle when the terminal individuals come in contact and mate (Eales, 1921; MacGinitie, 1934).

Aplysia spawns during late spring and early summer. During this time, *A. brasiliana* is said to migrate to the grass flats of inner bays for spawning (Fotheringham, 1980; Hamilton *et al.*, 1982). Inshore spawning migrations have been questioned for other *Aplysia* species (Chambers, 1934), but Hamilton *et al.* (1982), present evidence which suggests that *A. brasiliana* moves into estuarine waters for spawning. Eggs are deposited in elongate, often tangled, yellowish strings. The details of the life cycle of *A. brasiliana* have not been studied, but there is considerable information available on a related eastern Pacific species, *A. californica*. Development proceeds in four phases: (1), embryonic, from fertilized egg to hatching, (2), larval, from hatching to metamorphosis, (3), metamorphosis, the change from larva to adult body form and (4), post metamorphic from juvenile to adulthood. Embryonic development usually requires about 14 days, during which time a trochophore stage passes within the egg capsule. A veliger larva emerges from the egg and enters the meroplankton for a period of about 34 days. The veliger feeds on a variety of microscopic algae and possibly bacteria and organic detritus. Metamorphosis requires about 3 days, during which time *Aplysia* does not eat and leaves the meroplankton to become a member of the epifauna. Postmetamorphic development of the juvenile is completed about 85 days after metamorphosis, or about 133 days following deposition of the fertilized egg (Kriegstein *et al.*, 1974; Kandel, 1979). The development of *A. brasiliana* and *A. dactylomela* is probably similar to that of *A. californica*. The former species usually lives about 1 year, and apparently dies after spawning.

The lower margins of hard shores throughout the world are usually delimited by one or more large spiny sea urchins which browse upon algae or sea grasses (Lawrence, 1975). Urchins are rare or absent on the northern Texas jetties, but two or three species may be encountered from Port Aransas southward. The most common is the reddish or blackish urchin, *Arbacia punctulata* (Figs. 3-1 I, and 3-4 E). It is most abundant on sheltered inlet-facing jetty shores in waters with a salinity near that of the open sea. It is usually absent on the more exposed outer rocks. *Arbacia* is easily recognized by its reddish body and numerous black-tipped spines. The only species with which it might be confused is the Caribbean rock-boring urchin, *Echinometra lucunter* (Figs. 4-1 E1; 4-2 P; 4-4 O), a smaller dark echinoid most commonly found on the southernmost Texas jetties in areas of maximum exposure. Another Caribbean echinoid, *Lytechinus variegatus* also sometimes occurs with *Arbacia* on the southern jetties (Fairchild & Sorensen, 1985), but its short greenish spines are easily distinguished from the red-spined urchin.

Despite its abundance on the inner jetty shores, daytime visitors to the jetties usually fail to see *Arbacia*. It lives out of sight, from just below the tide to the base of the jetty rocks. Like most urchins, it shuns daylight, seeking shelter in darkened crevices between jetty boulders, emerging only at night to feed.

Arbacia moves with the combined effort of articulating spines and dozens of tube feet, each emerging from a tiny pore in the echinoid test between the spines. The tube feet terminate in small suction disks, and enable *Arbacia* to cling to the substratum. As it moves over the mats of algae of the lower shore *Arbacia* indiscriminately crops thallus pastures with an efficient and uniquely echinoid sickle located in the mouth. It consists of an intricately designed set of five trigonal articulating plates bearing calcareous teeth and associated structures. When one of these mouth parts was excised intact from an Aegean urchin by the Greek philosopher and biologist Aristotle, it reminded him of a kind of lantern then in use throughout the Ancient world (Thompson,1947). Appropriately, modern biologists have designated the echinoid mouthparts as "Aristotle's lantern." Muscles attach to each

of the five plates on the "lantern" and to the teeth on the plates, enabling the structure to be protracted or retracted from the mouth and the teeth to be opened or closed, much like the bit jaws on a power drill. As it feeds, the urchin can perform a variety of pulling, shredding, scraping, or tearing movements.

Arbacia is primarily a herbivore, but usually will ingest anything it is capable of removing from the substratum on its nocturnal forages. For example, it has been known to feed upon sponges, coral polyps, mussels, sand dollars, and other *Arbacia* (Harvey, 1956) and even moribund fishes (Parker, 1932). As an indiscriminate grazer on sheltered rocks, *Arbacia* may be an important biologic factor in the distribution of algae on the Texas jetties as are other urchins on other shores (Lawrence, 1975). Algal species susceptible to cropping by *Arbacia* on sheltered rocks are likely to be free of herbivory by this urchin on exposed shores. Unfortunately, there have been no studies quantifying the impact of *Arbacia* on floral density or diversity.

In many American classrooms, this sea urchin has been the model for studies of fertilization and early embryology. Entire books have been devoted to *Arbacia* reproductive and developmental biology (e.g., Harvey, 1956), so only a brief synopsis will be given here. *Arbacia* is dioecious, although there is no obvious external dimorphism between the sexes. Sex can be determined only by an examination of the gametes or by artificial stimulation of gamete release. Eggs are reddish and can usually be differentiated as tiny spheres by the naked eye. Sperm are discharged from gonopores in a white fluid, but individual spermatozoa are indistinguishable except with the aid of a microscope. Reproduction is by free-shedding of gametes into the sea. *Arbacia* ranges from New England to the Caribbean, and its period of gravidity varies with latitude. In New England, ripe gametes appear from late spring to mid-summer, whereas on the Gulf coast, ripe gametes are usually present throughout the winter and are spent by late spring (Harvey,1956). When one urchin releases gametes, nearby urchins somehow detect the spawn, and quickly follow suit. Soon, the sea is filled with eggs and sperm. Fertilization occurs as male and female gametes contact randomly in the sea.

Development also occurs in the sea. Three to four days following fertilization, a free-swimming echinopluteus larva is formed. In cool-temperate seas, the larvae may remain in the meroplankton 3 to 4 months, but development may proceed more rapidly in warmer waters. While in the plankton, the echinopluteus feeds on a variety of microscopic phytoplankton and undergoes a gradual change in body form. Eventually the modified echinopluteus settles to the bottom, where it quickly completes metamorphosis into the adult. At this stage, the juvenile urchin may be about 6 mm in diameter (Harvey, 1956).

Sessile Animals of the Subtidal and Sublittoral Fringe

The asphalt cap along several sections of the southern Aransas Pass jetty has eroded away, leaving the crevices between the underlying boulders visible and awash in moderate seas. Young oyster shells, *Crassostrea virginica* or *Ostrea equestris* (Fig. 3-2 Q), cover the rocks at the base of these narrow breaks. They attach during the cooler months, but by mid-summer few if any are alive. None exceed about 6 cm in length. A similar fate awaits oysters on other Texas jetties. Oysters attach to subtidal, sublittoral fringe, or surf-swept rocks and grow for a short time. Invariably, they perish at a young age. The reason oysters fare so poorly on the jetty is not known, but several factors may be involved. Oysters are not found amid the lush growth of attached macrophytes, so the algae or jetty fauna may out-compete the oysters for space. *Crassostrea* does not tolerate the higher salinities of the open Gulf, nor does *Ostrea* survive in the lower estuarine waters of the bays. The seasonal salinity fluctuations of the tidal inlets may effectively exclude both species from these shores, except for short periods when recruitment is possible, to be quickly followed by post-juvenile mortality. Both species may be affected by thermal stress, predation, disease, parasites, or other unsuitable environmental conditions unique to the jetties. For whatever reason or reasons, oysters, which require a hard bottom on which to settle, find it on the jetties, but rarely survive to maturity.

There are a few kinds of anemones on the jetties. The most common species is *Bunodosoma* (= *Phymactis*) *cavernata* (Fig. 3-2 T), found from Sabine Pass to the South Padre jetties. It is a greenish anemone found just below the mid-littoral in sheltered water-covered crevices between boulders. The oral disk can expand to a diameter of about 40 mm and is provided with 5 cycles of about 96 pale green sticky tentacles. The inner tentacles bear a pale blue stripe on the oral side and a light red stripe on the opposite surface. A fully extended *B. cavernata* can reach 9 cm in height. The surface of the columnar body below the tentacles is covered with numerous tiny wart-like pale blue vesicles which align in vertical rows. Like many intertidal anemones, *Bunodosoma* attaches bits of shell debris and other objects to its body for protection from sand abrasion or excessive solar illumination.

As with most cnidarians, the tentacles of *Bunodosoma* are provided with numerous microscopic stinging organelles, the nematocysts, which assist the tentacles in obtaining food. *Bunodosoma* has several different types of nematocysts, and they serve to distinguish this species from other similar anemones. The sting of *Bunodosoma* is almost imperceptible to humans. Only the "stickiness" of the tentacles provides the clue that nematocysts are present. *Bunodactis texaensis* is very similar to *Bunodosoma cavernata*, and like the latter, it occurs along the entire Texas coast. Reliable identification of this species requires microscopic examination of nematocysts and other structures.

Aiptasiomorpha texaensis is a small anemone, rarely attaining a basal diameter of 5 mm. Oyster reefs are probably its primary habitat, as it is tolerant of lowered salinities. *Aiptasiomorpha* reproduces sexually, but it also readily clones new individuals by asexual budding. A mature specimen may bear several new polyps developing from the body wall (Fig. 3-2 V). These tiny buds will eventually drop free of the parental body and take up independent existence nearby. It is because of the budding tendency that *Aiptasiomorpha texaensis* is usually found in clusters of a few to several dozen individuals in the lower sublittoral fringe.

Anthopleura krebsi (Fig. 3-2 U) is normally a tropical species sometimes found on the jetties from Port Aransas and southward. The disk may be 3 cm across and surrounded by a few greenish or rust-striped tentacles. The column is pale rusty green and covered with pink warts arranged in regular vertical rows. *Anthopleura krebsi* is more easily removed from the rocks than most of the other jetty anemones.

In addition to the relatively conspicuous anemones, polypoid cnidarians are also represented on the jetties by a number of small colonial hydroids. To the naked eye, hydroids are often mistaken for "seaweed," and in fact live among many of the lower intertidal algae. Careful examination with a hand-lens may be required to distinguish the hydroids from algae. The most common jetty hydroids are *Obelia adichotoma* (Fig. 3-5 B) and *Bougainvillia inaequallis* (Fig. 3-5 A), both of which occur on subtidal rock surfaces or in protected crevices of the lower littoral zone, especially at the seaward ends of the jetties. *Bougainvillia* is the more conspicuous of the two, growing in bushy colonies up to about 10 cm in diameter. Unlike the algae with which it is associated, the surface of the *Bougainvillia* colony appears very rough or wrinkled, and close inspection will reveal the characteristic tentacle-bearing polyps absent in any kind of algae. *Obelia* colonies are always much smaller than those of *Bougainvillia*, rarely extending more than about 2 cm in diameter.

Like most colonial hydroids, these species employ a free-swimming, sexually reproducing stage for dispersal to new environments. Tiny asexually-produced medusa buds develop in specialized reproductive polyps and are eventually released from the colony. The mature free-swimming hydroid medusa bears either male or female gametes and reproduces sexually by free shedding of sex cells into the sea. Fertilization occurs by chance encounters between egg and sperm, although as in other invertebrates, a triggering mechanism may regulate gamete release. A successfully fertilized egg will eventually develop into a ciliated larva, the planula, which then seeks a suitable substratum for attachment. If one is found, the planula develops rhizoid-like holdfasts and undergoes cellular differentiation into a new hydroid colony.

There are several additional hydroids which occur on the jetties. *Zanclea costata* (Fig. 3-5 G), *Clytia cylindrica* (Fig. 3-5 F) and *Sertularia inflata* (Fig. 3-5 D) are *Sargassum* epiphytes seen on jetty rocks. *Gonothyraea gracilis* (Fig. 3-5 C) and *Tubularia crocea* (Fig. 3-5 E) occur more frequently on subtidal rocks.

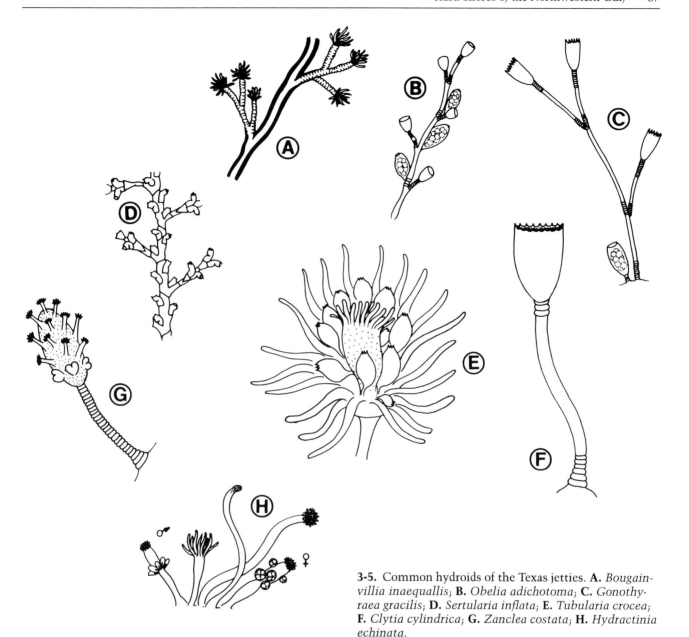

3-5. Common hydroids of the Texas jetties. **A.** *Bougainvillia inaequallis;* **B.** *Obelia adichotoma;* **C.** *Gonothyraea gracilis;* **D.** *Sertularia inflata;* **E.** *Tubularia crocea;* **F.** *Clytia cylindrica;* **G.** *Zanclea costata;* **H.** *Hydractinia echinata.*

Present, but not as common on the Texas coast as along cool-temperate Atlantic shores, is *Hydractinia echinata* (Fig. 3-5 H), an interesting hydroid that is usually found on gastropod shells inhabited by hermit crabs. As the crabs may move from sand flats to jetty rocks, *Hydractinia* is not restricted to the jetties. Nor is the association obligatory, for *Hydractinia* can also be found on unoccupied shells or attached to other firm substrata (Hyman, 1940).

Hydractinia, like most colonial hydroids, is polymorphic, i.e., there are several different kinds of polyps in the colony. Feeding polyps or gastrozooids are most conspicuous. Nematocyst-bearing tentacles on the gastrozooids capture a variety of microscopic animals for food, including nematodes, copepods and other microcrustaceans, and even certain kinds of detritus

(Christensen, 1967). Dactylozooids are the next most abundant polyp in the colony. These are defensive structures lacking tentacles but armed with terminal batteries of nematocysts. They are associated with gastrozooids and probably also assist prey capture. *Hydractinia* also bears two types of sexually dimorphic reproductive polyps, the male and female gonozooids (Fig. 3-5 H).

Two larger sessile cnidarians live upon the basal rocks of the jetties, and on the rocks and shells of the inlet floor and offshore. Neither are intertidal species. They are usually seen alive only by divers, but beachcombers often encounter their skeletons which wash ashore. *Astrangia poculata* (Fig. 10-2 T; Plate 11-3 C) and *Occulina diffusa* (Plate 11-3 D) are the only common shallow water stony corals on the Texas coast, the latter especially abundant on the rocks of southern Texas jetties. Compared to the massive Caribbean reef-forming species, they are poor representatives of the Scleractinia. Like their tropical relatives, both are colonial animals, but their colonies are usually small. Specimens attached to basal jetty rocks rarely consist of more than a few dozen calices, each no more than a few mm in diameter. Both species form slightly larger colonies offshore (Chapter 10). The *Astrangia poculata* colony grows into a stubby, irregularly branching shape, partially encrusting the substratum to which it is attached. Its calices usually lie closely adjacent and often touching. In contrast, *Occulina diffusa* produces a more delicate, erectly branching colony with widely spaced, elevated calices.

Gorgonian octocorals are another group of largely tropical cnidarians that are poorly represented on the Texas coast. There are only two conspicuous species: *Leptogorgia virgulata* (Fig. 10-1 Q) and *L. setacea*, both of which are called sea whips. They are found attached to hard substrata in shallow subtidal waters. The skeleton of these octocorals is not solid, but consists of numerous spicules embedded in a coenenchyme which surrounds a central protein axis. The latter is thickened at the base of the colony so as to function as an organic skeleton. The protein axis becomes progressively thinner and more flexible toward the tips of the branches. Sea whip colonies bend with the currents, and are especially well adapted for life in strong currents as occur in tidal inlets. The largest *Leptogorgia* populations, however, occur offshore (see Chapter 10). In addition to the small corals, sea whips and sea urchins, several species of sponges and tunicates are conspicuous sessile invertebrates on subtidal jetty rocks, often comprising more than 50 percent of the attached biota (Rabalais, 1982).

Mobile Epifauna of the Lower Jetty

Several errant members of the lower jetty fauna have already been discussed, including *Arbacia*, *Menippe*, *Stramonita* and *Aplysia*. There are a number of additional but less conspicuous animals here, including many small crustaceans which deserve mention. *Petrolisthes armatus* (Fig. 3-2 H) occurs commonly on all Texas jetties. It belongs to a group of anomuran crustaceans commonly known as porcelain crabs, so-called because of the characteristically polished, almost porcelain-like shell. *Petrolisthes* is a distinctive little crustacean, rarely exceeding 20 mm in width. Its flattened body enables it to crawl between narrow crevices, and, when threatened by beak or hand, seems able to almost meld with the jetty stones, making it difficult to pick up. *Petrolisthes* thrives on hard shores where it lives under stones or small cobbles in the mid-littoral zone. It infrequently leaves these shelters, so one must turn over stones to find it. Any attempt to capture *Petrolisthes* will usually produce a number of claws and few whole crabs. Porcellanids readily autotomize the large flattened chelae, an obvious defense mechanism which provides the would-be predator with a morsel but not the entire crab. Lost chelae can be restored in subsequent molt.

Petrolisthes is primarily a filter feeder, although it supplements the diet with bits of algae or carrion found among the rocks. Filter feeding is accomplished by the third maxillipeds, a pair of appendages located to either side of the mouth and provided with numerous setae. The maxillipeds are rapidly waved through the water, trapping small particles among the setae. Maxillae periodically clean the maxillipeds of their collected debris, passing it into the mouth for ingestion.

Several other brachyuran or anomuran crabs occur on or near the jetties, but as with so much of this jetty fauna, they are just as likely to be encountered in other habitats. These include the common intertidal hermit crab *Clibanarius vittatus* (Fig. 3-2 I) and the not-so-common subtidal species *Petrochirus bahamensis*, *Pagurus pollicaris* (Fig. 7-6 X) and *P. longicarpus* (Fig. 7-6 P). The small grapsids *Pachygrapsus transversus* (Fig. 5-2 S) and *P. gracilis* occur intertidally, the former being common on the northern jetties.

A number of relatively small (usually less than 1 cm) amphipod and isopod crustaceans live among the macrophytes and wave-cast debris of the lower jetty. There are too many to mention all of them: McKinney (1977) lists about 32 species of gammaridean amphipods which are known to occur on the jetties of the western Gulf region. Furthermore, few are restricted to jetties, as many are commonly found among macrophytes or decaying vegetation in a variety of coastal habitats. Among the more common amphipods are *Gammarus mucronatus* (Fig. 9-2 T), *Hyale frequens* (Fig. 3-3 D1) and the skeleton shrimp *Caprella equilibra* (Fig. 3-3 S). Many of the amphipods are detritivores or herbivores. The influence of their herbivory upon the algae is just beginning to be appreciated. For example, Brawley & Adey (1981) demonstrated that in a closed reef system, a significant percentage of the algal biomass consisted of filamentous species in the absence of amphipod herbivores. An increase in the numbers of amphipods was coupled with a decline in the biomass of filamentous algae and an increase in the biomass of large thallus forms.

A few of the microcrustaceans are predators. For example, skeleton shrimps like *Caprella equilibra* are amphipod versions of a praying mantis. They cling motionless to hydroid or bryozoan colonies in wait for an unsuspecting copepod or amphipod to pass. When one comes near, the caprellid seizes it with pincer-like gnathopods. Not all caprellids are predatory. Many species employ feathery antennae for suspension feeding or graze upon the diatoms and detritus which attach to the organisms upon which they live (Keith, 1969; Caine, 1974).

A few additional predatory gastropods prowl the macrophyte jungle, all smaller than *Stramonita haemastoma*. *Anachis semiplicata* (Fig. 3-3 J) and *Cantharus cancellarius* (Fig. 10-1 V) occur on all Texas jetties, whereas *Pisania tincta* (Fig. 10-2 P) rarely ranges north of Port Aransas. *Anachis semiplicata* is also a common snail on the grass beds of the Texas bays (Chapter 7), whereas the other snails frequent offshore sands and banks (Chapter 10).

Fishes and Cephalopods

A variety of fishes occur in the waters around the jetties, but most are not permanent residents. A great variety of sport and rough fishes are caught by anglers from the inlet or Gulf waters adjacent to the jetty. They include the spadefish, *Chaetodipterus faber* (Fig. 7-11 B); the gray snapper, *Lutjanus griseus* (Fig. 3-6 G); the sheepshead, *Archosargus probatocephalus*; the Florida pompano, *Trachinotus carolinus* (Fig. 3-6 B); the jacks *Caranx crysos* (Fig. 7-13 E), *C. latus* (Fig. 3-6 C), and *C. hippos*; and the hardhead catfish, *Arius felis* (Fig. 7-12 E). The tripletail, *Lobotes surinamensis* (Fig. 3-6 D) is occasionally seen from the jetties as it lazily floats on its side near the surface. In contrast, large schools of agile redfish, *Sciaenops ocellatus* (Fig. 3-6 H) migrate through tidal inlets in the spring and fall, attracting hundreds of anglers to the jetties. These and many other kinds of fishes are caught using a variety of baits, including shrimps, fiddler crabs, barnacles, worms and squid.

The spotted jewfish, *Epinephalus itajara* (Fig. 3-6 I), frequents rocky crevices in the deeper waters of the outer jetty, and is the most common nearshore grouper in Texas waters during the summer. Most specimens are less than a meter in length, but a few grow very large, over 1 m in length and weighing up to 700 lbs. Although rare, these large jewfish occasionally "terrorize" divers swimming along the base of the outer jetties.

Two common non-sportfish are frequently seen swimming near the surface near the jetty rocks. The Atlantic needlefish, *Strongylura marina* (Fig. 3-6 A), is usually seen during the day, and the halfbeak, *Hyporhampus unifasciatus* (Fig. 3-6 F), is usually seen only at night. Both species are widely distributed throughout the western Gulf and Caribbean region, where they readily enter estuaries containing waters of considerably reduced salinity.

Several additional fishes are more intimately associated with the jetty rocks, seeking protection among them or feeding on invertebrates, algae, or detritus which occur there. The hairy blenny, *Labrisomus nuchipinnis* (Fig. 3-6 J), and the crested blenny, *Hypleurochilus geminatus* (Fig. 3-6 E), stay close to the rocks and are seldom seen by most jetty visitors. On the southern jetties, a damselfish, the sergeant-major, *Abudefduf saxatilis* (Fig. 3-2 M and 3-4 C) may be locally abundant. Damselfishes and blennies often feed upon macrophytic algae, but we know little of the effect of their herbivory on the jetty community (Montgomery & Gerking, 1980).

Octopus vulgaris (Fig. 3-2 N) is a cosmopolitan species distributed throughout temperate and tropical seas. It occurs in Gulf waters from the intertidal to the continental shelf, taking shelter in the crevices of the jetties, as well as in empty shells, cans, and other debris which litter the sea floor.

GULLS AND TERNS

Shorebirds of the Texas coast often frequent more than one habitat. Gulls and terns, for example, are found near the jetties, but also range widely throughout the coastal zone from the open Gulf and barrier island beaches to localities far inland. They noisily perch on pilings beside ferry landings, jostle for a favorable position above a shrimper's wake, strut on the barrier strand and, gulls especially, congregate at municipal garbage dumps, scavenging what morsels appear in the debris. Gulls and terns are among the most conspicuous birds of the Texas shores.

Gulls are usually larger than terns. They also differ by having a rounded tail and a hooked bill which is directed forward in flight (the pointed tern bill is held downward in flight, and the tail is decidedly forked). Terns seek live prey, whereas gulls are much less choosy.

The laughing gull, *Larus atricilla* (Fig. 3-2 F), is the most common gull on the Texas coast. It is resident throughout the year, nesting in the summer on small islands or bayshores. It is a large bird with a black head and black-tipped wings. The herring gull, *Larus argentatus* (Fig. 3-2 E), is a winter resident, but a few nonbreeding stragglers may sometimes be seen in the summer. It is the largest gull of the Texas coast, identified by its white head and flesh-colored legs. Four other gulls make regular seasonal appearances (Table 3-3).

Gulls are largely scavengers. Some may dive into the sea for fish, but most are content to seek easier prey or plunder, often as much on land as at sea. Gregarious flocks easily walk, run or hop into the air in pursuit of an edible morsel. They may aggressively engage in aerial piracy (kleptoparasitism) to force another bird to drop its food, or, on the ground, steal food from a neighbor's beak. They are especially adept at scavenging rough fish and invertebrate debris discarded from shrimper's nets. The search for food is a loosely organized (almost accidental) group endeavor. A flock will fan out dozens of square kilometers to survey a shore, a bay or the open sea. When one spies a source of food, its actions bring in other nearby gulls, which, in turn, attract still other birds. Soon, the area is filled with screaming gulls, all competing for the meal. When the resource is depleted, the gulls vanish just as quickly as they arrived to begin the search anew.

Terns are smaller and more streamlined than the gulls, but like their larger cousins, many species (including those most common on Texas shores) are distributed widely throughout the world. Forster's tern, *Sterna forsteri* (Fig. 3-2 C), and the royal and Caspian terns, *Sterna maxima* (Fig. 3-2 B) and *Sterna caspia*, (Fig. 3-2 D), are common year-around residents of the Texas coast. Seven other terns make regular seasonal visits (Table 3-3). All but Forster's tern are birds of the

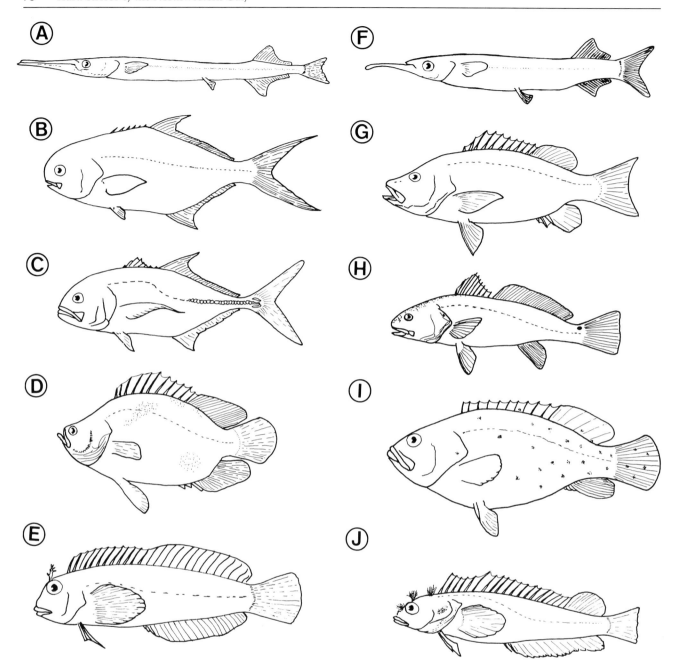

3-6. Fishes of Texas tidal inlets and jetties. **A.** Needlefish, *Strongylura marina*; **B.** Florida pompano, *Trachinotus carolinus*; **C.** Horse-eye jack, *Caranx latus*; **D.** Tripletail, *Lobotes surinamensis*; **E.** Crested blenny, *Hypleurochilus geminatus*; **F.** Halfbeak, *Hyporhampus unifasciatus*; **G.** Gray snapper, *Lutjanus griseus*; **H.** Redfish, *Sciaenops ocellatus*; **I.** Jewfish, *Epinephalus itajara*; **J.** Hairy blenny, *Labrisomus nuchipinnis*.

Table 3-3. Gulls and terns of Texas

		Texas Occurrence	Frequency	Texas Nesting
Subfamily Larinae (Gulls)				
Larus argentatus	Herring gull	Winter, entire	Common	No
Larus atricilla	Laughing gull	All year, entire	Common	Yes
Larus californicus	California gull	Winter, north	Rare	No
Larus delawarensis	Ring-billed gull	Winter, entire	Common	No
Larus pipixcan	Franklin's gull	Spr/Fall, south	Migrant	No
Larus philadelphia	Bonaparte's gull	Winter, entire	Rare	No
Subfamily Sterninae (Terns)				
Chidonias niger	Black tern	Spr/Fall, entire	Migrant	No
Sterna albifrons	Little tern	Summer, entire	Rare	No
Sterna caspia	Caspian tern	All year, entire	Common	Yes
Sterna dougallii	Roseate tern	Spring, entire	Rare	No
Sterna forsteri	Forster's tern	All year, entire	Common	Yes
Sterna fuscata	Sooty tern	Summer, south	Occasional	Yes
Sterna hirundo	Common tern	Spr/Fall, entire	Migrant	No
Sterna maxima	Royal tern	All year, entire	Common	Yes
Sterna nilotica	Gull-billed tern	Summer, south	Common	Yes
Sterna sandvicensis	Sandwich tern	Summer, south	Common	Yes

outer coast. Forster's tern tends to remain near the inner bays and marshes.

Terns are skillful, agile aerial acrobats. Although they are fast fliers, some can hover in the air over a single spot in the sea where they await the appearance of an unsuspecting fish or crustacean. Upon sighting a silvery flash, they will fold their wings and plunge headlong into the water (Fig. 3-2 C). As often as not the tern emerges from the water holding a small fish in the beak. Some, like the sooty tern, *Sterna fuscata* (Fig. 3-2 A), rarely enter the water. They fly low over the sea, dipping only the beak below the surface to catch an unwary swimming morsel. Others, like Forster's tern, patrol the air over bays and marshes for flying insects. Terns almost always take live food, and are rarely seen foraging on the shore.

One gull and seven terns nest in Texas (Table 3-3). All but one of these nest on sandy bayshores, spoil banks and along the more isolated portions of the barrier islands. Forster's tern nests among mats of vegetation in the bays and marshes. The nests of most species consist of shallow scrapes on grass or bare sand,

sometimes with a mat of grass or twigs added. Gulls and terns form large nesting colonies frequently composed of several different species. Terns are generally amicable nesting neighbors respecting the boundaries of nearby nesting territories. The sooty tern, however, vigorously defends its nest, and will kill hatchlings of other birds which stray into its territory. Gulls are even less magnanimous, and many resort to nest robbing. The only nesting gull in Texas, *Larus atricilla*, is not as aggressive as some of the other species (notably *L. argentatus*) but it is known to rob eggs from unattended nests (Bent, 1921).

The nesting season for gulls and terns in Texas is primarily from April to June. A typical nest may hold 2 or 3 eggs, although the sooty tern usually lays but one, and Forster's tern may lay as many as five. Hatching occurs 20 to 26 days after laying. Both sexes usually incubate the eggs. Hatchlings remain on the ground for 6–8 weeks before developing flight plumage. Gulls often require 3 years to develop adult color patterns.

4. The Hard Shores of Eastern Mexico

INTRODUCTION

As in Texas, the majority of Mexico's Gulf margins are sandy beaches. There are, however, three categories of hard shores on the Gulf coast of Mexico: (1), jetties, groins, and other man-made hard shores which, as in Texas, line tidal inlets and protect natural soft shores, (2), natural volcanic or limestone mainland outcroppings, the former along a limited portion of the central mainland shore, and the latter primarily along the southwestern margin of Yucatan, and (3), emergent limestone reefs or banks which primarily lie off the mainland. We will treat the latter category in Chapter 11, and describe the first two here.

MAN-MADE HARD SHORES

There are a number of tidal inlets along Mexico's Gulf coast which are now protected by massive granite or limestone jetties. Rock sea walls, such as at Veracruz, Campeche or Rio Lagartos (Yucatan), also provide a hard surface for attachment, and numerous minor rock groins and breakwaters interrupt the shore at most coastal towns. We will begin with the larger jetties and then briefly consider some of the minor man-made hard shores.

The biota on Mexican jetties nearest the Rio Grande, such as at La Pesca (Fig. 4-1 [1]), is similar to that seen in Texas. *Nodilittorina lineolata* (Fig. 4-1 A) continues as the only littorine on the upper shore. The barnacle, *Chthamalus fragilis* (Fig. 4-1 I), and the false limpet, *Siphonaria pectinata* (Fig. 4-1 K), occupy the middle shore and are joined here by the nerite, *Nerita fulgurans* (Fig. 4-1 P). The latter is found most commonly among small boulders, and in greatest numbers near the more sheltered mainland termination of the jetty and where sand accumulates in crevices.

The algal flora includes an increasing percentage of tropical species, but the dominants remain those previously discussed for south Texas jetties. Notably, the brown alga, *Padina vickersiae* (Fig. 4-1 U), a species particularly well adapted for shallow heated marine waters, thrives among the shallow subtidal boulders. *Gelidium crinale* (Fig. 4-1 T) remains the most common red alga. *Enteromorpha clathrata* paints wave-swept upper littoral rocks vividly green most of the year, and the sea lettuce, *Ulva fasciata* (Fig. 4-1 S), seasonally blankets the surf zone. The urchin, *Arba-*

cia punctulata (Fig. 4-1 D1), occurs on the La Pesca jetty, and persists in other habitats (see Chapter 11). It largely disappears from rocky intertidal shores south of La Pesca, where it is replaced by the tropical intertidal black rock-boring urchin, *Echinometra lucunter* (Fig. 4-1 E1).

The jetties or rocky breakwaters of northwestern Yucatan, as at Chelem (near Progreso) (Fig. 4-1 [5]) or to the east at Celestun (Fig. 4-1 [4]) have faunal elements similar to those further north, but the algal components have become decidedly more tropical in character. The numbers and diversity of both fauna and flora on the many man-made hard shores of Yucatan seem impoverished in comparison to those of Texas, in part the result of nearshore sand scour, and also possibly organic pollution from nearby municipalities. At the Celestun jetty (Fig. 4-1 [4]) in October, for example, we failed to find any species of littorine, whereas at the same time on the lighthouse breakwater at Chelem (Fig. 4-1 [5]) two littorines, *Nodilittorina lineolata* and *Littoraria nebulosa* (Fig. 4-1 B) occurred sparsely. The latter is poorly adapted to survive high surf conditions, so its presence on this jetty is indicative of the relatively sheltered nature of this shore.

In contrast to the few numbers of littorines, the barnacles, especially *Chthamalus fragilis* [or *C. proteus* Dando & Southward, 1980] (Fig. 4-1 I) and *Balanus amphitrite* (Fig. 4-1 J), were especially abundant at Celestun, forming dense, distinctive bands on the midlittoral rocks. A few *Siphonaria pectinata* (Fig. 4-1 K) occurred among the barnacles, occupying areas of bare rock between the cirripedes. Barnacles were much sparser at Chelem, and with *Chthamalus* sp. being the most common. At both localities, the lower shore was poorly colonized by algae, possibly the result of sand scour, pollution effects, or seasonal die-off during the summer. Species of red algae clearly dominate the flora. For example, numerous sand-trapping clumps of *Centroceras clavulatum* (Fig. 4-1 Z) mark the sublittoral fringe on the Celestun rocks. *Gracilaria debilis* (Fig. 4-1 A1) is another common red alga here. A closely cropped film of filamentous green algae, e.g., *Cladophora* sp. (Fig. 4-1 X), lines the rocks below the barnacles at both localities.

Smaller breakwaters along Mexico's Gulf shores follow a similar pattern to those of the jetties. Along southwestern Yucatan shores, however, a curious admixture of biota occurs on the man-made seawalls which lie naturally protected from prevailing winds. The rock breakwater along the northwestern side of the city of Campeche is an excellent example. It extends for several kilometers and is composed primarily of small boulders and large cobbles set in place to retard coastal erosion. The breakwater directly faces the Gulf of Mexico, or, more accurately, faces the broad, shallow Campeche Banks extending dozens of kilometers offshore.

Species more commonly associated with protected estuarine habitats seem to prevail on the Campeche breakwater, often in large numbers. We observed no littorines here, although one or two species may be present in small numbers as they are common on natural rock shores only a few km away. Barnacles are represented by two typically estuarine species, *Balanus improvisus* and *B. amphitrite* (Fig. 4-1 J). *Nerita fulgurans* (Figs. 4-1 P; 4-2 K; 4-3 N) is often very common, but the numerically dominant mid-littoral gastropod is *Cerithium lutosum* (Figs. 4-3 K; 4-4 B). The latter finds shelter among the small rocks and stones of the breakwater, and ample supplies of microscopic algae and detritus upon which it feeds. *Modulus modulus* is another common grazing gastropod, likely a recruit from nearshore turtle grass beds (Chapter 11, Fig. 11-4 N). The scorched mussel, *Brachidontes exustus* (Figs. 4-2 E; 4-3 E) and the yellow mussel, *B. modiolus* attach by byssus threads to the larger stones and boulders. The latter is especially abundant among the barnacles. The xanthid crab, *Panopeus lacustris* (of the *P. herbstii* complex, see Williams, 1983), takes shelter among the rubble and feeds upon many of the shelled invertebrates which also occur here. There are few large algae on the Campeche breakwater rocks, but numerous small filamentous species, especially Chlorophyta.

NATURAL MAINLAND HARD SHORES

Apart from a minor limestone protuberance at Punta Jerez, Tamaulipas, the northernmost natural rocky shore on the eastern coast of Mexico lies approximately 75 km north of Veracruz, extending from Punta del Morro to Punta Villa Rica. Here, the southern volcanic range of Mexico, which traverses the country from Pacific to Atlantic near the latitude of Mexico City, reaches the eastern sea. Seven prominent igneous outcrops, some 60 m in height, provide a natural hard substratum along the shore. A second area south of Veracruz, the San Andres Tuxtlas Mountains, presents a similar face to the sea. We will focus upon shores near Punta del Morro, north of Veracruz, as a model for this habitat (Figs. 4-1 [2] and 4-2).

Natural hard shores also occur along portions of Yucatan, but here the rocks are limestones. From Campeche to Champoton uplifted Eocene reefs form occasional headlands along the arcing coastline, separated by long, narrow sandy beaches. South of Champoton to Laguna de Terminos, which marks the eastern boundary of the Yucatan Peninsula, headlands are

generally reduced to occasional areas of limestone beachrock. A small outcrop of limestone also occurs at Punta Yalkupul, near the center of the northern coast of Yucatan. The dominant mainland shore of eastern Yucatan is also uplifted reef limestone, but inasmuch as this area lies within the Caribbean province, we will discuss its biota only briefly at the end of this chapter. We will use as our model for a western Yucatan limestone shore an unnamed site along Punta Mastun Grande, less than 20 km south of Campeche (Figs. 4-1 [3] and 4-3).

The Igneous Shore of Punta del Morro

The shoreline of the Punta del Morro region varies from steep, vertical headland cliffs to cobble tidepools, providing a variety of rocky habitats. The simplified zonal pattern of this shore is illustrated in Fig. 4-1 [2], but we also present a more detailed view of this shore in Fig. 4-2. Faunal and floral affinities here are distinctly tropical, and communities, although impoverished, resemble those of rocky shores on the central Caribbean islands. Wiley *et al.* (1982) have provided a list of the molluscan fauna identified from this region, and include notes on common members of other groups.

4-1. Patterns of zonation on Mexico rocky shores. **1.** The jetty at La Pesca, Tamaulipas; **2.** Rocky shores at Punta del Morro, Veracruz; **3.** Limestone platform at Punta Mastun Grande, Campeche; **4.** The jetty at Celestun, Yucatan; **5.** The jetty at Progreso, Yucatan; **6.** Ironshore (limestone) at Cancun, Quintana Roo. The scales indicate meters. **A.** Lined periwinkle, *Nodilittorina lineolata*; **B.** Cloudy periwinkle, *Littoraria nebulosa*; **C.** Angulate periwinkle, *Littoraria angulifera*; **D.** Beaded periwinkle, *Cenchritis muricatus*; **E.** *Echininus antonii*; **F.** Common prickly-winkle, *Nodilittorina tuberculata*; **G.** Zebra periwinkle, *Nodilittorina ziczac*; **H.** *Nodilittorina angustior*; **I.** Fragile barnacle, *Chthamalus fragilis*; **J.** Striped barnacle, *Balanus amphitrite*; **K.** False limpet, *Siphonaria pectinata*; **L.** False limpet, *Siphonaria alternata*; **M.** Knobby keyhole limpet, *Fissurella nodosa*; **N.** *Chiton squamosus*; **O.** Tessellate nerite, *Nerita tessellata*; **P.** Antillean nerite, *Nerita fulgurans*; **Q.** Four-toothed nerite, *Nerita versicolor*; **R.** Bleeding tooth, *Nerita peloronta*; **S.** Sea lettuce, *Ulva fasciata*; **T.** *Gelidium crinale*; **U.** *Padina vickersiae*; **V.** *Enteromorpha lingulata*; **W.** *Laurencia poitei*; **X.** *Cladophora* sp.; **Y.** *Caulerpa racemosa*; **Z.** *Centroceras clavulatum*; **A1.** *Gracilaria debilis*; **B1.** *Turbinaria turbinata*; **C1.** *Dictyota dichotoma*; **D1.** Red sea urchin, *Arbacia punctulata*; **E1.** Rock-boring urchin, *Echinometra lucunter*; **F1.** Cayenne keyhole limpet, *Diodora cayenensis*; **G1.** Sea lettuce, *Ulva lactuca*; **H1.** Gulfweed, *Sargassum filipendula*.

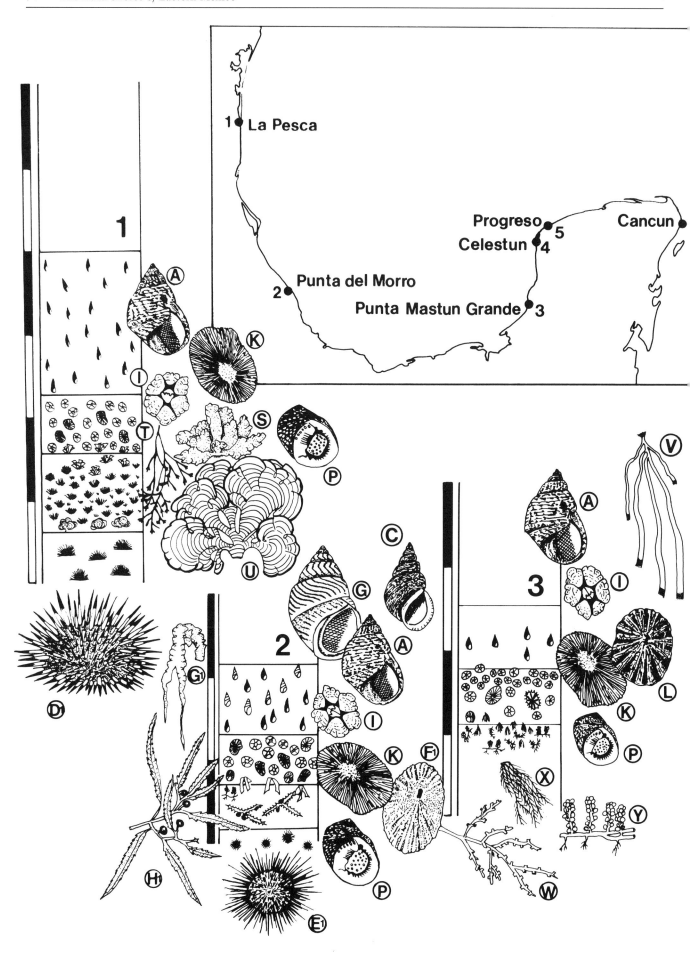

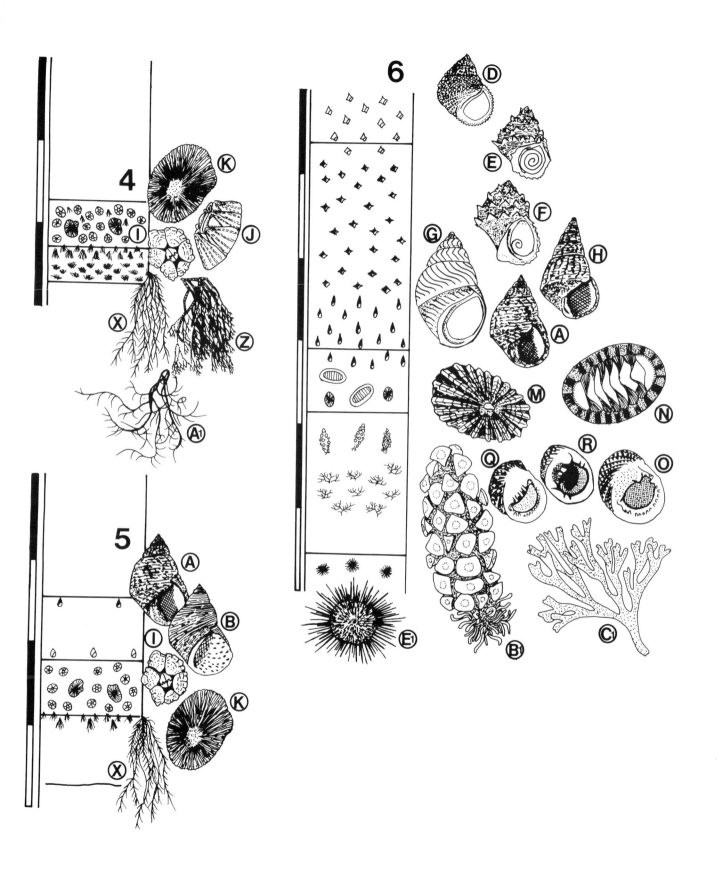

The supralittoral fringe of exposed headland rocks is characterized by two littorines, *Nodilittorina lineolata* (Figs. 4-1 A; 4-2 G) and *N. ziczac* (Figs. 4-1 G; 4-2 H). *Littoraria nebulosa* (Figs. 4-1 B; 4-5 C) is also occasionally found here (Wiley *et al.*, 1982). A fourth species, *Fossarilittorina meleagris* (Fig. 4-5 B) is found lower on the shore and often in association with algae.

Nerita fulgurans (Figs. 4-1 P; 4-2 K; 4-3 N) is common among the intertidal boulders and cobbles in somewhat more protected locations. Two other tropical Atlantic nerites, *Nerita versicolor* (Fig. 4-1 Q) and *N. tessellata* (Fig. 4-1 O) are less common, but when present usually frequent rocks adjacent to tide pools. Notably absent is the largest tropical Atlantic nerite, *N. peloronta*, a distinctive snail with an orange flair upon the columellar plate. Nor, according to published accounts, is this species recorded from many other natural mainland hard shores within the Gulf of Mexico (Wiley *et al.*, 1982; Vokes & Vokes, 1983). This is but one more indication of marginal tropical affinities along the central Mexico coast.

The agile grapsid crab, *Grapsus grapsus* (Fig. 4-2 I), moves easily from the sea to supralittoral rocks. It is an algal grazer and opportunistic scavenger. Called the Sally Lightfoot crab by sailors of previous centuries, this crustacean tiptoes across rocky intertidal crags or clings to vertical wave-splashed sea cliffs in search of food or shelter. It can bolt into the sea in an instant, effectively using land or water as a refuge from human or fish. The omnipresent sea roach, *Ligia exotica* (Fig. 3-1 A) shares the supralittoral fringe with *Grapsus*, being especially common where debris or seaweed wash ashore.

Barnacles, especially *Chthamalus fragilis* (Fig. 4-2 J), thrive in the mid-littoral. They share the habitat with some other familiar species such as *Siphonaria pectinata* (Fig. 4-2 F) and *Stramonita haemastoma* (Fig. 4-2 O), and several new tropical recruits, including the keyhole limpets *Diodora cayenensis* (Fig. 4-2 C) and *Fissurella barbadensis* (Fig. 4-2 B), the muricid *Plicopurpura patula* (formerly *Purpura patula*)(Fig. 4-2 N), the relatively large (20 mm) black snail, *Supplanaxis nucleus* (Fig. 4-2 L), and the smaller (5 mm) related *Angiola lineata* (Fig. 4-2 M), bearing a cream ground color upon which are dark spiral lines. The two planaxid species occur under stones at the tide line, emerging at night or on incoming tides to graze upon microscopic attached algae (Houbrick, 1987). *Supplanaxis nucleus* prefers relatively well-oxygenated, higher energy shores, whereas *Angiola lineata* is more common among rock rubble in more sheltered situations. It is not unusual, however, to find both on the same beach. This represents the northernmost regular occurrence of both species, although occasional specimens of *S. nucleus* appear on the Brazos-Santiago jetties of southern Texas. Neither species has been reported from the limestone shores of southwestern Yucatan.

The keyhole limpets are algal grazers relying especially upon fine filamentous green algae for suste-

nance. *Plicopurpura patula* is a predator. Unlike *Stramonita haemastoma*, which prefers to live in more sheltered habitats and to feed upon the numerous barnacles of the middle shore, *P. patula* prefers to feed upon the molluscs, especially nerites, of more wave-swept shores. It inserts a slender proboscis beneath the operculum of its prey and uses its radula to rasp flesh from inside the victim's shell. The process can take several hours to accomplish. Visitors to the shore often encounter *P. patula* feeding upon a nerite, the two apparently locked together and remain so even when picked up. If the disturbance is prolonged, the predatory snail releases the nerite and, upon additional provocation, will secrete a cream-yellow liquid which stains human skin and other proteins purple.

Stramonita haemastoma occurs commonly on the limestone rocks of southwestern Yucatan. *Plicopurpura patula* does not. This probably reflects the different habitat preferences of the two species, with the hard shores of southwestern Yucatan lying largely sheltered from the prevailing southeasterly winds, and providing the calmer shores preferred by *S. haemastoma*.

A few specimens of chitons, including *Tonicia schrammi*, occur among boulder debris and within tide pools in the vicinity of Punta del Morro. The polyplacophorans, though not abundant, are another indication of the increasing influence of neighboring tropical communities upon the region, with more than sporadic recruitment from them, but with adult survival still seasonally tenuous, inhibiting establishment of perpetually viable endemic populations.

The lower shore of many of these volcanic rocks near Punta del Morro is covered by *Sabellaria vulgaris*, a tube-dwelling sabellariid polychaete (Fig. 4-2 F1). These worms construct and live within sand tubes which they cement to a substratum of rock, concrete, or more often the tube of a neighboring worm. Sabellariid colonies sometimes grow to the size of boulders, but on this shore their 2 to 10 cm thick colonies only encrust mid-intertidal horizontal limestone platforms. The head of the sabellariid bears two setose appendages which effectively form an operculum by which the upper end of the sand tube can be plugged during low tide. The worms partially emerge on the incoming tide and filter the water for food. Several molluscs live in association with the sabellariid colonies, including the gastropods *Caecum vestitum* (Fig. 4-2 D1), a minute snail, and the similarly tiny but more snail-like *Fossarus orbignyi* (Fig. 4-2 E1). The nestling bivalve *Sphenia antillensis* (Fig. 4-2 G1) is also found commonly among the worm tubes.

Petaloconchus varians (Fig. 4-2 Q) is another tube-builder, but its "tube" is a convoluted shell, as this species is a gastropod mollusc. It is especially common along and within the tide pools along the south side of the northern headland at Punta del Morro (J.W. Tunnell, personal communication). Here, numerous colonies, each consisting of several dozen shells cemented together, lie in tangled calcareous masses. The snails also employ opercula to close their shells, but theirs are concave, chitinous, multispiral disks secreted by a modified foot. They are also filter feeders, active during the higher tides.

Wiley *et al.* (1982) indicate that the lower littoral and sublittoral shore in the vicinity of Punta del Morro is dominated primarily by brown algae, especially *Sargassum* cf. *filipendula* (Fig. 4-2 X) and *Padina vickersiae* (Fig. 4-2 Y), although red and green species also occur. *Caulerpa racemosa* (Fig. 4-2 C1) and *Ulva lactuca* (Fig. 4-2 A1) are mentioned as the most common species of green algae. The former is a highly variable species, and accordingly we illustrate several different growth forms on various figures in this book. No species of red algae have been reported from the Punta del Morro region, but they are undoubtedly present and likely diverse and abundant.

Several molluscs are commonly found in association with the lower shore algae and take refuge under the rocks of this zone. *Tricolia affinis* (Fig. 4-2 V) is a small grazing snail which apparently feeds upon algal epiphytes. Another minute *Caecum*, *C. pulchellum* (Fig. 4-2 Z) is usually present among the algae, but requires close inspection to be seen. The attractive *Nitidella laevigata* (Fig. 4-2 U) is another algal grazer common on the lower shore. The byssally-attached bivalves *Brachidontes exustus* (Fig. 4-2 E) and *Isognomon bicolor* (Fig. 4-2 D) live on intertidal rocks or among the algae. The arcids *Barbatia candida* (Fig. 4-2 R), *B. domingensis* (Fig. 4-2 T) and *Arcopsis adamsi* (Fig. 4-2 S) also cling to rocks by byssal threads, but these bivalves are more commonly encountered on the undersurfaces of rocks rather than upon the upper exposed faces.

The tectibranchs *Aplysia brasiliana* (Fig. 4-2 W) and *A. dactylomela* (Fig. 4-2 B1) and the black rock-boring sea urchin *Echinometra lucunter* (Fig. 4-2 P) are among the prominent macroscopic algal grazers. The latter is also common on emergent offshore coral reefs at Isla de Lobos between Tampico and Tuxpan, and sometimes occurs on northern Mexico and southern Texas jetties. Unlike the temperate *Arbacia punctulata*, which simply seeks shelter by wedging between boulders, *Echinometra* literally excavates small depressions in the rock, into which it retreats when not foraging. More will be said of this species in Chapter 11.

Shallow subtidal rocks on high wave energy shores along Punta del Morro are often heavily covered by the colonial zoanthid, *Palythoa mammillosa* (Fig. 4-2 A). During the day and at low tide, *Palythoa* colonies appear as fleshy, many-dimpled leathery coverings on rocks and boulders. A polyp emerges from each "dimple" at night during high tides to feed (inset, Fig. 4-2 A).

Despite recording 55 living molluscs (from a total of 121 species) from Punta del Morro and vicinity, Wiley *et al.* (1982) characterize the molluscan assemblage of these igneous shores as "depauperate Caribbean." It should be clear from our survey of Gulf of Mexico

hard shores that there is considerably greater faunal (and possibly floral) diversity here than on any of the man-made hard shores of the region. Yet to appreciate the depauperate nature of western Gulf of Mexico hard shores, one should at least compare them to a true Caribbean limestone "ironshore," which we will describe later.

Limestone Hard Shores of Western Yucatan

A few prominent limestone cliffs brush the Gulf of Mexico in the vicinity of Campeche, but most of the limestone shores of western Yucatan are low, narrow platforms which rise little more than 2 m above a surrounding sand veneer (Fig. 4-3). Maritime vegetation comes very close to the sea, with several species of trees commonly marking the rear margin of the rock platform. The edge of each platform contributes rock debris upon the adjacent sand, providing a secondary habitat for cobble shore species (Fig. 4-3, inset at upper right). The close proximity of vegetation to the shore, the generally impoverished nature of the fauna, and the presence of several "shelter" adapted species clearly indicate that the limestone shores of western Yucatan are relatively well protected from heavy surf.

The characteristic zoning species are few here (Fig. 4-1 [3]) and other common members of the community are equally sparse (Fig. 4-3). We found only one littorine, *Nodilittorina lineolata* (Figs. 4-1 A; 4-3 F) on the rock platforms of Punta Mastun Grande, south of

4-2. Biota at the rocky shore of Punta del Morro, Mexico. **A.** *Palythoa mammillosa*, including portion of a colony with contracted polyps and a single expanded polyp; **B.** Knobby keyhole limpet, *Fissurella barbadensis*; **C.** Cayenne keyhole limpet, *Diodora cayenensis*; **D.** Tree oyster, *Isognomon bicolor*; **E.** Scorched mussel, *Brachidontes exustus*; **F.** False limpet, *Siphonaria pectinata*; **G.** Lined periwinkle, *Nodilittorina lineolata*; **H.** Zebra periwinkle, *Nodilittorina ziczac*; **I.** Sally Lightfoot crab, *Grapsus grapsus*; **J.** Fragile barnacles, *Chthamalus fragilis*; **K.** Antillean nerite, *Nerita fulgurans*; **L.** Supplanaxis nucleus; **M.** *Angiola lineata*; **N.** *Plicopurpura patula*; **O.** Rock snail, *Stramonita haemastoma*; **P.** Rock-boring urchin, *Echinometra lucunter*; **Q.** *Petaloconchus varians*; **R.** *Barbatia candida*; **S.** Miniature ark, *Arcopsis adamsi*; **T.** *Barbatia domingensis*; **U.** Smooth dove shell, *Nitidella laevigata*; **V.** Checkered pheasant shell, *Tricolia affinis*; **W.** Sooty sea hare, *Aplysia brasiliana*; **X.** Gulfweed, *Sargassum filipendula*; **Y.** *Padina vickersiae*; **Z.** *Caecum pulchellum*; **A1.** Sea lettuce, *Ulva lactuca*; **B1.** Spotted sea hare, *Aplysia dactylomela*; **C1.** *Caulerpa racemosa*; **D1.** *Caecum vestitum*; **E1.** *Fossarus orbignyi*; **F1.** *Sabellaria vulgaris*; **G1.** *Sphenia antillensis*. The scale indicates meters.

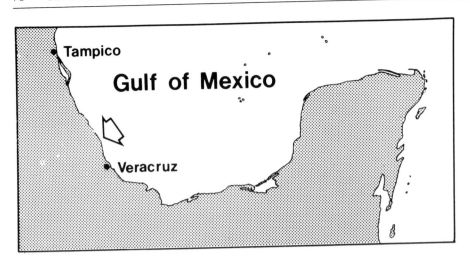

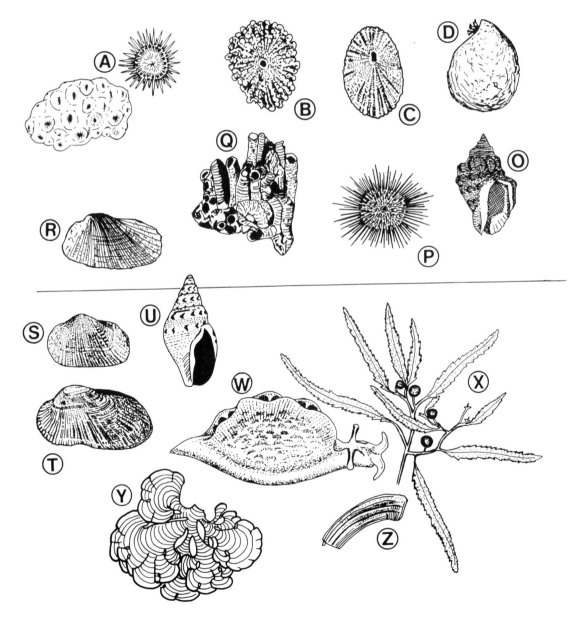

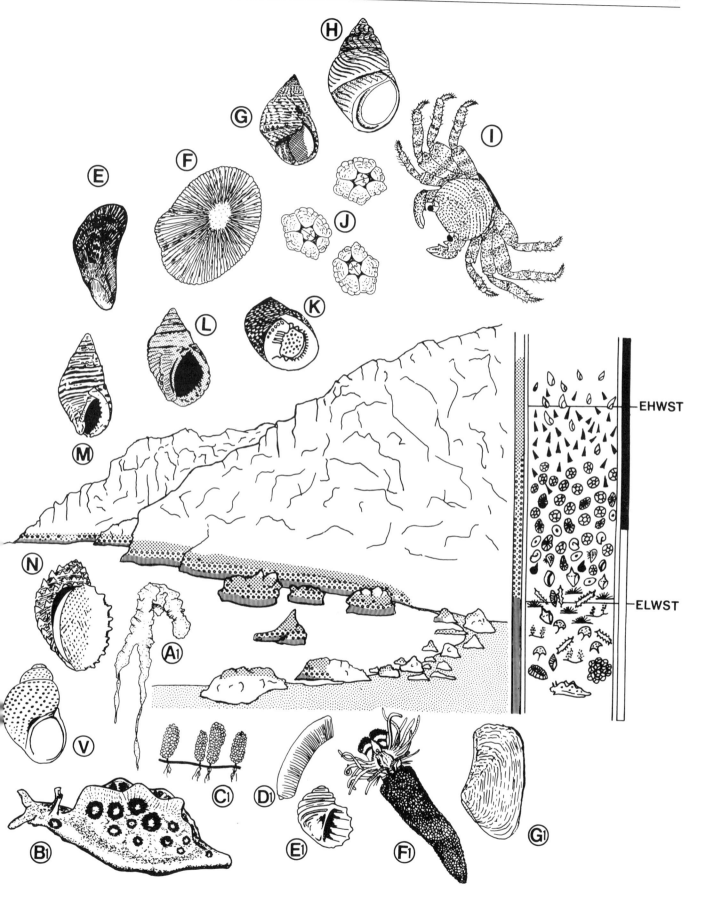

EHWST

ELWST

the city of Campeche, and Vokes & Vokes (1983) confirm that it is the most common littorine of the region. It is the high-zoned marine species characteristic of this habitat. *Chthamalus fragilis* (Figs. 4-1 I; 4-3 G) is the only barnacle here, but thousands of individuals effectively blanket the rocks of the upper mid-littoral. The scorched mussel *Brachidontes exustus* (Fig. 4-3 E) and the yellow mussel *B. modiolus* occur among the barnacles along the lower margin of their zone, and are equally common within small crevices in the boulder fields adjacent to the rocky platform. *Siphonaria pectinata* (Figs. 4-1 K; 4-3 H) is joined by *S. alternata* (Figs. 4-1 L; 4-3 I) on the rocks just below the area of greatest barnacle density. *Siphonaria alternata* is one of a number of marine animals found from North Carolina to Florida and on Yucatan shores, but is otherwise absent from the western Gulf. Numerous shallow tide pools dot the lower rock ledges, and most of these contain a thin film of loose sand. *Cerithium lutosum* (Fig. 4-3 K) occurs by the hundreds in these tide pools, apparently feeding primarily upon the microscopic algae and detritus which accumulates there. The gastropod predator of the rock platform is *Stramonita haemastoma* (Fig. 4-2 O), indicated by Vokes & Vokes (1983) to be common in this region.

As on the man-made western Yucatan hard shores, macrophytic algae are also sparse on the natural rock platforms, no doubt in part due to the ample amount of sand available to provide abrasion on the lower rock surfaces. A few species are sufficiently common to mention, including the red alga *Laurencia poitei* (Figs. 4-1 W; 4-3 J) which forms reddish-brown tangled clumps on the lower shore, and the green alga *Caulerpa racemosa* (Figs. 4-1 Y; 4-3 B), with its rhizomatous filaments forming mats on sandy tide pool floors, and *Cladophora* sp. (Figs. 4-1 X; 4-3 D), appearing as frazzled, unkempt tufts of closely cropped green "hair" seemingly growing out of the rock. All of these species appear to be decidedly sheared as if they were well grazed, cropped or sand abraded.

The boulder fields which lie adjacent to the rock platforms of Punta Mastun Grande are the source for several additional species which are uncommon upon the rock platform. *Nerita fulgurans* (Figs. 4-1 P; 4-3 N) finds refuge in fissures between rocks or in protected crevices near the base of boulders. Large numbers of *Mitrella ocellata* (Fig. 4-3 L) occur under the stones, and the similarly predatory snail, *Pisania tincta* (Fig. 4-3 M) also takes refuge under rocks. The flattened body of the porcelain crab, *Petrolisthes armatus* (Fig. 4-3 C), is particularly well adapted to live under rocks. Like other porcellanids, it has perfected the art of autotomy, and will readily relinquish a claw or leg to an attacker. *Cerithium lutosum* is also common among the boulders and represents one species successful on both the platform and the adjacent rock field. Of all of the fauna of the boulders, the gammaridean amphipods are numerically dominant. Several species are probably represented, but due to small size and difficult taxonomy, we have not attempted to illustrate them.

Along some parts of Punta Mastun Grande, groove-like cuts dissect the ironshore platforms (Fig. 4-3, inset, upper right). Their floors are largely devoid of sand. Beach veneer consisting of flat rocks and cobble fragments eroded from the walls of each channel lie upon a bedrock surface awash at all but the lowest tides. The red sea star, *Echinaster sentus* (Fig. 4-3 A), is common beneath these rocks and among the offshore grass beds.

We cannot conclude this section without mention of the vegetation which lies so close to the shore. We will expand this discussion in Chapter 6, but a few plants are worthy of mention here. Prominent among these are several trees. The buttonwood, *Conocarpus erectus* (Fig. 4-3 P), often stands along the back rim of the rock platform and provides at least some shade for the rock fauna. Where the platform is lower and the sand burden greater, it is not unusual to find black mangroves, *Avicennia germinans* (see Chapter 9) growing close to the shore. Higher on the beach, and usually in association with sand, the sea grape, *Coccoloba uvifera* (Fig. 4-3 Q) often occupies dense groves of small trees. The sea grape is unmistakable for any other tree with its large, broad distinctive leaves and clumps of green, grapelike fruits.

The back half of many rock platforms is carpeted by mats of fleshy-leafed sea purslane, *Sesuvium portulacastrum* (Fig. 4-3 O). Where there are considerable accumulations of sand, *Sesuvium* shares the habitat with several grasses and sedges. Further shoreward, a complex flora becomes established. Many elements of this community are described in Chapter 6.

TOWARD THE TROPICAL HARD SHORES

It would be unfulfilling to conclude our survey of the hard shores of the Gulf of Mexico with the low limestone platforms of western Yucatan. We have repeatedly spoken of impoverished communities, low species diversities, and shores which only hint at the richness of the tropical Caribbean. This richness lies outside of our self-imposed geographic limits, but just barely. It is appropriate, therefore to move a few kilometers around the northeastern margin of Yucatan and into the Caribbean province at Cancun (Fig. 4-1 [6]). We will not dwell upon all biota of tropical Caribbean hard shores, but focus instead upon a few key groups to show how these diversify in the tropics, where hard shores are more often the rule rather than the exception. Finally, we will examine one group in particular, the gastropod family Littorinidae, and by assessment of its total diversity throughout the Gulf and Caribbean basins, put into perspective its representation on Gulf shores.

There are a number of reasons why hard shores seem to dominate so much of the Caribbean region, including eastern Yucatan. Perhaps most importantly, the Caribbean basin is much more "open" than the Gulf of Mexico, providing a considerably greater area for waves to form and considerably lesser protection against wave attack. Sandy beaches are less common in the Caribbean, and when present, usually lie on the western sides of islands or headlands in the lee of prevailing winds. Eastern Caribbean shores, including those of eastern Yucatan, are frequently dominated by sea cliffs or rocky platforms composed of a grotesquely weathered limestone that has come to be known as ironshore.

"Ironshore" is neither hard nor contains any significant amount of iron. It is in fact uplifted or exposed reef limestone, the outer layer of which has been tempered by weathering to a brittle, brownish-black, often microkarsted state. When struck by a hammer it resonates like an anvil. Hence, ironshore. Inside the weathered core, ironshore is often white, soft, and easily crumbled, revealing its true limestone nature. Even the exterior is easily penetrated by boring organisms such as blue-green algae, barnacles or date mussels.

Carbonate ironshore occurs widely throughout the Caribbean from the Lesser Antilles to Central American shores, but the use of the term generally indicates a limestone shore in the western Caribbean, such as at Jamaica, Grand Cayman, Belize, Cozumel, or, in our case, Cancun, Mexico. Cancun will serve as a suitable example of a Caribbean shore due to its close proximity to the Gulf of Mexico, but keep in mind that Cancun ironshores are marginal, not central Caribbean habitats. The remarks which follow are more for comparison with the shores already described rather than a complete treatment of a very complex system.

The Cancun ironshore is an exposed reef platform rising as much as 6 m above the sea (Fig. 4-4). The width of the platform under maritime influence, consisting of poorly vegetated, microkarsted rock, varies according to position and elevation, ranging from little more than a few to as much as several dozen meters. It directly faces the prevailing southeasterly wind, receiving maximal wave energy generated across the broad Caribbean fetch. Limited tidal range, which inhibits the vertical zonation of intertidal organisms, is tempered at Cancun by a broad splash zone which effectively expands vertical zonation (Figure 4-1 [6]). Only the pattern of zonation observed on the La Pesca jetty (Fig. 4-1 [1]) approaches that at Cancun. In comparison, the jetties at Celestun or Chelem and the limestone platform at Punta Mastun Grande, in the lee of Yucatan, experience limited wave exposure from the prevailing winds, and accordingly have exceedingly narrow zonation bands. Even at Punta del Morro, the remote Yucatan peninsula helps shelter the shore. Recall a similar, although less dramatic, example of the effect of disparate wave exposure upon the two sides of the Texas jetties discussed in Chapter 3.

Despite the considerably greater vertical range of the intertidal region on the Cancun shore, the rich biota is frequently overlooked by the casual observer. Most of the fauna, especially the higher-zoned species, is small and blend cryptically with the weather-pitted ironshore. Close examination, however, will reveal

a much greater diversity than seen on any Gulf hard shore.

The littorine component has increased to six species, all zoned within the supralittoral fringe. *Cenchritis muricatus* (Figs. 4-1 D; 4-4 J; 4-5 I) lives highest upon the shore, sometimes (although not at Cancun) living 12 m above the sea. Two spinose littorines, *Nodilittorina tuberculata* (Figs. 4-1 F; 4-4 K; 4-5 L) and *Echininus antonii* (Figs. 4-1 E; 4-4 L; 4-5 K) appear next upon the shore, the former usually more abundant than the latter. The shells of these two periwinkles are quite similar, making discrimination difficult. The whorl patterns of the opercula are the most reliable method of distinguishing them, with the operculum of *N. tuberculata* consisting of a few small, tight, angular whorls and that of *E. antonii* having several broad, open circular whorls. The zebra-striped littorines previously encountered on some other Gulf shores also occur here: *Nodilittorina ziczac* (Fig. 4-1 G), *N. lineolata* (Fig. 4-1 A), and a third species, *N. angustior* (Fig 4-1 H), which sometimes is encountered on southern Gulf shores. The vertical range of these species overlaps those of the spinose *N. tuberculata* and *E. antonii* at the upper end, but they usually extend well into the mid-littoral zone, whereas the spinose littorines usually do not.

The absence, or at least paucity, of stony barnacles on western Caribbean ironshores is so pervasive as to be strikingly enigmatic! Barnacles were described by Stephenson & Stephenson (1972) as universally characterizing the rocky mid-littoral zone. One must question why at Cancun, the Cayman Islands, Roatan, Jamaica and elsewhere in the Caribbean there are so few balanoid barnacles on microkarsted mid-littoral limestone. (Rock-boring barnacles, however, are common within the rock fabric of the lower portions of these shores.) Several possibilities come to mind, but none are sufficient to explain the problem adequately. Temperature is suspect, especially when the few barnacles which live upon intertidal ironshores often attach to rocks in shaded refugia, or, like the volcano barnacle, *Tetraclita*, possess a shell suited for thermoregulation. The limited tidal range of the region is often mentioned, but one has only to examine the jetty shores of Texas or Celestun to quickly realize that limited tidal range may narrow the mid-littoral barnacle zone, but does not eliminate it. Perhaps it has something to do with the ironshore substratum, riddled and permeated as it is with large colonies of endolithic algae. Unfortunately this hypothesis has not been tested. So, for whatever reason, the universally characterizing group for the mid-littoral according to the Stephensonian scheme of rocky intertidal zonation is, more often than not, poorly represented on western Caribbean ironshores.

Instead, the mid-littoral of the tropical Caribbean tends to be dominated by a variety of molluscs, especially snails and chitons. The latter are the most conspicuous, with as many as five or six species occurring here. Most common are the large fuzzy chiton, *Ancan-*

thopleura granulata, the West Indian chiton, *Chiton tuberculatus*, the squamose chiton, *C. squamosus* (Fig. 4-1 N), and the marbled chiton *C. marmoratus*. All are intertidal grazers, feeding primarily upon the algal pastures of the lower intertidal. Three nerites are present: *Nerita versicolor* (Fig. 4-1 Q), the darkly operculate *N. tessellata* (Fig. 4-1 O), and the bleeding tooth shell *N. peloronta* (Fig. 4-1 R). Their common predator, *Plicopurpura patula*, also patrols the ironshore. Large specimens of the West Indian top shell, *Cittarium pica*, were once abundant in eastern Yucatan and throughout the Caribbean. Today they are rarely encountered. Humans harvest the larger specimens for food, leaving only the smaller shells. Keyhole limpets, including *Fissurella nodosa* (Fig. 4-1 M), *F. barbadensis* (Fig. 4-2 B), *F. fascicularis*, *Diodora listeri*, and *D. cayenensis* (Fig. 4-2 C) are also found on intertidal ironshores. Of the 14 species of keyhole limpets common on eastern Yucatan shores, only two or three are found with any regularity on mainland shores of the western Gulf of Mexico. Other common animals of the intertidal rocks include several grapsid crabs, e.g., *Grapsus grapsus* (Fig. 4-4 I), and the sea roach, *Ligia exotica*.

The diversity of intertidal and subtidal algae is too great to enumerate here, except to mention but a few of the more characteristic species. The green algae have become less important upon these shores. *Ulva* and *Enteromorpha*, for example, are largely replaced by various creeping *Caulerpa* species, although mild seasonal changes are sufficient for restoration of these populations during the winter months. The brown alga, *Padina vickersiae* (Fig. 4-1 U) continues to thrive in shallow, heated high-energy waters. Several species of *Sargassum* now occupy the lower ironshore, and intermingle with *Dictyota dichotoma* (Fig. 4-1 C1), a brown alga which shimmers iridescent blue in the receding surf. Numerous species of fuzzy branching rhodophytes carpet the rocks between clumps of *Sargassum*, and pink encrusting species coat rocks assaulted

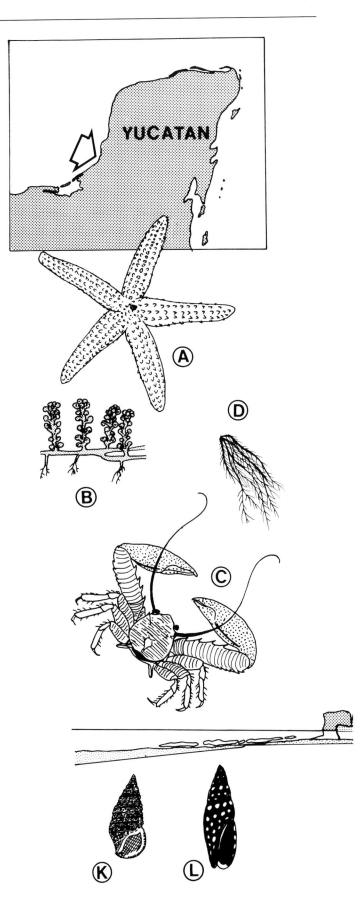

4-3. Limestone platform at Punta Mastun Grande, Campeche, Mexico. **A.** Red sea star, *Echinaster sentus*; **B.** *Caulerpa racemosa*; **C.** Porcelain crab, *Petrolisthes armatus*; **D.** *Cladophora* sp.; **E.** Scorched mussel, *Brachidontes exustus*; **F.** Lined periwinkle, *Nodilittorina lineolata*; **G.** Fragile barnacle, *Chthamalus fragilis*; **H.** False limpet, *Siphonaria pectinata*; **I.** False limpet, *Siphonaria alternata*; **J.** *Laurencia poitei*; **K.** Dwarf cerith, *Cerithium lutosum*; **L.** White-spotted dove shell, *Mitrella ocellata*; **M.** Tinted cantharus, *Pisania tincta*; **N.** Antillean nerite, *Nerita fulgurans*; **O.** Sea purslane, *Sesuvium portulacastrum*; **P.** Buttonwood, *Conocarpus erectus*; **Q.** Sea grape, *Coccoloba uvifera*. Inset: **1.** Ironshore platform; **2.** limestone rubble; **3.** sand beach; **4.** vegetated region dominated by *Sesuvium*. The scales indicate meters.

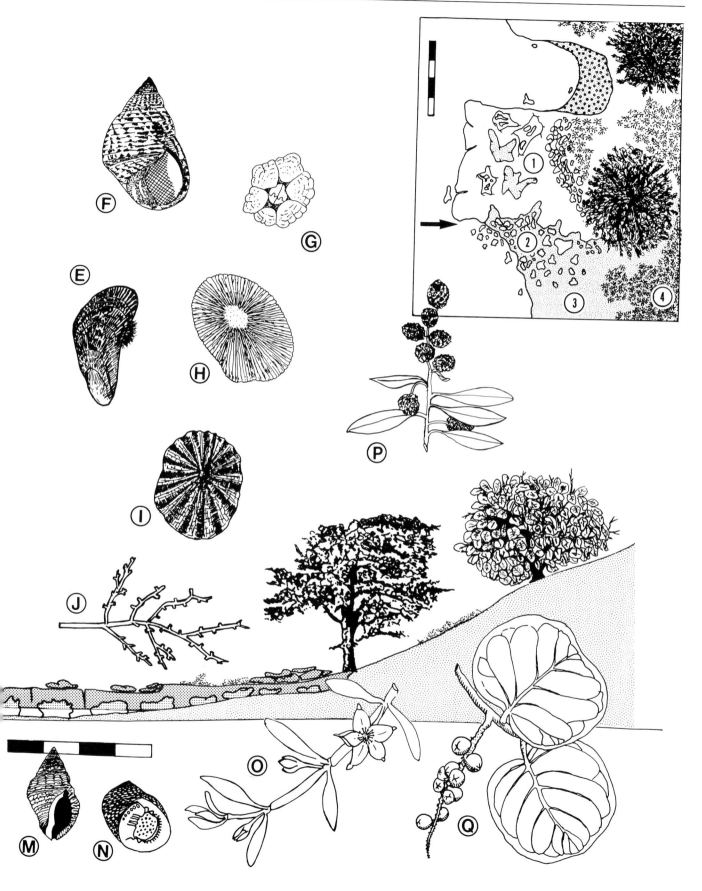

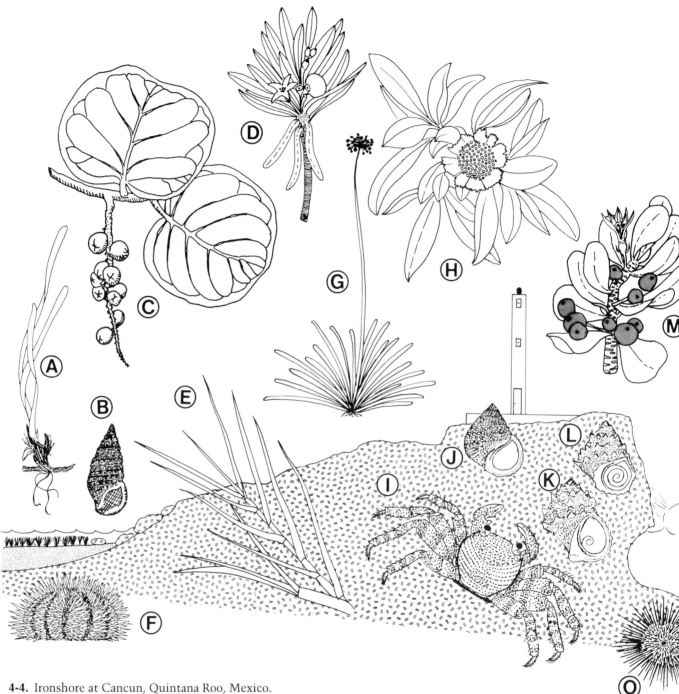

4-4. Ironshore at Cancun, Quintana Roo, Mexico.
A. *Turtle grass, *Thalassia testudinum*; **B.** *Dwarf cerith, *Cerithium lutosum*; **C.** Sea grape, *Coccoloba uvifera*; **D.** *Strumphia maritima*; **E.** Coastal dropseed, *Sporobolus virginicus*; **F.** *Sea egg, *Tripneustes ventricosus*; **G.** Bullrush, *Scirpus* sp.; **H.** Sea ox-eye, *Borrichia arborescens*; **I.** Sally Lightfoot crab, *Grapsus grapsus*; **J.** Beaded periwinkle, *Cenchritis muricatus*; **K.** Common pricklywinkle, *Nodilittorina tuberculata*; **L.** False pricklywinkle, *Echininus antonii*; **M.** *Scaevola plumieri*; **N.** Bay cedar, *Suriana maritima*; **O.** Rock-boring urchin, *Echinometra lucunter*; **P.** *Turbinaria turbinata*. The scale indicates meters.

*Bayside occurrence.

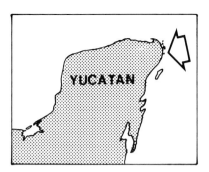

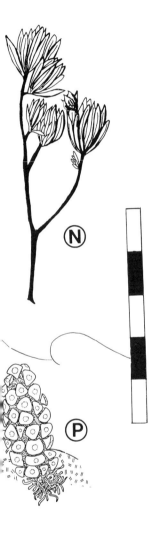

by the most intense wave surge. Slightly lower, on less wave-intense shores, trumpet-shaped "leaves" of *Turbinaria turbinaria* (Figs. 4-1 B1; 4-4 P) sway gracefully below the surface with the incoming swells. In the sheltered bays on the western side of Cancun, turtle grass, *Thalassia testudinum* (Fig. 4-4 A) thickly carpets subtidal flats. The algal gardens of the exposed shores and the turtle grass beds of the protected flats shelter a wealth of tropical biota that would require chapters to describe. A few, such as the sea egg, *Tripneustes ventricosus* (Fig. 4-4 F), are especially conspicuous here but absent from many Gulf shore grass beds. In contrast, *Cerithium lutosum* (Fig. 4-4 B), is abundant here and occupies similar habitats throughout the western Gulf of Mexico.

Higher on the shore, above the splash zone, the maritime flora also reflects the tropical transition. Ironshore is a difficult habitat for colonization, but several plants have been able to penetrate the rigid crust to the softer, moist carbonate core, or find pockets of sand in which to insinuate their roots. Several succulent or semi-succulent shrubs often lie closest to shore, including the bay cedar, *Suriana maritima* (Fig. 4-4 N), *Scaevola plumieri* (Fig. 4-4 M) and the low, woody *Strumphia maritima* (Fig. 4-4 D). Bay cedar is usually the largest of these shrubs. It bears small yellow flowers within clumps of velvety succulent leaves. The leaves of *Scaevola* are dark green and more leathery than succulent. It produces an unusual asymmetrical white flower open along one side, and which develops into a dark berry-like fruit. *Strumphia* is the smallest of these shrubs, and, although it can be found on dry rock shores throughout much of the Caribbean, unlike the other two, it does not occur within the Gulf of Mexico. It bears white or faintly pink flowers, but is most readily identified by the distinctly curled leaves and the small (5 mm) creamy white axillary fruits.

Sedges and herbs grow in ironshore depressions which accumulate moderate amounts of sand. A bullrush, *Scirpus* sp. (Fig. 4-4 G), and a Caribbean species of sea ox-eye daisy, *Borrichia arborescens* (Fig. 4-4 H), commonly occupy these areas. *Borrichia* is also common on the sandy beaches of southern Texas, but as we will see in Chapter 6, it is represented there by a different species. The ubiquitous *Sporobolus virginicus* (Fig. 4-4 E) and sand burs of the genus *Cenchrus* are present if the sandy cover is adequate. The rear of the ironshore is usually marked by a line of low trees, most commonly consisting almost exclusively of sea grapes, *Coccoloba uvifera* (Fig. 4-4 C).

These few examples from a tropical Caribbean hard shore should provide an indication of the complexity of this community. Some elements typical of temperate climates, specifically the barnacles, have disappeared. In their place appear new species: nerites, chitons, keyhole limpets, and others. They are not simply filling niches vacated by the barnacles, being neither sessile nor suspension feeders. They exploit the space vacated by the barnacles, and move from the midshore to forage the rich algal gardens of the sublittoral fringe.

The higher rocks are also home to new species of littorine snails, tenacious in their ability to survive on the weathered and sun-drenched ironshore, but provided the opportunity to live here because of the greater degree of wave exposure. The Littorinidae are particularly well adapted for life in this difficult environment, and have responded by specializing in surviving a variety of supralittoral niches, not all of them on hard shores.

We began Chapter 3 with an explanation of the taxonomic difficulty afforded by the Littorinidae, so it is fitting that we conclude our survey of the exposed shores of the western Gulf of Mexico with an enumeration of all of the presently recognized Gulf and Caribbean species and their geographic ranges. You should recall that when *Nodilittorina lineolata* was first introduced in Chapter 3, we indicated that this and many other striped littorine species were once lumped into the single taxon "*Littorina ziczac*." The number of striped littorine species in the western Atlantic has increased from one to at least six during the last 20 years, based in part upon differences in shell characters, soft body form and/or anatomy, radula structure, and the nature of the egg case (some of which are illustrated with the shells in Fig. 4-5). Many other littorines, previously lumped together in the genus *Littorina*, are now known to be sufficiently distinctive to warrant separate generic status. Much of this information has appeared in a recent monograph of western Atlantic *Nodilittorina* (Bandel & Kadolsky, 1982), although our taxonomy follows the suggestions of David Reid of the British Museum (Natural History), who is presently studying all western Atlantic Littorinidae. Accordingly, the nomenclature presented here does not correspond with that of many popular identification guides. Thus, we will provide "old" or alternate names following the designations employed herein.

Throughout all Gulf and Caribbean hard shores, *Cenchritis muricatus* (= *Tectarius muricatus*) (Fig. 4-5 I), is the highest zoned littorine. It is mostly confined to and widely distributed within the Caribbean region. It lives primarily upon limestone rocks sometimes as much as 30 m away from the sea. *Cenchritis muricatus* can survive at least 6 months out of water. Also very high-zoned, but usually ranging below *C. muricatus* are the spinose littorines, *Echininus antonii* (= *Echininus nodulosus* of authors or *Nodilittorina antonii* fide Bandel & Kadolsky, 1982) (Fig. 4-5 K) and *Nodilittorina tuberculata* (Fig. 4-5 L). These species are mostly pan-Caribbean in distribution on the same shores with *Cenchritis*. Bandel & Kadolsky (1982) recognize a third species, *N. dilatata*, which is very similar to *N. tuberculata*, except with a broader columella and ranging from Florida, the Bahamas, and along the northern shores of the Greater Antilles. Accordingly, *N. tuberculata* is considered by these authors to be a southern Caribbean species.

The striped littorines present a confusing taxonomy.

Nodilittorina ziczac (= *Littorina ziczac*) (Fig. 4-5 G) is usually the largest, most easily recognized species. It occupies rocky shores throughout the Caribbean and is occasionally found in similar habitats in the southern Gulf of Mexico. The dark, narrow stripes on the shell of *N. ziczac* frequently appear faded. The species is readily distinguished by having numerous (15 to 30) finely incised lines which spiral around each whorl of the shell, sometimes fading to oblivion. *Nodilittorina interrupta* (Fig. 4-5 N) is slightly smaller than *N. ziczac* with fewer finely incised spiral lines. It consistently displays two light bands on the inner surface of the shell. It is primarily a species of the central Caribbean basin.

Nodilittorina angustior (Fig. 4-5 J) is also reasonably easy to distinguish, for it has a few (usually less than 8) distinctly incised spiral lines on each shell whorl and the shell aperture is decidedly less than one-half the height of the shell. It also occurs throughout the central Caribbean region. Three other striped species bearing only a few incised spiral lines are much more difficult to distinguish, and usually require examination of the radula. All have a large aperture, one-half or more the length of the shell. They are: *Nodilittorina mordax* (Fig. 4-5 H), primarily a species of Florida and the Bahamas; *N. glaucocincta* (Fig. 4-5 M), ranging from Jamaica to Puerto Rico; and *N. riisei*, from Florida and Cuba. At least one of these species also occurs on the emergent offshore reef rocks (Arrecife Lobos) off central Mexico (see Chapter 11).

The last striped littorine is the most enigmatic, and it is also the one we cited first in Chapter 3. Bandel & Kadolsky (1982) maintain that *Nodilittorina lineolata* (Fig. 4-5 A) is a South American species restricted to the coast of Brazil. They did not examine the littorines of the Gulf of Mexico, and thus overlooked a widespread striped littorine which matches perfectly the description for *N. lineolata*. Until this taxonomic problem is resolved, we will continue to employ this epithet for the dominant littorine of the Gulf of Mexico.

The remaining western Atlantic littorines are distinctive, but not entirely rocky shore species. *Fossarilittorina meleagris* (= *Littorina meleagris*)(Fig. 4-5 B) is a "striped" littorine, but the stripe pattern is so bold as to appear to define numerous white spots between the dark stripes. It occurs on intertidal rocks throughout the Caribbean and occasionally appears in the Gulf of Mexico. *Fossarilittorina mespillum* (= *Littorina mespillum*)(Fig. 4-5 O) is a tiny, globose, and typically brown species commonly found in tide pools on rocky Caribbean shores. It is rare in the Gulf of Mexico. *Littoraria nebulosa* (= *Littorina nebulosa*)(Fig. 4-5 C) is a large (up to 2 cm), unstriped littorine with numerous fine spiral lines incised over the entire outer surface of the relatively thin shell. It is widely distributed in the Gulf and Caribbean, occurring on rocks and wooden pilings, particularly on sheltered shores. *Littoraria angulifera* (= *Littorina angulifera*)(Fig. 4-5 D) is another large, relatively thin-shelled species

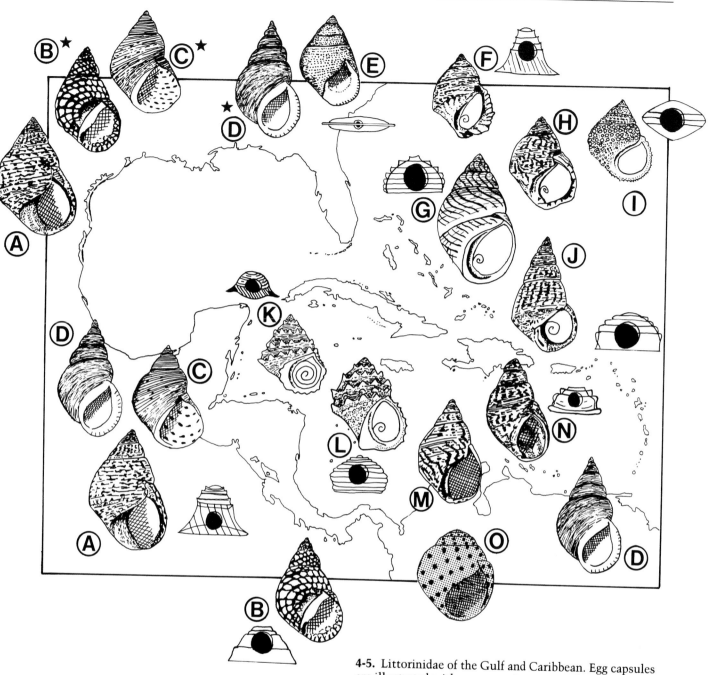

4-5. Littorinidae of the Gulf and Caribbean. Egg capsules are illustrated with some species; stars indicate primarily estuarine species. **A.** Lined periwinkle, *Nodilittorina lineolata*; **B.** White-spotted periwinkle, *Fossarilittorina meleagris*; **C.** Cloudy periwinkle, *Littoraria nebulosa*; **D.** Angulate periwinkle, *Littoraria angulifera*; **E.** Marsh periwinkle, *Littoraria irrorata*; **F.** *Nodilittorina riisei*; **G.** Zebra periwinkle, *Nodilittorina ziczac*; **H.** *Nodilittorina mordax*; **I.** Beaded periwinkle, *Cenchritis muricatus*; **J.** *Nodilittorina angustior*; **K.** False prickly-winkle, *Echininus antonii*; **L.** Common prickly-winkle, *Nodilittorina tuberculata*; **M.** *Nodilittorina glaucocincta*; **N.** *Nodilittorina interrupta*; **O.** Dwarf brown periwinkle, *Fossarilittorina mespillum*.

most commonly found on mangroves from southern Texas to the shores of South America. The marsh periwinkle, *Littoraria irrorata* (= *Littorina irrorata*)(Fig. 4-5 E), has perhaps the thickest shell of all western Atlantic littorines. It occurs exclusively in association with marsh grasses fringing protected estuarine shores from New York to Texas. It is generally absent from Caribbean shores.

Having now documented the 15 species of western Atlantic littorines, we can consider their importance on Gulf shores. Only one species, *Nodilittorina lineolata*, is common on most rocky shores throughout the region. *Littoraria nebulosa* can be expected on sheltered rocks throughout the western Gulf. At least one spotted and two other striped littorines are occasional inhabitants of some natural rocky shores. Thus, the Gulf of Mexico can claim a maximum of about 5 species of Littorinidae on its sparse rocky shores. In contrast, the tropical Caribbean hard shores are home for at least 12 species.

A FINAL PERSPECTIVE

The Cancun rocky shore, at the northern margin of the western tropical Caribbean province, clearly is richer in life than those we have described from the western Gulf of Mexico. Based upon the hardshore biota, the northeastern tip of Yucatan, therefore, seems a logical point to separate the western Gulf of Mexico biogeographic province from that of the western Caribbean. Biogeographers have long debated this point. Briggs (1974) summarizes much of the literature. In fact, he recognizes Cabo Rojo (just below Tampico) as the northern boundary of the Caribbean province. Here, or actually at Isla de Lobos just off the mainland shore, occurs the northernmost emergent coral reef in the western Gulf (see Chapter 11). As we will see, it includes an impoverished Caribbean reef biota, just as the jetties and natural mainland hardshores of the area include a few members of the Caribbean ironshore community. The presence of this emergent reef apparently had some influence upon Briggs' decision to place a biogeographic provincial boundary here.

Mainland shores of the tropical western Caribbean, if not dominated by igneous outcrops or ironshore limestone, certainly include a high percentage of them. Rocky headlands dominate the margins of most

western Caribbean islands. The western Gulf of Mexico has a paucity of natural hard substrata, but an abundance of largely uninterrupted sandy beaches. These differences in dominance of shore types and a corresponding difference in biotic diversity speak for including the entire western Gulf of Mexico within a single biogeographic province, albeit one in latitudinal transition.

Hardshore communities from Galveston Island to Cancun, Mexico clearly express a temperate to tropical transition accompanied by increasing biotic diversity from north to south. The seasonal expression of temperate flora decreases across the latitudinal gradient, just as the recruitment of tropical flora and fauna increases to the south. Northern jetties frequently receive tropical recruits, but rarely do southern shores recruit temperate species. Despite the complex wind and current patterns in the western Gulf basin, they favor northward, not southward, drift. The farther away the shore lies from the diverse tropical realm, the less likely it will derive recruitment from it. In a similar respect, as a shore comes to lie more within a temperate climate, the less likely it can provide a tropical species a suitable place to live. Finally, as a temperate shore such as Galveston or Port Aransas becomes increasingly isolated from other temperate habitats, such as those northeast of the Florida peninsula, the less likely the latter will or can contribute biota to the former. The rock jetties of Galveston are remote from tropical sources of recruitment, climatically unsuitable for most potential tropical recruits, and also remote or isolated from other Atlantic hard shores. All of these factors contribute to the isolation and extreme impoverishment of the northern Texas jetty biota.

The Texas jetties have been in place about 100 years. Their fauna and flora have come from the eastern Gulf, northern Caribbean, and from oyster reefs within the Texas bays. Perhaps a century from now, if additional species are transported from these sources, diversity may increase. The natural hard shore biota of central Mexico suggest that any increase in diversity on Texas jetties by natural processes of recruitment likely will be slight. Climate, remoteness and abrading sand will keep many species at bay. This shore is, after all, dominated by sand (Chapter 6).

5. Bay Hard Shores

INTRODUCTION

The primary depositional nature of the western Gulf of Mexico precludes extensive or even moderate development of natural rocky shores within any of the estuaries, bays or lagunas of the region. Some natural rocks occur at the mouth of Baffin Bay, Texas, for example, but they are not extensive. Further, the hypersaline waters of this bay largely inhibit the recruitment of a typical rocky shore biota. A few man-made breakwaters line some portions of the bays, especially near tidal inlets, and these have developed a characteristic fauna closely resembling that of the jetty rocks. Similarly, the concrete or wooden wharf pilings along most bayshores provide a habitat for a variety of sessile and wood-boring invertebrates. We will consider these man-made "shores" in the first section of this chapter.

The bays are not entirely devoid of natural hard substrata. In Chapter 9 we will consider a special kind of "hard shore," the stems and aerial roots of tropical mangroves. In this chapter, however, we will focus on one of the enigmas of both temperate and tropical estuaries, the oyster community that, in Texas and the southeastern United States, often develops into substantial reefs. Although largely subtidal in Texas waters, and primarily restricted to the northern bays (oyster reefs are much more extensive in Louisiana), they provide an interesting counterpoint to the faunistically less diverse intertidal hard shores and a contrast with tropical oyster communities, which are more poorly developed and usually intimately associated with the mangroves.

The oyster community of the Texas estuaries deserves separate treatment from other bay and lagoon biota for several reasons. First, it is dependent upon the survival of a single species, the oyster, which, in turn, exists in delicate balance with the sedimentary environment. Increased sedimentation can smother the reef, killing the oysters and depriving other members of the community of essential habitat. There is evidence that this has occurred in Texas bays frequently in the geologic past. In contrast, a coral reef could lose a dozen key species and probably still survive as an important habitat for a large variety of other life-forms. The survival of the oyster community, therefore, is intimately linked with the survival of the oyster itself.

Second, the Texas oyster community is, like many other aspects of the Texas marine biota, one in transition. The American oyster approaches the southern limit of its range in Texas. Large living reefs are virtually absent south of Port Aransas (Copeland & Hoese, 1966), and the hypersaline Laguna Madres immediately north and south of the mouth of the Rio Grande are essentially devoid of oysters. *Crassostrea virginica* is replaced in Mexico by a smaller, related species, *C. rhizophorae*. We will consider several factors contributing to the decrease in *C. virginica* and their associates along a latitudinal gradient in the northwestern Gulf.

Finally, the oyster is an important food source for humans and, as such, has attained considerable economic importance. It is harvested throughout its range, including several of the north and central Texas bays. Because of its economic value, *Crassostrea* has been one of the most intensively studied marine invertebrates. Several books and many thousand research papers have been written about the American oyster, a literature far too extensive to cover here. Much of this material is annotated in two bibliographies (Baughman, 1947 and Joyce, 1972) and a monograph (Stenzel, 1971). We will review some of the general aspects of oyster biology, and show how *Crassostrea*, in providing an estuarine habitat suitable for its own survival, also creates an environment utilized by a variety of other organisms. We will examine the oyster community, and enumerate many of its more prominent members.

BAY BREAKWATERS

Man-made rock or cobble breakwaters line many bayshores, created primarily to reinforce or stabilize the soft, often shifting shoreline. As on the jetties, the rocks provide shelter and living space for a number of animals and plants that otherwise would not be found on the natural bayshore. Community composition on artificial substrata varies, depending upon the location of the shore within the bay, especially in relationship to the distance from a tidal inlet or a major river channel and the local conditions of salinity, currents, exposure and tide.

We have selected a breakwater at Port Isabel, Texas, near Brazos-Santiago Pass (Fig. 5-1) near the historic lighthouse, as an example of a man-made cobble bayshore. Being near the tidal inlet, it has a biota similar to that found on the jetties, including the snails *Nodilittorina lineolata* (Fig. 5-1 D) and *Siphonaria pectinata* (Fig. 5-1 E), the barnacle *Chthamalus fragilis* (Fig. 5-1 F), the anemone *Bunodosoma cavernata* (Fig. 5-1 L), the filter feeding anomuran crab *Petrolisthes armatus* (Fig. 5-1 M), and the bivalve *Isognomon bicolor* (Fig. 5-1 G). The algae, including *Enteromorpha clathrata* (Fig. 5-1 O), *Solieria tenera* (Fig. 5-1 R), *Callithamnion byssoides* (Fig. 5-1 Q), *Digenia simplex* (Fig. 5-1 J) and *Centroceras clavulatum* (Fig. 5-1 P), similarly are species that we have previously encountered on the jetties (Chapter 3). With increasing distance away from the tidal inlets and concurrent decreasing salinity, these species gradually disappear from the cobble or boulder breakwaters, usually without replacement by estuarine ecological equivalents (see Chapter 8).

A few wide ranging species persist a considerable distance across this estuarine transition. For example, *Ligia exotica* (Fig. 5-1 C) is a common shore invertebrate on artificial cobble or boulder breakwater shores along Copano Bay where we have measured salinity at 8 ppt. Other euryhaline species include the rock snail, *Stramonita haemastoma* (Fig. 5-1 H), and the hermit crab, *Clibanarius vittatus* (Fig. 5-1 S), the latter capable of tolerating both hypo- and hypersaline conditions.

There are also a few distinctly estuarine-adapted species, primarily adapted for salinities between 12 to 25 ppt. They include the barnacle, *Balanus eburneus* (Fig. 5-1 K), the crab, *Eurypanopeus depressus* (Fig. 5-1 N) and the snail, *Cerithium lutosum*, (Fig. 5-1 I). When salinities drop below about 10 ppt, even these species usually disappear. One barnacle, *Balanus subalbidus*, seems to thrive in the lowest salinities of the bay, surviving salinities down to almost freshwater.

Patterns of zonation on the rocky bayshores are, at best, poor. At Port Isabel, for example, the littorines, barnacles, *Siphonaria*, and subordinate biota intermingle indiscriminately in the narrow splash zone. Texas bay tides are almost nonexistent, and most bayshores are relatively well protected from significant wave exposure. The shore-protecting rocks frequently lie on a gently sloping incline, partially covered in sand and silt, and rarely extend very far above the water level. In the absence of most of the physical elements contributing to zonation, there is little evidence that it occurs. Snails, false limpets and barnacles take refuge on the larger boulders, while small crabs, anemones, and other subordinate biota take shelter in crevices and under stones. Algae coat the lower rocks, whereas the upper shore, consisting mostly of a salty sandy soil, supports a sparse assemblage of angiosperm halophytes, including *Salicornia virginica* (Fig. 5-1 A) and *Borrichia frutescens* (Fig. 5-1 B). These and other supralittoral plants are typical of the flora of the upper sandy bayshore (Chapter 7).

PILINGS

Concrete or wooden pilings, the latter usually treated with tar or creosote to retard the destructive activities of marine borers, support a variety of man-made structures—piers, wharves, trestles, bridges and buildings—over Gulf and bay waters. Individually the pilings seem insignificant habitats, but they are so numerous, especially along some bayshores, as to collectively provide substantial living space for a variety of sessile biota and their associates. Pilings set in the sea quickly develop a growth of encrusting organisms, and, eventually, even the treated wooden pilings succumb to attack by wood borers. Concrete piles are less susceptible to borer damage, but a few rock borers are known to attack some kinds of concrete structures (see Chapter 11).

Piling biota is influenced by both the rising and falling tide and by the effects of waves or wakes. Accordingly, they follow the general patterns of zonation seen on other hard surfaces, but new piling surfaces usually have two important special properties: they are typically vertical and relatively smooth. The former minimizes the tidal factor in zonation (which, except near tidal inlets is already significantly dampened within Texas bays), and the latter reduces the availability of microhabitats. Both properties inhibit species diversity. As encrusting biota (especially barnacles) colonizes the piling, its surface texture is transformed from smooth to increasing irregularity, providing new surfaces and spaces which can be occupied by other organisms. Thus, only a few hardy colonists occupy new pilings, whereas older pilings may harbor a much richer diversity of life.

The piling biota offers few components unique to this habitat. We have already seen or will soon be introduced to most species found here. We illustrate, for example, an oyster-encrusted concrete piling in Figure 5-2, but this community, with some exceptions, is

5-1. Bayshore breakwater at Port Isabel, Texas. **A.** Glasswort, *Salicornia bigelovii*; **B.** Sea ox-eye daisy, *Borrichia frutescens*; **C.** Sea roach, *Ligia exotica*; **D.** Lined periwinkle, *Nodilittorina lineolata*; **E.** False limpet, *Siphonaria pectinata*; **F.** Fragile barnacle, *Chthamalus fragilis*; **G.** Tree oyster, *Isognomon bicolor*; **H.** Rock snail, *Stramonita haemastoma*; **I.** Dwarf cerith, *Cerithium lutosum*; **J.** *Digenia simplex*; **K.** Ivory barnacle, *Balanus eburneus*; **L.** Anemone, *Bunodosoma cavernata*; **M.** Porcelain crab, *Petrolisthes armatus*; **N.** Mud crab, *Eurypanopeus depressus*; **O.** *Enteromorpha clathrata*; **P.** *Centroceras clavulatum*; **Q.** *Callithamnion byssoides*; **R.** *Solieria tenera*; **S.** Hermit crab, *Clibanarius vittatus*. The scale indicates meters.

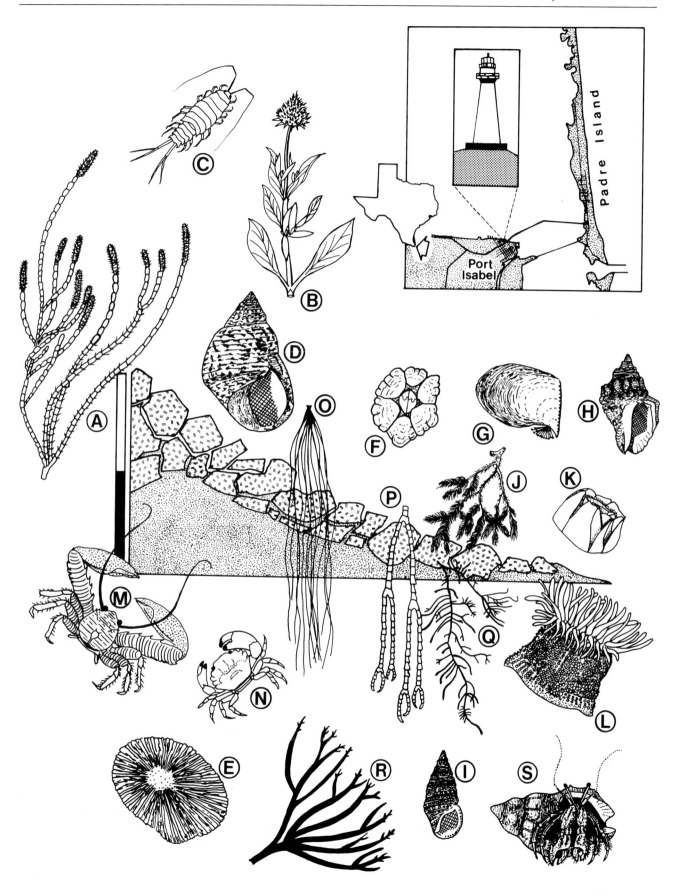

composed primarily of species recruited from an oyster reef. We will mention the common animals and plants usually associated with pilings, but we will not dwell upon them here. Also, we will point out some of the differences between the biota found on concrete pilings and that found upon wood.

The most conspicuous high-zoned animal of either concrete or wooden pilings is usually the sea roach, *Ligia exotica* (Fig. 5-1 C). It runs freely along the vertical piling face and, as on other shores, readily moves from submersion to emersion. The tiny striped littorine, *Nodilittorina lineolata* (Fig. 5-1 D and indicated on the piling diagram in Fig. 5-2), clings to concrete pilings near tidal inlets. It is usually uncommon or absent on wood, and progressively disappears within the bays.

The mid-littoral is indicated on pilings, as on the jetties, by barnacles. Hundreds of *Chthamalus fragilis* (Fig. 5-1 F) form encrusting mats near the top of the tidal range, whereas *Balanus eburneus* (Figs. 5-1 K; 5-2 T) and *Balanus amphitrite* (Fig. 5-2 R) occur lower. The two balanoid species are commonly found upon or among small oyster shells. Here, as upon the jetty, oysters rarely grow more than a few centimeters before they die. Pilings may be covered with hundreds of oyster shells, but few are living and fewer still are large. Oysters, especially *Crassostrea virginica*, occur in greater numbers on concrete structures than upon wooden pilings.

Lower down, near the sublittoral fringe, a variety of marine algae find suitable substrata for attachment. These tend to be the same suite of species that we encountered on the jetties, with density and diversity decreasing as one moves from pilings near inlets to those within the bays.

Barnacles, oysters and algae are the primary surface colonizers of the pilings. Their shells or thalli provide the surfaces required for the attachment or development of a variety of additional associates. Serpulid worms such as *Hydroides dianthus* (Fig. 5-2 N) often cement their long, twisted tubes to the sides of dead oyster shells, and employ a calcareous operculum to close the end of the tube when danger threatens. Soft-bodied sea squirts such as *Molgula manhattensis* (Fig. 5-2 I) occupy crevices between oyster shells. Many small amphipods and isopods take refuge within empty barnacle shells. The amphipods *Corophium louisianum* (Fig. 5-2 F), *C. lacustre* and *Jassa falcata* (Fig. 5-2 G) construct and live within mud tubes, which can blanket older pilings by the thousands. *Sphaeroma quadridentatum* (Fig. 5-2 Q), the most abundant isopod of the northern Texas coast (Clark & Robertson, 1982), occurs with equal frequency on both concrete and wooden pilings, and also favors the shelter of empty barnacle shells. The wood-burrowing *Sphaeroma terebrans* is similar, but bears four distinct tubercles on the last thoracic segment which are absent in *S. quadridentatum* (Heard, 1982a).

Several small crabs are common associates of well colonized piling communities. Notable among these are the xanthids *Eurypanopeus depressus* (Figs. 5-1 N; 5-2 J), *Rhithropanopeus harrisii* (Fig. 5-2 K) and the semiterrestrial *Pachygrapsus transversus* (Fig. 5-2 S). On wooden pilings *Rhithropanopeus harrisii* is often found within cracks and holes caused by the burrowing of *Sphaeroma*. The small anemone, *Aiptasiomorpha texaensis* (Fig. 5-2 H), occurs within the confines of empty oyster shells.

In addition to the attached and errant biota, wooden pilings can support several species of bivalve and arthropod borers, all of which weaken the wood and hasten its destruction. The wood-boring isopod or gribble, *Limnoria tripunctata* (Fig. 6-8 C) is especially destructive. It riddles wooden supports with tunnels running along the grain of the wood. Each tunnel is perforated at intervals with respiratory holes and occupied by a pair of gribbles. The *Limnoria* digestive tract secretes enzymes that can digest cellulose, but gribbles also derive nutrition from bacteria and fungi in rotting wood. The bivalve shipworms *Teredo* and *Bankia* (see Chapter 6) are also commonly found within older or untreated wooden pilings throughout the Gulf of Mexico.

5-2. Texas oyster community and piling biota. **A.** Brown pelican, *Pelecanus occidentalis*; **B.** White pelican, *Pelecanus erythrorhynchos*; **C.** American oystercatcher, *Haematopus palliatus*; **D.** Double-crested cormorant, *Phalacrocorax auritus*; **E.** Olivaceous cormorant, *Phalacrocorax olivaceus*; **F.** Tube-building amphipod, *Corophium louisianum*; **G.** Amphipod, *Jassa falcata*; **H.** Anemone, *Aiptasiomorpha texaensis*; **I.** Sea squirt, *Molgula manhattensis*; **J.** Flat mud crab, *Eurypanopeus depressus*; **K.** Mud crab, *Rhithropanopeus harrisii*; **L.** Stone crab, *Menippe adina*; **M.** Scorched mussel, *Brachidontes exustus*; **N.** Serpulid worm, *Hydroides dianthus*; **O.** Hooked mussel, *Ischadium recurvum*; **P.** Variable bittium, *Bittium varium*; **Q.** Gribble, *Sphaeroma quadridentatum*; **R.** Striped barnacle, *Balanus amphitrite*; **S.** Mottled shore crab, *Pachygrapsus transversus*; **T.** Ivory barnacle, *Balanus eburneus*; **U.** Slipper limpet, *Crepidula fornicata*; **V.** American oyster, *Crassostrea virginica*; **W.** Snapping shrimp, *Alpheus estuariensis*; **X.** Molly miller, *Scartella cristata*; **Y.** Naked goby, *Gobiosoma bosci*; **Z.** Pea crab, *Pinnotheres ostreum*; **A1.** Oyster shell with *Hydroides*, *Cliona* holes and *Crepidula*; **B1.** Blister worm, *Polydora websteri*; **C1.** Oyster piddock, *Diplothyra smithii*, juvenile; **D1.** *D. smithii*, adult with callum; **E1.** Parasitic snail, *Odostomia impressa*; **F1.** Rock snail, *Stramonita haemastoma*; **G1.** Flatworm, *Stylochus ellipticus*; **H1.** Flatworm, *Stylochus frontalis*.

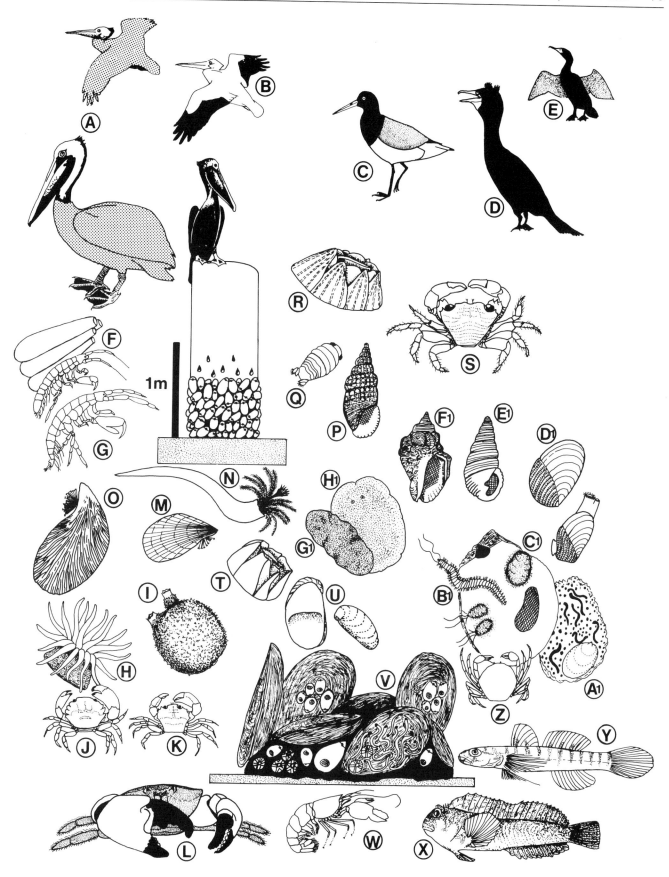

1m

THE OYSTER COMMUNITY

The American oyster, *Crassostrea virginica* (Fig. 5-2 V) is perhaps the most improbable success of the estuary, living as a sessile invertebrate on a bayfloor of mud. Few other life styles and habitats are more irreconcilable than these. Yet *C. virginica* thrives in bays from Canada to Texas, needing only small bits of shell to gain purchase upon the estuary floor. As it grows, its shell creates additional substrata for other oysters. Eventually, as shell grows upon shell, a broad massive oyster reef may develop which profoundly changes the local estuarine environment and the biota which occurs there. A variety of new organisms, many of which cannot live on the bare muddy bay floor, attach to or seek shelter within the oyster reef.

The Oyster

Members of the superfamily Ostreacea are monomyarian filibranchiate bivalve molluscs which normally live permanently attached by the left valve to a firm substratum. They are widely distributed, occurring in temperate to tropical seas from latitudes 64°N to 44°S, and having a relatively continuous fossil record from at least the upper Triassic (Stenzel, 1971). There are over 450 named living species (Harry, 1981), of which perhaps no more than 30 percent are biologically valid. The Gryphaeidae, including numerous fossils and two genera with living species, are exclusively euhaline oysters. The Ostreidae tend to be more euryhaline, with one genus, *Crassostrea*, living in salinities as low as 15 ppt. There are 6 living genera of Ostreidae (Stenzel, 1971; 8 genera *fide* Harry, 1981), of which three—*Crassostrea*, *Ostrea* and *Lopha*—occur in Western Atlantic waters. Table 5-1 lists the distinguishing features of the western Atlantic genera.

The most common temperate oyster is *Crassostrea virginica*, a brackish-water euryhaline species; whereas *C. rhizophorae* is the closely related tropical mangrove oyster. The geographic distributions of *C. virginica* and *C. rhizophorae* are almost mutually exclusive, although there is a zone of overlap along the subtropical margins of each species range, including southernmost Texas and northern Mexico. A few authors consider *C. virginica* and *C. rhizophorae* to be conspecific. *Ostrea equestris* is a steno-euhaline oyster found throughout the region, but less commonly than either of the other two. *Lopha frons*, the frons oyster, occurs attached to mangrove prop roots or gorgonians in the intertidal and shallow subtidal waters of the warm temperate and tropical estuaries. We will discuss *C. virginica* and *O. equestris* in this chapter, and consider *C. rhizophorae* and *L. frons* in Chapter 9.

All oysters regardless of species share a number of common features. For example, adult oysters lack the typical bivalve foot, although it is present in the larva. The foot is a superfluous organ for the permanently sessile adult; but it is essential for the transition from free-swimming larva to attached and metamorphosed juvenile spat. The larval foot and associated byssal gland are responsible for the initial permanent attachment of the young oyster to a substratum. Free-swimming larvae leave the plankton to seek a suitable attachment site on the bottom of the sea or bay. Finding it, a larval oyster places its left valve against the substratum, extends the foot and associated byssal gland to the area of contact, and secretes from the gland a sticky fluid between the shell and the substratum. The secretion hardens rapidly into conchiolin, which firmly bonds the larval shell to the bottom, and thereafter the foot and byssal gland are no longer needed. As the oyster undergoes metamorphosis to the adult, these organs degenerate and disappear.

Like most bivalves, oysters are filter feeders, employing ciliated ctenidia to create water currents, collect food particles from the plankton, and transport them to the mouth via specific ciliated pathways. The ctenidia are fused to portions of the mantle and to each other in such a way as to create two separate chambers, the inhalant and exhalant mantle chambers. Water is circulated from the inhalant chamber through ctenidial ostia to the exhalant chamber. Particulate inclusions unable to pass with the water through ctenidial ostia are subjected to the sorting activities of ctenidial cilia. Some of this material is unsuitable for ingestion and accumulates in the mantle cavity as pseudofeces, which are periodically expelled to the exterior. The remainder is transported from ctenidia to labial palps where final sorting occurs prior to ingestion.

Adult oysters possess only a single adductor muscle (i.e., they are monomyarian). Most bivalves possess a pair of adductors (dimyarian), one anterior and one posterior, functioning together to close the shell valves. Larval oysters possess paired adductor muscles, but the anterior one atrophies during metamorphosis, leaving only the posterior muscle which migrates to a relatively central location in the body as the adult form develops. This muscle becomes large in proportion to body size, and is divided into two separate physiological components, the "quick" and "catch" elements. Quick muscle lies proximal to the umbo and is employed for rapid action; it can contract quickly but is unable to maintain prolonged contraction. The catch muscle cannot respond quickly but is capable of sustained contraction for long periods. The two muscular elements lie adjacent to one another and act in concert to provide the range of actions required by the oyster. Quick and catch portions of the oyster adductor can be easily distinguished in fresh specimens. Catch muscle fibers appear opaque white or cream, whereas the quick fibers are a semitranslucent fleshy shade.

The process of reproduction in oysters varies according to genus or species. Members of the genus *Ostrea*, including *O. equestris*, are usually larviparous and ambisexual. Young *Ostrea* develop male gonads, but alternately produce gonads of the opposite sex. Eggs of *O. equestris* are fertilized and developmental stages proceed at least to the trochophore larvae before re-

Table 5-1. Features of Living Oyster Genera in the Gulf of Mexico (after Gunter (1951), Menzel (1955) and others cited in text)

Feature	*Crassostrea*	*Ostrea*	*Lopha*
Shell shape	Usually elongate	Subcircular	Globular to elongate
Average adult size	Larger	Smaller	Smaller
Valve margins	Neither plicate nor minutely papillate; without shelly claspers	Neither plicate nor minutely papillate; without shelly claspers	Plicate and minutely papillate; with shelly claspers
Muscle scar	Nearer valve margin; usually pigmented	Nearer center of valve; not pigmented	Nearer hinge of valve; not pigmented
Promyal chamber	Present	Absent	Absent
Gill ostia	Small	Large	Large
Reproduction	Non-incubatory; gametes shed into water where fertilization occurs	Incubatory; fertilization occurs in the mantle cavity and gills	Incubatory; fertilization occurs in the mantle cavity and gills
Egg size	Smaller	Larger	Larger
Fecundity	Often > 50 million eggs per spawn	Less than 2 million eggs per spawn	Less than 2 million eggs per spawn
Salinity preference	Estuarine	Near euhaline	Near euhaline

lease from the mantle cavity.

In contrast, *Crassostrea virginica* is oviparous and dioecious. The sexes are usually separate and fixed for life, although occasional hermaphrodites are known to occur. The sex of an oyster can be determined only by examination of gonads, as there are no external secondary sexual characteristics. Eggs and sperm are shed freely into the water, where fertilization occurs.

Spawning by *C. virginica* is initiated in the spring with increases in temperature, and varies with latitude. For example, Chesapeake Bay oysters spawn when water temperatures reach about 20°C, whereas Gulf oysters delay spawning until temperatures reach about 25°C (Galtsoff, 1964). The differences are due to local acclimation and not genetic differences, for oysters transported from one region to another will rapidly assume the spawning behavior typical of the new habitat (Butler, 1955).

The precise timing of gamete release is critical, for without some degree of synchrony, wastage of gametes can be immense. Several pioneer studies were conducted to determine what triggers a spawn (e.g., Nelson, 1928; Hopkins, 1931; Loosanoff & Engle, 1942). Generally, males are more easily stimulated to release gametes than females and can be induced to spawn by rising temperatures and a variety of chemical substances, many of which are not normally found in seawater (Galtsoff, 1938a; 1940). Females, on the other hand, usually require the presence of oyster sperm in the water to initiate egg release (Galtsoff, 1938b). The spawn of one male in a group of oysters triggers its neighbors to release gametes, and they, in turn, set off

a crescendo of spawning which can spread throughout an oyster reef. Millions of gametes released simultaneously into the water insure that at least some eggs will be fertilized. Larvae reside in the plankton for two to three weeks before seeking a place for settlement and metamorphosis.

Oyster Ecology

The relationships between the oyster and its environment are among the most intensely researched areas of marine and estuarine biology. Despite the tremendous interest, spurred by the economic importance of the oyster, some aspects of its ecology are still poorly understood, possibly because the oyster, especially *Crassostrea virginica*, is a highly adaptable organism. The geographic range of *C. virginica*, from cold Canadian waters to the subtropical Gulf of Mexico, suggests a strong potential for adaptability. A number of factors influence the local abundance of oysters. These include the nature of the substratum, intensity of sedimentation, water circulation, salinity, temperature, competition, predation, disease, and pollution (to name a few). We will consider several of these factors as they influence Texas oysters, and refer when necessary to populations of other geographic areas. Unless otherwise noted, the paragraphs which follow pertain to *C. virginica*.

Oysters require at least some hard substratum or cultch upon which to settle, or set. Growing shells of a successful set become additional cultch for later generation oysters. Shell material, especially oyster shell, seems to be the most desirable surface for attachment by juvenile oysters. They can and do attach to other hard structures, including rocks, concrete pilings, gravel, and even metal, but the greatest concentrations of oysters are found in large reefs where individuals attach shell to shell.

Thriving oyster reefs commonly rise from the muddy bottoms of Texas bays (Fig. 5-3 A). It is not difficult to visualize that these reefs were derived from small rocky protuberances or shell accumulations on the bay floor which coalesced as succeeding generations of oysters enlarged the original sites. Yet, the reefs are not located haphazardly in the estuaries, but arise through a successional series of complex physical and biological interactions (Marshall, 1954a). Oyster reef succession includes at least five stages: (1), initial colonization; (2), clustering; (3), accretion; (4), maturation and (5), senescence (Bahr & Lanier, 1981).

Initial reef formation begins as oysters settle and attach to isolated cultch materials in the lower intertidal and shallow subtidal zones of the estuary. The bottom upon which the cultch rests is important, for some substrata such as shifting sands or very soft muds are undesirable for oysters and rarely support reefs (Galtsoff, 1964). Almost any other bottom type from firm muds to bedrock is suitable for initial colonization, provided that some cultch is present. Colonization is inhibited in areas of high sedimentation (Hsiao, 1950; Butler, 1955; Galtsoff, 1964), high predation (Marshall, 1954b), prolonged lowered salinity (Butler, 1952; Andrews *et al.*, 1959; May, 1972; Burrell, 1977), and reduced water circulation (Galtsoff & Luce, 1930; Manning & Whaley, 1955).

A number of subtle factors influence initial colonization of a substratum, and subsequent clustering and accretion of clusters to form a reef. For example, cultch position can influence the success of initial colonization and subsequent clustering. Although Butler (1955) and Shaw (1967) present inconclusive data on cultch surface selectivity by oyster larvae, most others who have studied the problem report heavier sets on the underside of shells and test panels (Nelson, 1928; Pomerat & Reiner, 1942; Sieling, 1950; Medcof, 1955; Crisp, 1967). In laboratory experiments, bottommost layers of the cultch attract significantly more setting larvae than higher layers (Hidu, 1969). Ritchie & Menzel (1969) have shown that the tendency to set in secluded areas is in part a photonegative response by the larvae. Recently settled spat also stimulate additional spat to settle nearby, as if *C. virginica* has a tendency toward gregarious setting (Crisp, 1967; Hidu, 1969; Prytherch, 1929). Thus, initial colonization of cultch facilitates clustering, which in turn facilitates accretion of clusters.

Isolated cultch settled by several spat will eventually form a cluster, consisting of a colony of from one to several generations of oysters. As the cluster grows, the larger, lower oysters die from overcrowding or suffocation by more recently settled shells. Clusters growing upon mud bottoms frequently contain many oysters with elongate shells (Galtsoff, 1964), an adap-

tation to facilitate filter feeding upon an otherwise difficult substratum as well as maximize cultch surface area for the settlement of new spat. Storms break or scatter fragments of clusters, multiplying the availability of cultch in the local environment. Eventually, the bottom is littered with numerous cluster nuclei, each of which grows laterally and vertically and eventually coalesces to form the mature oyster reef (Grinnell, 1971; Wiedemann, 1972). The mature reef may persist several hundred years in an estuary, but remains a dynamic system, continually changing form in response to environmental factors (Marshall, 1954b).

A mature oyster reef usually extends into the intertidal zone. The degree to which living oysters can tolerate intertidal conditions is mediated by the local tidal range, seasonal temperature extremes, exposure, and other factors (see below). In *Spartina*-protected salt marsh estuaries (such as those along much of the Atlantic shores from Massachusetts to Georgia) oysters form small tidally-exposed reefs adjacent to the grass beds. Here the highest densities of living oysters often occur intertidally (Bahr & Lanier, 1981). In large, open, less-protected bays, mature reefs may attain immense sizes. Several oyster reefs in the Texas bays have lengths of 6 to 8 km (Price, 1954). The intertidally exposed upper portions of these large reefs, called

5-3. The Texas oyster fishery. During the last 35 years, the Galveston Bay area has produced a greater oyster harvest than all other Texas estuaries.

A. Galveston Bay and vicinity, with the primary public oyster reefs marked by numbers. Although oyster harvest has been temporarily suspended in many parts of the bay due to coliform contamination, the shaded areas have been closed almost continuously since 1950. The dotted lines indicate ship channels or the Intracoastal Waterway. Oyster reefs: 1. Fisher's; 2. Beezley's; 3. Dow; 4. Yacht Club; 5. Red Bluff; 6. Scott's; 7. Bayview; 8. Smith's; 9. Houston Ship Channel spoil; 10. Todd's Dump; 11. North Redfish; 12. Bart's Pass; 13. Vingtune; 14. Sheldon; 15. Possum Pass; 16. East Redfish; 17. South Redfish; 18. Dickinson; 19. Dollar; 20. Half Moon; 21. Hanna's; 22. Moody's; 23. Elm Grove; 24. Frenchy's; 25. Carancahua; 26. Confederate (after Hofstetter, 1977).

B. Salinity in Galveston Bay and Trinity River discharge since 1950. The upper graph (●) shows annual Trinity River discharge (1 cubic hectometer = 811.3 acre ft). The lower graphs illustrate mean annual salinity as follows: (○) Upper Galveston Bay; (□) Middle Galveston Bay; (●) East Bay (after Hofstetter, 1977; 1983 and data from the U.S. Geological Survey).

C. Oyster harvest as annual kilograms of shucked meat. Dark bars indicate Galveston Bay oyster harvest; white bars indicate harvest in all other parts of the state (after Hofstetter, 1977; 1983). Note the decline in oyster harvest correlated with years of lowered salinity and high river discharge.

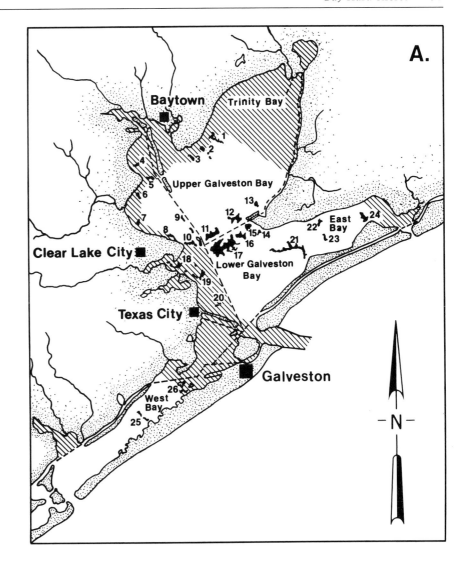

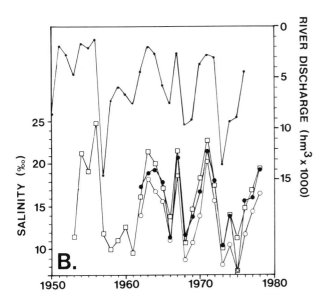

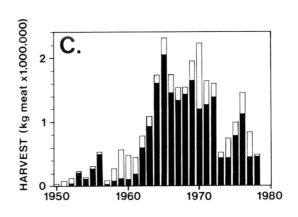

"flatland surfaces" (Grinnell, 1971) or "hogbacks" (Gunter, 1972, 1979b), are commonly devoid of living oysters. The hogbacks contain large quantities of coarse to finely divided shell debris easily moved by waves and tides. This "grit" (Gunter, 1979b) influences the distribution of living oysters around the mature reef. Waves keep the grit in motion, with individual particles constantly abrading against one another and effectively prohibiting the settlement of larvae, or destroying juveniles which have settled (Ortega, 1981). Reef flanks also receive some of this grit, but only enough to keep larger shell surfaces sufficiently clean to permit larval attachment. Thus, the large mature open-bay reef, the most common type along the Texas shore, is characterized by a barren central intertidal hogback flanked and surrounded by a largely subtidal living reef community (Price, 1954). This reef type differs significantly from the smaller, relatively more sheltered oyster reefs associated with *Spartina* marsh estuaries (most common in the southeastern United States). The latter fail to develop the large central hogbacks, lack the intertidal abrasive grit, and, accordingly, produce some of the highest densities of living oysters in the intertidal region (Bahr & Lanier, 1981).

Oysters are profoundly influenced by sedimentation, and can be destroyed under a naturally accumulating sediment burden (Norris, 1953) or a catastrophic burial by storms, floods, channel dredging or a variety of other phenomena (Engle, 1948; Ingle, 1952). They can withstand temporary covering, but survival is mediated by temperature. Oysters survive under 7.5 cm of sediment for 5 weeks at 5°C, but only 2 days at 25°C (Dunnington, 1968).

When partially buried or covered with only thin layers of sediment, oysters can remove much of the fouling material from mantle margins. Coarse sand is most easily removed; fine sand is least effectively eliminated (Dunnington, *et al.*, 1970). Mixed sediments consisting of various sand- and mud-sized particles are also more effectively removed than fine sand. Oysters clear sediments more effectively when in a vertical (umbo downward) position.

Burial is not the only adverse effect of sediment on living oysters. Highly turbid, sediment-laden water can clog the filter feeding machinery of these bivalves. Oysters live in constant danger of this kind of sediment stress, as high turbidity is a common occurrence in estuaries, especially during periods of high winds or floods. Accordingly, oysters have developed adaptations such as interlocking papillae on the mantle margins to minimize or prevent large particles from entering the mantle cavity. Furthermore, when waters become highly turbid, oysters decrease or cease feeding activity (Hsiao, 1950). Sustained heavy sediment loads in the water cannot be tolerated and will eventually smother the oysters.

Oysters must also contend with a sediment source of their own making. Oyster feces and pseudofeces contribute significantly to the sediment burden of the estuary. Even in waters of relatively low turbidity, oysters collect considerable amounts of suspended solids and redeposit them in concentrated form (Lund, 1957a). During the summer in a Virginia estuary, for example, oysters produced over 2000 kg of feces and pseudofeces per hectare per week (Haven & Morales-Alamo, 1966). Although the production of this biogenic silt varies seasonally (decreasing in the winter), oysters are always in danger of smothering themselves, especially if they have settled in an area of limited water circulation. In the absence of currents, oysters will smother themselves much more quickly than normal gravity-influenced sedimentation can bury them (Lund, 1957b). Experiments show that oysters cultured in still water of low turbidity and covering 50 percent of the bottom can produce enough silt to cover themselves completely in 36 days (Lund, 1957b).

Water currents are the sole means by which immobile adult oysters obtain food and by which waste is removed from the colony. Still or sluggish backbay areas are poor habitats for development of oyster reefs. The ideal *C. virginica* habitat occurs within a continuous but nonturbulent water flow. In most estuaries, these conditions are frequently associated with tidal exchange cycles, although not necessarily directly within main tidal channels. High density oyster beds occur where there is optimal water flow to deliver adequate food for all members of the population, while not being sufficiently turbulent to produce excessive turbidity by bottom agitation. Accordingly, large crowded oyster reefs are usually located in or near rapid tidal streams (Galtsoff, 1964). The large Redfish Bar reefs, located between Trinity and Galveston bays (Fig. 5-3 A) clearly demonstrate the importance of tidal currents on the development of oyster reefs.

Water currents also are directly responsible for the distribution of oyster larvae in estuaries (Manning & Whaley, 1955). Rapidly beating cilia on the larval velum keep young oysters suspended in the water with other plankton, but they generate insufficient thrust to move the larval oyster upstream against a current. Thus, the complex tidal and wind-generated currents usually found in estuaries influence where adult oysters will be found. Water currents also influence the success or failure of larval settlement. Fine sediments forming thin (< 2 mm) films on hard substrata in still waters may be enough to inhibit larval settlement (Galtsoff, 1964). A certain degree of microbiological fouling seems to aid settlement of larvae (Drinnan, 1969).

Crassostrea virginica, like its tropical Caribbean counterpart *C. rhizophorae*, can live intertidally. The American oyster is most successful as an intertidal bivalve in the central portion of its range. From Massachusetts to northern Florida, some of the more productive oyster reefs lie upon semi-protected intertidal mudflats at the margins of *Spartina* marshes. Relatively large tidal fluctuations move water and nutrients from the marshes over the oyster beds and back again, providing the necessary food and currents to the thriving oyster community.

Intertidal *C. virginica* at the extremes of the natural range fare much less successfully. In waters subjected to prolonged winter freezes oysters are excluded from the intertidal (Galtsoff, 1964), in part due to effects of exposure and in part due to ice abrasion. In subtropical and tropical estuaries, intertidal oysters are somewhat more successful, but do not produce thriving populations. Intertidal oysters occur in the northern Texas estuaries, but from the Brazos River southward, if *C. virginica* is present at all, it more commonly lives subtidally. Several factors are probably responsible. We have already discussed Gunter's "grit principle," which accounts for the absence of sessile biota from the intertidal reef crest on the basis of mechanical abrasion. Oysters also can face adverse competition from mussels at exposed intertidal localities (Ortega, 1981). The slight tidal fluctuation in Texas bays reduces habitable range for a variety of intertidal species, including oysters, and this, coupled with the general lack of protection from intense summer heat, also inhibits a thriving intertidal oyster community.

Oysters exposed at low tide in central and southern Texas bays suffer severe summer mortalities due to thermal stress (Copeland & Hoese, 1966). Unlike *C. rhizophorae*, which is sheltered from direct insolation by the mangrove vegetation upon which it normally sets, tidally exposed *C. virginica* in Texas receive full solar illumination. During the heat of a summer day mantle cavity temperatures can increase to between 46 to 49°C (Galtsoff, 1964). Highest mortalities of intertidal and shallow water oysters occur in July and August, and few specimens from these habitats live more than one year (Copeland & Hoese, 1966). Despite the high mortalities, growth of oysters living in the marginal environments is rapid. Copeland & Hoese (1966) report net production of soft tissue in Redfish Bay to be 5.2 gm/m²/day from March 24 to June 16, 1965. Rapid growth and early maturation apparently compensate for the shorter lifespan.

Sessile estuarine organisms cannot escape normal diurnal, seasonal, or annual salinity variations, although they may be able to isolate their tissues temporarily from the external medium. The effects of salinity changes upon such biota depend in part upon the suddenness, magnitude and duration of the changes (Wells, 1961). Other factors such as temperature, exposure, or disease can influence the degree to which estuarine organisms can survive large or prolonged changes in salinity (Galtsoff, 1964). Oysters illustrate these principles especially well.

Oysters usually have wide salinity tolerances, but different species have different optimal salinity preferences. *Ostrea equestris*, for example, is best adapted for the higher salinities of outer shores or the open sea. It is a common offshore fouling pest, attaching to buoys and drilling platforms in salinities up to 36 ppt (Menzel, 1955, 1956; Galtsoff & Merrill, 1962). It occurs in the tidal inlets of the Texas coast (e.g., Aransas Pass and Lydia Ann Channel) and often settles on jetty

rocks. *Ostrea equestris* is usually absent in the reduced salinities of inner bays. During drought years, when bay salinities increase significantly above normal levels, *O. equestris* enters the bays and displaces *Crassostrea virginica* (Parker, 1955; Gillard, 1969; Hofstetter, 1977). Under drought conditions, some reefs of the inner bays may be composed of 50 percent *O. equestris*, whereas in normal years the species is absent.

Crassostrea virginica is an exceptionally euryhaline species, tolerating lower salinities than any other living oyster (Hopkins, 1978). It lives in salinities from 5 to 30 ppt (Galtsoff, 1964; Castagna & Chanley, 1973), and even survives brief exposures above and below these extremes. Living populations have been reported from offshore reefs in oceanic salinities (Wells & Gray, 1960). The optimum salinity range for adult *C. virginica* is usually cited as being between 12 to 28 ppt, although Ladd (1951) and Gunter (1953) prefer 12 to 19 ppt. Within the optimum range, *C. virginica* is an osmoconformer. It conforms more slowly at lower salinities (4 to 8 ppt) and dies before attaining osmotic equilibrium below 4 ppt (Anderson & Anderson, 1974).

Crassostrea virginica is especially noted for its ability to tolerate and survive rapid, drastic salinity changes (e.g., 15 to 20 ppt within a few minutes), provided that the change does not exceed normally lethal limits (Loosanoff, 1953). It does so by cessation of water flow within the mantle cavity (perhaps related to the physiological effects of a different salinity on ciliary activity, see Dean & Paparo, 1981), temporary shell closure, and presumed gradual adjustment to the new salinity, usually within six hours of the change. *Crassostrea virginica* can survive and grow under even greater salinity fluctuations, provided the changes occur more slowly. For example, oysters attain harvestable sizes in Apalachicola Bay, Florida, where salinities range from freshwater to 42.5 ppt (Ingle & Dawson, 1952). Oysters acclimated to low salinities (3 to 10 ppt) can also survive transfer to high salinity (27 ppt) with minimal mortality (Loosanoff, 1950). *Crassostrea virginica* is less tolerant of rapid salinity changes in summer and more tolerant of similar changes in cool seasons (Galtsoff, 1964).

Crassostrea virginica endures depressed salinity to 5 ppt with little apparent physiological stress, although oxygen consumption increases as oysters experience lower salinities (Percy *et al.*, 1971; Bass, 1977). Below 5 ppt oysters cease feeding, close their valves, inhibit various metabolic processes (e.g., gonad development), and isolate their tissues from the unfavorable salinity of the external environment (Chestnut, 1946; Loosanoff, 1948; Loosanoff, 1953; Andrews *et al.*, 1959). This is a short-term survival mechanism, protecting oysters against brief freshwater surges. Prolonged freshwater dilution, especially in warmer seasons, usually results in high oyster mortality (Fig. 5-3 B & C). Long-term changes can alter oyster productivity more significantly, as can be estimated by fishery yields. For example, water which normally flowed into Delaware Bay twice was diverted for use by New York City (in 1929 and 1953). With each diversion, the mean salinity of oyster-producing areas of the bay increased, and was followed by a rapid decrease in oyster productivity (Gunter, 1975).

Low salinities are most commonly encountered in estuaries following late winter or spring floods. Low winter temperatures aid survival of oysters subjected to prolonged low salinities (Loosanoff, 1948; Owen & Walters, 1950; Loosanoff, 1953). Below about 6°C, oysters enter torpor, with metabolic activities (e.g., heartbeat, ciliary motion, and general sensitivity) reduced to very low levels (Stauber, 1940). Oysters usually resume normal metabolic activity when temperatures rise about 6 to 7°C, but torpor may persist if external conditions are not conducive for normal metabolic activity. At salinities below 5 ppt, oysters will remain in torpor, even when temperatures rise above 20°C. Torpor can persist several months, until external conditions reach acceptable levels (Andrews, *et al.*, 1959). Once broken, torpor is not easily regained, its onset apparently triggered by gradually decreasing temperatures (Andrews *et al.*, 1959). Furthermore, torpor cannot be maintained indefinitely. Persistent freshets will eventually bring about extensive oyster mortality (Andrews *et al.*, 1959; Butler, 1952; Gunter, 1953). Ironically, these same freshets indirectly assist surviving oysters by destroying some pest organisms (e.g., gastropods, flatworms, or asteroids) which prey upon oysters (Gunter, 1955; Shearer & Mackenzie, 1961; Wells, 1961; Galtsoff, 1964; Menzel *et al.*, 1966; May & Bland, 1970, May, 1972).

The optimum salinity for the development of oyster eggs and larvae seems to be dependent upon the salinity at which parent oysters live (Davis, 1958). In Long Island Sound, for example, the optimum salinity for development of *C. virginica* eggs is 22.5 ppt, with some normal development occurring as low as 12.5 ppt. At near optimum salinities, *Crassostrea* larvae survive and grow over a wider range of temperatures than at salinities near their lower limits of tolerance (Davis & Calabrese, 1964). At 10 ppt oyster larvae grow more slowly than similarly aged oysters at 12.5 ppt (Davis, 1958), and below 5 ppt, growth virtually ceases (Loosanoff, 1948).

Just as *C. virginica* is euryhaline, it is also eurythermal, occurring in water temperatures that range from a minimum of about 1°C in Canadian estuaries to as much as 36°C in Texas lagoons and bays (Galtsoff, 1964). Despite a broad general thermal tolerance, temperature profoundly affects oyster metabolism in many ways (rates of feeding, respiration, water transport and gonad maturation to name a few). Maximum ciliary effectiveness of oyster ctenidia, for example, is achieved at about 25°C; above 32°C ciliary activity rapidly declines, affecting the oyster's ability to obtain food. Nearly all body functions cease at 42°C (Galtsoff, 1964).

When either or both temperature and salinity increase above optimum limits, mortality rates of oysters increase. The greatest declines in harvestable oysters on the Texas coast are invariably linked to salinity perturbations, either the result of extreme drought (e.g., during the 1950s) or excessive flooding (e.g., 1973) (Hofstetter, 1977). A number of factors in addition to environmental stress also affect the degree of mortality. For example, as salinity and temperature increase, *C. virginica* becomes more susceptible to disease organisms, e.g., *Perkinsus* (= *Labyrinthomyxa* = *Dermocystidium*) *marinus* (Gillard, 1969; Ray *et al.*, 1953), and experiences increasing numbers of pests and predators (Gunter, 1955).

Parasites and Shell Pests

Oysters are plagued by a variety of parasites and pests that attack soft tissues or shells. The number of pests which plague *Crassostrea virginica* seems large, but it is probably no more than encountered by many other invertebrates (Overstreet, 1978). Over the years we have learned much about the oyster pests largely because of the economic importance of the oyster and a desire to attempt to minimize pest impact on shellfisheries. Despite this knowledge, humans have been unable to exert much control over pest infestations in natural oyster populations.

The microscopic *Perkinsus marinus* (not illustrated) is a damaging parasite of oysters that has received considerable study. It is an important contributing cause of summer mortality in *Crassostrea virginica*, especially among populations living in salinities near the upper limits of tolerance (Mackin, 1951; Dawson, 1955; Mackin, 1961; Andrews, 1962a, 1962b; Ray, 1966). It is an example of a pest that was detected because of the economic importance of its host, for it was discovered as a result of studies to explain high oyster mortalities on commercially harvested reefs. In most other invertebrates lacking the economic importance of the oyster, this parasite might easily be overlooked, for it requires a powerful microscope and sophisticated techniques even to be seen (Ray, 1952; 1966). The taxonomic affinities of *Perkinsus marinus* are still debated. For many years it was considered a fungus, first assigned to the genus *Dermocystidium*, and later *Labyrinthomyxa*. Recent studies (Perkins, 1976a, 1976b; Levine, 1978) place it among the protozoa, but this assignment has not received complete acceptance.

Perkinsus marinus invades cells, tissues and blood of the oyster, causing extensive lysis, fluid accumulation, and tissue weight loss. It is particularly destructive during periods of summer drought, when higher salinity waters move far into the estuaries. Even during relatively normal years, it is reported to be responsible for as much as 50 percent mortality of marketable oysters (Hofstetter, 1977).

The pyramidellid, *Odostomia impressa* (Fig. 5-2 E1) is an ectoparasite of the oyster. It rarely grows larger than 6 mm, but is very abundant on oyster reefs. It inserts an elongate proboscis bearing a piercing stylet between valves of the oyster and from which it sucks mucus and tissue fluids. Although many parasitic Pyramidellidae are host-specific, *Odostomia impressa* feeds upon several molluscs including oysters, *Stramonita*, *Bittium*, *Crepidula* and *Polydora* and a variety of polychaetes (Allen, 1958; Wells, 1959). It deposits clear, gelatinous egg masses containing 15 to 40 transparent eggs upon oysters and other shells during the warmer months, and especially in late spring and early summer. The snail apparently lives one year, dying after producing a spawn (Wells, 1959).

The crab, *Pinnotheres ostreum* (Fig. 5-2 Z), is a common pest which lives within the mantle cavity of the oyster. It is not unusual if more than half of the oysters in a bed are infested with them (Christensen & McDermott, 1958). Called pea crabs because they are about the size and shape of a pea, these crustaceans also frequent the mantle cavities of bivalves other than oysters (Chapter 10). An oyster usually harbors but one or two adult crabs, although oyster spat may contain several juveniles. *P. ostreum* was once thought to be a commensal of oysters, but it is now recognized as an oyster parasite, at least during later life stages (Stauber, 1945; Flower & McDermott, 1953; Christensen & McDermott, 1958; and Haven, 1959). The crab occurs throughout the range of *C. virginica* and extends into the Caribbean where it also parasitizes *C. rhizophorae* (Powers, 1977).

Young male and female pea crabs enter the mantle cavities of oyster spat in late summer or early fall. Upon initial invasion, as many as half a dozen soft-bodied, first instar post-larval juvenile crabs occupy the mantle cavity of an oyster. They over-winter within the host, during which time both sexes pass through several more soft instars. By late spring both sexes eventually molt into a hard-bodied stage which signals the onset of reproduction, as the hardened carapace is a functional necessity for copulation. At this point, males range in size from about 1.5 to 4 mm and females from 1.3 to 2.7 mm carapace width (Stauber, 1945; Christensen & McDermott, 1958).

Hard-carapace male pea crabs become restless wanderers, leaving their original host in search of mates inhabiting other oysters. Females rarely leave, but will do so if more than one female crab occurs within an oyster (Christensen & McDermott, 1958). Mating occurs within the mantle cavity of the oyster, usually in the early summer. Sperm are transferred in spermatophores and the female can retain these sperm packages some time after copulation before using them for fertilization. Fertilized eggs are incubated on the female abdomen for three to five weeks; thereafter larvae emerge from the egg mass and enter the plankton. The crab passes from a hatchling larva to a first instar crab in 25 days or less (Sandoz & Hopkins, 1947), at which time it is ready to occupy the mantle cavity of an oyster or other bivalve. First instar crabs preferentially seek oyster spat for invasion rather than adult oysters (Christensen & McDermott, 1958). Spat of 10 mm or more are most commonly entered, but pinnotherids are known to occur in spat as small as about 5 mm.

Males do not survive beyond the hard-carapace stage (a total lifespan of usually less than one year), but females persist up to three years, molting to produce several subsequent soft-carapace instars, and perhaps additional hard stages (Christensen & McDermott, 1958). Following the first hard stage, female crabs remain intimately associated with the oyster ctenidia.

The preceding account of life history was taken largely from Christensen & McDermott (1958), who studied pea crabs in Delaware Bay. There have been no studies on the life history of *Pinnotheres* in warm-temperate to tropical waters. Inasmuch as *C. virginica* grows best during the winter months in Texas bays (Gunter, 1942), growth and reproductive behavior of *P. ostreum* in Texas and more southerly localities may not correspond exactly to the pattern just described.

Most of the Pinnotheridae are commensal crabs living in association with a variety of invertebrates, including bivalve molluscs, burrowing crustaceans, echinoderms, and polychaetes and other worms. Few of these crustaceans are parasites. They derive sustenance from food material acquired by the commensal associate. *Pinnotheres ostreum* carries the association one step further, to become a partial parasite of its bivalve host. The feeding behavior of *P. ostreum* apparently changes as the crab matures. The relationship begins as a typically commensal one, with young crabs feeding on food-laden mucous strands formed by the filter feeding oyster. Parasitism of host tissue does not seem to be important at this stage. As the crabs grow larger, they begin to feed upon the ctenidial tissue, causing localized lesions and impairing the function of this important mantle organ.

The incidence of *P. ostreum* in oysters decreases as salinity decreases. In salinities of 20 ppt and greater, the incidence of *Pinnotheres* in oysters ranges from 35 to 50 percent, whereas in salinities below 20 ppt, the incidence of pea crabs is generally less than 20 percent (Flower & McDermott, 1953).

A variety of invertebrates live within the shells of oysters. They infrequently molest soft tissues, but may drain the strength of infested oysters by demanding constant energy for shell repair. Several species of boring sponges, *Cliona* sp. (not illustrated), riddle oyster shells with tiny tunnels, filling them with bright yellow tissues. Sponge larvae initiate the tunnels when they settle on the exterior of the oyster shell. Amoebocytes employ a combination of chemical and mechanical means to loosen tiny chips of shell, which are then discarded (Cobb, 1969). The sponge derives no nutrition from the oyster, but simply employs the shell as a habitat. Boring sponges can significantly weaken shells of living oysters, but the incidence of *Cliona* is usually much greater on unoccupied rather than living oyster shells (Fig. 5-2 A1). *Cliona* also bores into the unoccupied shells of a variety of other molluscs, and is important in the process of shell decomposition and sediment accumulation.

Larvae of the mud blister worm, *Polydora websteri* (Fig. 5-2 B1) settle upon the margins of young oyster shells and employ chemical secretions to etch U-shaped depressions into them. The worm dissolves calcium carbonate and the organic conchiolin to form its burrow, both ends of which lie open to the exterior (Zottoli & Carriker, 1974). As worm and oyster increase in size, *Polydora* maintains and enlarges its burrow within the shell, adding mud and other debris within the "U." The oyster responds by roofing over the tube with new shell material, forming an unsightly but functional semitransparent "blister." Like other spionids, *Polydora* employs a pair of palps for feeding. Particles of food adhere to the mucus-laden palps as they extend into the water from the blister burrow entrance.

The oyster piddock, *Diplothyra smithii* (Fig. 5-2 C1; D1) is a bivalve borer of the family Pholadidae, and one of the largest invertebrates to infest oyster shells. *Diplothyra* is generally thought of as a mechanical borer. Ridges on the anterior face of the shell bear abrasive spines that scratch at the host shell to create a globular burrow. Siphons project from the burrow aperture. As with *Polydora*, the oyster reacts to the activities of the growing bivalve by laying down additional blister-like shell material. *Diplothyra* continues to bore until it is sexually mature, often within a year of settlement. During the period of active boring the foot, the bracing and attachment organ essential for successful boring, protrudes through a wide pedal gape (Fig. 5-2 C1). When boring ceases, the pedal gape is closed by secretion of extra shell material, the callum (Fig. 5-2 D1), along the shell margins. The callum so effectively closes the pedal gape that it prevents further boring. The mature adult is now protectively encapsulated within its own shell, which, in turn, lies within the protective confines of the host shell. Callum formation and sexual maturity can commence over a range of shell sizes. It appears to be triggered when the actively boring juvenile runs out of host shell within which to develop. Such unusual metamorphoses seem to be typical of the Pholadidae, but not of the closely related wood boring shipworms (Teredinidae).

Sessile Epifauna

Not only do oysters find other oyster shells a suitable substratum for attachment, but a number of other sessile invertebrates also settle upon them. The balanoid barnacles *Balanus amphitrite* (Fig. 5-2 R), *B. eburneus* (Fig. 5-2 T) and *B. improvisus* (Fig. 9-3 I) are common associates, as are many of the other animals associated with bay pilings. These include the sea squirt, *Molgula manhattensis* (Fig. 5-2 I), the tube dwelling amphipods, *Corophium louisianum* (Fig. 5-2 F), and *Jassa falcata* (Fig. 5-2 G), and the gribble *Sphaeroma quadridentatum* (Fig 5-2 Q). The mussels *Brachidontes exustus* (Fig. 5-2 M) and *Ischadium recurvum* (Fig. 5-2 O) attach by byssal threads to oysters, the latter prevalent on oyster reefs in salinities below 20 ppt, but often replaced by the former in higher salinities (Menzel, 1955). The small anemone, *Aiptasiomorpha*

texaensis (Fig. 5-2 H) clings by a basal adhesive disk to the smooth inner surfaces of abandoned oyster shells.

The slipper limpets, *Crepidula fornicata* (Fig. 5-2 U), the smaller, flatter *C. plana* (Fig. 10-6 K), and tiny, mottled *C. convexa* (not illustrated) cling to oyster shells with a broad muscular foot. Although not permanently attached, each species is relatively immobile after larval settlement. The shells of these unusual gastropods have a characteristic ledge or shelf at about half the length of the ventral surface. All *Crepidula* are suspension feeders, moving water by cilia across an enlarged gill and trapping food particles among great quantities of mucus (Johnson, 1972). Their digestive tracts, equipped with a crystalline style rotating against a gastric shield in the stomach, are remarkably similar to that of most filter feeding bivalves.

Crepidula plana and *C. convexa* usually live solitary lives on other shells, but *C. fornicata* is remarkably gregarious. Larval *C. fornicata* preferentially settle upon living shells of their own kind, thereby accumulating "stacks" of a dozen or more individuals. The larger, older specimens on the bottom are females, whereas the smaller, younger specimens on the top are males. Reproduction is by copulation, which is facilitated in this relatively immobile gastropod by the stacking behavior. *Crepidula fornicata* is a protandric hermaphrodite, for as a male grows larger and older, or if it falls off the stack, its male reproductive system degenerates and is replaced by a female system (Coe, 1936). This provides for continuing reproduction in a relatively fixed stack of snails. When a larva must settle upon a shell other than another *Crepidula*, it will usually abort the male phase and develop directly as a female (Bandel, 1976).

Predators

Two of the most common predators of the oyster reef are also the conspicuous predators of the Texas jetties, and were obviously recruited from the oyster beds to the man-made environment. The powerful claws of the stone crab, *Menippe adina* (Fig. 5-2 L) are adapted for chipping oyster shells, and the boring apparatus of the rock snail, *Stramonita haemastoma* (Fig. 5-2 F1) is efficient for penetrating shells of both barnacles and small oysters (Chapter 3). *Stramonita haemastoma* has been cited as the most destructive predator of oysters in Galveston Bay, although its numbers are periodically controlled by spring freshets (Hofstetter, 1977). The ubiquitous blue crab, *Callinectes sapidus* (Chapter 7) not only takes shelter among the oyster reef, but will also feed upon small oysters.

Several xanthid crabs, including *Panopeus simpsoni* and *P. obesus* (Chapter 7) and the smaller *Eurypanopeus depressus* (Fig. 5-2 J) and *Rhithropanopeus harrisii* (Fig. 5-2 K), take refuge among clumps of oysters. *Eurypanopeus depressus* has black-tipped chelae with tiny spoon-shaped depressions on the tips and a red spot on the inner surface of the largest segment of each outer maxilliped. The chelae of *Rhithropanopeus harrisii* are neither black-tipped or spooned and it lacks the red spots on the maxillipeds.

Eurypanopeus depressus prefers oyster reefs to other estuarine habitats but also occurs on wharf pilings or in salt marshes (Chapter 7). Males reach a carapace width of about 25 mm, with females somewhat smaller. This crab attains sexual maturity at a carapace width of about 5 to 6 mm (Ryan 1956). Ovigerous females are present throughout warmer months of the year (Williams, 1984), and contribute large numbers of zoea larvae to the estuarine plankton. *Eurypanopeus depressus* is an omnivore, but its diet includes oyster spat and other juvenile bivalves.

Rhithropanopeus harrisii is an adaptable mud crab that occurs in many estuarine habitats from Quebec, Canada to Veracruz, Mexico, and has been introduced into estuaries in Oregon, California and parts of Europe. It frequents *Spartina* marshes and subtidal grass beds (Chapter 7), and mangrove shores in addition to oyster reefs.

Two predatory flatworms of the genus *Stylochus* patrol the oyster beds and can inflict significant damage to oysters, barnacles and other shellfish. They slip into the oyster mantle cavity through slightly gaping valves and, once inside, feed upon the unprotected soft tissues. *Stylochus frontalis* (Fig. 5-2 H1) grows to 50 mm in length and preys almost exclusively upon oysters. *Stylochus ellipticus* (Fig. 5-2 G1) reaches about half this size. It feeds upon barnacles and other bivalves in addition to oysters. Both species bear numerous simple eyes, some located upon the tentacles but many along the outer margin of the dorsal body surface. The latter circle the entire body of *S. frontalis*, but are restricted to the front third of the body in *S. ellipticus*.

Other Fauna

Many members of the subtidal estuarine biota (Chapter 7) also frequent the oyster reefs. For example, the tiny bittium snail, *Bittium varium* (Fig. 5-2 P), which is probably more at home on the subtidal grass beds, is almost as common on Texas oyster reefs.

If you walk along a tidally exposed oyster bar, you will undoubtedly notice pops or snapping sounds emanating from within the shell debris. These are made by the burrowing shrimps *Alpheus estuariensis* (Fig. 5-2 W). Both sexes bear disproportionate chelae on the first pair of legs, the larger being much more than twice the size of the smaller. Snapping shrimps are sexually dimorphic with respect to total body size: adult males are about half the size of adult females. Mating pairs are frequently found together in complex burrows below the shell debris.

Both sexes make snapping sounds with the large claw. It consists of a massive basal section terminating in an immovable spike and a smaller hinged claw. The base of the movable unit is formed into a tuberculate "hammer" which just fits into a disk or socket on the immovable spike. *Alpheus* can open or "cock" the movable finger. By muscular contraction, the hammer on the movable joint is forcefully snapped against the disk, producing a popping noise and a jet of water. *Alpheus* employs the snapping sound primarily as a means of inter- and intraspecific communication, especially for establishing and maintaining a territory (Nolan & Salmon, 1970). The snaps indicate to other alpheids the presence, size and location of the sound maker, and identify at least the genus and probably the species (Schein, 1977).

Alpheus estuariensis is an omnivore that probably relies more upon detritus and vegetable matter than living prey (Odum & Heald, 1972), but copepods and amphipods are also part of the diet. This species is commonly encountered throughout the Gulf and Caribbean, and can be found on coral reefs and among mangroves, as well as in association with oysters.

FISHES

The oyster reef provides shelter for numerous small estuarine fishes, some of which are discussed in Chapter 7. Here we will mention only two, as representative of two important bottom-dwelling fish families, the Blenniidae and Gobiidae, each containing many species in estuarine and shallow marine habitats throughout the region. We have previously encountered other blennies in association with the jetties (Chapter 3), and later we will encounter other gobies (Chapters 8 & 9).

Blennies and gobies are usually relatively small demersal fishes. Blennies are scaleless and bear a long dorsal fin which extends from just behind the head almost to the tail and is sometimes continuous with it. Most species live in association with reefs, rocks, or other hard substrata. The molly miller, *Scartella cristata* (Fig. 5-2 X), is a typical blenny found as frequently among oysters as it is among rocks at the base of the Texas jetties.

The gobies are fishes often thought of as inhabitants of tropical coral reefs, but there are also a number of temperate species. All bear a sucker below the head formed by the union of the margins of the pelvic fins, typically brought forward to lie below the pectorals. They may or may not have scales on the body but are easily distinguished from the blennies by their two dorsal fins. Gobies also tend to be more secretive and cryptic than the blennies. For example, the naked goby, *Gobiosoma bosci* (Fig. 5-2 Y) is a common fish on Texas oyster reefs, but because it remains hidden among the shell debris, is rarely seen.

PELICANS, CORMORANTS AND THE OYSTER CATCHER

Two species of pelicans occur in North America, and both may be found throughout the Gulf region. The brown pelican, *Pelecanus occidentalis* (Fig. 5-2 A), being exclusively marine or estuarine in its habits, is more commonly encountered. It is particularly abundant along the western and northern coasts of Yucatan, where large colonies roost and nest in mangroves or atop rows of coconut palms which line the shore. Brown pelicans were once equally numerous along Texas shores, but almost disappeared during the late 1950s and 1960s, victims of the accumulation of the pesticide DDT in the food chain. By the early 1970's they had become depleted to almost extinction. It was estimated that fewer than 50 birds comprised the entire Texas population (King & Flickinger, 1977; Blacklock *et al.*, 1978). Today, brown pelicans have made a noticeable comeback, but are still by no means as common as they once were along this shore.

Brown pelicans are solitary diving fishermen. From a height of 20 to 40 m, a pelican will fold its wings, pull the neck and head over the back of the body, and plunge breast-first into the sea. It enters the water with a resounding crash sufficient to stun a shoaling fish until it can be captured. Despite the normally solitary feeding habits, brown pelicans are gregarious in roosting and nesting. A late afternoon sun backlights memories of a group of a dozen or more brown pelicans flying to roost near Campeche, Mexico, one behind another with synchronized wing strokes and less than a meter above the sea. This impressive sight, once common in Texas, will, hopefully, be possible again as breeding stocks continue to increase.

White pelicans, *Pelecanus erythrorhynchos* (Fig. 5-2 B), are even more gregarious than the brown pelicans, feeding as well as roosting and nesting in flocks. The only breeding colonies of white pelicans on the United States Gulf coast are found in northern Laguna Madre, although they also occur in several of the Mexican estuaries. Unlike brown pelicans, the white birds are equally at home in freshwater lakes and marshes. Large inland populations occupy North American waters from northern California to the central plains from Saskatchewan to Nebraska.

White pelicans are cooperative fishermen. Groups of birds align themselves so as to drive schooling fishes toward shallow water, or, alternately, to encircle and close in upon them. Their behaviors are remarkably synchronized, even to the moment that each member of the group dips its bill into the water to capture trapped fishes, which are held temporarily within the voluminous pouch below the bill until they can be swallowed.

Two cormorants occur along the northwestern Gulf coast. The double-crested cormorant, *Phalacrocorax auritus* (Fig. 5-2 D) winters in the region, but spends summers in the Canadian marshlands. The olivaceous cormorant, *Phalacrocorax olivaceus* (Fig. 5-2 E) is a tropical species abundant on Mexico Gulf shores and once common in the northwestern Gulf, especially in the summer. Its numbers have declined greatly in Louisiana and Texas since the 1950's, in a manner that strikingly parallels that of the brown pelican (Rappole & Blacklock, 1985).

Cormorants pursue and capture fishes underwater but refrain from swallowing them until they surface. Unlike most other water birds, cormorant feathers are not water repellent. After feeding, they emerge from the water and stand with wings spread to allow the flight feathers to dry (Fig. 5-2 E).

The American oystercatcher, *Haematopus palliatus* (Fig. 5-2 C), with its black and white plumage, pink legs and distinctive, elongate red bill, is difficult to confuse with any other shorebird. It occurs upon estuarine shelly beaches in the western Gulf region throughout the year, but rarely in large numbers. Oystercatchers seem to be more abundant along the southeastern United States, where tidal fluctuations are greater than upon the Gulf coast. This is apparently important with respect to the feeding behavior displayed by these birds.

Oystercatchers typically feed on the ebbing tide. As receding waters expose oyster or mussel beds, oystercatchers drive their strong, laterally flattened beaks deeply into the slightly gaping shells of the bivalves. Using the beak somewhat like an oyster knife, the bird opens the oyster or mussel and scoops out the flesh inside. They will also turn over stones exposed at low tide and impale small crabs hiding there with the chisel-like tip of the beak. The limited tidal range of the western Gulf of Mexico is less than ideal for oystercatcher foraging, perhaps accounting for their somewhat patchy distribution throughout the region.

A PERSPECTIVE ON OYSTERS

The American oyster, *Crassostrea virginica*, lives precariously in an environment of its own making and in a habitat that is, more often than not, poorly suited to its needs. Drought, floods, unsuitable substrata, sedimentation, predators, parasites and perhaps a dozen other factors interact to the detriment of bay oysters. Yet their incredibly high fecundity, rapid growth and adaptability in the face of adversity provide populations of sufficient size that they can be commercially harvested as a favored seafood.

The Texas oyster fishery is modest in comparison to that of Louisiana or Chesapeake Bay, but from Galveston to Corpus Christi, Texas bays support large reefs suitable for commercial harvest. Prior to 1950, Galveston Bay rarely provided more than 10 percent of the annual Texas harvest, but since then it has usually provided more than 75 percent of Texas oysters (Fig. 5-3 C). During the 1980s, a rather sizable fishery also has developed in San Antonio Bay.

The oyster fishery in Texas is regulated by the state, which sets the season, harvestable areas and catch limits. The state recognizes two types of oyster reefs. The majority of oysters are taken from "public" reefs (Fig. 5-3 A), defined as any "natural reef containing more than 5 barrels of oysters per 2500 square feet or one having been exhausted in the last eight years" (Hofstetter, 1977). Private oyster leases of limited size in bay environments exclusive of the public reefs can be obtained from the state by payment of appropriate fees.

Since 1900, oyster harvest has fluctuated widely in Texas. Despite unmistakable variations in productivity based upon environmental perturbations, especially spring flooding or droughts, there was little indication of a trend toward depletion of the fishery until the late 1960s. Since then, many of the previously productive reefs have shown progressive declines in harvest (Fig. 5-3 C). Equally disturbing is the number of public reefs which have been closed to harvesting as a result of contamination by organic pollutants, especially municipal sewage (Fig. 5-3 A). Many formerly productive reefs in Galveston and Trinity bays are today unharvestable and/or dying because of this contamination.

Oysters naturally concentrate microorganisms within their tissues as a result of the filter feeding behavior. In addition to the large variety of harmless marine microbiota, feeding oysters can accumulate toxic red tide dinoflagellates or human pathogens. Dinoflagellate toxicants have little effect upon oysters, but, because they are concentrated in oyster tissues, may be present in sufficient quantities to be fatal to humans eating the shellfish (Chapter 12). Oysters in waters contaminated by sewage can also accumulate waterborne human pathogens, including those causing dysentery, hepatitis, and cholera. Again, the presence of these pathogens is not deleterious to the oyster, but

can be readily transmitted to anyone eating it. A constant monitoring program for the presence of coliform bacteria in bay waters and enforced closure of contaminated beds is essential for a safe oyster fishery. Yet, we increasingly hear news reports of people becoming ill from eating contaminated oysters, apparently obtained from poachers working polluted reefs.

The adaptable oyster can tolerate a lot of abuse, but there are clear signs, in Texas and elsewhere (Krantz & Meritt, 1977; Haven *et al.*, 1978) that human interference within the estuaries and bays is beginning to take its toll upon this species. The effects are not limited to depletion of an economic resource, for, as we have shown, the oyster is the basis of a complex estuarine community. As the oyster goes, so goes this community. Without continued annual oyster repopulation, reefs are naturally buried in mud and the community dies. For estuaries surrounded by high-density human populations, such as Trinity and Galveston bays, the next few decades will be critical. Careful monitoring of reefs in these areas is essential and will provide the information necessary to manage and conserve the American oyster and its community during the next century.

PART THREE Soft Shores

6. Gulf Beaches and Barrier Islands

INTRODUCTION

Sand dominates the shores of the western Gulf of Mexico. For most of Texas and northern Mexico, sandy beaches fringe the outer faces of barrier islands. Even in the absence of a barrier island, sands blanket the mainland margin, as near High Island, Texas or the Mexico coast from La Pesca to Tampico. Sands are harsh habitats, and the sandy surf zone is a particularly difficult environment for life. Breakers keep the sand in constant motion, filling burrows, abrading shells, and exposing the few organisms living here to surf and sun. Conditions are more stable below the surf zone, where diversity increases. On the beach above the surf, the environment is more extreme. Winds dry, move and pile sand into dunes. Summer sun sears the dunes, and, in the north, winter cold occasionally freezes them. Animals of the upper beach must burrow deeply or go elsewhere for refuge. Few plants occur on the foreshore, backshore or dune fronts. Those that do have adaptations which enable them to cling to the unstable substratum, compensate for sand burial, and conserve water.

Despite these difficulties, a number of soft-bottom communities occur on or near the outer Gulf shores. A diverse assemblage of burrowing animals which are rarely exposed by the tide characterizes the shallow subtidal nearshore sand banks (Chapter 10). In contrast, the intertidal foreshore community in the sandy surf zone comprises only a few species. This habitat is the most prevalent intertidal environment in the western Gulf of Mexico, but the least diverse. A mudbank habitat facing the Gulf breaks the sands continuity along some portions of the central Texas shore, as at Sargent Beach near Freeport (Fig. 6-16). The mudbank is exposed by beach erosion brought about by wave action and longshore transport. It and the associated backshore accommodate relatively few species in a unique assemblage blending typical outer coast biota with that most commonly found on bay shores. The backshore and dune front communities of the barrier islands, composed of semi-terrestrial and terrestrial components, are also relatively low in diversity. A similar assemblage occupies dune crests, and another considerably more diverse community characterizes protected back dune areas. The vegetation associated with these higher beach communities provides us with another excellent example of the temperate to tropical transition that characterizes Gulf shores.

We begin this chapter with a brief discussion of the physical environment and especially that of the barrier island. Then our survey of sand communities begins with a consideration of the biota of that part of the shore to which the eye is immediately drawn—the intertidal surf strand. From this focus, we will proceed landward upon the shore, and, generally, from temperate to tropical beaches. The subtidal components of the sandy seafloor are considered in Chapter 10.

SANDS, SPITS AND BARRIER ISLANDS

Broad, straight, low relief beaches fringe most of the western margin of the Gulf of Mexico. Despite local exceptions (e.g., see the end of this chapter), regional sediment deposition usually exceeds erosion along these shores, as indicated by the presence of such features as spits and barrier islands. A spit is a beach peninsula tied to the coast at one end and free at the other. It usually forms along moderately irregular shorelines, and grows in the direction of the prevailing longshore drift parallel to the mainland coast. Bolivar Peninsula is a large spit along the northern Texas coast, whereas Cabo Catoche is an even larger one in northern Yucatan. Barrier islands characterize lowland coasts having limited tidal range and relatively low wave energy. They dominate the coastal topography of the northwestern Gulf of Mexico.

A variety of agents, including winds, waves, storms, and tidal and longshore currents, move beach sands (Chapter 2). Gulf tidal currents are of minimal significance with respect to the movement of sediments, except within restricted tidal inlets. Waves move sand along a beach by the localized process of littoral drift, contributing to such common beach features as berm formation, cusping, and local beach cutting. Tropical storms and hurricanes move massive amounts of sand, but are episodic. Longshore drift is the most consistent process by which coastal sand is transported in the western Gulf. Longshore currents are essential to the formation and maintenance of narrow peninsulas, spits and barrier islands and are the basis of the fundamental dynamism characteristic of these shores.

Gulf Barrier Islands

Barrier islands are the most conspicuous coastal feature of Texas and northern Mexico and constitute the most important sand beach environment of the region.

Seven primary islands fringe the Texas mainland (Fig. 6-1): Galveston, Follets, Matagorda, San Jose, Mustang, Padre and Brazos. Two sand spit peninsulas, Bolivar and Matagorda (distinct from the island), were formed by processes similar to those responsible for the barrier islands. Tidal inlets breach many of the barriers, permitting tidal exchange with the enclosed bay waters of the mainland shore. There are seven major natural inlets cutting Texas barrier islands or peninsulas, and a few additional man-made cuts which permit water exchange from the Gulf to a bay or lagoon (Fig. 6-1). Other passes, (e.g., Corpus Christi Pass) have recently closed by natural processes.

Barrier islands are absent along portions of the northeastern Texas coast, as between Sabine Pass and Gilchrist, and between Freeport and Sargent Beach. Galveston and Follets Islands are relatively short, but the islands become increasingly more elongate to the south. Most islands are widest near their northern or eastern ends and diminish in width toward the south or west. Matagorda and San Jose Islands are the widest barriers in the United States. Padre Island, dominating the south Texas coastline, is the longest barrier island in the world. It extends 181 km (113 mi) from its junction with Mustang Island near Corpus Christi to Brazos Santiago Pass, interrupted only once by a man-made cut near Port Mansfield.

The Rio Grande delta interrupts the course of barrier islands for a few dozen kilometers south of the present river mouth. Thereafter, several narrow sandy barriers enclose the Laguna Madre de Tamaulipas, extending from the southern termination of the Rio Grande delta to La Pesca, Mexico. South of La Pesca, the mainland shore courses for many kilometers as a narrow sandy ribbon without an offshore island. South of Tampico, Cabo Rojo extends a sandy elbow into the Gulf. The outer face of this tombolo-like barrier has many features in common with the barrier islands, including the highest dunes of the region.

Cabo Rojo is the last major sandy barrier of the central Mexico coast, although there are still many small, short islands, spits or peninsulas which protect equally small estuaries from Cabo Rojo to Yucatan. Mainland sandy shores dominate the northern face of the Yucatan peninsula. The largest sandy barriers of the Yucatan region are Isla de Carmen, protecting the entrance of Laguna de Terminos on the southwestern coast of Yucatan, and Cabo Catoche, off the northeastern margin.

Origin of the Texas Barrier Islands

Several sets of barrier islands have formed along the northwestern Gulf coast during the last million years. Their birth and demise are associated with successive rises and falls of sea level, and the concurrent changes in the position of the shoreline. The present islands were formed 5,000 to 8,000 years ago at the end of the Holocene marine transgression (the last rise in sea level). Remnants of an even older (Pleistocene) mature barrier island chain (Fig. 6-2 A-D) fringe the mainland margin. The Live Oak Ridge, situated between San Antonio and Corpus Christi bays, is the best developed remnant. Even it is discontinuous, dissected by several embayments and sometimes eroded to the underlying Beaumont clay. The Live Oak Ridge is especially evident in the vicinity of Rockport and along portions of the Aransas National Wildlife Refuge. It varies in width from 5 to 16 km and rises to a maximum elevation of 9 m above sea level. Another segment, known as Flour Ridge, lies along the coast near Robstown. Dense groves of live oak, *Quercus virginiana*, thrive on the well-drained sandy ridge soils. So characteristic are live oaks upon these ridges that their striking dark green foliage, and hence the position of the ridge, shows clearly in infrared satellite photography (Finley, 1979).

These and other segments of the ancient barrier system extend almost 100 miles from a point west of the mouth of the Brazos River to Baffin Bay. Additional remnants occur along the east Texas coast near Chocolate Bay, east of Trinity Bay, and near Beaumont (Price, 1947). Barrier dune sands also probably extended farther south. From near Kingsville to the Rio Grande, the semi-arid climate, reduced vegetation cover, and prevailing southeasterly winds allowed Pleistocene dunes to be blown inland. Sand was scattered over hundreds of square kilometers, creating the south Texas aeolian plain (Fig. 6-2 C). Even today, sands from Padre Island are being carried landward, filling Laguna Madre and contributing to soils of the south Texas fields and ranchlands. Aeolian transport is even more acute in northern Mexico, where Laguna Madre de Tamaulipas is at an advanced stage of being filled by this process.

The origin of the modern Texas barrier island complex is related to the last rise of sea level, from about 14,000 to 9,000 years ago (Otros, 1970a,b). At the peak of the Wisconsin or last glaciation, about 20,000 years ago, sea level was about 120 m lower than present.

6-1. Barrier islands, peninsulas, tidal inlets, and major embayments of the northwestern Gulf of Mexico. Islands and peninsulas are indicated by larger type; tidal inlets by smaller type. Embayments are indicated by numbers as follows: **1.** Sabine Lake; **2.** Galveston Bay; **3.** East Bay; **4.** West Bay; **5.** Matagorda Bay; **6.** Tres Palacios Bay; **7.** Lavaca Bay; **8.** Espiritu Santo Bay; **9.** San Antonio Bay; **10.** Copano Bay; **11.** Aransas Bay; **12.** Corpus Christi Bay; **13.** Nueces Bay; **14.** Alazan Bay; **15.** Baffin Bay; **16.** Laguna Madre of Texas; **17.** Laguna Madre de Tamaulipas, cuenca septentrional (northern basin); **18.** Laguna Madre de Tamaulipas, cuenca meridional (southern basin).

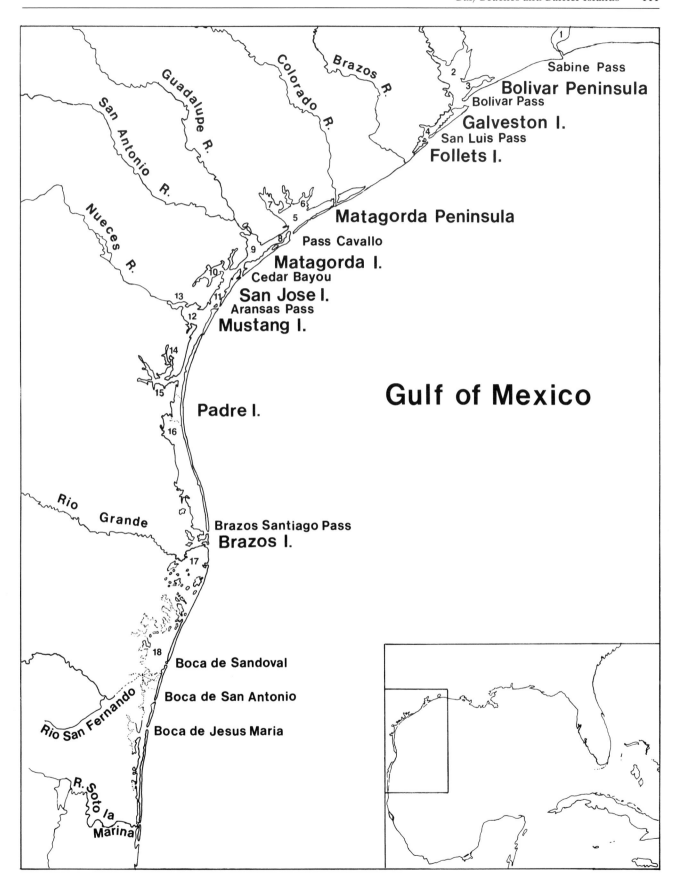

Sabine Pass

1

2

3

Bolivar Peninsula
Bolivar Pass

Galveston I.
San Luis Pass

4

Follets I.

Colorado R.

Brazos R.

Guadalupe R.

San Antonio R.

Nueces R.

7

6

5

Matagorda Peninsula

8

Pass Cavallo

9

Matagorda I.
Cedar Bayou

10

San Jose I.
Aransas Pass

11

12

Mustang I.

13

14

15

Padre I.

16

Gulf of Mexico

Rio Grande

Brazos Santiago Pass
Brazos I.

17

18

Boca de Sandoval

Boca de San Antonio

Rio San Fernando

Boca de Jesus Maria

R. Soto la Marina

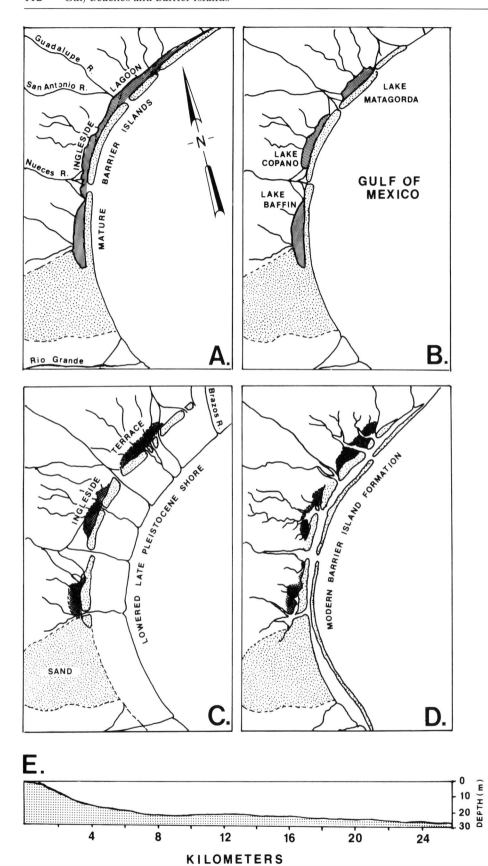

The Texas coast lay from 80 to 220 km seaward of its present position (LeBlanc & Hodgson, 1959) (Figs. 6-2 C; 6-3 A). Texas rivers cut deeply into the exposed, soft coastal sediments. When sea level began to rise, it did so in a series of fluctuating stands (Shepard, 1960). During this time the course of Texas and Gulf coast rivers and the distribution of their sediment loads underwent several changes (Fig. 6-3 E). The deeply cut river valleys filled with seawater and became coastal estuaries (Fig. 6-3 B, C, D). Then, about 5,000 years ago, sea level reached the position near that which it occupies today (Fig. 6-3 D). Soon thereafter, the largest Texas rivers, the Rio Grande and Brazos, carried sufficient sediment seaward to fill their once extensive estuaries (LeBlanc & Hodgson, 1959; Nienaber, 1963), and began depositing sediments directly into the Gulf of Mexico (Curray, 1960). The smaller rivers, with less sediment load, are still contributing material to their estuaries at accumulation rates of less than 1 m per century (Shepard, 1960). The Colorado River is nearing the terminal stages of filling its estuary.

About the time sea level approached its present height, conditions were right for formation of the modern barrier islands. Their development and maintenance involve a dynamic balance between sediment (sand) supply, longshore currents, bottom topography, and wave and tidal activity. Sands were derived from two primary sources: (1), subtidal Pleistocene and Holocene deposits on the Gulf shelf and (2), river sediments, and probably in that order. Wilkinson (1975) described events leading to the formation of Matagorda Island. As most of the other Texas barrier islands probably experienced similar formative steps, we will use Wilkinson's study as a model for barrier island formation in the northwestern Gulf.

6-2. Pleistocene sea level fluctuations and barrier island formation (after Price, 1933). Sea level fluctuations during the last geologic epoch have probably produced a succession of barrier island systems along the northwestern Gulf of Mexico. Two of these are conspicuous along the Texas coast: the present barrier island system and a former system indicated by the Live Oak Ridge (see text).

A. The mature Live Oak Ridge barrier island system, during a preceding interglacial; note resemblance to the modern barrier island system (D).

B. Initiation of Wisconsin glaciation and early stages of sea level subsidence. Note extensive delta filling by most major rivers, independent of the falling sea level.

C. Peak of Wisconsin glaciation, with sea level as much as 120 m below the present level. Rivers cut deep channels into the soft sedimentary deposits exposed by the falling sea level.

D. Sea level rises as the Wisconsin glaciation ends, eventually resulting in the modern barrier island system.

E. A depth profile of the floor of the northwestern Gulf of Mexico from a barrier island shore to 26 km offshore. Note the relatively gentle slope of the sea floor.

Matagorda Island encloses the Guadalupe Estuary, consisting of San Antonio, Espiritu Santo, and Mesquite bays and others. Prior to inundation by the rising sea, this area was a river delta. Wilkinson estimates it was flooded when sea level reached about 13 m below the present level. At this time, the drowned delta began to be blanketed with a thick layer of mud, over which Matagorda Island lies today (Fig. 6-4 D). San Antonio Bay sediments give no indication that they were ever subjected to normal marine conditions. As inundation of the delta proceeded, there was probably some form of barrier, however small, separating what would become bay waters from the open Gulf (Fig. 6-4 A). Embryonic Matagorda Island probably was a series of intermittently emergent sandy shoals traversed by numerous tidal inlets. Shoal sands were derived largely from shallow, recently submerged Pleistocene and Holocene sources on the Gulf shelf. The shoals moved shoreward with the rising sea, in part pushed by storms which deposited well graded washover fans upon the finer estuarine sediments. Shoreward migration of offshore sands ceased about 5,000 years ago when Pleistocene and Holocene offshore deposits came to lie at such a depth that they could no longer be moved landward by normal onshore processes.

With sea level at stillstand, longshore drift became the dominant factor contributing to the accumulation of sand along the existing shoals. It began to contribute sand to the developing barrier island when sea level reached about 8 m below the present level. Storm transport of sand to back island washover fans still occurred, although probably at a rate much less than that prior to sea level stillstand (Andrews, 1970). Sand accumulated along the Gulf face of the growing barrier island faster than it could be removed, and the island prograded seaward (Fig. 6-4 B). The specific manner of progradation probably differs from the northeastern islands (e.g., Galveston) to southwestern Padre Island shores. To the north, it likely occurred in steps, culminating with a series of dune ridges or beach ridges. The nucleus of each probably was deposited by successive hurricanes (Price, 1956; Andrews, 1970). The more southerly islands, with less vegetation cover, were transformed into vast active dune fields.

Fossil shells deposited in San Antonio Bay about the time sea level reached its present approximate position indicate that the bay waters, although not of normal marine salinity, were slightly more saline than at present. *Ostrea equestris*, for example, rather than *Crassostrea virginica*, was the dominant oyster (the former capable of living in higher salinities than the latter). This strengthens the hypothesis that the embryonic barrier island was breached by numerous tidal inlets. Sand deposition by longshore drift and island progradation following stillstand closed all but the largest channels (Fig. 6-4 C). The Texas barrier islands attained their approximate present configurations at least 2,000 years ago. Galveston Island has had its approximate modern outline for at least 3,000 years (Bernard *et al.*, 1959).

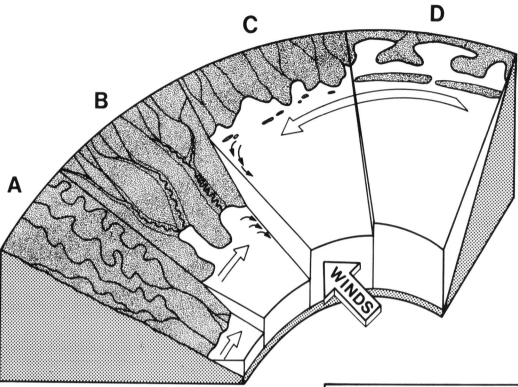

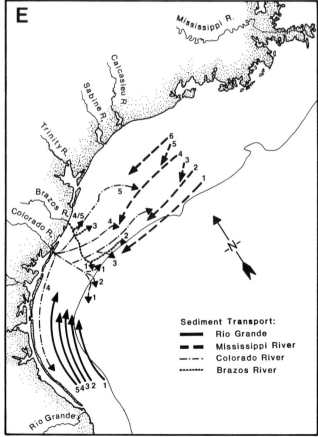

6-3. Coastal inundation, sediment transport and barrier island formation. The left figure demonstrates the effect of a rising sea level and coastal currents along a coastal arc such as the northwestern Gulf of Mexico. In the face of prevailing southeasterly winds, the coastal arc imposes northerly longshore currents along its lower (southern) margin (short open arrows) and southerly longshore currents along its upper (northerly) margin (elongate open arrow). The latter is reinforced by seasonal northerly wind shifts. The opposing longshore current systems produce a region of convergence where currents are erratic and tend to move offshore (small dark arrows).

A. At the height of the Wisconsin glaciation, sea level was as much as 120 m lower than at present and rivers cut deeply into the exposed sediments.

B. As glacial ice melted, the dissected river valleys were filled first by the rising sea.

C. Longshore currents delivered sand to form a string of small sandy shoals, the precursors of the modern barrier islands. The process occurred along the entire coastline, not just in the position indicated.

D. Sea level reaches the approximate modern stillstand, with the coastline attaining its present configuration.

E. Sediment sources and the direction of transport during the Holocene transgression. Numbers represent successive events during the period of rising sea level with dates approximated. 1, 19,000 years before present (ybp); 2, 16,000 ybp; 3, 14,000 ybp; 4, 12,000 ybp; 5, 9,000 ybp; 6, 3000 ybp. Compare with the diagram to the left. (After van Andel & Pool, 1960.)

Barrier Island Sands

The seemingly monotonous sand of Gulf-facing beaches is not all the same. Sands differ in mineral composition and grain size along the Texas coast, whereas Yucatan beach sands differ in origin from those of the northeastern Gulf. Texas beach sands are primarily lithogenous in origin, derived from processes of erosion on land and delivered by rivers to the sea. Along northeastern beaches, the sand is derived mostly from Mississippi and Sabine River sediments. It is a very fine sand, readily suspended with the slightest agitation. As a result, the surf on these beaches sometimes resembles a brownish muddy broth.

From the Nueces River to central Padre Island, coastal sands are derived mostly from the central Texas rivers. The Brazos and Colorado, with mouths opening directly to the Gulf, are the main contributors (Bullard, 1942; Shepard & Wanless, 1971). Beach sands of this region are better sorted (the grains more uniform in size, and with fewer small grains) than those of the northeastern coast. Sands of the southern half of Padre Island and near the mouth of the Rio Grande are derived from the latter drainage. Grains are small and well sorted. Little of the very fine sand that characterizes the northern Texas beaches is present. Accordingly, waters off South Padre Island are less turbid, almost turquoise, especially in comparison with the brownish waters off the northeastern Texas coast.

Beach sands of Yucatan are mostly of biogenous origin, derived from the shells or skeletons of a variety of marine plants and animals. This sand is more coarse than that of the northwestern Gulf, and usually better sorted.

Beach and Barrier Island Morphology

Biotic zonation effectively partitions hard shores and provides us a means to describe distinctive regions upon them (Chapter 3). Life zones on soft shores, although present, are not as easily perceived. Soft shore biota, and especially burrowing species, disappears from view within sediments, leaving large, important components of the community essentially unavailable as readily characterizing benchmarks. Soft shores, on the other hand, are easily molded by prevailing conditions of wind and water. This provides a number of distinctive, easily recognizable features independent of biological attribution. Thus, although hard shores are easily described in terms of the biota characterizing zones related to tidal benchmarks, soft shores, and especially sand beaches, are best described in terms of physical features.

Geologists refer to the gently sloping subtidal sand bottom just off the Gulf beach as the inner shelf. It extends many kilometers offshore, gradually becoming deeper toward the continental shelf (Fig. 6-2 E). Inner shelf biota is described in Chapter 10.

Features of a typical sand beach are illustrated in Figure 6-5. They occur on most sandy beaches regardless of location, whether mainland shore or barrier island. Waves approach the beach from offshore. The nearshore region through which waves break is called the breaker zone or inshore. The inshore and nearby offshore floors are typically rippled with a series of elevated bars and depressed troughs lying parallel to the long axis of the beach. They are formed by wave dynamics and longshore currents. Rip channels lying perpendicular to the shore periodically interrupt the bars. The troughs, bars, rip channels and longshore and rip currents interact as a system, transporting sand and other materials onto, off, and along the shore.

The foreshore lies between the upper limit of wave wash at high tide and the low-water swash mark. It is also characterized as the sloping beach face at the upper portion of the surf zone. Landward of the foreshore lies the backshore, usually marked nearest the sea by one or more nearly horizontal ridges or berms. A berm is formed by sediment deposition from receding constructive waves. The beach may have one, several, or no berms at all. Multiple berms, when present, lie at succeedingly higher elevations on the backshore, separated by beach scarps, or low, almost vertical escarpments caused by beach erosion. Berm crests stand slightly higher than the backshore behind it and typically cap each berm scarp. On gently sloping beaches, narrow water-filled shallow troughs or runnels may lie behind the most seaward berm crest. Most runnels are temporary features created by unusually high tides or storm waves, but sometimes they persist for a considerable time.

The backshore is the landward termination of the beach. A variety of coastal features occur behind it, including dunes, forests, coastal plains, or sea cliffs, depending upon the specific beach location. Dunes predominate on the Texas barrier islands. On the northeastern islands (e.g., Galveston), these dunes are a series of low, vegetation-stabilized mounds or beach ridges (Bernard *et al.*, 1959; Bernard *et al.*, 1962). The southern barrier island dunes, especially those on Padre Island, are much higher and often divided into two sets (Hayes, 1967). Typically, the foredunes are separated from a group of backdunes by a sparsely vegetated barrier flat. The bay shores of the northern islands usually adjoin the barrier island beach ridge system directly. On the southern islands, however, the backdunes are separated from the lagoon or bay by a broad tidal flat. Barrier island bayshores in the tropical zone are usually fringed by mangroves.

THE FORESHORE: INTERTIDAL SAND

The sandy surf strand is depauperate in life. Waves keep sands in constant turmoil, refreshing them, but delivering sufficient destructive power to exclude all except the most remarkably hardy biota. Few plants occur here naturally, except microscopic diatoms living among the sand grains. The productivity of this shore is based primarily upon input of offshore detritus held in motion by the breaking waves. Birds are

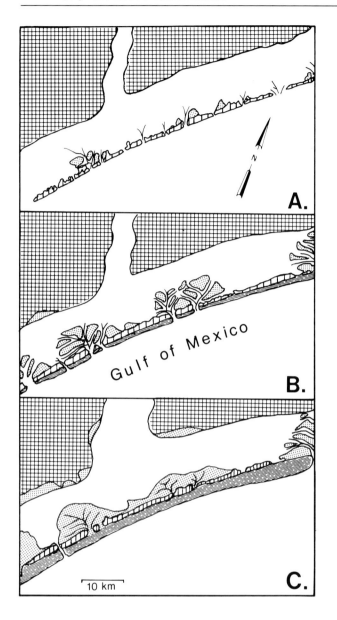
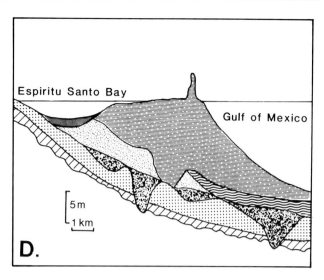
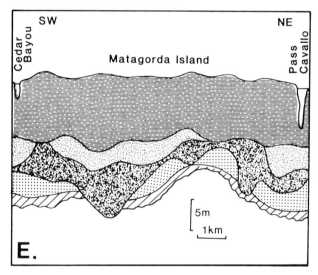

A.

Gulf of Mexico

B.

C.

10 km

D.

Espiritu Santo Bay

Gulf of Mexico

5m
1 km

E.

SW   NE

Cedar Bayou   Matagorda Island   Pass Cavallo

5m
1km

 Pleistocene sand

 Marsh

 Back-island sand

Fore-island sand

 Soil zone (P)

 Ingleside sand (P)

 Fluvial-deltaic sand (MH)

 Bay-estuarine mud (MH)

 Barrier island sand (LH)

 Bay-estuarine mud (LH)

Lower shoreface mud (LH)

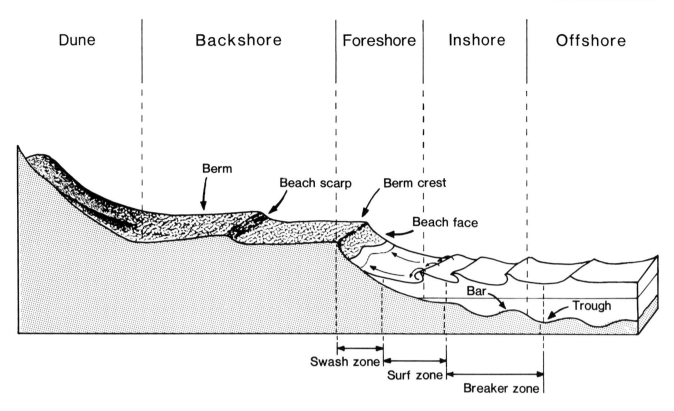

| Dune | Backshore | Foreshore | Inshore | Offshore |

6-5. Features of a typical sandy beach.

6-4. Barrier island formation along the Texas shore (after Wilkinson, 1975). Barrier islands form as a result of the interactions of complex coastal processes. Longshore currents deliver sand from offshore sources where they accumulate in spits, bars, and eventually a series of disjunct small sandy islands (**A**). The islands coalesce and rise higher as new sands are deposited from offshore sources upon the island foreshore, and old foreshore sands are moved by winds to central or back island dunes (**B, C**). Tidal currents deposit fine particulates along the margins of inlets, leaving marsh habitats (**B**). Storms transport sand to the rear of the developing island, where it accumulates in washover fans (**C**). Continued supply of offshore sand delivered by longshore drift eventually close all but the most active tidal inlets, and the island reaches approximately a modern configuration (**C**). The sedimentary composition of Matagorda Island (**D**, cross section; **E**, longitudinal section) indicates several features important in barrier island development. The underlying soil zone indicates a mainland terrestrial episode during a period of lowered sea level. It is followed by sand (indicating inundation), fluvial-deltaic sand (indicating riverine influence), and a mud interval (**E**, indicating a former bay environment), and the present barrier island sand.

the most obvious animals on sandy beaches, but they are not the permanent residents. Like us, they are temporary visitors. They visit the beach to scour backwash for nutritious morsels provided by the few permanent members of this most difficult habitat.

Few animals spend their adult lives in the unstable surf-swept sands of barrier islands. Mainland sandy beaches usually have a higher percentage of fine sands and muds, and species diversity and richness are slightly higher on the mainland Texas beaches, whereas mean density of individuals and dominance of particular species are higher on barrier island shores (Shelton & Robertson, 1981). The larger, more conspicuous species, to which we direct this discussion, often occur on both kinds of beaches. The commonly observed surf fauna from central Texas barrier islands are illustrated in the lower right corner of Figure 6-6. Surf-dwelling animals from other localities are illustrated on appropriate figures throughout this chapter.

At a Gulf beach, stand still in the shallow surf and stare at the nearby sand washed by waves. As each wave recedes, it seems to expose several dozen small clams that tumble down the beach slope in the backwash and, just as quickly, vanish into the sand. Using an agile muscular foot for burrowing, the bivalves are rapidly able to disappear into the protection of the surf-washed sand. These are the coquina (or surf) clams, *Donax*, represented by several species which occur in suitable sandy beach habitats throughout the Gulf of Mexico.

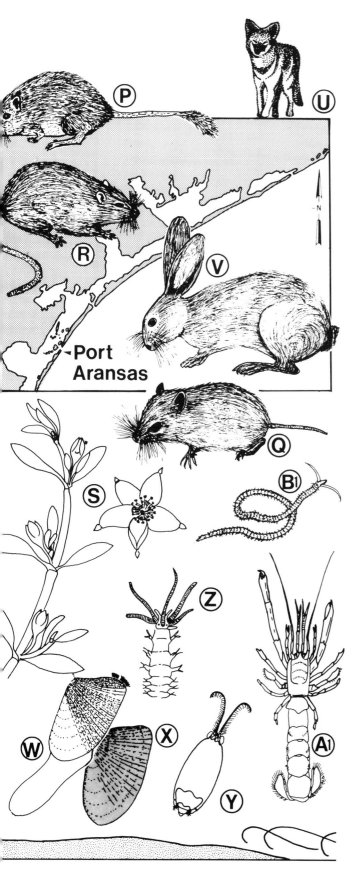

Two species commonly occur on western Gulf beaches from central Texas to central Mexico. During warmer months, *Donax variabilis roemeri* (Figs. 6-6 W; 6-12 U; 6-16 V) uses the surf to maintain its position within the intertidal zone, migrating upward with the incoming tide and seaward at the ebb. Morrison (1971) proposed calling this species *Donax roemeri roemeri*, but the International Commission of Zoological Nomenclature has conserved the more familiar *D. variabilis* (Melville, 1976; Pulley, 1979a, 1979b). A second species, *D. texasiana* (Figs. 6-6 X; 6-12 V), lives year round just below the surf zone in knee-deep water. In winter on temperate shores, *D. variabilis* may migrate seaward, intermingling with *D. texasiana* (Loesch, 1957), although Morrison (1971) insisted that *D. variabilis* lives intertidally year round, and Vega & Tunnell (1987) find *D. texasiana* migrating to the intertidal zone from May to August. A third, smaller species, *Donax dorotheae*, reaches the westernmost portion of its range in western Louisiana and eastern Texas to Bolivar Peninsula, where it coexists with both *D. variabilis* and *D. texasiana*. To the south, these two species are replaced by a fourth, *Donax denticulatus*, in the Cabo Catoche region of Quintana Roo, Mexico. The latter is primarily a Caribbean species, extending into the Gulf of Mexico only along its southeasternmost margins.

Population densities of *D. variabilis* and *D. texasiana* on central Texas beaches seem to peak in the late spring or summer (Loesch, 1957). Vega & Tunnell (1987) found *D. texasiana* most abundant on Mustang and Northern Padre Island during May and June,

6-6. The sandy beach at Mustang Island, Texas. **A.** Seaside goldenrod, *Solidago sempervirens*; **B.** Coastal pigweed, *Amaranthus greggii*; **C.** Sea ox-eye daisy, *Borrichia frutescens*; **D.** Partridge pea, *Cassia fasciculata*; **E.** Camphor daisy, *Machaeranthera phyllocephala*; **F.** Camphorweed, *Heterotheca subaxillaris*; **G.** Beach evening primrose, *Oenothera drummondii*; **H.** Silverleaf sunflower, *Helianthus argophyllus*; **I.** Sea oats, *Uniola paniculata*; **J.** Bitter panicum, *Panicum amarum*; **K.** Bushy beardgrass, *Andropogon glomeratus*; **L.** Beach tea, *Croton punctatus*; **M.** Spotted ground squirrel, *Spermophilus spilosoma annectens*; **N.** Ghost crab, *Ocypode quadrata*; **O.** Railroad vine, *Ipomoea pes-caprae*; **P.** Padre Id. kangaroo rat, *Dipodomys compactus*; **Q.** Pygmy mouse, *Baiomys taylori*; **R.** Norway rat, *Rattus norvegicus*; **S.** Sea purslane, *Sesuvium portulacastrum*; **T.** White morning glory, *Ipomoea stolonifera*; **U.** Coyote, *Canis latrans*; **V.** Blacktailed jackrabbit, *Lepus californicus*; **W.** Coquina clam, *Donax variabilis roemeri*; **X.** Coquina clam, *Donax texasiana*; **Y.** Mole crab, *Emerita portoricensis*; **Z.** *Onuphis eremita oculata*; **A1.** Ghost shrimp, *Callichirus islagrande*; **B1.** *Scolelepis squamata*. Vertical scale indicates meters.

whereas *D. variabilis* populations peaked at the same locations in August. Distributions are markedly clumped, with peak numbers usually located within beach cusps. As many as 100 clumps per mile of beach are common in the early summer, each containing thousands of individuals. A few meters from each clump, the sand may be devoid of *Donax*. Following the late spring or summer peaks, both species undergo density declines, with *D. texasiana* populations declining in midsummer. *D. variabilis* declines more slowly, with sizable but diminishing densities persisting throughout the summer and lowest densities occurring in the late fall and winter (Loesch, 1957; Vega & Tunnell, 1987).

Donax relies upon the constant activity of the surf to stir and bring diatoms and other microphytes into the water from which they can be filtered. So dependent are they upon constant water movement that they cannot survive without it. *Donax* extends and withdraws short, partially fused, inhalant and exhalant siphons into the water with each passing wave. Each siphon is equipped with a complex musculature which enables independent movement. Water and any suspended food enter the mantle cavity via the postero-ventral inhalant siphon and thence to fields of collecting and sorting cilia on ctenidial (gill) filaments and palp surfaces, respectively. Material accepted as food is passed to the mouth and ingested.

Waves not only deliver food to *Donax*, but uncover and leave the bivalve exposed on the otherwise bare intertidal sand. *Donax* actively migrates up and down the shore with the rising and ebbing tide. In this way they exploit the surf-lifted material upon which they feed. The agile bivalves quickly bury themselves, but not before they attract a number of shorebird predators. Willets (*Catoptrophorus semipalmatus*, Fig. 8-3 D), sanderlings (*Calidris alba*, Fig. 8-3 E) and plovers (*Pluvialis squatarola*, Fig. 8-3 K) are known to eat *Donax*. These birds are often seen running seaward behind a receding breaker in pursuit of *Donax* or *Emerita* tumbling in the wave-disturbed sand. Burrowing fails to provide *Donax* with complete protection against predation, for several of the offshore sand-dwelling carnivorous snails (e.g., *Polinices duplicatus* and *Oliva* spp.) will feed upon them. Even the rock snail, *Stramonita haemastoma*, has been known to drill *Donax* shells when the two occupy closely adjacent habitats. At least three crabs (*Callinectes sapidus*, *Ocypode quadrata*, and *Arenaeus cribrarius*) have been observed eating *Donax*. Several fishes including the drum (*Pogonias cromis*), the spot (*Leiostomus xanthurus*), the Florida pompano (*Trachinotus carolinus*) and the whiting (*Menticirrhus* sp.) are also *Donax* predators.

Several crustaceans share this dynamic sandy shore habitat with *Donax*. Most obvious are the rotund mole crabs of the genus *Emerita*, and which, like *Donax*, are active, agile burrowers. Three species are reported from Texas: *E. talpoida* (Figs. 6-7 A & b), *E. benedicti* (Fig. 6-7 a & c) and *E. portoricensis* (Figs. 6-6

Y; 6-7 a & d; 6-10 D1; 6-16 W). *Emerita talpoida* is near the southern limit of its distribution in Texas, although it has been reported from Progreso, Yucatan, Mexico. This report and records of its occurrence on Texas beaches were mostly made before the other species were recognized. If it occurs in the western Gulf, it is probably restricted to northern beaches. *Emerita benedicti* and *E. portoricensis* occur throughout the region, share many similar features, and are believed by some to be the same species. They differ primarily in the nature of carapace ornamentation (Felder, 1973a). The former has incised lines extending to the posterior ventral margin (Fig. 6-7 c), whereas these lines terminate well above this point on the latter (Fig. 6-7 d). *Emerita benedicti* is predominant and perhaps the only mole crab on the Texas coast (R.W. Heard, personal communication).

Emerita is found at the surf line. It usually maintains this position by migrating landward with rising tides and seaward at tidal ebb. If some individuals become stranded high on the beach, they burrow several centimeters into the sand and wait for the next high tide. *Emerita* has developed a specialized feeding behavior which requires that it live high upon the shore. It relies upon breaking waves to suspend interstitial phytoplankton or detritus; but rather than feed upon it in the high energy, abrasive breaker environment, *Emerita* waits until wave energy has been largely dissipated by the swash. When exposed by a strong wave, the mole crab faces the sea and enters the sand backward, positioning its body at a 45° angle just below the surface. It waits in this position for each receding wave. As the backwash flows over it, the crustacean extends a pair of elongate second antennae above the sand (Fig. 6-7 A). They are fitted with a dense fan of long filtering setae which, when extended, form a V-shaped filter. Diatoms, other phytoplankton, and suspended detritus are trapped in the setal basket (Snodgrass, 1952). With each passing wave *Emerita* rapidly withdraws the antennae from the flow and wipes them across the mouth, extracting the particles trapped on the setae (Efford, 1967).

Emerita talpoida lives one (Wharton, 1942) or two years (Edwards & Irving, 1943), and Texas species likely have similar life expectancies. Mature females carry developing eggs on abdominal segments during the summer. Just prior to hatching they are released to the sea, the first entering the plankton in July (Wharton, 1942). Zoea and megalopa larvae remain in the plankton about 4 weeks before they return to the beach as juveniles (Rees, 1959).

Mole crabs are eaten by a number of organisms. Sandpipers, sanderlings, other shorebirds and ghost crabs (Fales, 1976) are common predators. The carapace of *Emerita* sometimes serves as an attachment site for filamentous algae, e.g., *Enteromorpha* (Williams, 1947), as does the shell of *Donax*.

Other mole crab relatives sometimes occupy the surf zone. *Lepidopa benedicti* (Fig. 6-7 E) is relatively common on northern Gulf sandy beaches from the

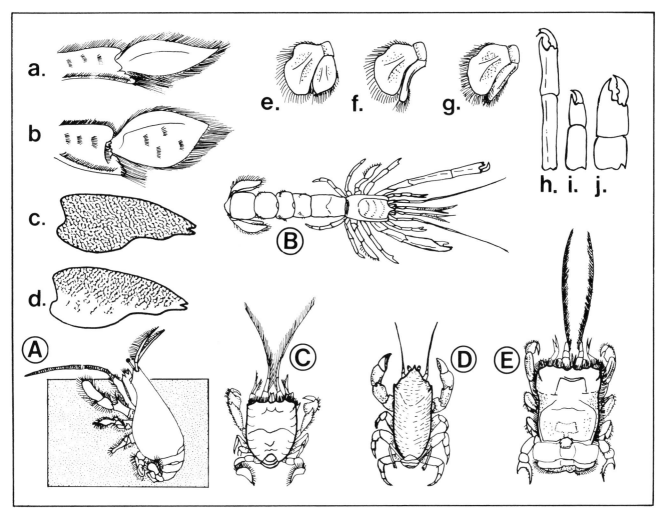

6-7. Sand-dwelling Crustacea. **A.** Mole crab, *Emerita talpoida*; **B.** Ghost shrimp, *Callichirus islagrande*; **C.** *Albunea paretii*; **D.** *Euceramus praelongus*; **E.** *Lepidopa benedicti*; **a & c.** *Emerita benedicti*; **a & d.** *Emerita portoricensis*; **b.** *Emerita talpoida*; **e & j.** *Callianassa louisia-nensis*; **f & h.** *Callichirus islagrande*; **g & i.** *Callichirus major*. Illustrations **e.**, **f.** and **g.** depict left uropods; illustrations **h.**, **i.** and **j.** depict major chelae and the associated carpus (after Felder, 1973a).

surf to a depth of about 1 m. The closely related *Lepidopa websteri* (Fig. 10-1 J) occurs in deeper water, usually 1 to 2 m. *Lepidopa benedicti* has decidedly rectangular eyestalks with rounded edges that bear a darkly pigmented spot on each outer margin; *Lepidopa websteri* has ovate eyestalks which lack the spots (Felder, 1973a). *Albunea paretti* (Figs. 6-7 C; 6-16 X) and *Euceramus praelongus* (Fig. 6-7 D) sometimes stray into the surf zone, but are more commonly encountered in the offshore sands (see Chapter 10).

Among the least observed of the sandy beach animals are the ghost or mud shrimps of the Callianassidae (Rabalais *et al.*, 1979). There are two common species in the western Gulf region; *Callichirus islagrande* (Figs. 6-6 A1 and 6-7 B, f & h), which seems to prefer the moderate surf of the outer barrier island beaches, and *Callianassa louisianensis* (Figs. 6-7 e & j), which occurs on the outer beaches but is more common in the protected bayshore sands. *Callichirus major* (Figs. 6-7 g & i) is a temperate water species reported from but uncommon on Texas beaches.

Callichirus islagrande constructs deep burrows in the lower foreshore and shallow nearshore sand. Below the surface, the burrows are stable, well-formed cylinders, often with turning chambers and several branches, some of which extend downward more than 1 m. They narrow near the surface, where they are indicated either by simple openings in the case of *Callichirus islagrande* on surf beaches, or by low (2 cm) conical mounds in the case of *Callianassa louisianensis* in more protected areas.

Ghost shrimps employ abdominal appendages (pleopods) to pump water through the burrows. Thoracic appendages (pereopods) are tipped with long hair-like setae which catch phytoplankton, detritus and other particles suspended in the flowing water. Trapped particles are transferred to maxillipeds and thence to the mouth. The shrimps emerge infrequently from burrows. When danger threatens, they move rapidly downward. Ghost shrimps are elusive crustaceans rarely seen by even the most observant biologist. Their abundance is indicated along the central Texas coast (Mustang and northern Padre Island) by hundreds of burrow openings exposed by the receding surf. Conical mounds, when present, hold their shape even in moderate swash. Like *Donax*, the distribution of the ghost shrimp is patchy, with some parts of the beach having several burrows per m², whereas nearby sands have none.

Polychaetes are less conspicuous than the other inhabitants of wave-swept sand, but are at least as common. The spionid *Scolelepis squamata* (Fig. 6-6 B1) is one of the best indicator species of the clean sandy swash zone in the northern Gulf. The bright red tube-dwelling polychaete *Onuphis eremita oculata* (Fig. 6-16 Z) lives within a thin membranous tube, from which its head emerges to scavenge tiny edible particles washed in by the surf. Its long, thin fragile body is easily broken, so specimens are rarely collected intact. This worm occupies the swash zone of sandy beaches as well as offshore current-swept subtidal banks and bars. Several additional polychaetes may also be found here (see Shelton & Robertson, 1981).

We cannot conclude this section without acknowledging the numerically dominant amphipods of the sandy beach. As most of the species found here are small and difficult to identify, we have not illustrated them, but this should not minimize their importance to the habitat. At least 10 species have been recorded from the intertidal sands of Texas beaches and account from 30 to 60 percent of the total number of individuals living here (Shelton & Robertson, 1981). The numerical advantage is not carried over to biomass dominance, for amphipods account for less than 15 percent of the total biomass of the intertidal fauna, reflecting their small size. Species of *Haustorius, Lepidactylus*, and other amphipods which occupy the central intertidal are, like the coquina clams, mole crabs and ghost shrimps, suspension feeders relying upon the sea to provide them nutrition.

THE STRAND LINE

Many of the organisms commonly seen on the sandy Gulf of Mexico beaches are not inhabitants, but castaways from a richer offshore fauna. This is the strand biota, the organisms deposited upon the upper beach by high tides or storm waves and left there to dry in the wind when the tide ebbs or the storm dissipates. Strand biota is derived from two sources. The shells, sea whips, sea pens, sand dollars, worm tubes, and similar forms are largely storm-deposited offshore benthos. This bottom-dwelling component is described in Chapter 10 in the context of the habitat in which it lives. The remaining strand biota is mostly beached flotsam, organisms which normally live afloat at sea.

We will describe the flotsam component of the strand biota here, and discuss some aspects of the lives of its constituent species.

Pelagic Biota

The Portuguese Man-o-War, *Physalia physalia* (Fig. 6-8 E), is one of the more conspicuous strand flotsam species on Gulf and Caribbean shores. Its appearance may be seasonal, blowing ashore in greatest numbers in the early spring. When present on shore, it is easily identified by the membranous, cylindrically elongate, sail-crested, float carrying a knot of blue or lavender tissue and tentacles which become covered with sand.

Although *Physalia* has a jellyfish-like appearance, it differs from true jellyfishes in many respects. Most important, *Physalia* is not a single individual, but a complex colony consisting of several kinds of polyps and medusae. Using the crenulated float as a sail (which can be raised, lowered or twisted to adjust to the wind), *Physalia* drifts with the surface currents of the open sea. Several elastic fishing tentacles trail the float, sometimes extending many meters below the water surface. These tentacles are armed with thousands of potent toxic stinging structures (nematocysts) capable of paralyzing fish or bringing excruciating pain to any swimmer or child on the beach that touches them. Even after several days on the beach, the brittle, sun-dried and dehydrated *Physalia* tentacles still contain nematocysts which can discharge and deliver a painful sting.

At sea, fishing tentacles (dactylozooids) are used primarily for food capture. Their nematocysts stun or immobilize a variety of pelagic fishes, ranging in size from a few mm to over 25 cm. The fishing tentacles move captured prey to batteries of feeding polyps (gastrozooids) located in the mass of tissue below the float. Each gastrozooid distends its mouth over a part of the prey, bringing enzyme-secreting tissues in contact with it. Digestion proceeds rapidly, and a 20 cm fish can be consumed by a large *Physalia* within several hours.

Physalia physalia is a cosmopolitan species, found worldwide in warm-temperate and tropical waters. It is also the largest of the Siphonophora, a group of pelagic hydrozoans which are particularly abundant in lower latitude seas. Two other smaller pelagic hydrozoans which superficially resemble *Physalia* may be washed ashore on Gulf beaches. The By-the-Wind Sailor, *Velella velella* (Fig. 6-8 J), vaguely resembles a very small Portuguese Man-o-War. *Velella* has an elliptical, more flattened float bearing a distinctive flattened, diagonal, triangular sail. The circular float of *Porpita porpita* (Fig. 6-8 K) lacks a sail. Both species belong to the hydrozoan order Chondrophora (Disconantha), which differ from the Siphonophora in that the former have chitinous floats, numerous short blue reproductive polyps, a large central feeding polyp bearing a single mouth and marginal tentacles that extend less than 2 cm below the float. The Chondrophora feed primarily upon zooplankton at the surface of the sea, so their nematocysts require significantly less potent toxins than those of *Physalia*. Neither possess locomotor abilities, and if tipped over they are unable to right themselves. Chitinous chondrophore floats differ not only in composition from the membranous float of *Physalia*, but are also capable of persisting long after the animal has died. After a storm, Gulf beaches may be littered with thousands of empty *Velella* floats.

Porpita is not as common on Texas beaches as *Velella*, but it is seen regularly on Mexico shores. It is primarily a tropical species occurring in greatest abundance to the south.

Several animals prey upon siphonophores and chondrophores, and these appear occasionally among the strand biota. The pelagic nudibranch mollusc *Glaucus atlanticus* (Fig. 6-8 F) is possibly the most spectacular but the least likely seen on the beach strand. This blue, shell-less gastropod floats upside down near the surface, relying upon gas-filled pockets within frilly lobes for buoyancy. It is an active swimmer uncommonly found near shore. It feeds upon all of the pelagic hydroids, especially *Velella* and *Porpita*.

The purple sea snails, *Janthina* sp. (Fig. 6-8 G), are unlikely pelagic species. Despite a very thin shell, *Janthina* will sink if submerged in water and lacks any internal flotation mechanism that can return it to the surface. It stays afloat by clinging to a mucous raft containing hundreds of trapped air bubbles. Lacking any means of directing its course, *Janthina* floats randomly on the surface of the sea, occasionally encountering a siphonophore or chondrophore and upon which it quickly begins to feed. *Janthina* can dispose of a *Velella* or *Porpita* rapidly, and a pair of these gastropods have been known to consume a moderate-sized *Physalia* in less than a day.

Three species of *Janthina* occur within the warm-temperate and tropical western Atlantic: *J. janthina* (Fig. 6-8 H), *J. globosa* (= *J. prolongata*) (Fig. 6-8 I), and *J. pallida*, the latter distinguished from *J. globosa* by having a somewhat more flaring, less pointed aperture. Though never abundant, they are most often found stranded on Gulf beaches in the spring following a strongly blowing southeasterly wind.

The most common true jellyfish found among the beach strand is the large cabbage head, *Stomolophus meleagris* (Fig. 6-8 A). It is closely related to the upside-down jellyfish, *Cassiopea*, which we will encounter later in tropical bays and mangrove swamps. *Stomolophus meleagris* is a cosmopolitan pelagic species attaining a bell diameter of 30 cm. It is naturally translucent white and has a waxy gelatinous consistency. The interior of the cabbage head may appear reddish or brownish due to the presence of ripening gametes or ingested zooplankton. *Stomolophus* lacks tentacles, but employs numerous short oral arms surrounding a many-divided mouth to capture copepods and other zooplankters. As the nematocysts borne on the oral arms are needed only to subdue very small prey, this jellyfish is harmless to humans. During the summer and fall it is a common sight to see numerous "cabbage heads" floating through tidal inlets beside the Texas jetties, and just as many stranded upon the shore.

Some of the strand biotas are not what they first appear to be. The fragile *Spirula spirula* shell (Fig. 6-8 B) is a case in point. This loosely coiled shell is commonly mistaken for a snail, but, in fact, is the internal gas-filled skeleton of a cosmopolitan pelagic cephalopod. *Spirula* have rarely been seen alive, as they inhabit the region of perpetual twilight and darkness of the deep midwater sea. *Spirula* floats head down in waters between 400 to 1200 m in depth, using gas secreted into chambers within the shell for buoyancy. By varying the gas content, *Spirula* can control buoyancy and adjust its vertical position in the sea. When the animals die, the gas-filled shells relieved of the tissue burden rise to the surface and are moved by currents to beaches throughout the world.

A variety of other animal parts or products appear among the beach strand. Some sharks, for example, produce floating egg cases (Fig. 6-8 L) which are stranded occasionally. Similarly, whelk and moon snail egg cases (see Chapter 10) sometimes wash ashore.

Attached Flotsam and Borers

Several strand biota come ashore within or attached to flotsam. Gooseneck barnacles, e.g., *Lepas anatifera* (Fig. 6-8 M), are perhaps the most obvious. This species floats near the surface attached to wood, bottles, cans, pumice, *Janthina* shells, shark egg cases or any other buoyant object. A similar species, *L. fascicularis*, secretes a bubble raft to which several specimens usually cling. Both are common among the strand of sandy beaches throughout the world. The pelagic gooseneck barnacles feed upon various zooplankton which they filter from the water by use of typical cirripede appendages. They are also known to prey upon siphonophores and small fishes such as juvenile flying fishes (Howard & Scott, 1959; Jones, 1968).

Marine wood boring molluscs and crustaceans are less conspicuous but common among the flotsam strand. All timber or wood floating at sea will come under eventual attack by these organisms, as will untreated wharf pilings and other wooden structures built along the shore. There are many wood-boring species, but here we will mention only some of the most common.

Two groups of bivalve molluscs bore into wood, the Pholadidae or piddocks (e.g., *Martesia*) and the Teredinidae or true shipworms (e.g., *Teredo* and *Bankia*). The boring method of *Martesia* is similar to that described for *Barnea* and *Cyrtopleura*, the pholads commonly found in stiff bayshore clay banks. The Teredinidae have further perfected the wood-boring habit, becoming considerably more specialized for this way of life.

The shipworm body consists mostly of a naked pallial tube up to 10 cm long (Fig. 6-8 D1), and from which project the usual bivalve siphons. The tube is divided horizontally into inhalant and exhalant chambers separated by the ctenidium (gill). The terminal end of the tube is attached at the opening of the wood burrow, and is protected by two shelly, retractable pallets (Fig. 6-8 D3 & D4). The siphons grow more elongate as the shipworm enlarges its burrow. The diminutive unhinged bivalve shell (Fig. 6-8 D2) is confined to the anterior end where it surrounds a small body and from which anteriorly projects the disk-shaped foot. Rasp-like shell margins abrade wood at the head of the tunnel, achieved as asymmetric contractions of the adductor muscles rock the valves about dorsal and ventral fulcra while the foot pulls the shell to the end of the burrow. Shipworms obtain food by both filtering water and ingesting wood fragments, the latter digested by cellulolytic enzymes (Morton, 1978). The identification of shipworm species is difficult, with taxonomy dependent upon shell and pallet structure and soft body morphology (Clench & Turner, 1946; Turner, 1966).

The gribble, *Limnoria tripunctata* (Fig. 6-8 C), is one of the most commonly encountered wood-boring crustaceans (see Menzies, 1957, for a survey of the wood boring Limnoriidae). Like most of the pelagic biota we have already described, this isopod is a cosmopolitan species, living in wood in all temperate and tropical seas. *Limnoria* bores by use of asymmetrical chewing mandibles. The left mandible is a rasping file, whereas the right is a sharply pointed awl. Burrows usually follow the grain of the wood. *Limnoria* can digest cellulose (Ray and Julian, 1952; Ray, 1958) and thus wood is the major source of nutrition (Ray, 1959a; b), although fungal hyphae and bacteria also likely contribute (Schafer & Lane, 1957).

Sargassum Biota

The final group of strand biota is associated with floating Gulfweed, the brown alga *Sargassum*, for which the Sargasso Sea is named. *Sargassum* normally lives attached as a lower intertidal and shallow subtidal hard-bottom macrophyte in shallow warm-temperate and tropical seas. Storm waves dislodge it and other macrophytes from the rocks to which they cling. Most of these algae fare poorly when cast afloat, but at least two species of Gulfweed, *Sargassum fluitans* and *S. natans* (Fig. 6-9 I & J), not only survive, but actually grow and reproduce as pelagic species. Floating clumps of Gulfweed (*S. natans* is the most common in the Gulf of Mexico; Parr, 1939), aggregate with other clumps to form large mats. These mats in turn attract a unique assemblage of animals which find food, shelter, or a surface upon which to attach. Many of these animals mimic the shape or color of *Sargassum* so effectively that they represent classic examples of cryptic subterfuge.

There are two components of the *Sargassum* community: (1), the sessile biota which lives attached to the algae and (2), the motile biota which, although it might cling to the plants, is capable of an independent existence (Shulman, 1968). The former includes a variety of encrusting species which add weight to the *Sargassum* mat and reduce the photosynthetic surface area. However, as *Sargassum* growth usually exceeds that of the encrusting biota, rarely, if ever, will biofoulants cause the entire mass to sink (Woodcock, 1950).

Among the sessile biota, *Aglaophenia latecarinata* (Fig. 6-9 P) and *Gonothyraea gracilis* (Fig. 6-9 R) are the most common hydroids which attach to Gulf of Mexico *Sargassum*. Several other hydrozoans may be present, including *Clytia* sp., *Plumularia* sp., and *Sertularia* sp. Bryozoans such as *Membranipora tuberculata* (Fig. 6-9 Q) or *Aetea* sp. often encrust *Sargassum* fronds. The gooseneck barnacles (*Lepas* sp.) also colonize *Sargassum* mats. Hundreds of coiled *Spirorbis* shells secreted by tiny suspension feeding polychaetes (Fig. 6-9 C) can line a single blade of Gulfweed. At least one anemone, *Anemonia sargassensis* (Fig. 6-9 O), lives exclusively upon floating *Sargassum*. This anemone is easily overlooked due to its small size (the pedal disk is only about 5 mm in diameter) and cryptic color.

The largest, although not necessarily the most conspicuous, member of the motile component of the *Sargassum* community is the sargassum fish, *Histrio histrio* (Fig. 6-9 H). This bizarre relative of angler and frog fishes is an ideal example of cryptic *Sargassum* biota. Not only is its body misshapen in the pattern of branching Gulfweed, but it is colored in a mottled pattern of browns and creams that mimic the light and dark patches of floating *Sargassum*. Its pectoral fins are formed into hand-like appendages used to crawl through the Gulfweed. *Histrio* stalks small unsuspecting fishes (including other sargassum fishes) and crustaceans. It creeps upon them with plodding certainty and ingests them with a forceful slurp. Occasionally, *Histrio* uses the dorsally projecting snout appendages as lures, attracting prey closer with wiggles of the terminal barbel. This behavior indicates the close relationship between *Histrio* and bottom-dwelling angler fishes.

There is apparently no fixed spawning season for *Histrio* in tropical seas, although spawning activity may cease during the cooler months in warm-temperate climates (Adams, 1960). The presence of ripe gametes in sexually mature specimens apparently suppresses normally cannibalistic tendencies (Mosher, 1954). Females produce prodigious quantities of eggs which, when extruded, float on the surface in a scroll-like mass. Egg masses are produced every three or four days for a period of two or three weeks. As each new mass of eggs develops within the female body, the buoyancy of the mass causes a shift in her center of gravity. Just prior to egg release, the gravid female must only swim snout down, tail high. A few hours before egg release, the female becomes relatively inactive. She is attended by the male, who apparently will defend her from danger or other males. Immediately prior to spawning, both sexes begin to swim actively, with the male swimming immediately behind the fe-

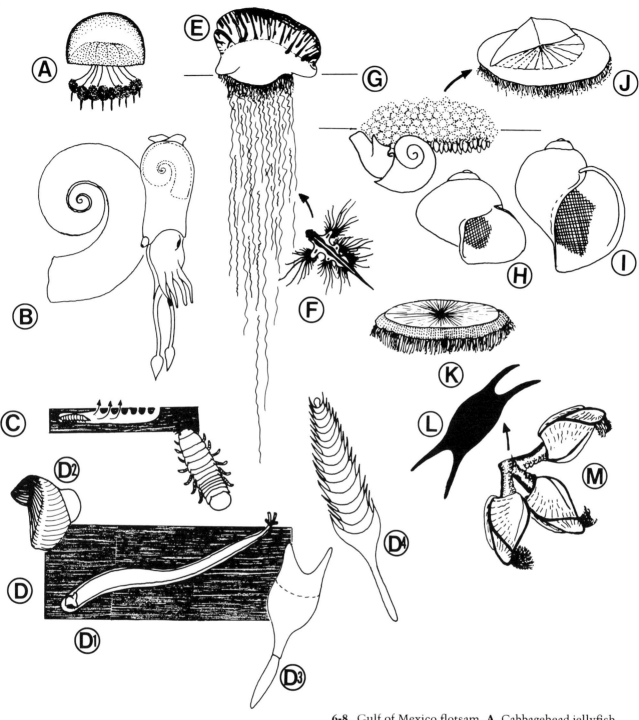

6-8. Gulf of Mexico flotsam. **A.** Cabbagehead jellyfish, *Stomolophus meleagris*; **B.** *Spirula spirula*; **C.** Wood-boring isopod, *Limnoria tripunctata*; **D.** Teredinidae: D1, habitat; D2, shell; D3, *Teredo navalis* (pallet); D4, *Bankia gouldi* (pallet); **E.** Portuguese Man-o-war, *Physalia physalia*; **F.** Blue sea slug, *Glaucus atlanticus*; **G.** Purple sea snail, *Janthina* sp., attached to bubble raft; **H.** Purple sea snail, *Janthina janthina*; **I.** Purple sea snail, *Janthina globosa*; **J.** By-the-wind sailor, *Velella velella*; **K.** *Porpita porpita*; **L.** Shark egg case; **M.** Gooseneck barnacle, *Lepas anatifera*. Arrows indicate predation (**F** to **E**; **G** to **J**) or attachment (**M** to **L**).

male, snout to vent. This short swim culminates in an extraordinarily brief spawn that begins as the female moves (or is pushed by the male) toward the surface. In less than a second he sweeps by her, releasing sperm and breaking the water's surface. She continues to the surface, where she releases an 8 to 10 cm egg raft. The entire process usually takes less than 10 seconds (Mosher, 1954). A raft contains thousands of fertilized eggs, each of which undergoes development for four or five days and hatch as larval *Histrio*.

The *Sargassum* pipefish, *Syngnathus pelagicus* (Fig. 6-9 G), is another cryptic species whose closest relatives are shallow benthic fishes. Its shape mimics a blade of *Sargassum*, although usually not as effectively as the mottled skin of *Histrio*. This slender planktivore selectively devours various copepods, ostracods and shrimps swimming within the clump of Gulfweed. Pipefishes are in the same family (Syngnathidae) as seahorses, and, like them, females deposit eggs in male brood pouches, where fertilization and development occur.

The brown sargassum snail, *Litiopa melanostoma* (Fig. 6-9 N) is most often collected among *Sargassum* beach strand. Little is known about this cerithiid except that it seems to be restricted to floating *Sargassum* upon which it deposits egg capsules. The sargassum nudibranch *Scyllaea pelagica* (Fig. 6-9 M) feeds upon hydroids and other cnidarians. The mottled brown color and two pairs of swimming fins along the back readily distinguish this species from other flotsam nudibranchs such as *Fiona pinnata*, which is found occasionally among the floating Gulfweed.

There are several arthropods which crawl or swim among the floating Gulfweed mats. Tiny gammaridean amphipods, isopods, and other small crustaceans are especially common. The small crab *Portunus sayi* (Fig. 6-9 D) is shaped like the common edible blue crab. Its carapace, with 4 marginal teeth between the eyes, rarely exceeds 5 cm in width and, like other members of the *Sargassum* community, it is cryptically orange-brown. *Portunus sayi* can swim but usually crawls through the Gulfweed mats. Like other portunids, it is a scavenger or predator. The tiny grapsid crab *Planes minutus* (Fig. 6-9 E) is unable to swim, but clings to *Sargassum*, sea turtles, or flotsam. White, black, and yellow chromatophores and hypodermis pigmentation provide this crab with a mottled camouflage. It is a herbivore, foraging upon the epiphytes that attach to dead or encrusted portions of the Gulfweed mat. It is rare in the Gulf of Mexico.

The spindly sea spider (Pycnogonida), *Endeis spinosa* (Fig. 6-9 A) is a chelicerate arthropod, more closely related to the predominately terrestrial spiders and mites (Arachnida), but in this case restricted exclusively to pelagic *Sargassum*. The anterior head or cephalon of most sea spiders usually bears three pairs of ventral appendages: chelicerae, palps and ovigerous legs, but *Endeis* lacks the first two, and only males bear the latter. Females deposit eggs, but males carry and brood them on the ovigerous legs during their de-

velopment. The cephalon of both sexes is equipped with a proboscis which is employed to feed upon bryozoans, hydrozoans and other *Sargassum* associates. The trunk bears 4 pairs of thin, jointed walking legs.

Several shrimps live among floating *Sargassum*. *Latreutes fucorum* (Fig. 6-9 B), with a characteristic upturned rostrum nearly as long as the carapace, is usually the most common. This shrimp is variously attired in yellows, reds and spots of blue. The similar shrimps *Hippolyte coerulescens* and *Leander tenuicornis* are sometimes also found in floating Gulfweed.

In addition to the sessile *Spirorbis*, two additional errant polychaetes are usually present in the *Sargassum*. Adult *Platynereis dumerilii* (Fig. 6-9 K) or *Harmothoe aculeata* (Fig. 6-9 L) are neither restricted to the pelagic realm nor characteristic of this habitat. The latter are found more often on tropical reefs, whereas the former more often occur among intertidal or subtidal grasses along western and eastern Atlantic shores and throughout the Mediterranean basin. *Sargassum* helps raft *P. dumerilii* throughout the Atlantic, but another aspect of its life cycle plays an important role in providing the species with a broad geographical distribution.

Platynereis dumerilii reproduces by epitoky, a process which transforms otherwise bottom-dwelling polychaetes into swimming worms adapted for carrying large quantities of gametes. During the reproductive season (usually summer), normal (nonreproductive) individuals undergo transformation into a "heteronereis" reproductive stage. The heteronereis worms are smaller in size, develop enlarged eyes, and the parapodia on the rear half of the body become flattened and produce numerous setae adapted for swimming. Internal organs degenerate at the expense of developing gametes.

6-9. Sargassum community. **A.** Sea spider, *Endeis spinosa*; **B.** Sargassum shrimp, *Latreutes fucorum*; **C.** Spirorbis sp.; **D.** Sargassum crab, *Portunus sayi*; **E.** Gulfweed crab, *Planes minutus*; **F.** Flatworm, *Gnesioceros sargassicola*; **G.** Sargassum pipefish, *Syngnathus pelagicus*; **H.** Sargassumfish, *Histrio histrio*; **I.** Gulfweed, *Sargassum fluitans*; **J.** Gulfweed, *Sargassum natans*; **K.** Platynereis dumerilii; **L.** Scaleworm, *Harmothoe aculeata*; **M.** Sargassum nudibranch, *Scyllaea pelagica*; **N.** Brown sargassum snail, *Litiopa melanostoma*; **O.** Sargassum anemone, *Anemonia sargassensis*; **P.** Hydroid, *Aglaophenia latecarinata*; **Q.** Bryozoan, *Membranipora tuberculata*; **R.** Hydroid, *Gonothyraea gracilis*.

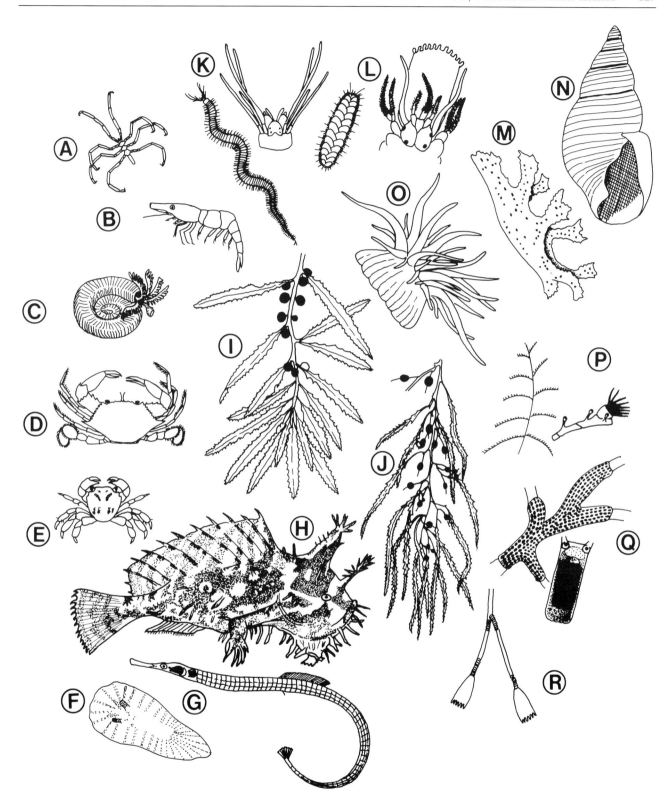

When the transformation is complete, benthic *P. dumerilii* emerge from grassbeds at night during the dark of the moon. Pelagic specimens living in *Sargassum* presumably emerge from the Gulfweed mats. They swim near the surface of the sea, where males and females intertwine. Unlike most nereids which rupture at this stage, dispersing gametes into the sea, *P. dumerilii* females grasp males, ingesting sperm through the mouth. Sperm bore through the flaccid tissues of the digestive tract to fertilize eggs lying within the body cavity. Shortly thereafter, the female body disintegrates, releasing fertilized eggs into the sea. After a brief period of development, the eggs become planktonic trochophore larvae in the open sea, where they remain until a suitable habitat is encountered for metamorphosis into the adult. Benthic grassbeds or pelagic *Sargassum* apparently serve as equally suitable substrata.

Just as the errant *Sargassum* polychaetes are actually benthic species, many of the other animals in this community are derived from families or groups normally found in shallow subtidal habitats. All frog fishes (Antennariidae) except *Histrio histrio* are sedentary inhabitants of shallow tropical seas. The pipefishes and sea horses (Syngnathidae), except for *Syngnathus pelagicus*, similarly prefer shallow grass beds. Most portunid crabs, despite swimming abilities, usually take refuge in shallow sandy bottoms. *Portunus sayi* is an exception. Grapsid crabs characteristically occupy intertidal or shallow subtidal habitats, except for the pelagic *Planes minutus*. *Spirorbis* worms similarly thrive on intertidal and shallow subtidal macrophytes. Cerithiid snails usually occupy shallow subtidal grass beds. Again, the cerithiid *Litiopa melanostoma* is an exception. The Gulfweed polyclad flatworm, *Gnesioceros sargassicola* (Fig. 6-9 F), is restricted to pelagic *Sargassum*, but its nearest relative (*G. florida*) lives among shallow seagrasses from the Carolinas to Florida. The pattern is clear. Many of the animals living among pelagic *Sargassum* were derived originally from a shallow benthic stock, typically with but one representative from each group obtaining for itself a niche in this floating mass of weed.

THE BACKSHORE

We now turn away from the dynamic foreshore to look landward towards the backshore, dunes, and maritime coastal strand. A hardy community of halophytic plants tolerant of habitats strongly influenced by salt, surf and sand becomes increasingly dominant here. Only a few species occupy the backshore, but floral diversity increases rapidly upon and behind the dunes or dune ridges. Marine and terrestrial animals find the backshore an almost intolerable environment. Yet a few sometimes occur here, and fewer still even help characterize the backshore biota. Figures 6-6, 6-10, 6-12, 6-14, and 6-15 present an array of backshore and dune life proceeding from warm-temperate central Texas (Mustang Island, Fig. 6-6), sub-tropical southern

Texas (southern Padre Island, Fig. 6-10), near-tropical central Mexico (Cabo Rojo, Fig. 6-12), and distinctly tropical Yucatan (Figs. 6-14 and 6-15). We will discuss each of these localities, beginning with an examination of backshore biota and its almost Gulf-wide constancy. As we move inland from the backshore, species diversity and latitudinal biogeographic differences become sufficiently pronounced that we must separate the discussions of the upper shore and maritime zones by region.

Vegetation

The backshore varies considerably in width on Gulf shores. It is usually a broad belt of gently sloping sand between 50 to 100 m wide along many of the barrier islands of the northwestern Gulf region, but Yucatan beaches vary greatly in width and slope (Fig. 6-13), some being no more than 3 m wide. The backshore is characterized by sparse "pioneering" vegetation which typically grades into the greater floral diversity and cover on the landward dunes or dune ridges. Here we will consider only the most seaward coastal plants, and defer discussion of the more diverse dune, dune ridge, and central barrier island or coastal mainland flora to later sections. Backshore flora throughout the Gulf is characterized by fleshy succulents, a few grasses, and prostrate creeping vines.

The sea purslane, *Sesuvium portulacastrum* (Figs. 6-6 S; 6-10 V; 6-12 L; 6-14 D; 6-15 K), rarely attains the prominence on Gulf beaches that it enjoys throughout much of the Caribbean, but small sprawling clumps can usually be located on the backshore near dunes. The fleshy green leaves, green or orange stems, and the solitary pink, apetalous flowers distinguish this plant from any other on the seaward beach. *Sesuvium* is a predominantly tropical species, becoming increasingly more common toward the south. On South Padre Island, it is second in importance only to *Uniola* on the backshore flats (Judd *et al.*, 1977), and it forms thick mats on appropriate beaches in Mexico.

Bitter panicum, *Panicum amarum* (Figs. 6-6 J; 6-10 Y; 6-12 G), usually dominates the backshore and lower foredune slopes, and extends over the dunes toward the leeward vegetated flats. It favors exposed areas where windblown sand accumulates (Dahl *et al.*, 1974). Here it grows vigorously, stimulated perhaps by the sparse influx of nutrients delivered with the sand, or by the need to avoid burial. This panicum has an extensive below-ground rhizome system from which leaves sprout. In areas of heavy sand accumulation, only a small fraction of the entire plant may be exposed. Leaves extend as much as 0.4 m above the sand, but usually are only half that height. Bitter panicum flowers in the fall, from September to December, but the seeds are largely sterile (Palmer, 1972). Reproduction is primarily by vegetative processes. It is a favorite livestock forage and was eliminated along some portions of the Texas barrier islands by grazing. When livestock are removed, this grass reestablishes rapidly along the backshore.

Two morning glories commonly occur on the backshore and foredune slopes of Gulf beaches. The railroad vine, *Ipomoea pes-caprae* (Figs. 6-6 O; 6-10 X; 6-12 Q; 6-14 A), is a broad-leafed creeper producing prominent rose or lavender flowers, while the beach morning glory, *I. stolonifera* (Figs. 6-6 T; 6-10 W; 6-12 P), has narrower, more irregularly lobed leaves and bears large white to yellowish flowers. Both species are perfect examples of the trailing creeper lifeform. Leaves and flowers are borne on prostrate stems which lie directly on the sand and extend as much as 30 m in length. Roots emerge at numerous nodes along the stem and anchor the plant to the substratum. The prostrate plant is at the mercy of blowing sand, and portions are often covered. Survival is dependent upon the length of the stem, for blowing sand rarely covers all of the plant. Buried leaves die, but somewhere along the stem, there are exposed leaves which generate new runners. In this way, morning glories creep across the dune fronts and backshore, not actually moving, but literally growing to stay alive.

The backshore may harbor thin stands of several grasses or sedges more commonly encountered elsewhere. The cordgrass, *Spartina patens* (Fig. 6-16 P), grows here, especially along the northern coast, but it is more characteristic of bayshores. Seacoast bluestem, *Schizachyrium scoparium littoralis* (Fig. 6-10 M), and the sedge *Fimbristylis castanea* (Figs. 6-12 N; 6-16 E), both more typical of the protected vegetated flats, sometimes occur on the backshore. Sea oats, *Uniola paniculata* (Figs. 6-6 I; 6-10 K; 6-12 I), also occur on the backshore, especially upon coppice dunes, where they become a significant element of the backshore vegetation (Judd *et al.*, 1977). They are more conspicuous, however, upon larger barrier island dunes.

With one exception, the backshore strand flora changes little from temperate to tropical beaches. The bay bean, *Canavalia maritima* (Figs. 6-12 O; 6-14 H), is a pantropical legume which only occasionally grows on the south Texas barrier island backshore strands, but is common on the sandy beaches of Mexico. It occupies the same habitat and exhibits the same growth form as the beach morning glories. It is easily recognized by its large trifoliate leaflets, rose purple pendulous flowers and the large, distinctly ribbed, legume pods.

The Ghost Crab

When the backshore is a broad sandy apron separating dunes from the foreshore, as along many of the Texas barrier beaches, there are even fewer permanent animal residents to be found here than occur in the intertidal foreshore. Apart from the shorebirds which are sporadic visitors, the most conspicuous inhabitant is the ghost crab, *Ocypode quadrata* (Figs. 6-6 N; 6-10 C1; 6-12 S; 6-14 K; 6-16 U), found on exposed sandy beaches from Rhode Island to Brazil, and throughout the Gulf of Mexico. The common name seems most appropriate for this agile, largely nocturnal, pale white or straw-yellow crab that blends so well with the color of the sand in which it lives. *Ocypode* is exceptionally fleet-of-foot. When approached, it scurries sideways with unexpected speed to disappear into the nearest burrow. Adults are rarely seen during the day, but juveniles are more commonly encountered, particularly when the sky is overcast.

On Texas beaches *Ocypode quadrata* is active from March to early December. It spends the winter dormant within a sand-sealed burrow. Within the tropics, however, it remains active year round. Haley (1972) estimates the average ghost crab survives about three years. Females mature in their second year. Mating, larval brooding and release by *Ocypode* is similar to that described for *Gecarcinus*, except females do not migrate *en masse* to the sea. Males of some *Ocypode* species construct complex "copulation burrows" where mating occurs. *Ocypode quadrata* may mate within a burrow, but this species also is known to copulate on the beach (Hughes, 1973). Copulation and larval release likely occur throughout the summer, with larval density in the meroplankton peaking in late spring and early fall. Most juveniles appear on the beach in July and late October (Haley, 1972).

Ocypode is one of a number of semi-terrestrial crustaceans, although the only one which regularly inhabits the sandy backshore. Like all of these crustaceans, their larvae are dependent upon the sea for later development, but juveniles return to the beach, where they spend their adult life. The ghost crab is rather poorly adapted for life on land in comparison with some of the other semi-terrestrial crustaceans. It can never be

6-10. The sandy beach at southern Padre Island, Texas. **A.** Western diamondback, *Crotalus atrox*; **B.** Keeled earless lizard, *Holbrookia propinqua*; **C.** Six-lined racerunner, *Cnemidophorus sexlineatus*; **D.** Glasswort, *Salicornia virginica*; **E.** Key grass, *Monanthochloe littoralis*; **F.** Swordgrass, *Scirpus americanus*; **G.** Sedge, *Cyperus surinamensis*; **H.** Prickly pear, *Opuntia lindheimeri*; **I.** Seaside spurge, *Chamaesyce maculata*; **J.** Coastal dropseed, *Sporobolus virginicus*; **K.** Sea oats, *Uniola paniculata*; **L.** Whitetop sedge, *Dichromena colorata*; **M.** Seacoast bluestem, *Schizachyrium scoparium littoralis*; **N.** Bushy beardgrass, *Andropogon glomeratus*; **O.** Beach evening primrose, *Oenothera drummondii*; **P.** Partridge pea, *Cassia fasciculata*; **Q.** Gulfdune grass, *Paspalum monostachyum*; **R.** Snoutbean, *Rhynchosia minima*; **S.** Beach tea, *Croton punctatus*; **T.** Deer fly, *Chrysops* sp.; **U.** Tiger beetle, *Cicindela* sp.; **V.** Sea purslane, *Sesuvium portulacastrum*; **W.** White morning glory, *Ipomoea stolonifera*; **X.** Railroad vine, *Ipomoea pescaprae*; **Y.** Bitter panicum, *Panicum amarum*; **Z.** Sea ox-eye daisy, *Borrichia frutescens*; **A1.** Mangrove crab, *Cardisoma guanhumi*; **B1.** Red land crab, *Gecarcinus lateralis*, also illustrating sand plug at burrow entrance and capillary transfer of water droplets from base of walking leg to gill; **C1.** Ghost crab, *Ocypode quadrata*; **D1.** Mole crab, *Emerita portoricensis*.

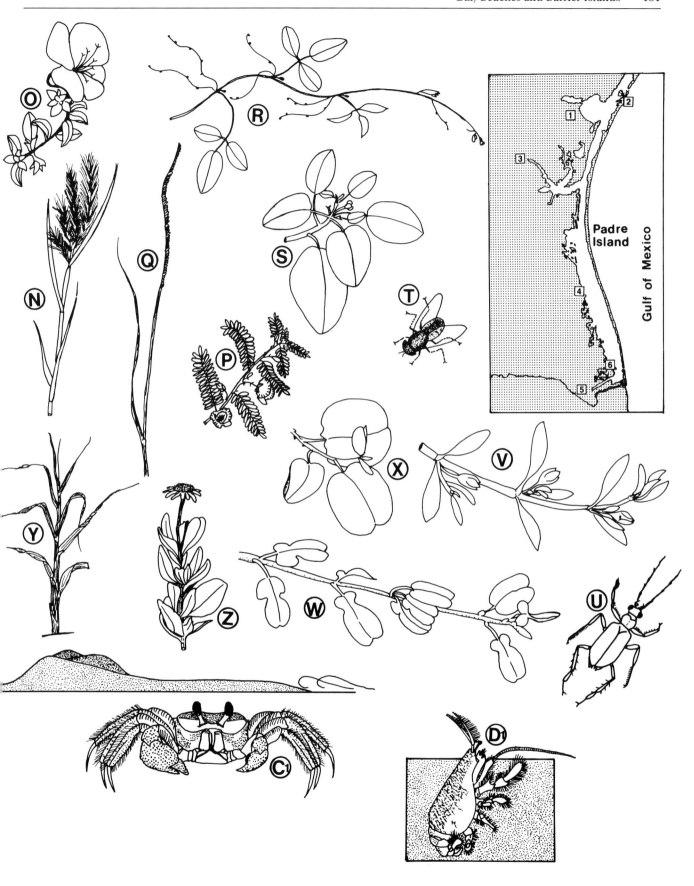

far from a source of seawater, for its gill chambers lose water easily and must be moistened frequently. *Ocypode* does this by running through the surf, or digging a burrow to the water table. Except on the larger dunes, the latter rarely lies more than 1 m below the surface and approaches the surface seaward along the foreshore (Judd *et al.*, 1977). Large numbers of small-diameter *Ocypode* burrows are common on the foreshore behind the surf zone. These are constructed by juvenile and young adult crabs, and reflect their dependency upon a ready, shallow, source of seawater. The backshore has considerably fewer burrows, but these increase in length and diameter away from the foreshore. The longest (1 m or more), largest (200 mm diameter), and most complex burrows occur among the foredunes, reflecting the tendency of larger, older, animals to live farther away from the sea and their need to burrow deeper to reach the water table (Hill & Hunter, 1973).

Ghost crabs are the primary predators or scavengers of the foreshore. As predators, they hunt at night in the upper intertidal, digging for *Donax* and *Emerita*. When mole crabs and coquina clams are abundant, they constitute the primary food source (Wolcott, 1978), but *Ocypode* are also opportunists. In the absence of the preferred food, they are excellent facultative scavengers. They will feed upon a variety of carrion and decaying vegetation, including dead fish, insects, *Sargassum*, *Physalia*, other ghost crabs, turtles, and even the carcass of a cow (Teerling, 1970). They are especially opportunistic in the presence of humans. Ghost crabs thrive anywhere human refuse accumulates on the beach. Their populations swell near garbage dumps, fishing piers, restaurants, or other centers of human activity. Unlike many other Ocypodidae, *O. quadrata* is not especially noted for sand-sifting, although juveniles rely upon this method of feeding more than adults. Nevertheless, when humans spill refuse on beach sands, adult *O. quadrata* exploit the resource. They have been observed sifting sand soaked with either beer, coffee, dishwater, gravy, milk, or toothpaste (Teerling, 1970).

THE UPPER SHORE

So far, our surveys of the foreshore and backshore habitats of exposed sandy Gulf beaches have revealed few differences in the flora and fauna of temperate and tropical Gulf shores. Coquina clams and mole crabs are the conspicuous biota of the foreshore, whereas *Sesuvium*, *Ipomoea*, *Panicum*, *Sporobolus* and ghost crabs characterize the backshore. Beginning at the rear margin of the backshore, however, the nature of the beach and its biota vary strikingly according to latitude. The northern Gulf, and especially the semiarid southern Texas coast, consists mostly of sandy barriers with broad backshores behind which lie large dunes. The southern Gulf shores have few barrier islands and narrower backshores. Low, vegetation-stabilized, dune ridges commonly replace the high, active,

dunes and tropical maritime or terrestrial vegetation extends much closer to the sea (Fig 6-13). It is not uncommon, for example, to observe large agave plants within 5 m of a Yucatan beach.

We cannot generalize for the entire region with respect to the maritime biota at the rear of the beach; nor can we ignore it. The biota of these areas is intimately bound directly or indirectly to the ecological dynamics of the sea. Thus, we divide the remaining discussion of sandy shores into several parts. First, we will consider the temperate and subtropical Texas barrier islands, with their dunes, barrier island flats, and other special habitats (Figs. 6-6; 6-10; 6-11). Next, we will compare the Texas barrier islands with those of Mexico (Fig. 6-12), especially with respect to maritime vegetation. Finally, we will examine the Yucatan beaches (Figs. 6-13, 6-14, and 6-15) as examples of tropical mainland shores.

Barrier Island Dunes of Texas and Northern Mexico

On most Gulf sand beaches, the backshore ends at the base of large aeolian (wind-deposited) mounds, the coastal dunes. On northeastern Texas barrier islands and along southern Mexico mainland shores, dunes are usually low rounded ridges, well stabilized by vegetation. From San Jose Island, Texas, northward, sets of two to eight successively higher dune ridges rise toward the interior of the island and parallel the barrier island shore. They are especially well developed on Galveston Island, lying atop an ancient forebeach ridge. Similar dune ridges fringe much of the mainland shore of northern Yucatan. In both localities, the presence of numerous successive dune ridges indicates that the shore has accumulated sediment by seaward progradation.

Larger dunes and dune fields occupy the barrier islands from Mustang Island, Texas to La Pesca, Tamaulipas, Mexico. Southward of Aransas Pass, vegetation cover on the barrier islands progressively diminishes, reflecting an increasingly arid climate. With less stabilizing vegetation, the dunes rise higher. The largest dunes of Texas reach 12 m in height on Padre Island. Active moving dune fields a km or more in width are common on this island, as on its counterparts of northern Mexico. The local topography on much of Padre Island changes frequently due to shifting dunes and storm-induced changes.

There are often two areas of massive sand accumulation, a foredune field and a set of backdunes, the latter often including the highest dunes of the island. The two sets of dunes are separated by a low, broad, sparsely vegetated barrier flat (Fig. 2-11 A). The barrier flat is created and maintained by hurricane surge-water flooding, and this process also provides sand for backdune accumulation (Hayes, 1967). Much of Padre Island consists of foredune and backdune morphology separated by the barrier flat. There are two areas where this pattern is noticeably interrupted. At the center of the island, along a 16 km strip inland from Big Shell Beach, well developed backdunes are absent. Near the southern termination of Padre Island, all dunes diminish in size. This has, in part, allowed the development of South Padre Island, the Gulf shore resort town of south Texas.

The northernmost barrier strand fringing Laguna Madre de Tamaulipas, being the largest and best developed barrier of the Tamaulipas system, has a reasonably well developed dune field arising 100 to 200 m behind the forebeach and reaching 8 m in height. Dunes also occur on the smaller, narrower southern islands. Here they rise immediately behind the forebeach, diminishing in size toward the south.

Dunes, especially the unstabilized active dunes of south Texas and northern Mexico, are at the mercy of winds. Seasonal windshifts frequently bring about changes in dune shape and movement. The western Gulf coast is influenced by three wind components. Persistent spring and summer winds blowing from the southeast mostly during times of fair weather and dry sands are the major dune formers of Texas and northern Mexico (Price & Kornicker, 1961; Andrews, 1970). Sands deposited by longshore currents along barrier foreshores are sun-dried and lofted landward by these winds, accumulating in the dune field behind the beach. As they accumulate sand in the spring and summer, the dunes drift northwesterly, pushed by the prevailing southeasterly winds. Several years might pass before a growing dune reaches 12 m in height.

The second wind component arrives with winter northers, accompanied by cold, gusty, and often rainy weather. The northerly winds are intermittent. Each arctic front eventually passes, with the restoration of the prevailing southeasterly windflow. Northerly winds recur on roughly a five to eight day cycle throughout the winter. Rains often precede arctic fronts along the Texas coast, saturating and compacting barrier island sands. Wet sand grains resist wind lofting, and are moved only by the strongest gusts. Texas dunes move only slightly seaward during the winter. Despite the sometimes extended duration of dune adolescence and the typically plodding movements of a large mature dune, the third major wind component of the Gulf coast, the tropical storm or hurricane can destroy the dune in less than a day (see Chapter 2).

Primary dunes form a natural windbreak for central vegetated flats and constitute a source of sand for one or more active or stabilized secondary dune fields if the latter are present. Vegetational zonation is prominent on the primary dunes, with distinctive windward and leeward plant communities. Vegetation cover grades from sparse to moderate across these zones. Vegetation shelters less than 15 percent of the windward slopes of primary dunes, but cover increases to between 25 to 50 percent on the leeward side, or even higher on the northeastern islands (e.g., Galveston and Follets). When present, stabilized secondary dunes, lying in the protection of the primary dunes, have communities more like those of the leeward face of the primary dunes or vegetated flats. The latter have the greatest floral diversity of all the terrestrial barrier island communities. Here, vegetation cover approaches 100 percent.

From Virginia to Mexico and throughout parts of the Caribbean, the most conspicuous and characteristic dune crest plant is the sea oat, *Uniola paniculata* (Figs. 6-6 I; 6-10 K; 6-12 I). Sea oats occur along the entire Texas coast, ranging from the backshore to the central vegetated flat of the barrier islands. They are especially prevalent on the upper slopes of the dunes. *Uniola* is the tallest of the dune grasses, easily recognized by the dense nodding clusters of compressed spikelets (Fig. 6-10 K, detail) produced in the late summer and early fall. These tall clumps give the impression that *Uniola* is a bunchgrass, but adjacent clumps are often interconnected by an extensive underground rhizome system. There is almost as much of the plant underground as appears above the surface. Rhizomes and roots anchor and interconnect emergent leaves and culms and thereby help stabilize the dunes. So effective are the rhizomes in holding sand that following severe storms, coppice mounds of *Uniola* may be all that remain of former dune fields.

Only a few other plants occur with *Uniola* on the most exposed dune slopes and crests. Bitter panicum, *Panicum amarum* (Figs. 6-6 J; 6-10 Y; 6-12 G), often occurs here, but is replaced by shoredune panicum (*P. amarulum*) on leeward slopes and in protected depressions. The morning glories are relatively common on windward and leeward dune slopes. Beach tea, *Croton punctatus* (Figs. 6-6 L; 6-10 S; 6-12 H; 6-15 H), a low spreading shrub with a woody base and silvery leaves, is also common on Gulf-facing primary dune slopes, especially on South Padre Island. The light green erect heads of *Amaranthus greggii* (Figs. 6-6 B; 6-14 C) are usually conspicuous along the seaward dune margins in late summer and fall. It is most prevalent along the southern half of the Texas coast and ranges far southward, to the northern Yucatan coast of Mexico (Fig. 6-14 C). Camphor daisy, *Machaeranthera phyllocephala* (Figs. 6-6 E; 6-16 N), and seacoast bluestem, *Schizachyrium scoparium littoralis* (Fig. 6-10 M), are locally common.

All of the plants of the windward slope of the primary dunes also occur on the leeward face, but the relative frequencies of the species are slightly different (Hartman & Smith, 1973; Judd *et al.*, 1977). The relative importance of the morning glories, especially *Ipomoea pes-caprae*, and *Uniola* begin to wane, whereas seacoast bluestem, *Schizachyrium scoparium littoralis*, assumes a somewhat more prominent position in the community, especially on the lower leeward slopes and swales. Bluestem rarely occurs upon the higher dune slopes, having a greater moisture requirement than either *Panicum* or *Uniola* and less tolerance to salt spray than either of the other grasses (Oosting & Billings, 1942; Wagner, 1964).

A number of new plant species are encountered for the first time on the leeward dune slope, significantly increasing floral diversity. Most conspicuous of the ad-ditions include the partridge pea, *Cassia fasciculata* (Figs. 6-6 D; 6-10 P), the snoutbean, *Rhynchosia minima* (Fig. 6-10 R), the beach evening primrose, *Oenothera drummondii* (Figs. 6-6 G; 6-10 O; 6-12 D), and the gulfdune grass, *Paspalum monostachyum* (Fig. 6-10 Q). The sedge, *Fimbristylis castanea* (Figs. 6-12 N; 6-16 E), is locally common in swales. Dense stands of the silverleaf sunflower *Helianthus argophyllus* (Fig. 6-6 H) are common behind the dunes of Mustang and northern Padre Islands. When present, the 2 m tall sunflowers may cover dozens of square meters of sand.

Shoredune panicum (*Panicum amarulum*) is very similar to bitter panicum (*P. amarum*), and considered by some (Palmer, 1972) to be conspecific. It differs, however, in growth habits and ecology. It is only weakly rhizomatous, being primarily a tall (up to 2 m) bunchgrass. Its growth is not stimulated by sand accumulation, preferring instead the protection afforded by moist lowland sites behind the dunes where it readily germinates from seeds. It is especially common leeward of the primary dunes on South Padre Island.

Many insects occur among the dune vegetation, but few of them are wholly beach species. The beach tiger beetles, *Cicindela* sp. (Fig. 6-10 U) are fast flying predators, hunting other smaller insects along the backshore and primary dunes. The larvae are also beach-dwellers, occupying open burrows and feeding upon smaller insects that wander past. Several species of *Cicindela* occur on Texas beaches, and identification usually requires the assistance of an entomological specialist. Mosquitoes are often encountered behind dune ridges, especially in the summer, but a persistent sea breeze in front of the dunes usually keeps these insects off the beach. Similarly, biting flies (Tabanidae) are sometimes encountered among the vegetation behind the dunes. Female horseflies, *Tabanus* spp., and deer flies, *Chrysops* spp. (Fig. 6-10 T), bite a variety of mammals, including humans, and ingest their blood. The male diet is generally restricted to nectar and pollen. The aquatic and semi-aquatic larvae of these flies are predaceous on other insects.

A few other animals occur among the primary dune fields. Larger ghost crabs are often found here, as are specimens of the red land crab *Gecarcinus lateralis* (Figs. 6-10 B1; 6-12 R). The latter is a tropical species reaching the northwesternmost limit of its range along the southern half of Padre Island. When prolonged or particularly cold winter conditions supplant the normally mild south Texas climate, *Gecarcinus* populations are significantly reduced. For example, in December 1983, a particularly severe winter storm pushed icy gusts deep into northern Mexico. Air temperatures at South Padre Island hovered near or below freezing for several days. In August 1984, a census of *Gecarcinus lateralis* from the dunes north of the town of South Padre Island disclosed that the density of this crab had been reduced 80 percent from values determined two years before.

Gecarcinus can avoid brief episodes of cold weather.

Like the ghost crab, it will plug the burrow entrance with sand for insulation (Fig. 6-10 B1). This may be only a temporary solution, especially for *G. lateralis* living high upon the dunes. The reason is related to the method by which this crab respires and the way it has become adapted for terrestrial life.

Gecarcinus respires by gills, but the gill chamber has become highly vascularized and almost like a lung (Bliss, 1968). Nevertheless, the chamber (which lies under the lateral walls of the carapace) remains functionally external and must be kept moist by an external source of water. Many other crabs, including *Ocypode* and the blue land crab *Cardisoma guanhumi* (Fig. 6-10 A1) access water by having a burrow which penetrates the water table. *Gecarcinus* burrows may not reach the water table because, under appropriate conditions, this crab can replace gill cavity water without immersion. Hair-like setae on the bases of the walking legs absorb moisture from water droplets on vegetation and transfer it by capillary action to the gills. In suitable environments such as tropical shores with frequent rains and humid nights that drench vegetation with dew, this nocturnal crab can remoisten its gills each time it forages for food. It can pass many days or even weeks without complete submersion of the gills in standing water.

The adaptations which permit *Gecarcinus* to live far from the sea in tropical climates compromise this species on temperate shores experiencing even mild winters. Dry cold air hastens desiccation, and robs *Gecarcinus* gill chambers of moisture needed for respiration. Crabs in burrows which do not reach the water table must either dig deeper to reach it or leave the underground shelter to seek moisture for their drying gills. The latter places the crab in triple jeopardy. Normal nocturnal foraging will expose the crab to numbing winter cold. If it emerges, it must do so during the relatively warmer day. This exposes the crab to even more rapid desiccation and to predators from which it is hidden by night. Clearly, the respiratory adaptations to free this gill-breathing crustacean from dependence upon standing water operate much more efficiently on the perpetually warm moist tropical shore and in the absence of a winter season.

Gecarcinus lateralis must struggle for existence on Texas barrier islands. It is appropriate, therefore, that we defer additional details concerning the biology and ecology of this land crab to the section on Mexico shores later in this chapter, an environment more typical for the species.

Two lizards are common on the dunes, the keeled earless lizard, *Holbrookia propinqua* (Fig. 6-10 B) and the six-lined racerunner, *Cnemidophorus sexlineatus* (Fig. 6-10 C). *Holbrookia propinqua* is particularly well adapted for the dune habitat, occurring on mainland aeolian sand as well as the barrier island dunes from central Texas to Mexico (Dixon, 1987). It thrives best on the leeward slopes of the primary dunes in densities of about 100 individuals/hectare (Judd, 1976a). Like many lizards, *Holbrookia* defends a territory. Males defend about 300 m² against transgressions by other males, whereas females defend only about 100 m². *Holbrookia* is most common on sands with a 30 to 70 percent vegetation cover; if the sands are bare or cover approaches 100 percent, *Holbrookia* is usually absent. It moves from shade to bare sand, feeding upon insects when in the latter, but seeking the shelter of shrubs and clump grasses to avoid predators and heat. It is an opportunistic insectivore, waiting passively on an exposed dune until an insect comes within reach (Judd, 1976b). Barrier island specimens are cryptically colored to blend with the sand, except during the summer reproductive season when females develop blotches of red and yellow on the sides of the body and hind legs. *Holbrookia* is most active in the morning and late afternoon, although occasionally individuals hunt at midday. During the winter, activity is usually restricted to the warmer afternoons. On cold days they lie inactive, buried in the sand.

A variety of animals feed upon *Holbrookia*, including coyotes, ground squirrels, racerunners, the Rio Grande racer, and several species of gulls. Adult *Holbrookia* are also cannibalistic upon their own juveniles. As a result of heavy predation, the mean life expectancy for this lizard is only about one year.

Cnemidophorus sexlineatus, the six-lined racerunner, is readily distinguished from *Holbrookia* by shape and behavior. It has a more elongate body, protruding snout, and a longer tail than the earless lizard, and is decorated with at least six distinctive lines on the back which course from the neck to the base of the tail. *Cnemidophorus* is most active during mid-morning, constantly flitting from sand to shade as it seeks insects or other small prey. It is not a sit-and-wait predator like *Holbrookia*. Nor does it defend a fixed territory, as its nervous hunting takes it far across the sands. The racerunner is an excellent burrower, and when not hunting insects, it remains inactive under the sand. This lizard occurs with *Holbrookia* on the leeward sides of primary dunes, but it is more common on the central barrier island flats. The tendency for the two species to favor slightly different habitats may be the result of competition for similar resources in a difficult environment.

Texas Barrier Island Flats

Barrier island "flats" occupy the region extending from behind the barrier island dune fields to the bayshores. The distance across an island ranges from a few hundred meters at hurricane washover flats to several kilometers, as at northern Padre Island. The area is not always flat, and actually consists of several different environments. Wind deflation flats, active back-island dunes and washover channels and flats are formed and/or maintained by dynamic atmospheric or hydrologic processes. These areas are characterized by little or no vegetation. In contrast, the vegetated barrier flats and stabilized secondary dunes usually have the densest vegetation cover and greatest floral diversity of the barrier islands. Weise and White (1980) provide an over-

view of the physical processes which create these environments. We will emphasize the biota.

There have been several floral surveys of the Texas barrier islands (Gillespie, 1976, Mustang Island; Hartman & Smith, 1973, Matagorda Island; and Lonard *et al.*, 1978 and Lonard & Judd, 1980, South Padre Island). About 200 plant species occur on each of these islands. Lonard and Judd (1980) list 117 species on South Padre Island introduced by humans. They consider an additional 99 species native to the island, brought there by birds (54.5 percent), oceanic drift (22.2 percent), the wind (3.0 percent) or a combination of these (20.2 percent). About 28 percent of the native South Padre flora are derived from the tropics, and this percentage decreases slightly as one moves northward along the Texas coast. There are only two possible endemics on western Gulf barrier islands (South Padre Island and the Tamaulipan barrier islands of northern Mexico), the grass *Sporobolus tharpii* and the composite *Flaveria brownii*.

The vegetation of the Texas barrier island flats is overwhelmingly dominated by annual and perennial herbs, especially grasses such as seacoast bluestem, *Schizachyrium scoparium littoralis* (Fig. 6-10 M), or coastal dropseed, *Sporobolus virginicus* (Figs. 6-10 J; 6-14 F; 6-15 A), and the sedges *Fimbristylis castanea* (Figs. 6-12 N; 6-16 E), *Dichromena colorata* (Fig. 6-10 L), *Eleocharis albida* (Figs. 6-12 M; 6-16 C) and *E. obtusa*. Bushy beardgrass, *Andropogon glomeratus* (Figs. 6-6 K; 6-10 N; 6-11 F) is common in the lower areas. Marsh grass, *Spartina patens* (Fig. 6-16 P), and sea oats, *Uniola paniculata* (Figs. 6-6 I; 6-10 K; 6-12 I) are locally abundant. Low shrubs such as the partridge pea, *Cassia fasciculata* (Figs. 6-6 D; 6-10 P) are common among the vegetation-stabilized inner dunes. The spindly sea lavender, *Limonium nashii* (Fig. 6-11 N), with its characteristic small pastel purple flowers and spreading basal leaves provides sparse cover on more barren lowland flats. The snoutbean, *Rhynchosia minima* (Fig. 6-10 R), is easily recognized by trifoliate leaves, legumose yellow flowers which develop into seed pods, and a trailing or twining growth form. Several other herbs provide showy yellow flowers, including beach evening primrose *Oenothera drummondii* (Figs. 6-6 G; 6-10 O; 6-12 D), seaside goldenrod *Solidago sempervirens* (Fig. 6-6 A), camphor weed *Heterotheca subaxillaris* (Fig. 6-6 F), camphor daisy *Machaeranthera phyllocephala* (Figs. 6-6 E; 6-16 N), and sea ox-eye daisy *Borrichia frutescens* (Figs. 6-6 C; 6-10 Z). Large prickly pears, *Opuntia lindheimeri* (Fig. 6-10 H), and *O. macrorhiza*, are occasional but conspicuous plants on the southern barrier islands.

There is a striking absence of trees or large woody shrubs on central and southern Texas barrier islands. This is not typical of all barrier islands, as those of comparable size on the Atlantic and eastern Gulf shores usually support oak- or pine-dominated woodlands. The arid climate of central and southern Texas is certainly one factor limiting the development of an extensive shrub or forest climax, but this is probably

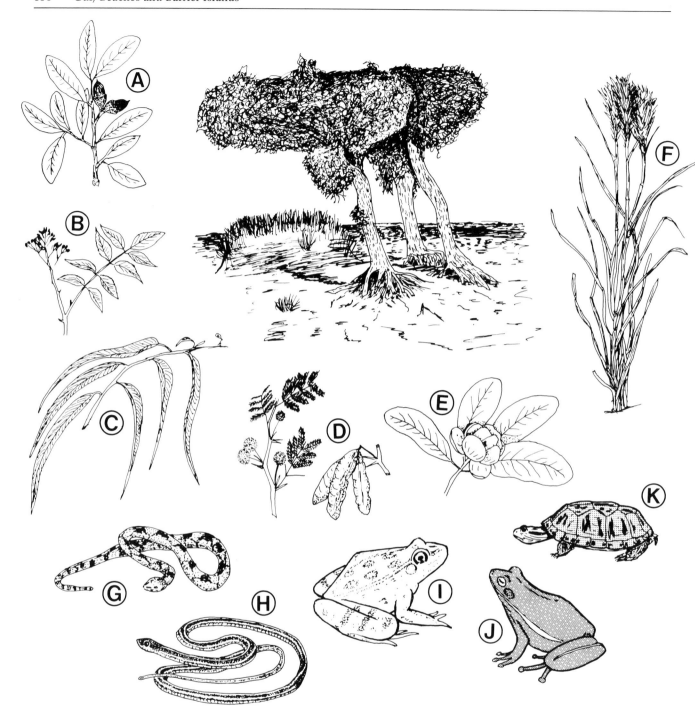

6-11. Biota of a Texas barrier island flat. **A.** Live oak, *Quercus virginiana*; **B.** Prickly-ash, *Zanthoxylum clavaherculis*; **C.** Black willow, *Salix nigra*; **D.** Huisache, *Acacia farnesiana*; **E.** Sweet bay, *Magnolia virginiana*; **F.** Bushy beardgrass, *Andropogon glomeratus*; **G.** Diamond-back water snake, *Nerodia rhombifera*; **H.** Gulf coast ribbon snake, *Thamnophis proximus orarius*; **I.** Rio grand leopard frog, *Rana berlandieri*; **J.** Green tree frog, *Hyla cinerea*; **K.** Red-eared turtle, *Chrysemys scripta elegans*; **L.** Pocket gopher, *Geomys personatus*; **M.** Hispid cotton rat, *Sigmodon hispidus*; **N.** Sea lavender, *Limonium nashii*. Habitat: Oakmotte.

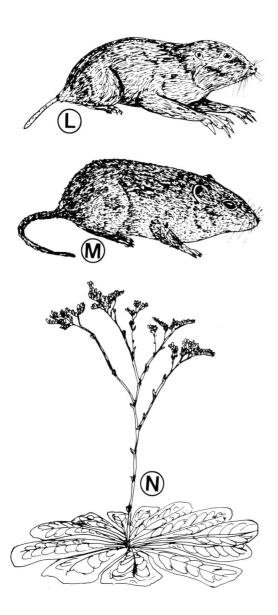

not the only responsible factor, as trees are not absent from barrier islands of the region. For example, moderately dense stands of mesquite (*Prosopis* sp.) reaching heights of 3 m occur on the barrier islands of northern Mexico (Selander *et al.*, 1962). Mesquite likely was introduced on the Tamaulipan islands as propagules spread by livestock. Cattle also grazed many of the Texas islands for at least 100 years, but mesquite never became established here, despite its abundance on the adjacent mainland. Clearly, the Texas island habitat is not conducive for the development of the mesquite-dominated thorn-scrub woodland, nor do other trees fare well here.

The earliest records of exploration along the Texas coast emphasize a general absence of trees, although a few live oak mottes (oak groves surrounded by sandy grasslands) are occasionally mentioned. These mottes, although never extensive, may have been somewhat better developed prior to the present century. On Padre Island they seem to have been best developed on the north end, diminishing in number and size southward (Dahl *et al.*, 1974). Live oak, *Quercus virginiana* (Fig. 6-11 A), was the largest, most conspicuous tree of the motte, but the woodland also included prickly-ash, *Zanthoxylum clava-herculis* (Fig. 6-11 B), sweet bay, *Magnolia virginiana* (Fig. 6-11 E), huisache, *Acacia farnesiana* (Fig. 6-11 D), and occasional black willows, *Salix nigra* (Fig. 6-11 C). If they were ever extensive during the late Pleistocene or early Holocene, by historical times the mottes were no more than minor island habitats (Fig. 6-11). During the last 100 years, they have almost disappeared, reduced to only a few living oaks and sand-covered stumps. Humans or livestock probably contributed to the decline of the mottes, but the record is not clear on this point. Suffice it to say that oak mottes of Texas barrier islands were ephemeral oases waxing and waning in a marginal habitat, and today they are virtually gone.

Few marine animals find suitable living conditions on the barrier island flats, save the semi-terrestrial crabs. The red land crab, *Gecarcinus lateralis*, was discussed in the previous section, and when present, it is equally at home on the barrier island flats as among the vegetation-stabilized dunes. The mangrove crab, *Cardisoma guanhumi* (Fig. 6-10 A1), is much less common, but a few of its burrows sometimes fringe marshes on southern Padre Island or lie along suitable southern Texas bayshores. The burrows may exceed 20 cm in diameter, and are frequently mistaken as the work of a large mammal. The excavator is rarely seen, for this nocturnal crab is extremely shy.

Like *Gecarcinus*, *Cardisoma* lives on Padre Island at the extreme edge of its range. Its burrows are always near water, for it must moisten its gills at least once each day by submersion. Thus, *Cardisoma* burrows always penetrate the water table. The mangrove crab is rare on Padre Island, in part due to unsuitable winter chills, but also because this island provides much less vegetational shelter than the crab normally prefers. Large *Cardisoma* communities are common on southern Gulf and Caribbean shores where mangroves merge with the terrestrial forest, close enough to the sea that burrows easily reach water, but where the land stays dry for all but the highest tides. There are no large *Cardisoma* communities on Padre Island. Isolated individuals exiled here by chance larval dispersal roam the flats at night, but rarely stray far from the protection of their gaping burrows. *Cardisoma* is the largest semi-terrestrial crab of the western Gulf and Caribbean region, sometimes reaching a carapace width of 18 cm. We will consider additional aspects of its biology in Chapter 9.

Amphibians and Reptiles

A remarkable diversity of typically terrestrial animals occupies the barrier island flats, despite the generally inhospitable nature of this environment. Several reptiles and amphibians are commonly found near shallow marshes or pools of standing water. The Rio Grande leopard frog, *Rana berlandieri* (Fig. 6-11 I), red-eared turtle, *Chrysemys scripta elegans* (Fig. 6-11 K), and diamond-backed water snake, *Nerodia rhombifera* (Fig. 6-11 G), are often seen in the water, whereas the green tree frog, *Hyla cinerea* (Fig. 6-11 J), and Hurter's spadefoot toad, *Scaphiopus holbrooki hurteri*, are usually nearby. The Gulf coast ribbon snake, *Thamnophis proximus orarius* (Fig. 6-11 H) and eastern checkered garter snake, *T. marcianus marcianus*, are important predators of the adult amphibians and their tadpoles.

Three venomous snakes are permanent residents of the barrier islands. The western diamondback rattlesnake, *Crotalus atrox* (Fig. 6-10 A), and western massasauga, *Sistrurus catenatus tergeminus*, are usually more common than their infrequent human encounters indicate. The true abundance of these pit vipers becomes apparent following a tropical storm or hurricane, when high water drives hundreds of them from their underground shelters. Both rattlesnakes feed primarily upon rodents. The only other poisonous reptile, the Texas coral snake, *Micrurus fulvius tenere*, is an occasional inhabitant of the barrier islands, decreasing in abundance from north to south and east to west.

Several other species of nonvenomous snakes occur commonly on the central barrier island flats. The western coachwhip, *Masticophis flagellum testaceus*, one of the fastest snakes in North America, actively chases prey, capturing lizards and small rodents. The Mexican racer, *Coluber constrictor oaxaca*, has a similar diet, but also relies upon insects for food. Two snakes, the Mexican milk snake, *Lampropeltis triangulum annulata*, and the Mexican glossy snake, *Arizona elegans arenicola*, rely upon an acute sense of smell to track down sleeping lizards buried in the sand. Both will also take small or juvenile rodents. The flathead snake, *Tantilla gracilis*, is primarily a burrower, feeding upon soil insects. The slender glass lizard, *Ophisaurus attenuatus*, a legless lizard, looks like a snake, and lives in the soil below the vegetation of the barrier flat.

Mammals

Lagomorphs and rodents dominate the native mammalian fauna of the barrier island flats. The former is represented by the black-tailed jackrabbit, *Lepus californicus* (Fig. 6-6 V), on the central and southern islands, and by the cottontail, *Sylvilagus floridanus*, and swamp rabbit, *S. aquaticus*, in eastern Texas. The most conspicuous rodents are the ground squirrels. The spotted ground squirrel, *Spermophilus spilosoma annectens* (Fig. 6-6 M), occurs from central Padre Island northward to Mustang Island, whereas the Mexican ground squirrel, *S. mexicanus*, is restricted to the southern half of Padre Island. Ground squirrels occur throughout central island habitats and even dig burrows on the windward slopes of the primary dunes. Perhaps the most successful rodents of the central flats are the pocket gophers, *Geomys*. Three species occupy the Texas coastal zones, *G. personatus* (Fig. 6-11 L) on Padre and Mustang Islands, *G. attwateri* along the central Texas coast, and *G. breviceps* from the mouth of the Colorado River eastward. All spend most of their lives underground in shallow burrows constructed in the loose sandy soil.

Several species of rats and mice occupy the vegetation-stabilized dunes and flats, including the Padre Island kangaroo rat, *Dipodomys compactus* (Fig. 6-6 P), the hispid cotton rat, *Sigmodon hispidus* (Fig. 6-11 M), the marsh rice rat, *Oryzomys palustris*, the pygmy mouse, *Baiomys taylori* (Fig. 6-6 Q), and the short-tailed grasshopper mouse, *Onychomys leucogaster*. The ubiquitous rodent pest of human habitations, the Norway rat, *Rattus norvegicus* (Fig. 6-6 R), is, of course, also present.

The coyote, *Canis latrans* (Fig. 6-6 U) is the most common mammalian carnivore on the Texas islands. As elsewhere, it has adapted well to the influx of humans. It is as at home on the treeless flats of central Padre Island as it is in the shadows of multistory condominiums on the outskirts of the towns of Port Aransas or South Padre Island. While researching this book, the authors observed a coyote for several minutes early one autumn morning from the window of a hotel room overlooking a south Padre Island barrier flat. The young coyote was obviously tempted to investigate a nearby kitchen dumpster, but eventually decided the dawn was too far advanced. Doubtless it would return the next evening. Local island residents testify that coyotes are common on the fringes of barrier island towns.

Mexico Barrier Islands

The dunes, flora and fauna of the sandy barrier islands separating Laguna Madre de Tamaulipas from the Gulf of Mexico are similar to those just described for Texas, so we will not dwell upon them here. Southward from La Pesca, Mexico, at the southern termination of the Laguna Madre system, the coastal vegetation increasingly reflects tropical dominion, but temperate influences persist far into Mexico. Arctic cold fronts or "nortes" sweep deeply into tropical Mexico each winter, pulsing strong gusty winds through the region. Rains are left behind in subtropical Texas. From Tampico to Veracruz, winter is a dry, sometimes windy season. The nortes remind us that the central Gulf lies within a transitional zone, or climatic convergence. High, destructive waves pushed ashore by the northerly winds are more important in sculpting Mexico's sandy Gulf beaches than the gentle breakers which arise from the persistent prevailing southeasterlies. The seasonal windshifts also induce temporary directional changes in nearshore currents. These and other factors contribute to the geomorphological complexity of Mexico beaches and the diversity of the coastal vegetation upon them. For example, many of the coastal strand plants colonize new shores by wind- or water-borne seeds. The shifting winter winds and currents insure that the central Gulf of Mexico beaches are supplied from both temperate and tropical sources. Thus, the coastal vegetation of central Mexico retains much of the flora of the Texas barrier islands and adds several new tropical components which are rarely seen on Texas shores.

The largest sandy barrier of eastern central Mexico is Cabo Rojo (Fig. 6-12). We will focus upon its vegetation as our example of a coastal flora in the temperate-to-tropical transition. Cabo Rojo arises as a sandy spit immediately south of Tampico and extends toward the southeast for a distance of about 90 km. The extreme eastern point of the cape lies about 30 km off mainland Mexico. Here the shore makes an abrupt bend, trending just west of north for about 40 km until it again approaches the mainland, but remains separated from it by a tidal inlet. The cape is narrowest to the north, immediately after it departs from the mainland. Here it is but a few hundred meters wide. The greatest width of about 4 km occurs just north of the easternmost point.

Gulf-facing shores of Cabo Rojo consist primarily of unconsolidated sands. They persist across half to two-thirds of the barrier strand. Eventually, the substratum changes from sand to organic clays and silts, the latter produced by mangroves along the shores of Laguna de Tamiahua (Cruz, 1968). We will restrict this discussion to those areas nearest the Gulf beach and dominated by a substratum of nutrient-poor, relatively unconsolidated sands.

The beach slope and morphology of Cabo Rojo varies considerably according to its location and degree of exposure. Foreshores along much of the cape grade into elevated, poorly vegetated backshore flats ranging in width from 10 to more than 100 m. Dunes are common behind the backshore. Sands are lofted upon these dunes along the northern sections of Cabo Rojo by the prevailing east-southeasterly winds of spring and summer. The gusty nortes move these sands southward in the winter. Since the strongest winds and waves striking Cabo Rojo (aside from tropical storms or hurricanes) are produced by the winter nortes, the northern beaches have steep slopes, rela-

tively coarse sands and low dunes. The latter increase in size toward the south, until they reach maximum elevations of about 30 m just north of the Cabo Rojo elbow. The southern limb of Cabo Rojo angles back toward the mainland. It is shielded from accumulating sands during winter nortes by the mangrove forest fringing Laguna de Tamiahua. Beaches composed of relatively fine sands rise gradually from the sea along the southern limb of Cabo Rojo. They often grade into broad, low, nearly barren backshores. The southern beaches provide a monotonous face generally devoid of a diversity of microhabitats, whereas the northern beaches are geomorphologically diverse with numerous microhabitats (Poggie, 1963). These differences are reflected in the flora.

Only a few species of plants characterize the southern beaches of Cabo Rojo, most of which also occur on the Texas beaches. *Ipomoea pes-caprae* (Fig. 6-12 Q), *Ipomoea stolonifera* (Fig. 6-12 P) and *Croton punctatus* (Fig. 6-12 H) are the most common. These plants are well adapted for life upon the unprotected barren sands of the southern beaches. Trailing morning glories approach the foreshore much closer than the more shrub-like *Croton*, but rarely closer than about 30 m. The sedges *Eleocharis albida* (Fig. 6-12 M) and *Fimbristylis castanea* (Fig. 6-12 N) and the grasses *Paspalum distichum* (Fig. 6-12 F) and *Sporobolus virginicus* are commonly associated with backshore swales. The partridge pea, *Cassia cinerea* (Fig. 6-12 E; a different species from that of Texas beaches), the beach primrose *Oenothera drummondii* (Fig. 6-12 D), and the tropical *Hibiscus tiliaceus* are occasionally found on slightly elevated ridges. The larger shrubs or small tropical trees common on the northern beaches are uncommon on the southern portion of Cabo Rojo.

Poggie (1963) found only 12 species of plants on the southern beaches of Cabo Rojo, but 25 species on the northern shores, including several not found to the south. The increased habitat diversity of the northern beaches apparently accounts for the increased species diversity. More importantly, 60 percent of the plants on the northern beaches of Cabo Rojo, especially those of the dunes and back-dune areas, are tropical species rarely found on the Texas beaches. The backshore flats of the northern beaches are usually as sparsely vegetated as those of the southern beaches. *Ipomoea pes-caprae* and *I. stolonifera* are the first encountered, lying 30 to 50 m from the foreshore. Several additional plants occur near the base of the dunes, including the creepers *Sesuvium portulacastrum* (Fig. 6-12 L) and *Canavalia maritima* (Fig. 6-12 O), the grasses *Uniola paniculata* (Fig. 6-12 I), *Sporobolus virginicus*, and *Panicum amarum* (Fig. 6-12 G), and the herbs *Croton punctatus* and *Oenothera drummondii*. These plants are not as abundant as the list might suggest, as any specific locality will yield only a few species.

On temperate Gulf shores *Uniola paniculata* usually is the dominant plant of the dune crests, but on Cabo Rojo this grass yields to several tropical woody shrubs or small trees. Among these, the sea grape *Coc-*

coloba uvifera (Fig. 6-12 A) is the most common on the northern cape. The sea grape is a tree growing to heights of 10 m on central Caribbean shores, but on Cabo Rojo, it rarely exceeds 2 m in height. Fan-like leaves and reddish woody branches usually form a low, dense tangle along seaward dune crests. This coastal thicket provides excellent cover for large colonies of the land crab *Gecarcinus lateralis*, which riddle the sand with numerous burrows. The sea grape is dioecious, bearing elongate racemes of small, fragrant tubular male or female flowers on separate plants. The flowers on female trees produce green, fleshy grape-like edible seeds.

Sea grapes may be the only plants on the Cabo Rojo dune crests, but more frequently they share this habitat with several other woody plants. Notable among these are the box-briar, *Randia laetevirens* (Fig. 6-12 K), with persistent opposite leaves and spiny branches; *Scaevola plumieri* (Fig. 6-12 J), with asymmetrical white flowers and black, olive-sized fruits; the cocoa plum, *Chrysobalanus icaco* (Fig. 6-12 C), with small white flowers and large (3–5 cm diameter) white to purplish edible fruits; and the buttonwood, *Conocarpus erectus* (Fig. 6-12 B), with characteristic clusters of spherical cone-like fruits on the tree at all seasons. Each of these plants are tropical species rarely encountered on temperate Gulf shores.

The marine fauna on Gulf-facing beaches of the Mexico barrier islands is similar to that of Texas shores. *Donax, Emerita,* and *Callichirus* dominate the foreshore, and *Ocypode* is the primary inhabitant of the backshore. *Gecarcinus lateralis* (Fig. 6-12 R), no longer at the limit of its geographical range, is represented by large populations in suitable areas on the dunes or vegetated flats. This land crab prefers sandy ground with at least moderate cover (Britton *et al.,* 1982). The stunted sea grape thickets on the dunes

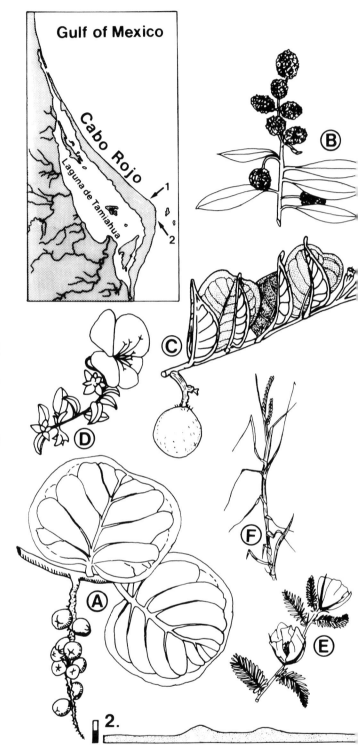

6-12. The sandy beach at Cabo Rojo, Veracruz, Mexico. **A.** Sea grape, *Coccoloba uvifera;* **B.** Buttonwood, *Conocarpus erectus;* **C.** Cocoa plum, *Chrysobalanus icaco;* **D.** Beach evening primrose, *Oenothera drummondii;* **E.** Partridge pea, *Cassia cinerea;* **F.** Knotgrass, *Paspalum distichum;* **G.** Bitter panicum, *Panicum amarum;* **H.** Beach tea, *Croton punctatus;* **I.** Sea oats, *Uniola paniculata;* **J.** *Scaevola plumieri;* **K.** Box-briar, *Randia laetevirens;* **L.** Sea purslane, *Sesuvium portulacastrum;* **M.** Sedge, *Eleocharis albida;* **N.** Sedge, *Fimbristylis castanea;* **O.** Bay bean, *Canavalia maritima;* **P.** White morning glory, *Ipomoea stolonifera;* **Q.** Railroad vine, *Ipomoea pescaprae;* **R.** Red land crab, *Gecarcinus lateralis;* **S.** Ghost crab, *Ocypode quadrata;* **T.** Mole crab, *Emerita portoricensis;* **U.** Coquina clam, *Donax variabilis roemeri;* **V.** Coquina clam, *Donax texasiana.* Locations of shore profiles (1, 2) are indicated on regional inset map. Scales indicate meters.

along northern Cabo Rojo are ideal habitats, but *Gecarcinus* can be found under a variety of other low trees or shrubs. It avoids most of the backshore except during reproductive migrations, and thereby minimizes overlap with *Ocypode.*

Gecarcinus mates during the summer months. The female does not require a molt prior to copulation with a male, and probably mates two or three times each year. After the female receives spermatophores from the male, each egg is fertilized within the maternal body and enclosed within a chitinous capsule. They are then transferred from the female reproductive system to abdominal pleopods, where they are carried for two to three weeks and undergo the early stages of development. Gravid females are easily recognized by the large masses of eggs held beneath the abdomen. The eggs darken to a reddish brown as development proceeds.

Mating, early development and the release of eggs from the female abdomen apparently are regulated by lunar cycles. Female *Gecarcinus* migrate to the surf during darkness of the new moons of summer to release eggs into the sea (Bliss & Sprague, 1958; Bliss *et al.*, 1978). Unlike other closely related species (e.g., the larger *Gecarcinus ruricola* of the tropical Caribbean) the seaward movements of female *G. lateralis* rarely focus on specific beaches or involve large aggregations of crabs. Instead, individuals apparently move to the nearest available shore. Upon entering the surf, the female vigorously agitates her abdomen with each incoming wave, freeing thousands of eggs into the sea. Contact with water stimulates the egg capsules to rupture, releasing zoea larvae which are swept seaward with the backwash. As with all meroplankton, there is high mortality among these larvae while at sea. The survivors continue development for several weeks, and, eventually, when the appropriate developmental stage is reached, juvenile crabs return to the shore.

THE SANDY GULF BEACHES OF YUCATAN

The Yucatan peninsula is composed primarily of limestone bedrock originally deposited by a variety of carbonate-secreting organisms in a tropical sea. The sands formed by these rocks are fundamentally different from any we have discussed so far. Texas beach sands and those of central Mexico contain some limestone shell debris, but most is derived from erosion of terrestrial rocks consisting of siliceous particles or heavy minerals fragmented by riverine transport. The source rocks of northern Gulf beach sands often lie far inland from the shore and are usually geologically ancient. The source rocks for most Yucatan sands are formed by marine processes that are still active in the region today and, thus, are geologically young. Many of the sand grains on northern Yucatan beaches were the skeletons of a variety of plants or animals just a few years before. The carbonate framework of several species of calcareous green algae (e.g., *Halimeda*), Foraminifera, Scleractinia, Mollusca and Echinodermata contribute greatly to the Yucatan beach sands. Particle sizes are larger and the beach fabric more coarse than usually encountered on northern Gulf beaches.

Yucatan is poorly supplied with rivers or unconsolidated alluvium. Its soils are thin, chalky and often hardened by surface weathering. Sandy beaches are thin veneers of unconsolidated debris over a bedrock base. Even in the absence of sand the coastal strand is typically narrow. Sandy beaches are widest and steepest along the southwestern and northeastern margins of the peninsula (Fig. 6-13 A & F). Beaches facing the Bay of Campeche along Isla del Carmen and Isla Aguada typically are 12 m or more in width, have a slope in excess of 7°, and are composed of coarse sand and, near tidal inlets, considerable shell debris (Fig. 6-13 F). From Isla Aguada to Champoton the sandy shore narrows significantly (Fig. 6-13 E), eventually yielding to a narrow limestone platform and a thin veneer of sand near Campeche (Fig. 6-13 D). From Campeche to Celestun the shore is dominated by mangroves (Fig. 6-13 C).

Northeastward from Celestun to Cabo Catoche, a distance of well over 200 km, the beach is again primarily a veneer of sand over limestone bedrock. Along the western half of northern Yucatan, the beach rarely exceeds 6 m in width (Fig. 6-13 B), except where it has been artificially widened by clearing vegetation from dune ridges and redistributing the sand, as at the resort community of Progreso. Along most of the northern Yucatan shore, a distinctive vertical escarpment, created by wave activity acting at the highest part of the tide, rises 0.3 to 1.3 m and demarcates the foreshore from the natural backshore beach margin. The latter is eventually succeeded shorewards by the vegetation-stabilized dune ridges (Figs. 6-13 A & B, 6-14, and 6-15).

Eastward toward Cabo Catoche, the beach gradually becomes wider, and steeper. At Las Coloradas, for example, the beach has a width of about 20 m and a slope of about 5° (Fig. 6-13 A). Here a distinctive vegetation-stabilized dune ridge rises to about 4 m above sea level. Although active dunes are generally absent along most of the Yucatan shore, one to several low, sandy ridges frequently persist inland from the beach.

6-13. Shore profiles of the Yucatan Peninsula, Mexico. **A.** Sandy beach at Las Coloradas, Yucatan, Mexico (see Fig. 6-15); **B.** Sandy beach about 2 km E. of Chicxulub Puerto, near Progreso, Yucatan, Mexico (see Fig. 6-14); **C.** Mangrove-fringed shore about 20 km N of Campeche, Campeche, Mexico; **D.** Low limestone platform about 20 km S of Campeche, Campeche, Mexico (see Fig. 4-3); **E.** Narrow sandy beach about 35 km SW of Champoton, Campeche, Mexico; **F.** Sandy beach about 1 km NE of termination of Isla Aguada peninsula, Campeche, Mexico. Vertical scales indicate meters.

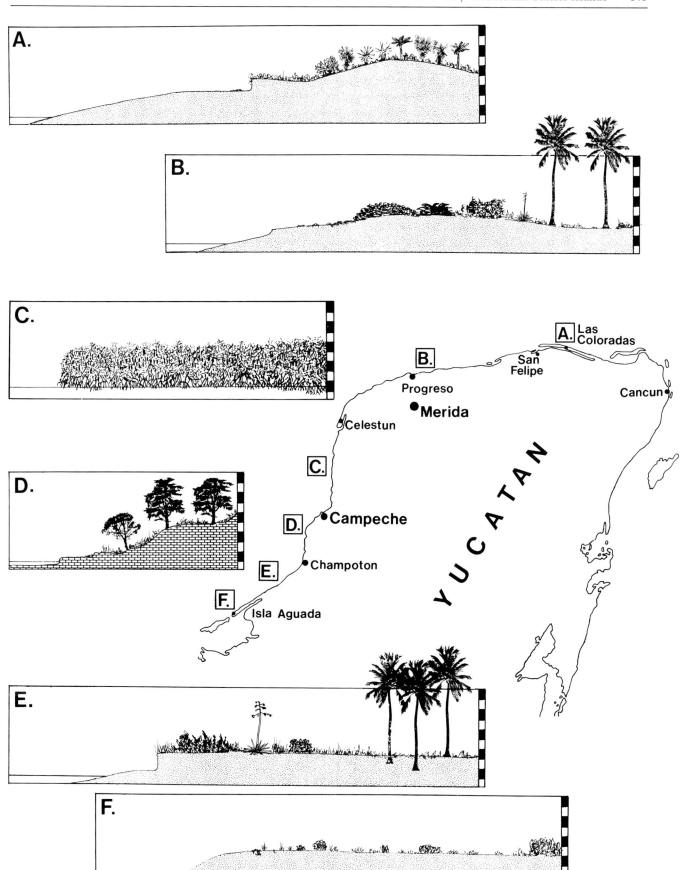

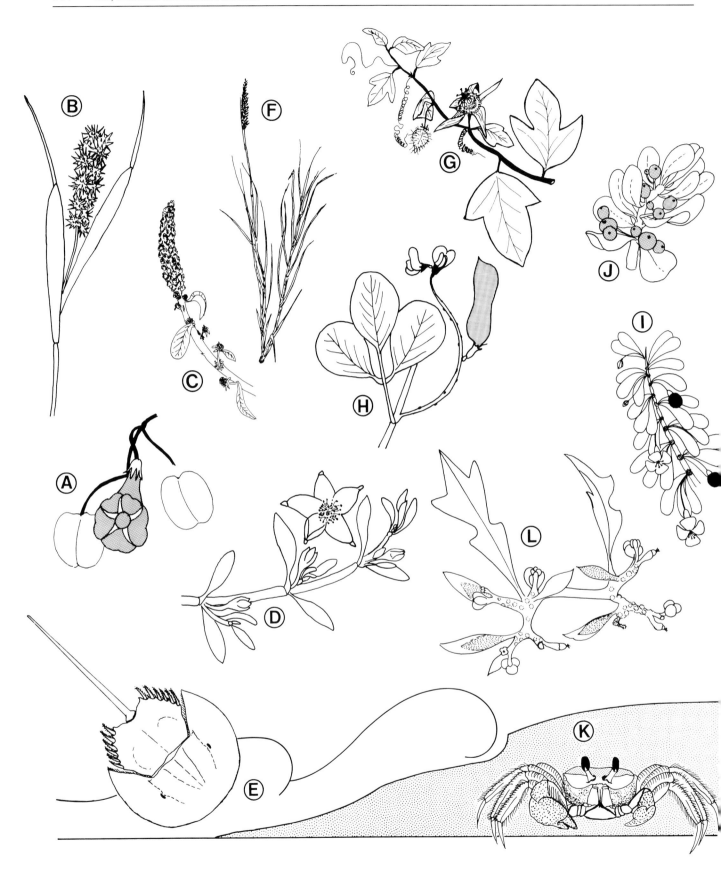

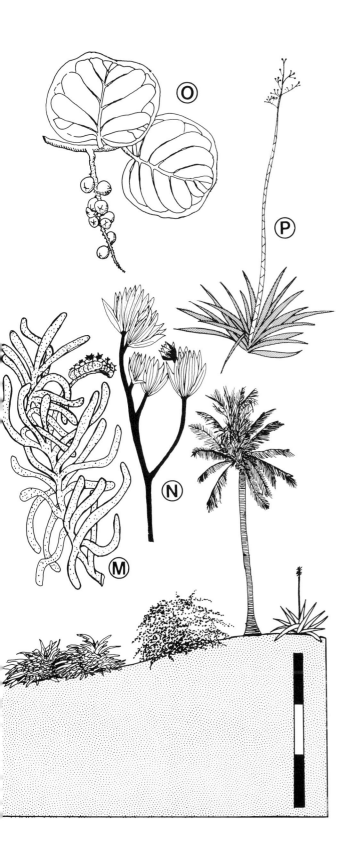

These features are readily apparent from the air, especially along the northeast and northwest margins of the peninsula, but are almost impossible to recognize from the ground because they are well covered and stabilized by maritime and/or terrestrial vegetation.

Maritime floral diversity landward from the unvegetated coastal strand is high. There is a subtle transition of species, especially among the secondary floral elements, from the south central coast (e.g., Isla del Carmen) to the northeastern region (Cabo Catoche or Las Coloradas). Yet, the Yucatan flora has received insufficient comprehensive modern treatment (Standley, 1930; Sauer, 1967), and the identification of some of even the most common plants is, at best, tentative. With a few exceptions, we will emphasize the most common, easily identifiable species that occur on or near northern Yucatan beaches. Despite this limitation, the dominance of tropical plants over temperate species will be obvious, although a few of the latter (e.g., *Sporobolus virginicus*, *Amaranthus greggii*, or *Lycium carolinianum*) persist on these shores.

The trailing vines or creepers such as *Ipomoea pes-caprae* (Fig. 6-14 A), *I. stolonifera* and *Sesuvium portulacastrum* (Figs. 6-14 D; 6-15 K) remain the seaward-most pioneer plants of Yucatan beaches. The morning glories seem to be more common from Isla Aguada to Progreso than along the northeastern barrier islands of Yucatan. Near the rear of the backshore, they are often joined by the coastal dropseed *Sporobolus virginicus* (Figs. 6-14 F; 6-15 A), the sand bur *Cenchrus incertus* (Fig. 6-14 B), and the bay bean *Canavalia maritima* (Fig. 6-14 H). Carpet weeds of the Euphorbiaceae are locally abundant.

The Yucatan backshore often terminates in a zone of halophytic herbs and shrubs. This zone is relatively diffuse along Isla del Carmen and Isla Aguada, arising 10 m shoreward of the surf zone and at an elevation of 3 m above sea level (Fig. 6-13). From Celestun to San Felipe along the northern coast, the backshore rises little more than 1.5 m above sea level and terminates abruptly in a definite escarpment, ranging from 0.5 to 1.5 m in height (Fig. 6-13 B). A relatively dense vegetation cover, consisting of many shrubs, herbs, and a few woody plants, arises landward of the escarpment.

6-14. The sandy beach near Progreso, Yucatan, Mexico. **A.** Railroad vine, *Ipomoea pes-caprae*; **B.** Sand bur, *Cenchrus incertus*; **C.** Coastal pigweed, *Amaranthus greggii*; **D.** Sea purslane, *Sesuvium portulacastrum*; **E.** Horseshoe crab, *Limulus polyphemus*; **F.** Coastal dropseed, *Sporobolus virginicus*; **G.** Passion flower, *Passiflora foetida*; **H.** Bay bean, *Canavalia maritima*; **I.** Wolfberry, *Lycium carolinianum*; **J.** Scaevola plumieri; **K.** Ghost crab, *Ocypode quadrata*; **L.** *Poinsettia cyanthophora*; **M.** Sea lavender, *Tournefortia gnaphalodes*; **N.** Bay cedar, *Suriana maritima*; **O.** Sea grape, *Coccoloba uvifera*; **P.** *Agave* sp. Vertical scale indicates meters.

Light green stands of *Amaranthus greggii* (Fig. 6-14 C) frequently line the seaward margin of the shrub zone. Thereafter, large clumps of the tropical shrubs *Scaevola plumieri* (Fig. 6-14 J), *Tournefortia gnaphalodes* (Fig. 6-14 M) and/or *Suriana maritima* (Fig. 6-14 N) are prominent and differentiated easily. *Scaevola* has glossy, dark, mostly alternate green leaves, numerous white flowers which are open to the base on one side, and black spherical drupes (fruits) about 1 cm in diameter. Branches of the sea lavender, *Tournefortia gnaphalodes*, are densely covered by light gray-green, succulent leaves bearing a velvety pubescence. The branches terminate in recurving cymes bearing numerous tiny white flowers along one side. Sea lavender fruits are also black drupes about half as large as those of *Scaevola*. Bay cedar, *Suriana maritima* occurs on sandy beaches throughout the tropical Gulf and Caribbean. Its fleshy pubescent leaves form crowns at the ends of branches and often conceal small yellow flowers. *Jacquinia aurantiaca* (Fig. 6-15 I) is a small tree of inland Yucatan and Central America, but is commonly encountered within the shrub zone along the northern coast, where it rarely grows over 2 m tall. It bears orange flowers, ovate, spine-tipped leaves, and spherical fruits containing many seeds.

Other, somewhat smaller, shrubs also occur here. Beach tea, *Croton punctatus* (Fig. 6-15 H) is among the most common. The sea rocket, *Cakile lanceolata* (Fig. 6-15 F) and the sea blite, *Suaeda linearis* (Fig. 6-15 B) are occasionally found here. Numerous other small trailing, creeping or low-standing plants occupy the areas between the larger shrubs. The wolfberry or Christmas berry, *Lycium carolinianum* (Figs. 6-14 I; 6-15 G), is a sprawling woody shrub with long branches that often trail upon the sand. The spiny branches bear pale blue flowers in the summer that develop into bright red berries in the fall. The bright green lacy leaves of the coastal ragweed, *Ambrosia hispida* (Fig. 6-15 E), are especially apparent, arising from prostrate stems that extend 3 or 4 meters across the sand. A relative of the partridge pea seen on Texas shores also occurs here, *Cassia* sp. (Fig. 6-15 C).

Other plants found between the shrubs are derived primarily from inland habitats. Among these are the passion flower, *Passiflora foetida* (Fig. 6-14 G), the euphorb, *Poinsettia cyanthophora* (Fig. 6-14 L), and the distinctive Turk's cap, *Malvaviscus arboreus* (Fig. 6-15 D). Passion flowers are prostrate vines that cling by tendrils to other plants. This species bears trilobed leaves and ornate white or lavender flowers. The fruits are sheathed by a fuzzy membranous capsule that contains seeds and a mucilaginous pulp. When new, the fruits are green, but age to red. *Poinsettia cyanthophora* is a spindly herb reaching a meter or more in height. Like many of the euphorbs, it weeps a milky sap when leaf petioles or branches are broken. The upper lanceolate leaves often bear bright red blotches near their basal portions, but this species never attains the uniformly red leaves of the closely related poinsettia of horticulture. The Turk's cap is a native Cen-

tral American plant which has been spread widely throughout the world by horticulturists. It is a close relative to the hibiscus, its bright red flower differing from the latter in being smaller, and having its petals clasping around the distinctive elongate style. In addition to these three examples, several dozen additional species could be cited as occasional residents of the shrub-dominated sandy coastal ridges.

The shrub zone sometimes terminates in woody thickets of sea grapes, *Coccoloba uvifera* (Figs. 6-14 O; 6-15 J). Under favorable conditions, these trees attain normal dimensions on northern Yucatan beaches, growing to as much as 7 m in height. More commonly, however, they are stunted like the sea grapes of Cabo Rojo, and even occur intermingled among the smaller shrubs. Near population centers, sea grape thickets have been removed to make room for coastal development. A number of ornamental plants have been relocated here, especially a variety of palms including coconuts.

The coastal strand of Yucatan, like that of most of the Gulf beaches, is largely a disturbed shoreline, altered significantly from its original condition by human activity. There is one area, only recently been made accessible by highway, that still offers a glimpse of Yucatan shores as the Mayans before Columbus might have seen them. At Las Coloradas, near San Felipe and Rio Lagartos in northeastern Yucatan (Fig. 6-15), Mexico has established a national park and seashore. Except for a large salt mine near its center, the barrier island lies relatively undisturbed. Broad dune ridges are covered by a tropical xerophytic plant community dominated by several small palms and large succulents. The sisal or hemp agave *Agave sisalana* (Fig. 6-15 L), intensely cultivated for its fiber throughout central Yucatan and the principal cash crop of the region, grows wild at Las Coloradas. It shares the upper dune ridges with other agaves (e.g., *Agave* sp., Fig. 6-14 P), sea grapes, thatch palms, *Thrinax* sp. (Fig. 6-15 O), and an attractive short palm, *Pseudophoenix sargentii* (Fig. 6-15 N), the most conspicuous plant of the region. Smaller succulents including the cacti *Opuntia dillenii* (Fig. 6-15 R) and *Cereus pentagonus* (Fig 6-15 Q) are also common here. Growing between the palms and succulents, *Lantana involucrata* (Fig. 6-15 M) is the dominant shrub on the dune ridges behind the beach. Many of the shrubs and vines mentioned in preceding paragraphs are also here. This unique community at Las Coloradas offers exciting opportunities for ecological investigation, but unfortunately it has received virtually no study.

The fauna of the sandy beach strand offers little that we have not discussed before. In addition to the two species of *Donax* which characterize the northern Gulf shores, a third species, *Donax denticulatus* (Fig. 6-15 S), appears on the easternmost beaches of Cabo Catoche. This is the primary *Donax* species of the Caribbean, and it rarely makes an appearance on Gulf beaches. Mole crabs are present here, but seem to be less common than we have previously observed. Ghost crabs are as common on these shores as they are on other Gulf beaches, and the land crab *Gecarcinus lateralis* is locally abundant. At Las Coloradas, a small lizard, *Sceloporus* sp. (Fig. 6-15 P), lives on the sand below the vegetation. It likely occupies a niche similar to that of *Holbrookia propinqua* on the Texas barrier islands.

There is one animal often seen on Yucatan beaches that we have not previously encountered. The horseshoe crab, *Limulus polyphemus* (Fig. 6-14 E), is a common inhabitant of sandy Atlantic shores from Nova Scotia to Florida, except that it is absent from southern Florida, the Caribbean, and the northwestern Gulf of Mexico east of Mobile, Alabama. (A small population has become established in Galveston Bay, Texas, as a result of an introduction by humans.) Thus, it is somewhat surprising to find horseshoe crabs along the Mexico shore. They occur just off the entire northern Yucatan coast and southward at least to Isla de Carmen. They normally occur subtidally, just offshore, but briefly congregate on protected intertidal beaches for mating and egg laying in the spring and summer (Rudloe & Herrkind, 1976; Rudloe, 1978; Cohen & Brockmann, 1983).

Female horseshoe crabs come ashore during the highest spring tides to lay their eggs. In some localities, the shoreward migration usually occurs at night, especially during a new moon (Rudloe & Herrkind, 1976; Rudloe, 1978), but we observed this migration one mid-afternoon in early January just north of Champoton, Campeche, not only confirming the report by Cohen & Brockmann (1983), but also suggesting a longer or different breeding season for tropical populations.

As the females reach shallow water, smaller males seek, climb upon and cling to them. Each female then crawls with the attached male to a place on the foreshore touched only by the highest spring tides. Here she excavates shallow depressions in the sand into which she deposits thousands of eggs. Until this point, the male has been a passive partner, but as the eggs are deposited, he fertilizes them. With the completion of egg laying and fertilization, which may take an hour or more, the male releases the female, and both return to the sea.

A few waves of the spring tide bury the eggs under a couple of centimeters of sand, but as the tide recedes, the clutch is left to develop undisturbed by most waves. Development proceeds for a fortnight within the sun-warmed sandy incubator. The next spring tides release them from burial and wash them to sea where seawater stimulates the eggs to hatch. Tiny trilobite larvae (so-named because of their resemblance to an ancient, now extinct, arthropod group) emerge and remain near the bottom as they grow and develop through a series of molts into adult horseshoe crabs.

Limulus is an omnivorous scavenger, feeding upon what it can find on the shallow offshore sand banks. Common food items include molluscs, worms, crustaceans, and bits of algae.

SARGENT BEACH

Before we consider bayshores of the western Gulf of Mexico, there is one other outer shore of the Texas coast that we must discuss. It shares many of the components of shores already described, but also includes elements similar to those found along bay margins. It is a transitional community not readily classified according to the generally accepted shore types nor easily partitioned into foreshore and backshore components. We have left its description until now, in part because of its unique attributes, and in part because it serves as a fitting transition to bayshore communities.

Soft shores wax and wane at the mercy of currents. Over the last several thousand years, shores of the northwestern Gulf of Mexico have expanded seaward and grown upward as river-deposited sands from offshore banks were captured by longshore currents and deposited on coastal spits, peninsulas, and ultimately barrier island dunes. The depositional process, however, is not uniform in time or space. While most Texas shores are slowly growing seaward by longshore drift, some are rapidly eroding away.

During the last two decades, several miles of Texas State Highway 87, between Sabine Pass and High Island along the eastern coast, have washed into the sea. Similarly, significant portions of the beach at South Padre Island are being moved offshore, undercutting a sea wall and threatening beachfront property. But perhaps the most dramatic erosion on the Texas coast is focused along a small portion of mainland outer shore between Freeport and Matagorda, specifically from Sargent Beach to the vicinity of Cedar Lake.

In 1850, the Sargent Beach shoreline lay more than 1000 m seaward of its present location. Since 1850, this coast has lost an average of 3 to 4 m of foreshore per year (Morton & Pieper, 1975b). Most of the sand that once covered this beach has been stripped away, especially in the aftermath of a hurricane, leaving only a low sandy berm and large patches of exposed bedrock. But the local "bedrock" consists not of stone, but rather of a hard, compact but unlithified clay originally deposited at the bottom of a Pleistocene bay. To-

6-15. The beach at Las Coloradas, Yucatan, Mexico. **A.** Coastal dropseed, *Sporobolus virginicus*; **B.** Sea-blite, *Suaeda linearis*; **C.** Partridge pea, *Cassia* sp.; **D.** Turk's cap, *Malvaviscus arboreus*; **E.** Coastal ragweed, *Ambrosia hispida*; **F.** Sea rocket, *Cakile lanceolata*; **G.** Wolfberry, *Lycium carolinianum*; **H.** Beach tea, *Croton punctatus*; **I.** Joe-wood, *Jacquinia aurantiaca*; **J.** Sea grape, *Coccoloba uvifera*; **K.** Sea purslane, *Sesuvium portulacastrum*; **L.** Sisal hemp, *Agave sisalana*; **M.** Lantana, *Lantana involucrata*; **N.** Hog cabbage palm, *Pseudophoenix sargentii*; **O.** Thatch palm, *Thrinax* sp.; **P.** Spiny lizard, *Sceloporus* sp.; **Q.** Dildoe cactus, *Cereus pentagonus*; **R.** Prickly pear, *Opuntia dillenii*; **S.** *Donax denticulatus*. Horizontal and vertical scales indicate meters.

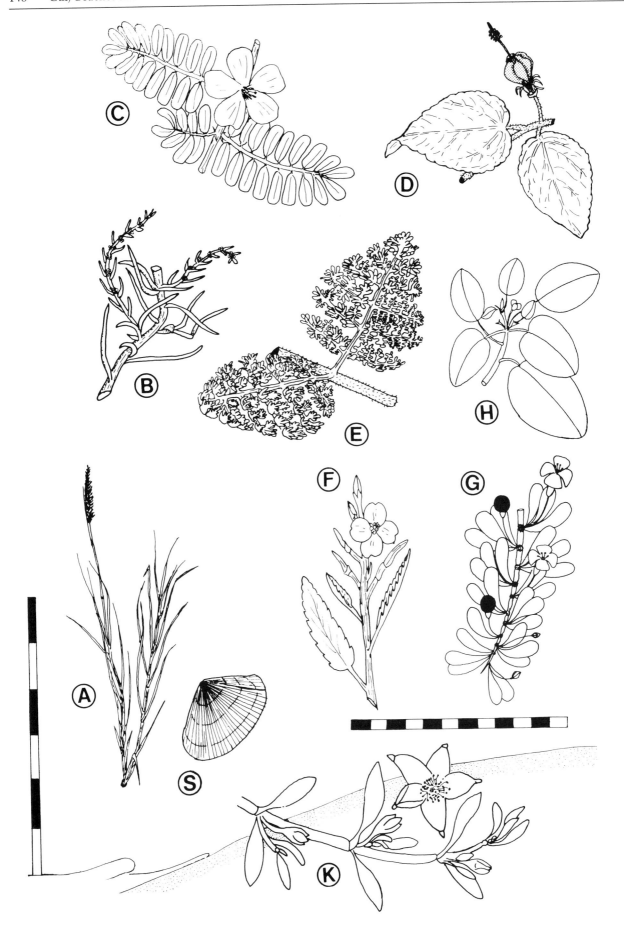

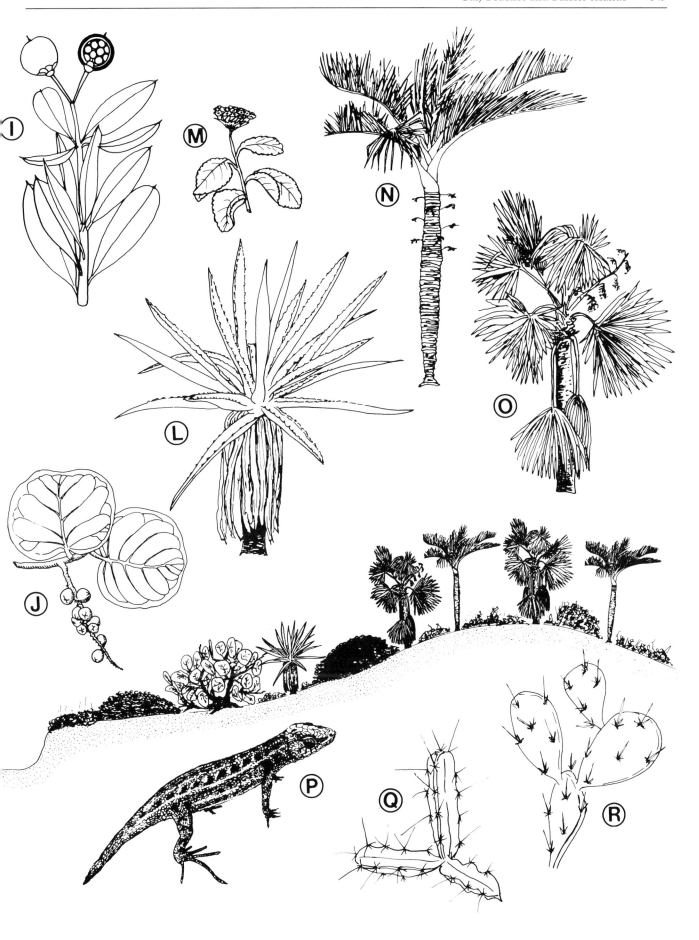

day the clay is exposed at the foreshore, where waves have molded it into raised, seaward-projecting mudbank fingers thrusting into cusps of sand. Moderate amounts of sand will accumulate at Sargent Beach in the summer and between major storms or hurricanes, but the passage of a storm is sufficient to remove most of it, exposing and eroding the mudbanks again. The paucity of sand, the presence of an intertidal mudbank, and the generally low relief of the shore provide a unique environment on the outer coast where bayshore and barrier island biota intermingle unlike anywhere else in the western Gulf.

The mudbanks at Sargent Beach consist of two layers of clay. The lower, thicker layer consists of a hard clay easily distinguished by its dark, pitted surface. It constitutes the bulk of the mudbank, rising as much as 50 cm above the sand. In the absence of a bank, as in cusps between banks or along broad expanses of gently sloping foreshore, the black clay underlies a thin blanket of sand. A thinner, less compacted red clay overlies the dark clay along some parts of the shore. It is most prominent on top of the banks, where it is exposed along a 2 to 3 m wide zone, before it is covered by berm sand. It holds a thick network of deteriorating woody roots, presumably the remnant of a once-extensive vegetation cover similar to that presently found in the swale behind the berm.

Intertidal clay banks provide an unexpected harbor for life (Fig. 6-16). The fiddler crab, *Uca spinicarpa* (Fig. 6-16 T), is perhaps the most unusual mudbank inhabitant, or at least its occurrence on a Gulf-facing shore is unusual. Fiddler crabs usually inhabit protected bay and tidal inlet mud flats, where wave energy is minimal and salinities are moderate. Yet, at Sargent Beach, in the face of normal oceanic salinity and the pounding surf of an exposed shore, *Uca spinicarpa* occupies mudbank burrows and apparently leads a fairly typical life. There are, however, mediating circumstances which may account for this unusual situation.

A large population of *Uca spinicarpa*, much larger than that on the mudbank, occupies the swale behind the Sargent Beach berm. Despite its present close proximity to the outer shore, the swale is actually a typical *Uca* habitat that, less than 100 years ago, was a marsh more than a kilometer away from the Gulf shore. Because of the rapidly eroding coastline, the intertidal mudbank undoubtedly once was the base of a similar marshy swale. As the shoreline receded, onshore winds pushed the low, sandy beach berm progressively landward, burying and compacting this part of the swale. Berm displacement kept pace with shoreline erosion until the "fossil" swale (now the mudbank) was exposed at the surf line. Woody *Batis* roots and "fossil" fiddler crab burrows testify to the nature of the mudbank prior to sand burial.

Fiddler crabs from the crowded modern swale have reoccupied some of the relic burrows, deepening or enlarging them as necessary. It is difficult to determine if the mudbank *Uca* population consists of permanent

residents or transient squatters. The environment suggests the latter. In either case, *Uca* burrowing activity weakens the intertidal bank and hastens the ultimate erosion of the shore.

Several other organisms weaken the mudbank by their burrowing or boring activity. The bivalve angel wing, *Barnea truncata* (Fig. 6-16 Y) bores deeply into the stiff dark clay. Like *Uca*, it is not usually found on exposed outer shores. It is more commonly encountered in hard clays along eroding bayshore margins where it grows to 75 mm in length. Specimens are smaller at Sargent Beach, rarely exceeding 50 mm. The shell of this piddock (Pholadidae) is remarkably thin, yet designed to facilitate boring. The valves permanently gape at two locations: at the posterior end where a pair of long fused siphons extend from between the valve margins, and along the anteroventral margin, where the disk-shaped foot is exposed within a spacious pedal gape. Elsewhere, the mantle is entirely fused. The ligament is significantly reduced, such that the valves are in contact as fulcra only near the umbos and the anteroventral margin, and are held together primarily by the large adductor muscles, and protected by complex shelly plates. Contraction of the posterior adductor muscle around the dorso-ventral fulcra separates the anterior valve margins. Relaxation of the posterior and adduction of the anterior adductor closes the anterior valve margin so that the two valves rock about the umbo and provide a mechanism for boring. This is accomplished by the outer surface of the shell which is sculptured with concentric ridges and strong radial ribs, forming prominent imbrications, especially anteriorly. The shell ornamentation acts as an abrasive auger, powered by the alternate opening and closing of the anterior gape, permitting deep boring of stiff clays or soft rocks.

Barnea bores by first attaching the foot like a sucker to the anterior borehole wall and pulling the shell forward. The posterior adductor contracts, applying the valves firmly against the borehole wall, and the shell is rocked by asymmetrical contractions of pedal retractor muscles. Dislodged sediment passes through the pedal gape to the mantle cavity where it is collected and eliminated as pseudofeces. After several passes, the foot relaxes and repositions a few degrees away from its original point of attachment and the process is repeated. In this way, *Barnea* bores a symmetrical circular tunnel.

The false angel wing, *Petricola pholadiformis* (Fig. 6-16 E1), is another mudbank borer. It is smaller than *Barnea*, and is readily distinguished by the lack of pedal or siphonal gapes and the ability to wholly withdraw all soft parts within the shell. The slender clam may reach 50 mm in length, but most specimens on Sargent Beach are much smaller. Like *Barnea*, it utilizes its shell to rasp the borehole.

The small (8 mm) isopod *Sphaeroma quadridentatum* (Fig. 6-16 C1) seems to be another misplaced inhabitant on the mudbank. It is common within the numerous burrows and crevices in the black clay, but apparently is more at home among the dense algal mats of the Texas jetties where it is easily lost among the vegetation. *Sphaeroma* is one of the few marine isopods which, when threatened, rolls into a ball in a manner similar to its distant terrestrial relatives, the pill bugs. This defensive habit serves to distinguish it from other small Texas marine crustaceans.

Juvenile stone crabs, *Menippe adina* (Fig. 3-4 F), take refuge within mudbank crevices. Many larger claw and carapace fragments wash ashore, suggesting that there may be a sizable *Menippe* population in off-shore mudbanks.

Broad shallow water-filled depressions on top of the mudbanks harbor tangled tufts of the green filamentous alga *Enteromorpha* (Fig. 6-16 A1) attached to decaying *Batis* root fragments (the latter originally put down when the mudbank was a back-berm swale). The bright green algal tufts are strikingly highlighted against the red clay. Blue green algae (Fig. 6-16 B1) also sometimes form filamentous mats on the red mudbank.

The thin veneer of intertidal sand at Sargent Beach is rarely more than a few cm thick, but it provides shelter for several species more typical of the barrier island beaches. *Donax variabilis roemeri* (Fig. 6-16 V) occurs here, as does the mole crab, *Emerita portoricensis* (Fig. 6-16 W). *Albunea paretii* (Fig. 6-16 X), although more typically found offshore, is fairly common in the lower intertidal. We did not find *Lepidopa benedicti* or *L. websteri* here, but they are likely inhabitants. The red tube-dwelling polychaete *Onuphis eremita oculata* (Fig. 6-16 Z), also is common in the wave-swept sand. Above the surf, beachhoppers, especially *Orchestia platensis* (Fig. 6-16 D1), congregate under driftwood or within the decaying flotsam. Ghost crabs, *Ocypode quadrata* (Fig. 6-16 U), occur throughout the upper beach.

Like the fauna, the floral community of Sargent Beach consists of a mixture of outer shore and bay margin species. The marsh grass, *Spartina patens* (Fig. 6-16 P), is the most noticeable plant on the foreshore. Clumps of this grass rise above the sand along the berm crest, marking the highest elevation along the shore. Sparse vegetation occurs seaward of the berm crest, but several species are represented. A few struggling sprigs of sea purslane, *Sesuvium portulacastrum*, are in evidence, as are small clumps of *Tidestromia lanuginosa* (Fig. 6-16 S). Neither attains the size or prominence that they enjoy on San Jose, Mustang, or Padre Islands to the south. A few sprouting leaves of *Ipomoea pes-caprae* are sometimes seen on the foreshore, but the morning glory appears to fare poorly here. The spurge, *Chamaesyce polygonifolia* (Fig. 6-16 K) is somewhat more successful. It is not uncommon seaward of the berm crest, and forms large prominent prostrate mats on the sand behind it. Elongate leaves, milky sap, tiny inconspicuous flowers, and a creeping habit serve to distinguish this species from others on the berm sand. Other spurges, including *C. maculata* (Fig. 6-10 I), also occur here.

The density and diversity of vegetation increase significantly on the landward slope of the beach berm, despite the fact that this slope is less than about 4 m wide and eventually grades into the back berm swale, which contains predominantly only three plants, *Batis maritima* (Fig. 6-16 J), *Salicornia virginica* (Fig. 6-16 M), and the grass *Monanthochloe littoralis* (Fig. 6-16 Q). Plants of the upper sandy slope include the sea oxeye, *Borrichia frutescens* (Fig. 6-6 C), the camphor daisy, *Machaeranthera phyllocephala* (Fig. 6-16 N), the seaside heliotrope, *Heliotropium curassavicum* (Fig. 6-16 O), the glassworts *Salicornia bigelovii* (Fig. 6-16 F) and *S. virginica* (Fig. 6-16 M), and occasionally the sea rocket, *Cakile geniculata* (Fig. 6-16 R). Several sedges occur lower on the berm slope along the swale margin, including *Cyperus odoratus* (Fig. 6-16 B), *Eleocharis albida* (Fig. 6-16 C), *Cyperus surinamensis* (Fig. 6-16 D), *Fimbristylis castanea* (Fig. 6-16 E), and *Scirpus americanus* (Fig. 6-16 G). The grass *Distichlis spicata* (Fig. 6-16 I), forms a dense border just above the swale. Several plants occasionally rise above this grassy border, including the sea blite, *Suaeda linearis* (Fig. 6-16 H), the composites, *Pluchea odorata* (Fig. 6-16 A) and *Eclipta alba*. The long creeping legume *Strophostyles helvola* (Fig. 6-16 L) grows atop plants of the swale margin, readily identified by its trifoliate compound leaves and creamy to lavender pea flowers.

TOWARD BAYSHORES

Before leaving the Gulf beaches, it is appropriate that we reflect for a moment upon what we have found. The fauna of these shores is, at best, sparse and the marine intertidal flora virtually nonexistent. The total diversity of beach biota is significantly increased by the influx of flotsam or the remains of offshore benthos (Chapter 10). As neither of these sources has members capable of surviving on the beach, they cannot be considered a part of the beach community. The biota living in sand between the rise and fall of the tide is markedly deficient in species, as are similar communities throughout the world.

Despite its paucity, there is remarkable correspondence in the major elements of the beach fauna of the western Gulf as one traverses the temperate to tropical transition. *Donax*, *Emerita* and *Ocypode* are represented by the same species throughout most of the region, except that the temperate *Emerita talpoida* approaches the southern limit of its range in Texas and the tropical *Donax denticulatus* barely extends into the Gulf of Mexico. The land crab *Gecarcinus lateralis* is a tropical species with little more than a foothold on the southern Texas temperate fringe. But it is not a true beach inhabitant. It lives among the maritime vegetation behind the beach and, as we will soon see, the biota here more effectively reflects latitudinal change. Similarly, *Limulus polyphemus* is not a beach resident, but a brief visitor to the shore from offshore sands. The reason for its natural absence along Texas beaches or bays is unknown, but clearly it is not the

6-16. The clay banks at Sargent Beach, Texas. **A.** Marsh fleabane, *Pluchea odorata*; **B.** Sedge, *Cyperus odoratus*; **C.** Sedge, *Eleocharis albida*; **D.** Sedge, *Cyperus surinamensis*; **E.** Sedge, *Fimbristylis castanea*; **F.** Glasswort, *Salicornia bigelovii*; **G.** Swordgrass, *Scirpus americanus*; **H.** Sea-blite, *Suaeda linearis*; **I.** Saltgrass, *Distichlis spicata*; **J.** Saltwort, *Batis maritima*; **K.** Seaside spurge, *Chamaesyce polygonifolia*; **L.** Fuzzy bean, *Strophostyles helvola*; **M.** Glasswort, *Salicornia virginica*; **N.** Camphor daisy, *Machaeranthera phyllocephala*; **O.** Seaside heliotroph, *Heliotropium curassavicum*; **P.** Marshhay cordgrass, *Spartina patens*; **Q.** Key grass, *Monanthochloe littoralis*; **R.** Sea rocket, *Cakile geniculata*; **S.** *Tidestromia lanuginosa*; **T.** Fiddler crab, *Uca spinicarpa*; **U.** Ghost crab, *Ocypode quadrata*; **V.** Coquina clam, *Donax variabilis roemeri*; **W.** Mole crab, *Emerita portoricensis*; **X.** *Albunea paretii*; **Y.** Angel wing, *Barnea truncata*; **Z.** *Onuphis eremita oculata*; **A1.** *Enteromorpha* sp. attached to woody debris; **B1.** Filamentous blue-green algae; **C1.** Gribble, *Sphaeroma quadridentatum*; **D1.** Amphipod, *Orchestia platensis*; **E1.** Boring clam, *Petricola pholadiformis*. Note the thin sand veneer which covers the mudbank on the lower parts of the beach. Fiddler crab burrows (indicated within the marshy area on the left side of the shore profile) also riddle the mud in the surf zone. The dark line and vertical hatching on the profile indicate different mud horizons.

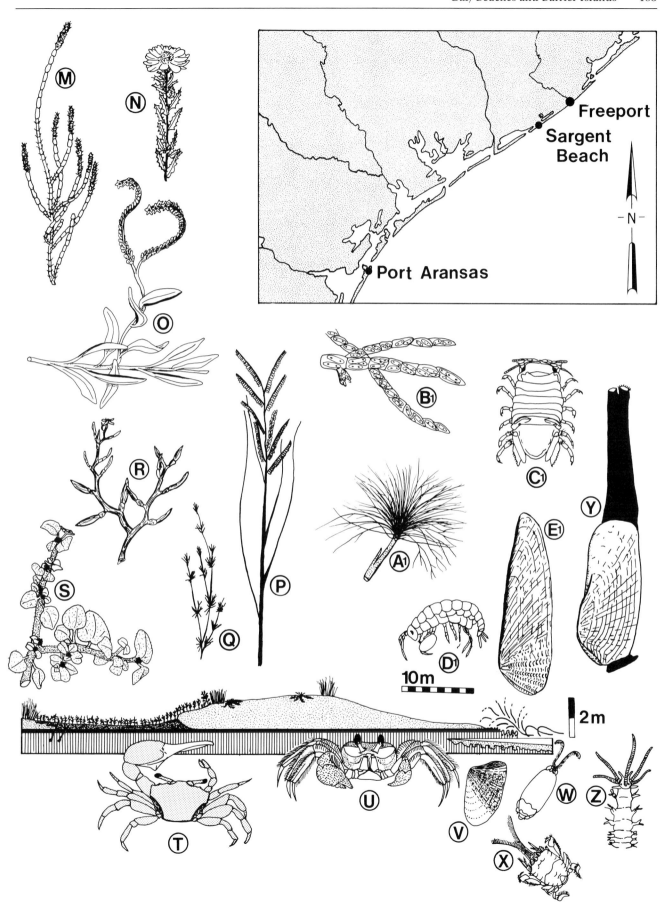

result of the climatic gradient, for flourishing populations exist north and south of Texas. Smaller beach crustaceans, especially the amphipods and isopods, more adequately demonstrate species change from northern to southern Gulf shores (Dexter, 1976) than the larger fauna.

Maritime vegetation expresses more diversity than any other component of the beach community and provides us some of the clearest patterns of change from temperate to tropical shores (Table 6-1). Those plants living closest to the sea display the broadest geographic ranges among the western Gulf flora. The pioneering succulents (*Sesuvium*), creepers (*Ipomoea*) and grasses (*Sporobolus, Spartina patens*) of the backshore are usually found on most Gulf beaches. (Indeed, *Ipomoea pes-caprae* and *Sporobolus virginicus* occur in similar habitats throughout the world.) To this as-

semblage is added another creeper, *Canavalia maritima*, restricted to frost-free shores.

A few larger plants are able to exploit the back edge of the beach throughout the region. Most notable of these is *Croton punctatus*, growing as tall (1 m) perennial shrubs on the dune fringes of south Texas and northern Mexico, but being considerably smaller in the face of much greater competition on the outer dune ridges of Yucatan. *Amaranthus greggii* is another tall pioneer plant common throughout the region, exploiting suitable backshore sites as an annual herb.

Vegetation undergoes a transition at the backshore margin. The demands of surf, salt and shifting sand slowly subside, providing additional habitats for slightly less adaptable species. A few plants provide shelter for several more, and these in turn eventually establish microrefugia for a large number of species.

Table 6-1. Distribution of Common Sandy Beach Flora in the Western Gulf of Mexico

Plant	Common Name	Family	Sargent Beach, Texas, USA	Mustang Island, Texas, USA	South Padre Island, Texas, USA	Cabo Rojo, racru Mexi (1)
Sesuvium portulacastrum	Sea purslane	Aizoaceae	AB	ABC	ABC	ABC
Chamaesyce polygonifolia	Seaside spurge	Euphorbiaceae	BCD			
Ipomoea stolonifera	White morning glory	Convolvulaceae	BC	BCD	BCD	BCI
Ipomoea pes-caprae	Railroad vine	Convolvulaceae	BC	BCD	BCD	BCI
Sporobolus virginicus	Coastal dropseed	Gramineae	BC	BCD	BCD	BCI
Panicum amarum	Bitter panicum	Gramineae	BC	BCD	BCD	BCI
Paspalum monostachyum	Gulfdune grass	Gramineae	BC	BCD	BCD	
Amaranthus greggii	Coastal pigweed	Amaranthaceae	BC	BC	BC	
Spartina patens	Marshhay cordgrass	Gramineae	BC	CDE	CDE	CI
Croton punctatus	Beach tea	Euphorbiaceae	BC	CD	CD	CI
Fimbristylis castanea	Sedge	Cyperaceae	CD	CDE		
Borrichia frutescens	Sea ox-eye daisy	Compositae	CD	DE	DE	I
Cakile geniculata	Sea rocket	Cruciferae	CD	DE	DE	
Philoxerus vermicularis	Silverhead	Amaranthaceae	CD			
Cassia fasciculata	Partridge pea	Fabaceae	D	DE	DE	
Andropogon glomeratus	Bushy beardgrass	Gramineae	DE	DE	DE	
Eleocharis albida	Sedge	Compositae	DE	DE		
Oenothera drummondii	Beach evening primrose	Onograceae	DE	DE	DE	I
Machaeranthera phyllocephala	Camphor daisy	Compositae	DE	DE	DE	
Cyperus surinamensis	Sedge	Cyperaceae	DE	DE		
Suaeda linearis	Sea-blite	Chenopodiaceae	DE	DE	DE	
Cyperus odoratus	Sedge	Cyperaceae	DE	DE	DE	
Heliotropium curassavicum	Seaside heliotrope	Boraginaceae	DE			
Batis maritima	Saltwort	Bataceae	E	E	E	
Monanthochloe littoralis	Key grass	Gramineae	E	E	E	
Schizachyrium scoparium	Little bluestem	Gramineae	E	E	E	

(1) As reported by Poggie (1963)
(2) As reported by Sauer (1967)
* Usually restricted to bayshores in Texas
** Usually restricted to habitats with some limestone bedrock
NOTE: Many of these plants are also common on bayshores.

A: Backshore pioneer habitats
B: Backshore near dunes or dune ridges
C: Windward slopes of dunes or dune ridges
D: Leeward slopes of dunes or dune ridges
E: Vegetation-stabilized sands and flats

This transition is spread over a wide distance on southern Texas and northern Mexico shores, in part aided by the natural aridity of the region. At Cabo Rojo, the unvegetated or sparsely vegetated beach also can be very wide, suggesting that winds, blowing sands, salt spray, or a combination of these influence the patterns of distribution of the maritime vegetation. On the more sheltered sandy shores of Yucatan, the transition is often more abrupt. One step can take you from bare sand to dense vegetation.

In addition to the obvious local, physically mediated vegetational transition at the back of the shore, there is another, more subtle latitudinal transition only observable on a regional scale. The plants which fringe the rear margin of the backshore are not as widely distributed as the pioneering species. Some of these plants occur intermittently here and there, but cannot be considered as ubiquitous as most of the backshore pioneers. Others are simply restricted by the climatic gradient. Examples of plants with intermittent distributions include *Philoxerus vermicularis*, *Suaeda linearis*, *Uniola paniculata* and *Lycium carolinianum*. The irregular distribution of these species more likely reflects the presence or absence of specific microenvironments, rather than a more general climatic transition. For example, *Uniola paniculata* rarely occurs in the absence of dunes and *Suaeda linearis* is usually found on moderately open sites but with at least some protection afforded by other, often taller, plants. Sometimes the distribution patterns are difficult to explain. *Lycium carolinianum* marks the backshore boundary on many Yucatan beaches facing the open Gulf, but this woody creeper occurs only on bayshores in Texas (Chapter 7).

The differences between temperate and tropical sandy beaches become most apparent in the maritime province behind the backshore. The common plants found behind Texas and Yucatan beaches are almost mutually exclusive of the respective opposite shores (Table 6-1). Grasses, sedges, and small shrubs dominate the maritime vegetation of arid south Texas, and form a significant component of the backshore even in the regions of adequate or abundant rainfall (Freeport, Texas and eastward). In contrast, small trees and large tropical shrubs commonly fringe the sandy beaches of Cabo Rojo and even the relatively arid shores of Yucatan. The difference in the regional flora can only be explained by the climatic transition that has occurred from north to south. On Gulf sandy beaches the increasingly tropical influence is poorly expressed by beach fauna and pioneering beach flora, but becomes strikingly obvious landward from the rear margin of the backshore.

A special point must be made about the vegetation lying behind the dune ridge at Sargent Beach. These plants are not representative of the vegetation of most Gulf-facing shores. As will be seen in the next chapter, they are clearly the flora of a bay margin. We will defer a general assessment of their position along the climatic gradient until the complete estuarine-fringing flora is described.

Most of the western Gulf region is provided with adequate sand supply and winds, waves and currents that enable the development of a typical sandy beach morphology. But when sand supply is deficient, or when the shore is protected from even moderate wave activity, the outer shore assumes at least some of the characteristics of bayshore margins. To the north, Sargent Beach serves as the example, whereas to the south, the narrow sandy beaches of western Yucatan frequently yield to mangroves (Chapter 9). The latter can occur here because the area lies protected from prevailing winds in the lee of the Yucatan peninsula. In both instances, special circumstances have permitted communities with characteristics of sheltered bay margins to develop on the outer coast. It should be

Barra ncha, Veracruz, Mexico (2)	Isla Aguada, Campeche, Mexico	Progreso, Yucatan, Mexico	Las Coloradas, Yucatan, Mexico
C	ABC	ABC	ABC
CD			
CD	BCD	BCD	
CD	BCD	BCD	
CD	BCD	BCD	BCD
	BC	BC	
	CDE	CDE	CDE
CD	CD	CD	CD
DE			
		CD	
	DE	DE	DE
E			
	E	E	E

continued on following pages

Table 6-1, *continued*

Plant	Common Name	Family	Sargent Beach, Texas, USA	Mustang Island, Texas, USA	South Padre Island, Texas, USA	Cab Rojo, racru Mexi (1)
Tidestromia lanuginosa	Espanta vaqueros	Amaranthaceae	E	E	E	
Quercus virginiana	Live oak	Quercaceae	E	E	E	
Scirpus americanus	Swordgrass	Cyperaceae	E	E	E	
Solidago sempervirens	Seaside goldenrod	Compositae	E	E	E	
Pluchea odorata	Marsh fleabane	Compositae	E	E	E	
Strophostyles helvola	Fuzzy bean	Fabaceae	E	E	E	
Limonium nashii	Sea lavender	Plumbaginaceae	E	E	E	
Distichlis spicata	Saltgrass	Gramineae	E			
Salicornia bigelovii	Glasswort	Chenopodiaceae	E			
Salicornia virginica	Glasswort	Chenopodiaceae	E			
Uniola paniculata	Sea oats	Gramineae		CD	CD	CI
Lycium carolinianum	Wolfberry	Solanaceae		*		
Dichromena colorata	Whitetop sedge	Cyperaceae		DE	DE	
Heterotheca subaxillaris	Camphorweed	Compositae		DE	DE	
Helianthus argophyllus	Silverleaf sunflower	Compositae		DE	DE	
Rhynchosia minima	Snoutbean	Fabaceae		E	E	
Magnolia virginiana	Sweet bay	Magnoliaceae		E	E	
Acacia farnesiana	Huisache	Fabaceae		E	E	
Zanthoxylum clava-herculis	Prickly-ash	Rutaceae		E	E	
Salix nigra	Black willow	Salicaceae		E	E	
Opuntia lindheimeri	Prickly pear	Cactaceae		E	E	
Paspalum distichum	Knotgrass	Gramineae				BCL
Canavalia maritima	Bay bean	Fabaceae				BC
Scaevola plumieri	Beach lobelia	Goodeniaceae				C
Coccoloba uvifera	Sea grape	Polygonaceae				CI
Tournefortia gnaphalodes	Sea lavender	Boraginaceae				CI
Suriana maritima	Bay cedar	Surianaceae				CI
Cassia cinerea	Partridge pea	Fabaceae				I
Malvaviscus arboreus	Turk's cap	Malvaceae				I
Chrysobalanus icaco	Cocoa plum	Chrysobalanaceae				I
Conocarpus erectus	Buttonwood	Combretaceae				I
Passiflora foetida	Passion flower	Passifloraceae				
Randia laetevirens	Box-briar	Rubiaceae				
Cenchrus incertus	Sand bur	Gramineae				
Cocos nucifera	Coconut	Palmaceae				
Opuntia dillenii	Prickly pear	Cactaceae				
Ambrosia hispida	Coastal ragweed	Compositae				
Cakile lanceolata	Sea rocket	Cruciferae				
Jacquinia aurantiaca	Joe-wood	Theophrastaceae				
Cereus pentagonus	Dildoe cactus	Cactaceae				
Thrinax sp.	Thatch palm	Palmaceae				
Agave sp.	Agave	Agavaceae				
Poinsettia cyanthophora	Spurge	Euphorbiaceae				
Lantana involucrata	Lantana	Verbenaceae				
Cassia sp.	Partridge pea	Fabaceae				
Agave sisalana	Sisal hemp	Agavaceae				
Pseudophoenix sargentii	Hog cabbage palm	Palmaceae				

(1) As reported by Poggie (1963)
(2) As reported by Sauer (1967)
* Usually restricted to bayshores in Texas
** Usually restricted to habitats with some limestone bedrock
NOTE: Many of these plants are also common on bayshores.

A: Backshore pioneer habitats
B: Backshore near dunes or dune ridges
C: Windward slopes of dunes or dune ridges
D: Leeward slopes of dunes or dune ridges
E: Vegetation-stabilized sands and flats

clear, then, that the outer beaches of the western Gulf of Mexico, even in the face of active coastal erosion, tend toward the lower energy side of the category of "exposure." We now turn our attention to the category of "shelter," as we examine the estuaries, bay margins, and mangrove communities of the western Gulf region, and we will find that these sheltered shores, like the zone of maritime vegetation behind outer shore beaches, beautifully demonstrate the biotic consequences of a temperate to tropical transition.

rra icha, ra- uz, xico 2)	*Isla Aguada, Campeche, Mexico*	*Progreso, Yucatan, Mexico*	*Las Coloradas, Yucatan, Mexico*
CD	CD	CD	CD
CD	BCD		
C	BC	BC	BC
	C	C	C
	CD	CD	CD
	CD	CD	CD
	CD	CD	CD
	DE		
	DE	DE	DE
	E	E	E
DE	**DE	**DE	**DE
	E	E	E
	E		
C	ABC	ABC	ABC
DE	DE	DE	
E	E	E	E
	BCD	BCD	BCD
	CDE	CDE	CDE
	DE	DE	DE
	DE	DE	DE
	DE	DE	DE
	E	E	E
	E	E	E
	E	E	E
		DE	DE
		E	E
			DE

7. Texas Primary Bays

INTRODUCTION

Coastal estuaries are ephemeral basins—intermediate successional stages of a geologic continuum. The present Gulf estuarine embayments were born from 14,000 to 5000 years ago during the Holocene transgression following the Wisconsin glaciation. Water from melting glaciers caused sea level to rise as much as 60 m, inundating coastal river valleys. Shortly thereafter, many of these drowned valleys were separated from the open sea by barrier islands, effectively forming the bays and lagoons of the present shoreline.

From the time of their creation, bays receive and accumulate sediments from the land, usually brought there suspended in turbulent river waters, and sometimes by winds. Sediment accumulation, especially of the finer silts and muds, is facilitated in the presence of barrier islands which restrict the amount of sediment that can be deposited directly into the Gulf of Mexico. Broad, shallow, protected bays also rapidly dissipate the energy of already rather sluggish rivers, and encourage settling of suspended silts and muds on the bay floor.

The estuary is a successional environment, becoming shallower and smaller as it fills with sediments. But unlike the many terrestrial successional habitats which achieve a climax in a few dozen years, estuarine succession is usually measured by centuries. Sediment accumulation is slow, perhaps a few centimeters per 100 years. Also, river and tidal currents influence sedimentation rates. Here, strong currents rapidly erode a mudbank, while there, sediments accumulate faster than sea grasses can grow. Rates of accumulation or erosion are not constant throughout the basin. A variety of habitats develop in the estuary based upon the stability of the substratum, rates of sedimentary accumulation or erosion, water depth, current flow, and other variables. Habitats shift from place to place as parameters change. The grassbed that was here a few years ago is a mud bank today. Succession may seem an inappropriate description of these habitat oscillations, and indeed it is if measured only over a few years. Despite the give and take, the balance sheet of all estuaries eventually shows a net accumulation of sediments, a shallowing of the basin, and a reduction in the size of the estuary over the centuries.

Any enclosed basin can receive only so much sediment; eventually it will fill to the brim. "Climax"

bays are not bays at all, but flat low-lying coastal plains, like the now-filled deltas of the Brazos River and the Rio Grande. Both rivers once emptied into extensive estuaries, and both have filled them. The Brazos and Rio Grande estuaries are gone, transformed into the coastal plain farmlands that today produce cotton, milo, and vegetable crops. The Colorado River, Texas, is in a late stage of filling the Matagorda estuary, as was the Rio San Fernando of northern Mexico, before climate interceded. Other rivers of the western Gulf, the Sabine, Trinity, Lavaca, San Antonio, and Nueces in Texas and the Rios Palizada, Chumpan, Candelaria and smaller streams in Mexico, to name a few, still flow into basins behind barrier islands. Yet, they too are depositing copious quantities of silts, muds, and relatively fine sands, most of which are settling in the bays. These basins are already partially filled, and some will climax as new lands within a few hundred years.

In the next few pages we will consider some of the physical characteristics of western Gulf estuaries. Then, we will review bayshore and shallow bay communities of Texas primary bays. We will begin with the most conspicuous plants and animals from barrier island and mainland bayshores, and then, in turn, consider the less common intertidal species, the biota of shallow estuarine grassbeds and mud banks and finally some of the biota living in the waters of the bay. We are mostly concerned here with the biota of Texas primary bays— the larger, higher salinity (15 to 35 ppt) estuaries which mostly lie immediately behind the barrier islands. In the next chapter we will discuss the biota living in more difficult estuarine situations, including the low salinity secondary and tertiary bays, and the hypersaline lagoons where salinity often exceeds 35 ppt. Finally, in Chapter 9, we will consider tropical bayshores and their unique community of mangroves.

PHYSICAL FEATURES OF TEXAS ESTUARIES

An estuary is defined as a semi-enclosed coastal body of water having a free connection with the sea and being measurably diluted by freshwater (Pritchard, 1967). Large semi-enclosed embayments are unequally distributed along the western Gulf of Mexico, and not all of them correspond to this definition of an estuary (Fig. 7-1). Nine broad, shallow basins lie behind the

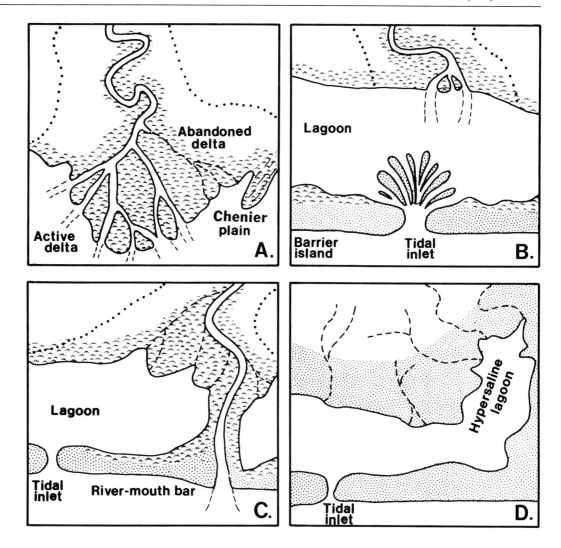

7-1. Estuarine types of the western Gulf of Mexico.

A. River delta. A river-dominated allochthonous estuarine system, e.g., the Mississippi River delta.

B. Barrier island estuary. A wave and current-dominated autochthonous estuarine system, e.g., Galveston Bay, Texas fringed by salt marshes; Laguna de Terminos, Mexico fringed by mangroves.

C. Composite river and wave-dominated system, e.g., the Colorado River-Matagorda Bay, Texas complex.

D. Hypersaline lagoon. Waves and currents create barrier island enclosing a lagoon, but evaporation exceeds precipitation. With little freshwater input from the land, salinity rises above normal marine conditions, e.g., the Laguna Madres of Texas and Mexico.

barrier islands of the Texas coast (Table 7-1). In contrast, the Gulf coast of Mexico has only a few large embayments, the most prominent being Laguna Madre de Tamaulipas, Laguna Tamiahua (Cruz, 1968), and Laguna de Terminos (Yanez, 1963). The location and physical characteristics of the western Gulf embayments strongly reflect the climate of the region.

The humid, forest-covered coastal plains of northeastern Texas receive abundant precipitation. Much of it accumulates as surface water and is delivered via rivers into the embayments protected from the Gulf by barrier islands. In normal years river discharge markedly decreases salinities in the bays (Fig. 7-2), and the basins conform exactly to the definition of an estuary. In years of drought, freshwater discharge is greatly diminished, and bay salinities approach that of normal seawater. Seasonal or yearly variations are usually so great as to render "mean salinities" only rough approximations of the actual conditions in a bay or lagoon at any particular time. Organisms living in estuaries must be capable of tolerating these considerable salinity fluctuations.

Table 7-1. Major Estuarine Systems of the Western Gulf of Mexico

Intracoastal System	Type	Area (km²)	Major Rivers	Net Inflow or Discharge (m³/sec)	Passes (*Constructed) (+Now closed)	Primary Bays	Max. Depth (m)
Texas							
Sabine-Neches Estuary	Embayments	259	Sabine-Neches	510.80	Sabine Pass	Sabine Lake	2.0
						East Bay	2.0
Trinity-San Jacinto Estuary	Embayments	1600	Trinity-San Jacinto	389.57	*Gilchrist Cut Bolivar Pass San Luis Pass	Galveston Bay	1.3
						West Bay	1.3
Brazos Estuary	River mouth	—	Brazos	143.00	NA	NA	
Lavaca-Tres Palacios Estuary	Embayments	910	Lavaca Navidad	102.80	Pass Cavallo *Matagorda Cut	Matagorda Bay	4.0
						Matagorda Bay	2.6
Colorado Estuary	River mouth	—	Colorado	67.00	NA	NA	
Guadalupe Estuary	Embayments	579	Guadalupe San Antonio	80.70	Cedar Bayou	Mesquite Bay	1.3
						Espirito Santo Bay	1.8
Mission-Aransas Estuary	Embayments	447	Mission Aransas	6.88	Aransas Pass	Aransas Bay	3.1
						Redfish Bay	2.9
Nueces Estuary	Embayments	485	Nueces	16.16	Aransas Pass *+"Fish" Pass +Packery Pass	Redfish Bay	3.1
						Corpus Christi Bay	3.1
Laguna Madre Northern Basin	Hypersaline lagoon and embayments	321	No permanent streams	<5.00	NA	NA	
Laguna Madre Southern Basin	Hypersaline lagoon	1036	None	<3.00	*Port Mansfield Cut Brazos-Santiago Pass	N. Laguna Madre	1.0
Rio Grande Estuary	River mouth	—	Rio Grande	77.00	NA	S. Laguna Madre	1.0
Mexico						NA	
Laguna Madre de Tamaulipas	Hypersaline lagoon and embayments	2000	San Fernando Soto la Marina	low	Boca de Sandoval Boca de San Antonio Boca de Jesus Maria	L. M. Septentrional	2.8
						L. M. Meridional	1.3
Rio Panuco Estuary	River mouth	—	Panuco Santa Maria	548	NA	NA	
Laguna de Tamiahua	Embayment	4116	None, but many small streams and canals	—	Boca de Corazones	Laguna de Tamiahua	5.1
Laguna de Alvarado	Embayment	NA	Papaloapan Tuxtepec	1240	1	Laguna de Alvarado	—
Laguna del Carmen	Embayment	NA	None	—	1	Laguna del Carmen	—
Rio Grijalva Estuary	River mouth	—	Grijalva	200	None	NA	
Rio Usumacinta Estuary	River mouth	—	Usumacinta	1730	None	NA	
Laguna de Terminos	Embayments	2400	Palizada Chumpan Candelaria	—	Paso del Carmen Paso Real	Laguna de Terminos	3

Secondary Bays	Max. Depth (m)	Tertiary Bays	Max. Depth (m)
None	—	None	—
Trinity Bay	3.1	Many	2.1
NA		NA	
		Chocolate Bay	1.0
Lavaca Bay	2.1	Cox Bay	2.1
Caranchahua Bay	1.6	Keller Bay	2.0
Tres-Palacios Bay	2.1	Turtle Bay	1.7
		+ others	
NA		NA	
San Antonio Bay	2.0	Hynes Bay	1.0
Copano Bay	2.6		
St. Charles Bay	1.3	Mission Bay	
Nueces Bay	1.0		
Baffin Bay	3.1	Alazan Bay	2.8
None	—	None	—
NA		NA	
None			
Bahia de Catan	—	None	—
NA		NA	
None	—	None	—
None	—	None	—
			—
None	—	None	
NA		NA	
NA		NA	
Laguna de Panlau	1	several small embayments	1
L. de Puerto Rico			
Laguna del Este			

Mean annual precipitation decreases toward the southeastern Texas coast. From Corpus Christi southward, evaporation becomes an increasingly important climatic factor, often exceeding precipitation for months or years at a time. The Rio Grande Valley thrives as an agricultural breadbasket only because of irrigation water derived from the river and its reservoirs. Lands not under irrigation receive an excess of water only during major storms, and most of it is lost in flash floods which bring surges of water and sediment to the coastal lagoons.

There are no permanently flowing rivers along the Texas coast from the Nueces River to the Rio Grande, but the Baffin/Alazan Bay complex suggests that during the late Pleistocene or early Holocene, the region experienced a more pluvial climate. Laguna Madre, occupying the basin behind Padre Island, is the southernmost major semi-enclosed coastal body of water in Texas. A similar system, Laguna Madre de Tamaulipas, fringes the northern coast of Mexico. Neither of these embayments conforms to the definition of a typical estuary. The waters of both are rarely more dilute than those of the Gulf of Mexico, and frequently they are more saline. The Laguna Madres are hypersaline lagoons, produced by the arid climate and paucity of freshwater input. Because of their unique characteristics, we will defer discussion of these basins to Chapter 8.

Bays along the Texas coast are considered primary, secondary, or tertiary according to their position in relation to the barrier islands and tidal inlets (Table 7-1). The primary bays are closest to the tidal inlets. They usually exchange water directly with the Gulf of Mexico, and are typically broad basins. They include most of the largest and deepest bays of Texas, such as Galveston, Matagorda, and Corpus Christi (although in comparison with other bays, all in Texas are relatively shallow).

Secondary bays adjoin the primary bays but are usually smaller and somewhat isolated from them (e.g., the entrance to Copano Bay, a secondary bay, is markedly restricted from Aransas Bay, a primary; Fig. 7-2). They are more distantly removed from the tidal inlets and less influenced by Gulf of Mexico waters. Precipitation and river discharge along the northeastern and central coasts are usually sufficient to cause a marked reduction of salinity in the secondary bays, where it typically ranges from 8 to 15 ppt. Those of the more arid southwestern coastal sections, however, may have salinities equal to or in excess of the primary bay. Salinities of Baffin Bay, for example, often exceed 50 to 60 ppt.

Tertiary bays are one step further removed from the sea. They are well enclosed and usually small basins which contribute to and exchange with the secondary bay. Their proximity to stream and river mouths usually results in their waters ranging from fresh to slightly brackish. Often, their shorelines resemble freshwater marshlands. Not all of the Texas estuaries have tertiary bays, and some of the secondary bays

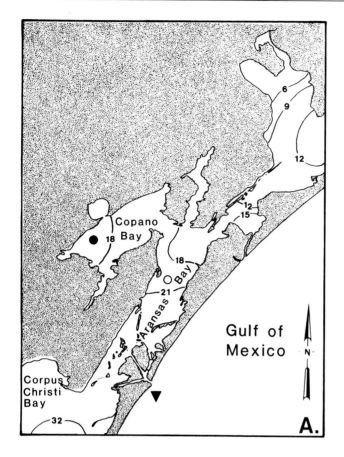

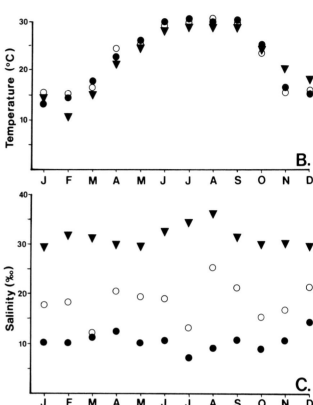

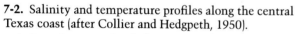

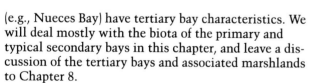

7-2. Salinity and temperature profiles along the central Texas coast (after Collier and Hedgpeth, 1950).

A. Location map. Symbols correspond to points plotted in B and C. Port Aransas is indicated by the triangle. Numbers are mean salinity values and are subject to variation according to season and climate.

B. Seasonal fluctuation of mean water temperatures (°C) at Port Aransas (triangle), Aransas Bay (light circle), and Copano Bay (dark circle).

C. Seasonal fluctuation of mean salinities at Port Aransas (triangle), Aransas Bay (light circle), and Copano Bay (dark circle).

(e.g., Nueces Bay) have tertiary bay characteristics. We will deal mostly with the biota of the primary and typical secondary bays in this chapter, and leave a discussion of the tertiary bays and associated marshlands to Chapter 8.

Estuaries are born following an erosional process, but they mature and die by deposition. During the last Pleistocene glaciation, Texas rivers cut deep broad valleys through the soft coastal sands on their way to Gulf shores lying far seaward of their present positions (Chapter 6). Modern estuaries reflect the position of these ancient valleys. Since the last rise in sea level, bays have filled with more than just water. Drilling records show that most of the northern and central bays have received as much as 25 m of sediment during the last 9,000 years (Shepard & Moore, 1960), and the process of silting will continue until, like the Brazos and Rio Grande estuaries, they are completely filled. Shepard & Moore (1960) estimate the mean rate of shoaling

in Texas estuaries is 38.4 cm/century. They point out that the actual sedimentation rate may be even greater, as the Texas coast has undergone moderate subsidence since the early Tertiary.

Texas rivers transport considerable sand in their upper and middle reaches. About 48 km (30 miles) upstream from their mouths, most of the Texas riverbeds almost "level out." They encounter the slight gradient of the low, flat coastal plain. With less energy to move it, sand settles out, and only the smaller, finer particles remain suspended in the water. (The Rio Grande, Colorado, and Brazos Rivers are exceptions; with their much greater flow they can carry considerable sand across this barrier and deposit it in the coastal zone.) Large quantities of fine silty sediment reach the broad, shallow sluggish waters of the estuaries. No longer suspended by the turbulent streamflow characteristic of the river channel, the silts settle out. They are often rich in nutrients (and in modern times, also pollutants). Estuaries are natural settling basins where sediments, nutrients, and pollutants are deposited. Estuaries have the potential to develop a rich biota, on one hand continually nourished by the incoming flow, and, on the other, under constant danger of eventually being smothered by the sediments.

Texas bays are shallow, most averaging depths of 3 m or less. All are deepest near their mouths. Tidal currents entering primary bays have scoured natural channels to depths of 9 to 12 m (Shepard & Moore, 1960). The deeper Texas bays (e.g., Matagorda Bay) usually lack significant river input.

Texas bay floors are usually flat, dominated by thick accumulations of soft mud and silt. Oyster reefs occur in all of the estuaries, although they are best developed in Copano, Galveston, and San Antonio bays (Chapter 5). The larger reefs form elongate ridges dividing the bays into sections and interfering with water circulation and sediment transport within the bay system. Oyster reefs are the only large natural hard-bottom substrata on the Texas coast.

Water circulation in bays is influenced by a number of factors. Fresh water from river and stream discharge encounters a density barrier as it enters a bay. The lighter river waters override the more dense saline waters of the bays, with only limited mixing. Thin freshwater surface layers extend far into even the largest bays. At the opposite extreme, waters of oceanic salinity enter the bay from tidal inlets and are forced to creep on the bay floor, held down by waters of lower salinity above. Texas bays are so shallow that the bottom saline wedge, usually characteristic of most estuaries, is poorly expressed. Nevertheless, it does exist especially within the deeper natural basins or dredged channels. It tends to pulse with the tides, moving up the estuary into shallower waters on the flood, and retreating to the deeper basins and channels with the ebb. The saline wedge allows many marine benthic species to live in parts of the estuary outside the immediate influence of the tidal inlets. In dry years, the bottom salinity wedge moves into shallow waters far up the estuary, even carrying brine several kilometers up rivers and streams.

Winds are more important than tides and river discharge in creating circulating currents in the shallow waters of Texas bays. Generally, currents in the central bay flow in the direction of the existing wind, and localized countercurrent eddies commonly form near shore. Northerly winter winds pile waters on the south sides of bays, covering north and central Texas barrier island bayshore marshes with water as much as 0.5 m above normal. This seiche effect also forces water and sediments through the tidal inlets. The prevailing southeasterly winds move bay waters in the opposite direction, against the mainland and away from the inner barrier island shores. Southerly winds usually blow more gently, so the seiche effect is less pronounced. Shallow waters and short fetches usually keep wave heights in the bays less than half a meter. Most bay waves "touch bottom," i.e., water particles

set in circular motion by the waves make a frictional contact with the bottom. Sediments are suspended by this process, rendering waters a turbid muddy brown. It is the rare day to find clear water in any of the Texas bays. The more southerly estuaries and lagoons with higher percentages of coarse-grained sediments seem somewhat clearer than the northeastern bays.

Sediment distribution in an estuary is influenced by a number of factors, including (1), the nearness to entering streams, inlets, bayshores, or narrows, (2), water depth, (3), climate, and (4), the number and position of oyster reefs in the bay system. Several sedimentary environments or facies are recognized in Texas estuaries and lagoons according to the manner in which the above factors interact. The sedimentary facies help determine the structure and composition of benthic estuarine biotic communities. Shepard and Moore (1960) list the most common sedimentary facies in the Texas estuaries: (1), bay margins, (2), shallow bays without stream inputs, (3), rivermouths and rivermouth bays, (4), oyster reefs, (5) inlet-influenced bottoms, and (6), deep central bays far removed from the immediate influence of inlets and rivers.

Bay Margin Sediments. The bottom slope along bay margins is slight, usually less than one percent. For a distance of about 0.8 km into the bay, sediment is characterized by having a high proportion (80 percent) of sand-sized grains, with small amounts of silt and clay. Sediment composition changes abruptly at the edge of the bay margin bank. The deeper central bay sediments consist almost exclusively of poorly sorted silts and clays. Organic remains are poorly represented on most bay margin banks, although the bayshores themselves may have a well developed tidal marsh community.

Sediments of the Shallow Bays Lacking Entering Streams. Few bays along the north and central coast fall into this category, but there are some, such as Redfish Bay near Aransas Pass. Laguna Madre is the best example (Chapter 8). Less sand occurs in these sediments than is found on the bayshore margins, but shell debris, especially gastropod shells, becomes an important sediment component (28 percent of the coarse material in Redfish Bay). Marine algae and sea grasses often carpet the shallow bay floors and contribute to the organic component of the sediments.

Sediments of Bays Near Rivers and Rivermouth Estuaries. Sand fractions are variable in these sediments, but typically low for reasons discussed above. Wood fragments and red, iron-stained aggregates often constitute a high percentage of the coarse sediment fraction. Clays are the dominant sediments, and are usually high in calcium carbonate, apparently eroded from upstream beds. Rivermouth sediments usually present a laminated texture, reflecting the differential nature of stream deposition. Shells are uncommon except in storm drifts where large quantities of land snail casts often accumulate.

Oyster Reef Sediments. Oyster reefs constitute a biogenous sediment, yielding the only significant concentrations of cobble or boulder-sized particles in the bay. Despite the dominance of large shells, there is also a sizable fraction of fine-grained detritus interspersed among the shells. This accumulates in part by the settling of silt from bay waters, but most is probably derived from the feeding activities of oysters and other filter feeders living on the reef (Chapter 5). Storms can transport shells from existing reefs into other portions of the bay, contributing to the coarse sediment fraction and providing a nucleus upon which new reefs can develop.

Sediments of Inlet-influenced Bottoms. Areas near barrier island inlets or adjacent to narrow passageways connecting adjoining bays are subject to tidal transport. Sediments in these areas are well sorted and high in coarse-grained fractions, especially sand. There is also a fair percentage of clays. Silts are virtually absent. Sediments in the barrier island inlets are usually characterized as sandy clays, whereas they are typically clayey sands in the narrow passes between inner bays. The barrier island inlets are also characterized by waters of higher salinity. A variety of normally offshore species find a home in the inlet sediments. For example, echinoderms, which are almost absent in the low salinities of the inner bays, seem to thrive on the floor of barrier island inlets. Echinoderm spines and tests are often a common component of coarse sediment fractions taken here.

Deep Central Bay Sediments. Central bay areas receive little direct influence from either river discharge or tidal sorting. The dominant sediments are silts and clays which can be carried most easily by weak bay currents. A large variety of burrowing organisms live in these fine sediments, and continually rework it. Foraminifera tests are the only large particles found in significant quantities in the deep bay basins. Their presence apparently reflects a slow but constant accumulation unobscured by the deposition of sands which are too heavy to be transported here by the weak bay currents.

ESTUARINE LIFE

Estuarine biota, and especially that of barrier island estuaries, lives in a slowly dying coastal environment. They even contribute to its ultimate demise with their tissues, skeletons, shells, and feces. These organisms must cope with the constant rain of sediments that can clog their gills, snuff out their lives, and entomb them in a muddy grave. They must be able to tolerate the rapidly fluctuating salinities and temperatures that are characteristic of the shallow bays but which never occur in the deeper offshore banks. Estuarine biota must be hardy, quick, or both.

The best adapted bay fauna are the active swimmers, crawlers and burrowers that can respond readily to adverse conditions. If sedimentation rates are high, industrious burrowers dig or plow their burrows clean. Active infauna push through the soft bottom, moving to the surface at will. If torrential rains dilute bay wa-

ters, swimmers or crawling forms migrate toward higher salinity waters near bay mouths or tidal inlets. If summer temperatures heat the bay shoals to intolerable levels, errant animals move to deeper, cooler, tidally flushed basins.

In contrast, the sessile biota, by virtue of its immobile lifestyle, finds the estuary a difficult place in which to live. Unlike errant forms, they cannot move to avoid unfavorable conditions. They are always in danger of being smothered by the accumulating sediments, stressed by low (or excessively high) salinities, or fried or frozen in estuarine shoals. Sessile biota usually requires a solid substratum upon which to attach. In estuaries hard objects are often rare and, when present, quickly buried. Exposed rocks or shells are premium sites for the settlement of sessile estuarine biota. There is often intense competition for the limited living space. Thus, sessile biota is often poorly represented in estuaries. That it occurs at all is testimony to its tenaciousness and to either the slowness of depositional processes and/or the fact that rates of deposition are not everywhere constant in the estuary.

There are fewer species of attached plants in estuaries than occur on hard shores, but those that live here are remarkably well adapted to the habitat. For example, few flowering plants occur in the sea, but of these, several species (*Thalassia testudinum, Halodule wrightii, Ruppia maritima* and *Syringodium filiforme*) have evolved adaptations specifically for life in estuaries. Extensive "grassbeds" carpet shallow bay floors, anchored by rhizomes buried deeply within the sediment. Emergent green grass-like blades provide a refuge for a great diversity of life. Yet, for their success, they contribute to their own demise. The seagrass beds encourage the further accumulation of sediment and hasten the basin-filling process.

Even more remarkable than the attached estuarine plants are the few sessile animals that occupy the bay. For example, the American oyster, *Crassostrea virginica*, has been able not only to survive in the estuary, but to characterize a major habitat within it (Chapter 5).

BAYSHORE VEGETATION

Vegetation of the upper intertidal and supratidal bayshore demonstrates both subtle and marked transitions from the northern Texas coast to Laguna Madre. Some plants (e.g., *Batis, Salicornia, Distichlis, Monanthochloe,* and *Spartina spartinae*) commonly occur throughout the region, each occupying approximately the same relative zone or level upon the shore (Figure 7-3). Other plants, although present throughout, are decidedly favored in one region. For example, the marsh grasses *Spartina patens* (Figs. 7-3 C; 7-6 C) and especially *S. alterniflora* (Figs. 7-3 B; 7-6 B) form extensive intertidal marshlands in Texas estuaries from the Sabine River to Rockport (although these seem pale in comparison with similar marshes on the Atlantic coast from Virginia to Georgia). *Spartina* marshes begin to wane from Freeport to the Corpus Christi Bay complex. In Laguna Madre, *S. alterniflora* all but disappears, no doubt the result of increasing aridity and hypersalinity. *Spartina patens* persists locally along southern Laguna Madre shores and also ranges into Mexico and Caribbean estuaries. Its occurrence is patchy, and never with the lush extravagance it enjoys in temperate North America.

Regional trends are also evident among mid- to higher-zoned plants. *Baccharis halimifolia* (Fig. 7-3 A) is a common shrub along Galveston Bay and West Bay shores, and decreases in abundance southward. The lightly thorned wolfberry, *Lycium carolinianum* (Fig. 7-3 G), also occurs high on the bayshore, but seems to be best developed as a Texas coastal plant along Matagorda and San Antonio bays. The black mangrove, *Avicennia germinans* (Fig. 9-1 C), is restricted to bayshores from Aransas Pass southward. Sea lavender, *Limonium nashii* (Figs. 7-3 N; 7-8 K), occurs on the northern shores, but usually lies hidden among dense vegetation. Southward, especially along Laguna Madre, sea lavender becomes more conspicuous as competing vegetation disappears. Indeed, the percentage of total ground cover diminishes from north to south, being greater than 90 percent along the shores of Galveston Bay and less than 30 percent along some Laguna Madre margins.

Vegetation patterns from several different bayshore localities along the Texas coast are illustrated diagrammatically in Figure 7-3, where the trends suggested above are clearly evident. Bay margin vegetation is relatively lush along the northern shores, as at Galveston Island State Park (Fig. 7-3 [1]) Here, *Spartina alterniflora* and *S. patens* occupy broad bands of tidally inundated flats which extend bayward 100 m or more. *Spartina* may occur in monoculture, or consist of mixed stands of *S. alterniflora* and *S. patens*. Nearer shore, *Salicornia virginica* (Figs. 7-3 D; 7-8 J), *Batis maritima* (Figs. 7-3 P; 7-6 F; 7-8 L), and, less commonly *Salicornia bigelovii* (Figs. 7-3 O; 7-8 M) intermingle with *Spartina*. These succulent halophytes are frequently washed by the higher tides, but are indicative of the bayshore supratidal margin. As one proceeds further shoreward, *Spartina* gradually disappears, replaced by *Paspalum* sp. and other grasses which intermingle with the succulent halophytes or stand alone in small erect clumps. When ground cover is light, *Monanthochloe littoralis* (Figs. 7-3 L; 7-6 J; 7-8 N), marks the zone above which tidal inundation rarely occurs. With heavier cover and taller vegetation, this zone is indicated by *Borrichia frutescens* (Figs. 5-1 B; 6-6 C; 6-10 Z; 7-6 H), which also occurs commonly in shallow swales behind low beach ridges. Globose clusters of *Spartina spartinae* (Fig. 7-3 H), mark the first prominent shore ridge. This cord grass rarely experiences tidal inundation and often occupies vast lowland meadows on barrier island or mainland shores. A second slight elevation provides sufficient drainage for *Baccharis halimifolia* (Fig. 7-3 A), where it forms prominent hedgerows in suitable localities.

The wolfberry, *Lycium carolinianum* (Fig. 7-3 G), occurs between *Baccharis* shrubs and *S. spartinae* clumps.

Only a few kilometers south of Galveston Beach State Park, the trend of diminishing dominance of intertidal *Spartina* becomes apparent. About 5 km north of Surfside on Follets Island (Fig. 7-3 [2]), intertidal *Spartina* is patchy. Emergent grass flats rarely extend more than 50 m into Drum Bay, and more commonly the *Spartina* zone is less than 20 m wide. The pattern of vegetation zonation on the shore is similar to that just described for Galveston Beach State Park, except that *Baccharis* is mostly absent, ground cover is often less than 50 percent permitting development of more extensive beds of *Monanthochloe*, and the high zoned *Limonium* is more apparent.

The trend of diminishing bayshore vegetation is by no means consistently progressive along central Texas estuaries. It waxes and wanes. At the Aransas National Wildlife Refuge on San Antonio Bay, for example, highly productive *Spartina* flats extend dozens of meters into the water. Visitors to the refuge glimpse some of these marshes from an observation tower near Mustang Lake, where, from November to March, they may also be able to see wintering whooping cranes, *Grus americana* (Fig. 7-3 I). These and many more intertidal flats along San Antonio Bay harbor a variety of invertebrates upon which the cranes and other wading birds feed.

7-3. Vegetation profiles along Texas bays. **1.** Galveston Island State Park, West Bay. **2.** Drum Bay from Follets Island. **3.** Aransas National Wildlife Refuge, San Antonio Bay. **4.** Laguna Salada. **5.** Laguna Madre from Padre Island. The biota (profile codes in parentheses): **A.** Groundsel-tree, *Baccharis halimifolia*, (Bc); **B.** Cordgrass, *Spartina alterniflora*; **C.** Marshhay cordgrass, *Spartina patens*; **D.** Glasswort, *Salicornia virginica*, (Sa); **E.** Sandhill crane, *Grus canadensis*; **F.** Osprey, *Pandion haliaetus*; **G.** Wolfberry, *Lycium carolinianum*, (Ly); **H.** Gulf cordgrass, *Spartina spartinae*, (Ss); **I.** Whooping crane, *Grus americana*; **J.** Clapper rail, *Rallus longirostris*; **K.** Sea-blite, *Suaeda linearis*, (Su); **L.** Key grass, *Monanthochloe littoralis*, (Mn); **M.** Saltgrass, *Distichlis spicata*, (Ds); **N.** Sea lavender, *Limonium nashii*, (Li); **O.** Glasswort, *Salicornia bigelovii*; **P.** Saltwort, *Batis maritima*, (Ba); **Q.** American coot, *Fulica americana*. Other vegetation indicated on profiles: Bo, *Borrichia frutescens*; Ms, *Machaneranthera phyllocephala*; Pp, *Paspalum* sp. and other grasses; Qu, Live oak, *Quercus virginiana*; Sp, *Spartina alterniflora*, *S. patens*, or both, depending upon location (see text).

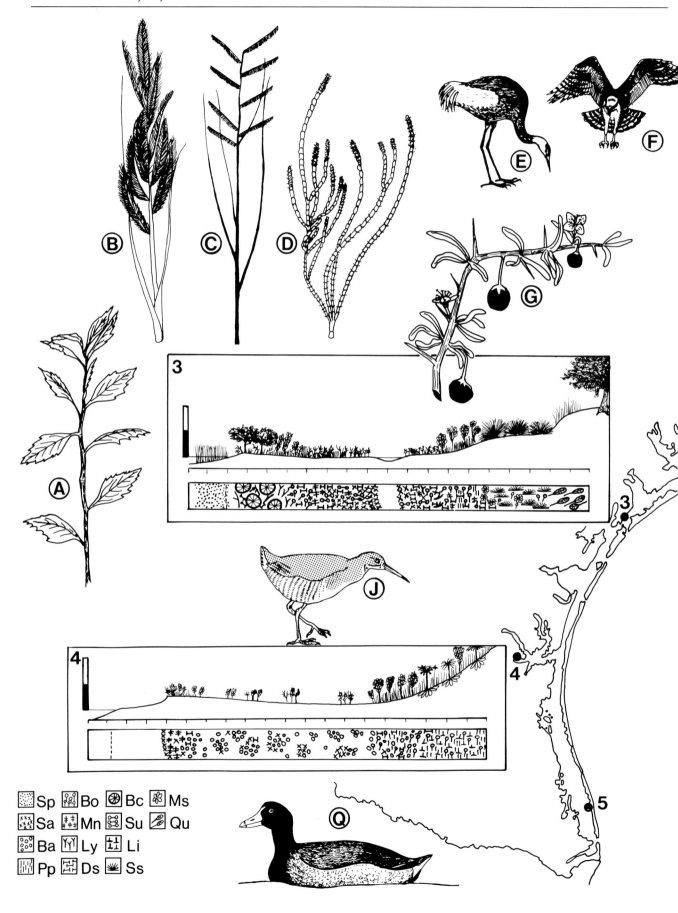

Sp   Bo   Bc   Ms
Sa   Mn   Su   Qu
Ba   Ly   Li
Pp   Ds   Ss

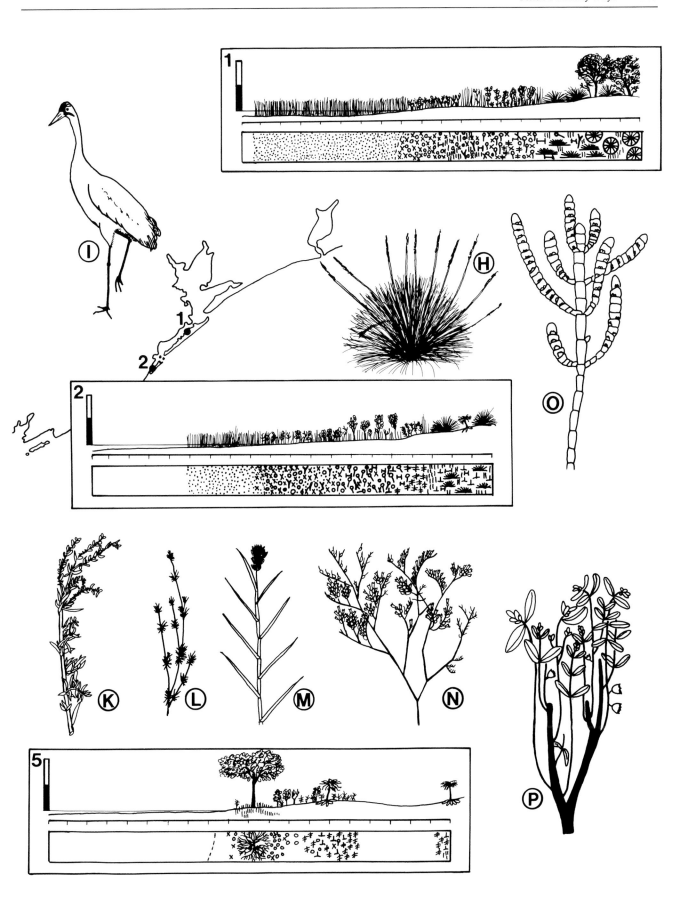

Near the observation tower, the Fish and Wildlife Service has constructed a boardwalk extending onto the marsh and providing visitors easy access to it. At the end of the boardwalk, intertidal *Spartina* is sparse (Fig. 7-3 [3]), due to a sharply sloping shore which faces the prevailing winds blowing across the widest fetch of San Antonio Bay. Just behind the tide line a small sandy ridge extends along the shore. Small *Baccharis* shrubs dominate the ridge, but wolfberry, sedges (e.g., *Scirpus americanus*, Figs. 6-10 F; 6-16 G), grasses, and other plants also occur here. Several small tidal inlets breach the ridge near the boardwalk, and each quickly branches into smaller tidal rivulets which dissect the flats behind the ridge. The walkway traverses these flats, permitting easy observation of typical bayshore vegetation zonation patterns and salt marsh biota.

At the lowest level of the tidal flat, broad, thin algal mats grow in and around stagnant pools. Algal mats occur increasingly more commonly on tidal flats from central Texas shores southward. They usually consist of several different kinds of filamentous blue-green algal species (Fig. 9-2 S)—*Schizothrix*, *Oscillatoria*, and *Scytonema* are common genera—growing upon the moist surface of the tidal flat. Blue-green algal filaments are surrounded by sticky gelatinous sheaths that readily trap sand grains washing upon them. With each tidal surge or bout of rain, a thin layer of fresh sand washes upon the mat, and the whole structure thickens in a layered arrangement. In dry seasons the mats frequently dry out, forming darkened, cracked blocks with curled margins.

On moist algal mats hundreds of tiny shore flies (Ephydridae) feed on the algae and deposit eggs within the mat. In turn, they attract predatory tiger beetles (Cicindelidae), which feed upon the flies. The insect community associated with the algal mats is a rich but little known microcosm deserving additional study.

Salicornia, *Batis*, and the annual *Suaeda linearis* (Figs. 7-3 K; 7-6 I; 7-9 A) or the perennial *Suaeda conferta* fringe the Aransas tidal basins, and sometimes occur standing in water. *Monanthochloe* and *Distichlis spicata* (Figs. 7-3 M; 7-6 E) occur slightly higher, and eventually grade into stands of *Borrichia*, various grasses and occasionally *Limonium* on the drier portions of the lowland flat. An abrupt 30 cm rise occurs at least 80 m shoreward of San Antonio Bay and marks the edge of the tidal flat. The additional elevation provides the drainage necessary for *Spartina spartinae* to become established. Attractive globose clumps of this grass are especially well developed on elevated flats throughout the Aransas Refuge. Another, more abrupt elevation, 1.5 to 2 m above sea level marks the position of the fossil dunes of the Live Oak Ridge (Chapter 6), upon which now grow live oak, red bay, and a variety of other trees and shrubs. At the observation tower, the oak motte lies at least 100 m from shore, but a kilometer to the north, where the shore is rapidly eroding, trees from a similar motte are falling into

the bay as the dunes are undercut by waves.

The decrease in vegetation cover along Texas bayshores becomes pronounced south of Corpus Christi Bay. Diminished shore vegetation is especially apparent along parts of the Laguna Madre and the Baffin Bay systems. The shore of Laguna Salada, a subunit of Baffin Bay, provides a good example. Salinities in Laguna Salada may exceed 60 ppt, especially during dry summers. Accordingly, many halophytes capable of standing in lower salinity brackish waters (e.g., *Spartina*, *Batis*, and *Salicornia*) cannot survive the hypersaline brine. These plants are either absent (e.g., *Spartina alterniflora*) or persist supratidally. Shore vegetation does not extend into Laguna Salada (Fig. 7-3 [4]). There are no roots or rhizomes to bind the substratum and protect the shore. Moderate wave action scours the beach, producing low but distinctive notches or ridges rising about 20–30 cm above the mean tide. Shore vegetation grows upon this ridge, consisting of a tight band of *Salicornia*, *Batis*, *Monanthochloe*, and *Distichlis*. Behind the ridge, the shore sometimes drops into a gently sloping swale. Vegetation is sparse here, consisting mostly of small clumps of *Batis*, *Salicornia*, and occasionally *Sesuvium portulacastrum* (Figs. 7-8 I; 7-9 B). The swale can persist landward for a distance of 50 to 60 m, then the land rises upon a hillside reaching 4 m above sea level. The lower hillside consists of *Borrichia* and mixed grasses, which grade upslope into a dense cover of *Limonium*. Many of the plants encountered on northern bayshores are no longer present here.

Laguna Madre flats (Figs. 7-3 [5]; 7-8) are characterized by even less total ground cover. It is not unusual for large areas of the low-relief Laguna Madre shore to be almost devoid of vegetation. When halophytes are present, *Salicornia* is often the dominant nearshore plant, and *Batis* also occurs here. Both *Salicornia virginica* (Figs. 7-3 D; 7-8 J), characterized by branching rhizomes and relatively small diameter erect stems, and *S. bigelovii* (Figs. 7-3 O; 7-8 M), lacking rhizome junctions and providing generally larger-diameter erect branches, are common here. Both species live under stress on the shores of Laguna Madre, and reflect this by bearing distinctive reddish or brownish branches. Thin, patchy stands of *Monanthochloe* and *Distichlis* can be found a little higher upon the shore, and small clumps of *Sesuvium* or *Philoxerus vermicularis* (Fig. 7-6 G) are not uncommon. *Limonium nashii* is a frequently encountered high-zoned plant. Eventually, the lower shore halophytes grade into mainland or barrier island vegetation.

Near tidal inlets, the black mangrove *Avicennia germinans* (Fig. 9-1 C) may be locally abundant, where it stands on the shore behind thin bands of *Spartina patens*. This is the only common mangrove on Texas bayshores, although a few red mangroves, *Rhizophora mangle*, occasionally appear in extreme south Texas. *Avicennia* is most easily recognized by the prominent pneumatophores that rise from the ground beneath the leaf canopy. These effect gaseous exchange via lenticels, and thus provide a source of oxygen for roots anchored in anaerobic muds. Black mangroves rarely exceed a height of 2 m in Texas, although specimens in Caribbean estuaries grow to 10 m or more. Mangroves are at the extreme northern limits of their range in Texas and are frequently subjected to catastrophic mortalities during winter freezes. The severe 1983 winter freeze destroyed almost all black mangroves in Texas. The following summer, a few new sprouts emerged from the base of an otherwise dead crown, but many trees did not recover. Most new mangrove growth during the summer of 1984 was from seedlings. Apparently black mangrove seeds are better able to withstand winter freezes than the established trees. The few red mangroves that grew on the South Padre Island bayshore were killed without immediate replacement.

Before concluding this discussion of bayshore vegetation, it is appropriate to reconsider the flora of the Texas barrier islands as a unified system. For purposes of clarity, we have, until now, arbitrarily partitioned the barrier islands into three major vegetated regions. The first consists of vegetation communities facing or primarily influenced by the waters and waves of the Gulf of Mexico (Chapter 6). These communities become established upon shifting, unstable sand and typically consist of a few species with special adaptations which enable them to live under relatively harsh conditions. The bayshore and its flora, which we have just described, constitutes a second vegetated region comprising but a few species of halophytes especially adapted for life on the sheltered leeward shores of the barrier island. The third region, the barrier island flat, separates the other two and consists of a diverse and primarily terrestrially derived flora dominated by herbs, grasses and small shrubs (Chapter 6).

The barrier island is, in fact, a large continuous habitat extending from Gulf sands to bayshores and comprising a number of biotic elements zoned somewhat like the biota of the intertidal rocky shore. Vegetational zonation patterns on the barrier island, however, are not so sharply defined as that seen on hard shores, in part because of the vastly different sizes of the respective habitats. The division of the barrier islands into vegetated regions is possible because of specific habitat preferences of a few of the shoreward pioneering species, either in favor of the exposure of the Gulf beach or the shelter of the bayshore. The closer to the shore, the more demanding is the environment and the more pronounced vegetational zonation becomes. The diversity of flora on the barrier island flat is possible in the relative absence of extrinsic zoning factors.

The continuity of the barrier island flora and the distribution of the more distinctly zoned species are diagrammed in Figure 7-4. Begin at the left side of the figure with the Gulf shore in the foreground and proceed to a dune crest along the left margin. The back of the figure follows a similar trace from a dune crest to a point near the bayshore. The right side of the figure continues from this point to waters of the bay, again represented in the center foreground. Thus, by beginning at the center foreground and following the illustration in a clockwise direction, the conspicuously zoned plants of most Texas barrier islands will be encountered, as if you made a trip across the barrier island from Gulf beach to bayshore.

The exposed Gulf beaches present a broad face of unvegetated sand, eventually colonized at the rear margin of the backshore by trailing vines (*Ipomoea*) and succulent creepers (*Sesuvium*). Both of these kinds of plants are also encountered on the leeward faces of dunes, although less extensively. Grasses such as *Uniola* dominate the dune crests and backdune flanks, with sedges and broadleaf plants such as *Suaeda* occurring where conditions are appropriate. These continue to increase in diversity on the central barrier island flats, especially when protected behind high dunes (Chapter 6). Eventually the relative shelter of the flats yields to the more rigorous environment of the bayshore. Wind and wave exposure is minimal here, but other factors such as salinity and substratum limit the kinds of plants which can grow. The bayshore flora consists of a few species of distinctly zoned plants.

The grasses *Monanthochloe littoralis* and *Distichlis spicata* provide a high zoned ground cover, above which project heads of the sea oxeye, *Borrichia frutescens*. The glassworts, *Salicornia virginica* and *S. bigelovii*, lie nearer the shore, sometimes immersed by tidal waters. The remaining bayshore plants usually experience regular tidal inundation. *Batis maritima* is the shortest and highest zoned of these plants. It is followed on southern Texas bayshores by stands of the black mangrove, *Avicennia germinans* (Chapter 9). In the absence of mangroves, *Batis* grades into stands of *Spartina*. When *Spartina* and *Avicennia* coexist, as near the causeway at South Padre Island, *Spartina* is the most bayward-dwelling plant, forming a grass fringe around the more shoreward mangrove trees.

FAUNA OF THE BAYSHORES
Cranes and Rails

A rich variety of birds occurs on Texas bayshores, and few of these are restricted to one particular habitat. Many species are permanent residents, but many more make only seasonal appearances, either as winter residents or passing migrants from the north or south. As a result of the large number of migratory species, the Texas coast ranks high as a favored locality among bird watchers. In this and the next two chapters, we include some of the more common species that may be encountered. There are many detailed sources available for those interested in more information on the birds and waterfowl of Texas and Mexico shores.

Two cranes (Gruidae) winter along the Texas coast. The sandhill crane, *Grus canadensis* (Fig. 7-3 E) occurs commonly on the coastal prairies from November to March. The whooping crane, *Grus americana* (Fig.

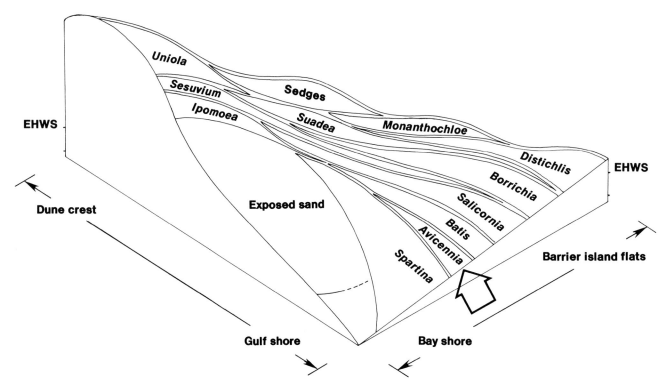

7-4. Patterns of vegetation dominance on southern Texas barrier island Gulf and bayshores. The left profile extends from the swash zone of a barrier island Gulf shore (center) to a dune crest (far left); the right profile extends from a bayshore (center) to a vegetated barrier island flat (far right); the rear of the diagram suggests a profile from dune crest (left) to a low-lying vegetated barrier island flat. The indicated positions for various genera are not absolute; considerable variation occurs on all barrier islands. For example, *Sesuvium* and *Ipomoea* sp. commonly interchange positions or intermingle within a zone, and the mangrove (*Avicennia*) is increasingly sparse or absent north of Port Aransas.

7-3 I) once wintered in salt marshes along most of the north central Gulf coast, but today this endangered species winters at only one locality, the Aransas National Wildlife Refuge near Rockport, Texas, since 1937 a reserve set aside specifically for the protection of whooping cranes. Reduced by humans to a total population of less than two dozen, this largest member of the North American avifauna breeds during the summer in western Canada. The winter census of whooping cranes at the Aransas refuge is now an annual ritual which reflects the success of the preceding breeding season and the hazards of the 3800 km migration.

The Rallidae include both ground-dwelling birds (the rails and crakes) and waterfowl (gallinules and coots). The American coot, *Fulica americana* (Fig. 7-3 Q) is one of the most common birds throughout the Texas coastal zone. It is readily found on most lakes, ponds, marshes and bays. It is a year round resident, but numbers swell in the winter when additional birds arrive from the north. Two gallinules, *Porphyrula martinica* (the purple gallinule) and *Gallinula chloropus* (the common gallinule) may also be seen among marsh grasses. The former is most common in the summer whereas the latter winters in southern Texas and northern Mexico. Both prefer freshwater marshes to estuaries.

Rails are among the most reclusive birds and the species which occupy the Texas marshes are no exceptions. All of the Gulf of Mexico rails can fly, but mostly prefer to stay on the ground, relying upon cryptic coloration and stealth to disappear among marsh vegetation. Their presence is more often indicated by their rattling voice than by a sighting of the bird. The clapper rail, *Rallus longirostris* (Fig. 7-3 J) is the most common rail of Texas salt marshes, and, although elusive, the species that is most likely to be seen. It is a year round resident of estuarine marshes throughout the Gulf of Mexico. Clapper rails forage along the shore for fiddler crabs and other crustaceans during summer months, but rely upon snails for food in the winter when the crustaceans are less abundant (Heard, 1982). The similar king rail *Rallus elegans* (not illustrated) prefers freshwater marshes. Two other rails, the yellow rail, *Coturnicops noveboracensis*, and the black rail, *Laterallus jamaicensis* have been recorded from Gulf marshes, but are so extremely reclusive that little is known about them.

The Osprey

The osprey, *Pandion haliaetus* (Fig. 7-3 F) is the sole representative of the Family Pandionidae, and is distributed throughout the temperate and tropical zones of the world. It is a large bird, almost as large as an eagle. It feeds exclusively upon fish, diving for them feet-first from high in the air. For this reason, it is also known in some parts of the world as the fish-hawk.

The osprey is migratory in North America, and most commonly encountered in the spring and fall along the northwestern Gulf of Mexico. There are always a few birds which remain as permanent residents, especially along the northern Texas estuaries. Several nests are known from the shores of Galveston Bay. Nests are most often constructed near the tops of dead trees. They are large, elaborate structures, reused year after year.

Mosquitoes

Four hundred years ago, Cabeza de Vaca, stranded on a Texas barrier island and living among the Karankawa Indians, remarked in simple understatement, "mosquitoes are in great plenty." Today, the Karankawas are gone, brought to extinction by the pestilence of European diseases. But they are survived by the hordes of mosquitoes that must have made life miserable for the Karankawas and continue to plague modern bayshore visitors especially every summer.

A number of species of mosquitoes occur along western Gulf bayshores. We illustrate the salt marsh mosquito, *Aedes sollicitans* (Fig. 7-6 A), but several additional species of *Aedes*, *Culex*, *Psorophora* and *Anopheles* also occur here. Male mosquitoes feed upon flower nectar and fruit juices, and are thus important pollinators for a variety of wildflowers. Females may also feed upon nectar, but usually require a meal of vertebrate blood prior to egg production. Males are usually easy to distinguish from females, as they typically bear frilly antennae, whereas the antennae of females are sparsely plumose.

Females deposit eggs in standing water, where they hatch into larvae (Fig. 7-6 A, lower right). The coastal lowlands of the western Gulf provide innumerable ponds and puddles suitable for the development of mosquito larvae. Frequent tidal inundation inhibits larval development in many (but not all) species of mosquitoes, so coastal areas with relatively broad tidal ranges tend to have fewer species of mosquitoes than those areas where tidal range is narrow. Accordingly, it is not surprising to find both numerous species and numerous individuals of mosquitoes on Texas bayshores where tidal fluctuation is slight.

After a few days the larvae metamorphose into pupae (Fig. 7-6 A lower left). Both juvenile stages are active swimmers which frequently rise to the surface and breathe air through a pair of tubes or spiracles. In the larva these are located at the end of the abdomen, but are at the top of the thorax in the pupa. Because of the air breathing habitat, one method of mosquito control is to place a light film of oil on standing bodies of water which can harbor mosquito larvae. The oil acts as an impenetrable barrier to the breathing tubes of larva and pupa, inhibits the exchange of atmospheric oxygen into the water, and provides a hindrance to the emergence of adult mosquitoes from the pupae.

The life cycle is completed in 4 to 10 days, depending upon the species. Adults emerge from the pupae to take up their aerial existence. Actually, much of the adult life is spent resting among grasses, shrubs or other vegetation. Females emerge in the evening when the air is still in search of a blood meal, or whenever the vegetation upon which they are resting is disturbed.

Bayshore Crustacea
Fiddler Crabs

The most conspicuous crustaceans of the Texas bays are the fiddler crabs of the genus *Uca*. These small crabs (carapace width 2 to 3 cm) produce burrows that dot almost every bayshore from the tide line to as much as one meter above sea level. Burrows bearing crabs are often punctuated with tell-tale round balls of mud formed during excavation and neatly piled at the entrance. Burrows nearest the water are 20 to 30 cm in length, unbranched, and shaped like a curved L. Those occurring higher on the shore are similarly shaped, but extend downward as much as 1 m to the water table.

Male fiddler crabs, bearing one grotesquely enlarged claw, are easily differentiated from females, with small equal-sized chelae. The large claw serves as a defensive weapon and is used with much pushing and shoving to keep intruders from a burrow. Just as importantly it is used by males to gesture territorial rights or to attract a mate. The gestures are species-specific; those made by one species are usually ignored by a second (but see Aspey, 1971). This reduces interspecific conflicts, especially when, as is common, two or more species share a shore.

Most fiddler crabs emerge from burrows at low tide to feed or seek a mate. The rhythmicity of activity and quiescence is remarkably predictable for most species, reflecting tidal and diurnal cyclic components (Barnwell, 1966; 1968). Those living high upon the shore, however, may restrict foraging and socialization to cloudy days or at night. In addition to the tidal activity rhythm, most species also display conspicuous color changes on a daily cycle, darkening during the day and becoming lighter at night. Color changes are caused by expansion or contraction of melanophores (pigment cells) associated with the integument.

Uca is predominantly a detritivore. Food is obtained by foraging excursions away from the burrow. Some species stray only one or two meters, whereas others (e.g., *U. spinicarpa*) wander dozens of meters as they feed. Food is usually extracted from sand, mud and detritus on the surface of the tidal flat. With tips shaped like narrow spoons and fringed with short comb-like setae, the small chelae are ideally suited for scooping small bits of sediment and passing them to maxillae and maxillipeds (the large male claw is useless for feeding), which sift sand from edible materials and pass the latter to the mouth. Fiddler crabs also will feed on vegetation and carrion when it is present.

A pair of compound eyes located at the ends of movable eyestalks provides fiddler crabs excellent visual acuity. Unexpected movements will send them scurrying back into burrows—their own if handy, or any unoccupied burrow or the sea if not. At least some species have perfected contact proprioreceptive memory (precise retracing of one's steps) within short distances of their burrow (Herrnkind, 1972). When within range, they can proceed directly to the burrow, even in total darkness. Despite their circumspection, countless fiddler crabs nevertheless fall prey to wading birds, fishes, larger crabs, and other bayshore predators.

Reproductive activity of many species of fiddler crabs is cyclic during the warmer months of the year, with peaks of male display activity immediately preceding fortnightly spring tides (Christy, 1978). Male displays include claw waving, color changes and, in some species, auditory signals made by drumming the large claw or walking legs against the ground (Salmon & Stout, 1962; Salmon 1965, 1967; Salmon & Atsaides, 1968). The displays are performed to attract females for mating (Crane, 1957) and as territorial signals to competing males (Crane, 1967). The males of most species will actively and ritualistically defend a territory.

(*Uca pugilator*) females mate once each month, with about half of the local population seeking males every two weeks. A male who successfully attracts a female entices her into his burrow for mating. The male closes the entrance of the burrow, and the mating pair remains secluded together for between 1 to 3 days. Females do not molt immediately prior to copulation. After the female deposits eggs on her abdomen for brooding, the male leaves the burrow. The female remains in the burrow for about 10 to 12 days while the eggs undergo development.

Females leave their burrows the night eggs are to hatch, move to the water's edge and release the larvae. This typically occurs about 5 to 7 days prior to the next spring tide. Christy (1978) suggests that the timing of larval release occurs to take advantage of tidal characteristics in the estuary thereby helping to insure that the majority of larvae are not swept out to sea. Early larval stages occur near the surface, but later stages are most abundant near the bottom where they apparently take advantage of a net landward non-tidal drift (Sandifer, 1973; 1975). Under favorable conditions *Uca* larvae spend about 22 days in the plankton.

The pattern of reproduction for most *Uca* species is similar to this model, but differs in details. We have already mentioned differences between species with respect to male display patterns (Crane, 1941, 1943, 1957). In some species, males entice females into their burrows; in other species, the female leads the male to her burrow (Crane, 1957). Not all species require the

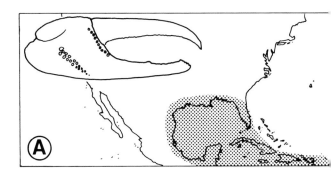

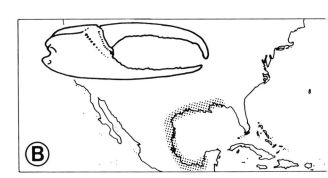

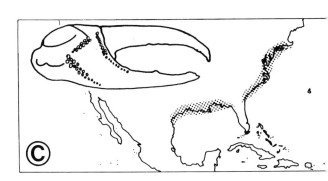

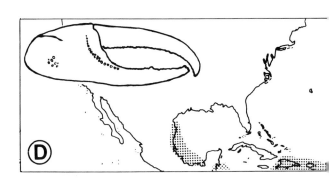

7-5. Fiddler crabs of the Gulf of Mexico and their approximate geographic distributions. **A.** *Uca rapax*; **B.** *Uca panacea*; **C.** *Uca minax*; **D.** *Uca vocator*; **E.** *Uca subcylindrica*; **F.** *Uca pugilator*; **G.** *Uca spinicarpa*; **H.** *Uca rapax*; **I.** *Uca marguerita*; **J.** *Uca leptodactyla*; **K.** *Uca burgersi*; **L.** *Uca speciosa*.

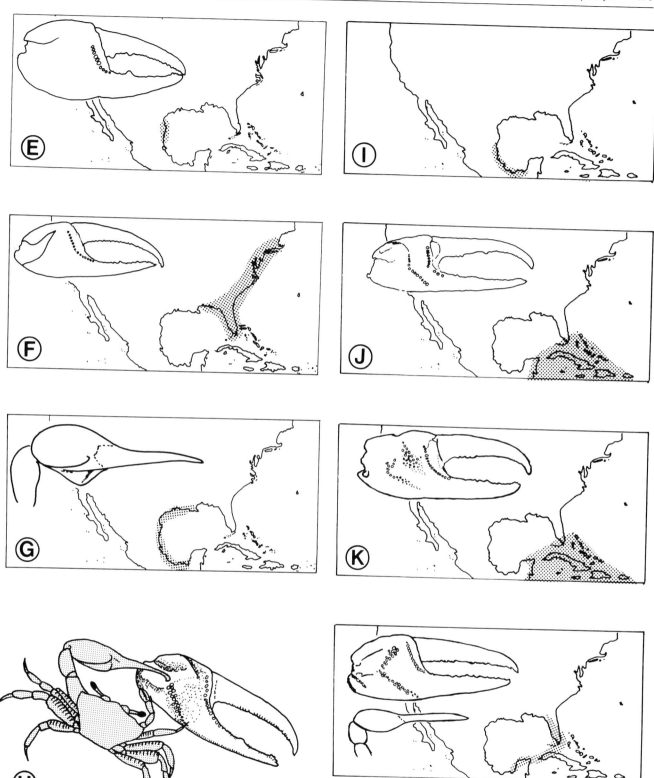

seclusion of the burrow for mating, especially at night.

Thirteen species of fiddler crabs occur in the Gulf of Mexico. Five of these are Gulf of Mexico endemics (Barnwell & Thurman, 1984). Seven species occur in Texas, including four of the Gulf endemics, one species of Carolinian affinity, and two whose range extends throughout the tropical Caribbean. The remaining species of Gulf of Mexico fiddler crabs include one endemic to central Mexico shores, and four predominantly Caribbean species which are occasionally encountered in the southern Gulf of Mexico.

The most common fiddler crab of the more temperate shores of the eastern United States, *Uca pugilator* (Fig. 7-5 F), has been widely reported as occurring on the Texas coast, especially in the literature prior to 1974. Most of these records are erroneous, referring instead to the similar but only recently recognized *U. panacea* (Figs. 7-5 B; 7-6 R) (Barnwell & Thurman, 1984). *Uca pugilator* is at the extreme western margin of its range in northwestern Florida, and, except for a few chance migrants, does not occur in Texas.

Uca panacea is one of the endemic fiddler crabs in the Gulf of Mexico and one of the most common on Texas shores. It ranges from western Florida to Campeche, Mexico, occurring upon bayshores composed primarily of terrigenously derived sediments. Adult males usually have a carapace width of between 17 to 22 mm. Like *U. pugilator*, this species lacks tubercles on the lower portion of the inner surface of the large claw, and is further distinguished from other Texas *Uca* by (1), a lack of pubescence on walking legs and (2), the segmented portion of its antennae extend almost to the pigmented portion of the eyestalk. It undoubtedly is closely related to *U. pugilator* (Selander et al., 1971).

Uca minax (Fig. 7-5 C) is another primarily temperate species, but whose range includes portions of the northern and central Texas coasts. This is the only North American fiddler crab displaying a disjunct Carolinian distribution, ranging from Cape Cod to near Daytona Beach, Florida and along the northern Gulf of Mexico shores, but absent from southern Florida and Mexico. It seems to prefer lower salinity bayshores (Mace & McGraw, 1985). We found *U. minax* especially common on the shores of Drum Bay about 5 km east of Surfside, Texas. *Uca minax* males can be recognized by having a heavily tuberculated ridge on the inner surface of the chela, grooves on the carapace just behind the eyes, and a distinctive red spot near the large joint of the chelae. This is a relatively large species with males having a carapace width of between 30 to 40 mm.

Uca rapax (Figs. 7-5 A and H; 7-6 T) and *U. vocator* (Fig. 7-5 D) are predominantly tropical species commonly encountered on most Mexico shores and approaching the northern limits of their range in Texas. The latter is easily recognized as the only fiddler crab in this region to possess a dense pubescence on the dorsal surface of the carapace and the uppermost surfaces of the walking legs. The transverse tuberculated ridge of the male chela is restricted to the inner basal third of the palm. *Uca rapax* lacks pubescence on the carapace, although it is often present on the upper portions of the walking legs. A tuberculated ridge on the male chela extends completely across the palm. *Uca rapax* is the most widely distributed fiddler crab in the western Gulf of Mexico, occurring commonly on bayshores composed of either terrigenous or carbonate dominated sediments. The related Gulf endemic, *U. longisignalis* (not illustrated), ranging from northwestern Florida to Texas, is very similar in appearance to *U. rapax*, except that pubescence extends over much of the walking legs, including the lower surface of the merus. *Uca longisignalis* is primarily restricted to sediments of terrigenous origin.

Uca subcylindrica (Fig. 7-5 E) and *U. spinicarpa* (Fig. 7-5 G) are the two other fiddler crabs endemic to Gulf shores and which also occur in Texas. The former is a small crab (male carapace ranging from between 15 to 20 mm) with a rounded (subcylindrical) body. Males are most readily identified by the very narrow gonopods, whereas the female gonopore is correspondingly small compared to that of other fiddler crabs. The largest populations of *U. subcylindrica* occur on shores of the hypersaline Laguna Madre system of Texas and northern Mexico (Barnwell & Thurman, 1984), suggesting that this species is primarily adapted for a hypersaline environment. It is an extremely euryhaline species, occurring in freshwater drainage ditches as well as hypersaline waters of up to 90 ppt salinity (Thurman, 1984).

Uca spinicarpa is a moderate-sized species (adult male carapace width ranging from 15 to 20 mm). The males are easily distinguished from other fiddler crabs in Texas by the large prominently projecting tooth on the inner surface of the large claw. In the southern portion of its range it can be confused with *Uca speciosa* (Fig. 7-5 L), a predominantly tropical Caribbean species. *Uca spinicarpa* seems to be restricted to predominantly terrigenously derived shores, whereas *U. speciosa* is restricted to habitats within the tropical carbonate sedimentary province. We have previously encountered *U. spinicarpa* on the unusual habitat of Sargent Beach, Texas (Chapter 6), where it is found in great numbers burrowing in clay. Its preference for a clay substratum is not restricted to Sargent Beach, for this crab typically occurs on Texas and Mexico bayshores dominated by hard packed clays.

The remaining Gulf of Mexico fiddler crabs are restricted to Mexico bayshores. *Uca marguerita* (Fig. 7-5 I) is found from the southern margin of Laguna Madre de Tamaulipas to the Rio San Pedro in the state of Campeche, Mexico. Prior to 1980, this species had been confused with several other species, especially *Uca burgersi*, but is distinguished by an absence of pubescence from the carapace and upper portions of the walking legs, a well developed oblique ridge across the palm of the large claw, a short body, and additional subtle details of anatomy and behavior (Thurman, 1981).

Uca burgersi (Fig. 7-5 K), *U. major* (not illustrated), *U. thayeri*, (not illustrated), and *U. leptodactyla* (Fig. 7-5 J) are occasionally recruited onto southern Mexico shores from Caribbean sources. *Uca burgersi* is perhaps the most widely distributed species of this group.

Other Crustaceans

In addition to the fiddler crabs, many other crustaceans occur at or near the water's edge. Some, like hermit crabs, take refuge in abandoned gastropod shells, and retreat into them for protection. Others are more secretive and thus more difficult to locate. Some hide among the shore vegetation or among the sea grass beds just offshore. Others take temporary refuge just below the mud, emerging frequently to search for food. Still others construct permanent burrows where they spend most of their lives. In this section we will describe a number of bay crustaceans which occur near shore. Because many of these species are equally common throughout the bays, not just in one habitat along the shorelines, we discuss them collectively here. Some species have typical salinity preferences which we will indicate when appropriate. Later, when we consider specific bay habitats, we will indicate some of these crustaceans that are particularly abundant there.

The striped hermit crab, *Clibanarius vittatus* (Figs. 7-6 Q; 7-8 E; 7-9 O) is the only intertidal hermit crab on Texas shores. The common name refers to light longitudinal stripes on the walking legs, a diagnostic feature for this crab in Texas. This species is more efficient in resisting desiccation than most of its near relatives (Young, 1978). It frequents jetties, mud flats, oyster bars and bayshores, where it scavenges for food just below the water line. It remains near the shore most of the year, retreating into the sublittoral only to avoid lethal winter cold (Fotheringham, 1975). When air temperatures drop below freezing, the crabs bury into sublittoral muddy bottoms, where temperatures are near 4°C. Larger, mostly male, specimens migrate to deeper waters first and return to the shore last during a migration cycle. In the summer, this crab is remarkably tolerant of high temperatures. It is one of the few animals that can be found regularly on heated shoals in July and August. It is also exceptionally tolerant of variations in salinity, occurring in waters ranging from 10.5 to 34.5 ppt.

Clibanarius vittatus occupies a variety of gastropod shells, especially those of *Stramonita haemastoma*, *Polinices duplicatus*, and *Littorina irrorata*. Availability of suitable empty shells limits the size of hermit crab populations, and a scarcity of larger shells can inhibit growth (Fotheringham, 1976a, b, c).

Reproduction occurs during the summer. Development requires water temperatures in excess of 15°C. Metamorphosis to the adult has been observed in salinities of 25 ppt or greater (Young & Hazlett, 1978). Even at 25°C, there is a prolonged larval life, with zoeal stages persisting two months or more. Accordingly, this is a warm temperate to tropical species.

Distribution is dependent upon appropriate conditions for larval development. Other hermit crabs which occur in Texas bays include *Pagurus longicarpus* (Fig. 7-6 P), *P. pollicaris* (Fig. 7-6 X), and *P. impressus*, all of which are more common offshore.

Callinectes sapidus (Fig. 7-7 K) is the most common large crab in eastern North American estuaries. It ranges from Maine to Argentina and has been introduced into European and Japanese waters. The blue crab is better known than any other North American brachyuran. The fishery value of this species (it is taken as a commercial product throughout its range) has stimulated intense research and resulted in a vast literature. Here, we will emphasize the ecology of the species, leaving fishery aspects to other authors (e.g., Pearson, 1948; Van Engel, 1962; More, 1969; Powers, 1977).

Although *C. sapidus* larvae are restricted mostly to the relatively stable conditions of neritic seawater, adult blue crabs are extremely tolerant of environmental extremes. Normally found in waters from 1 to 27 ppt salinity (Copeland & Bechtel, 1974), they range from freshwater to hypersaline basins such as Laguna Madre de Tamaulipas where salinities can exceed 100 ppt (Hildebrand, 1958). They prefer temperatures between 10 to 35°C, but can survive below bay ice (Scattergood, 1960) or on shoals heated to 45°C. Powers (1977) has observed blue crabs leaving 40°C waters at midday for the shade of *Salicornia* patches near shore,

7-6. *Spartina* marsh at Port Lavaca, Texas. **A.** Salt marsh mosquito, *Aedes sollicitans*, with stages of life cycle indicated; **B.** Cordgrass, *Spartina alterniflora*; **C.** Marshhay cordgrass, *Spartina patens*; **D.** Marsh periwinkle, *Littoraria irrorata*; **E.** Saltgrass, *Distichlis spicata*; **F.** Saltwort, *Batis maritima*; **G.** Silverhead, *Philoxerus vermicularis*; **H.** Sea ox-eye daisy, *Borrichia frutescens*; **I.** Sea-blite, *Suadea linearis*; **J.** Key grass, *Monanthochloe littoralis*; **K.** Lunar dove shell, *Mitrella lunata*; **L.** Mud snail, *Nassarius vibex*; **M.** Tulip mussel, *Modiolus americanus*; **N.** Ribbed mussel, *Genkensia demissa*; **O.** Paper mussel, *Amygdalum papyrium*; **P.** Hermit crab, *Pagurus longicarpus*; **Q.** Hermit crab, *Clibanarius vittatus*; **R.** Fiddler crab, *Uca panacea*; **S.** Marsh crab, *Sesarma reticulatum*; **T.** Fiddler crab, *Uca rapax*; **U.** Purple tagelus, *Tagelus divisus*; **V.** Buttercup, *Lucina pectinata*; **W.** Portunid crab, *Portunus gibbesii*; **X.** Hermit crab, *Pagurus pollicaris*; **Y.** Mud crab, *Panopeus obesus*; **Z.** Lug worm, *Arenicola cristata*; **A1.** Terebellid worm, *Amphitrite* sp.; **B1.** *Capitella* cf. *capitata*; **C1.** Clam worm, *Nereis succinea*; **D1.** Egg cockle, *Laevicardium mortoni*; **E1.** *Macoma tenta*; **F1.** Flat mud crab, *Eurypanopeus depressus*; **G1.** Mud crab, *Neopanope texana*; **H1.** *Cirratulus* sp.; **I1.** *Eteone heteropoda*; **J1.** *Loandalia americana*; **K1.** Grass shrimp, *Palaemonetes pugio*; **L1.** Mud crab, *Rhithropanopeus harrisii*; **M1.** Ribbon worm, *Cerebratulus lacteus*.

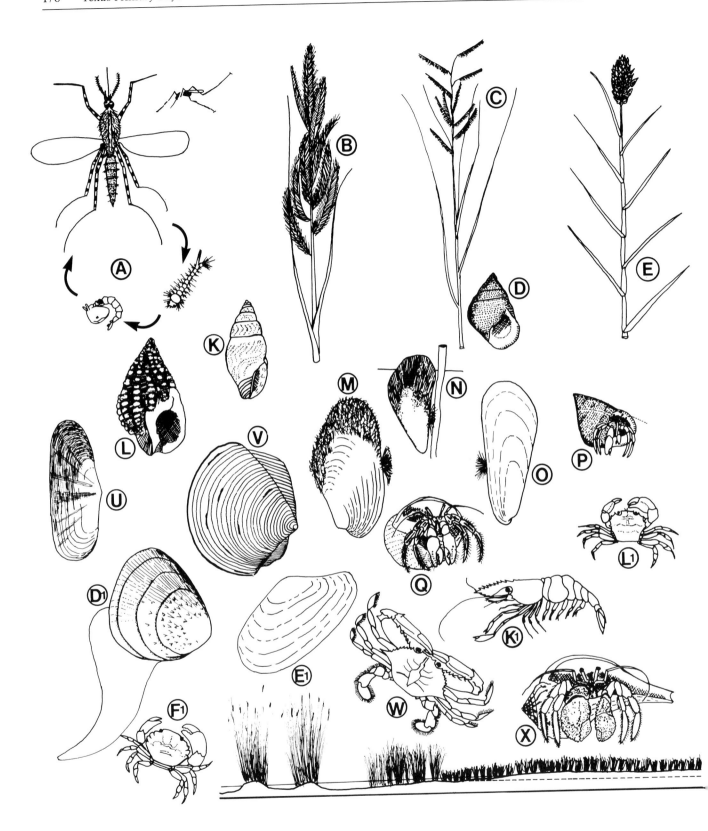

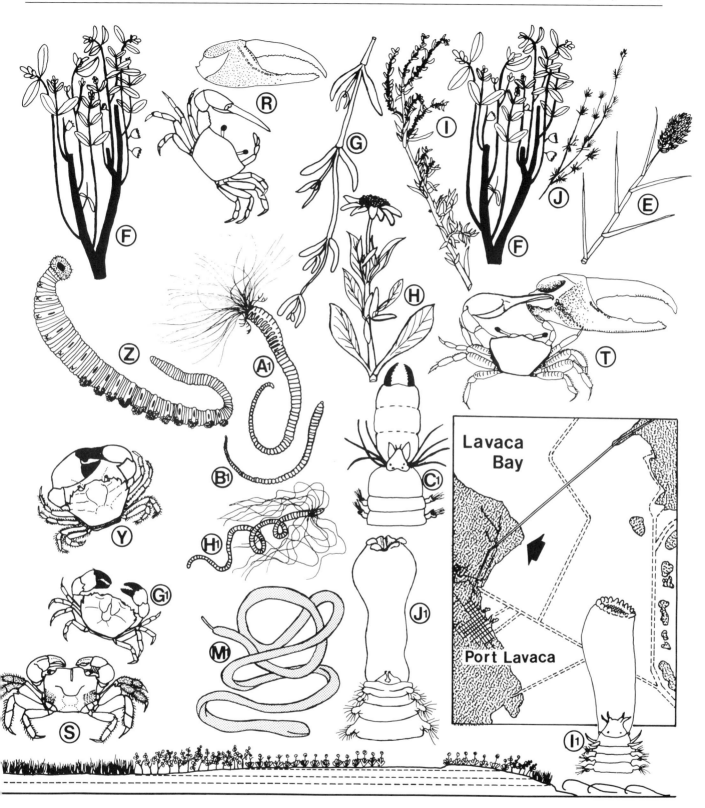

where they remain for two to four hours in the cooler (30 to 35°C) humid air. They are known to occur in polluted sewage where mean oxygen levels are well below 1 mg/l (Smith, 1971). Large males even have been taken from salt springs in the St. Johns River, Florida over 180 miles from the sea (Williams, 1984). Few other marine crustaceans display the tolerance of *Callinectes sapidus* to environmental extremes.

The typical habitat of the blue crab is the shallow waters throughout moderately saline estuaries. We have illustrated it as a member of the central bayfloor community, but it is an active animal and can be expected in all parts of the bay. When on the unvegetated bayfloor, the blue crab seeks shelter by burrowing into the soft mud, but it just as readily finds refuge among tangled vegetation on subtidal grass beds. As with all portunids, the fifth pair of limbs are flattened paddles modified for swimming (Spirito, 1972).

Blue crabs are omnivores and scavengers. They are attracted to carrion, and will feed upon almost any dead animal on the sea floor. Commercial fisheries employ the scavenging activities of *C. sapidus* to advantage by baiting crab traps with fish parts. The normal diet is equally varied (Darnell, 1959, 1961; Dunnington, 1956; Hamilton, 1976; Menzel & Hopkins, 1956; Odum & Heald, 1972; Tagatz, 1968). They are known to capture fishes, medusae, gastropods, mussels, oysters, tunicates and a variety of additional soft-bodied benthic invertebrates. Virstein (1977) has shown *C. sapidus* to be a major predator on estuarine infauna. Crabs obtain shallow burrowing infauna from the bayfloor by searching just below the surface with the chelae. Some dig as much as 12 cm into the sediment for deeper burrowing species (Orth, 1977). Blue crabs will ingest plant material, and will extract the epibiota from sea grass blades by passing the leaves through the mandibles (Williams, 1984).

Blue crabs are among the most active and aggressive brachyurans. They forage both day and night. When threatened, they will respond in kind (Jachowski, 1974), confronting the attacker with flailing chelae that promise (and can deliver) flesh-severing snips. Like other portunids, *C. sapidus* bears dimorphic chelae. One (usually the right) is adapted for crushing, whereas the other is designed for cutting. Variations in this pattern are known (Hamilton *et al.*, 1976).

Reproduction in *C. sapidus* involves a complex migratory sequence, presumably to insure that the planktonic larval stages are provided optimal conditions for development. Males congregate in the lower salinity portions of estuaries, where they spend the majority of their adult lives. Females join the males here for mating. Copulation is possible only immediately following a molt by the female. In anticipation of molting, a male crab will carry a female beneath its body. Other males often challenge this male for possession of the female. Copulation involves transfer of spermatophores to the female. They are not employed immediately for fertilization, but are held in the female body for later release.

Soon after mating, females migrate to higher salinity portions of estuaries near tidal inlets or just offshore where most will stay the remainder of their lives. Here they lay the eggs, attaching them to abdominal pleopods. They brood the eggs for about two weeks. Ovigerous (berried) females occur in Texas bays almost year round, but peak during June and July. Females usually move seawards just prior to the eggs' hatching (Daugherty, 1952; King, 1971). The larval zoea pass through several instars in the offshore marine plankton. Eventually, they reach the megalops stage and begin to migrate back into the estuary with the surface plankton (King, 1971; More, 1969; Naylor & Isaac, 1973; Williams, 1971). Crabs reach sexual maturity in about one year.

Blue crabs usually experience a final molt at sexual maturity, but survive one or two years thereafter. The shells of these older crabs become attachment sites for a variety of epizoites. For example, the barnacles *Balanus amphitrite* and *Chelonibia patula* (Fig. 7-7 L) commonly encrust the carapace. The parasitic barnacle, *Octolasmis lowei* (= *mulleri*) (Fig. 7-7 M), attaches to gills. It resembles a miniature gooseneck barnacle with highly reduced calcareous valves. Hundreds may occupy *Callinectes* gill chambers. Young crabs control barnacle infestations by molting, but specimens beyond the final molt gradually succumb to this and other epizoites.

Other parasites plague the blue crab. The rhizocephalan *Loxothylacus texanus* is a most unusual barnacle (Wass, 1955), which invades the internal tissues of the crab. The adult is unrecognizable as a barnacle; its phylogenetic position is revealed only in the planktonic larval stage. *Loxothylacus texanus* lives partly within and partly outside the crab body. The portion within the host consists of highly branching nutritive roots which unite at a pore formed at the base of the crab abdomen. The external body emerges from this

7-7. Biota of the Texas bays. **A.** Paper bubble, *Haminoea succinea*; **B.** Variable bittium, *Bittium varium*; **C.** *Pyrgocythara plicosa*; **D.** Paper bubble, *Haminoea antillarum*; **E.** *Rictaxis punctostriatus*; **F.** Atlantic assiminea, *Assiminea succinea*; **G.** *Odostomia laevigata*; **H.** *Odostomia gibbosa*; **I.** *Vitrinella floridana*; **J.** *Caecum johnsoni*; **K.** Blue crab, *Callinectes sapidus*; **L.** Barnacle, *Chelonibia patula*, which frequently lives attached to the carapace of a blue crab; **M.** Parasitic barnacle, *Octolasmis lowei*; **N.** Mantis shrimp, *Squilla empusa*; **O.** *Macoma tageliformis*; **P.** *Cumingia tellinoides*; **Q.** *Macoma mitchelli*; **R.** *Macoma constricta*; **S.** Contracted corbula, *Corbula contracta*; **T.** Gem clam, *Gemma gemma*; **U.** Pointed nut clam, *Nuculana acuta*; **V.** *Pandora trilineata*; **W.** Dwarf surf clam, *Mulinia lateralis*; **X.** Mud-burrowing heart urchin, *Moira atropus*: *left*, view from the side with spines intact, *right*, view of test from above, lacking spines.

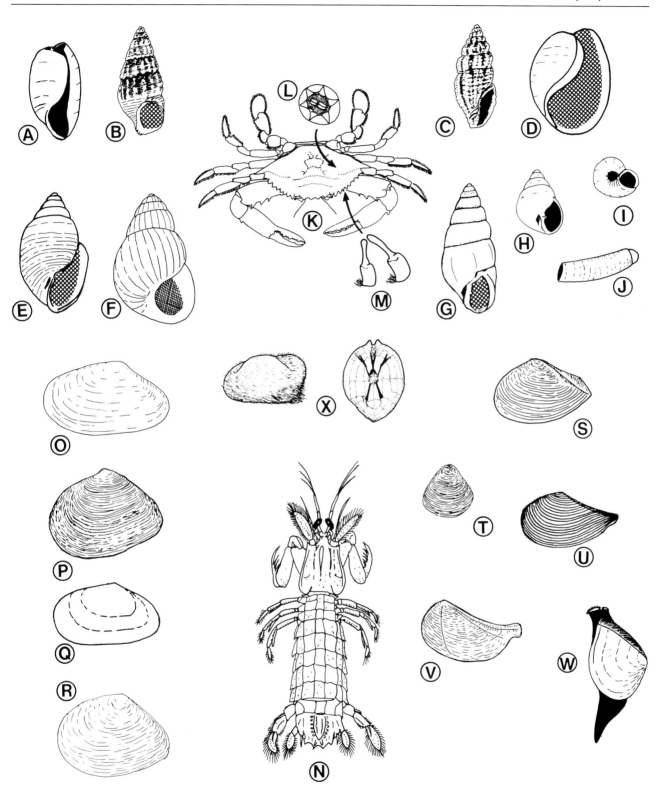

pore as a rounded chitinous gonadal sac beneath the host abdomen. Effects of the rhizocephalan parasite on *Callinectes* are severe. Infested crabs are inhibited from molting and experience a loss of sexual organs (parasitic castration).

The parasitic nemertean *Carcinonemertes carcinophila*, which occurs on the gills of female blue crabs, exhibits two color phases. Large red worms are found on ovigerous female crabs or those which have already spawned, whereas only light-colored worms are present on mature females which have never spawned (Hopkins, 1947).

Callinectes sapidus is the most common portunid within Texas bays, but two additional species, *Callinectes similis* and *Portunus gibbesii* (Fig. 7-6 W), sometimes appear. The former frequents higher salinity (but not excessively hypersaline) bays and offshore areas. The latter, a predominantly offshore species, occasionally occupies tidal inlets and the deeper portions of the outer bays. *Callinectes rathbunae* ranges along the central Mexican coast, and rarely ventures into extreme south Texas waters.

Sesarma reticulatum (Fig. 7-6 S) is a small crab which frequents the muddy bottoms of *Spartina* marshes. It seems to prefer moderate salinities from 10 to 25 ppt. It is essentially a temperate species, occurring along the northern portion of the Texas coast to about Port O'Connor. It constructs elaborate deep burrows (80 to 90 cm below the surface) with several openings, shallow interconnecting corridors and vertical shafts (Crichton 1960, 1974; Allen and Curran, 1974). The burrows usually contain a male and from two to several females. At low tide on sunny days, the crabs remain in or near the burrows, but actively forage upon *Spartina* at high tide or on cloudy days (Teal, 1959). *Sesarma reticulatum* is also known to capture and eat fiddler crabs (Crichton, 1974).

Sesarma cinereum (Fig. 9-2 E1) is a similar marsh crab, but tends to prefer higher salinity marshes than *S. reticulatum*, and also frequents jetties, wharves, cobbles and mangrove shores. It occurs along the entire Texas coast and as far south as Veracruz, Mexico. It is particularly resistant to desiccation, and capable of spending months in damp areas with only small amounts of standing freshwater available (Oler, 1941; Duncker, 1934; Gray, 1957). The primary food for *S. cinereum* is *Spartina* (Seiple, 1979), but it is also a scavenger and occasionally cannibalistic. This species also burrows, but unlike *S. reticulatum*, apparently constructs solitary burrows (Duncker, 1934).

Both *Sesarma* species produce larvae during the summer. Captive female specimens of *S. cinereum* isolated from contact with males during their life in captivity have produced several successive egg masses which develop viable larvae (Duncker, 1934). As in other brachyurans, mating may be necessary only once in this genus, with the females capable of holding viable spermatophores for three years or more.

Several species of small xanthid (mud) crabs, most bearing stout, black-tipped chelae, commonly hide un-

der shells or among the subtidal bay vegetation. *Neopanope texana* (Figs. 7-6 G1, 7-9 Z) occupies a variety of habitats from grass beds, mud and sand flats, among shell debris and oyster reefs, and even on subtidal gravel banks. Its diet is probably varied, but oyster spat and juvenile bivalves (<10 mm) are known to be preferred.

Panopeus herbstii was once considered a wide-ranging species occupying even more variable habitats than *N. texana* and displaying several morphotypes. Reames & Williams (1983) have shown that two of the morphotypes, *P. h. simpsoni* and *P. h. obesus*, occupy distinctly different habitats in the Mobile Bay, Alabama region and also are separable morphometrically. This has prompted Williams (1983) to elevate several of the "forms" of *P. herbstii* to species. *Panopeus herbstii sensu stricto* now refers to populations occupying Atlantic oyster reefs from Massachusetts to eastern Florida. It is absent from the Gulf of Mexico. Two new species are recognized in the northwestern Gulf: *Panopeus obesus* (Fig. 7-6 Y) and *P. simpsoni*. The two are very similar, differing in coloration, ecology and subtle aspects of morphometry (Reames & Williams, 1983; Williams, 1983).

Adult *Panopeus* spp. of the northwestern Gulf are 40 to 50 mm wide across the carapace, not as large as *Menippe adina*, but larger than most of the other Texas xanthid crabs. *Panopeus obesus* lives intertidally along undercut mudbanks or marsh margins, where it produces burrows consisting of numerous honeycombed galleries. *Panopeus simpsoni* occurs intertidally or subtidally in association with rock rubble, and especially among oyster shells. It excavates shallow depressions beneath the rocks or shells, and will occupy *P. obesus* habitats if there is sufficient cover available. Both feed upon shelled invertebrates such as oysters, barnacles and other crabs, including smaller specimens of their own species. They employ the chelae to chip away parts of the prey shell. They are the only other xanthids in Texas, in addition to *Menippe*, sufficiently large enough to crack open adult oysters (Menzel & Nichy, 1958). *Panopeus obesus* is a more aggressive feeder than *P. simpsoni*, and more capable of chipping away shells to attain the enclosed flesh. Accordingly, it also preys upon *Littorina irrorata*, causing noticeable reductions in the numbers of the marsh snail in areas having large populations of the crab (Reames & Williams, 1983).

Panopeus obesus and *P. simpsoni* contribute zoea to the bay and offshore plankton during the warmer months, in Texas likely from April to November. Larval development in *P. herbstii* is accelerated as salinities approach normal seawater and water temperature increases from 20 to 30°C (Costlow & Bookhout, 1961). Similar stimuli likely influence the *Panopeus* spp. of the northwestern Gulf. Both are polyhaline to euhaline in distribution (Fig. 8-2 A), with salinities below about 15 ppt insufficient to support either species.

Rhithropanopeus harrisii (Fig. 7-6 L1), unlike many of its other xanthid relatives, does not possess black-tipped chelae. It is also one of the smaller xanthids, with carapace widths of adult males usually less than 20 mm. *Rhithropanopeus* prefers the upper reaches of estuaries in salinities less than 20 ppt, although it can and does range into the higher salinity bays. It tends to be absent on bare sand or mud, requiring some form of surface irregularity (e.g., shells, grass beds, mangrove roots or debris) in which it finds shelter.

Rhithropanopeus harrisii is an omnivore deriving considerable sustenance from leaf detritus when it is available (Odum & Heald, 1972). Smaller specimens feed upon amphipods and copepods.

Larval development of *Rhithropanopeus* is best adapted for estuarine conditions. Christiansen & Costlow (1975) tested larval survival to the early crab stage in a variety of salinities and temperatures, finding greatest survival in 20 ppt salinity at a temperature of 20 to 25°C. Field evidence (e.g., Herman, *et al.*, 1968; Sandifer, 1973) corroborates the laboratory evidence, with greatest numbers of *Rhithropanopeus* zoea occurring in the upper reaches of estuaries.

Eurypanopeus depressus (Fig. 7-6 F1) prefers shelter among oyster shells, and may be found on intertidal oyster reefs and shell bank shores. It also occurs on wharves, pilings, and sometimes in grass beds.

The shores of estuaries frequently accumulate piles of *Spartina* leaves and other decaying vegetation. A variety of small amphipods and isopods are likely to be found among the debris. The sea roach, *Ligia exotica* (Figs. 3-1 A; 5-1 C) is sometimes found here, especially if rocks, bricks, or concrete blocks also line the shore. Several species of amphipods, including *Gammarus mucronatus* (Fig. 9-2 T), frequent this habitat, obtaining both food and shelter from the mass of decaying vegetation.

Bivalves

The only truly intertidal bivalve of Texas bayshores is the ribbed mussel *Geukensia demissa* (Fig. 7-6 N). It is also one of the largest bivalves of the northwestern Gulf (although not always the most conspicuous). Many individuals exceed 100 mm in length. The mussel lives in clumps at the base of *Spartina* stands near the mean tide line, especially along the margins of tidal channels. It secures a position by means of byssus threads attached to *Spartina* rhizomes. *Geukensia* seems to thrive where *Spartina* fares well, but tends to be absent when *Spartina* stands are sparse. It is more prevalent in northern Texas bays and is uncommon or absent in the southern estuaries.

As this mussel lives tidally exposed at least half of its life (Kuenzler, 1961a,b), it has developed some interesting adaptations for survival in air, for example, valve gaping, providing for aerial respiration. This is most effective when the mussel lives under the protection of dense vegetation cover, which helps to maintain relatively high subaerial humidity and reduce desiccation stress. *Geukensia* has broad thermal and salinity tolerances, surviving temperatures from -22°C to 40°C (Kanwisher, 1955; Lent, 1969) and salinities

from 5 to 75 ppt (Wells, 1961; Lent, 1969). It is especially tolerant of subfreezing temperatures, and capable of surviving with as much as 71 percent of its tissue water frozen (Lent, 1969). Large specimens are less tolerant of high temperatures (<36°C) than smaller ones.

Geukensia is an important biological contributor to sedimentary processes. It is an efficient filter feeder, removing considerable particulate material from the water and depositing it as solid feces or pseudofeces on the floor of the marsh. Kuenzler (1961a, b) estimates this species can remove as much as one-third of the particulate phosphorus from the water of a *Spartina* marsh, and Jorden & Valiela (1982) demonstrate its ability to process equally significant amounts of nitrogen. Nutrient binding and deposition by the ribbed mussel provides an otherwise unavailable concentration of nutrients to deposit or detritus ingesting worms and other organisms.

Geukensia demissa lives 10 years or more in well protected estuarine habitats (Bertness, 1980). It spawns in the late summer or early fall, but details of the reproductive cycle of this species, especially in Texas, are wanting.

Most other bivalves of the Texas bays live subtidally or at least protected within the sediments as infauna. Several species are encountered so frequently near the shore that they can be considered a part of the bayshore fauna. For example, apricot or bleached white shells of *Lucina pectinata* (Fig. 7-6 V) are often found strewn over unvegetated tidal flats, especially in the vicinity of Port Aransas and in some portions of Corpus Christi Bay and Laguna Madre. A tidal flat may yield many unattached valves, but apparently no living specimens. The living lucine clams lie deeply buried in the subtidal but nearshore mudbanks. Unlike other deeply buried bivalves which communicate with surface waters by a pair of posterior siphons, *Lucina* has only a single posterior siphon used for the elimination of filtered water and feces from the mantle cavity. Inhalant water enters the clam anteriorly via an inhalant tube constructed by an elongate vermiform foot. Water flow in the lucinid mantle cavity is thus from anterior to posterior, unlike that of most bivalves.

Other bivalves whose shells litter unvegetated tidal flats throughout the entire coast are the razor clams *Tagelus divisus* (Figs. 7-6 U; 7-8 B), the larger *T. plebeius* (Fig. 8-3 A1), and the narrower jackknife clam, *Ensis minor* (Fig. 7-8 A). The *Tagelus* species are also deep burrowers, but with the characteristic paired posterior siphons. They possess a large digging foot which constructs a semi-permanent burrow in muddy sand and in which the clam resides. Their burrows extend vertically downward to a distance of approximately five or six times the length of the shell. Unfused siphons emerge on the surface at different locations, giving the impression that the clam has two openings to its underground burrow. When in feeding position, the body lies about one shell length below the surface, but

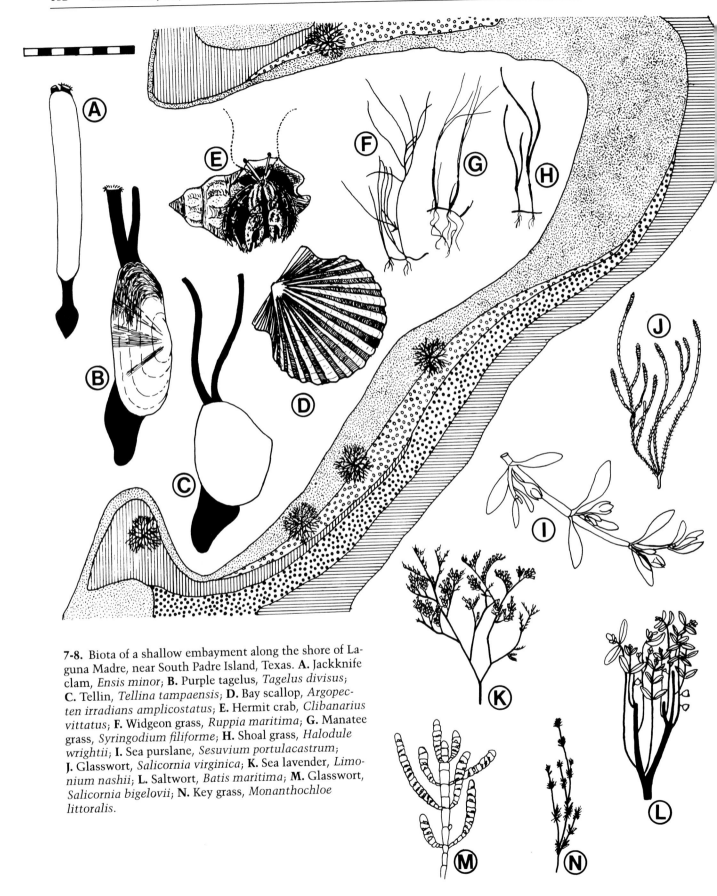

7-8. Biota of a shallow embayment along the shore of Laguna Madre, near South Padre Island, Texas. **A.** Jackknife clam, *Ensis minor*; **B.** Purple tagelus, *Tagelus divisus*; **C.** Tellin, *Tellina tampaensis*; **D.** Bay scallop, *Argopecten irradians amplicostatus*; **E.** Hermit crab, *Clibanarius vittatus*; **F.** Widgeon grass, *Ruppia maritima*; **G.** Manatee grass, *Syringodium filiforme*; **H.** Shoal grass, *Halodule wrightii*; **I.** Sea purslane, *Sesuvium portulacastrum*; **J.** Glasswort, *Salicornia virginica*; **K.** Sea lavender, *Limonium nashii*; **L.** Saltwort, *Batis maritima*; **M.** Glasswort, *Salicornia bigelovii*; **N.** Key grass, *Monanthochloe littoralis*.

can rapidly move downward within the burrow when danger threatens (Wardle, 1970). The ligament of *T. divisus* exerts such force upon the valves that, outside the burrow, the clam must expend significant amounts of energy to maintain valve closure. The counterpressure exerted by the walls of the burrow relieve the clam of much of this burden, for, if maintained in water outside of the burrow for 24 hrs or more, the clam is rendered so weak by the attempt at valve closure that it often is unable to dig back into the substratum (Fraser, 1967).

Unlike most of the Tellinacea which are deposit feeding bivalves employing their inhalant siphons to sweep the bayfloor, *Tagelus* is not a strict deposit feeder (Fraser, 1967; Wardle, 1970). It can take in loose sediment and other coarse material stirred up by currents and wave action, but it does not apply the inhalant siphon directly upon the substratum to obtain this material.

The two species of *Tagelus* are not difficult to distinguish. *T. divisus* is the smaller of the two, rarely exceeding a shell length of 40 mm. It has a slightly arched ventral margin and a weak internal radial rib which divides the valves into two parts (and from which the scientific name is derived). In contrast *T. plebeius* attains a length of up to 100 mm. It has almost parallel dorsal and ventral margins and lacks the internal radial rib.

Both species have extremely broad salinity tolerances, living in waters ranging from 5 to 35 ppt. Both species also suffer considerable mortality in Texas bays during the late summer. Wardle (1970) suggests that the mortality is due, in part, to weakened conditions brought about by fungus infections in ctenidial and mantle tissues which are especially noticeable during the warmer months.

Spawning occurs at all times of the year, but is most prevalent from December to March for *T. divisus* in Biscayne Bay, Florida (Fraser, 1967) and presumably about the same time period for *T. plebeius* in Galveston Bay (Wardle, 1970). The duration of the larval stage is unknown, but probably between one week and one month. Juvenile specimens are found in the sediment at all seasons, but peaks for both species occur in early spring.

With its elongate (but considerably more slender) shell, the jackknife clam *Ensis minor* superficially resembles *Tagelus*. The resemblance involves little more than adaptation to a common habitat, for *Ensis* differs from *Tagelus* in so many respects that it is placed in a separate superfamily, the Solenacea. The siphons of *Ensis* are very short, the shell gapes at both ends, and the ventral margin is fused along most of its length. The long foot (occupying at least half of the mantle cavity) protrudes from the anteriorly located pedal gape and is exceedingly well adapted for digging. But *Ensis* does not construct a subterranean burrow. When feeding, it lies near the surface with the long axis of the shell vertical. If threatened, it is able to dig rapidly into the sediment, pushing sand into the position it

formerly occupied. So adept is this bivalve at digging that it relies primarily upon its agility to escape predation by the numerous shore birds which feed upon it. If stranded in water, it may leap or swim away from the immediate vicinity of the threat before seeking shelter in the substratum (McMahon & McMahon, 1983). Fraser (1967) reports a similar behavior for *Tagelus divisus*.

There are several species of deposit feeding tellinids commonly found in the shallow sediments near Texas bayshores. *Tellina tampaensis* (Fig. 7-8 C) and *Macoma tenta* (Fig. 7-6 E1) are particularly common in the shallow hurricane washover channels and hypersaline lagoons of southern Texas. *Tellina tampaensis* occupies shallow unvegetated sandy bottoms, often in large numbers. It is easily recognized by the ovate subtrigonal translucent shell with a slight pink or peach blush. *Macoma tenta* occurs on both bay margins and in hypersaline lagoons.

Gastropods

The marsh periwinkle, *Littoraria irrorata* (Figs. 7-6 D and 9-2 N) is the most conspicuous snail of the bayshore. Its stout, light tan or gray shell can be confused with no other snail in the region. It climbs blades of *Spartina* with the rising tide. It rests by attaching to the grass, spire down, above the high tide mark by means of a dried mucous holdfast formed along one margin of the outer lip of the aperture. The holdfast is just that, for *L. irrorata* relies upon a thickened chitinous operculum to retard water loss during the period of attachment. Decreasing relative humidity or excessively low (< 10 ppt) or high (> 45 ppt) salinity stimulates holdfast formation (Bingham, 1972a). A snail remains attached several hours or days, but eventually descends the grass blades during low tide to feed upon the lichens and algae which occur on the base of the grass. The littorine also will forage on the mud floor of the *Spartina* bank at low tide (Teal, 1962). With the return of the tide, *L. irrorata* returns to the grass and climbs above the rising water, as submersion augments a strong negative geotaxis in this species. Other than the upward movement when covered by the tides, *L. irrorata* displays no other synchrony with tidal or lunar periodicity (Bingham, 1969 & 1972b). High air temperatures or being wetted after a period of desiccation will cause *L. irrorata* to move downward.

Foraging *L. irrorata* demonstrate a distinctive tendency to follow mucous trails made by other periwinkles of the same species. Trail-following occurs without regard to sex or direction, and, although ease of travel in the path of a trail-blazer has been suggested as one reason for the behavior (Hall, 1973), the actual reason has yet to be conclusively demonstrated.

Littoraria irrorata is dioecious. Copulation occurs during the warmer days of summer, and rarely on cooler, overcast days. Mating occurs while the partners are on the marsh grass out of water (Bingham, 1972c). Spawning by the female usually occurs about a day after mating, at a time corresponding to just after high tide. Most females position themselves along a *Spartina* stalk at the interface between water and air to spawn. Eggs are expelled continuously at the rate of four or five per second for a period of as much as four hours. Each spawn includes from 40,000 to 85,000 disk-shaped planktonic egg capsules, each of which contain a single gray egg. Planktonic egg capsules are of obvious adaptive value for this marsh-dwelling species in lieu of the benthic egg capsules produced by many other marine snails.

The shell color pattern of *Neritina virginea* (Fig. 7-9 I) is so variable that, on first inspection, you may consider each specimen to be a different species. This small (to 15 mm) herbivorous snail ranges from Bermuda to Surinam, and occurs along shores throughout the Gulf of Mexico. In the northwestern Gulf it is most commonly encountered on intertidal flats along bayshores or on sparsely vegetated tidal flats just offshore. Intertidal grass beds in the vicinity of Port Isabel, Texas, for example, often yield numerous specimens. It also occurs on tidal banks adjacent to small streams or freshwater inflow into the sea or higher salinity estuaries. Look for *Neritina* in this environment on shallow flats with sediments consisting of a mixture of mud, sand and gravel. Many shores of northern and western Yucatan provide this habitat.

Neritina virginea has a high tolerance for both temperature and salinity extremes. We have collected the snail alive in 40°C waters. When exposed to hypersaline conditions, the colors and patterns on shells of this nerite become more subdued (Andrews, 1940). *Nerita virginea* spawns during the winter. Females deposit yellowish gelatinous egg masses, which often adhere to other *Neritina* shells.

The mud snail, *Nassarius vibex* (Fig. 7-6 L), is a common scavenger on the intertidal mud flats of tidal inlets and higher salinity bays, where it is most frequently observed. It is also common subtidally offshore. It has chemoreceptors capable of detecting even faint odors given off by decaying flesh (Carr, 1967a, b). These snails are easily attracted by a stranded fish carcass or decaying bait left behind by anglers (Hurst, 1965). They are, in turn, fed upon by predatory whelks (e.g., *Fasciolaria*, see Chapter 10). When contacted by a predator, *Nassarius* evades capture by leaping or somersaulting away (Gore, 1966). Mud snails also avoid areas of recent contact by predatory gastropods or sea stars.

The small ellobiid, *Melampus bidentatus* (Fig. 9-2 P) is often found crawling on the lower stalks of *Spartina* and on the muddy floor of the marsh. In southern Texas, is also occurs commonly in association with stands of black mangrove, but in Mexico, the species is mostly replaced in mangroves by *M. coffeus*. However, it persists throughout the tropical Gulf and Caribbean in marshes dominated by grasses. *Melampus bidentatus* is smaller, rarely more than 10 mm high, thinner shelled, and with fine incised spiral lines on the body whorl above the shoulder; *M. coffeus* can attain a height of 15 mm, is heavier shelled, and lacks

the incised spiral lines. Both species bear two prominent elevations on the columella and several lirae on the inner surface of the outer lip.

BIOTA OF THE SUBTIDAL GRASSBEDS

Many of the bayshore species discussed above, especially the crustaceans, also occur in the shallow grassbeds of the Texas bays. Here we emphasize those species which are most frequently found among the sea grasses, and we will start with a discussion of the flora of the grass beds.

Algae and the Sea Grasses

The majority of species of subtidal marine plants are algae, most of which live attached to hard substrata or upon other plants. A moderate number of algal species occur in estuaries, especially in association with shell debris, and particularly among oysters. Prominent among these are *Acetabularia crenulata* (Fig. 8-6 E), *Cladophora dalmatica*, *Dictyota dichotoma* (Figs. 3-3 G; 4-1 C1), *Ectocarpus siliculosus*, *Giffordia rallsiae*, *Hypnea cornuta*, and *Polysiphonia* sp. Although a number of tropical algae have adaptations to survive on soft sediments (see Chapter 11), few temperate species are capable of prolonged survival on sands or muds in the absence of a suitable substratum for the holdfast. Those that do, such as *Laurencia poitei* (Figs. 4-1 W; 4-3 J), *Chondria cnicophylla* and *Gracilaria verrucosa*, are attached species which have broken free and survive a nomadic existence floating about the estuary without permanent attachment.

Algae are at a disadvantage on soft sands or muds. They cannot drive holdfasts or rhizomes deeply into the submarine soil, for they lack conducting tissue necessary to provision distantly buried cells. Algae must live on or very near the surface, where each cell provisions just itself or its most immediate neighbors.

7-9. Laguna Madre grassbeds, near Port Isabel, Texas. **A.** Sea-blite, *Suaeda linearis*; **B.** Sea purslane, *Sesuvium portulacastrum*; **C.** Shoal grass, *Halodule wrightii*; **D.** *Rissoina catesbyana*; **E.** Turtle grass, *Thalassia testudinum*; **F.** Arrow shrimp, *Tozeuma carolinense*; **G.** Broken back shrimp, *Hippolyte pleuracanthus*; **H.** Sea grass, *Halophila engelmannii*; **I.** Virgin nerites, *Neritina virginea*; **J.** Cross-barred venus, *Chione cancellata*; **K.** Bubble shell, *Bulla striata*; **L.** Dove shell, *Anachis semiplicata*; **M.** *Phoronis architecta*; **N.** Bamboo worm, *Clymenella torquata*; **O.** Hermit crab, *Clibanarius vittatus*; **P.** Blood worm, *Glycera americana*; **Q.** Plumed tube worm, *Diopatra cuprea* and tube chimney; **R.** Sea cucumber, *Thyone mexicana*; **S.** Burrowing anemone, *Nematostella vectensis*; **T.** Ghost shrimp, *Callianassa louisianensis*; **U.** Spider crab, *Libinia dubia*; **V.** Grass shrimp, *Palaemonetes vulgaris*; **W.** White shrimp, *Penaeus setiferus*; **X.** Spider crab, *Libinia emarginata*; **Y.** Grass shrimp, *Palaemonetes pugio*; **Z.** Mud crab, *Neopanope texana*.

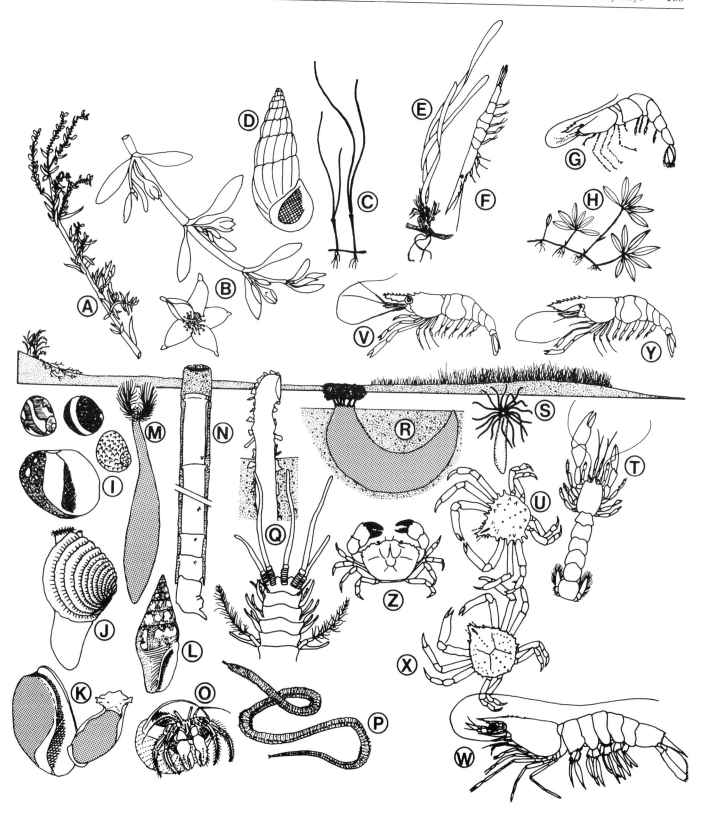

Only the more advanced plants which have developed conductive or vascular tissues can effectively sink roots or underground stems (rhizomes) deeply into the sediment. Ironically, conductive tissues evolved presumably as one of the adaptations for life on land. But having developed vascular tissues, a few of the more advanced plants, belonging to the flowering angiosperms, returned to live in the water and eventually upon the soft bottoms of the shallow sea.

There are three families of marine sea grasses in the western Gulf of Mexico (but see below), comprising at least five species, none of which belongs to the Gramineae, the family of true grasses. They are called grasses because they bear grass-like leaves and rhizomatous stems. All are limited to depths within the bays between about 0.3 to 2 m, the limit controlled primarily by turbidity of the water and depth to which sufficient light can penetrate for photosynthesis. Most species employ hydrophilous pollination and have developed specific anatomical adaptations to facilitate this type of sexual reproduction: *Halophila* and *Halodule* have long styles, *Cymodocea* and *Syringodium* produce long stigmata, and *Thalassia* and *Halophila* bear elongate hypanthia. Moreover, the spherical pollen grains of *Halophila* and *Thalassia*, arranged in coherent moniliform chains, increase their floating capacity.

Collectively, the sea grasses provide refuge, substrata, or sustenance for a variety other plants and animals. Accordingly, the species diversity and total biomass of the grass beds is often very high. We will deal with only the larger, more conspicuous species. As with other plants and animals, the sea grasses of the Texas coast include a blend of temperate and tropical species, both groups generally near the limits of their respective ranges.

The Zosteraceae include most of the temperate species of sea grasses. The best known member of this family, the eelgrass, *Zostera marina*, is a cool-temperate species and does not occur in the western Gulf of Mexico. The family is represented in Texas bays by widgeon grass, *Ruppia maritima* (Fig. 7-8 F), characterized by thread-like, sharply pointed leaves which arise directly from an almost equally thin rhizome. This narrow-bladed sea grass ranges along the Atlantic coast of North America from northern Canada to northern Mexico in the lower salinity portions of estuaries. It is relatively common in the shallow grass beds of northern and central Texas bays, but diminishes in importance southward. It thrives best in shallow areas where the leaves remain submerged at the lowest tides, but is uncommon in the deeper grassbeds or within especially turbid estuaries, apparently having a relatively high requirement for light.

Unlike most of the other sea grasses which rely primarily upon vegetative processes for reproduction, *Ruppia* abundantly produces small clusters of tiny flowers at the tips of elongate slender peduncles. The peduncles lift the flowers above the water surface where they are pollinated. Following fertilization, the peduncle recoils, bringing the developing seeds again below the surface. Because of these and several other unique characteristics, some botanists place *Ruppia* in the monogeneric family Ruppiaceae. Widgeon grass, alone and in combination with the other sea grasses, provides excellent shelter for a variety of estuarine animals. It is eaten by a variety of waterfowl and shore birds.

The Cymodoceaceae are a small family of warm temperate to tropical species which rely more upon asexual vegetative reproduction than the sexual process of flowering for propagation. Flowers are produced during the summer months, but they are small, obscure, and probably contribute little to reproductive success in this family. Two species of Cymodoceaceae occur throughout the western Gulf region, both of which have narrow leaves similar to those of *Ruppia maritima*. The Cymodoceaceae can be easily distinguished from *Ruppia* as their leaves are always enclosed in a basal sheath. The flattened leaves of the shoal grass, *Halodule wrightii* (Figs. 7-8 H; 7-9 C), are only slightly wider than those of *Ruppia*, but they are not sharply pointed. When examined under a hand lens, the leaf tips are distinctly toothed. Shoal grass also prefers waters of higher salinity than normally occupied by widgeon grass.

Manatee grass, *Syringodium filiforme* (Fig. 7-8 G), is widely distributed throughout the warm temperate and tropical western Atlantic, ranging from Bermuda to South America. Like the above species, its leaves are narrow (2 mm or less), but easily distinguished by their sheathed bases, terete or cylindrical form and blunt tips. It is a common shallow subtidal seagrass along western Gulf shores, often surviving situations that other plants cannot tolerate. It grows, for example, on nearshore subtidal flats where summer afternoon water temperatures often exceed 40°C. It also grows in deeper waters and readily shares a habitat with other sea grasses. Waves and currents frequently detach leaves from the rhizomes. They rise to the surface and often float ashore. Many Texas bay margins and Yucatan Gulf shores are thickly carpeted by mats of decaying *Syringodium* leaves.

The Hydrocharitaceae are predominantly tropical aquatic plants consisting of both fresh and salt water species. There are two marine species in the western Gulf region. *Halophila engelmannii* (Fig. 7-9 H) is the least "grass-like" of the sea grasses, bearing rosettes of six elliptical leaves arising at the tips of short stems, which, in turn, arise from a slender creeping rhizome. It lives in deeper water than most of the other sea grasses, so it is not as commonly encountered. In contrast, turtle grass, *Thalassia testudinum* (Fig. 7-9 E), is the dominant sea grass of the tropical Atlantic. With broad flattened blades and thick, extensively branching rhizomes, turtle grass cannot be confused with any other marine angiosperm.

Turtle grass is a tropical plant, but is capable of surviving mild winter freezes. It occurs in the higher salinity bays of the northern Texas coast, especially in the summer, but becomes increasingly more common from central Texas southward. It is the predominant sea grass carpeting the shallow floors of the higher salinity portions of most Mexico estuaries. Turtle grass thrives best in salinities at or near normal seawater, although it is uncommon in the Gulf of Mexico off most of the Texas coast. In the tropical Gulf and Caribbean, it forms vast offshore meadows in waters ranging in depth from the intertidal to as much as 30 m. Its network of rhizomes and roots extend 10 to 15 cm into the sediment and overlies a considerably thicker accumulation of "peat" or organic debris produced by previous stands of turtle grass. This rhizome and peat network serves to stabilize the sediment and provides refuge for a large variety of burrowing marine animals. Similarly, the leaf stock at the top of the grass bed provides shelter for another assemblage of epifaunal or epiphytic biota. Each older blade of turtle grass may be encrusted with serpulid worms of the genus *Spirorbis* (Fig. 6-9 C). A large variety of sessile diatoms, bryozoans and hydroids also attach to the leaves of this and other sea grasses.

Grassbed Crustacea

Many previously mentioned crustaceans, including the hermit crab, *Clibanarius vittatus* (Fig. 7-9 O), the spider crabs *Libinia dubia* (Fig. 7-9 U) and *Libinia emarginata* (Fig. 7-9 X), and the blue crab, *Callinectes sapidus*, also frequent the grass beds. Several additional crustaceans are also found here. Two families of small grass shrimps, the Palaemonidae and Hippolytidae, are abundantly represented in the grass beds. The former bear chelae on only the first pair of pereopods, whereas the latter bear chelae on the first two pairs of pereopods.

Three closely related species of Palaemonidae live among intertidal *Spartina* and especially in the sea grass beds just offshore. *Palaemonetes vulgaris* (Figs. 7-9 V & 9-2 J) is most common in the mid- to upper salinity portions of the estuary, preferring salinities between 15 to 35 ppt (Nagabhushanam, 1961; Wilson, 1969). *Palaemonetes pugio* (Figs. 7-6 K1; 7-9 Y)) is most abundant when salinities range between 10 to 20 ppt (Wood, 1967; Thorpe & Hoss, 1975), but also occurs in higher salinities. A third species, *P. intermedius*, occupies similar habitats and salinities. These three species are difficult to differentiate. Consult Holthuis (1952), Fleming (1969) or Williams (1984) for distinguishing characteristics. There is a considerable body of literature prior to 1952 on "*P. vulgaris*" from Texas and elsewhere which is now of marginal value because of the confusion of this species with the other two.

Palaemonid grass shrimps are important intermediaries in the complex food web of a tidal marsh or sea grass bed. They are detritivore shredders, taking chunks out of moderate to large detritus particles, and thereby contributing to the food chain in two ways. The voids left on detrital particles after shrimp grazing serve as attachment sites for diatoms and other micro-

flora and fauna, which, in turn, serve as food for other species. Also, the particles they ingest are not completely assimilated as they pass through their digestive tracts. Grass shrimp fecal pellets provide additional nutrition to other marsh dwellers which require small-sized detrital particles but are themselves incapable of shredding (Johannes & Satomi, 1966; Welsh, 1975).

Palaemonids begin reproduction in spring and continue to produce offspring throughout the summer. Males seek recently molted females to transfer spermatophores (Burkenroad, 1947). Like other shrimps, female *Palaemonetes* lack seminal receptacles, so spermatophores are cemented to the ventral surface of the abdomen. The male transfers encapsulated packets of sperm to the female, but is not present when the sperm are discharged for external fertilization. Decapod sperm are nonmotile (they lack flagella). The release of the eggs from a pair of oviducts must be perfectly timed with the release of sperm from the spermatophore. Eventually, fertilized eggs adhere to the setae of abdominal pleopods. The female carries the eggs containing developing embryos two or three weeks before zoea emerge to enter the plankton. During the summer, adult females will produce a new brood within two or three days of releasing zoea. The larvae are remarkably tolerant of temperature and salinity variations, permitting development within the estuary. They also seem to vary with respect to the number of larval instars, depending upon environmental conditions and the availability of food (Broad, 1957; Knowlton, 1965; 1974).

The broken-back shrimp, *Hippolyte pleuracanthus* (Fig. 7-9 G) (Hippolytidae), is primarily restricted to subtidal grass beds. It possesses numerous chromatophores which enables it to change color from green to brown, depending upon the color of the vegetation in which it has taken refuge. Another member of this family, the arrow shrimp, *Tozeuma carolinense* (Fig. 7-9 F), attaches to grass blades, or other solid substrata and also relies upon chromatophores to provide the cryptic coloration necessary to "blend" with the background. *Tozeuma* grazes upon the epiphytes and sessile invertebrates which attach to grass blades (Bryce, 1961).

In addition to the smaller grass shrimps, juveniles of all of the commercially harvested Penaeidae utilize the grass beds and *Spartina* marshes as nursery areas. We illustrate the white shrimp, *Penaeus setiferus* (Fig. 7-9 W) as one example, but the brown shrimp, *P. aztecus* and the pink shrimp, *P. duorarum* are also here. These species are treated in more detail in Chapter 10.

Grassbed Gastropods

The cerithiid, *Bittium varium* (Fig. 7-7 B) is the most abundant gastropod of the central and southern Texas estuarine grass beds, and ranges southward along the entire Mexico coast and into the tropical Caribbean. Because it is a tiny snail, rarely more than 6 mm in length, it is overlooked by most seashore visitors. Yet, hordes of *B. varium* graze upon the microflora associated with blades of turtle, manatee, and widgeon grasses just below the tide. Its apparent abundance seems to decrease in the tropics, but this may simply be a reflection of increasing diversity. *Bittium varium* often is cited as *Diastoma varium*, but Houbrick (1981) has clearly demonstrated the genus *Diastoma* is represented by a single south Australian species not a member of the Cerithiidae.

The larger cerithiid, *Cerithium lutosum* (Figs. 4-3 K; 4-4 B; and 5-1 I) is also a grass bed inhabitant from the central Texas coast southward. Three other tiny herbivores, *Rissoina catesbyana* (Fig. 7-9 D), *Assiminea succinea* (Fig. 7-7 F), and *Zebina browniana* (not illustrated), all members of the Rissoidae, comprise a group of microgastropods less than 5 mm in height which graze the epiphytes of the grass beds.

Although not a large snail (length up to about 16 mm), the dove shell, *Anachis semiplicata* (Fig. 7-9 L) (Columbellidae), is one of the most commonly observed gastropods of the grass beds. It clings to grass blades or shell debris by a mucous thread. It is not restricted to the grass flats, for it often occurs among oyster reefs or upon the rock jetties. *Mitrella lunata* (Fig. 7-6 K), is another columbellid much smaller than *A. semiplicata*, attaining a shell length of only about 5 mm. Like its larger relative, it searches for prey, probably hydroids, on intertidal grass beds and among shell debris. It ranges from Massachusetts to Brazil.

Grassbed Bivalves

The Mytilidae, or mussels, are often regarded as bivalves of exposed shores. Certainly the subfamily Mytilinae are cosmopolitan rocky shore bivalves with a triangular body and an epibyssate, gregarious life style. The Modiolinae are just as important upon soft sediments, and close relatives and possible ancestors of the Mytilinae. Modiolinae live partially or completely buried in sands or muds. They have open mantle margins with no discrete inhalant siphon, and are especially susceptible to fouling of the mantle cavity by sediment. We have already discussed one high-zoned species, *Geukensia demissa*, which lies partially buried, attached by a tangle of byssal threads to *Spartina* roots. Two other species of byssate mussels occur subtidally. *Modiolus americanus* (Fig. 7-6 M), is a typically offshore species which occurs in bays near tidal inlets. The small paper mussel, *Amygdalum papyrium* (Fig. 7-6 O), is a predominantly bay-dwelling species but also occurs offshore. The former is more triangularly "mussel" shaped, the latter more modioliform, elongate and thin-shelled. *Modiolus americanus* is solitary and does not build a nest of byssal threads, attaching instead to stones and gravel. *Amygdalum papyrium* achieves protection by cocooning itself within a nest of fine byssal threads which are woven around the shell by the greatly extensible foot. Safely ensconced, further security is attained by attachment to *Ruppia* roots and leaf blades.

Chione cancellata (Fig. 7-9 J) is perhaps the most abundant infaunal grass bed bivalve from central Texas southwards. It also occurs on bare sand or mud, although it is less abundant in these habitats. It prefers waters near normal salinity, and is largely excluded from the lower salinity estuaries of the northern Texas coast (Calnan, 1980). During periods of drought, *C. cancellata* has temporarily occupied estuaries such as Copano, Aransas, St. Charles, and Mesquite bays (Ladd, 1951; Parker, 1959), but living populations disappear when normal precipitation patterns are reestablished. The numerous *Chione* shells which accumulate on bayshores suggest that periodic occupation of these bays has occurred many times in the last few thousand years.

Chione cancellata is easily distinguished from other bivalves by its distinctive shell ornamentation. Thin concentric blades rise prominently above the numerous, short radial ribs lying between them. On bare sand, *Chione cancellata* lies buried as much as 30 cm below the surface (Moore & Lopez, 1969), but on the grass beds, most specimens lie near the surface with the posterior margins of the valves exposed. *Chione* has well developed siphons by which it distributes water through the mantle cavity for suspension feeding and respiration.

The mean life expectancy of *Chione* is between 2 to 3 years, with a maximum life span of about 4 years. It reaches sexual maturity in the first year at a shell length of about 15 mm. In southern Florida there are two spawning periods, winter and summer, and presumably this reproductive periodicity is maintained in other portions of the range where temperatures are conducive for gonad development (Moore & Lopez, 1969). D'Asaro (1967) details the larval and postlarval development of *Chione cancellata*.

The Atlantic bay scallop *Argopecten irradians amplicostatus* (Fig. 7-8 D) is a common estuarine bivalve from central Texas to Veracruz, Mexico. It is a common associate of subtidal grass beds and frequently observed in the very shallow lagoons along barrier island bayshores. It also occurs on sandy bottoms throughout the bays of the northwestern Gulf. The scallop lifestyle is very unlike the attached or burrowing estuarine bivalves. Juveniles retain a byssal gland by which they secrete a byssus for attachment to stones or shells, but the adult bay scallop forgoes attachment for swimming freedom, albeit only occasionally in brief spurts. The *Argopecten* shell is slightly unsymmetrical, with the right valve more deeply cupped than the left valve and lighter in color, often entirely white. The bivalve lies on its side with the right valve resting upon the sandy bayfloor. If turned over, the scallop will reposition itself so as to place the right valve against the substratum.

Bay scallops feed upon microflora from the phytoplankton and benthic diatoms, bacteria and sedimentary detritus kept in suspension by waves and tidal currents (Davis & Marshall, 1961). They are efficient filter feeders with relatively high filtration rates (Chipman & Hopkins, 1954).

Argopecten excavates a shallow resting depression

by pumping jets of water from the mantle cavity toward bayfloor sand. If disturbed or threatened, it will employ the water jets to propel it away in several erratic jerks. The water jets are created by repeated rapid closures of the valves, forcing water to exit the mantle cavity on either side of the hinge. The scallop moves upward in the water largely because the left mantle margins overlap those of the right side, thereby directing water downward toward the bottom. The bivalve cannot maintain a constant jet, but must frequently open the valves for more water. During each recharge, gravity causes the scallop to begin to settle. Scallop "swimming" is erratic but effective in eluding slow-moving predators (Peterson *et al.,* 1982).

One of the most prominent features of bay scallops are the numerous blue eyes along the mantle margins. They are not image-forming eyes, but are capable of detecting shades of brightness or darkness. The eyes are certainly useful in predator detection and may also serve additional unknown functions.

Argopecten irradians commences spawning at the age of about one year (Gutsell, 1930), has an annual reproductive cycle and lives about two years (Sastry, 1961). Gonad development is correlated with increasing temperature and peak phytoplankton production in early summer. Spawning usually occurs in the fall from September to November (Sastry, 1961; 1963).

Argopecten irradians is the common edible scallop of the western Atlantic. The subspecies of the northwestern Gulf, *Argopecten irradians amplicostatus,* rarely occurs in sufficient numbers for commercial harvest. Two subspecies of eastern North America, *A. i. irradians,* from Cape Cod, Massachusetts to New Jersey, and *A. i. concentricus,* from Maryland to the northeastern Gulf of Mexico (Clarke, 1965), are more commonly taken in commercial fisheries and are amenable to mariculture (Castagna & Duggan, 1971). A smaller, superficially similar scallop, *Argopecten gibbus,* is an offshore species of relatively deep water sands which occasionally washes ashore on Texas beaches (see Sastry, 1962, for a comparison). It is more common in the eastern Gulf of Mexico.

Other Grassbed Biota

A variety of soft bodied invertebrates live within the shelter of the grass beds, or the nearby tidal flats. Polychaete worms are well represented, often by many of the species which are also common on the offshore sands and unvegetated sediments within the estuary. These include *Nereis succinea* (Fig. 7-6 C1), *Clymenella torquata* (Fig. 7-9 N), *Glycera americana* (Fig. 7-9 P) and *Diopatra cuprea* (Fig. 7-9 Q), all of which are discussed in Chapter 10.

Echinoderms are poorly represented in the Texas estuaries, but one species usually can be found in association with the grass beds. The sea cucumber, *Thyone mexicana* (Fig. 7-9 R), is a small dendrochirote species, rarely more than 3 cm in length. It is a suspension and indirect deposit feeder, obtaining food by sweeping the oral circlet of tentacles through the water or across the

surface of the bottom. Plankton or detritus particles adhere to mucous secretions on the tentacles. As each tentacle becomes loaded with debris, it is inserted into the mouth and wiped clean. *Thyone* is a relatively sedentary holothurian settling within bare sand or mud between patches of sea grass. It lies mostly buried within the sediment with only the oral tentacles and aboral end of the body exposed.

The small burrowing anemone, *Nematostella vectensis* (Fig. 7-9 S) lives among the grass beds, extending its ring of tentacles from the burrow for feeding at night and retreating within the burrow during the day. *Phoronis architecta* (Fig. 7-9 M) is another small mud burrower about 1.5 cm in length. Although it superficially resembles an anemone, it is, in fact, a member of the phylum Phoronida, a small group of relatively complex invertebrates. Unlike the anemones, *Phoronis* has a complete, U-shaped digestive tract with mouth, anus and excretory pores at the upper end of the body, a circulatory system employing hemoglobin as a respiratory pigment, and a capacious body cavity or coelom. The "tentacles" or lophophore at the oral end of the body are highly branched extensions of the body wall which contain portions of the anterior coelom or mesocoel.

Phoronis is a suspension feeder, living in a vertical, chitin-lined, tube constructed on the floor of the grass bed. The tube is open at only one end, necessitating the concentration of all body orifices at one end of the phoronid body. Cilia on the lophophore create water currents which sweep first over the mouth and thence over the anus and excretory pores. Suspended particles are trapped in mucous sheets, which are moved by other cilia into the mouth, while the excurrent flow of water insures that excretory products flow away from the lophophore and mouth.

The ribbon worm, *Cerebratulus lacteus* (Fig. 7-6 M1), is a predator of the grass beds. This soft-bodied, unsegmented, ribbon-shaped animal can reach a length in excess of 1 m. Its ciliated epithelium is also equipped with numerous mucous-secreting glands which provide a layer of slime upon which the worm moves by a combination of muscular contractions and beating cilia. *Cerebratulus* captures polychaetes, crustaceans, molluscs and other invertebrates by means of an eversible proboscis housed in a unique internal cavity, the rhynchocoel. McDermott (1976) reports *Cerebratulus* pursuing and feeding upon *Ensis directus* in Chesapeake Bay, so it is probable that the nemertean also feeds upon the smaller *E. minor* in Texas.

UNVEGETATED SUBTIDAL BAYFLOORS

Subtidal Texas bayfloors consist largely of unvegetated sedimentary deposits. Sands dominate near shore and in the vicinity of tidal inlets, but the deeper estuarine basins are often lined by very fine silts and clays. A few sparse clumps of algae occasionally appear on this substratum, but macroscopic vegetation is generally absent. As on the offshore banks, infaunal and epi-faunal herbivores rely primarily upon the phytoplankton as the base of the food chain. The habitat is populated primarily by filter feeders, detritus feeders, predators and scavengers.

Crustacea

We have already discussed the most abundant large crustacean of Texas subtidal bayfloors, the blue crab, *Callinectes sapidus*. This portunid is equally at home on the unvegetated muds of the deeper estuarine basins as it is among sea grass beds or scavenging in the shallows near piers or wharves.

The Stomatopoda, or mantis shrimps, are primarily tropical crustaceans, but a few species are found in temperate waters (Manning, 1969). *Squilla empusa* (Fig. 7-7 N) is one of these, ranging from Cape Cod to Texas. It is common on offshore shrimp banks and on the muddy bottoms of higher salinity bays. *Squilla empusa* is large, frequently exceeding 16 cm in length. It cannot be mistaken for any other crustacean in the Texas bays, having a distinctive elongate, dorsoventrally flattened abdomen bearing abdominal gills, a broad armored telson, a relatively short head and thorax, and a pair of large thoracic appendages resembling the scythe-like arms of a praying mantis.

Mantis shrimps are predators, employing the large anterior raptorial appendages to capture prey. Different species use these appendages in different ways (Chapter 11). *Squilla empusa* waits in ambush at the mouth of its burrow for small fishes, shrimps and other invertebrates to pass within striking range. Lightning-fast jabs of the raptorial appendages impale the prey upon inward-facing spines. As the prey struggles for freedom, it wedges tighter against the spines and is also held by the leverage applied between the two limbs of each appendage united by a joint. Holding the prey in this manner, the mantis shrimp leisurely ingests it.

Squilla empusa is not only an effective burrower, but also a modestly capable swimmer. Abdominal pleopods are used as oars, and the telson and other body parts serve as a rudder.

Two spider crabs, *Libinia dubia* (Fig. 7-9 U) and the slightly more common *L. emarginata* (Fig. 7-9 X) are equally at home on the shallow soft beds of Texas higher salinity bays, the offshore shrimp banks (Hildebrand, 1954) and on the turtle grass beds off western Yucatan. A globose spiny carapace and spindly walking legs easily distinguish these species from most other Texas bay crabs. It is difficult to differentiate species among juveniles (Wass, 1955), but adults are easier to separate. *Libinia dubia* is slightly smaller (carapace length about 100 mm) and has only about 6 spines along the carapace midline. The carapace of *Libinia emarginata* may reach 125 mm in length and bear about 9 medial spines (Felder, 1973a). Both are sluggish, fostered in part by a small gill area relative to body size (Gray, 1957). They are also poorly adapted for intertidal exposure (Pearse, 1929), preferring to remain in deeper estuarine basins (Ayers, 1938) or

burrowing into shallow subtidal bay muds. Tabb and Manning (1961) reported smaller specimens of *L. dubia* more common in *Thalassia* beds than larger specimens, which frequented the deeper waters of Florida Bay.

Both species produce eggs and larvae during the warmer months, with the reproductive period longer in the southern part of each species range. Ovigerous females are known from the western Gulf of Mexico in February and are common in July (Powers, 1977). Hinsch (1968) has studied the mating behavior of *L. emarginata*. Females produce 3 or 4 broods each season, carrying developing embryos on abdominal pleopods for about 25 days before releasing zoea. Males ignore females with eggs in early stages of development, but readily seek females which are ready to or have just released zoea. Copulation occurs despite a fully hardened female exoskeleton (it is not known if mating also accompanies the final female molt). If a male grasps a female which has not released zoea, he will not attempt to mate, but assists and protects her as she discharges zoea. Within 12 hours of releasing larvae during the reproductive season, a female will have usually mated and produced a new brood.

As with most spider crabs, there are two planktonic zoeal stages and a megalops. The duration of each larval stage varies with temperature and salinity, but molting to the first crab stage usually occurs within two weeks (Sandifer & Van Engel, 1971; Johns & Lang, 1977).

Small specimens of both *L. dubia* and *L. emarginata* are known to occur upon several scyphozoan medusae. The cabbage head, *Stomolophus meleagris*, is a frequently mentioned host of both species (Corrington, 1927; Gutsell, 1928; Hildebrand, 1954), whereas *L. dubia* is also known to occur upon *Chrysaora quinquecirrha*, *Chiropsalmus quadrumanus*, and *Aurelia aurita* (Phillips *et al.*, 1969). The habit aids in dispersal for both species, and provides a source of food, at least for *L. dubia*, which has been observed feeding upon the medusae.

Bivalves

A number of bivalve molluscs are associated with the unvegetated bayfloors. Most of these live as infauna within the soft sediments, but a few species spend much of their lives exposed on the surface. The most ubiquitous infaunal bivalve in Texas estuaries is the diminutive mactrid, *Mulinia lateralis* (Figs. 7-7 W; 8-3 B1; 8-4 C). Because it rarely exceeds 10 mm in length, many visitors to Texas shores are unaware it even occurs here. Small size does not diminish its importance to the economy of the estuary. One common name of the species, coot clam, suggests its value as a link in the food chain. Many of the diving waterfowl and some species of shore birds feed upon *Mulinia* extensively each day, as do many bottom feeding fishes (e.g., the black drum). With a short generation time (about 60 days) and exceedingly high fecundity (3 to 4 million eggs with each spawning according to Calabrese,

1969), the coot clam is easily able to keep up with the high predation. It consistently is found to be the most numerous bivalve in subtidal Texas estuarine faunal surveys.

Mulinia lives in salinities from 5 to 80 ppt (Parker, 1975), permitting it to occur in a variety of subtidal habitats from the low salinity marshes to hypersaline Laguna Madre. It is most commonly found alive in mud (Calnan, 1980) where it lies buried just below the surface. *Mulinia* is a suspension feeder, but obtains additional organic material by suspending surface deposits with water discharge from the exhalant siphon, and filtering the material thus suspended in the typical manner (Parker, 1975). This mactrid is not as tolerant of high temperatures as some other bivalves. During the summer it migrates to deeper water and occurs on nearshore banks only when there is relatively good water circulation. During the winter, *Mulinia* moves shoreward in extremely large numbers, providing overwintering waterfowl a ready source of food.

The semelid *Cumingia tellinoides* (Fig. 7-7 P) is another mud-dweller, superficially resembling some of the tellinids, but differing largely with respect to feeding habits and internal anatomy. It is a suspension feeder adapted for life on shallow, turbid muddy bottoms, and thus relies upon the environment to provide a ready supply of suspended detrital organics. Like other semelids, it has very large labial palps (larger than the gills) which facilitate sorting of the detrital particulates.

Two species of deposit feeding Nuculanidae, relatively primitive protobranch bivalves, commonly occur in the higher salinity bays, tidal inlets and offshore sands of the western Gulf of Mexico. Both are easily identified by their elongate, posteriorly tapering shells and a flexed hinge containing anterior and posterior rows of numerous chevron-shaped hinge teeth. *Nuculana acuta* (Figs. 7-7 U; 8-3 R; 10-3 H) is the smaller of the two, usually with deeply incised concentric lines on the shell exterior. *Nuculana concentrica* (Fig. 10-3 I) is larger with more numerous, faintly incised concentric lines. Both species prefer waters of near normal salinity. Bird (1970) reports an optimum salinity of 35 ppt for *N. acuta* and both species occur in offshore sands and in the higher salinity bays. *Nuculana concentrica* is commonly found in the central sediments of large bays, whereas *N. acuta* is more widely distributed, occurring in bay centers, sandy bay margins, or within tidal inlets (Calnan, 1980). McGowan & Morton (1977) record large numbers of *N. acuta* living in the lower portion of Laguna Madre, Texas.

The feeding and respiratory behavior of the nuculanids is unique among bivalves. Water enters the mantle cavity via a pair of elongate posterior siphons, typically oriented with the ventral siphon inhalant and the dorsal one exhalant. The gills are much smaller than those of the eulamellibranch bivalves, yet are more extensively developed than the simplest protobranch type. They are expanded and dilated so as to effectively form a porous partition between inhalant and exhalant mantle chambers. At regular intervals muscles within the gill axes contract, moving the gills upwards and effectively pumping water out the exhalant siphon, to be replaced by recharge through the inhalant siphon. Water entering the ventral mantle cavity is moved to the exhalant chamber above the gill by cilia on the gill filaments. The water flow is primarily for respiration, and only incidentally contributes to feeding.

The primary nuculanid feeding organs are the palps, which are considerably larger and more elongate than those of many other bivalves. They arise on either side of the mouth at the anterior end of the body and sweep backward, flanking both sides of the visceral mass. Near the posterior shell margin, they taper into slender palp processes, the structures which initially acquire the food. Palp processes are extremely contractile, and can extend far beyond the posterior margin of the shell.

Feeding is achieved as the nuculanid lies partially buried in soft sediment, with the tapered posterior margin of the shell protruding above the surface. Palp processes are extended through the gaping valves just below the siphons, and moved over the surface of the bottom where they collect organic detritus and sediment. This material is transported along mucous-lined ciliated grooves on the palp processes toward the expanded central portion of the palps. Here, sorting tracts and cilia reject larger particles, but convey finer, food-laden particles toward the mouth.

A number of deposit feeding tellinids thrive in the organically rich bayfloor muds (see Chapter 10 for a description of their feeding behavior). *Macoma mitchelli* (Figs. 7-7 Q; 8-3 C1) is the most commonly encountered in the lower salinity estuaries such as Copano and Nueces bays. It fares poorly in the higher salinity bays and experiences significant dieoffs when higher salinity water invades the upper reaches of estuaries during prolonged droughts (Parker, 1956; Calnan, 1980). In contrast, *Macoma constricta* (Fig. 7-7 R) is an exceedingly euryhaline and eurythermal species, occurring in a variety of salinities and temperature conditions. *Tellina texana* (not illustrated) is more commonly associated with deeper estuarine basins, but is capable of tolerating relatively low salinities. It ranges far into the secondary Texas bays. *Macoma tageliformis* (Fig. 7-7 O) occurs in soft sediments along the margins of tidal inlets, and is also found offshore in the Gulf.

The small egg cockle, *Laevicardium mortoni* (Fig. 7-6 D1) is a common subtidal bivalve of inlet-influenced sand banks and hypersaline lagoons. Like all cockles, it lives primarily upon the surface of the bottom, or lies only partially buried. It possesses an elongate, muscular foot by which it hops about with remarkable agility (Baker & Merrill, 1965). It eludes predators by leaping away.

Corbula contracta (Fig. 7-7 S) is one of several infaunal species of *Corbula* which occupy unvegetated sandy bottoms of the primary bays and offshore sands.

Corbula is characterized by inequal valves, the right valve is larger than and distinctly overlaps the left. It lies shallowly buried on the larger right valve at an angle, with short siphons projecting upwards toward the water above. The thick overlapping shell valves confer considerable protection, but even more protection is provided, particularly from boring naticiid snails by a unique shell structure. Organic conchiolin layers embedded between shell layers prevent penetration by shell borers such as *Polinices duplicatus* which employ chemical dissolution of the shell (Lewy & Samtleben, 1979).

The venerid, *Gemma gemma* (Fig. 7-7 T), is one of the smallest bivalves of the northwestern Gulf. This sand dweller rarely exceeds 3 mm in length or height. The species ranges from Nova Scotia to Yucatan, and bears a variety of subspecific epithets which require revisionary clarification (Abbott, 1974; Andrews, 1977). Most ecological studies have been conducted on temperate populations (Bradley & Cooke, 1959; Sellmer, 1967). These studies suggest that *Gemma gemma* is an ovoviviparous bivalve producing juveniles throughout the warmer months. The mean life expectancy is a little over two years with a maximum life span of about 4 years. It is a nocturnal suspension feeder that preferentially occupies sandy tidal channels. It is reported to be relatively tolerant to high water temperatures (Kennedy & Mihursky, 1971).

Pandora trilineata (Fig. 7-7 V) is an unusual laterally flattened bivalve which lives upon muds or sands of the higher salinity bays and tidal inlets (Ladd, 1951; Parker, 1956 & 1959). It is epifaunal and always lies upon its left side. The left valve is larger than and slightly overlaps the right. Neither valve is particularly inflated. Little is known about the ecology of this curious bivalve.

Gastropods

In addition to several of the offshore gastropods (Chapter 10) which also occur in the tidal inlets and higher salinity portions of coastal estuaries, there are a number of additional gastropods, most of them minute in size, which occupy the unvegetated bottoms of estuaries. Little else is known about the majority of these species, other than that they occur here.

The Pyramidellidae, a group of primitive yet specialized opisthobranchs, are well represented in the northwestern Gulf. They are primitive in the sense that they retain an external, whorled shell and bear an operculum, both features which tend to be lost among the more advanced opisthobranchs. They are specialized in that the majority are ectoparasites. Most species are small and difficult to distinguish from one another by shell features. The largest pyramidellid in Texas waters, the notched pyram, *Pyramidella crenulata*, has a shell length of about 1 cm, but most of the other two dozen species are considerably smaller. For example, *Odostomia laevigata* (Fig. 7-7 G) has a shell length of 3 to 5 mm, whereas *Odostomia gibbosa* (Fig. 7-7 H) is 3 mm or less in length. The ectoparasitic pyr-

amidellids attach to a variety of host species, including other bivalves, gastropods, or sedentary polychaetes by means of the foot or an oral sucker. They employ a buccal stylet at the end of an extendable proboscis to pierce the flesh of the host and ingest its body fluids. The hosts for many species, including most Gulf species, have yet to be determined. Because of the relatively wide distribution of most species within coastal estuaries, they probably parasitize more than one host (Calnan, 1980).

Bubble shells (Acteonidae) are another group of shelled opisthobranchs which are well represented in the subtidal sands of higher salinity bays and inlets, especially those southwards from Aransas Pass. Their anatomical characteristics are less primitive than those of the pyramidellids, although the presence of the shell suggests that they are not among the most advanced opisthobranchs. All are predators on other invertebrates. *Bulla striata* (Figs. 7-9 K; 10-6 F) is the most commonly encountered. It can be found in the unvegetated sands adjacent to grass beds, and is also relatively common offshore. The paper bubbles, *Haminoea succinea* (Fig. 7-7 A) and *H. antillarum* (Fig. 7-7 D) have smaller, more fragile shells. Their bodies cannot be withdrawn entirely within the shell, and when active, the soft tissues completely envelop it. *Rictaxis punctostriatus* (Fig. 7-7 E) is another tiny (3 to 6 mm) Acteonidae, but with a more characteristically snail-like shell. It preys primarily upon polychaetes.

Ceacum johnsoni (Fig. 7-7 J) is one of about a dozen species of Caecidae which occur in the shallow waters of the northwestern Gulf. The caecids are tiny cylindrical gastropods, most of which rarely exceed 5 mm in length. They begin life with a typically coiled gastropod shell, but soon begin to grow from it an uncoiled, slightly curved tube. As the tube elongates, the early coiled shell breaks away, and the broken end of the tube is sealed with a shelly septum. The Caecidae includes many species especially abundant in the grass beds, but *C. johnsoni* is more commonly encountered on unvegetated muds or in the vicinity of oyster reefs.

Vitrinella floridana (Fig. 7-7 I) (Vitrinellidae) is another extremely small (less than 2 mm) gastropod. It usually is found clinging to the undersides of shells on sandy or muddy bottoms near shore.

The reddish brown plicate mangelia, *Pyrgocythara plicosa* (Fig. 7-7 C) is common in the hypersaline waters of Laguna Madre, where it occurs on unvegetated muds or within grass beds. It apparently belongs to that group of turrid gastropods equipped with poison glands and a highly modified radula. Being no more than 6 to 8 mm in height, its poison is designed to subdue minute invertebrate prey.

Mudflat Burrowers and Their Commensals

Many infaunal inhabitants of anoxic intertidal mud flats have perfected mechanisms to pump water through permanent or semipermanent burrows or subterranean tubes for oxygenation and respiration. The majority of these animals are also filter or deposit feeders which have developed various techniques to remove food particles from the incoming water or sediment. Unwanted sediments and feces (or pseudo-feces) often are removed from the burrows in an excurrent water flow. The incoming water thus serves several functions—oxygenation, cleansing and a source of nutrition.

The animals of high energy, well sorted sandy shores, such as *Emerita* and other hippid and oxystomatid crabs, usually build only temporary burrows which have no special form and are created for use only as temporary retreats as, for example, at low tide. Other inhabitants of less dynamic shores, experiencing only moderate wave action and where the mixture of sand and silt is less well sorted, build semi-permanent burrows, but possess the ability to reburrow when dislodged, as for example after a storm. Many bivalves fall into this category.

On muddy, fully protected shores, permanence of occupation is largely assured and elaborate permanent burrows are created. The inhabitants of such burrows are typically soft-bodied and notably include many annelid worms. Some crustaceans, such as *Callianassa*, *Callichirus* and *Upogebia* also construct such structures and all have the propensity for deep retreat into their burrows, either to maintain contact with the falling water table when tidal levels fall exceptionally low, as, for example, at the times of spring tides, or to escape predation.

Predation is often insignificant on the deep burrowers, as only highly specialized predators with specific adaptations, such as the long-billed curlews, godwits and avocets, can effectively prey upon them. Shallow-burrowing animals are prone to the greatest predation pressures. Many of these seek protection from stoutness of form, as in shallow burrowing cardiid and venerid bivalves, or fast retreat, as in the razor clams. Many gastropods (e.g., *Polinices*), fishes (e.g., *Callionymus*), crabs (e.g., *Calappa*) and birds (e.g., oyster-catchers) have adapted their feeding strategies to cope with such animals.

For the deep burrowing inhabitants of mud flats, life has become secondarily sedentary. Specialized sense organs are not needed within such protective confines. Accordingly, the highly cephalized "heads" of deep burrowers may become degenerative organs, much like the human appendix, for the rich supply of nutrients entering the burrow make few sensory demands upon the animal. Such burrows and their occupants make ideal refugia and companions for commensals.

Many roving epifaunal organisms seek temporary retreat from the desiccating effects of a falling tide or from aerial predators, in the myriad of burrows that dot the shore. Flatworms, crustaceans, polychaetes and gastropods find temporary refuge therein. From such simple interactions it is easy to envisage how more permanent relationships have come to be established—leading eventually into commensalism and ultimately parasitism. We deal here with those groups of animals that can be broadly defined as commensal,

in that the host obtains little or no benefit from the partner, though for the latter, life is to lesser or greater degrees bound up with the former. Two broad categories of commensalism can be identified: facultative in which the benefitting partner occurs with a range of burrowers and obligate where it is host specific.

Two important animal groups are typically commensal. These are the leptonacean bivalves and the pinnixid decapod crabs. This is not to say that others are not commensal, indeed representatives from a wide range of phyla have adopted this life mode and on coral reefs, in particular, enhanced niche diversity has led many into complex symbiotic relationships. On mud flats, however, the Pinnotheridae are most obvious. *Pinnixa* species are primarily suspension feeders, employing setose maxillipeds to remove particles from the water flowing through the host tube or burrow.

The deposit feeding echiuran, *Thalassema hartmani* (Fig. 7-10 B) builds cavernous burrows in mud and shares its home with the obligate filter feeding bivalve *Paramya subovata* (Fig. 7-10 A) (Jenner & McCrary, 1970) and the facultative *Pinnixa lunzi* (Fig. 7-10 C). The latter has also been reported to occur with the polychaetes *Clymenella torquata* and *Pherusa affinis*, the cnidarian *Ceriantheopsis americanus*, the amphipod *Ampelisca vadorum*, the sipunculan *Golfingia margaritacea* and the holothurian *Caudina arenata* (Boesch, 1971). The report of *P. lunzi* from the stomach of a red snapper (Felder, 1973b) supports the idea that it may live outside the protection of a burrow, and hence is a facultative commensal. *Thalassema hartmani* is a relatively abundant inhabitant of mud banks adjacent to tidal inlets along the northern Texas coast (Henry, 1976).

The highly specialized polychaete *Chaetopterus variopedatus* (Fig. 7-10 E) builds long U-shaped burrows in mud through which water and sediment are pumped. The latter is trapped in a mucous web to be then bound up and eaten. Co-occurring with it is *Pinnixa chaetopterana* (Fig. 7-10 D), which seems somewhat more specialized than *P. lunzi* in that it has only, hitherto, been recorded by Williams (1984) as also occurring with one other polychaete, *Amphitrite ornata*, though a small form of the crab also occurs with *Callianassa louisianensis* (Fig. 7-9 T) in the northeastern Gulf (Biffar, 1971a,b).

Experiments have demonstrated that *P. chaetopterana* is not restricted to host tubes or burrows, but is capable of entering and leaving at will. If the "chimney" of a *Chaetopterus* tube is too small for the passage of a crab, it will cut a hole large enough to permit movement through it (Gray, 1961).

In addition to the pinnotherid, the *Chaetopterus* tube may be occupied by another commensal, the porcellanid crab *Polyonyx gibbesi* (Fig. 7-10 F). The filter feeding porcellanids are more widely known as inhabitants of rocky beaches (e.g., *Petrolisthes*), though many others associate themselves with sponges, anemones and corals in coral habitats (e.g., *Pachy-*

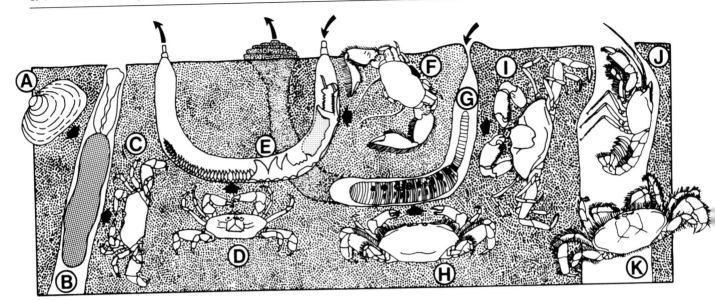

7-10. Mud burrowers and commensals. **A.** Commensal clam, *Paramya subovata*; **B.** Echiuroid worm, *Thalassema hartmani*; **C.** Commensal crab, *Pinnixa lunzi*; **D.** Commensal crab, *Pinnixa chaetopterana*; **E.** Tube worm, *Chaetopterus variopedatus* **F.** Commensal crab, *Polyonyx gibbesi*; **G.** Lug worm, *Arenicola cristata*; **H.** Commensal crab, *Pinnixa cylindrica*; **I.** Commensal crab, *Pinnixa cristata*; **J.** Mud shrimp, *Upogebia affinis*; **K.** Commensal crab, *Pinnixa retinens*.

cheles and *Porcellana*). *Polyonyx gibbesi*, however, seems to be obligate with *Chaetopterus* (Gore, 1974). It rarely ventures outside the worm tube, and usually a male and female are found together. *Pinnixa* rarely occurs in association with a *Chaetopterus* tube occupied by both male and female *Polyonyx* (Gray, 1961). The breeding season for *P. gibbesi* in Texas is from June to August (Rickner, 1975).

The dark green lug worm, *Arenicola cristata* (Figs. 7-6 Z & 7-10 G) is a deposit-feeding polychaete which constructs an L-shaped burrow in sandy muds. It draws water into the burrow through the vertical shaft, providing oxygen to eleven pairs of reddish gills located on the central portion of its body. The water is then forced to flow into the sediment at the closed end of the horizontal mucous-lined shaft. The flow of aerobic water into anoxic substrata oxidizes the reduced organics normally found there and changes the color of the sediments from black to light yellow or tan. *Arenicola* ingests this reoxidized sediment, extracting the sparse nutrients it can provide.

The process of forcing water into the adjacent sediment from the underground burrow can force a small mound of sediment to rise at the surface (Fig. 7-10 G, left). Ingested sediment is defecated into a small mound around the entrance to the burrow (Fig. 7-10 G, right). After considerable sediment has been removed by the deposit feeding polychaete, the original bulge created by the water flow becomes a conical depression.

Three pinnotherid species have been recorded as occurring with *Arenicola cristata*. *Pinnixa cristata* (Fig.

7-10 I) occurs with *Callianassa* and other burrowers including *Arenicola* (Felder, 1973a). *Pinnixa cylindrica* (Fig. 7-10 H) occurs with *Arenicola* and other large polychaetes from Massachusetts to Pensacola, Florida (Wass, 1955; McDermott, 1963), but it has yet to be recorded from the western Gulf. Wass also records *P. retinens* (Fig. 7-10 K) commensal with the filter feeding mud shrimp, *Upogebia affinis* (Fig. 7-10 J). The *Pinnixa* spp. of the northwestern Gulf are now under taxonomic revision, and new names for the regional representatives of this genus are likely (D.L. Felder, personal communication).

Upogebia affinis is locally common in some Texas bays. It is usually found in soft muds and muddy grass beds in high salinity estuaries, although it is not common in Laguna Madre. It is especially abundant in the *Halodule* beds of Aransas Bay, just off Aransas National Wildlife Refuge (Hedgpeth, 1950). *Upogebia* lives most of its adult life in a deep burrow with one or several narrow chimneys opening at the surface and containing many spacious subterranean branches. Several mud shrimps may occupy a burrow, one male and a harem of females (Jenner, 1977), each keeping to a branch of the network (Pearse, 1945). Mud shrimps are suspension feeders. They move water through the burrow by the sweeping motions of the pleopods and trap incoming particles on setose mouthparts and walking legs.

Upogebia affinis zoea appear in the estuarine plankton during the summer (Hay & Shore, 1918; Standifer, 1973), with the reproductive period shorter in northern populations (Fish, 1925, at Woods Hole) and longer in southern locales (Rouse, 1970, southwestern Florida).

Callianassa louisianensis (Fig. 7-9 T) is a hardy mud shrimp tolerant of prolonged exposures to aquatic and aerial anoxia (Felder, 1979) and variable salinities (Felder, 1978). It commonly burrows in estuarine muds where salinities drop below 5 ppt. Larval development is entirely estuarine, consisting of two free-swimming zoeal instars and a postlarva. The larvae osmoregulate in lower salinities in a manner similar to that of the adult. (Felder *et al.*, 1986).

It seems clear that the deep burrowing inhabitants of more stable muddy shores provide accommodation for a wide range of variously adapted organisms. It is significant that the majority of the hosts are either deposit or filter feeders and that the commensals can capitalize upon the water currents engendered for these feeding and respiratory purposes. In later chapters, especially with regard to coral reefs we shall see yet further examples of these intimacies.

A number of additional burrowing polychaetes also live within the unvegetated muds, but these usually lack distinctive commensal associations. They include many of the same species encountered on the grass beds or offshore sand banks (Chapter 10). They also occupy several different feeding niches. For example, *Capitella* cf. *capitata* (Fig. 7-6 B1), is a direct deposit feeder, everting a papillose sac-like pharynx and producing a mucus that agglutinates sand grains and selects organic particles of low specific gravity. The cirratulids, e.g., *Cirratulus* sp. (Fig. 7-6 H1), and terebellids, e.g., *Amphitrite* sp. (Fig. 7-6 A1) are equipped with a series of long extensile tentacles which they utilize to directly accumulate detritus from the sea floor. Several errant predatory polychaetes, such as the clam worm, *Nereis succinea* (Fig. 7-6 C1), the paddle worm, *Eteone heteropoda* (Fig. 7-6 I1), or the pilargiid, *Loandalia americana* (Fig. 7-6 J1), occupy temporary burrows when resting, but crawl about the muds in search of prey. Each of these species possesses an eversible proboscis equipped with chitinous jaws by which they grasp their prey. The polychaete feeding guilds are discussed at length in Chapter 10.

BAY MACROPLANKTON

The biota of the water column of the sea comprises two basic and broad categories: the nekton, which is capable of moving against a current, and the plankton, which cannot. Both of these categories can be divided into several subgroups, based upon their taxonomy, size, stage of life or preferred place in the sea. The nekton consists primarily of the fishes, marine mammals, cephalopods, and a few birds (such as the penguins), all of which are active swimmers in the sea. As the nekton is largely peripheral to the general thrust of this book, we will not subdivide this category in any other manner except along taxonomic lines. Thus, we review some of the more prominent members of

the nekton in appropriate sections of this and other chapters.

The plankton requires some additional explanations. The term plankton usually engenders thoughts of microscopic plants and animals adrift in the vastness of the sea. Although the latter is correct, the size of planktonic organisms varies from the ultramicroscopic bacteria, fungi, and coccolithophores to enormous jellyfishes weighing almost a ton. Size does not determine membership in the plankton, but the inability to swim against a current does. Although large jellyfishes are able to regulate their orientation and depth in the water, they lack sufficient musculature to "swim" against a current. So membership in the plankton is not determined entirely by size, but also by anatomical development.

In this book we have been primarily concerned with the benthic organisms that comprise the mosaic of myriad shore habitats. Many of the primary consumers, notably the filter feeders, are dependent upon the permanently floating plankton of the sea and inshore waters for their sustenance. Ultimately, even the benthic grazing primary consumers are dependent upon provision from the plankton. Algal sporelings afloat in the sea must settle and develop to provide the rich algal harvest of the shore. Furthermore, benthic species, whether plant or animal, usually disperse themselves following the reproductive process to ensure that they have the opportunity to exploit all of the survivable and accessible habitats that make up their total range. Thus, we can recognize two components of the plankton based upon residency.

The holoplankton are permanent members of the plankton which spend their entire lives floating in the sea. They include plants (the phytoplankton) and animals (the zooplankton), both of which can be exploited by benthic filter feeders for food.

The meroplankton are the temporary floating residents of the sea which occupy the waters primarily for purposes of dispersal. The progeny of more specialized ovoviviparous species never contribute to the meroplankton, but the majority of marine benthic species spend at least part of their lives floating in the sea. The most common pattern of reproduction involves the production of gametes, followed in stages by fertilization, larval development, metamorphosis and recruitment to the habitats of the parental generation. At times, inshore plankton will predominately comprise the eggs and larval stages of species which are non-planktonic as adults.

In the plankton, as elsewhere, intra- and interspecific competition and predation regulate numbers without regard to the length of time a plankter remains in the plankton. For those meroplankton fortunate enough to survive planktonic life, subjected to the vagaries of wind, wave and current and the biotic demands of competition, predation, and simply staying afloat, there are yet further problems to be overcome upon metamorphosis. Suitability of settlement site, competition from species adapted for the same or

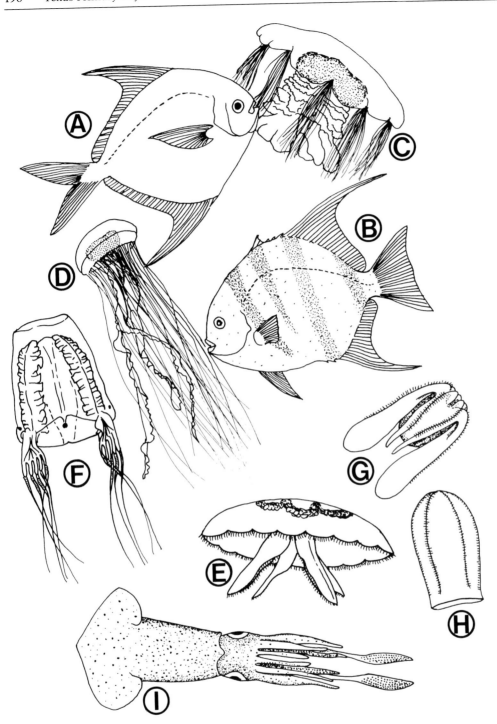

7-11. Bay macroplankton, fish associates and the bay squid. **A.** Harvestfish, *Peprilus alepidotus*; **B.** Atlantic spadefish, *Chaetodipterus faber*; **C.** Lion's mane jellyfish, *Cyanea capillata*; **D.** Sea nettle, *Chrysaora quinque-cirrha*; **E.** Moon jellyfish, *Aurelia aurita*; **F.** Sea wasp, *Chiropsalmus quadrumanus*; **G.** Lobed comb jelly, *Mnemiopsis leidyi*; **H.** Sea walnut, *Beroe ovata*; **I.** Bay squid, *Lolliguncula brevis*.

similar niches and predation from a new group of predators are only some of the perils faced by recently metamorphosed benthos.

In preceding pages and those which follow we suggest some of the larval stages through which particular benthic plants and animals must pass before they restore the adult form and behavior. In Chapter 6, we discussed some of the offshore macroplankton which usually spend their entire lives at sea. Because these holoplankters frequently wash ashore, and are encountered by the visitors to the seashore, we are justified in including them in this book. They are important in other ways, not the least of which is that they typically represent the apex of a holoplanktonic food chain that is fed, in part, from the vast reproductive resources of the shore. A few additional macroscopic holoplankters commonly encountered within the coastal estuaries also deserve attention.

Jellyfishes are pelagic cnidarians belonging to the Class Scyphozoa. They are always predatory, capturing their prey by means of nematocyst batteries and exploiting a wide range of planktonic and other nektonic life. In inshore waters, two orders are important. Members of the Cubomedusae have bells with four flattened sides and simple margins. Most Cubomedusae bear highly toxic nematocysts. *Chiropsalmus quadrumanus* (Fig. 7-11 F) prefers high salinities. It is usually uncommon in Gulf bays, but may occur in them in large numbers during periods of drought when salinities are elevated. It feeds on shrimp and crab larvae.

The majority of inshore jellyfish belong to the Semaeostomae. Common bay representatives include the moon jellyfish, *Aurelia aurita* (Fig. 7-11 E), the sea nettle, *Chrysaora quinquecirrha* (Fig. 7-11 D) and the lion's mane jellyfish, *Cyanea capillata* (Fig. 7-11 C). *Aurelia* is rather flat, some 20 cm across and feeds on small plankters. Large numbers may occur in bay waters in mid-summer, and often become stranded on shore. The sea nettle has long trailing marginal tentacles and four equally long oral arms. It is usually pale yellow or pink and is a summer species, ranging widely into inner bays where salinities can fall to as low as 3 ppt. The lion's mane jellyfish, *Cyanea capillata* is one of the largest found in the inshore waters of the Gulf of Mexico. The bell diameter can approach 2 m, although individuals with a bell diameter of 0.3 m are considered large in waters of the western Gulf. Its size and abundant clusters (typically 8) of marginal and oral tentacles gives it its name.

The most conspicuous jellyfish of Texas coastal waters is the large cabbagehead, *Stomolophus meleagris* (Fig. 6-8 A). It is primarily an offshore species, but seasonally enters the bays via tidal inlets in very large numbers. During the late summer and early fall, jetty fishermen watch thousands float by, either into or out of the bay, depending upon the direction of the tides.

Ctenophores are sometimes confused with jellyfish, and, indeed, they have an obvious if uncertain relationship with them. The Ctenophora, or comb jellies, are transparent globular planktonic predators in which locomotion is achieved by eight rows of ciliary comb plates, instead of bell pulsations as in the Scyphozoa. Ctenophores such as *Mnemiopsis leidyi* (Fig. 7-11 G) possess tentacles set between two body lobes. *Mnemiopsis* is brightly luminescent, occurs in bay waters in summer and is a voracious predator of zooplankton and many kinds of planktonic larvae. The egg-shaped *Beroe ovata* (Fig. 7-11 H) is about the same size as *Mnemiopsis* but lacks tentacles. It is more common in bays in winter and luminesces slightly when disturbed. It feeds on smaller members of the plankton. The ctenophores and smaller jellyfish are the predators of zooplankton, but they in turn are fed upon by the large jellyfishes *Chrysaora* and *Cyanea*.

BAY FISHES AND CEPHALOPODS

Murdy (1983) lists almost 550 species of fishes from the marine and estuarine waters of Texas. Although many live exclusively offshore, a considerable number enter at least the higher salinity portions of Texas bays. Some spend their entire lives in the estuaries. We cannot list all of the bay fishes here, but refer the reader to guides which provide a more complete treatment, including the books by Hoese & Moore (1977), Murdy (1983) and Robins, *et al.* (1986). We will, however, discuss some representative families and species from the perspectives of abundance, habitat or trophic level, and, to a lesser degree, taxonomic position. We realize that several prominent game species are omitted from these discussions, not because they are considered unimportant, but because another fish adequately serves as an example of the biological position the family or group occupies.

The most commonly observed fish in bays throughout the western Gulf of Mexico is the striped mullet, *Mugil cephalus* (Fig. 7-13 H). This species swims in schools and frequently leaps from the water when threatened by a predator. Mullets occur in a variety of salinities from the freshwaters of Texas and Mexico rivers to the hypersaline brine of Baffin Bay or Laguna Madre de Tamaulipas. They can survive in salinities of 75 ppt or more. Mullets leave the bays in the fall to spawn in the open sea. In addition to the striped mullet, at least three other species of Mugilidae occur in the western Gulf region. All are bottom feeding detritivores which disturb and suspend large quantities of sediment as they grub along the bottom.

Fishes which live upon or in close association with the bottom are said to be demersal. They include a variety of species representing several different groups of cartilaginous and bony fishes. The families of cartilaginous demersal fishes include the guitarfishes (Rhinobatidae), the electric rays and torpedo fishes (Torpedinidae), the skates (Rajidae), the stingrays (Dasyatidae), the butterfly rays (Gymnuridae), and the eagle rays and kin (Myliobatidae). We illustrate only three species from two of these families to represent this group.

Sharks excepted, stingrays are among the most dreaded fishes of sandy beaches and bayshores of the Gulf coast. All possess one to several serrated barbs on the tail which can inflict a painful wound in human flesh. Some species have a toxin associated with the barb which serves to intensify the pain, and wounds are often prone to infection. Stingrays only use the barbs for self defense. They have a habit of resting buried within the sand or mud, often in shallow water, with only eyes and spiracles (gill openings) exposed. If surprised or stepped upon by a swimmer or angler, they lash the armed tail toward the presumed attacker. If given sufficient warning, they will swim harmlessly away. Anyone wading in coastal waters should always be aware of the possible threat of stingrays, and with a knowledge of their habits should be able to easily avoid harm from them.

At least six species of stingrays are known to occur in Texas waters, but two are common. The Atlantic stingray, *Dasyatis sabina* (Fig. 7-12 I) is found throughout Texas bays and also occurs in shallow nearshore waters of the Gulf of Mexico. It is distinguished from the southern stingray, *Dasyatis americana* (Fig. 7-12 H) in that it has a more pointed snout, the sides of the disk are more rounded (less angular) and the top and bottom of the tail displays slightly elevated fin folds. In contrast, the snout of the southern stingray is angular but not drawn out to a point, the sides of the disk are more angular, and there is an elongate and prominently elevated fin fold on the ventral surface of the tail. Both species are bottom feeders, collecting clams, crabs, a variety of other invertebrates, and even small fishes which they crush within toothed jaws.

The cownose ray, *Rhinoptera bonasus* (Fig. 7-13 A) (Myliobatidae), attains a width of almost 1 m. Like the stingrays, it is equipped with a barb near the base of the tail, and is also a bottom feeder, collecting the same kind of prey. It differs from the stingrays in being a powerful schooling swimmer and is noted for its ability to jump out of the water. The cownose ray is migratory, visiting the northwestern Gulf in the summer, but departing for warmer waters in the winter. When present in the region, it is common offshore and can sometimes be seen within the higher salinity portions of the Texas bays.

The most obvious demersal bony fishes of sandy and muddy bottoms are the flatfishes (Pleuronectiformes). They are well represented in the western Gulf with at least 28 species in three families: the lefteye flounders (Bothidae), the soles (Soleidae) with eyes and body pigmentation on the right side of the body, and the tonguefishes (Cynoglossidae) with a teardrop shaped body and eyes and body pigmentation on the left side. All are demersal carnivores. Many of the flatfishes are summer residents in the primary bays, where they are frequently taken in trawls over sandy or muddy bottoms. It is not uncommon to find several different species in a single summer trawl, but most

leave the bays for offshore banks and spawning during the winter.

The southern flounder, *Paralichthys lethostigma* (Fig. 7-12 A), occurs on soft, unvegetated mud bottoms. Another flounder, the bay whiff, *Citharichthys spilopterus* (Fig. 7-12 B), is perhaps the most common flatfish in the northwestern Gulf region. Soles are easily distinguished from the flounders as their eyes are positioned on the opposite side of the body. The hogchoker, *Trinectes maculatus* (Fig. 7-12 C), is one of the most euryhaline of the flatfishes. Juveniles are often found far upriver in almost freshwater, but the adults seem to have somewhat more restricted salinity tolerances. They are nevertheless common in middle to higher salinity bays, especially during the summer. The lined sole, *Achirus lineatus* (Fig. 7-12 D) is similar in appearance to the hogchoker, but lacks the vertical pigmented bars and its body is covered by small tufts of hairlike cirri. It is much less tolerant of brackish water but will enter the higher salinity portions of all primary bays in Texas.

Tonguefishes are less likely to be found in the bays than the flounders or soles, but one species, the blackcheek tonguefish, *Symphurus plagiusa* (Fig. 7-12 G), is a common bay resident. All of the tonguefishes are noticeably smaller than the flounders and soles.

The demersal fishes most frequently encountered by anglers are probably members of the Ariidae, or sea catfishes. They are often caught on a baited line, and have more than once inflicted a painful hand wound with the stiff spines on the dorsal and/or pectoral fins. They are edible but rarely eaten, being considered a rough fish by most coastal fishermen. Two species occur in the region. The hardhead catfish, *Arius felis* (Fig. 7-12 E), is the more common. It is characterized by four barbels on the chin, only short barbels at the corner of the mouth, well developed spines without fleshy filaments in the dorsal and pectoral fins, and a deeply forked caudal fin. It is frequently taken by anglers on inlet jetties or bay fishing piers. The similar, although less common, gafftop catfish, *Bagre marinus* (Fig. 7-12 F), has elongate flattened barbels at each corner of the mouth, only 2 barbels on the chin, and very long fleshy filaments extending from the spines on the dorsal and pectoral fins. Both species are omnivorous scavengers.

Several species of planktivorous fishes are present in the Texas estuaries, often in very large numbers. Most belong to either the anchovy family (Engraulidae) or to the herring family (Clupeidae). Most anchovies are offshore fishes, but the bay anchovy, *Anchoa mitchelli* (Fig. 7-13 D), is exceedingly common in most of the Texas bays. It moves in large schools, providing food for many of the bay predators. With a length of only about 10 cm, this anchovy is considered to be too small for commercial harvest. In contrast, the Gulf menhaden, *Brevoortia patronus* (Fig. 7-13 J), a member of the herring family, is heavily harvested off the Gulf coast, primarily for fish meal and oil. The adults,

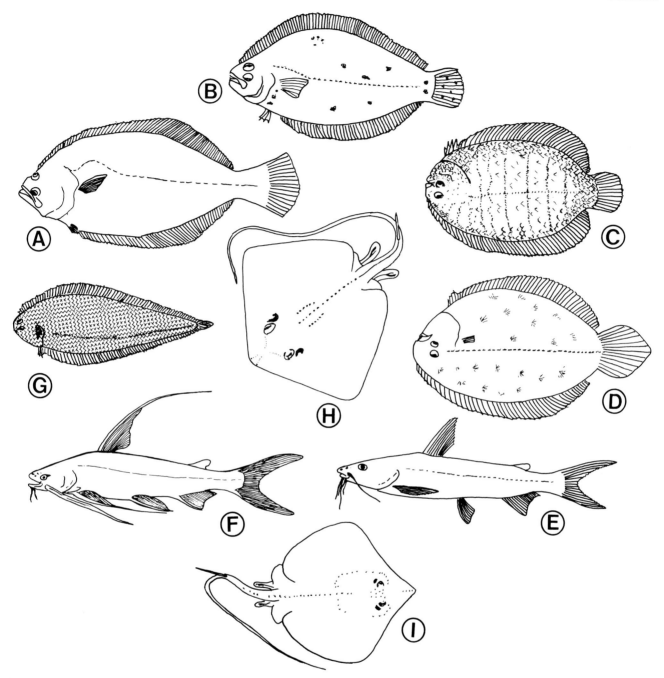

7-12. Demersal bay fishes. **A.** Southern flounder, *Paralichthys lethostigma*; **B.** Bay whiff, *Citharichthys spilopterus*; **C.** Hogchoker, *Trinectes maculatus*; **D.** Lined sole, *Achirus lineatus*; **E.** Hardhead catfish, *Arius felis*; **F.** Gafftop catfish, *Bagre marinus*; **G.** Blackcheek tonguefish, *Symphurus plagiusa*; **H.** Southern stingray, *Dasyatis americana*; **I.** Atlantic stingray, *Dasyatis sabina*.

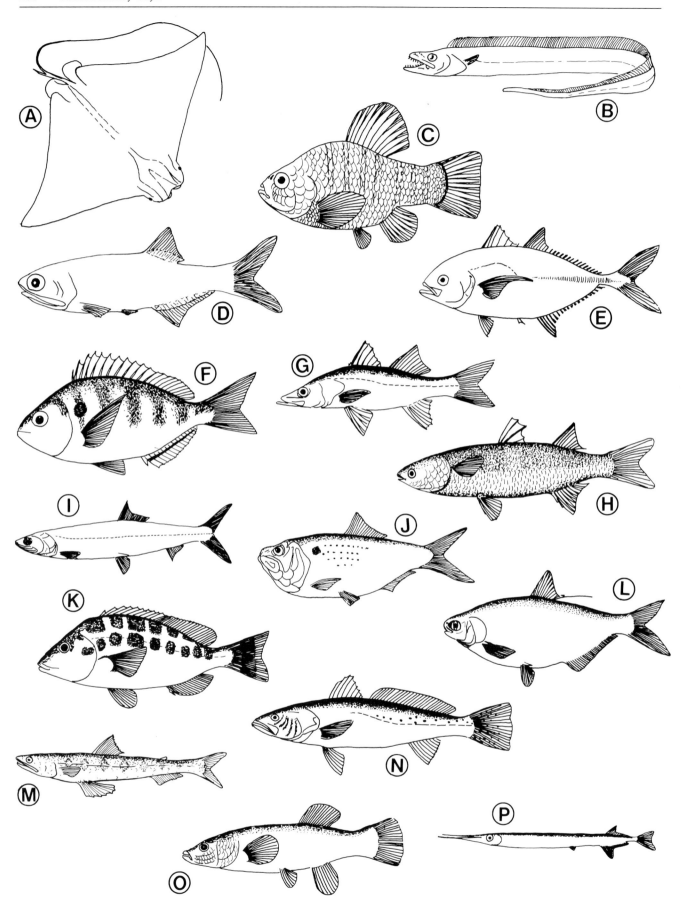

which reach 25 cm in length, occur in large nearshore schools. Juveniles come within the bays to occupy low salinity marshes. Two other members of the herring family, the gizzard shad, *Dorosoma cepedianum* (Fig. 7-13 L), and the threadfin shad, *Dorosoma petenense* (Fig. 8-4 W) are freshwater species which frequently enter the lower salinity waters of estuaries.

There are a great variety of predatory fishes in the Texas estuaries, including all of the sport and game species. For example, the sand trout or white trout, *Cynoscion arenarius* (Fig. 7-13 N), is a favorite of bay anglers. It belongs to the drum or croaker family (Sciaenidae), so named because many species produce a croaking sound with special muscles which move against the swim bladder. This family includes more inshore species than any other along the northwestern Gulf, and, together with the mullets and anchovies, comprise the majority of the fish biomass in bay waters within this region (Hoese & Moore, 1977). The sand trout can be found in all of the Texas bays. Adults are piscivorous, feeding upon a variety of the smaller bay fishes. Spawning occurs in the tidal channels, deeper bay basins or on shallow offshore banks. Young sand trout seem to prefer waters over unvegetated muds, whereas the closely related spotted seatrout, *Cynoscion nebulosus* (Fig. 8-6 T) spawns in the shallower portions of the bays and the young usually occupy grassbeds.

The snook, *Centropomus undecimalis* (Fig. 7-13 G) (Centropomidae) is another important sportfish. It is a warm water species which occurs from central Texas southward, but is more common in the bays and offshore waters of Mexico. It frequents waters around river mouths and mangroves, especially along limestone shores, and is rare or absent where there is little freshwater runoff. It leaves the bays to spawn offshore.

The jacks (Carangidae) are a large family of fast-swimming, mostly offshore fishes, many of which move about in schools. Some, such as the blue runner, *Caranx crysos* (Fig. 7-13 E), will enter tidal inlets and the Texas primary bays. They are commonly taken by fishermen on the jetties or fishing piers. *Caranx* feeds upon smaller fishes, shrimps, crabs, and other crustaceans. It spawns offshore and the juveniles develop there. Only adults enter shallow coastal waters.

7-13. Representative bay fishes. **A.** Cownose ray, *Rhinoptera bonasus*; **B.** Ribbonfish, *Trichiurus lepturus*; **C.** Sheepshead minnow, *Cyprinodon variegatus*; **D.** Striped anchovy, *Anchoa mitchilli*; **E.** Blue runner, *Caranx crysos*; **F.** Pinfish, *Lagodon rhomboide*; **G.** Snook, *Centropomus undecimalis*; **H.** Mullet, *Mugil cephalus*; **I.** Skipjack, *Elops saurus*; **J.** Gulf menhaden, *Brevoortia patronus*; **K.** Pigfish, *Orthopristis chrysopterus*; **L.** Gizzard shad, *Dorosoma cepedianum*; **M.** Inshore lizardfish, *Synodus foetens*; **N.** Sand seatrout, *Cynoscion arenarius*; **O.** Longnose killifish, *Fundulus similis*; **P.** Atlantic needlefish, *Strongylura marina*.

The tarpon, *Megalops atlanticus* (Fig. 8-4 Z), is a large fish (up to 2.5 m) which frequents moderate to low salinity estuarine habitats (Chapter 8). It is a member of the Elopidae, which also includes another estuarine species, the ladyfish or skipjack, *Elops saurus* (Fig. 7-13 I). The latter is smaller, but still grows to a length of 1 m. Its scales are smaller and more numerous than those of the tarpon, but both fishes reflect a luminous silvery sheen. The ladyfish feeds upon smaller fishes and shrimp, and is prized by anglers as a fierce fighter and jumper.

The Elopidae are relatively primitive fishes which produce an unusual pelagic larva, the leptocephalus. It is an elongate, ribbon-like transparent larva similar to that produced by eels but differing from them by having a forked rather than rounded caudal fin.

The pinfish, *Lagodon rhomboides* (Fig. 7-13 F) of the porgie family (Sparidae) is a small perch-like fish which frequents sea grass beds and waters around wharves. It is a notorious bait thief, but when caught, rarely attains a sufficient size to warrant keeping. The shoulder spot is distinctive.

Many of the predatory fishes are too small or too specialized to be sought by anglers. For example, we have already mentioned the needlefish, *Strongylura marina* (Fig. 7-13 P), in Chapter 3. Not only is this elongate specialized predator common near the jetties, but it is found throughout the higher salinity portions of bays and mangrove areas. It feeds by slashing fish prey with dozens of tiny teeth in the needle-like jaws.

The grunts (Haemulidae) are primarily a family of offshore fishes, which include many important reef predators. The pigfish, *Orthopristis chrysopterus* (Fig. 7-13 K) is one of the few members of this family that occur in the more restricted bays. It is a night feeder in the higher salinity estuarine waters. Juveniles are common on the grass beds.

The killifishes (Cyprinodontidae) are minnow-sized predators which frequent shallow waters and include many freshwater species. The sheepshead minnow, *Cyprinodon variegatus* (Fig. 7-13 C), has the greatest salinity tolerance of any known fish. It occurs in small freshwater pools, grassbeds, restricted portions of hypersaline lagoons, and a myriad of shallow water habitats in between. The longnose killifish, *Fundulus similis* (Fig. 7-13 O), is another member of the Cyprinodontidae, but rarely ventures into low salinity habitats. It feeds upon small benthic invertebrates on shallow water flats, and is especially common near mangroves.

The lizardfishes (Synodontidae) and the ribbon fish (Trichiuridae) represent two additional predatory fish families. Lizardfishes are benthic predators with a streamlined body, an elongate head and a large mouth bearing numerous sharp teeth. We illustrate the inshore lizardfish, *Synodus foetens* (Fig. 7-13 M), but several species occur in the area. They are occasionally caught by fishermen on hook and line, but are more frequently encountered in shrimp trawls. They are capable of inflicting a painful bite upon careless hands.

The ribbonfish, *Trichiurus lepturus* (Fig. 7-13 B), is more frequently taken on hook and line, and has the reputation for being a bait thief.

Squid are torpedo-shaped cephalopod molluscs well suited for darting through the water in search of prey. Their shell has all but disappeared, being only an internal chitinous "pen" within the dorsal wall of the muscular mantle. They possess a spacious mantle cavity fitted with a funnel-like siphon below the head. Water drawn into the mantle cavity is forcefully ejected through the siphon, producing a jet of water which pushes the squid in a direction opposite that of the water jet. If rapid escape is needed, the movement is usually backwards, but in most species the direction of the siphon can be adjusted and the force of propulsion controlled to provide a wider range of motion.

Large well developed eyes lie on each side of the head. One pair of elongate tentacles and four pairs of shorter arms project forward from the head and encircle a beaked mouth. The tentacles are used to capture prey and draw it to the arms where it is held during feeding. The diet usually consists of various fishes and shrimp.

Two species of squid are common in shallow Gulf waters. The bay squid, *Lolliguncula brevis* (Fig. 7-11 I) is common in Texas and Louisiana bays, and *Loligo pealei* (not illustrated) usually frequents shallow offshore waters. Large, broad fins serve to distinguish the bay squid from its offshore counterpart. *Loligo* fins are about half as wide as the length of the body (excluding

tentacles), but those of *Lolliguncula brevis* approach 80 percent of the body length.

THE HARVESTFISH

The juvenile stages of a number of pelagic fishes associate themselves with floating objects in the sea, such as logs and thereby gain some measure of security. Others, such as carangiids also take up with jellyfishes and take advantage of the protection afforded by the stinging tentacles. Theirs is a loose association, and is readily disrupted by the availability of more reliable shelter. Other fishes such as the spadefish, *Chaetodipterus faber* (Fig. 7-11 B) actively feed on ctenophores and jellyfish.

The association between fish and scyphozoan is more permanent with respect to the harvestfish, *Peprilus alepidotus* (Fig. 7-11 A). Harvestfish regularly gain sanctuary within the bell and tentacles of several species of jellyfishes. The preferred host is the large filter feeding cabbagehead, *Stomolophus meleagris* (Fig. 6-8 A) which it occupies primarily for protection. It may nibble on host tentacles and definitely feeds on the tentacles of other jellyfish such as *Cyanea*. The fish has some measure of immunity from jellyfish nematocysts. The relationship between harvestfish and jellyfish can be regarded as a form of commensalism, brought about through familiarity of contact and advantage, and in the process of leading to a more adversarial relationship.

8. Secondary Bays, Lower Salinity Marshlands and Hypersaline Lagoons

INTRODUCTION

The aquatic environment is an enigma for life. Normal seawater is the most compatible medium, with its ions similar in quantity and composition to that of most body fluids. Seawater and cell water exist near equilibrium, with neither making osmotic demands upon the other. Waters with salinities above or below that of normal seawater are more demanding upon aquatic life, for their salt concentrations are different from those within living cells. Under these conditions, water will move by osmosis across cell membranes from a region of low salt concentration to one which is higher (i.e., one which is more saline).

Despite the tendency of freshwater to invade cells, its osmotic pressure is predictable and constant. A large variety of plants and animals have perfected ways to deal with this osmotic stress. Most osmoregulate over only a narrow range (see below), but one sufficient for removing excess water and maintaining relatively constant internal ionic concentrations. Many protozoans, for example, simply employ vacuoles to accumulate and bale water flooding the cytoplasm. Some aquatic insects have thick cuticles to retard water uptake. Others, like the freshwater mussels, have a relatively dilute blood to minimize the osmotic gradient. More advanced multicellular invertebrates develop coelomoducts and nephridial systems to remove the excess water and tissues to reabsorb salts before they are excreted. Freshwater vertebrates employ complex kidneys and salt reabsorption to regulate internal osmotic concentrations.

At salinities higher than normal seawater, from about 40 ppt and above, cells face the opposite osmotic challenge. Hypersalinity robs the cells of water. But hypersaline waters vary significantly with respect to their ionic concentrations and, accordingly, their osmotic demands. Few organisms have developed ways to cope with the challenging demands of hypersalinity.

Aquatic biota is not uniformly distributed in aquatic systems (Fig. 8-1). Significantly fewer kinds of life can survive hypersaline waters than can survive in either the sea or in freshwater. The diversity of life also decreases as salinity decreases, but increases again as freshwater replaces seawater (Remane, 1934). More than twice as many marine species tolerate a salinity of 10 ppt as 5 ppt. Those which disappear in the lower salinities are not replaced by freshwater-adapted species. Few of the latter can survive in salinities above about 3 ppt. As a result, there is a depauperate biota in salinities permanently ranging from between 3 to 6 ppt (but see below). A variety of names have been applied to this saline desert (Remane, 1934; Kinne, 1971), but perhaps the most descriptive is the "brackish water paradox" (Khlebovich, 1969). Only a few osmotically hardy species are able to traverse it.

Disparity in the diversity of life between different aquatic habitats is related to the variable abilities of organisms to cope with ions and osmotic water movements across cell membranes. Euhaline species, living in salinities between 30 to 40 ppt (Fig. 8-2 A), tend to be osmoconformers. Water concentration within their body varies with that of the external medium. As long as they live in the open sea, salinity (and thus the amount of water in relation to the dissolved salts) varies but slightly. The modest changes which do occur impose almost no osmotic demands upon these species. If placed in freshwater or the upper reaches of an estuary, they will die, for they cannot cope with the flood of water that will enter their cells. Many euhaline osmoconformers also have narrow tolerances for salinity change. In this respect they are said to be stenohaline.

Estuarine species, on the other hand, are typically euryhaline; that is, they are tolerant of broad salinity fluctuations. They do this in one of two ways. They may simply conform osmotically to the broad variations of estuarine salinity, with their cellular fluids fluctuating as the external medium changes. The clam *Polymesoda maritima* is a good example, as illustrated in Figure 8-2 B. In this figure, the salt concentration of the external medium is indicated on the x-axis and that of an animal's blood is given on the y-axis. Physiologists measure these concentrations in several different ways, but here we show it as the amount by which a certain ionic concentration depresses the freezing-point of water (°C). These values are correlated with actual salinities at the top. The diagonal line that traverses the figure from lower left to upper right represents the points where the ionic concentration of the external medium equals that of the internal body fluids. Plots depicting the relationship between external and internal ionic concentrations can be determined when animals are exposed to various known external salinities, and the salt concentrations of their body fluids are determined following this exposure. These lines and curves tell much about how the animals cope with a changing aquatic environment. In the case of *P. maritima*, internal fluid salt concentration varies almost precisely in concordance with salt concentration of the external medium. The length of the line, which usually indicates tolerance limits, suggests that *P. maritima* is an extremely euryhaline osmoconformer. Few other marine animals can osmoconform over such an extreme range. In comparison, the mussel *Modiolus modiolus* is a moderately stenohaline osmoconformer, although some stenohaline animals have even narrower salinity tolerances than this.

Some of the species indicated on Figure 8-2 B deviate significantly from the diagonal conformity. These are the osmoregulators, and they employ several different mechanisms of osmoregulation. The freshwater cladoceran, *Daphnia magna*, is a hyperosmotic regulator. It maintains or regulates the ionic concentration within its cells higher than that of the medium in which it normally lives, and holds this internal concentration relatively constant until the external medium exceeds it. Thereafter it is a conformer with a low tolerance to increasing salinity. Most freshwater fishes are hyperosmotic regulators with tolerances similar to that displayed by *Daphnia*. They employ, however, several different means to achieve this end.

Hyperosmotic regulation is not limited to freshwater species. *Rhithropanopeus harrisii* is a marine crab that essentially conforms to the external medium from the lower limits of normal seawater to about 12 ppt. Thereafter, it regulates the internal ionic concentration at a level equivalent to about 10 ppt, even when the salinity of the external medium drops below this. Near its lower limit of tolerance, at a salinity of about 1 ppt, its osmotic curve indicates that it is beginning to lose the ability to regulate. Many estuarine animals, especially those which live in the lower salinity portions of estuaries, are hyperosmotic osmoregulators.

Some species regulate hyposmotically; that is, they maintain an internal ionic concentration below that of the external medium. The brine shrimp, *Artemia salina*, is a good example. *Artemia* is one of the few animals that can live in extremely hypersaline brines, such as that of the Great Salt Lake where salt concentrations can exceed 200 ppt. Near the lower limits of tolerance, at a salinity of about 5 ppt, *Artemia* is an osmoconformer. But from 10 ppt to salinities far in excess of 45 ppt, *Artemia* regulates its internal ionic concentration significantly below that of the external medium. Many shrimps and prawns, especially those that migrate from the sea to brackish waters, are also hyposmotic regulators, although not to the extreme degree of *Artemia*.

Some marine species are hyper-hyposmotic regulators; that is, they maintain a relatively constant internal ionic concentration whether the external medium is above or below this level. *Uca crenulata*, a fiddler crab of Pacific North America, is a good example. Mi-

gratory fishes such as the catadromous eel *Anguilla* (which breeds at sea but matures in fresh waters) and the anadromous salmon (breeds in freshwater but matures at sea) are other examples.

The examples we have just given are but a few of the numerous combinations of osmotic conformity and regulation which occur in nature. In this chapter, we deal with the biota occupying Gulf environments of osmotic extremes. There are no stenohaline osmoconformers here, for the variability of these environments will not permit their survival. But for this exception, the species we will discuss in the next few pages belong to one or more of the osmotic patterns we have described, depending upon the environment and the conditions prevalent at the time.

SALINITY PROFILE OF A TYPICAL ESTUARY

A typical normal or "positive" estuary is one with relatively free access to the open sea and in which seawater is measurably and progressively diluted by freshwater. Salinity gradually decreases as one traverses the estuary from its mouth to its major freshwater source. Few bays along the western Gulf of Mexico conform exactly to the typical estuary model, but the deviations, especially with respect to lower salinity and hypersaline waters, are best understood in relation to the typical. Accordingly we briefly digress to explain some of these features.

Several saline regimes occur within the normal estuary (Fig. 8-2 A, left side). Near its mouth and offshore, the euhaline environment is a region of osmotic uniformity and little osmotic stress. The greatest species diversity is typically found here. Within the estuary, salinity and species diversity gradually decrease through polyhaline and mesohaline environments. The central estuarine environment is one of saline and osmotic variability (Chapters 5 & 7). Animals like oysters survive normal spring floods by biding time, protecting their tissues from the environment until the crisis passes and a measure of normality returns. If the flood is prolonged, they and many other members of their community perish. Conversely, in drought, polyhaline or even euhaline conditions deeply invade the estuary. *Crassostrea* may be replaced by *Ostrea*, or attacked by a swarm of predators typically more euhaline in their salinity preferences. *Ostrea* and euhaline predators survive only to the next freshet.

Few marine organisms can tolerate permanent oligohalinity (salinities within the region of the brackish water paradox), but few parts of the estuary are permanently oligohaline because of tidal flux (see below). Eventually the estuary becomes a river with freshwater discharge. A new suite of plants and animals occupy its waters and live upon its shores. The uniform hypotonicity of the freshwater environment harbors a diversity of osmotically adaptable freshwater species, just as the uniform isotonicity of the shallow open sea harbors a diversity of predominantly stenohaline marine species. The variable environment of the central

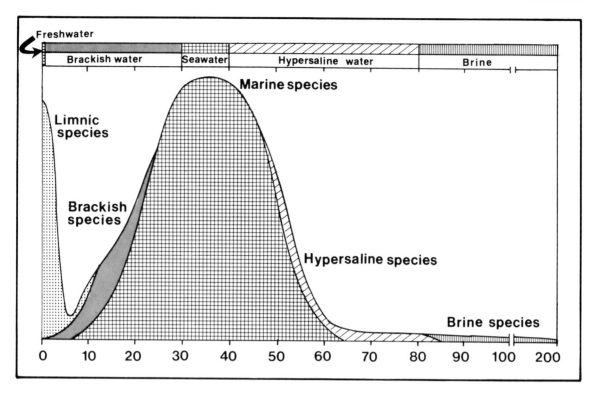

Freshwater

Brackish water | Seawater | Hypersaline water | Brine

Marine species

Limnic species

Brackish species

Hypersaline species

Brine species

0 10 20 30 40 50 60 70 80 90 100 200

8-1. Numbers of species in aquatic habitats. Approximations of relative species abundance in aquatic habitats from freshwater (left) to hypersaline brines (right). The low number of species in the region between freshwater and seawater represents the brackish water paradox. After Remane (1934), Hedgpeth (1959) and Kinne (1971).

estuary demands a degree of adaptability greater than many stenohaline marine and freshwater animals can achieve. Accordingly, it is a habitat of reduced diversity and population flux.

Despite the brackish water paradox, the upper reaches of normal estuaries are not devoid of life. Interestingly, marine organisms (or at least those with closer phylogenetic ties to the sea) tend to dominate even these lower salinity regions. Few estuaries have regions of permanent oligohalinity. River mouths are provided saline variability by tidal flux, reinforced by density differences between bodies of water. With sufficient agitation or prolonged contact, freshwater and seawater will mix, and eventually do. But where they first meet, at the head of the estuary, fresh and brackish waters tend to stay apart, the denser brackish water on the bottom and the lighter freshwater on the surface. The position of contact between these two bodies of water moves up and down the estuary according to the stage and strength of the tides and the volume of fresh water discharge which varies with precipitation in the river catchment. Flood tides inhibit river flow and push a deep, bottom-hugging wedge of

saline water far into the estuary (Fig. 8-2 C). A thin sheet of fresh, less dense river water often rides above the encroaching salt water wedge. This effect is especially pronounced just as the flood tide crests and begins to ebb. A receding tide releases the river water and allows it to flow far into or out of the mouth of the estuary (Fig. 8-2 D). Freshwater displaces the salt water wedge far seaward, itself displaced again by the next rising tide. This ebb and flow of alternating saline and fresh bottom water can move many kilometers up and down the estuary.

Marine organisms take advantage of the benthic saline incursion. Even near the head of the estuary, especially in regions with a broad tidal range where its effect is strongest, biota can expect meso- or polyhaline water near the bottom with every tidal cycle, although it may alternate with fresh or oligohaline water at the ebb. Sediments also help to bind salt water. Animals commonly take refuge within them during tidal freshets. Even without sedimentary assistance, marine biota more readily tolerates brief incursions into the brackish water paradox than do those from freshwater habitats. The upper reaches of estuaries are dominated

A.

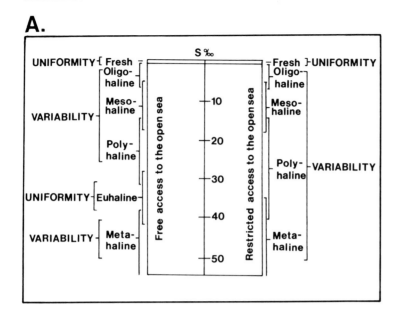

B.

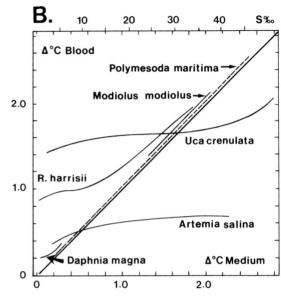

C.

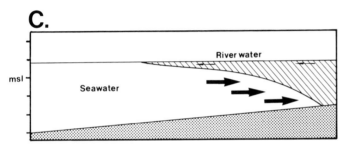

D.

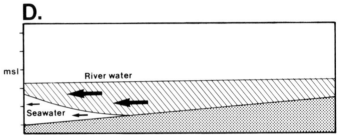

8-2. Salinity relationships.

A. Salinity regimes in "normal" estuaries (left) and hypersaline lagoons (right); modified after Dahl (1956) and Carpelan (1967).

B. Osmotic relationships of various aquatic invertebrates. See text for explanation.

C. A rising tide moves a seawater wedge upstream within an estuary, displacing the less dense river water.

D. A falling tide releases the impeded flow of river water, which moves the seawater wedge toward the mouth of the estuary.

by organisms derived from the sea.

The estuaries of the northwestern Gulf of Mexico differ in several respects from the typical estuary just described. First, their communication with the open sea is more restricted than the typical estuary, being confined to a few tidal channels which breach the offshore barrier islands. Secondly, Gulf shore estuaries are often partitioned into at least primary and secondary basins. The large embayments directly behind the barrier islands of the northwestern Gulf are described in the preceding chapter as the higher salinity or primary estuaries. It is into these basins that tidal waters from the Gulf of Mexico first flow. Yet, primary bays rarely receive land runoff directly from major river channels, although a number of minor tributaries flow into them. The major rivers either flow directly into the Gulf (e.g., the Brazos, Colorado and Rio Grande), or, more commonly, into the secondary or lower sa-

linity bays and associated marshlands, which are connected to the primary bays by a second restricted inlet (Fig. 1-3) maintained by runoff and tidal currents. Because of the separation of primary and secondary bays, distinctly different salinity regimes normally characterize the two basins. Primary bays vary in salinity from euhaline at the tidal inlets to polyhaline or upper mesohaline near their junctions with the secondary bays. The brackish to freshwater transition is completed within the secondary basins.

The tidal range of Gulf shores is relatively small. Accordingly, all estuaries in the Gulf of Mexico, regardless of morphology, do not benefit from the effects of tidal flux to the same degree as those shores with greater tides. The presence of a second restricted inlet at the entrance to the secondary bays further inhibits tidal distribution of saline water, but it does not halt it. Fiddler crabs and marine worms live in the muds of secondary bays and river banks, supplied with a wedge of saline bottom water once or twice a day. The deeper tidal channels in both the primary and secondary bays are refugia for the slightly more stenohaline biota. They cycle in and out of the estuaries with the tides or make brief incursions into the less saline shallows to feed.

With this background, we can now resume our discussion of the communities occupying the more extreme estuarine environments in the Gulf of Mexico, beginning with those of Texas secondary bays. It is followed by a section devoted to the logical conclusion of the estuarine progression, the near-freshwater marshlands. Finally, we conclude with a consideration of the opposite coastal extreme, the hypersaline lagoons where salinities sometimes exceed 100 ppt.

TEXAS SECONDARY BAYS

The best examples of primary-secondary bay systems on the Texas coast occur from Corpus Christi northwards, including the Trinity-Galveston, Copano-Aransas, and the Nueces-Corpus Christi bay systems. The main basins of Texas secondary bays are shallow (depths range from 0.3 to 2.0 m), with a floor comprising various combinations of silt and clay. Secondary bayshores often are bounded by extensive low lying marshlands bisected by numerous narrow drainage channels. Discharge currents in these bays are weak except near the rivers and drainage channels, as riverine energy is readily dissipated across the broad settling basin. Tidal influence is also minimal here, already having been dissipated significantly by the tidal inlet bottlenecks between the barrier islands and the broad expanse of the primary bays behind.

Under normal circumstances, the influence of seawater is similarly reduced within secondary estuaries, inhibited by the shallow bottoms, minimal tidal force, and restricted inlets. Average salinities usually range little above 10 ppt. Surface waters may be significantly fresher, but density gradients are present and help to maintain at least mesohaline salinities near the bottom. Nevertheless, the smaller, inner bays are more vulnerable to change than the larger, deeper primary bays, and are severely affected during floods or droughts.

Periods of increased, sometimes torrential, precipitation in the spring and fall often flush all brackish waters out of the secondary bays, killing many benthic invertebrates. Silts suspended in river waters settle out as the relative turbulence of river flow is dissipated in the broader expanse of the secondary bay. Nutrient loadings are enhanced at this time and oxygen levels become depleted. The sediments fan out to form vast mud flats, frequently covered by water depths measuring only a few centimeters. Water temperatures on these flats climb above 40°C in the summer and drop below freezing in the winter.

During prolonged drought, salinities in the secondary bays rise much higher than normal. When this oc-

curs the biota begins to resemble the communities of the higher salinity bays. Ladd (1951) considered Copano Bay to be a characteristic low salinity environment. Parker (1959), reporting upon the same area immediately following a prolonged drought, demonstrated that the typical low salinity bay community had been largely eliminated and replaced by a biota usually associated with the higher salinity bays. Clearly, the boundary defining a low salinity bay is dependent upon more than just physical barriers and fluctuates considerably as rainfall varies. Despite these climate-induced perturbations, we will consider the inner secondary bays in the context of their normal state, as representative of the lower salinity portion of the estuarine environment.

The prominent lower salinity embayments of the central coast of Texas include Rockport, Nueces, a small part of San Antonio and Copano bays. We take our example from Nueces Bay, which receives freshwater primarily from the Nueces River and which opens into Corpus Christi Bay through a shallow channel bounded by a narrow isthmus, across which Texas Highway 35 joins the city of Corpus Christi with eastern Texas (Fig. 8-3).

Flora

The natural margins of low salinity bays are fringed by mixed plant communities of *Spartina*, *Batis*, *Distichlis*, *Monanthochloe*, and *Salicornia* which transgress towards the head of the bay into the more typical marshland community based around *Typha* and *Scirpus*. Bay fringing floras differ little from those surrounding the primary bays and are dealt with in greater detail in Chapter 7.

Fauna

Other than the fiddler crabs and marsh periwinkles which we discussed in the previous chapter, there are few intertidal invertebrates along the shores of Nueces Bay. The water level of secondary bayshores varies little because of poor tidal flushing. Tidally mediated water levels may rise and fall by but a few centimeters—so little in fact that the casual observer fails to notice it. Moreover, wind can totally negate the tidal regime: onshore breezes banking the water on the shore, offshore gusts taking levels a few centimeters lower. The coastal vegetation is always lapped by bay water and sandy beaches are really no more than locally wave accumulated and sorted shell fragments. Even the fiddler crabs and marsh periwinkles must work to provide intertidal diversity, the former by digging burrows to insure a constant water supply and the latter by climbing upon blades of grass to insure emergence. The intertidal zone is naturally narrow, so much so that most of the fauna of the secondary bays are typically subtidal.

The low salinity, widely fluctuating temperature, and strongly sediment-managed environment of the inner bays is a difficult one for the survival of either freshwater or marine organisms. Oysters are absent

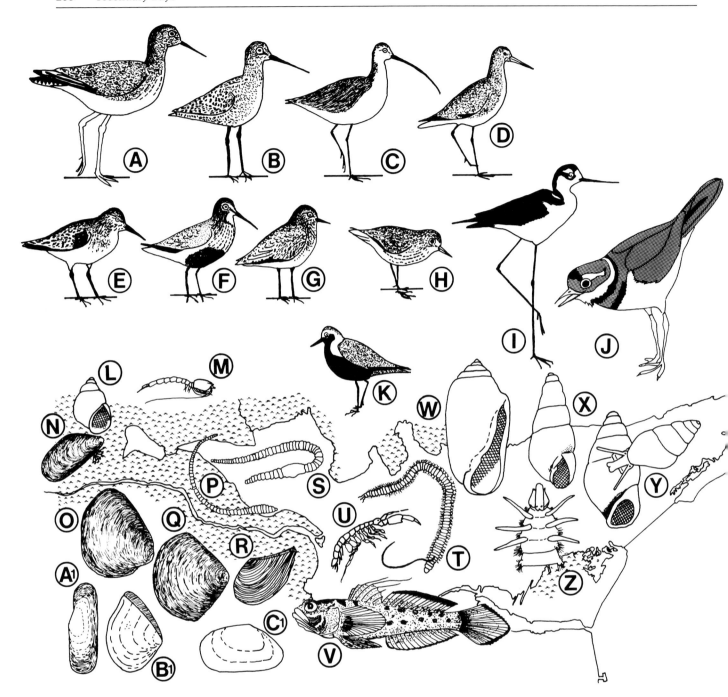

8-3. Fauna of Texas secondary bays. The underlying map is of Nueces Bay, Texas, with marshlands indicated by stippling. **A.** Greater yellowlegs, *Tringa melanoleuca*; **B.** Long-billed dowitcher, *Limnodromus scolopaceus*; **C.** Long-billed curlew, *Numenius americanus*; **D.** Willet, *Catoptrophorus semipalmatus*; **E.** Sanderling, *Calidris alba*; **F.** Dunlin, *Calidris alpina*; **G.** Western sandpiper, *Calidris mauri*; **H.** Least sandpiper, *Calidris minutilla*; **I.** Black-necked stilt, *Himantopus mexicanus*; **J.** Killdeer, *Charadrius vociferus*; **K.** Black-bellied plover, *Pluvialis squatarola*; **L.** *Littoridinops monroensis*; **M.** Cumacean, *Oxyurostylis smithi*; **N.** False mussel, *Mytilopsis leuco-phaeata*; **O.** Common rangia, *Rangia cuneata*; **P.** *Capitella* cf. *capitata*; **Q.** *Crassinella lunulata*; **R.** Pointed nut clam, *Nuculana acuta*; **S.** Oligochaete, *Enchytraeus albidus*; **T.** *Cossura* sp.; **U.** *Corophium* sp.; **V.** Clown goby, *Microgobius gulosus*; **W.** *Acteocina canaliculata*; **X.** *Odostomia* sp. (cf. *emeryi*); **Y.** *Texadina sphinctostoma*; **Z.** *Paraprionospio pinnata*; **A1.** Stout tagelus, *Tagelus plebeius*; **B1.** Dwarf surf clam, *Mulinia lateralis*; **C1.** *Macoma mitchelli*.

here, providing almost no solid substrata suitable for attachment by epizoic organisms. The community is characterized by an assemblage of euryhaline species of limited diversity, most of which are burrowing infauna or mobile epifauna, and all of which can be subjected to catastrophic mortalities. Drought can reduce freshwater input and raise salinities considerably, causing the periodic extinction of even the euryhaline species and establishing, if only temporarily, a community more typical of the hypersaline bays. Similarly some of the organisms to be found here are transients, in passage typically for breeding purposes. Perhaps the best example of this is the caridean prawn *Macrobrachium acanthurus* (Fig. 8-4 I). Females regularly migrate to the outer bays for egg laying.

There are three major groups of benthic invertebrates in the secondary bays: (1), the molluscs, including several infaunal bivalves and epifaunal gastropods, (2), amphipod crustaceans and (3), worms (euryhaline polychaetes and deposit feeding, interstitial, oligochaetes). We will discuss each of these groups in turn.

The Bivalves

Parker (1959) defined the Texas bays in terms of indicator species, and for the inner bays selected those components of the fauna which are most obvious if not necessarily the most numerous. He identifies the bivalves *Rangia cuneata*, *Mulinia lateralis* and *Macoma mitchelli* as indicative of such waters and it is therefore appropriate to begin discussion of these.

The infaunal bivalve fauna of the inner bays makes for an interesting mix of freshwater, estuarine and marine-derived species. The more typically freshwater species belong to the largely freshwater family Corbiculidae, specifically *Polymesoda maritima* (Fig. 8-4 U) and *P. caroliniana* (Fig. 8-4 V). As marshlands are their more typical habitat and occur in the bays only at their heads, we will consider them in more detail in the next section.

Parker's (1959) inner bay indicator species belong to two families. The Mactridae, including *Rangia cuneata* (Figs. 8-3 O and 8-4 D) and *Mulinia lateralis* (Figs. 8-3 B1 and 8-4 C), have short fused siphons and therefore live shallowly buried in the muds. The Tellinidae, including *Macoma mitchelli* (Fig. 8-3 C1), have long separate siphons and lie deeply buried at an angle. Both groups are generally considered to be deposit feeders and therefore presumably exploiting the rich film of microorganisms on the bay floor.

The posteriorly pointed nut clam, *Nuculana acuta* (Fig. 8-3 R), has a small shell with strongly impressed concentric lamellae. It, too, is a shallow burrowing deposit feeder belonging to the family Nuculanidae. It relies upon palp proboscides to collect food, but also with a ctenidium structure permitting some filter feeding. The primitive *Nuculana* is in many ways intermediate in morphology between the exclusively palp proboscide feeding of *Nucula* (Nuculidae) and more advanced filter feeding bivalves.

Crassinella lunulata (Fig. 8-3 Q) is a member of the

little understood Crassatellidae and has a characteristic triangular shell. With no siphons extending beyond the shell's edge, this species is another shallow burrower and possibly also a deposit feeder. The razor clam, *Tagelus plebeius* (Fig. 8-3 A1), has a thin, anteriorly elongate shell and lies vertically disposed in the sediment with long fused siphons extending upwards to the water above. On the line of evolution that has culminated in the grossly elongate razor clams of more high wave energy shores, *Tagelus* is a fast burrowing filter feeder.

Mytilopsis leucophaeata (Fig. 8-3 N), is a member of the fresh and brackish water family Dreissenidae. It has a mussel-like triangular shell and lives byssally attached to stones and shells of the fringing shallows. *Mytilopsis* is capable of tolerating a wide range of salinities, whereas the true mussels of the Mytilidae are mostly excluded from very low salinities, being more typical of cleaner, higher salinity waters. The high-zoned *Geukensia demissa* from marshes and mangroves is an exception.

Gastropods

The life histories and ecology of most of the small gastropods that inhabit the sediments of the inner bays are poorly known. All are small (up to 5 mm in shell length) and typically smooth and uncolored. *Littoridinops monroensis* (= *L.* sp. A, *fide* Andrews, 1977) (Fig. 8-3 L), *Texadina sphinctostoma* (Fig. 8-3 Y), *T. barretti* (Fig. 8-4 G) and *Probythinella* (= *Vioscalba*) *louisianae* (Fig. 8-4 H) are members of the Hydrobiidae, a family of mostly tiny gastropods which frequent marsh pools and feed upon surface films of microorganism-enriched detritus. *Texadina barretti* also occupies the upper parts of *Callianassa louisianensis* burrows (R.W. Heard, personal communication). Several additional unrecognized hydrobiid species probably occupy the nutrient rich tidal flats of the northern Gulf (Heard 1979 and 1982a). *Acteocina canaliculata* (Fig. 8-3 W) is a member of the Acteocinidae, closely related to other families of predatory snails, i.e., the Bullidae and Atyidae. It, too, is probably an infaunal predator. Finally, *Odostomia* cf. *emeryi* (Fig. 8-3 X) is tentatively placed in the Pyramidellidae and, if a member of this family, it is probably an ectoparasite of worms or bivalves.

Micro-crustaceans

Many species of micro-crustaceans inhabit the floors of the inner bays, but we will restrict our comments to only two species representative of two feeding groups. The Cumacea are typified by *Oxyurostylis smithi* (Fig. 8-3 M), an inhabitant of low salinity bays. There are over 700 species of cumaceans world-wide, most living in the sea at depths below 500 m. They typically lie buried in the sediment, head and tail projecting upwards into the water above. Filamentous gills developed on the epipodite of each first maxilliped function as a ventilating pump. The water current so created enters and leaves the branchial chamber from the front, facilitating the buried position. Some capitalize upon this current for filter feeding, while others scrape organic material from sand grains.

Most Amphipoda are detritus feeders or scavengers, but a few, like *Corophium* sp. (Fig. 8-3 U) are filter feeders. This amphipod occupies a tube in the sediment and strains fine detritus through filter setae on the gnathopods, the feeding current being created by the pleopods.

Worms

Benthic annelid worms in the inner bays fall into two groups—the Oligochaeta and the Polychaeta. We illustrate one example of the former class, *Enchytraeus albidus* (Fig. 8-3 S), which is a small white worm some 2.5 mm long and found among decaying leaf matter at the head of the bays and extending into the marsh channels. It is somewhat unrepresentative of the oligochaetes of Texas bays, as its length of about 3 cm is several times that of most estuarine species. We cite it, however, for it is the one estuarine oligochaete most likely to be seen. Oligochaetes are usually direct deposit feeders, ingesting mud and decaying organic matter. Individuals are hermaphroditic, copulation resulting in reciprocal sperm transfer.

The Polychaeta are better represented in inner bay sediments. The undistinguished looking *Capitella* cf *capitata* (Fig. 8-3 P) is usually present in considerable numbers. Its 100 mm earthworm-like body has poorly developed parapodia but lacks the typical oligochaete clitellum. *Capitella* is a burrowing animal which grows at a rate of about 30 mm per month, lives for but two years and produces mature gametes after the first year (Warren,1976). *Capitella* is easily cultured in the laboratory and has been extensively used as an indicator of pollution effects. However, the taxonomy of *Capitella* remains unsettled, and there is some evidence that Atlantic populations of *C. capitata* in reality represent a complex of sibling species (Grassle & Grassle, 1974, 1976).

Two other typically mud-dwelling polychaete families are well represented here. The monogeneric Cossuridae are represented by at least one species of the genus *Cossura* (Fig. 8-3 T). Members of this family are burrowers and apparently detritus feeders. They are readily distinguished by the single filamentous medial palp arising from an anterior segment of the body. The Spionidae are another family of ubiquitous polychaetes which can be found in a variety of environments but which are especially common in muds. We illustrate only one, *Paraprionospio pinnata* (Fig. 8-3 Z), but as many as a dozen spionid species likely occur here. This species is a selective deposit feeder.

Fishes

In addition to the bay fishes that we discussed in the last chapter, there are a few which are especially characteristic of the lower salinity bays. One of these is the clown goby, *Microgobius gulosus* (Fig. 8-3 V), a predator of benthic invertebrates in the bay shallows.

Wading Birds

The shores of the Texas inner bays and marshes support large flocks of sea and coastal birds. We will deal with the ducks and geese, more typical of marshlands later, but here draw attention to those birds of more open areas that patrol the shore and shallows in pursuit of burrowing invertebrates. They are collectively referred to as waders and largely belong to the family Scolopacidae. They are characterized by long legs, relatively short necks endowed with a bill that is slender and elongate. Bill length is usually an indication of the depth in the sediment to which they probe for their prey, and varies from species to species as each exploits an individual food resource.

Members of the Scolopacidae are most numerous and generally accumulate on the shoreline in gregarious, mixed, flocks. The willet, *Catoptrophorus semipalmatus* (Fig. 8-3 D), is a spring and autumn migrant on Texas bay shores. Its flashy black and white wing pattern makes this bird easy to identify. Bright yellow legs identify the greater yellowlegs, *Tringa melanoleuca* (Fig. 8-3 A), which is also a spring and autumn migrant. Sanderlings, dunlins and sandpipers are smaller, busier birds, with shorter legs and bills, running hither and thither over the shallows energetically probing for food. The dunlin, *Calidris alpina* (Fig. 8-3 F), is a migrant but winters along the coast from October to May. The sanderling, *Calidris alba* (Fig. 8-3 E), has a readily identifiable flashing white wing stripe and a habit of chasing in and out of retreating wavelets in search of prey. The western sandpiper, *Calidris mauri* (Fig. 8-3 G), has a somewhat longer and more solid bill than other sandpipers and forages in slightly deeper waters. The least sandpiper, *Calidris minutilla* (Fig. 8-3 H), is the smallest of the sandpipers, little bigger than a sparrow, and this "peep" is more active among the vegetation. All of the above, except the dunlin are spring and autumn migrants to Texas.

Two species of dowitchers or "snipe," the long-billed, *Limnodromus scolopaceus* (Fig. 8-3 B), and short-billed, *L. griseus* (not illustrated), are spring and autumn visitors and are identified by their feeding style in which the bill is rapidly and repeatedly jabbed perpendicularly into the sand, somewhat reminiscent of a sewing machine needle. The last member of the Scolopacidae illustrated is the long-billed curlew, *Numenius americanus* (Fig. 8-3 C), with its long characteristically downwardly curved bill. This bird is resident in Texas. It inserts its bill alongside a burrow, thrusts its head sideways, and strikes the prey at depth from the side.

The plovers and turnstones (Charadriidae) are more compactly built wading birds, with thicker necks, shorter legs and bills and large eyes. Plovers run across the ground in short starts and stops. The common resident plover on Texas shores is the killdeer, *Charadrius vociferus* (Fig. 8-3 J), so called because of its distinctive vocalizations. It is not restricted to the coastal region, but occurs throughout much of the

United States and Canada. This noisy bird has two black breastbands unlike the single band of the semipalmated plover, *C. semipalmatus* (not illustrated). By contrast, the black-bellied plover, *Pluvialis squatarola* (Fig. 8-3 K), has a black breast and a whitish back. These birds are spring and autumn visitors and at rest have a dejected, hunched appearance.

The stilts and avocets (Recurvirostridae) are characterized by slender bodies set upon long, delicate legs. The long bill is curved upwards in the American avocet, *Recurvirostra americana* (not illustrated), but is straight in the black-necked stilt, *Himantopus mexicanus* (Fig. 8-3 I). Dramatically black above and white below, the remarkably long legs are red. The bird is a central American species visiting Texas bays in summer where it wades the shallows as if on stilts.

COASTAL MARSHLANDS

Coastal marshlands are habitats of sedimentary accretion that mark the freshwater-oligohaline boundary, although temporary incursions of higher salinity waters are not uncommon here. They are dominated by stands of grasses, sedges and cattails partitioned by numerous drainage channels of varying widths and depths. The channels undergo continual change, with new tributaries opening as old ones are closed by silting. Moreover, the marshland habitat is successional in much the same way as are mangrove communities (Chapter 9). There are many differences between marshlands and mangroves beyond the obvious ones of vegetation size and composition. Mangroves are exclusively tropical, whereas low salinity marshlands occur in temperate or tropical climates. Temperate coastal marshlands are winter limited in much the same way as are temperate salt marshes; their underground rhizomes are, in part, adaptations to survive winter freezes. Mangroves are not so limited. The latter, especially *Avicennia* and *Rhizophora*, produce water borne seeds and fruits which provide these plants the capability of dramatic downshore range extensions. Marshland vegetation generally relies upon wind or insect borne seeds, which can be carried long distances. More often, community expansion is by adventitious shoots and runners from a rhizome stock.

Two plants are of overriding importance on the Texas marshes—the cattail, *Typha latifolia* (Fig. 8-4 A) and the bullrush, *Scirpus maritimus* (Fig. 8-4 B). *Typha* grows to a height of about l.5 m, whereas *Scirpus* stands only about l m. These two plants create fields of broad waving blades and inflorescences. In the rich basal layer of decomposing litter, hordes of mosquitoes and midges reside to rise up as clouds at sunset. In summer, the marsh is still and seemingly airless with only the buzz of insects, whereas in winter, winds turn the sedges and reeds into wave-like motion. Only occasionally wetted by water, the marshes themselves are anoxic and poorly inhabited except by insects and seed eating birds, e.g., the redwing blackbird, *Agelaius phoeniceus* (Fig. 8-4 J).

The mud banks and sand floors of the drainage channels support a rich interstitial and tube dwelling fauna of oligochaetes, polychaetes and amphipods such as *Corophium* (Fig. 8-4 E). Many of the euryhaline worms described elsewhere in this book occur here.

The caridean prawn *Macrobrachium acanthurus* (Fig. 8-4 I) is of particular importance. Some 20 cm long from rostrum to telson, this prawn is immediately recognized by the enormously elongate and chelate second pereopods which are held out from the body at right angles. It prefers the deeper channels and especially tidally influenced river areas, where it lives as an opportunistic scavenger or predator. Darnell (1958) has shown the stomach of a related prawn, *M. ohione*, to contain 50 percent finely ground detritus and bits of organic matter, 20 percent sand and 30 percent clam tissue and miscellaneous plant, invertebrate and fish remains. *Macrobrachium* breeds in the lower salinity channels and streams, but gravid females, eggs securely held by the pleopods, migrate downstream to release the developing young in the higher salinity bays. By subtle changes in the depth at which the larval shrimps swim, they avoid being washed out into the Gulf on the ebbing tide and eventually return to the marshes and streams where they will mature. Such migrations by both adult and young require a high degree of differential osmoregulation—an attribute characteristic of many other marsh inhabitants.

Molluscs

The hydrobiids mentioned in the previous section, including *Texadina barretti* (Fig. 8-4 G), *T. sphinctostoma* (Figs. 8-3 Y; 8-4 F), *Littoridinops monroensis* (Fig. 8-3 L) and *Probythinella louisianae* (Fig. 8-4 H), will also be found crawling over the channel muds and sands. None are more than 2 to 3 mm long. They make long trails over the richer organic muds of the drainage channel floors as they feed on the nutrient rich surface organic film.

In contrast to the small gastropods of the channels, two species of infaunally buried bivalves are much larger. *Polymesoda maritima* (Fig. 8-4 U) attains a length of 25 mm, *P. caroliniana* (Fig. 8-4 V) grows up to 40 mm. Both are members of the Corbiculidae—a group of largely tropical bivalves which are adapted to withstanding wide variations in temperature and salinity and, moreover, can tolerate extensive periods of emersion. At such times, the shell valves gape slightly posteriorly and aerial respiration occurs across a delicate strip of exposed mantle tissue. Exchange may also be maintained with subterranean waters in the mud. In this way *Polymesoda* can withstand extended periods of drought.

The ubiquitous bivalves characteristic of the lower salinity portions of bays, e.g., *Mulinia lateralis* (Figs. 8-3 B1 and 8-4 D) are equally at home in the subtidal portions of marshlands.

Fishes

A number of fishes occurring in the marsh drainage channels can be regarded as either more properly belonging to the freshwater domain or to higher salinity bays or marine environments. In either case, they occupy waters adjacent to the marshlands near the extreme limit of their more typical range. For example, the Alligator gar, *Lepisosteus spatula* (Fig. 8-4 Y), is normally a predator of freshwaters, whereas the tarpon, *Megalops atlanticus* (Fig. 8-4 Z), is a pelagic predator of the bays. The threadfin shad, *Dorosoma petenense* (Fig. 8-4 W), is a planktivorous fish of freshwaters, but commonly ventures into the lower salinity reaches of Texas bays. The "Bigmouth sleeper" goby, *Gobiomorus dormitor* (Fig. 8-4 A1), is a marine fish tolerant of a wide range of salinities. In the marsh channels it feeds on bottom invertebrates.

A few fishes regularly wander between fresh and salt water habitats. Anadromous species, such as salmon, move from the sea into freshwater to spawn. There are no salmon on the Texas coast, but there are catadromous species, which move from freshwater to the sea to spawn. Most notable of these is the American eel *Anguilla rostrata* (Fig. 8-4 X). Females and some males spend much of their adult lives in the freshwater domain of streams and rivers far inland from the sea. Adults will enter Texas marshland channels especially during the winter months as part of downstream migrations to the sea. Spawning occurs in the Sargasso Sea in the central Atlantic, and leptocephalus larvae remain here a year or more before they return to the marshlands and rivers previously occupied by their parents. Juvenile eels enter the estuaries as "elvers" which migrate to the marshes and where they reside for a while. The males may spend most of their inland lives here, but females typically move far up river where they can remain for several years.

In many ways, as we have seen first with *Macrobrachium* and now with *Anguilla*, the marsh channels are critical pathways to and from the sea from freshwater and an obstacle that must be traversed by the returning young.

Ducks and Geese

The Anseriformes comprise a discrete group of waterfowl, the ducks, geese, and swans, which, more than any other group of birds, characterize marshlands. All have short legs, with webbed feet giving them a waddling gait on land but making them proficient surface swimmers and divers.

The geese are much more at home on land and may often be seen on grasslands and in the marshes. Two species are illustrated—the snow goose, *Chen caerulescens* (Fig. 8-4 K), and the Canada goose, *Branta canadensis* (Fig. 8-4 L). The former is shown in its adult white plumage, but in the Texas marshes it more often occurs as an immature gray and speckled variant, formerly thought to constitute a separate species, the blue goose. The species breeds in the high Arctic tundra, but migrates to Gulf shores in winter.

The Canada goose is the most common and familiar goose in America. The black head and neck marked with a distinctive white chin-strap make it easily distinguishable. Canada geese breed in open or forested areas near water in Canada. The birds winter along the Texas coast, with large migrating flocks arriving in September and October, displaying the classic V formation as they swoop upon coastal marshlands. They remain in Texas until April, noisily honking to one another as they fly from roosts to feeding grounds on coastal meadows.

Except for the American widgeon, *Anas americana* (Fig. 8-4 M), which is a marshland forager, ducks are much more at home on the water than geese, and display a greater diversity of species. We illustrate eight species common to Texas shores, but there are twice that number which overwinter here. The male American widgeon is easily recognized in mixed flocks by his white cap ("baldpate").

The mottled duck, *Anas fulvigula* (Fig. 8-4 Q), is the only common year round resident on the marshes. Migratory species are usually present from October to April. Most can be expected from the Louisiana border to the Rio Grande, but some are more abundant than others. For example, the mallard, *Anas platyrhynchos* (not illustrated), is not as common as many other ducks, but it occurs along the entire coast in winter. The green-winged teal, *Anas crecca* (Fig. 8-4 O), and the blue-winged teal, *Anas discors* (Fig. 8-4 N) are much more common and also occupy the entire coast. The Gadwall *Anas strepera* (Fig. 8-4 P), prefers marshlands from central Texas southwards, as does the northern pintail, *Anas acuta* (Fig. 8-4 R). The latter is easily identifiable by the long black central tail feathers. The northern shoveler, *Anas clypeata* (Fig. 8-4 T),

8-4. Biota of Texas coastal marshlands. Cat-tails and bullrush flank channels through the marsh. **A.** Cat-tail, *Typha latifolia*; **B.** Bullrush, *Scirpus maritimus*; **C.** Dwarf surf clam, *Mulinia lateralis*; **D.** Common rangia, *Rangia cuneata*; **E.** Tube-building amphipod, *Corophium* sp.; **F.** Small-mouthed hydrobiid, *Texadina sphinctostoma*; **G.** Hydrobiid, *Texadina barretti*; **H.** *Probythinella louisianae*; **I.** Freshwater shrimp, *Macrobrachium acanthurus*; **J.** Red-winged blackbird, *Agelaius phoeniceus*; **K.** Snow goose, *Chen caerulescens*; **L.** Canada goose, *Branta canadensis*; **M.** American widgeon, *Anas americana*; **N.** Blue-winged teal, *Anas discors*; **O.** Green-winged teal, *Anas crecca*; **P.** Gadwall, *Anas strepera*; **Q.** Mottled duck, *Anas fulvigula*; **R.** Northern pintail, *Anas acuta*; **S.** Lesser scaup, *Aythya affinis*; **T.** Shoveler duck, *Anas clypeata*; **U.** Florida marsh clam, *Polymesoda maritima*; **V.** Marsh clam, *Polymesoda caroliniana*; **W.** Threadfin shad, *Dorosoma petenense*; **X.** American eel, *Anguilla rostrata*; **Y.** Alligator gar, *Lepisosteus spatula*; **Z.** Tarpon, *Megalops atlanticus*; **A1.** Bigmouth sleeper, *Gobiomorus dormitor*.

is characterized by the long spatulate beak which the animal uses to stir up small invertebrates on the floor of the estuary.

All the preceding ducks are generally termed "dabblers" and constitute the familiar "paddle ducks" of salt marshes. Except for the shoveler, dabblers feed by upending in the water to reach aquatic plants, snails and crustaceans. Dabblers require no running start for a take off but explosively spring directly into flight.

Mergansers and sea-ducks are less obvious in coastal bays, the former breeding in the far north and moving south in large flocks to overwinter, the latter as common inland on lakes and ponds as they are on the bays and the open Gulf of Mexico. The lesser scaup, *Aythya affinis* (Fig. 8-4 S), is a sea-duck or "pochard," a group characterized by legs set well back and far apart, facilitating diving. Unlike the dabblers which rarely dive, the pochards are excellent divers, disappearing below the water surface to search for food on the bay or sea floor. The lesser scaup is a common breeder in the Texas marshes and a year-round resident.

HYPERSALINE LAGOONS

Hypersaline lagoons are small, shallow coastal basins created in arid climates. They do not display the typical salinity pattern of a normal estuary (Fig. 8-2 A, right side). Deficient freshwater input, excess evaporation and limited communication with the open sea act in concert to modify the system. Saline excess and extreme osmotic variability rule hypersaline basins and mediate biotic diversity. Euhaline salinities occur in parts of the hypersaline system, but, except in tidal inlets, they are usually transitory, lacking the stability of the euhaline waters in the open sea.

There are three major hypersaline systems along western Gulf of Mexico shores, and perhaps several dozen minor hypersaline basins. The Laguna Madres of Texas and northern Mexico are the two largest. We will discuss these in this chapter. A complex system of salt pans and hypersaline lagoons also fringe the northern Yucatan shore, and unlike the more northerly basins, these are associated with a distinctly tropical flora and fauna. We will discuss the Yucatan basins in Chapter 9.

The coastal region and adjacent lands from Corpus Christi, Texas to La Pesca, Mexico are characterized by a climate of relatively high humidity and low precipitation. Net evaporation usually exceeds precipitation and runoff into the coastal bays, producing within them salinities in excess of that encountered in the open Gulf. The Laguna Madre system of Texas is the largest hypersaline basin in the United States, and Laguna Madre de Tamaulipas shares the same distinction for Mexico. We will first consider the physical characteristics of the Laguna Madres, and then examine how the hypersaline environment influences their biota.

The Physical Environment

The Laguna Madre of Texas (Fig. 8-5) is the best studied hypersaline lagoon in the world (e.g., Gunter, 1950; Collier & Hedgpeth, 1950; Breuer, 1957; 1962; Simmons, 1957; Parker, 1959; Copeland & Jones, 1965; Behrens, 1966; Carpelan, 1967; Hedgpeth, 1947, 1957, 1967; Fuls, 1974; Krull, 1976; Cole, 1980; Cornelius, 1984). It is a long, narrow basin located behind Padre Island and encompassing 1550 km². It was created by the formation of Padre Island, about 5000 years ago (Rusnak, 1960). At this time, the Rio Grande entered the sea north of its present mouth, where it flowed into the southern portion of Laguna Madre. About 4000 years ago, the river moved considerably to the south, creating the complex delta which now separates the Laguna Madre de Tamaulipas from its counterpart in Texas. During the last 4000 years, the Laguna Madre of Texas has been without significant river input.

For most of this time, and well into the early years of human discovery and exploration, Laguna Madre was a continuous water-filled basin extending from Corpus Christi Bay in the north to Brazos Santiago Pass near the mouth of the Rio Grande (Price, 1958; Fisk, 1959). About 150 years ago, a central region, which had been accumulating sediments for centuries, finally filled with sand. This created a broad tidal flat, dividing the Laguna into northern and southern sections. Unlike its twin to the south, the Texas Laguna Madre was not partitioned by accumulation of river sediments, but mostly by storm deposits and wind-blown sand. Today, the flat which separates northern and southern sections of the Laguna Madre of Texas is usually dry. It will cover with a few cm of water only on very windy days (Shepard & Wanless, 1971).

The northern Laguna basin has an area of about 320 km², not including the Baffin Bay system which adjoins it (Fig. 8-5 A). It is narrower (average width = 4 km) and shorter (75 km) than the southern basin. The latter is about 88 km long, with an average width of 8 km and has an area of about 1050 km². Both sections have an average depth of slightly less than 1 m (Rusnak, 1960). Distribution of sediments within Laguna Madre are as might be expected. Sand-sized particles dominate nearshore, but increasing percentages of finer-grained detrital silts are common in the deeper basins.

Although hurricane channels occasionally breach Padre Island, providing ephemeral communication between Laguna Madre and waters of the open Gulf, the Laguna is normally isolated from the sea along most of its length, or so it was prior to human intervention. In its natural condition, Laguna Madre was what some would call a stagnant basin. Sea water entered through the restricted inlets at the north and south ends of Padre Island, and through hurricane channels during and immediately following major storms. Once within the basin, water had difficulty exiting or circulating. The high summer temperatures characteristic of the area

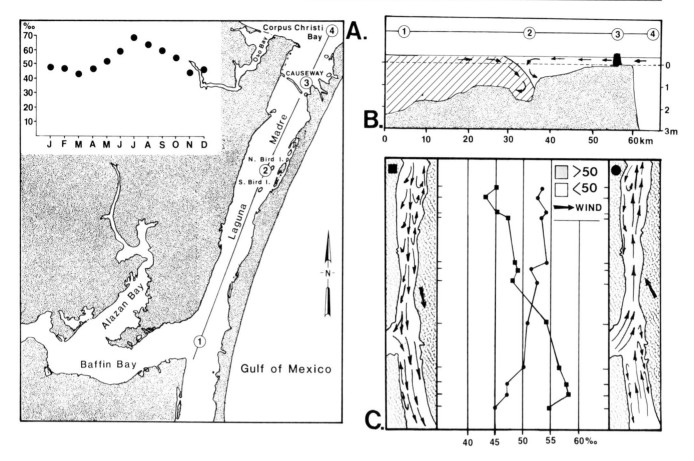

8-5. Hydrography of the Laguna Madre of Texas (modified from Rusnak, 1960).

A. Northern Laguna Madre. Numbers along the transect correspond to those on B. The inset shows mean seasonal salinity fluctuations (ppt) in Laguna Madre at a point about equidistant from 1 and 2.

B. Cross section of the northern entrance to Laguna Madre subsequent to causeway construction. Dense, higher salinity water is indicated between points 1 and 2 by cross-hatching. Point 2 represents the boundary between high salinity Laguna Madre water and the lower salinity water from Corpus Christi Bay. Point 3 represents the causeway, which now inhibits water exchange

between Laguna Madre and Corpus Christi Bay (4), except along specific channels.

C. Seasonal shifts of the hypersaline water mass in Laguna Madre near the entrance to Baffin Bay. Left margin, winter conditions; right margin, summer conditions; thin arrows indicate surface currents; thick arrows over land indicate the prevailing wind direction; shading within Laguna Madre indicates the hypersaline water mass (> 50 ppt). The plots in the central portion of the diagram indicate salinity values (ppt) in winter (squares) and summer (circles), correlated with the location in Laguna Madre marked by these symbols on the left and right maps.

evaporated some of the water, leaving behind a concentrated brine. As the salt concentration increased, the density of the water also increased, so the briny water sank to the bottom, further inhibiting circulation. Without permanent rivers entering the Laguna, there was little freshwater to dilute the brine. Thus, the waters became hypersaline. High salinities have been characteristic of parts of the Laguna for at least 4,000 years, since the Rio Grande changed course toward the south (Rusnak,1960). Oyster and *Macrocallista* shell middens along the shores of Baffin Bay radiocarbon dated at about 5,000 years b.p. suggest that lower salinities were present in the area about the time Laguna Madre was forming (Hedgpeth, 1957), and

support the idea that the region received more rainfall then than it does now.

Today, salinities in Laguna Madre range from about 2 to 86 ppt. The highest salinities are usually found in Baffin Bay and its associated embayments, although a few isolated parts of the Laguna have seen salinities in excess of 100 ppt for short times (Hedgpeth, 1953). Baffin Bay was created as a drowned river valley estuary during the pluvial episode prior to the formation of Laguna Madre. It is somewhat isolated from the northern Laguna basin, cut off by "rock reefs" and a narrow sill (Rusnak, 1960). The Baffin Bay system is a relic of an earlier river discharge which no longer makes a significant contribution to the coastal zone. Salinities from 60 to 80 ppt are common within the Baffin Bay system, but local cloudbursts can depress salinities to as low as 2 ppt in some parts of the bay (Gunter, 1945). The waters of the more restricted northern Laguna basin are more saline than those of the southern basin, although salinities commonly approach 70 ppt near the northern end of the southern section. Since the opening of the intracoastal canal in 1949 and the Port Mansfield channel in 1962, both of which have facilitated water circulation from the Gulf to the lagoon, salinity conditions in some parts of Laguna Madre have ameliorated, but the basin as a whole still trends toward hypersalinity.

Since 1940, human activities in the coastal zone have had a number of direct and indirect effects upon Laguna Madre. Beginning in 1940, several unsuccessful attempts were made to open Yarborough Pass, a man-made tidal inlet connecting the Gulf of Mexico with northern Laguna Madre. This channel could never be maintained, and today lies buried beneath Padre Island sands. In 1949, the Intracoastal Waterway, a 40 m wide, 3 m deep canal, was completed from Corpus Christi Bay to Brazos Santiago Pass. It joined the northern and southern Laguna basins across the central tidal flats, providing some water exchange between them. The prevailing southeasterly winds of spring and summer create northerly currents in the Laguna. Water enters Laguna Madre through Brazos Santiago Pass and sometimes flows its entire length via the Intracoastal Canal, exiting to Corpus Christi Bay. The currents transport new water into the lagoon system and aid the mixing of waters already there. The Intracoastal Canal also provides an escape route for fishes encountering excessive salinities in some parts of the lagoon (Simmons, 1957).

The moderating effects of the canal might have been even greater were it not for another man-made change. In 1950, a landfill causeway was completed, connecting Padre Island to the mainland at Encinal Peninsula near Corpus Christi. The causeway effectively blocked water exchange between the northern Laguna basin and Corpus Christi Bay, except for three 150 m wide inlets. One of these quickly filled with sand. Today, all water exchange between the northern Laguna basin and Corpus Christi Bay is limited to two narrow channels (Fig. 8-5 A-B).

The southern basin has also been subjected to modifications as a result of human activities. In 1962, the Port Mansfield Channel was opened through Padre Island. The channel remains open, in part due to the protection given it by jetties on the Gulf shore, and in part by periodic dredging. It provides another outlet for Laguna waters moved by southeasterly winds. Throughout much of the southern basin, salinities are now more like those of the adjacent Gulf, and the diversity of biota has been increasing (Hedgpeth, 1967). Nevertheless, there are still many stagnant pockets with poor circulation and high salinities.

The ultimate fate of Laguna Madre, like all coastal estuaries, is to fill with sediment. Unlike other estuaries, the Laguna is not being filled to any appreciable degree by sediments delivered by rivers. This is being achieved by aeolian and storm driven processes. Wind-blown sands are derived primarily from Padre Island. The most important sources of Laguna sediments, however, are hurricane washover fan deposits.

The Texas hypersaline system has received considerably more attention than that of Mexico, but the latter has not been overlooked (Hildebrand, 1958; Yanez & Schlaepfer, 1968; Schlaepfer, 1968). Much of what has just been said with respect to the Laguna Madre of Texas can be said again for Laguna Madre de Tamaulipas (Fig. 8-6), although the latter differs in some important respects from the former. It is a double basin hypersaline lagoon system, largely isolated from Gulf of Mexico waters by sandy barrier island strands. The barrier islands of Mexico are narrower and mostly lower than Padre Island, and are cut by several, normally sand-filled tidal inlets.

Basin filling has proceeded further in the Laguna Madre de Tamaulipas than in the Laguna Madre of Texas, and the source of these sediments is fundamentally different. Deltaic deposits of the Rio Grande cover hundreds of km^2 at the northern end of the Laguna, and no doubt occupy what was once a part of this basin. The central portion also is largely filled (except during the highest tides), in part by wind-deposited sands, but primarily by deltaic river deposition from the Rio San Fernando during a former pluvial period (Yanez & Schlaepfer, 1968). Fluvial deposition has influenced the Tamaulipas Laguna to a much greater degree than has occurred in the Laguna Madre of Texas, which has received deltaic sediments only during its earliest stages of development. Today, Laguna Madre de Tamaulipas, like its northern counterpart, receives little river discharge from any source due to the arid climate. On the central flats, numerous vegetated deltaic "islands" rise 2 to 3 meters above the surrounding barren, dry river-bed flats.

Brine-filled basins rimmed by extensive sun-baked and long-exposed tidal flats lie to the north and south of the Rio San Fernando delta. The northern basin is the largest and most isolated. It is about 20 km wide and 55 km long, with a maximum depth of a little more than 3 m. The southern basin is narrower and shallower (maximum depth about 1.3 m). It is widest (17 km) immediately south of the Rio San Fernando delta. The width diminishes to less than 3 km near the mouth of the Rio Soto la Marina.

Evaporation exceeds precipitation in the Laguna Madres of Texas and Tamaulipas, but to a greater degree along the Tamaulipas shore. Salinities vary seasonally, but tend to remain high. Salinities in excess of 110 ppt are common in the northern portion of the northern basin, and in excess of 130 ppt in the northern portion of the southern basin. As most of the tidal channels are normally filled with sand, there is little exchange of water with the Gulf of Mexico except after major storms, and even then ineffectually for only a short time. The Laguna Madre de Tamaulipas is a harsh environment in a harsh climate, and generally a poor habitat for most marine life.

Osmotic Factors and the Biota

Salinity is the primary factor limiting biotic diversity in a hypersaline lagoon. Life must be able to tolerate not only increased salinity, but often fluctuations significantly greater than any encountered in a normal estuary. If the lagoon waters could achieve a specific constantly elevated "maximum" salinity (like freshwaters achieve a relatively constant minimum "salinity"), perhaps species could evolve that are adapted to it. But the "norm" in a hypersaline system seems to be one of continual change. As day upon rainless day persists, water is slowly lost to the atmosphere by evaporation, and the brine becomes more briny. But one intense cloudburst can reduce salinity in a shallow local embayment by 60 ppt or more. Few aquatic organisms are capable of surviving this kind of drastic osmotic shock.

The only osmotically uniform environments of the hypersaline lagoon system are at the lower freshwater extreme (Fig. 8-2 A, upper right), and within the tidal channels which connect these lagoons with the open sea (not indicated on Fig. 8-2 A). Because of the aridity of the climate, reliable freshwater outflows are rare or ephemeral. The few which flow year round are usually small springs from mineral-rich groundwater sources. These waters are hardly "fresh" and will mix rapidly with the hypersaline brine. Even following dilution by a thunderstorm, evaporation of water in the upper reaches of the hypersaline lagoon quickly can restore the salinities of metahaline brines.

Unlike a normal estuary, salinity in a hypersaline lagoon *decreases* near the few tidal inlets (not illustrated in Fig. 8-2 A). Biota recruited from offshore faces increasing, not decreasing, salinity as it moves from the tidal inlet into the central portion of the lagoon. This is the reverse salinity profile of a normal estuary.

Even in a moderately hypersaline system, the osmotic imbalance between body fluids and the environment places a constant demand upon the organism to yield water. As external salinity increases, the intensity of this demand increases. At 40 ppt, osmotic stress is present. At 50 ppt and above, it becomes intense, with only a few of the hardiest of plants and animals capable of surviving the onslaught. Add to this the osmotic shock of rapid decreases in salinity during rare periods of intense rainfall, and it is little wonder that the more restricted hypersaline basins and coastal waters are characterized by low species diversity. These areas are biological deserts, not devoid of life, but containing a few hardy, adaptable species, often in surprisingly large numbers.

Despite tendencies toward high salinity and restricted circulation, large portions of the hypersaline lagoons are neither biologically stagnant nor excessively impoverished. Except for a few species uniquely adapted for the hypersaline environment, such as the crab, *Uca subcylindrica* (Fig. 8-6 J), an endemic of the

Texas and Mexico Laguna Madres, the majority of lagoon biota is derived from euryhaline components of the marine and estuarine environments. In some parts of each hypersaline system, notably in the vicinity of tidal inlets, salinity characteristics are about the same as those found in similar locations in normal estuaries. Furthermore, the construction of the intracoastal waterway and the Mansfield Cut facilitates circulation of normal seawater through much of the Laguna Madre of Texas. The biota in these portions of the Laguna Madres has already been discussed in the preceding pages. Seagrass meadows, for example, are more extensive in the Laguna Madre of Texas than in most other Texas estuaries, and account for exceptionally high biological productivity (Simmons, 1957; Breuer, 1962; Hellier, 1962; Conover, 1964; Pulich, 1980). Many of the invertebrates associated with seagrass beds in other Texas estuaries also occur in Laguna Madre. Redfish Bay, at the northern end of the southern Laguna Madre basin, harbors not only extensive sea grass beds, but also luxuriant stands of blue-green algae which thrive in the hypersaline medium. The algae and grassbed biota provide abundant food for grazing fishes which are, in turn, fed upon by sport and food fish species. During normal years, when salinities in Redfish Bay fluctuate between 40 to 60 ppt, the area is a highly productive fishing ground. In fact, Laguna Madre was once described as "producing more fish than all the remainder of the Texas coast" (Gunter, 1945). During dry years salinities rise above 70 ppt and bring about large fish kills within Redfish Bay. The fishery survives because many individuals migrate to waters of lower salinity near the inlets. Eventually the excessive brine in the deeper basins is flushed out, either by a hurricane or by drought-breaking rains which swell long-dry arroyos with angry white waters that surge into the lagoon. Fishes return from their inlet refugia to the basins and the fishery is quickly restored. For most of the last 50 years, more than 50 percent of the finfish catch from Texas bays has come from Laguna Madre (Diener, 1975). Since 1974, Laguna Madre has been second only to Galveston Bay for finfish landings (Osburn & Ferguson, 1987).

We will not dwell upon the Laguna Madre communities which are also well represented in other western Gulf estuaries, although we will point out some of the component species frequently encountered in Laguna Madre. Instead, we will focus upon the more extreme portions of the hypersaline system where excessive salinities limit biotic diversity. These conditions occur commonly in the upper restricted parts of the system, such as Baffin or Alazan bays in Texas or the northern basins of Laguna Madre de Tamaulipas in Mexico.

There are two readily definable categories of organisms which occupy hypersaline habitats: permanent residents and transitory residents; and a third group, the plankton, which is more difficult to place within this framework. Permanent residents are restricted to a specific geographic area largely because they lack

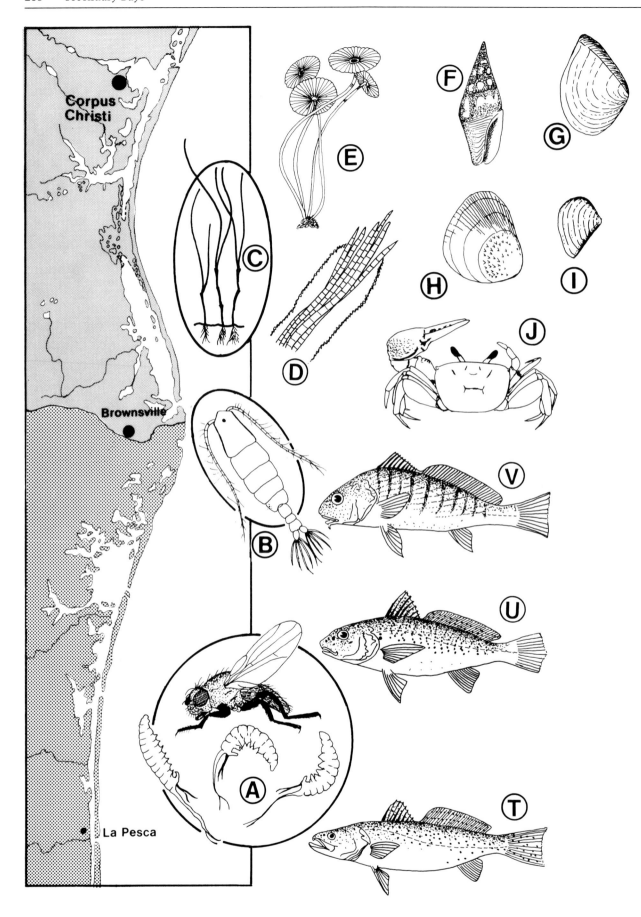

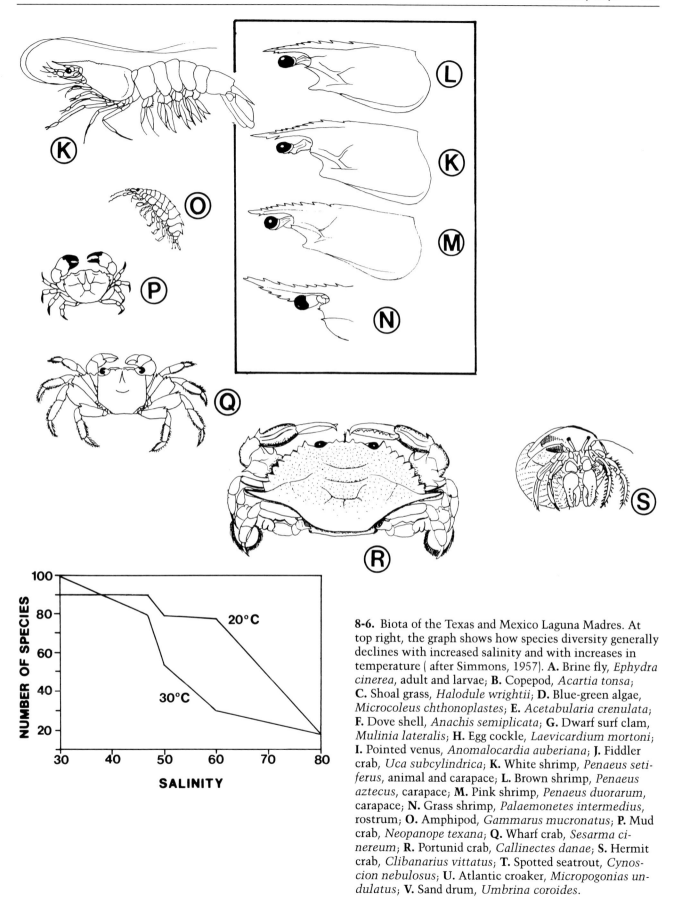

8-6. Biota of the Texas and Mexico Laguna Madres. At top right, the graph shows how species diversity generally declines with increased salinity and with increases in temperature (after Simmons, 1957). **A.** Brine fly, *Ephydra cinerea*, adult and larvae; **B.** Copepod, *Acartia tonsa*; **C.** Shoal grass, *Halodule wrightii* **D.** Blue-green algae, *Microcoleus chthonoplastes*; **E.** *Acetabularia crenulata*; **F.** Dove shell, *Anachis semiplicata*; **G.** Dwarf surf clam, *Mulinia lateralis*; **H.** Egg cockle, *Laevicardium mortoni*; **I.** Pointed venus, *Anomalocardia auberiana*; **J.** Fiddler crab, *Uca subcylindrica*; **K.** White shrimp, *Penaeus setiferus*, animal and carapace; **L.** Brown shrimp, *Penaeus aztecus*, carapace; **M.** Pink shrimp, *Penaeus duorarum*, carapace; **N.** Grass shrimp, *Palaemonetes intermedius*, rostrum; **O.** Amphipod, *Gammarus mucronatus*; **P.** Mud crab, *Neopanope texana*; **Q.** Wharf crab, *Sesarma cinereum*; **R.** Portunid crab, *Callinectes danae*; **S.** Hermit crab, *Clibanarius vittatus*; **T.** Spotted seatrout, *Cynoscion nebulosus*; **U.** Atlantic croaker, *Micropogonias undulatus*; **V.** Sand drum, *Umbrina coroides*.

sufficient mobility to leave. Transitory residents move into an area when conditions are favorable and leave it when they are not. High salinities in restricted basins are often strongly correlated with high temperatures. The decline in the number of species in the upper portion of Laguna Madre, Texas with an increase in temperature (Fig. 8-6, upper right), apparently reflects the departure of migratory species as conditions became less than optimum.

Plankton are neither permanent nor transitory, but opportunistic, thriving in good times and disappearing when they are bad. We will discuss each of these categories in turn, beginning with the group of permanent residents which are unable (or unwilling) to move elsewhere.

Permanent Residents of Hypersaline Systems

Most of the permanent members of the hypersaline community are benthic biota existing at the mercy of the environment and surviving only as long as physical conditions are within their limits of tolerance. They flourish when conditions are acceptable and perish when they are not. In this category are most macroscopic marine algae, rooted angiosperms, molluscs, worms, barnacles and other smaller crustaceans. The number of permanent resident species is small in hypersaline lagoons, but the numbers of individuals can be exceptionally high.

The flora which occupy the shores of hypersaline lagoons includes a variety of fleshy herbs and halophytic grasses common on other bayshores (Chapter 7). Numerous burrows of the fiddler crab, *Uca subcylindrica* (Fig. 8-6 J) often lie within the sparse cover of the shore vegetation (Rabalais & Cameron, 1985a,b). This fiddler crab digs its burrows relatively high upon the shore and extends them deeply into the sand to a depth that will reach the water table. In addition to the detrital food eaten by most fiddler crabs, *U. subcylindrica* has also been observed cutting and taking bits of *Batis* leaves and fruit into its burrow (Thurman, 1984).

Mats of decaying vegetation accumulating along the edge of the hypersaline lagoon attract dozens of beach hoppers, *Gammarus mucronatus* (Fig. 8-6 O), the same amphipod that is common in similar situations on the shores of normal estuaries. Each spring, the shallow hypersaline water just offshore crawls with millions of larvae and pupae of the brine fly, *Ephydra cinerea* (Fig. 8-6 A). This is one of the permanent residents of the hypersaline system which could go elsewhere, but seeks hypersaline brines for development. Tiny adult flies emerge from aquatic pupae, and often live in dense swarms near the shore. They and other insects are preyed upon by several species of tiger beetles (Cicindelidae, see Chapter 6).

Few of the sea grasses survive in excessively elevated salinities, but the shoal grass, *Halodule wrightii* (Fig. 8-6 C), is an exception. We have encountered it in the Baffin Bay system in salinities of 60 ppt, and presumably it can survive under even more concentrated brines. *Halodule* sometimes serves as an attachment

site for the epiphyte *Enteromorpha*, which coat each blade with thousands of green hair-like filaments. Another green alga, *Acetabularia crenulata* (Fig. 8-6 E) occurs on the subtidal floor of Laguna Madre in scattered but dense patches. Where tidal flats lie partially exposed, thick, moist, dark mats of blue-green cyanophytes, containing *Microcoleus chthonoplastes* (Fig. 8-6 D), *Lyngbya confervoides* and others, coat the sandy floor.

A large percentage of the subtidal permanent faunal residents of Laguna Madre are bivalve molluscs, including *Mulinia lateralis* (Fig. 8-6 G), *Anomalocardia auberiana* (Fig. 8-6 I), *Polymesoda floridana*, *Laevicardium mortoni* (Fig. 8-6 H), *Tellina tampaensis* and *Amygdalum papyrium*. *Mulinia lateralis* rarely survives in salinities in excess of 50 ppt, but it is such an efficient opportunist that it will quickly invade an area where salinities have dropped within its range of survival. When they rise again to excessive levels, *Mulinia* dies and its shells wash ashore by the millions. In contrast, we have already discussed the broad salinity tolerance of *Polymesoda floridana*, and *Anomalocardia auberiana* is capable of surviving salinities of 80 ppt. Fewer species of gastropods occur in hypersaline waters. However, *Anachis semiplicata* (Fig. 8-6 F) and *Bittium varium* are found in salinities up to about 50 ppt.

Cornelius (1984) found the most diverse invertebrate group in Alazan Bay, a subunit of the Baffin Bay complex, to be the polychaetes. The most abundant species were *Diopatra cuprea* (Fig. 7-9 Q), *Mediomastus californiensis* (Fig. 10-5 H), *Polydora* sp., and *Capitella* cf *capitata* (Fig. 8-3 P). In addition to these, 27 additional species were collected alive. Most species increased in abundance as rainfall and runoff dropped salinities in Alazan Bay from 55 ppt at the beginning of his study to the mid-20s a year later. The spionid *Polydora ligni* may be the most euryhaline of the Gulf of Mexico polychaetes, as it is reported surviving in salinities between 20 to 80 ppt (Hedgpeth, 1967).

The barnacles *Balanus eburneus* (Fig. 5-2 T) and *B. amphitrite* (Fig. 5-2 R) have similar salinity tolerances, although prolonged exposure to excess salinity is usually fatal. It is not unusual to find balanoid barnacles on wharf piles in moderate salinity waters of the lagoon, but they are usually rare or absent in the face of extreme conditions.

Several small crabs are sufficiently agile to move freely within a lagoon or estuary, but, because of size or habitat preferences, are probably incapable of removing themselves from hypersaline adversity. Included among these are the xanthid, *Neopanope texana* (Fig. 8-6 P), and the wharf crab, *Sesarma cinereum* (Fig. 8-6 Q). The latter is a common shore crab in the higher salinity portions of normal warm temperate and tropical Gulf and Caribbean estuaries, and will occur in moderately elevated but not extreme hypersaline waters. Hedgpeth (1967) cites the salinity range for the subtidal *Neopanope texana* as between about 30 to 50 ppt. When local salinities exceed these values, both species likely perish before they can find adequate refuge.

Transitory Residents of Hypersaline Systems

Transitory species are those with sufficient mobility to occupy a geographic area when conditions are within limits of tolerance and leave it when they are not. They have the ability to avoid the adverse conditions which bring mortality to permanent residents, although they sometimes perish for failing to leave in time or by becoming "trapped" within a restricted portion of the system. Most fishes are transitory species, as are the larger highly mobile crustaceans such as the penaeid shrimps and the portunid crabs.

Cornelius (1984) found the most common transitory invertebrate from salinities exceeding 40 ppt in Alazan Bay, Texas to be the blue crab, *Callinectes sapidus* (Fig. 7-7 K). A related species, the thicker-shelled and stockier *Callinectes danae* (Fig 8-6 R) occurs in the Lagunas from Port Mansfield, Texas to La Pesca, Mexico. Both portunids live in salinities up to 60 ppt, whereas *C. sapidus* can tolerate almost fresh waters but *C. danae* is rarely encountered in brackish water below 15 ppt (Williams, 1974).

The hermit crab, *Clibanarius vittatus* (Fig. 8-6 S) is a common nearshore crustacean around and within all tidal inlets, but rapidly disappears as salinities increase above about 45 ppt toward the interior of the lagoons. In pluvial seasons when salinities of central lagoon waters are depressed, *Clibanarius* migrates toward lagoon interiors, and slowly retreats back to the tidal inlets as evaporation concentrates the brine.

The shrimps are perhaps the best examples of transient invertebrates. All of the commercially important penaeid species occupy Laguna Madre habitats. The brown shrimp, *Penaeus aztecus* (Fig. 8-6 L) tolerates salinities in excess of 70 ppt, the pink shrimp, *P. duorarum* (Fig. 8-6 M), can occur in waters up to 60 ppt, whereas the white shrimp, *P. setiferus* (Fig. 8-6 K), rarely occurs in waters above 45 ppt. Each species will move as far into the lagoon as its salinity tolerance permits and will migrate to new localities as conditions change within the system. Not all shrimps should be characterized as transients, for habitat preferences of some species preclude their movement from adversity. The grass shrimp, *Palaemonetes intermedius* (Fig. 8-6 N), is a good example. It is so bound to grassbeds, especially *Halodule wrightii* in the Laguna, that it will not abandon the habitat as salinities continue to rise. This grass shrimp is able to osmoregulate in salinities exceeding 50 ppt (Dobkin & Manning, 1964) and will survive in waters up to 60 ppt (Hedgpeth, 1967).

The fishes more than the invertebrates are noted for their transient behavior. For a few species, transience is not necessary because of their extreme euryhaline tolerance. None can exceed that of the sheepshead minnow, *Cyprinodon variegatus* (Fig. 7-13 C). It is known to survive a salinity of 140 ppt (Hedgpeth, 1967). Other fishes have little difficulty in moderate hypersalinity. Cornelius (1984) found the most common fish in Alazan Bay to be the anchovy, *Anchoa mitchelli* (Fig. 7-13 D), and was most abundant in salinities from 41 to 50 ppt. Simmons (1957) lists 10 fishes in northern Laguna Madre which can survive up to 75 ppt, including the spotted seatrout, *Cynoscion nebulosus* (Fig. 8-6 T), and *Micropogonias undulatus* (Fig. 8-6 U). Both belong to the Sciaenidae, or croaker family, one of the most characteristic groups of inshore Gulf fishes. Another member of this family, the sand drum, *Umbrina coroides* (Fig. 8-6 V), is uncommon in Texas, but a prominent member of the transient biota in Laguna Madre de Tamaulipas.

Simmons lists an additional 10 species which survive in salinities up to 60 ppt, and 33 additional species which can occur in salinities from 25 to 45 ppt. Many of the species which disappear in warmer, higher salinity waters (Fig. 8-6 upper right) are these fishes moving to more optimal environments within or even outside the lagoon. Clearly, the transitory fishes occur in greater diversity and can exploit the hypersaline lagoons much more effectively than the relatively permanent benthos.

Plankton in Hypersaline Waters

The plankton constitute the third group of hypersaline biota and they are neither permanent residents nor transitory in the sense just defined. A remarkably large number of planktonic species can tolerate hypersaline conditions, including macroplanktonic species such as the jellyfishes *Stomolophus meleagris* (up to 60 ppt) and *Aurelia aurita* (up to 58 ppt) and the ctenophore *Beroe ovata* (up to 75 ppt). The microplankton are also well represented, as evidenced by large numbers of planktivorous anchovies within the hypersaline system (see also Breuer, 1957; Simmons, 1957; Ferguson Wood, 1963; Mackin, 1971; and Jensen, 1974). Copepods typically dominate the zooplankton, with *Acartia tonsa* (Fig. 8-6 B) comprising between 40 to 50 percent of the individuals in both Texas and Mexico Laguna. Like microplankton elsewhere, those in hypersaline lagoons are opportunists. They await optimum conditions in small numbers, and exploit them rapidly when they arrive.

9. Mangrove Shores

INTRODUCTION

Sedges, reeds and grasses comprise the primary vegetation along temperate bayshores. The grasses *Spartina alterniflora* and *S. patens* dominate salt marshes from New England to Texas (Chapter 7). Trees are virtually absent from tidally inundated temperate lowlands, but the reasons they are absent are not immediately obvious. Aquatic submergence is not a factor. Bald cypress, for example, is a tree of temperate climates which can live permanently submerged in standing freshwater. It is poorly adapted for prolonged survival in saline, tidally influenced estuaries. Yet, trees are not uniformly excluded from estuarine shores. Several kinds of tropical trees not only thrive in this habitat, but characterize it. Neither submergence nor salinity is sufficient to account for the absence of trees on temperate bayshores.

The combined freezing winter temperatures and tidal flux are sometimes cited as factors inhibiting tree colonization. Tides cause winter ice to rise and fall along bayshore margins, abrading objects fixed along the shore. Trees are fixed objects bearing essential conducting tissues just below the bark. On thin-barked seedling trees moderate abrasion is often sufficient to destroy the conducting tissues, and thereby the tree. Thus, tidally mediated ice scour has been implicated as capable of inflicting fatal damage to trees. In contrast, the marsh grasses have adaptations to avoid destruction by winter ice scour. Frosty autumn mornings kill exposed parts of *Spartina* and other marsh grasses, and these usually die back to form an insulating bed of straw. The stems of these plants lie underground, protected from the reach of scouring ice beneath layers of mud and straw. New growth arises from the underground stems with the spring thaw. Grasses like *Spartina* are ideally suited for life on temperate bayshores.

Ice does not form on tropical shores. From central Texas southward, shores experience increasing numbers of ice-free days, until freezing conditions disappear entirely. The *Spartina* marsh is progressively replaced (but never eliminated) across the temperate to tropical transition by a group of trees collectively known as mangroves. Mangroves are trees capable of tolerating periodic immersion or exposure to seawater. They are a diverse assemblage representing several different plant families having a range of adapta-

tions to the semi-aquatic tropical bayshore habitat. Mangroves are susceptible to freezing temperatures, and are generally absent on shores which experience more than an occasional winter frost. They probably evolved independently from rain-forest ancestors and represent the seaward fringe of a successional system that has spread from the tropical lowland forest onto protected estuaries of tropical rivers. Indeed, tropical river banks are flanked by tall trees from source to mouth. The definition of where a river ends and the sea begins is obscure, but, in the tropics, it is frequently defined by the presence of halophytic mangroves.

Mangrove communities reach their greatest development on tropical shores protected from exposure to high waves or strong currents. They usually occupy anoxic, muddy or silty substrata rich in organic debris to which the community makes a major contribution. These conditions are most commonly encountered along bays, but they also occur along a leeward coast protected by the mainland from the prevailing winds, such as along the western side of the Yucatan peninsula.

There are several species of mangroves, some with greater tolerance to salt water than others. When all mangrove species occur on a shore, they tend to segregate into distinctive bands or zones, reflecting their specific ecological tolerances. Collectively, they constitute a biological community which harbors many additional kinds of life, but they also are indicative of a set of specific physical conditions without which this community would be unable to exist.

The focus of mangrove evolution is in the tropical Indo-Pacific, where upwards of 44 species are recorded, representing 14 genera and 11 families (Walsh, 1974; Hutchings & Saenger, 1987). Mangrove diversity is low in the tropical western Atlantic, with only 9 species representing 4 genera and 3 families (Table 9-1). Only four species are common in the Gulf of Mexico. In all parts of the world, mangrove species diversity diminishes rapidly north or south of the tropics. In Japan and New Zealand the richness of Indo-Pacific mangroves eventually is depleted to a single species, *Avicennia marina*, which forms monospecific shrublike stands. A similar situation occurs in the Gulf of Mexico with *Avicennia germinans* essentially being the only species north of the Rio Grande. Mangroves also have a tenuous existence on lagoon shores south of the Rio Grande to about the vicinity of La Pesca at the southern termination of Laguna Madre de Tamaulipas. Thereafter, mangroves increase in importance to become the dominant shore habitat fringing most of the protected bays and lagoons. Tangles of leafy branches thrust seaward, occasionally exposing a dark, impenetrable thicket understory, as uninviting to Spanish explorers of the sixteenth century as they are to developers, tourists or casual adventurers of the modern age.

The mangrove shores of Mexico have remained largely as they were before Europeans colonized the New World and are among the least studied habitats of the western Gulf of Mexico. We will illustrate in this chapter the progressive increase in mangrove species diversity and habitat complexity along the temperate to tropical transition from Texas to Mexico.

THE PLANTS

The term mangrove refers both to the trees and to a habitat. To avoid confusion we will employ the word mangal to describe a habitat that is extraordinarily rich in life and exaggerated in dimensions, the latter provided by halophytic trees conferring a vertical component to an otherwise flat and uniform alluvial shore.

Mangroves comprise two broad categories, primary and secondary, according to the varying measure of adaptations that each shows to an amphibious existence. Primary mangroves are those which have a more seaward distribution. They are also often referred to as pioneers. Secondary mangroves are more landward in distribution and more terrestrial in their adaptations.

The term pioneer adequately describes the process by which mangrove plants extend the forest's influence seawards. Pioneer plants have a range of adaptations that permit the seaward colonization of mud, and, in so doing, deepen the tropical forest. The adaptations that permit the mangrove plants to be stabilized in mud (e.g., prop roots) also enhance accretion of marine and stream sediments, leaf litter and other organic debris, so that soil levels within the mangrove are progressively raised. The sedimentary accretion process is dramatically enhanced by fallen mangrove leaves and the complex food web based upon them. Leaf litter is broken down in a series of steps involving leaf shredders (e.g., isopods, amphipods, and decapod crustaceans) and decomposers (e.g., fungi and bacteria) on the floor of the mangal. The resulting detritus adds bulk and substance to the soil. Sediments continue to accumulate until eventually the sea can no longer wash over the raised mud. At this time, more terrestrial conditions prevail. Conditions which previously favored pioneer mangrove species are now no longer optimal. The transformed environment now favors the secondary mangroves, which replace the pioneering species shorewards.

The premier pioneer mangrove throughout the tropical Gulf and Caribbean is the red mangrove, *Rhizophora mangle* (Rhizophoraceae). It occupies the seaward mangal fringe, and, in many localities, does so in large monoculture stands. Elsewhere, it shares the intertidal shore with at least one additional species, the black mangrove, *Avicennia germinans* (Avicenniaceae). The secondary Gulf and Caribbean mangroves belong to the Combretaceae and include the white mangrove, *Laguncularia racemosa*, and the buttonwood, *Conocarpus erectus*. Several additional species of woody halophytes occur in association with the major mangrove species and help characterize the total environment, but we will deal in less detail with these.

Each principal mangrove species and the associated flora (grasses, sedges, herbs, and shrubs) have specific adaptations to the periodicity of tidal immersion and emersion, salt levels and sediment composition so that no two mangal stands are exactly the same. Nevertheless, fundamental principles of zonation dominate in this habitat as elsewhere (with the added complication of succession) and each principal species generally occupies a definable region. Mangrove communities attain their greatest development in the Gulf of Mexico along bayshores fringing the Bay of Campeche and along much of the western coast of Yucatan (Figure 9-1). The basic patterns of mangrove zonation are well expressed here. Other than the mangroves themselves, the mangal fauna of this region remains poorly studied. It will likely prove to be similar to the mangal fauna we will describe shortly, but until it becomes better known, it is fitting that we at least employ the region to characterize typical patterns of mangrove zonation.

From Tampico to Celestun, the red mangrove, *Rhizophora mangle* (Fig. 9-1 D), dominates the seaward fringe of well developed mangrove shores, forming a characteristic seaward zone (Fig. 9-1) of adult trees (area 5) and newly sprouting droppers (area 6). Distinctive tangles of dense prop roots support a bright green leafy canopy above tannic-black shallow waters near the shore.

Rhizophora mangle is one of the most easily identified tropical trees. It is statuesque, attaining a height of 4 to 5 m in the tropics and is characterized by prop roots which develop adventitiously from the main stem, arch downwards and root in the mud, thereby further stabilizing the tree. These aerial roots arise from the trunk and main branches of trees more than three years old. In addition to their obvious supportive function they bear superficial cells (lenticels) and internal tissues specialized for gaseous exchange. The prop roots can stand in meter-deep waters, and provide shelter for a variety of swimming and attached life. They can also stand out of water upon the shore, but here they receive competition from other mangrove species. None of the other Atlantic mangroves have a tolerance of water immersion equal to that of *Rhizophora*.

The red mangrove leaf is thick and fleshy, with a waxy, shiny, bright green upper face and a light yellow lower surface. Leaf stomata are few and sunken, both

Table 9-1. Western Atlantic Mangroves and their Distributions

Family Rhizophoraceae
    Rhizophora mangle. Central Caribbean Basin, Southern Gulf of Mexico and Panama to Trinidad
    Rhizophora racemosa. Panama to Brazil
    Rhizophora harrisonii. Central Caribbean Basin

Family Avicenniaeceae
    Avicennia germinans. Gulf of Mexico, Caribbean Basin, South America to Argentina
    Avicennia schauerana. Eastern Caribbean

Family Meliaceae
    Xylocarpus guianensis. Northern coast of South America within the Caribbean Basin

Family Combretaceae
    Laguncularia racemosa. Southern Gulf of Mexico, Caribbean Basin, South America to Brazil
    Conocarpus erectus. Southern Gulf of Mexico, Caribbean Basin

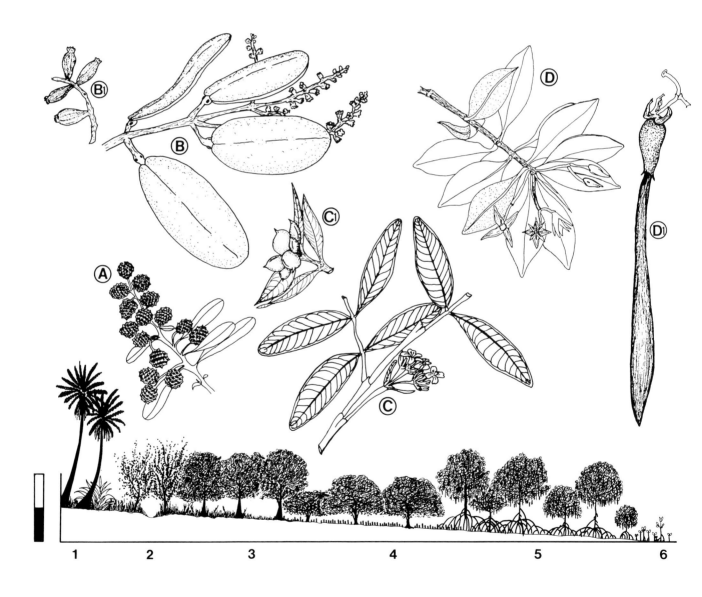

adaptations arising to reduce evaporative water loss. The leaves also bear salt glands to actively excrete salt that enters the plant via the roots. *Rhizophora* lives in a marine desert where the conservation of water and the maintenance of an osmotically acceptable cell sap pressure is important. Its physiological adaptations more resemble those of terrestrial xerophytes than those of freshwater macrophytes.

When the red mangrove grows in monoculture along the narrow band of intertidal shoreline, it forms the base of one of the most productive communities on earth. A Puerto Rican red mangrove forest was shown to have a gross productivity of more than 204 pounds of organic material per acre per day (Golley *et al.*, 1962). If most of this organic material could be stored, the observable net productivity would be astronomical. Still, there is relatively high net yield. Almost 2 tons of new wood per acre are added to the forest each year (Golley *et al.*, 1962) and almost 3 tons of leaves, twigs and seedlings per acre fall annually from the forest to the water or mud below (Heald, 1971). This rain of organic debris supports complex communities which live attached to mangrove roots or within the mud.

The fecundity of the red mangrove forest is also high. Small (2 cm) yellow flowers are produced throughout the year. They develop into brown viviparous seeds which germinate while still attached to the parental tree. A hypocotyl emerges from each seed and progressively elongates, resulting in the characteristic torpedo-shaped seedlings or "droppers" (Figs. 9-1 D1; 9-3 C1) which hang down like daggers from the tree, usually in great numbers. After several weeks or months, droppers attain a length of 30 cm or more and finally fall from the tree. If they fall while the tide is low, seedlings can impale into the mud just below the branch on which they were formed. The maze of *Rhizophora* along the tropical bayshore attests that this happens often. In this way the mangrove stand slowly creeps seaward, binding sediments under new prop roots, and eventually creating new land along the shore. If the droppers fall during high tide, they are carried by the water to new localities, either further

into the mangrove by the advancing tide or out to sea by the ebb. Droppers can survive afloat several weeks. Many will perish at sea, but a few are washed ashore, and a few of these take root. When this occurs on previously uncolonized shores, the dropper has contributed to the process of species dispersal. It is in this manner that small red mangrove trees occasionally appear upon southern Texas shores. They can survive only until the next hard freeze. In the tropics, however, the chance survivor often becomes the founding colonizer of a new mangal.

The black mangrove, *Avicennia germinans* (Fig. 9-1 C), derives its common name from the appearance of wet bark on the trunk of the tree. It lacks the aerial prop roots of the red mangrove, and, without these supports, it is poorly adapted for extending into permanently subtidal nearshore waters. In a well developed mangal, the black mangrove usually occurs just shoreward of *Rhizophora*, where it tolerates periodic tidal immersion but also lies exposed part of the time (Figure 9-1, area 4). *Avicennia germinans* is more tolerant of cold weather than the red mangrove, a feature of importance in the temperate to tropical transition (see below), but of little advantage within the fully developed tropical mangal.

Long underground cable roots radiate out from the base of the trunk and serve to anchor the plant in the mud. *Avicennia* is characterized by numerous erect aerial spikes called pneumatophores which arise from the cable roots and project as much as 35 cm above the mud. The pneumatophores form a link between the cable roots buried within anoxic bay sediments and the aerobic atmosphere, and it is through lenticels upon them that most gaseous exchange to the roots occurs (Scholander *et al.*, 1955). They also bear numerous salt-secreting glands which serve to remove excess salts from the root sap. In fact, *Avicennia* tissues passively absorb sea salts in substantial amounts, and the plant relies upon salt glands on pneumatophores and leaves to remove excess ions. As a result, *Avicennia* has one of the highest salt tolerances of all mangroves, and even concentrates certain ions (e.g., potassium) within its tissues (Walsh, 1974).

Black mangrove leaves are opposite, elongate (45 mm) and narrow (15 mm), and usually green above and gray below. The inflorescence consists of clusters of small white flowers that are insect pollinated. A single seed is produced within a 3 to 5 cm flattened green capsule (Fig. 9-1 C1), which begins to split open and germinate while still attached to the parent. Unopened capsules float in the sea, so waterborne dispersion is common.

The white mangrove, *Laguncularia racemosa* (Fig. 9-1 B), is a large tree (5 to 6 m) usually found behind or at the rear of the zone of black mangroves (Fig. 9-1, area 3). It will tolerate occasional tidal immersion, but not to the degree tolerated by *Avicennia*. The white mangrove prefers slightly dried, firmer soil rarely covered by standing water. Accordingly, it is properly considered a secondary mangrove.

9-1. Mangrove zonation. The basic pattern of mangrove zonation is diagrammed at the bottom of the illustration from shore (left) to sea (right). 1. Terrestrial vegetation; 2. Buttonwood (*Conocarpus erectus*) zone; 3. White mangrove (*Laguncularia racemosa*) zone; 4. Black mangrove (*Avicennia germinans*) zone; 5. Red mangrove (*Rhizophora mangle*) zone; 6. Pioneer zone of initial colonization by *Rhizophora mangle*. Vertical scale indicates meters. **A.** Buttonwood, *Conocarpus erectus*; **B.** White mangrove, *Laguncularia racemosa*; **B1.** White mangrove seeds; **C.** Black mangrove, *Avicennia germinans*; **C1.** Black mangrove seeds; **D.** Red mangrove, *Rhizophora mangle*; **D1.** Red mangrove dropper.

Laguncularia bears light yellow green leaves which are ovally rounded, the tip blunt and usually notched. They are also thick and semi-succulent, more so than any of the other Atlantic mangroves. A pair of large salt glands, one on each side of the petiole near its junction with the leaf blade, serve to distinctly characterize this species.

The accessory root system of *Laguncularia* is much like that of *Avicennia* in that pneumatophores arise from the subsurface root system but do not usually appear above ground. Rather, small deciduous structures, pneumathodes, arise from the blunt tip of the pneumatophores and extend upwards. Like pneumatophores, pneumathodes bear lenticels.

Small white flowers are borne on terminal clusters. Whereas those of *Avicennia* and *Rhizophora* have four petals, those of *Laguncularia* have five. The fruit is an elongate leathery capsule containing a single stonelike seed (Fig. 9-1 B1). Seeds do not develop while the fruit is attached to the tree. Ripened, wrinkled prunelike capsules fall from the tree, and are buoyant in water, facilitating waterborne dispersal.

The buttonwood, *Conocarpus erectus* (Fig. 9-1 A), is another secondary mangrove indicative of the mangal fringe beyond the direct influence of most tidal inundation. It marks the transition of the mangal and the terrestrial realms, at home on land beside the sea. On some exposed rocky shores, *Conocarpus* grows as a small shrub (Chapter 4), but at the rear of the mangal it usually occurs as a tree up to 5 m tall (Fig. 9-1, area 2). The foliage is smooth, each leaf some 2 to 10 cm long, oval or elliptical, though some are acute at the tip. There are two varieties of *Conocarpus erectus*, each displaying a distinctive leaf form. One has graygreen leaves and the other bears foliage colored a rusty olive drab. Both varieties are present in the tropical Gulf, often standing side by side. Buttonwoods bear green flowers 10 mm or less in width. The fruits are purple-green, drying to brown conelike spherical buttons and providing this tree its common name. Beyond the buttonwoods, one leaves the mangal and enters the exclusively terrestrial realm (Fig. 9-1, area 1).

The pattern just described is not everywhere apparent along the western coast of Yucatan. It is most obvious within coastal embayments such as Laguna de Terminos, but it sometimes occurs along Gulf shores, especially from Campeche to Celestun. Sometimes, one or more of the mangroves will be absent at a specific locality, and local topography will alter the typical pattern of zonation. Where shores rise rapidly from the sea or where salinities are exceptionally high, the red mangrove may be absent and the black mangrove appears to be the seaward pioneer. Where tidal lowlands are extensive, *Rhizophora* may seem to persist in broad bands of monoculture. Isolated mangrove trees are also common along the rocky Gulf shores from Campeche to Isla Aguada, and here buttonwoods may stand on limestone ledges less than 2 m from the sea. There are many variations upon these themes. In the next few pages, we will consider still other variations, but these are imposed by climate or salinity, and constitute exceptions to the normal patterns of mangrove distribution.

THE TEXAS MANGAL

Only one mangrove species, *Avicennia germinans*, is sufficiently tolerant of Texas winters to be able to survive and form a substantial mangal. *Rhizophora* droppers may come ashore, especially along southern Laguna Madre. The few that become established grow for no more than a few years, for they perish from exposure to even mild winter freezes. *Avicennia germinans* is slightly more tolerant. The populations which occur on Texas shores apparently belong to a genetic race of the species which is capable of surviving colder temperatures than those normally experienced by more tropical populations (McMillan, 1975).

The black mangrove is known to occur as far north as Galveston Island, but here the specimens are small, sparse, and readily succumb to hard winter freezes (McMillan, 1971; Sherrod & McMillan, 1981). Abundant stands occur in the vicinity of several tidal inlets, including Cavallo Pass, Aransas Pass (especially on Harbor Island), and in the vicinity of Brazos Santiago Pass and the Port Isabel area. Additional scattered mangrove stands occur from Cavallo Pass to the Rio Grande (Hartman & Smith, 1973; Sherrod & McMillan, 1981). *Avicennia germinans* occurs on Texas shores in both monospecific stands and, in association with *Spartina*, *Batis*, *Monanthochloe*, *Distichlis* and other bayshore vegetation, more complex communities. The black mangrove barely attains the dimensions of a tree in Texas. Near Port Aransas, it occurs as a shrub standing little more than a meter above the ground, but at South Padre Island it attains twice that size or more.

Our example of a Texas mangrove is taken from the Laguna Madre side of South Padre Island, near the highway causeway and fishing pier. Shore stabilization on the Padre Island end of these two structures has created a flat shore of stiff mud, overlying the South Padre sands. Seawards the mud becomes progressively more sloppy, so that a transect down the shore from land to sea exposes at low tide a progressive continuum from berm sand, stiff mid-littoral mud and soft subtidal silt (Figure 9-2). The backshore elements of this community are typical of bayshores described earlier (Chapter 7). Proximity of the community to the Brazos-Santiago Pass, however, creates an environment in which salinities fluctuate more typically in concordance with those of the Gulf. Algal mats consisting of blue-green cyanophytes and diatoms (Fig. 9-2 S) blanket the flat, unshaded mid-shore (Sorensen and Conover, 1962). The mats shrivel into unsightly, curling crusts during the dry days of summer, but swell and become an emerald-green shroud under tidal or rainwater immersion.

Vegetation and Shore Crustaceans

Grasses, such as *Digitaria insularis* (Fig. 9-2 C1), demarcate the supratidal bayshore and are replaced seaward by the coastal grass *Distichlis spicata* (Fig. 9-2 X) in combination with *Suaeda linearis* (Fig. 9-2 A1) and *Limonium nashii* (Fig. 9-2 Y). Lower down are isolated clumps of the sea ox-eye daisy, *Borrichia frutescens* (Fig. 9-2 B1), and the sprawling halophyte *Philoxerus vermicularis* (Fig. 9-2 Z).

The seaward margin of the back-of-beach community is defined by the fleshy-green upright herb *Salicornia virginica* (Fig. 9-2 U), the trailing *Sesuvium portulacastrum* (Fig. 9-2 W), and the bayshore grass *Monanthochloe littoralis* (Fig. 9-2 V). Here, at the upper extent of tidal influence, sediment composition changes as mud replaces sand. For 20 m or more, the shore appears to be bare of life, except for a coat of tolerant algae. Actually, the algal mat is rich in nutrients and supports a relatively rich crop of a few hardy algal species. Underneath clumps of algae and decaying strand vegetation are many side-leaping amphipods, such as *Gammarus mucronatus* (Fig. 9-2 T), which not only take refuge within but also feed upon the decaying vegetation. High-zoned, too, are the burrows of *Uca panacea* (Fig. 9-2 G1), and from which at low tide and in the noonday sun the crabs emerge to feed on the film of algae and detritus characterizing the algal flats.

Further seaward, the mid-tidal desert is fringed by a bank of the reddish and low-profiled *Salicornia bigelovii* (Fig. 9-2 R). Beyond these, the black mangrove, *Avicennia germinans* stands out above all else, rising to a height of 2 to 3 m, and obscuring the horizon to an observer beside the mangal. A black lichen called "sooty mold" (Fig. 9-2 M), attaches to the upper surfaces of the leaves of *Avicennia* where it utilizes the salt excreted from the salt glands. Inside the *Avicennia* clump, the air is hot and humid, the ground a miniature forest of pneumatophores which intermingle with the *Salicornia* and trap strands of algae and other debris washed in by the tide. Spring tides regularly inundate this area, depositing fine sediments which, together with progressively decomposing leaf litter, turn the water into a rich soup. In this region, the burrows of *Uca rapax* (Fig. 9-2 F1), warren the mud. Here and there, a few *Avicennia* seedlings struggle for light below their parental canopy. If winters have been mild for several seasons, a few small living red mangroves with their characteristic prop roots appear among the dominant *Avicennia*. More often, bare branches and decaying wood offer mute testimony that a recent winter freeze has destroyed the *Rhizophora*.

The seaward edge of this mangal is occupied by *Spartina patens* (Fig. 9-2 L), which here grows to a height of about 70 cm. The tide rarely rises more than about 20 cm above the bayfloor along the grass zone, and the bases of the clumps of *Spartina* are frequently exposed at low tide. If winters were milder, the zone of *Spartina* would surely be replaced by the mangrove pioneer *Rhizophora mangle*. Clearly, *Avicennia* does not encroach upon this position in the absence of *Rhizophora*, but maintains its normal position upon the upper portions of the intertidal realm.

The agile crab *Sesarma reticulatum* (Fig. 7-6), is common among the *Spartina* and within the mangal. It climbs among trees, pneumatophores and grasses, feeds upon mangrove leaves and detritus, and, when threatened, escapes down meandering burrows.

Molluscs

Mangals are often richly endowed with molluscs, especially gastropods which exploit the dank humus of the mangrove floor, graze upon the lichens that encrust the upper levels of the trees or browse among the strands of algae that festoon the lower stems, branches and pneumatophores. The Texas mangal, with but a single mangrove species, is similarly limited with respect to the molluscan fauna, and some species which are present here are clearly derived from other bay habitats.

9-2. A Texas mangal from the Laguna Madre shore, South Padre Island. The location of the site is indicated in the map insets. Numbers on the map refer to mangal zones as follows: **1.** grass-dominated supratidal bayshore; **2.** tidal flat and algal mats; **3.** *Avicennia* zone; **4.** *Spartina* fringe; and **5.** Laguna Madre. The vertical scale adjacent to the profile near the bottom of this figure indicates meters. **A.** Great blue heron, *Ardea herodias*; **B.** Green-backed heron, *Butorides striatus*; **C.** Little blue heron, *Egretta caerulea*; **D.** Louisiana heron, *Egretta tricolor*; **E.** Great white heron, a race of *Ardea herodias* (formerly *A. occidentalis*), a bird of the eastern Gulf and rare in Texas; **F.** Snowy egret, *Egretta thula*; **G.** Common egret, *Casmerodius albus*; **H.** Cattle egret, *Bubulcus ibis*; **I.** American bittern, *Botaurus lentiginosus*; **J.** Grass shrimp, *Palaemonetes vulgaris*; **K.** Pink shrimp, *Penaeus duorarum*; **L.** Marshhay cordgrass, *Spartina patens*; **M.** Black mangrove, *Avicennia germinans*, leaves with some sooty mold; **M1.** Relationship of tree crown to pneumatophores in the black mangrove; **M2.** Young black mangrove showing cable root (cr), geotrophic root (gr) and pneumatophore (pn); **N.** Marsh periwinkle, *Littoraria irrorata*; **O.** *Truncatella caribaeensis*; **P.** Eastern melampus, *Melampus bidentatus*; **Q.** Horn shell, *Cerithidea pliculosa*; **R.** Glasswort, *Salicornia bigelovii*; **S.** Algal mat; **T.** Amphipod, *Gammarus mucronatus*; **U.** Glasswort; *Salicornia virginica*; **V.** Key grass, *Monanthochloe littoralis*; **W.** Sea purslane, *Sesuvium portulacastrum*; **X.** Saltgrass, *Distichlis spicata*; **Y.** Sea lavender, *Limonium nashii*; **Z.** Silverhead, *Philoxerus vermicularis*; **A1.** Sea-blite, *Suaeda linearis*; **B1.** Sea ox-eye daisy, *Borrichia frutescens*; **C1.** Sourgrass, *Digitaria insularis*; **D1.** Ribbed mussel, *Geukensia demissa granosissima*; **E1.** Wharf crab, *Sesarma cinereum*; **F1.** Fiddler crab, *Uca rapax*; **G1.** Fiddler crab, *Uca panacea*.

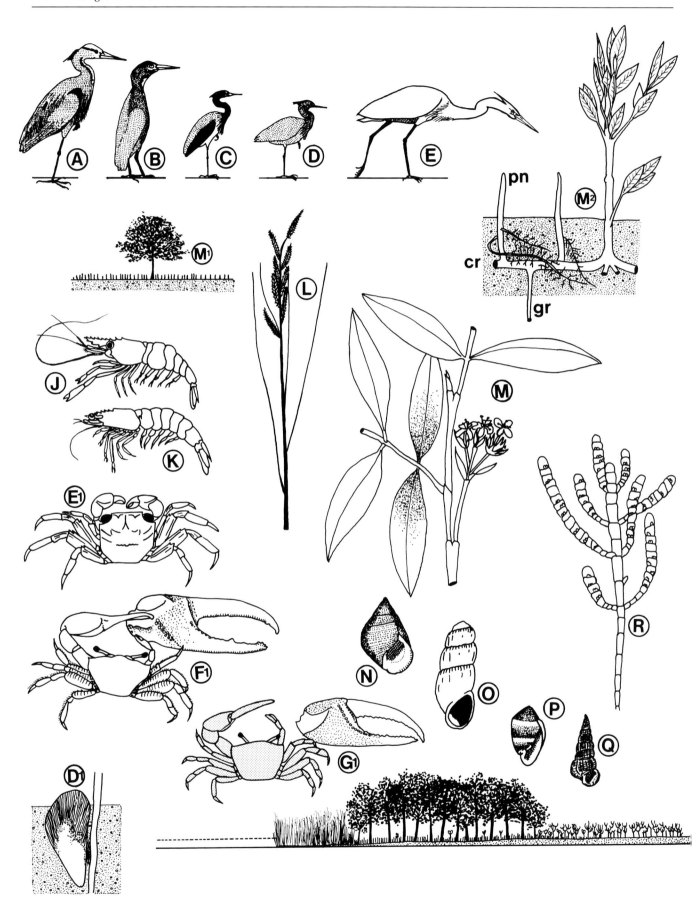

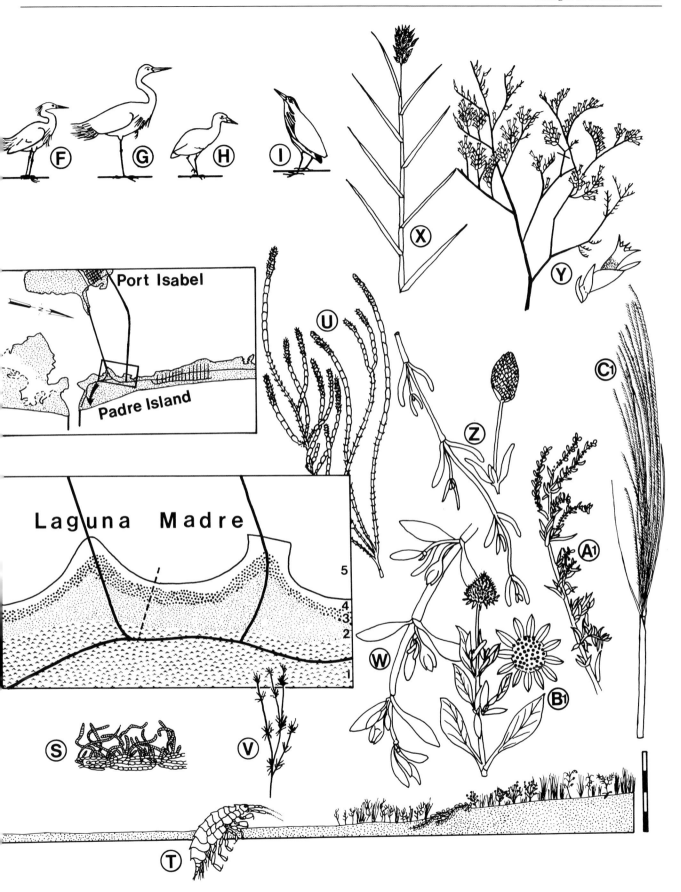

Port Isabel

Padre Island

Laguna Madre

The only littorine to occur in Texas mangroves, *Littoraria irrorata* (Fig. 9-2 N), is a case in point. This plump and unornamented snail is most at home in *Spartina* marshes (Chapter 7), but will inhabit the undersurface of the leaves, branches and stems of *Avicennia*. It attaches to a leaf by a mucous film, where it remains inactive at low tide. It emerges at high tide and crawls downwards to feed among moistened seaweed. Also in the trees is the elongate, spiralled *Truncatella caribaeensis* (Fig. 9-2 O), which is also a grazer but with an unusual method of locomotion. It extends a proboscis forwards and securely attaches it to the substratum. Once attached, the shell and foot are hunched forwards, rather like the looping gait of certain caterpillars and leeches.

Two snails are ground dwellers. The first is the air-breathing pulmonate, *Melampus bidentatus* (Fig. 9-2 P), with two distinctive circular whitish bands on an otherwise chocolate brown shell. It is a high intertidal algal grazer (Hausman, 1936; Apley, 1970), experiencing variable and usually short tidal submersions. Because of its position on shore, *Melampus* is often subjected to large fluctuations in salinity and temperature. It seeks refuge under rotting wood or other shore debris (Hausman, 1932), but also displays considerable physiological tolerances for extreme conditions (McMahon & Russell-Hunter, 1981). The elongate mud-snail, *Cerithidea pliculosa* (Fig. 9-2 Q) lives slightly lower on the floor of the mangal, where it experiences more frequent tidal inundation. *Cerithidea* is an indiscriminate feeder on mud and algal filaments. The mangrove bivalves of the Indo-Pacific and Western Atlantic have been reviewed by Morton (1983a). Relatively few species can tolerate life in this high-zoned habitat, and divide into two groups: those byssally attached or cemented to stems and aerial roots (e.g., *Crassostrea rhizophorae*, *Lopha frons* and species of *Isognomon*) and infaunal species (e.g., *Polymesoda caroliniana*). The bivalve fauna of Texas mangroves is, however, depauperate probably because *Rhizophora* is here absent and thus unable to provide attachment sites and the low canopy cover permits summer water temperatures to rise to extremes intolerable to most species.

The ribbed mussel, *Geukensia demissa* (Fig. 9-2 D1), is sometimes found in Texas mangals, but is more commonly associated with *Spartina* marshes to the north (Chapter 7). It is another example of a mollusc which may occur in the mangal but is not typically associated with it. It attaches by byssal threads to the underground roots of the grass, but will use *Avicennia* pneumatophores for this purpose in the absence of *Spartina*. It is positioned so only the posterior inflated edge of the shell projects above ground. Like the majority of bivalves, it is a filter feeder, but in its high-zoned position is able to feed only during tidal floods.

Shrimps and Prawns

In suitable localities along the fringe of the Texas mangals, as throughout all Gulf estuaries, various types of shrimps and prawns find suitable refuge. We illustrate only two, mainly to remind you that these and several other previously mentioned species (Chapter 7) may be here, too. Penaeid shrimps such as the pink shrimp, *Penaeus duorarum* (Fig. 9-2 K) and grass shrimps such as *Palaemonetes vulgaris* (Fig. 9-2 J) enter the Texas mangal on a flood tide, but are more commonly restricted to the subtidal bottoms that fringe it.

Herons, Egrets and Bitterns

The Ardeidae include the herons, egrets and bitterns, a family of wading birds with long legs, long necks and pointed dagger-like bills. Often secretive, they rely on stealth to capture their prey which will typically be small fish and other aquatic life such as frogs in freshwater. In flight the head is tucked back onto the shoulders in an S configuration, with the long legs trailing behind. At rest, the head may be erect, again in an S configuration or directed downwards and forwards when hunting. On the ground, movements are slow and deliberate. Most members of the Ardeidae (bitterns excepted), like the several other families of shore birds we have discussed in previous chapters, are not restricted to a particular habitat such as the Texas mangal, but are found along estuarine or wetland shores throughout the region. As before, we present examples of the entire family here only for convenience.

Several herons are common throughout the western Gulf region. The largest of these, the great blue heron, *Ardea herodias* (Fig. 9-2 A) is equally at home along the shores of inland waters as along coastal marshes, bays or mangrove margins. Its tall stature (1.2 m), blue-gray plumage, dark underparts, and whiter head and neck are distinctive. The "great white heron" (Fig. 9-2 E) was once regarded as a separate species, *A. occidentalis*, but ornithologists now consider it to be a morphotype of *A. herodias*. The white phase is restricted mainly to southern Florida, but a few have been seen on Texas and Mexico bayshores. The majority of white heron-like birds of the western Gulf are egrets.

The tricolored heron, *Egretta tricolor* (Fig. 9-2 D), is a smaller, snaky bird with a white belly, dark head, and a slender neck. It distinctly prefers bayshores, and is only rarely encountered along inland freshwater marshes. The little blue heron, *Egretta caerulea* (Fig. 9-2 C) is migratory, occupying coastal shores in greatest numbers during the winter. Many remain here year-round, but a large number of birds move northward to freshwater habitats and summer breeding grounds. The mature little blue heron has a slate-blue body and rust-brown neck, but juveniles are white and yearlings are mottled.

The green-backed heron, *Butorides striatus* (Fig. 9-2 B) is the smallest of the dark herons in Texas, and one of the least common along the coast. The short yellow or orange legs, deeply chestnut neck and streaked throat help to identify this bird, although the entire neck of immature specimens is streaked. This species prefers freshwater shores, and can readily be encountered during the summer along ponds near the coast. Like all herons, the nest is a loosely woven platform of twigs and sticks atop a tree or bush. It winters in Mexico and southward.

Egrets are typically white, often with head crests. Four species may be encountered, all of which are semi-permanent residents of coastal marshes, meadows and mangroves, and occasional visitors to more exposed bayshores. The great (common) egret, *Casmerodius albus* (Fig. 9-2 G), and the snowy egret, *Egretta thula* (Fig. 9-2 F) are the most common species. Rookeries of both species occur along the entire Gulf coast, in inland lowland forests along the northeastern Texas coast, or in mangrove forests along much of Mexico. The common egret is a large, slender, snowy white bird with black legs and feet and a yellow bill. The snowy egret is much smaller and has a blackish bill.

The cattle egret, *Bubulcus ibis* (Fig. 9-2 H), is not native to North America, but was introduced to the New World via South America. It first appeared in Texas in 1955. It is now a breeding resident throughout the western Gulf region, often in the company of snowy egrets. It is usually see in meadows or pastures, and is not restricted to the coastal region. It feeds upon insects flushed from hiding by cattle or other livestock. Unlike the great or snowy egrets which are entirely white, cattle egrets display a buff-colored plumage on the head, back and breast during the summer breeding season.

As its name implies the mature reddish egret, *Egretta rufescens* (not illustrated), is not white, but displays a tan body and rusty head and neck. This is the least common egret in Texas, but because it prefers salt water flats and marshes, it is more likely to be encountered along the more exposed bayshores than the other species. The red egret sometimes occurs in a white color phase which resembles the great and snowy egrets. The white phase of *E. rufescens* can be distinguished from the great egret by its pink, black-tipped beak (the great egret beak is yellow) and bluish legs (great egret legs are black). The snowy egret beak is black, as are its legs, and its feet are yellow.

Bitterns are usually absent on higher salinity bayshores or among mangroves. They may be found in the low-salinity freshwater marshes near the coast. We include them here because of their close relationship to the herons and egrets. The American bittern, *Botaurus lentiginosus* (Fig. 9-2 I), is a secretive bird, most commonly encountered in *Spartina* marshes where the vertically striped throat with the head held erect provides almost perfect camouflage in the grasses and reeds.

MANGROVES OF CENTRAL MEXICO SHORES

As we move south of the Rio Grande, the climate becomes progressively more tropical and the mangals along tidal bays, inlets and estuaries of Mexican shores are increasingly more luxuriant and diverse. We take our next example from near La Pesca, Tamaulipas, Mexico, located at the southern termination of Laguna Madre de Tamaulipas and north of Tampico (Fig. 9-3). Here, the climate is mostly tropical, but brief winter incursions of cold "norte" winds remind us that the area is not entirely so. Nevertheless, freezes are rare and most mangrove species can become established. The steeply sloped shores of a meandering river estuary near La Pesca are flanked by a sparse mangal consisting of a few large specimens of *Rhizophora*, *Avicennia* and *Laguncularia*.

The Mangal

Rhizophora assumes the typical position on the seaward flank of the shore. Several trees, some as much as 5 m tall, fringe the estuary. Large aerial prop roots arch over the water and spread downwards into the sediment. Shiny green leaves fill the crown of each tree, but some are marred by the attack of leaf miners (Fig. 9-3 D), the larvae of certain moths or beetles which tunnel within and feed upon leaf tissues, and produce meandering white scars upon the leaf surface. Clusters of droppers (Fig. 9-3 C1) hang from the branches of the leafy canopy. Some which have fallen from the tree lie impaled in the mud between the bases of the prop roots at the waters edge. Many of these have taken root and exhibit various stages of development. The *Rhizophora* zone here is not extensive, but distinctive.

Landward of *Rhizophora*, the steep slope of the shore forces smaller trees of *Laguncularia* and *Avicennia* to intermingle in a narrow band, demonstrating how a specific physical condition can alter the typical zonation pattern of these two species. Seaward of the *Rhizophora* fringe the estuary floor flattens out as an extensive mat of the manatee grass, *Syringodium filiforme* (Fig. 9-3 K).

Rhizophora Communities

Rhizophora mangle provides the basis for a complex community which, as we will see, can be subdivided into components based upon microhabitats. When *Rhizophora* forms a broad coastal boundary, the numbers of species which comprise this community may number in the hundreds, and the sheer quantity of species make it difficult to define relationships. In a simpler mangal, such as the shore at La Pesca, the basic elements of the community remain, but the diversity is not so great as to become an obstacle. We will consider elements of the *Rhizophora* community here, first with a brief consideration of energy relationships and then on the basis of habitat components.

Except for the mangrove trees themselves, the mangal community is mostly an allochthonous system.

Primary productivity within the mangal is confined largely to the leaves of the mangrove canopy, which absorb most of the light useful for photosynthesis. Additional productivity is derived from phytoplankton which is utilized by subtidal herbivores and filter feeders along the coastal fringe. Some light penetrates the canopy to provide photic energy for a few species of lichens or algae near the mangal floor, but this source of primary production is insignificant in comparison with the tremendous amounts of energy stored within carbohydrates produced by the mangrove leaves. These leaves, in turn, supply most of the mangal community, directly or indirectly, the energy required to sustain it. With few exceptions (filter feeders prominent among them), mangrove leaves are the base of the food chain in the mangal.

A few species, such as the leaf miners mentioned above, utilize the living mangrove leaves for sustenance, but most of the primary consumers wait until the leaves fall from the tree to harvest them. The primary consumers of the mangrove leaf litter are dominated by small crustaceans, especially amphipods, isopods, and juvenile shrimps. They are aided by decomposers, the bacteria and fungi, which help to break down complex carbohydrates and, in the process, add additional energy previously unavailable to the primary consumers. Primary consumers and decomposers are difficult to see and identify without special equipment or identification guides. But their small size does not minimize their importance to the community. They cut, shred, and pulverize the leaf litter and other organic debris into increasingly finer particles. They convert the carbohydrates bound in the leaf litter into the proteins of their own bodies, and, in turn, become the food of larger organisms. They act as trophic exchangers, converting generally unpalatable cellulose and polysaccharides of mangrove leaves into simple carbohydrates and proteins which are much more easily assimilated by the larger organisms.

The more conspicuous members of the *Rhizophora* community can be grouped into three categories: (1), a hard-bottom component, including biota which lives permanently upon and often attached to the mangrove roots, stems and branches; (2), a soft-bottom component, including biota which lives in or on the soft bottom sediments that accumulate around the base of the mangroves and (3), transients, including errant animals capable of entering and leaving the mangroves, via either water, land or air.

The Hard-bottom Component

Roots, stems and branches of *Rhizophora* provide an intertidal hard substratum in an otherwise alluvial environment. Organisms usually excluded from the soft floor of the estuary can find a place to cling or attach here, and, as on other hard shores, they often occupy distinctive vertical zones. Living high upon the roots and branches in a region roughly corresponding to the supralittoral fringe of a rocky shore is the angulate periwinkle, *Littoraria angulifera* (Fig. 9-3 G). Unlike

L. irrorata, which is a temperate littorine more at home in *Spartina*, *L. angulifera* is primarily adapted for life on mangroves. It is occasionally found on *Avicennia* in Texas, but becomes increasingly common on *Rhizophora* south of the Rio Grande. Like other littorines, it is a grazer, feeding upon the small lichens which grow on the bark of *Rhizophora*. The sea roach, *Ligia exotica* (Chapter 3) is another common high-zoned animal of the upper mangal, although a second species, *L. baudiniana* is also likely to occur here (R.W. Heard, personal communication).

The mid-tide level of the mangal is occupied by a variety of attached or encrusting biota. Prominent among them is the mangrove oyster, *Crassostrea rhizophorae* (Fig. 9-3 M), the frons oyster, *Lophia frons* (Fig. 9-3 A1) and the barnacles *Balanus eburneus* (Fig. 9-3 H) and *B. improvisus* (Fig. 9-3 I). Unlike *Crassostrea virginica*, which lives upon the estuarine floor attached to shells and other hard objects, *C. rhizophorae* and *L. frons* prefer mangrove roots for attachment, the latter producing characteristic encircling "claws" from the lower valve when attaching to aerial roots and twigs. *Crassostrea rhizophorae* rarely attains the size of its northern relative, but is nevertheless harvested commercially in some parts of the region. The irregularly shaped *L. frons* is usually too small for commercial harvest. The barnacles are the same species we have encountered previously on rocky and shell habitats. They attach to the mangroves opportunistically, not selectively, and will readily colonize any other suitable substratum when available.

9-3. A mangal of north-central Mexico, near La Pesca. **A.** White mangrove, *Laguncularia racemosa*; **B.** Black mangrove, *Avicennia germinans*, leaves; **B1.** *A. germinans*, fruit; **C.** Red mangrove, *Rhizophora mangle*; **C1.** *R. mangle* droppers; **D.** *R. mangle* leaf with miner trails; **E.** Mangrove crab, *Cardisoma guanhumi*; **F.** Red mangrove tree crab, *Goniopsis cruentata*; **G.** Mangrove periwinkle, *Littoraria angulifera*; **H.** Ivory barnacle, *Balanus eburneus*; **I.** Bay barnacle, *Balanus improvisus*; **J.** Tree oyster, *Isognomon alatus*; **K.** Manatee grass, *Syringodium filiforme*; **L.** Hooked mussel, *Ischadium recurvum*; **M.** Mangrove oyster, *Crassostrea rhizophorae*; **N.** Horn shell, *Cerithidea pliculosa*; **O.** Virgin nerite, *Neritina virginea*; **P.** Hermit crab, *Clibanarius vittatus*; **Q.** Spinycheek sleeper, *Eleotris pisonis*; **R.** Tellin, *Tellina tampaensis*; **S.** Marsh clam, *Polymesoda caroliniana*; **T.** Purple tagelus, *Tagelus divisus*; **U.** False mussel, *Mytilopsis leucophaeata*; **V.** Fiddler crab, *Uca rapax*; **W.** Wharf crab, *Sesarma cinereum*; **X.** Roseate spoonbill, *Ajaia ajaja*; **Y.** Wood stork, *Mycteria americana*; **Z.** White-faced ibis, *Plegadis chihi*; **A1.** *Lopha frons* attached to mangrove aerial root. Vertical scale indicates meters.

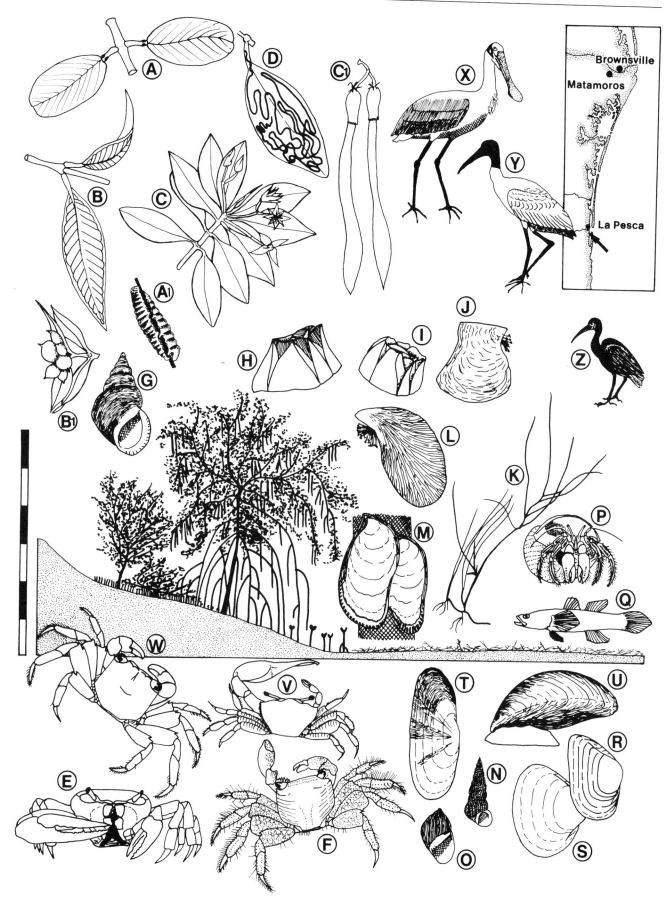

Nestling in the crevices among clusters of oysters is the black mytilid *Ischadium recurvum* (Fig. 9-3 L) and the flat tree oyster, *Isognomon alatus* (Fig. 9-3 J), both as tolerant as the mangrove oyster to fluctuating salinities. Despite its common name, *Isognomon* is not a true oyster (Ostreidae), as it does not cement a valve to the substratum. It belongs to the family Isognomonidae, which, like the mytilids, employs a byssus to attach to the mangrove.

A variety of soft-bodied or encrusting sessile epifauna are found lower down, on permanently submerged branches and prop roots. These include sponges, tunicates, bryozoans, tube worms and other invertebrates. This community attests to the true nature of mangrove trunks—a hard habitat in an otherwise soft environment but where adaptation to widely fluctuating salinities and high sediment loadings permit colonization by what would normally be regarded as rocky, mid-littoral species. As on other hard substrata, suspension or filter feeding is a common feeding strategy for the sessile fauna.

The Soft-bottom Component

This portion of the mangal community includes those organisms which are essentially permanent residents within or upon the soft bottom sediments at the base of the mangroves. The mangrove-dominated river banks are a perfect habitat for a variety of burrowing crabs. As in Texas, *Uca rapax* (Fig. 9-3 V), is zoned towards the lower fringe of the trees. Burrows of the large, blue-gray mud crab, *Cardisoma guanhumi* (Fig. 9-3 E) line the banks. The mud crab attains a carapace width of 20 cm and the large claw may reach 40 cm in length. *Cardisoma* is nocturnal and, except for brief foraging excursions, is reluctant to move far from the mouth of its burrow (Gifford, 1962; Henning, 1975). It belongs to the land crab family Gecarcinidae, but is one of the least tolerant gecarcinids with respect to aerial exposure (Fimple, 1975; Harris, 1977). It must frequently submerge its gills in water, and its burrow always reaches the water table (Herreid & Gifford, 1963). It feeds upon the detritus which accumulates at the base of the mangal.

Several kinds of molluscs occur on the floor of the mangal. As in Texas, large numbers of the horn shell, *Cerithidea pliculosa* (Fig. 9-3 N) live among the decaying leaf litter. Just offshore, among the beds of manatee grass are hundreds of the multicolored nerites, *Neritina virginea*, (Fig. 9-3 O), the similar *N. reclivata*, and the bright green emerald nerite *Smaragdia viridis* (Fig. 11-4 M). Stones on the sea grass bed are colonized by the false mussel, *Mytilopsis leucophaeata* (Fig. 9-3 U). Rarely more than 20 mm in length, *Mytilopsis* is usually found in clusters, each attached by a short byssus to the shell or stone.

Several infaunal bivalves occupy the mud. Prominent among these are the corbiculids, *Polymesoda caroliniana* (Fig. 9-3 S), and *P. maritima*. We have reported upon these bivalves from bayshores in Texas. The razor clam, *Tagelus divisus* (Fig. 9-3 T), is a deep-burrowing tellinacean of the family Solecurtidae. It is a deposit feeder with long separate siphons, the inhalant of which has a "hoovering" action over the mud surface. The smaller, thin-shelled *Tellina tampaensis* (Fig. 9-3 R) with its slightly pinkish blush on the center of the valves, is another infaunal deposit-feeding tellinacean of the unvegetated muds of the adjacent lagoon.

A few fishes such as the spinycheek sleeper, *Eleotris pisonis* (Fig. 9-3 Q) are permanent residents of the subtidal mangal. This secretive fish is commonly found among *Rhizophora* prop roots, but little else is known about it.

Transients

This component is much more difficult to characterize than the preceding because its members are constantly changing. Many are capable of entering or leaving the mangal, whereas others simply move from water to air within the mangal. Furthermore, they are obtained from two separate sources: those derived from essentially aquatic species and those which are primarily terrestrial. The former include a variety of fishes such as young tarpon, ladyfish (*Elops saurus*), snook, striped mullet, and small barracuda. All will enter the submerged tangle of prop roots for food or protection. The hermit crab *Clibanarius vittatus* (Fig. 9-3 P) is an invertebrate aquatic transient that ranges widely in the mangroves and onto the seagrass beds below. Portunid crabs, including *Callinectes marginatus*, take refuge here.

Several semiterrestrial crabs are primarily mangrove associates, but move from one habitat to another within the mangal. Prominent among these is *Sesarma cinereum* (Fig. 9-3 W) and the larger reddish grapsid crab, *Goniopsis cruentata* (Fig. 9-3 F). Both are frequently observed resting upon emergent prop roots or nimbly browsing upon thin filamentous algae clinging to the roots near the waterline. If approached too closely, they quickly scurry into the water, hiding among the maze of roots which lie there.

It requires little effort to imagine that ancestral sesarmids, grapsids and even gecarcinids may have taken to the land in part to avoid predators of the sea. A sheltered, secluded mangal is an excellent retreat for a threatened aquatic animal. Being motile, it is an easy step for a crab to leave the water, especially if pursued by a predatory fish or octopus. The dense canopy of mangrove leaves would provide protection from the drying effects of the tropical sun, and a place to rest until the danger passed. The tangle of timber would also provide cover to hide the animal from many terrestrial predators. But only for a while. Modern sesarmids travel back and forth from water to air to water, seeking food and shelter in both worlds, but finding neither totally free of danger.

In contrast to the aquatic transients, a number of terrestrial animals move into and out of the mangal. Prominent among these are the birds, including many that we have already discussed such as the brown pelican, snowy egret and the little blue heron. Ibises and spoonbills are other mangrove associates belonging to a tropical family of wading birds (Threskiornithidae) which we have not yet discussed. Ibises are long-legged marsh birds with sharp, recurved bills used to impale crustaceans and fishes. Spoonbills, as their name implies, have a terminally expanded beak which is used with sideways sweeps of the head to stir up small mud-dwelling invertebrates. Both move about in small flocks and, unlike herons, fly with their necks outstretched and legs trailing behind.

Several species of ibises frequent the mangrove-fringed bays of Mexico but we illustrate only the white-faced ibis, *Plegadis chihi* (Fig. 9-3 Z). The wood "ibis," *Mycteria americana* (Fig. 9-3 Y), is actually a stork (Ciconiidae) and hence more solitary. Like its more gregarious relatives, the wood stork also feeds on aquatic invertebrates and fishes which it sedately and deliberately stalks.

The roseate spoonbill, *Ajaia ajaja* (Fig. 9-3 X) is unmistakable in its pink plumage with a red flash along the shoulders and its highly characteristic bill. The side to side sweeps of the head during feeding, stir up bottom animals which are snapped at when touched by the bill. Spoonbills frequent many estuarine habitats, not just mangrove shores. Chapman (1982) summarizes the status of spoonbills in Texas.

NORTHERN YUCATAN MANGROVES

The mangal environment of the northern Yucatan peninsula of Mexico affords one of the most interesting intertidal bayshores of the Gulf. It is, in some places, similar to the hypersaline lagoons of southern Texas, yet it demonstrates new ways in which geology, hydrology and biology interact in an unusual combination to create a lagoon mangrove system of unique character.

The northern shore of Yucatan consists of a series of longitudinal beach ridges trending east-west from Cabo Catoche to south of Celestun. Undoubtedly created, or at least molded by prevailing longshore currents, the northern coast is prograding seaward as offshore sands are deposited on the mainland shore. Most of the ridges along the northwestern side of the peninsula have coalesced with the mainland, but are separated as barrier islands or capes toward the northeast (Fig. 9-4, upper right). The sandy ridges rise only a few meters above sea level and, except for the seaward-most ridge, are difficult to identify from the ground. They are separated from one another by lowlands which frequently lie under a thin layer of standing water. Near the sea, this water is derived from marine transgressions, but farther inland, it is derived from the numerous freshwater aquifers which emerge from the porous limestone bedrock of Yucatan.

Vegetational Zonation

A transect of the northern Yucatan shore from the Gulf beach (left), across saline lagoons and freshwater marshes, to the fringe of xeric forests on the mainland peninsula (right) appears at the bottom of Figure 9-4. The path traverses an integrated sequence of distinctive but linked plant communities. The same transect is shown from above on the far right of the figure with the seashore at the top. Our figure is diagrammatic in that it represents only one continuous ridge-to-marsh system, when, in fact, the 10 km distance from beach to xeric forest may actually demonstrate several ridges and depressions. At the specific area we describe, located about 8 km east of Progreso (line below the small arrow on the upper left map, Figure 9-4), the lowland lagoon system is very broad. Elsewhere along the northern shore of Yucatan, it may be divided by ridges into several distinct units. With this in mind, the description we provide is appropriate for much of the northern coast of Yucatan from Celestun to Cabo Catoche, with modifications for local conditions.

We begin the description of this transect at the shore and proceed (left to right and top to bottom) toward the xeric forest. Numbers refer to positions on the transect. The outermost community on the Gulf-facing dune (1) is described in Chapter 6. When there

9-4. The mangroves and hypersaline lagoons of northern Yucatan. The location of the transect at the bottom and right sides of the illustration is marked by a vertical line below the small arrow on the map at upper left. Vertical relief on the lower transect is illustrative, and not to scale. The map at upper right shows the presence of longshore bars along the northeastern coast of the Yucatan Peninsula. Transect numbers are as follows: **1.** Beach community along the Gulf of Mexico; **2.** scrub fringe landward of the beach dune crest; **3.** *Monanthochloe*-dominated grasses; **4.** *Conocarpus* zone; **5.** *Avicennia* hummocks in the hypersaline lagoon; **6.** *Rhizophora-Avicennia* hummocks in the hypersaline lagoon; **7.** *Salicornia* and associates along the lagoon fringe; **8.** *Typha* and *Spartina spartinae* marsh; **9.** tropical xeric forest. **S1:** Profile of an *Avicennia* hummock near the periphery of the lagoon. **S2:** Profile of a *Rhizophora-Avicennia* hummock at a central location within the lagoon. **A.** Brasiletto, *Caesalpinia vesicaria;* **B.** Hibiscus, *Hibiscus clypeatus;* **C.** Saltgrass, *Distichlis spicata;* **D.** Dildoe cactus, *Cereus pentagonus;* **E.** Glasswort, *Salicornia virginica;* **F.** Prickly pear, *Opuntia dillenii;* **G.** Buttonwood, *Conocarpus erectus;* **H.** Sea-blite, *Suaeda linearis;* **I.** Tiger beetle, *Cicindela* sp.; **J.** Saltwort, *Batis maritima;* **K.** Sea purslane, *Sesuvium portulacastrum;* **L.** Key grass, *Monanthochloe littoralis;* **M.** Pennywort, *Hydrocotyle bonariensis;* **N.** termite; **O.** Cat-tail, *Typha domingensis;* **P.** Gulf cordgrass, *Spartina spartinae;* **Q.** Fiddler crab, *Uca speciosa;* **R.** *Truncatella* sp.; **S.** Horn shell, *Cerithidea pliculosa;* **T.** Tellin, *Tellina tampaensis;* **U.** Pointed venus, *Anomalocardia auberiana;* **V.** Broad-ribbed cardita, *Carditamera floridana;* **W.** Mangrove warbler, *Dendroica erithachorides;* **X.** Greater flamingo, *Phoenicopterus ruber.*

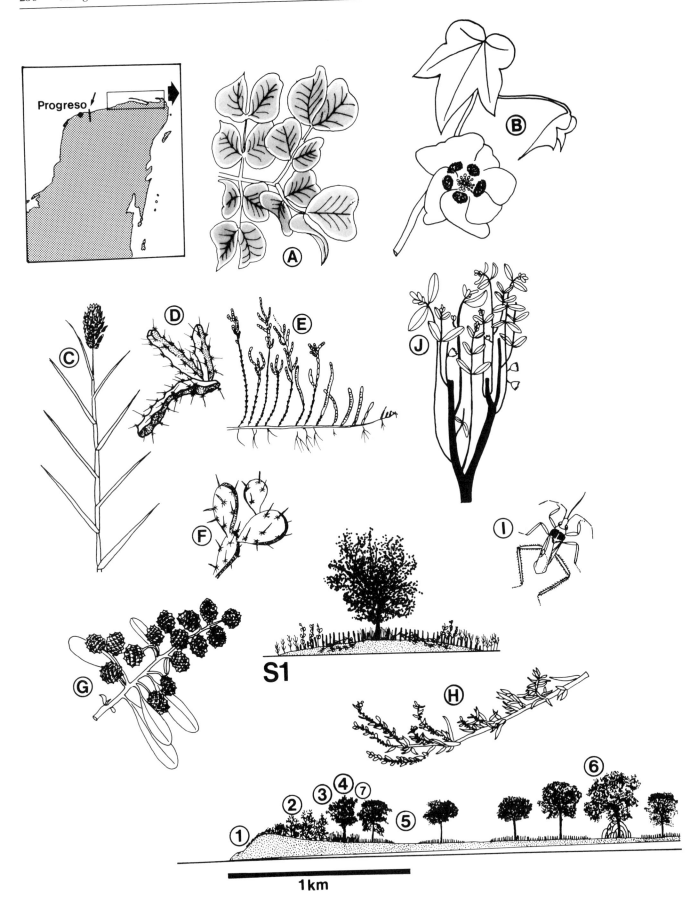

S1

1 km

S2

are a series of ridges, the one closest to the sea is usually the highest and broadest. It arises directly from the Gulf beach, reaches an elevation of from 3 to 5 m above sea level and extends as much as 1 km in width. The coastal villages, towns, and roads of northern Yucatan usually are built upon various limbs of the seaward dune ridge.

At intervals along the length of the Yucatan coast, the dune ridge is breached by shallow tidal channels, which lead to the inland lagoons. Many of the channels are silled and restrict water flow into or out of the lagoons, permitting the influx of only the highest tidal waters or wind-forced seiches. A few deeper channels lead to more typical coastal estuaries receiving regular tidal water exchange such as the embayments at Celestun and along the northeastern margin of the peninsula.

On the leeward (mainland) side of the dune ridge, the vegetation consists of disturbed scrub (2) rising above a carpet of the grasses *Monanthochloe littoralis* (Fig. 9-4 L) (3) and *Distichlis spicata* (Fig. 9-4 C). The most prominent tree is the buttonwood, *Conocarpus erectus* (Fig 9-4 G) (4), although most specimens here are more shrub-like. The two varieties of this secondary mangrove, one with olive drab leaves and the second with leaves gray-green, occur here side by side. Other vegetation commonly associated with the scrub border includes the legume *Caesalpinia vesicaria* (Fig. 9-4 A), distinguished by paired leaflets fringed by a narrow yellowish margin; the hibiscus, *Hisbiscus clypeatus* (Fig. 9-4 B), with its yellow-petaled, brown-centered flowers and distinctly lobed leaves; the small, wispy green shrub *Suaeda linearis* (Fig. 9-4 H); and the cactuses *Opuntia dillenii* (Fig. 9-4 F) and *Cereus pentagonus* (Fig. 9-4 D).

Lagoonward from the *Monanthochloe*/buttonwood fringe a band of *Salicornia virginica* (Fig. 9-4 E) and *Batis maritima* (Fig. 9-4 J) borders the flat unvegetated expanse of lagoon floor (7). The latter stretches at least 5 km north to south, and, in the vicinity of Progreso, at least 15 km east to west. The lagoon floor is inundated with seawater only during the highest tides or during strong winter "nortes." Most of the seawater which floods the lagoon is trapped there. It becomes hypersaline as a result of high evaporative water loss and low rates of replenishment or flushing. In the summer, the lagoon is often dry, exposing bare white sand covered by a thin crust of salt. In the winter it is frequently ankle-deep in water.

Numerous small hummocks of *Avicennia* (5) and *Rhizophora* (6) rise throughout the lagoon, most having dimensions of no more than a few dozen meters. We will expand on the ecology of these remarkable hummocks in a separate section below.

Eventually, the southern margin of the lagoon again gives way to a fringe of *Salicornia* and *Batis* (7), which, in turn, yields to the grass *Monanthochloe* (3) which, in turn, yields to the grass *Monanthochloe* (3) growing at the base of more stunted buttonwoods (4). The lagoon rim, therefore, is bounded by a community dominated by these four plants.

At some six to ten kilometers from the coast, freshwater springs wash away a shallow topsoil to expose limestone bedrock. Having little head or gradient to induce flow, the emergent groundwater accumulates at the surface, creating an extensive marsh habitat (8) dominated by the cattail, *Typha domingensis* (Fig. 9-4 O). This cattail is a coarse, stout plant that grows to a height of about 3 m. The leaves are essentially flat, with cylindrical pale or gray-green sheaths, overtopping the terminal spikes. The mature staminate spikes are above and distinctly separated from the pistillate spikes, both of which are pale brown. With *Typha*, along the fringes of the marsh, are *Spartina spartinae* (Fig. 9-4 P), the pennywort, *Hydrocotyle bonariensis* (Fig. 9-4 M), and several small trees and shrubs, sedges and other grasses that serve to link the marsh with the adjacent xeric forest (9).

The Hypersaline Lagoon

The lagoon system of northern Yucatan must be one of the most biologically depauperate tropical marine environments on Gulf shores. The interactions between climate, geology and hydrology have contributed to its creation. First, the climate is arid. Although relative humidity is usually high and rainfall can be seasonally or locally intense, annual precipitation is lower here than any other part of the Yucatan peninsula. This, combined with the intense solar radiation, produces an environment in which evaporation annually exceeds precipitation.

Strong longshore currents sweeping the northern Yucatan shore produce the dune ridge system we described above. These ridges enclose natural basins, which become the floors of the lagoons. The longshore currents also sill entrances to some of the basins, with tidal currents lacking sufficient energy to eliminate the sills. Only the highest tides, wind-driven seiches or intense cloudbursts can put water into the shallow lagoons, and once in, most of it cannot escape except by evaporation. Standing water slowly vaporizes to the atmosphere, and the remaining liquid is transformed into an increasingly hypersaline brine. We have measured salinities of 55 ppt in these silled lagoons in January, and they rise much higher in the summer as parts of the basins dry to form salt pans. Along Estero Rio Lagartos, east of Las Coloradas, the drying lagoon floor is covered by salt crystals to such a thickness that is can be mined here.

Few plants or animals can tolerate such extremes of salinity. For example, there is a striking absence of eukaryotic algae upon the lagoon floor. Small rounded mounds of the more tolerant blue-green algae (cyanophytes), reminiscent of stromatolites in a primordial sea, lie on the lagoon floor in some deeper basins where water stands most of the year. Hypersaline waters keep most herbivores at bay, so the uncropped cyanophytes accumulate in rounded concentric mounds. They are not as large or as well developed as the stromatolitic mounds at Shark Bay, Australia, but the fact that they develop at all is indicative of the harsh conditions encountered by most other forms of life within this lagoon.

In the absence of primary consumers, few nutrients are biologically transformed. Except for the occasional cyanophyte, the surface sands are mostly clean and detritus is largely absent. The influx of tidal water and runoff from the mangrove hummocks provides some nutrients, sufficient to support three burrowing bivalves: *Anomalocardia auberiana* (Fig. 9-4 U), *Tellina tampaensis* (Fig. 9-4 T) and *Carditamera floridana* (Fig. 9-4 V), all noted for their tolerance to hypersaline waters. *Anomalocardia* is a near-surface filter feeder, whereas *Carditamera* is an infaunal bivalve which employs a byssus to attach to buried stones or mangrove roots. *Tellina tampaensis* can burrow to a depth of 15 cm but moves to the surface and feeds by means of its elongate separate inhalant siphon upon the sparse detritus available on the lagoon floor. The only other fauna we observed from the lagoon floor were large numbers of tiger beetles, *Cicindela* sp. (Fig. 9-4 I), which were hunting other insects such as flies and midges on the moist sandy flats. It is likely that these lagoons support the larvae and pupae of one or more species of brine flies, but we have only encountered them further east at the Laguna dos Flamingos near Las Coloradas, where salinities are much higher than observed at Progreso.

Mangrove Hummocks in the Hypersaline Lagoon

In such a physical and biological desert, mangrove hummocks, scattered across the lagoon floor, stand out as oases of life. We use the term hummock instead of island because these topographic elevations within the lagoon are not always surrounded by water. Yet, even when the basin is dry, the hummocks are unmistakably distinctive. Two successional stages seem to prevail. The first (Fig. 9-4 S1) is most commonly encountered nearest the margins of the lagoon. *Avicennia germinans* fringe these hummocks, occupying small hillocks of accumulated sand and humus. The mangroves are surrounded by tufts of *Monanthochloe* and successive outwards-spreading bands of *Sesuvium portulacastrum* (Fig. 9-4 K), *Salicornia virginica* (Fig. 9-4 E) and *Batis maritima* (Fig. 9-4 J). Apparently *Avicennia* is better able to withstand the hypersaline and more sandy conditions prevailing in the lagoon than other mangrove species.

A further successional stage (Fig. 9-4 S2) is encountered on hummocks located toward the center of the lagoon. Here, larger masses of accreted sand and accumulated humus have developed. *Avicennia* still fringes the outer margins, but their center is occupied by *Rhizophora mangle*, and typically by one per hummock. An elongated trunk and long prop roots remove the crown of the tree from the extreme conditions this plant would otherwise be unable to tolerate. The *Rhizophora* focus is surrounded by smaller black mangroves, and its canopy shades a central ground cover of *Monanthochloe* among which are interspersed rooted *Rhizophora* droppers. Like the more peripheral *Avi-*

cennia-dominated hummocks, successive zones of *Sesuvium*, *Salicornia* and *Batis* radiate out from the central focus. Among these plants are a few stands of *Suaeda linearis*, (Fig. 9-4 H).

Nearly every hummock large enough to support a central red mangrove also contains a large brown mound of nest-building termites (Fig. 9-4 N), which derive nutrition by attacking the dead wood of the mangrove focus. They are the insect equivalents of the microorganisms in a more typical mangrove which are responsible for litter breakdown and nutrient recycling. Thus, the termites are of considerable ecological significance in the higher, central, mangrove hummocks.

Apparently few nutrients leave the hummock. In addition to the termites, a variety of small arthropods found among the leaf litter reduce this debris to humus. The *Monanthochloe* and the surrounding bands of low profile vegetation trap and exploit the nutrients from the humus on the hummocks before it can wash to the lagoon floor; whereas in a more typical mangrove much of this material would contribute to the general pool of nutrients within the bay—both in the water and on the mud surface. Accordingly, the mud snail, *Cerithidea pliculosa* (Fig. 9-4 S), everywhere abundant on mangrove frontage in Texas and elsewhere in Mexico, is here restricted to the hummocks, both by the hypersaline sands around and by the lack of appropriate food anywhere else, except on the hummocks. Occurring with *Cerithidea* are a few other snails such as *Truncatella* sp. (Fig. 9-4 R). Endogenously generated nutrients are locked up on the mangrove hummocks, leaf and wood fall being trapped by surrounding bands of grasses and other salt tolerant plants and broken down by leaf shredders and termites for local nutrient supply.

The more open portions of the hummocks provide habitat for small, isolated populations of the fiddler crab *Uca speciosa* (Fig. 9-4 Q), a close relative of *U. spinicarpa* which we previously encountered in Texas. The latter ranges from the northern Gulf to near Campeche, Mexico, whereas the former occurs along the northern Yucatan coast, southern Florida and on some Caribbean islands (Barnwell & Thurman, 1984). In Yucatan, *U. speciosa* is commonly found in association with mangroves.

Flamingos

The Yucatan lagoons are usually eerily silent places. Sometimes a bird such as the mangrove warbler, *Dendroica erithachorides* (Fig. 9-4 W), gently breaks the silence with a song. In the evening the hum of insects rises above the lagoon. But occasionally a rancorous noise shatters the solitude. Goose-like honks echo across lagoon desolation, made by the one bird above all others which characterizes tropical hypersaline lagoons. Flocks of the greater flamingo, *Phoenicopterus ruber* (Fig. 9-4 X), occupy some of the Yucatan lagoons, especially along the northeastern margin of the peninsula. Most of the flamingos live along the shores of Laguna Flamingos, east of Las Coloradas. Sometimes the birds cluster as one huge flock and at other times they break up into smaller feeding groups. Each bird is impressive, standing about 1 m high and, except for black flight feathers and a tricolored bill, is entirely pink, including the legs. The pigments are derived from caretenoids produced by blue-green algae, especially *Spirulina*, which also discolor the lagoon water, rendering it a bright pink as well.

Flamingos patrol lagoon waters, feeding upon that which they can filter from the water (Jenkin, 1957), using the unusual bill as a highly efficient strainer. The lower mandible resembles an expanded box and the upper a thin, profusely laminated lid that just fits into the lower. Both are sharply bent in front of the nostrils so that with the head down and the bill thus in an inverted position, it can be raked from side to side like a scoop, each sweep sieving small morsels from the lagoon floor. In essence, flamingos are filter feeders. The diet includes brine shrimp, small gastropods such as *Cerithidea pliculosa*, small bivalves, the larvae and pupae of brine flies, and even the filamentous blue-green algae from which its plumage color is presumably derived. Hurlbert *et al.* (1986) have suggested that the absence of planktivorous fishes which compete for invertebrate prey is important with respect to the distribution of flamingos. Although their work was done on the high Andean lakes of South America, the absence of fish predators in many of the Yucatan hypersaline lagoons supports the general applicability of the observation. At rest, flamingos strike a characteristic pose, standing upon one leg and the head tucked over one shoulder.

MANGROVES IN PERSPECTIVE

Of all the mainland shores encountered in the Gulf of Mexico, few offer more inspiration than those characterized by mangrove plants. Habitats consisting of richly organic muds, little sorted and aerated by sea waves, and subjected to local and seasonal flushing by freshwater drainages, provide few foci around which ecological stability can be sustained. The colonization of this habitat by higher plants with specific and highly specialized adaptations to it provides the much needed permanence of stasis. Of limited diversity, in comparison to the mangrove shores of the Pacific, or even other parts of the southern Gulf or tropical Atlantic, the Texas mangal is held in delicate balance. A single species of *Avicennia* occurs here. Occasionally droppers of *Rhizophora* wash ashore from Mexican beaches. They take root, grow and, for a while, add variety. Cold winters first kill the red mangroves, and eventually *Avicennia* during prolonged winter freezes, but not before they have added their measure of influence to these developing shores. The plants confer stability and in so doing extend a terrestrial influence seawards to counter the degradation of more open coasts by wave action. The intertidal balance they help sustain is important to the continued stability of the coast as a whole. Just as important is the stability they confer on the euryhaline community of associated plants and animals they encourage. The trunks provide a hard shore environment in a region where such habitats are usually absent. Moreover, the mud beneath receives marine flotsam and jetsam, allochthonous material from rivers and streams and is the recipient of locally engendered litter. Such material is degraded and recycled to contribute to the nutrient resources not only of the mangrove stand itself but for the benefit of other habitats nearby and unpossessing of the basis for productivity.

Mangrove diversity increases to the south in Mexican bays where succession (in addition to zonation) plays an enhanced role in natural reclamation processes. Of special importance is the red mangrove, *Rhizophora mangle* and its special reproductive attributes, the droppers, which are capable of dramatically extending the mangrove's influence seaward. *Avicennia* is now relegated to a successional component of the mangal. Succession is not an obvious feature of marine intertidal communities, so it is well to note that the mangroves are, in fact, a coastal extension of a typically successional tropical terrestrial habitat. As with other forests, the mangal is in peril from the ax or buzz saw. Throughout the Gulf and Caribbean, much has already been cut. Continued removal of the remaining protective fringe of mangroves will have important implications to shore stability, and hence the balance between erosion and shore accretion.

The best example of the mangrove's role in ecological stability has been seen in the Yucatan lagoons where the plants create and sustain oases of life in an otherwise hypersaline desert. That their role here is noticeably different from the more uniform and characteristic life style of mangroves in Texas illustrates the dynamic nature of the coastal zone and the adaptability of its biota.

PART FOUR Subtidal Sands, Banks and Coral Reefs

10. Subtidal Sands and Banks

INTRODUCTION

Having now examined the shore habitats of the western Gulf of Mexico, it is appropriate that we conclude this regional survey by considering some of the shallow offshore communities that flank the intertidal shore and whose representatives are often better known by virtue of their commercial value. Offshore communities are rich in species, including some which are harvested as seafood. But many offshore fauna are less well known than their coastal counterparts, and are considered strange curiosities when they occasionally wash ashore to die in the drift.

The intertidal Gulf has been, and remains, the focus and fulcrum of our survey. We began by examining the intertidal biota of hard and soft shores, and then proceeded landward via dunes, flats, lagoons or embayments to examine the biota of these habitats. It is now time that we move in the opposite direction, seaward, and examine the other side of the tide.

The landward terminations of our shoreward sojourns were often arbitrary. The discussion of a shore habitat ended when maritime influences waned. Similarly, we will be somewhat arbitrary in terminating the seaward extension of this investigation. Our primary interest in coastal processes and communities dictates that discussions of subtidal environments be restricted to those which strongly influence or are influenced by the intertidal shore. On barrier islands, for example, onshore waves may deposit sand on a foreshore, and winds may move this sand to a dune field. But storms or winter winds may redeposit dune sands in offshore bars. There is continual interplay between sediment distribution on berms, bars and dunes, and this interplay has a profound influence upon shore and subtidal life. It is in this aspect of interrelationship that we are interested. Where a supratidal or subtidal habitat is influenced by the shifting sands, the community associated with it must be within the purview of broad studies of Gulf shore ecology. We will not, however, consider the deeper shelf or slope environments, nor consider the abyssal basins of the Gulf of Mexico.

Subtidal communities begin just below the tide and continue seaward. Those within our horizon of interest may extend dozens of kilometers offshore, typically to water depths of less than 50 m. This offshore region encompasses several times the area of the intertidal shores and estuaries. It has the potential of developing numerous microhabitats that can be exploited by a large number of species. We are just beginning to understand the subtle variety of habitats that are found here. In this and the next chapter, we will emphasize only general bottom types (sands, muds, or hard banks) and the communities that they contain. The offshore bottoms, however, are not exclusively "sand," "mud" or "bank." Near river mouths, especially along the northeastern Texas coast, sand/mud mixtures are common and considerable debris (including rocks, logs, and garbage) is washed seaward and deposited offshore. A number of microhabitats can be differentiated according to the relative proportions of sands, muds and debris on the shallow sea floor. For example, Keith & Hulings (1965) recognized two distinct nearshore communities with almost mutually exclusive microfauna between Sabine Pass and Bolivar Point, Texas, and Hubbard (1977) recognized three polychaete assemblages which correlate well with substratum types. Differences between microhabitats are often subtle, and the transition from predominantly sandy mud to predominantly muddy sand is usually gradual. Such distinctions do become less pronounced toward southwestern Texas shores where the environment is more uniform. The carbonate sands of Yucatan, however, produce communities distinct from those in the quartz sands off Texas barrier islands. Although we will not attempt to make these fine distinctions, you should keep in mind that (1), critical work has and should continue to consider sediment composition as an important influence upon community structure and (2), each species has an optimum habitat and limits of tolerance with respect to sediment particle size and chemical composition that will influence its local distribution along the array of shallow offshore bars and banks that characterize Gulf nearshore waters.

We will begin our discussion of subtidal Gulf habitats with the communities that occupy unconsolidated sediments lying off the Texas barrier islands. In this region, over 90 percent of the bottom consists of loose, soft sediments. After consideration of this diverse assemblage, we will compare the northwestern subtidal sand biota with similar communities occupying the offshore subtidal carbonate sands in the Yucatan region.

There are some areas on the shallow northwestern Gulf continental shelf that are not covered by unconsolidated sands or muds. Here, hard carbonate hills or banks rise above the surrounding sediment blanket. The banks off the Texas and Louisiana coasts apparently originated at a time when sea level was considerably lower than today, and when mean water temperature was warmer (Parker & Curray, 1956; Curray, 1960). They are relic habitats providing refuge for a biota otherwise unrepresented in the region. As one moves southward along the continental shelf, the banks become more prominent and eventually rise to the surface as emergent reefs. In this chapter, we will consider the simpler bank communities of the northwestern Gulf, and in the next chapter we will discuss the height of their development, the subtidal bank reefs off Texas and emergent coral reefs of tropical Mexico.

TEXAS OFFSHORE SANDS

Snorklers surveying the surface of shallow sands off northwestern Gulf of Mexico beaches usually report a paucity of life. There are few sea grasses or macrophytic algae, for the longshore currents are too strong and the sediment too unstable for them to become established. The only blemish upon the monotony of otherwise endlessly undulating sand is the occasional shuffling hermit crab, scurrying portunid or settling sting ray. A surface survey belies the true faunal diversity, for most members of the community lie buried within the sand. In fact, a relatively rich assemblage of crustaceans, molluscs, cnidarians and echinoderms occur here, only a few of which are epifaunal. Some like the polychaetes *Diopatra cuprea* (Fig. 10-5 K) and *Onuphis eremita* (Fig. 10-1 O) construct and live within membranous, sometimes shell-lined tubes, but most lack permanent burrows. Scavengers such as the portunid crabs freely enter and leave the sand, disappearing backwards within it for protection when danger threatens. The molluscan predators (e.g., olive or moon snails) often seek bivalve prey without emerging. The faunal elements which do emerge (e.g., sand dollars and sea pansies) often do so at night.

Despite the lack of conspicuous plants, the offshore Gulf coast sands and overlying waters are highly productive, containing numerous microscopic diatoms, dinoflagellates and other algae. This phytoplankton, together with detritus derived from the land, form the base of the offshore bottom community food chain. The fauna is dominated by primary consumers which exploit these kinds of nutrients. There are many buried suspension feeders, such as bivalve molluscs and mole crabs, that rely upon siphons or body movements to bring phytoplankton-laden water to their biological screens. A few suspension feeders, such as the pen shells, lie partially exposed on the surface. A few more of the primary consumers are deposit feeders which derive nutrition from the sediments in which they live. All of these are pursued, in turn, by a variety of secondary consumers, the predators and scavengers, most of which also remain below the surface. We will discuss each of these groups in the paragraphs that follow.

Suspension Feeders

Infaunal suspension feeders, especially bivalve molluscs, constitute the primary herbivores of the subtidal sand community of the northwestern Gulf. At least 15 species of bivalves commonly occur in the nearshore sands and tidal inlets, with as many more occurring locally or sporadically. The sand-dwelling ark shells, *Anadara ovalis* (Fig. 10-1 B1), *A. brasiliana* (Fig. 10-1 C1), and *Noetia ponderosa* (Fig. 10-1 A1) are among the most common. Their stout, strong-ribbed shells characterized by a straight "taxodont" hinge containing a row of many vertically aligned parallel hinge teeth are common on the barrier island beaches, but the living arks are rarely seen. Many Arcidae live semi-permanently attached by numerous byssal threads to rocks and other hard substrata, especially within reef habitats (Chapter 11). The sand arks (i.e., *Anadara* and *Noetia*) forgo the byssus and live unattached just below the sublittoral sand. As primitive suspension feeders, they cannot burrow deeply, for they lack the discrete siphons of the more "advanced" bivalves. They are among the first sand-dwelling molluscs to be displaced during a storm. Many are brought ashore by hurricane tidal surges. The stranded arks die on the beach and the valves quickly separate, but the solidly built half-shells are not easily destroyed by even the most violent storms. This accounts for the large numbers of ark valves commonly found behind the storm berm of barrier island beaches. The large heavy-shelled venerid, *Mercenaria campechiensis* (Fig. 10-3 J), is a locally important contributor to beach drift (especially on southern Padre Island), but its offshore distribution seems to be patchy. It is more often encountered alive in the Texas bays where it hybridizes with *M. mercenana* (Craig & Bright, 1986).

The giant cockle, *Dinocardium robustum* (Fig. 10-1 S) is another shallow burrower in the offshore sand. Its large (up to 120 mm) shell is thinner and more fragile than that of *Mercenaria* or any of the arks. Unbroken *Dinocardium* valves are much less common on barrier beaches. Living cockles are usually abundant just offshore, where they employ a powerful dark red muscular foot to dig and, when attacked, to make spectacular leaps across the sand. They possess short siphons fringed with numerous finger-like papillae which help to prevent sand and other large particles from entering the mantle cavity. *Dinocardium robustum* is one of several sand-dwellers with a curious disjunctive geographic distribution. It occurs from the Florida panhandle to Yucatan and from Virginia to northern Florida, but is absent from central and southern Florida, despite an abundance of apparently suitable habitats, especially along the southwestern coast.

The venerid genus *Dosinia* is represented by two species in Texas, *D. discus* (Fig. 10-1 M), which occurs along the entire coast and *D. elegans*, restricted to south Padre Island. Both occur along the eastern Mexican coast to Yucatan. In Florida, *D. elegans* reaches sexual maturity at about 1 year of age and a length of 15 mm, and attains a maximum size of about 30 mm in 3 years (Moore & Lopez, 1970). In the western Gulf of Mexico, specimens commonly grow to 50 mm, probably indicating faster growth rates. There are two spawning periods each year, with about 50 percent of the tissue weight at each spawn invested in gametes. Moore and Lopez estimated annual mortality rates at about 80 percent. There is considerable loss to predation by moon snails, as most shells which wash ashore on Texas beaches have been drilled by *Polinices*.

Another venerid, *Cyclinella tenuis*, resembles *Dosinia*, but is smaller and not as common in offshore sands. It prefers very fine or muddy sands of tidal inlets and along bay margins. *Cyclinella tenuis* is predominantly a tropical Caribbean bivalve, but occurs throughout the Gulf and Atlantic to North Carolina. In southern Florida it seems to spawn throughout the year (Wright & Moore, 1970). Beached shells are usually more easily found in Texas waters than living adults.

The pen shells, *Atrina serrata* (Fig. 10-2 F) and *A. seminuda* (Fig. 10-2 D) are the largest subtidal bivalves of the Texas coast, as well as the entire Gulf and Caribbean region. The thin, fragile shells can attain 250 mm in length. Both species occupy sandy or muddy bottoms. They lie with the long axis vertical and the broad posterior third of the shell exposed above the substratum. When disturbed, the animal retracts to the lower half of the shell, an obvious adaptation to avoid a variety of curious or hungry swimming predators that, given the opportunity, would readily graze upon extended fleshy mantle lobes. The brittle, fluted, and sometimes spiny shell keeps most predators at bay, although numerous *in situ* living specimens with damaged posterior margins suggest that some predators try to penetrate the shelly armor. To compensate for the assault, pen shells firmly anchor to the sediment by a tangled network of byssal threads, and have an exceptional capacity to repair marginal shell damage, replacing as much as 10 mm in 24 hours (Grave, 1911; Yonge, 1953).

Atrina serrata, restricted to the outer subtidal sands, is the more common pen shell in Texas waters. *Atrina seminuda*, when present, occupies subtidal muds in inlet influenced bays as well as shallow muddy sands on the outer coast. The two species are difficult to distinguish, the former having thinner shells and larger nacreous areas than the latter. Both harbor commensal crabs (*Pinnotheres maculatus*) (Fig. 10-2 E) or shrimps (*Pontonia domestica*) (Fig. 10-2 G) within the mantle cavity.

Additional filter feeding bivalves of the offshore sands include the lucines *Lucina amianthus* (Fig. 10-2 K) and *Parvilucina multilineata*, the egg cockle, *Laevicardium laevigatum* (Fig. 10-6 P), the surf clam, *Spisula solidissima*, the channeled duck clam, *Raeta plicatella* (Fig. 10-6 Y), and the venerids *Chione intapurpurea* and *C. clenchi*. Several bivalves, more

typical of bay habitats, also occur on outer subtidal sands or along tidal inlets. These include *Mulinia lateralis* (Fig. 10-3 N), *Ervilia nitens* (formerly *E. concentrica*; de Rooij-Schuiling, 1973) and *Chione cancellata* (Fig. 10-3 G). All are common among beach drift on the barrier islands.

A few bivalves are mostly restricted to inlet channels along the Texas coast, although they occur in other habitats in other localities. Representative of this group are the lucines *Lucina pectinata* (Fig. 10-3 M) and the edentulate *Anodontia alba* (Fig. 10-3 L). Both are common shells on tidal inlet beaches, but living specimens are difficult to find, the former more common than the latter. The largely tropical Lucinidae are especially well suited for life in anaerobic reducing sediments. Typically they live below the redox potential discontinuity, but communicate with surface waters in an unusual manner. Lucines lack the typical posterior inhalant siphon. Instead, they rely upon an elongate vermiform foot to construct an anterior inhalant water tube, through which they bring water into the mantle cavity for feeding and respiration. Waste water and feces exit the body via an elongate posterior exhalant siphon. Living as much as 4 to 6 times the shell length below the surface and well within anaerobic muds, the lucine blood-vascular system has become enhanced for greater respiratory efficiency. Lucines often develop a large mantle blood vessel and some even possess hemoglobin as an accessory respiratory pigment.

10-1. Fauna of the Texas offshore sands. **A.** Tricolor anemone, *Calliactis tricolor*; **B.** Calico crab, *Hepatus epheliticus*; **C.** Speckled crab, *Arenaeus cribrarius*; **D.** Spiny-armed crab, *Portunus spinimanus*; **E.** Blue crab, *Callinectes sapidus*; **F.** Iridescent swimming crab, *Portunus gibbesi*; **G.** *Cronius ruber*; **H.** Shame-face crab, *Calappa sulcata*; **I.** *Persephona aguilonaris*; **J.** *Lepidopa websteri*; **K.** *Albunea paretii*; **L.** *Euceramus praelongus*; **M.** Disk dosinia, *Dosinia discus*; **N.** Sea pansy, *Renilla mulleri*; **O.** *Onuphis eremita*; **P.** Single tooth simnia, *Simnialena uniplicata*; **Q.** Sea whip, *Leptogorgia virgulata*; **R.** Lined tellin, *Tellina alternata*; **S.** Giant Atlantic cockle, *Dinocardium robustum*; **T.** Dwarf tellin, *Tellina versicolor*; **U.** Minute dwarf olive, *Olivella minuta*; **V.** Cancellate cantharus, *Cantharus cancellarius*; **W.** Giant eastern murex, *Muricanthus fulvescens*; **X.** Scotch bonnet, *Phalium granulatum*; **Y.** Common Atlantic auger, *Terebra dislocata*; **Z.** Olive snail, *Oliva sayana*; **A1.** Ponderous ark, *Noetia ponderosa*; **B1.** Blood ark, *Anadara ovalis*; **C1.** Incongruous ark, *Anadara brasiliana*; **D1.** Salle's auger, *Hastula salleana*; **E1.** Lined tulip shell, *Fasciolaria lilium*; **F1.** Giant hermit crab, *Petrochirus diogenes*; **G1.** Say's porcellanid, *Porcellana sayana*; **H1.** Atlantic distorsio, *Distorsio clathrata*; **I1.** Sand dollar, *Mellita quinquiesperforata*; **J1.** Sand dollar pea crab, *Dissodactylus mellitae*; **K1.** Banded luidia, *Luidia alternata*; **L1.** Two-spined starfish, *Astropecten duplicatus*.

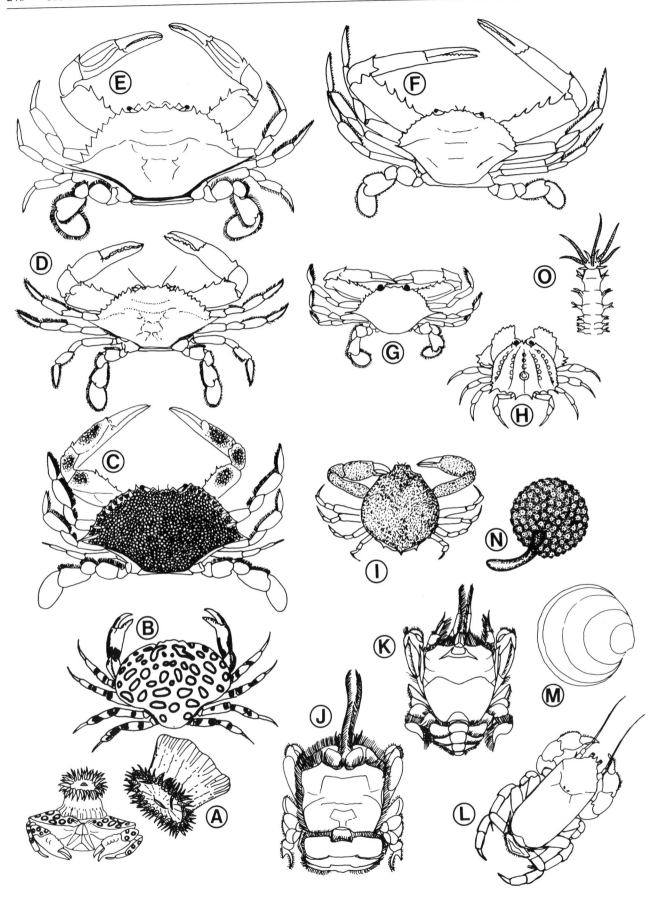

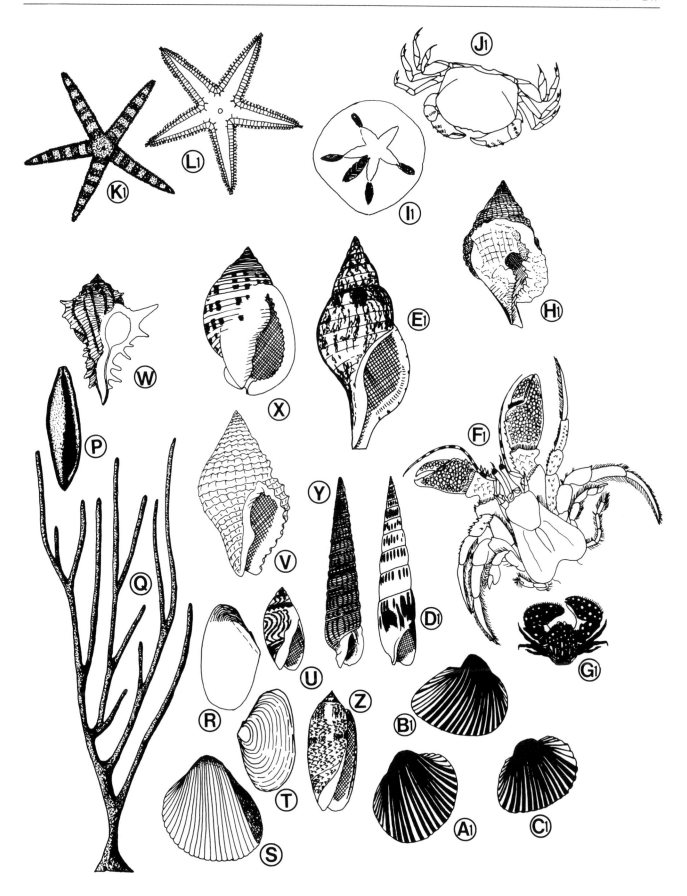

An even deeper-living bivalve, *Cyrtopleura costata* (Fig. 10-3 P) bores to a depth of almost 500 mm in hard clays along tidal inlets and the margins of outer bays. Like the closely related *Barnea truncata* (described in Chapter 6), the shell of this large piddock (Pholadidae) is relatively thin and adapted for boring, especially in firm clay banks. *Cyrtopleura* bores very much like *Barnea*, using the shell as an abrasive auger.

Other tidal inlet bivalves which also occur within the bays (Chapter 7) include the bay scallop, *Aequipecten irradians amplicostatus* (Fig. 10-3 E), the razor shells, *Tagelus plebeius* (Fig. 10-3 O) and *Ensis minor* (Fig. 10-3 Q), the nut clams *Nuculana acuta* (Fig. 10-3 H) and *N. constricta* (Fig. 10-3 I), the tellin *Macoma constricta* (Fig. 10-3 K), the latter three species feeding upon settled surface deposits.

Little is known about the ecology and life history of the tiny bivalve *Crassinella lunulata* (Fig. 10-2 I), but certain aspects of its anatomy and distribution suggest that it is not a typical infaunal filter feeding bivalve. It lacks an inhalant, but has a short exhalant siphon. It also has a curious scythe-shaped gland of unknown function on the anterior mantle margin. Although not a common shallow water species, *C. lunulata* shells often accumulate in shallow subtidal sediments. Living specimens seem to prefer coarse substrata, especially shelly deposits, where they apparently spend considerable time crawling upon the surface with the aid of a weak byssus (Harry, 1966). The species is rarely found alive in shallow Texas coastal waters, although it is known from some deep bay and shallow offshore bank habitats.

Deposit Feeders

In contrast to the suspension feeding bivalves just described, the Tellinidae and Semelidae have perfected a different feeding strategy. Tellinids possess two separate, elongate siphons that can be extended far beyond the posterior margin of the shell. The body lies within the sediment, somewhat or completely upon its side, with only the siphons emergent at the surface. This suggests a suspension feeding strategy, and, indeed, the tellinids may be derived from more typical suspension feeding bivalves. They are deposit feeders exploiting a niche unavailable to most other bivalves, that of the film of rich organic detritus that settles at the surface of the sea floor.

In most natural aquatic systems, a thin nutrient-rich layer usually accumulates at the sediment-water interface. Unless agitated by water movements this layer is inaccessible to strict suspension feeders. The tellinids can exploit it. Their ventral inhalant siphon becomes more elongate than the dorsal exhalant. As a result, the exhalant siphon extends from the body to the sediment surface, where it eliminates filtered water and feces. The inhalant siphon extends beyond the surface, arches, and can be applied to the thin sediment-water interface. Working like a vacuum cleaner, it gleans particulate nutrients from the surface of the sea floor. Tellinids also possess a large muscular foot

by which they can plow through the substratum to seek new feeding areas or to rapidly burrow when pursued by predators.

The Tellinidae occupy a variety of soft bottom situations, ranging from coarse sands to very fine muds. Three species commonly occur off Texas barrier beaches: *Tellina alternata* (Fig. 10-1 R), *T. versicolor* (Fig. 10-1 T), and the unusual *Tellidora cristata* (Fig. 10-2 J). *Tellina alternata* is the largest member of the family in Texas waters, often attaining a shell length of 60 to 70 mm. It occurs in fine sands or sandy muds on the outer shores, along inlets and outer bay margins. In southern Florida it apparently spawns twice yearly, with a spring brood being the more important. It probably lives about three years (Moore & Lopez, 1970). *Tellina versicolor* is much smaller than *T. alternata*, not exceeding 15 mm. Its tiny, fragile shell is often flushed with red or pink rays on a white shiny base. The compressed *Tellidora cristata* can be confused with few other bivalves. Its dorsally angular and ventrally rounded shape, combined with the distinctive dorsal extensions of concentric ornamentation and a flattened left valve, set it apart. Little is known about this tellin, apart from the fact that it usually inhabits predominantly sandy bottoms. It is occasionally dredged from the deeper portions of tidal inlets throughout the Gulf of Mexico. The purple semelid, *Semele purpurascens*, is a somewhat different tellinacean deposit feeder common in offshore sands.

Tusk shells have perfected a different method of deposit feeding, especially in relatively clean sand. Several species commonly inhabit Texas tidal inlets and offshore sands. All live subtidally and most are relatively small and thin, thus infrequently encountered and easily overlooked. The largest species, *Dentalium texasianum* (Fig. 10-2 L), reaches almost 4 cm in length.

10-2. Additional fauna of the Texas offshore sands. **A.** Brittle star, *Hemipholis elongata*; **B.** Brittle star, *Ophiolepis elegans*; **C.** Brittle star, *Ophiothrix angulata*; **D.** Pen shell, *Atrina seminuda*; **E.** Pea crab, *Pinnotheres maculatus*; **F.** Pen shell, *Atrina serrata*; **G.** Commensal shrimp, *Pontonia domestica*; **H.** Lesser sponge crab, *Dromidia antillensis*; **I.** *Crassinella lunulata*; **J.** White-crested tellin, *Tellidora cristata*; **K.** *Lucina amianthus*; **L.** Tusk shell, *Dentalium texasianum*; **M.** Wentletrap, *Epitonium angulatum*; **N.** Wentletrap, *Epitonium tollini*; **O.** *Turbonilla interrupta*; **P.** Tinted cantharus, *Pisania tincta*; **Q.** Mud snail, *Nassarius vibex*; **R.** Peanut worm, *Phascolion strombi*; **S.** Blood ark, *Anadara ovalis*; **T.** coral, *Astrangia poculata*; **U.** Moon snail, *Polinices duplicatus*; **V.** *Heterocrypta granulata*; **W.** "Pipe cleaner" sea pen, *Virgularia presbytes*; **X.** *Pteria colymbus*.

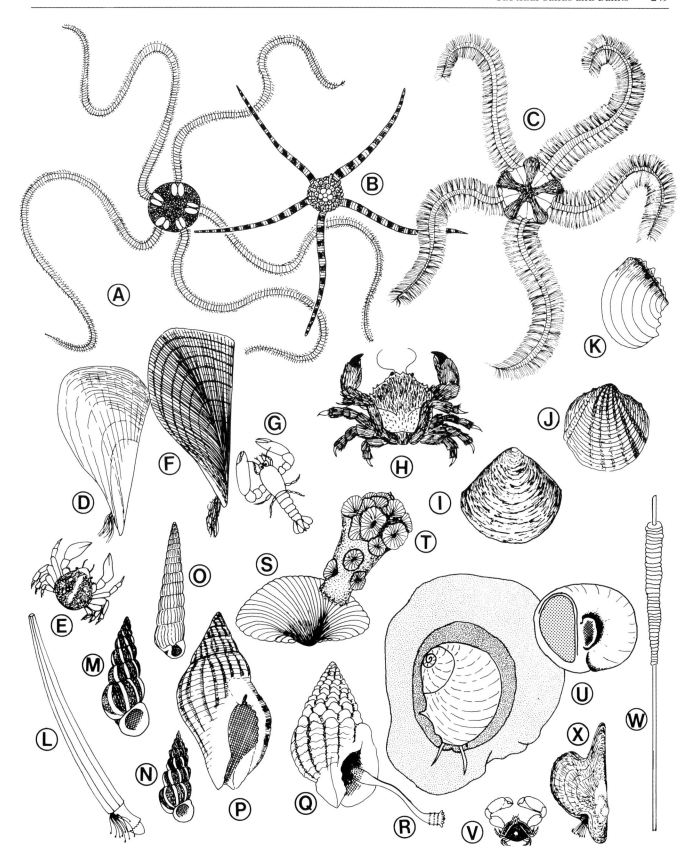

Tusk shells are scaphopod molluscs and differ in several significant respects from either bivalves or gastropods. They are enclosed within an elongate shell open at both ends. A reduced head and conical foot emerge from the larger end, whereas the smaller posterior end (through which water enters and leaves) opens into a rather spacious mantle cavity. Scaphopods live buried head-down with only the smaller tip protruding above the surface of the sand. In this position the tusk shell can provide mantle tissues with aerated water for respiration (there are no gills) and simultaneously search the sand for food. Scaphopods feed upon foraminiferans and other interstitial biota captured by numerous threadlike tentacles (captacula) which extend from two lobes on either side of the mouth.

Deposit feeding echinoderms are poorly represented in the shallow offshore sands. Several large, conspicuous species of sea cucumbers help to characterize similar habitats at other localities (e.g., Yucatan), but there are only two or three small species of Holothuroidea in the nearshore deposits of the northwestern Gulf. The best known of these, *Thyone mexicana*, is most frequently found in association with grass beds in the bays behind barrier islands (Chapter 7).

What they lack in diversity, the echinoderms make up for in numbers. The most common animal in the sands just off the barrier islands is the sand dollar, *Mellita quinquiesperforata* (Fig. 10-1 I1). Few other species are so dependent upon the clean, unvegetated sandy sea floor as is this discoid echinoderm. The dorso-ventrally flattened body and numerous extremely short spines are intimately adapted for passage through unencumbered sand. *Mellita* simply cannot live among cobbles or in grass beds, for it lacks the arms, feet, or other appendages that would enable it to move aside a stone or pass through a tangle of rhizomes or grass blades.

Beginning at about the third offshore trough, sand dollars occur in high densities, lying within the sand by day and emerging to feed at night. They spend many motionless hours just below the surface, sometimes with the posterior end slightly exposed. Occasionally, they move through sand, the motion restricted to only the anterior direction. If uncovered and placed on the surface, they will glide back into the sand by movements of very short spines on the oral body surface. Within 5 minutes they can rebury, but the rate at which they burrow is dependent upon light intensity. *Mellita quinquiesperforata* is negatively phototaxic. It burrows more rapidly as light intensity increases (Bell & Frey, 1969).

Like the tellinids, *Mellita* feeds from the organically rich sediment-water interface, although in a different manner. At night the surface of the offshore troughs and bars are covered by dense aggregations of feeding sand dollars. The feeding activity occurs primarily on the bottom or oral body surface. Many tiny tube feet remove food particles from the sediment, passing them into radiating ambulacral grooves which converge at the mouth. The edges of the grooves are lined by numerous short spines, arching above them, and loosely interlocking like a sieve. This arrangement permits the passage of only fine particles into the grooves. Ambulacral podia move the selected particles toward the mouth, where they are ingested (Bell & Frey, 1969). Although rare in Texas, a tiny crab, *Dissodactylus mellitae* (Fig. 10-1 J1), sometimes can be found living among the short spines of this sand dollar, and may extract bits of food during the feeding process.

The gregarious behavior of *M. quinquiesperforata* is important during the late spring and summer spawning season. Like most echinoids, sand dollars shed gametes into the sea. Fertilization occurs as spermatozoa randomly contact ova. A productive spawn is dependent upon the synchrony of shedding and the relatively close proximity of spawning sand dollars. Within two days the fertilized ova develop into echinopleuteus larvae, which remain in the meroplankton for 4 to 6 weeks before settlement and metamorphosis into the adult body form.

In addition to sand dollars, the offshore sands also harbor several species of brittle stars, including *Hemipholis elongata* (Fig. 10-2 A), *Ophiolepis elegans* (Fig. 10-2 B), and *Ophiothrix angulata* (Fig. 10-2 C). The ophiuroids are more properly characterized as scavengers or predators rather than deposit feeders, but most species derive some nutrition from the sediments. The brittle stars are not common near shore, but are found there occasionally. They are extremely agile echinoderms, using the narrow arms for efficient, rapid motion. Like the sand dollars, brittle stars shun light. During the day they lie below the sand with only the tips of the arms exposed. They emerge at night to forage. Brittle stars are considerably more common in the southern Gulf, and will be considered in more detail below.

Predatory Gastropods

Most of the common gastropods of the shallow offshore sands are predators or scavengers which burrow in search of prey. Many of these species also occur within tidal inlets and higher salinity bays. Despite subterranean habits, the moon snail, *Polinices duplicatus* (Figs. 10-2 U; 10-3 D), is one of the most conspicuous gastropods. Its trails crisscross lower intertidal beaches or the sand banks just offshore and, after the death of the snail, its shell is often occupied and carried about by hermit crabs. The globular *P. duplicatus* shell has a semi-polished exterior and distinctive brown spot on the columellar lip. The closely related but less common ear snail, *Sinum perspectivum* (Fig. 10-3 F) has an equally distinctive shell, being little more than an ear-shaped trinket into which the gastropod cannot possibly retract. Both are members of the family Naticidae, a prominent group of gastropod predators characteristic of clean shallow subtidal sands.

Naticids blindly seek their prey as they plow along just below the surface of the sand. The *Polinices* shell is not ideally shaped for streamlined movement, but soft tissues, especially the foot, anteriorly envelop the shell to provide a more efficient wedge-shaped design. The foot is divided into three lobes, a propodium, forming an anteriorly directed plow, a mesopodium, forming the central sole, and a metapodium, covering the rear of the shell and carrying the operculum. A fully expanded *P. duplicatus* is two to three times larger and heavier than when the body is contracted within its shell. It seems remarkable that all of this mass can even fit into the shell. (When the *Sinum* body is tightly contracted, it still remains mostly outside the small shell.) The remarkable fact, however, is the manner by which naticid tissues expand. The foot enlarges by taking considerable amounts of seawater into internal aquiferous canals. Water uptake is a slow process, so expansion of the *P. duplicatus* foot may take as much as 10 minutes to accomplish. On the other hand, water can be eliminated within a few seconds as the snail contracts into its shell.

Naticids are shell borers. They drill into the shells of living molluscs to feed upon the animal inside, and are largely responsible for the symmetrical countersunk holes apparent on many shells (mostly bivalves) that wash ashore on Texas beaches (Fig. 10-3 I). Prey is captured and held by the foot in preparation for feeding. Boring is accomplished by a combination of mechanical (radular) and chemical (accessory boring gland) processes similar to those described for *Stramonita* in Chapter 3. As with *Stramonita*, the drilling process may take from 2 hours to 2 days to accomplish, depending upon the thickness of the shell of the prey. The proboscis is inserted into the drilled hole and the radula cuts away flesh. *Polinices* is a significant predator of offshore bivalves, often consuming more than one per day. With an abundance of available prey, *Polinices* can be selective. It is not unusual for the snail to grasp one bivalve beneath the metapodium of the foot and carry it around while searching for another bivalve that might be easier to drill.

P. duplicatus probably remains in the expanded condition most of its life. Unless danger threatens, it plows just below the surface of the sand in search of or feeding upon suitable bivalve prey. It will also feed upon other gastropods, including members of its own species. On the other hand, other sand predators such as the predatory sea stars (e.g., *Astropecten*) seek naticids. In the presence of sea stars many naticids secrete profuse quantities of mucus (Yonge and Thompson, 1976). *Sinum perspectivum* will do the same when handled by humans. The mucus may contain some substance noxious to naticid predators, but experiments with sea stars suggest that more likely it renders the snail too slippery to be grasped by asteroid tube feet.

Naticid egg cases are distinctive, although they vary in size and shape according to the species. Commonly called sand collars, the broad, coiled nidus straps consist of mucus-bound sand and tiny egg capsules, the latter embedded along the underside of the collar and containing developing embryos. A collar is formed beneath the sand as eggs and mucus are extruded from the naticid mantle cavity in a long, continuous sheet. It is shaped by the outer surface of the snail body. The sticky mucus binds sand on the outer surface of the collar and eventually sets to an almost rubbery consistency. *Polinices duplicatus* sand collars (Fig. 10-3 D1) are about 50 mm wide and up to 150 mm in diameter. During the reproductive season they wash ashore in large numbers. Those that remain in the water eventually disintegrate as the larvae emerge from the egg cases to enter the meroplankton.

Olive snails of the family Olividae are equally adept as sand burrowers, and easily recognized by their highly polished, streamlined shells with slit-like apertures. The olivid mantle and foot envelop the shell, polishing and protecting it from the abrasive sand. The most common Texas olive, *Oliva sayana* (Fig. 10-1 Z), occurs on outer shores just below the tide. It glides beneath the sand, with only a narrow inhalant siphon protruding at the surface. It progresses by advancing its foot into the sand and pulling its shell forward. Two smaller olivids, *Olivella minuta* (Fig. 10-1 U) and *Olivella dealbata* occur in Texas, the former more common along inlets of the northeastern coast and the latter prevailing off southern beaches and inlets.

The olivids are nocturnal predators and scavengers. They are not shell borers, but apparently crack shells by use of the radula and foot. *Oliva sayana* is known to feed upon *Donax, Laevicardium, Tellina, Nassarius* and a variety of dead fishes, shrimp, and other animals. Scavenged flesh is often held in a foot pouch prior to eating. Some live prey such as *Laevicardium vitellinum* apparently sense the presence of *O. sayana* and try to evade capture. They "flip about energetically" in aquaria which also contain the snail (Olsson & Crovo, 1968).

Oliva sayana deposits unattached egg capsules on the surface of the sand in the late summer. These hatch into veligers in 3 to 5 days (Olsson & Crovo, 1968). Dispersal is not only by free-swimming veligers, but also by the egg capsules picked up from the sand and carried away by currents.

Auger shells of the family Terebridae are also common in the lower intertidal outer shores, though not as conspicuous as the larger naticids. This high spired family is represented by three common species in Texas, *Terebra dislocata* (Fig. 10-1 Y), usually found in sand just below the tide along inlets, *Hastula salleana* (Fig. 10-1 D1) and *H. maryleeae*, which occur in the lower intertidal and subtidal of the outer sandy beaches. Terebrids burrow in the sand in a manner reminiscent of many bivalves. Their elongate foot is extended into the sand and terminally dilated to form an anchor. Columellar and pedal muscles then contract, pulling the streamlined shell through the sand. None of the Texas terebrids burrow deeply, and *T. dislocata* always occurs in the upper, well oxygenated layer above the redox potential discontinuity.

In addition to using the foot for burrowing, *Hastula*

salleana has been observed using it as a water "sail" to migrate seaward (Kornicker, 1961). Snails finding themselves in the swash zone apparently move or are pushed landward with the rising tide, but are unable to crawl seaward rapidly enough to avoid being stranded by the receding tide. As an occasional stronger surge washes the recently exposed beach, *H. salleana* raises out of the sand and extends its foot upward to catch the retreating swash. In this position one wave can carry the snail several meters seaward.

Typically, the Terebridae are toxoglossid gastropod predators which possess a highly modified radula and an associated poison gland. The *Hastula* species fall into this category, as they paralyze small sand-dwelling polychaetes with the radular toxin and then ingest them intact. *Terebra dislocata* represents a second group of auger shells which lack both radula and poison glands (Mollick, 1973). The exact mode of feeding in this species is not clear, but there is some evidence that *T. dislocata* is a deposit feeder.

Phalium granulatum (Fig. 10-1 X), the scotch bonnet, is the only common cassid along the Texas coast, although the tropical *Cypraecassis testiculus* is found occasionally. *Phalium* preys upon sand dollars and burrowing sea urchins by rasping a 2 mm hole into the echinoderm skeleton and inserting a proboscis to obtain the soft tissues.

The distorted triton, *Distorsio clathrata* (Fig. 10-1 H1) occupies deeper offshore sands, where it, too, probably feeds upon echinoderms and infaunal bivalves. It possesses an elongate, muscular proboscis (Lewis, 1972) apparently useful in probing narrow spaces for food. The life history and ecology of *D. clathrata* is poorly known, although D'Asaro (1969) provided a rather complete description of the early embryology. Spawning apparently occurs in the late summer or early fall. Rows of white egg capsules are attached to hard substrata, and gradually become pigmented as development proceeds. Each capsule holds 20 to 40 embryos, and a snail can produce 1500 capsules in 24 hours. Veliger larvae emerge after about two weeks.

Wentletraps (Epitoniidae) are predators which specialize in feeding upon the tissues or body fluids of cnidarian polyps, especially anemones. Eight species have been reported from Texas (Andrews, 1977), including *Epitonium angulatum* (Fig. 10-2 M) and *E. tollini* (Fig. 10-2 N). Several of the names eventually may prove to be synonyms.

The pyramidellids have carried fluid feeding to its ultimate conclusion. There are a number of ectoparasitic *Turbonilla* in Texas (e.g., *T. interrupta*, Fig. 10-2 O), known primarily by their shells from beach drift. Little is known about the specific habits of most Texas *Turbonilla*, especially the identity of the hosts which they parasitize. It is likely that, like other pyramidellids, they feed upon the body fluids of a variety of polychaetes, bivalves or other gastropods.

A final group of gastropod predators, the whelks, occur offshore, along the base of the jetties, in tidal channels and within the higher salinity bays. Whelks are characterized by having thick-walled shells with few whorls. Some, like *Busycon*, grow to exceed 20 cm, but many in Texas waters are much smaller. There are several families of whelk-like gastropods including the Buccinidae, Melongenidae, Fasciolariidae, and the somewhat more distantly related Nassariidae and Muricidae.

The most familiar whelks in the Gulf of Mexico belong to the melongenid genera *Busycon* and the recently elevated *Busycotypus*. Two species occur in shallow Texas waters. *Busycotypus spiratum* (Fig. 10-3 B) is the smaller whelk with a dextral (right-handed) aperture. The second species is identified as either *Busycon contrarium* (Conrad 1840) or *B. perversum* (Linnaeus 1758), both names reflecting the unusual sinistral (left-handed) aperture of most specimens. Sinistral *Busycon* range from New England to the Caribbean and have developed several local conchological races with significantly different shell forms. The absence of planktonic larvae in the genus has likely contributed to the development of localized differentiation. Some malacologists group all of the predominantly sinistral *Busycon* races or subspecies into a single species complex, with *B. perversum* (Fig. 10-3 C) the valid name according to priority. *Busycon perversum* is much larger than *Busycotypus spiratum* (345 mm vs 135 mm shell length). *Busycon perversum* shells from Texas are less spinose than those from other parts of the species range, but always more spinose than *Busycotypus spiratum*. Both have a powerful muscular foot and a small head. A proboscis is everted from the head during feeding.

The whelks are normally found in association with beds of either shoal grass, *Halodule wrightii*, or turtle grass, *Thalassia testudinum*. They also occur in bays where scattered clumps of oysters intergrade with patches of sand and mud, but rarely are found upon the oyster reefs themselves. Whelks once were thought to be primarily carrion scavengers. Although carrion is a part of the diet, these gastropods rely primarily upon living bivalves for food. Unlike the nati-

10-3. Subtidal fauna of Texas offshore sands and tidal inlets. **A.** Lined tulip shell, *Fasciolaria lilium*; **B.** Pear whelk, *Busycotypus spiratum*; **C.** Perverse whelk, *Busycon perversum*; **D.** Moon snail, *Polinices duplicatus*; **D1.** *P. duplicatus* "sand collar" with eggs; **E.** Bay scallop, *Argopecten irradians amplicostatus*; **F.** Ear shell, *Sinum perspectivum*; **G.** Cross-barred venus, *Chione cancellata*; **H.** Pointed nut clam, *Nuculana acuta*; **I.** Concentric nut clam, *Nuculana concentrica*, shell with naticid (moon snail) drill hole; **J.** Southern quahog, *Mercenaria campechiensis*; **K.** Constricted macoma, *Macoma constricta*; **L.** Fragile lucine, *Anodontia alba*; **M.** Buttercup lucine, *Lucina pectinata*; **N.** Dwarf surf clam, *Mulinia lateralis*; **O.** Stout tagelus, *Tagelus plebeius*; **P.** Angel wing, *Cyrtopleura costata*; **Q.** Jacknife clam, *Ensis minor*.

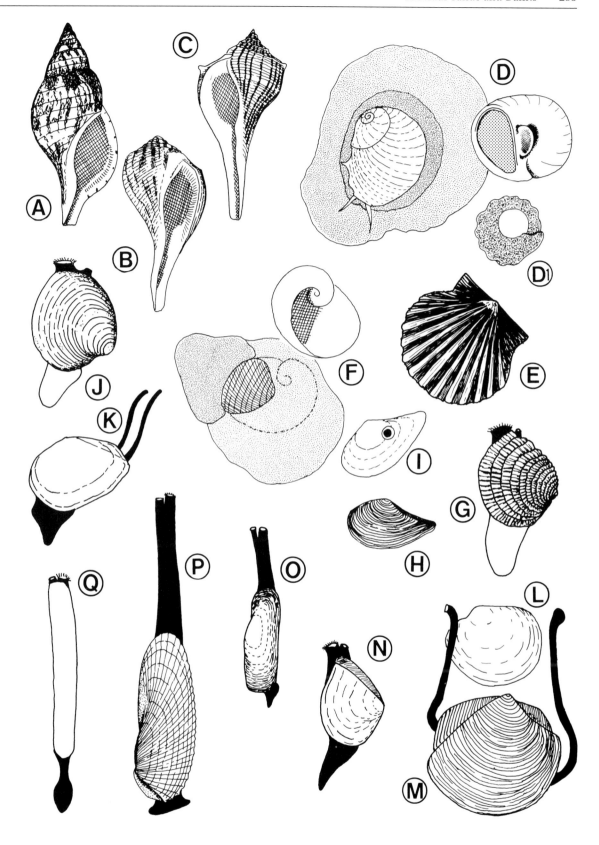

cids or muricids which drill their prey, the Melongenidae lack glands or a radula that can effect entry by boring through a shell. Rather, their small, delicate, stenoglossate radula located at the tip of the proboscis consists of many rows of three teeth, each row comprising a cuspate central tooth and a pair of laterals which are sharp and scissor-like in their cutting action.

Prey capture strategies adopted by these two whelks differ, with prey detection, stalking, inspection, grasping and attacking for each species following a highly ritualized sequence. Both grasp their bivalve prey with the muscular foot and inspect it with the head. *Busycon perversum*, with a large powerful foot, seeks "passive" bivalves as prey. It prefers shallow burrowing species such as *Chione cancellata* or *Carditamera floridana*, whose escape response is firmly to clamp valves together. A variety of other bivalves are also attacked less frequently. *Busycon perversum* opens a bivalve by wedging the lip of its siphonal canal between prey valves, forcing them open sufficiently to insert the everted proboscis. This large, powerful whelk can press its shell so firmly against the bivalve that pieces are chipped away from the valves until a hole is made large enough to allow the proboscis to be inserted (Magalhaes, 1948; Paine, 1962). *Fasciolaria lilium* (Fig. 10-1 E1) also is known to use its shell to pry open bivalve prey (Wells, 1958a), and *Muricanthus fulvescens* (Fig. 10-1 W) will use its short siphonal canal to chip bivalve shells (Wells, 1958b).

Busycotypus spiratum, with a smaller foot, seeks more "active" bivalves which possess gaping shells and which use flight as an escape mechanism. Common prey include the swimming scallop, *Argopecten irradians* or the rapidly burrowing razor shell, *Ensis minor*. It approaches the prey rapidly, grasping it by the foot, and dramatically inserting the proboscis between parted valves, although the siphonal channel or the shell may be inserted to prevent closure or escape (Magalhaes, 1948; Paine, 1962). The radula quickly begins scraping flesh from the surprised bivalve. *Busycotypus spiratum* also demonstrates a greater degree of opportunism than *B. perversum*, in that the former will also feed on conspecifics and other predatory snails such as *Polinices duplicatus*, *Fasciolaria lilium* and *Nassarius vibex*, as well as carrion.

With two sympatric species of closely related genera occupying similar habitats, it is natural to question how these species avoid resource overlap and competition. Certainly, the size difference between adults and their differential prey preference serves to minimize competition for food resources. Kent (1983a) has examined how juveniles of *Busycon contrarium* (= *B. perversum*) avoid resource overlap with *Busycotypus spiratum*. By manipulating field densities of these two species in Alligator Harbor, northwest Florida, he was able to show that competition was occurring between specimens of comparable size on grass flats but not among clumps of oysters. In choice experiments, *Busycon contrarium* preferred "active" prey, but was

both less efficient in capturing such prey and the loser to the more aggressive *Busycotypus spiratum* in contests over such food. Furthermore, competition between whelks along oyster bars is influenced by the stone crab, *Menippe*. The crab is a dominant predator of both oysters and whelks. The thinner shell of the normally more aggressive *Busycotypus spiratum* makes it more vulnerable to crab predation, thereby favoring survival of the sinistral species in this habitat.

Busycon perversum and *Busycotypus spiratum* are both slow growing and apparently long lived. Kent (1983b) has shown that *Busycotypus spiratum*, with a larger foot, crawls twice as fast as *B. perversum*. Reproduction occurs once a year in both species, copulation taking place in late autumn. Flask-shaped egg capsules are lain in March and crawling juveniles hatch in May.

There are several smaller whelks and related snails in Texas waters. The buccinids *Cantharus cancellarius* (Fig. 10-1 V) and *Pisania tincta* (Fig. 10-2 P) are predators of subtidal grass beds, rocks and shell mounds. They are often found alive by divers at the base of Texas jetties. The mud snail, *Nassarius vibex* (Fig. 10-2 Q), is most easily observed on mud flats in the higher salinity estuaries (Chapter 7), but it is equally abundant on subtidal offshore sands. It is a scavenger and, in turn, is fed upon by predatory whelks (e.g., *Fasciolaria*) or asteroids.

Two fasciolarids, *Fasciolaria lilium* (Figs. 10-1 E1; 10-3 A) and *F. tulipa* (Fig. 10-6 O) also occur in Texas, although the latter is relatively uncommon here. These two species constitute another sympatric species pair in the eastern Gulf of Mexico (Wells, 1970), usually avoiding direct competition by environmental partitioning. *Fasciolaria tulipa* lives subtidally in the grass beds where it searches for food day or night, whereas *F. lilium* is primarily nocturnal and commonly found in association with oyster beds or along the subtidal margins of tidal inlets and the higher salinity bays. *Fasciolaria lilium* is the smaller species, averaging about 60 mm in length; *F. tulipa* commonly exceeds 120 mm. The latter bears 25 to 40 interrupted spiral lines on the body whorl, whereas the former has only 4 to 8 uninterrupted primary lines.

Both species of tulip shells prey upon a variety of molluscs, including members of their own species. *Fasciolaria lilium* is especially fond of oysters (Wells, 1958a) and is known to occasionally prey upon the polychaetes *Diopatra* and *Onuphis*. When *F. lilium* encounters *F. tulipa*, it initiates a flipping escape response reminiscent of that performed by *Nassarius* in the presence of *Fasciolaria*. In turn, these snails are fed upon by other predatory gastropods, stone crabs (*Menippe* sp.), shame-face crabs (*Calappa* sp.) and sting rays (*Dasyatis* sp.).

Mating occurs in *F. lilium* during the early spring in western Florida (Wells, 1970). Even the receding tide which uncovers a copulating pair will not disturb the mating bond. After copulation, the female cements numerous flattened, trumpet-shaped capsules on shells or other hard substrata, each of which contain several dozen eggs. A few unfertilized eggs in each capsule are cannibalized by the developing embryos. Young snails crawl out of the capsules about a month after they are deposited. As with other whelks, there is no planktonic larval stage in *Fasciolaria*.

Muricanthus fulvescens (Fig. 10-1 W) is the largest muricid of the western Gulf of Mexico. Its spinose shell frequently exceeds a length of 130 mm, and is difficult to mistake for any other species. Large shells occasionally wash ashore, but they are more often dredged from offshore bars or tidal inlets. This species feeds upon a variety of bivalves. Unlike the related *Stramonita*, which enters bivalves by drilling, *M. fulvescens* employs the large foot to pry apart bivalve shells, providing a slit just large enough to enable a proboscis to be inserted (Wells, 1958b). It also spends considerable time buried motionless in the sand.

Predatory Starfish

Three predatory asteroids, *Luidia alternata* (Fig. 10-1 K1), *L. clathrata* and *Astropecten duplicatus* (Fig. 10-1 L1) are common in the offshore sands. The latter is usually smaller than the first two and readily distinguished from them by possessing rows of large plates along the margins of each arm. *Luidia alternata* is distinguished by alternating dark and light bands on each arm, whereas *L. clathrata*, although of similar size and shape, is uniformly light cream or flesh colored. Both species of *Luidia* attain a diameter of 25 cm. *Astropecten* is more common than *Luidia* in deeper offshore waters, but all are equally common near shore. These sea stars usually lie buried just below the surface, where they ingest benthic invertebrates and large amounts of bottom material. *Astropecten* feeds primarily upon small gastropods, whereas *Luidia alternata* ingests considerable numbers of Foraminifera in addition to gastropods (Hulings & Hemlay, 1963). Additional food items for all species include bivalves, small crustaceans, nematodes, ophiuroids, small echinoids, and at least some detritus. These are relatively primitive asteroids, having only a mouth but no anus. Indigestable material brought into the stomach must be regurgitated.

Cnidaria

In addition to the sessile Cnidaria that live attached to hard substrata (see below), there are a few species with adaptations that enable them to live upon the soft sands. The commensal anemone, *Calliactis tricolor*, (Fig. 10-1 A) has already been discussed. The sea pansy, *Renilla mulleri* (Fig. 10-1 N), is the most common colonial anthozoan on subtidal sands. This maroon pennatulid consists of a flattened disk joined to a short stalk or peduncle which anchors the colony in the sand. Several dozen polyps borne upon the upper surface of the disk emerge at night to feed upon microcrustaceans and other zooplankters. Shrimpers often collect large numbers of *Renilla* in their otter trawls.

The pipe cleaner sea pen, *Virgularia presbytes* (Fig. 10-2 W) is another pennatulid which has developed an even more effective way to keep its feeding polyps above the sand. Unlike *Renilla*, which has a relatively short, fleshy anchor stalk, *Virgularia* is equipped with a rigid, slender calcareous stalk or central rachis as much as 60 cm in length and upon which rows of polyps are borne near the top. The lower half to two-thirds of the rachis is barren, functioning only as a support to raise the sea pen polyps above the substratum. *Virgularia* litters a sandy bottom like hundreds of Roman candles awaiting a Fourth of July display. Storms occasionally uproot them, and currents wash them ashore in large numbers. *Virgularia presbytes* has been observed rarely in its living position offshore. Most of our knowledge of the pipe cleaner sea pen is from beach strandings, especially along the Texas coast from Galveston to northern Padre Island.

Decapod Crustaceans

A number of feeding strategies are employed by the great variety of decapod crustaceans on offshore sands and banks. It is more convenient to survey this diverse group according to taxonomic criteria than by the trophic levels or the feeding guilds that they occupy. Although we restrict our discussions of benthic crustaceans to the decapods, several other crustacean groups are equally or better represented in this habitat. The decapods, however, include the largest and most conspicuous species of shallow-water crustaceans.

Penaeids: The Shrimps

A great variety of shrimp-like crustaceans reside in the offshore waters of the northwestern Gulf. Many of these resemble each other although they are in reality classified into a number of different families and higher taxonomic categories. The caridean shrimps of the genera *Alpheus*, *Palaemonetes*, *Palaemon* and *Hippolyte* are characterized by the third legs not being chelate. They occur primarily in the sea, but also have a few estuarine and freshwater representatives. The penaeid shrimps, on the other hand, bear chela on the third legs and are more typically marine. They include the best studied and most economically important shrimp-like crustaceans. Many volumes have been devoted to their biology and fisheries. Consult Burkenroad (1934), Hildebrand (1954), Roberts & Pequegnat (1970), or Williams (1984) for information and references beyond the scope of this treatment.

Penaeid shrimps offer excellent examples of the continuity of habitat from the tidally influenced inshore waters to the more constant offshore benthic realm. Most penaeids have a similar life cycle involving offshore spawning, larval migration into shallow coastal bays, juvenile development in shallow salt marsh or mangrove nursery environments, and migration of adults back to the sea. Different species avoid competition by occupying estuarine habitats at different times, and having different substratum and depth preferences, especially offshore. The timing of spawning or movement also varies according to the species.

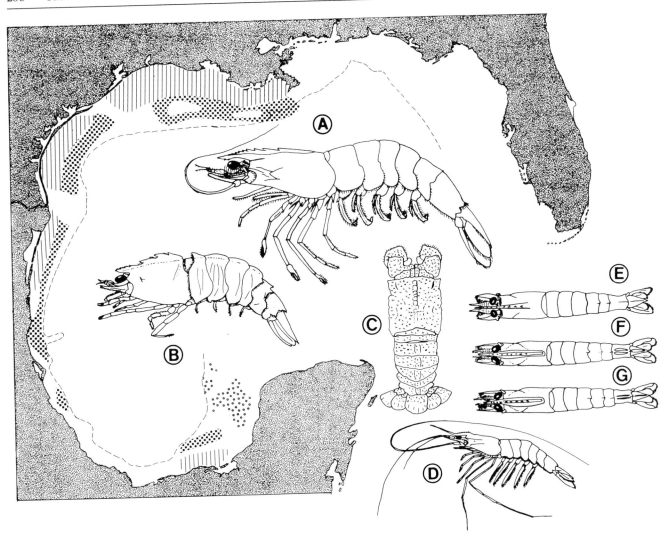

10-4. Shrimps and kin. Shrimp "grounds" are indicated on the map as follows (after Hildebrand, 1954):

   ▦ White shrimp (*Penaeus setiferus*)

   ▦ Brown shrimp (*Penaeus aztecus*)

   ▦ Pink shrimp (*Penaeus duorarum*)

A. Brown shrimp, *Penaeus aztecus*; **B.** Rock shrimp, *Sicyonia brevirostris*; **C.** Spanish lobster, *Scyllarides nodifer*; **D.** Seabob, *Xiphopenaeus kroyeri*; **E.** White shrimp, *Penaeus setiferus*; **F.** Brown shrimp, *Penaeus aztecus*; **G.** Pink shrimp, *Penaeus duorarum*.

Specific variations will be noted as each species is discussed in the paragraphs below.

The brown shrimp, *Penaeus aztecus* (Fig. 10-4 A & F), is the most important commercial shrimp of the northwestern Gulf, with the annual catch usually exceeding that of all other species. It occurs throughout the Gulf and Caribbean region and as far north as Massachusetts, but it seems to be most abundant along the Texas coast and on the Campeche Bank off Mexico. As adults, brown shrimps prefer silty substrata (Hildebrand, 1954, 1955; Springer & Bullis, 1954) in waters deeper than occupied by other commercially important penaeids (Fig. 10-4). Adult population densities peak in depths between 27 and 55 m (Williams, 1984). Brown shrimps are detritivores which feed upon the organic debris that accumulates on the surface of

the bottom. Feeding usually occurs at night. When not feeding, *P. aztecus* burrows for shelter.

The reproductive activity and life cycle of all commercially important penaeid species are similar, varying in certain minor details and timing. The life cycle of the brown shrimp will serve as a model, and descriptions of other species will emphasize differences from this model. Spawning occurs offshore year-round, especially in deeper waters, but there is a peak spawn in the fall. Males transfer spermatophores to the females in relatively shallow offshore waters. The females retain these encapsulated sperm bundles intact for varying periods of time as they continue to migrate offshore. Eventually eggs are discharged from the oviducts through gonopores at the base of the third pair of walking legs and fertilized by sperm released from the spermatophores. For brown shrimp, this typically occurs in water depths greater than 18 m. Significantly fewer males are found at these depths, suggesting that a female brown shrimp may not expend all spermatophores in a single spawning, but save some for later spawns (Burkenroad, 1939).

The buoyant fertilized eggs undergo rapid development as they rise toward the surface. Within 24 hours they hatch into planktonic nauplius larvae. Brown shrimps remain in the plankton for several weeks as they pass through a number of nauplius, protozoea, and mysis larval stages. Eventually they molt into a postlarval stage that begins a migration from offshore waters into the shallow coastal estuaries. Recruitment of juvenile shrimps on estuarine nursery grounds peaks during the spring months (Copeland & Truitt, 1966). Some studies suggest that postlarval migration into estuaries through tidal inlets peaks at night during spring flood tides (Copeland & Truitt, 1966; Williams & Deubler, 1968; Williams, 1969) but others find little correlation of peak migrations with tide or diurnal cycle (King, 1971). Brown shrimp grow rapidly on the shallow bayfloor nursery grounds during the summer. Their nursery areas are essentially the same as those of the pink shrimp, but as the majority of the respective populations occupy these areas at different times of the year, competition is minimized. As the juvenile brown shrimps increase in size, they migrate from the shallow nursery areas to progressively deeper water within the estuary, and eventually leave it for the offshore spawning grounds.

The white shrimp, *Penaeus setiferus* (Fig. 10-4 E), are the second most important commercial species of the northwestern Gulf. They range from New York to Yucatan, and are the primary commercial penaeid species in areas where brown shrimps are not abundant. Adult white shrimps are usually found in shallower waters closer to shore than brown shrimps, and the spawning grounds are correspondingly shallower, in depths from shore to 30 m. They prefer muddy substrata, both as adults offshore and as juveniles in the estuarine nurseries. White shrimps are less likely to burrow than the other penaeids. They are effective osmoregulators in lower salinity waters (McFarland & Lee, 1963), and populations increase following years of abundant rainfall (Hildebrand & Gunter, 1953; Gunter & Hildebrand, 1954).

White shrimps spawn at least once between March and September in the northwestern Gulf, and possibly twice, spring and fall. Larval development is temperature dependent, with postlarval stages reached within two weeks at 30°C but about 3 weeks at 22°C (Lindner & Cook, 1970). Migration into the estuarine nursery grounds occurs during the summer months, and usually following the peak migration of postlarval brown shrimps. Juvenile white shrimps seek shallower, lower salinity portions of bays for the initial nursery. They prefer somewhat muddier sediments than *P. aztecus*, but occupy shared nursery grounds later in the season, after most brown shrimps have moved to deeper waters. As they increase in size, white shrimps also move to deeper bay waters, and eventually back to the offshore spawning grounds.

The pink shrimp, *Penaeus duorarum* (Fig. 10-4 G), is common in the northwestern Gulf, but rarely in sufficient numbers for commercial harvest. It is much more common on Campeche Bank (Fig. 10-4), and is accordingly an important component of the shrimp fishery in that region. Pink shrimps prefer nearshore calcareous sands, muds, or sand-mud mixtures that often include shell debris, a habitat that is poorly represented off Texas or Louisiana coasts. They seem to be most abundant in water depths of less than 35 m. They usually spend daylight hours within a burrow, emerging at night to forage (Fuss, 1964; Fuss & Ogren, 1966). Like other penaeids, pink shrimps are opportunistic omnivores relying primarily upon superficial benthic detritus for food (Odum & Heald, 1972; Idyll et al., 1967). Feeding activity diminishes as water temperature decreases (Fuss & Ogren, 1966), yet this species is better able to withstand low salinity and low temperature than the other commercially important penaeids. It is not uncommon to find *P. duorarum* overwintering within lower salinity portions of some estuaries (Williams, 1984).

Pink shrimps spawn year-round in some tropical or subtropical localities (Jones, et al., 1970, describing spawning activity at Tortugas, Florida), but one spring peak characterizes spawning in temperate waters. Development from hatching nauplius to early postlarvae usually require less than three weeks. Postlarval migration into embayments occurs primarily during the summer at approximately the same time postlarval white shrimps are moving into the nursery areas. Pink shrimps prefer less muddy shoals of slightly higher salinity than those occupied by white shrimps. Like most penaeids, they develop rapidly and move to deeper parts of the bay as they grow larger.

White shrimps are easily distinguished from brown or pink shrimp, but the latter two are more difficult to differentiate. *Penaeus setiferus* has antennae which extend more than twice the length of the body. In comparison, the antennae of *P. aztecus* (Fig. 10-4 A) or *P. duorarum* are less than a third of the body length. The rostrum of *P. setiferus* arises near the middle of the carapace and is not flanked by a groove at its base (Fig. 10-4 E). *Penaeus aztecus* and *P. duorarum* have rostra which extend almost to the posterior termination of the carapace and are flanked by distinctive grooves (Figs. 10-4 F & G). These species also possess a pair of dorsal grooves on the sixth abdominal segment. These grooves are wide enough to receive a thumbnail in *P. aztecus*, but much narrower in *P. duorarum*. Adult pink shrimps also usually possess a distinct reddish spot between the third and forth abdominal segments, but this is not a reliable character for juveniles. Furthermore, a few adult brown shrimps sometimes also display a pigmented spot in this location. The differentiation of young brown and pink shrimps is often difficult.

Although the three foregoing species are the primary commercial shrimps of the Gulf of Mexico, there are several additional species, some of which have been harvested commercially. The seabob, *Xiphopenaeus kroyeri* (Fig. 10-4 D) is a nearshore species which sometimes ventures into the higher salinity portions of estuaries. It is easily distinguished from the other penaeids by its elongate, upcurved rostral spine and the extremely elongate third and forth pairs of walking legs. Seabobs are large enough to be used as a seafood, but they are rarely taken in sufficient quantities to make a commercial fisheries economically feasible. They are sometimes collected and sold for bait.

The rock shrimps *Sicyonia brevirostris* (Fig. 10-4 B) and the smaller *S. dorsalis* have a hard, thick integument which make these species less desirable as marketable shellfish than the penaeids. Nevertheless, the former species has become a moderately important commercially harvested shellfish within the last 20 years. Both occur offshore most commonly from shallow water to depths of about 70 m, but specimens have been taken from much deeper waters. *Sicyonia brevirostris* seems to prefer sandy or shell bottoms, whereas *S. dorsalis* is more common on mud. The latter is more common in the northwestern Gulf than the former. *Sicyonia brevirostris* seems to be especially abundant on sand banks off the northeastern tip of Yucatan. Like the penaeids, they are most active at night, but seem to be more predatory than omnivorous, feeding upon molluscs, other crustaceans, and polychaetes (Kennedy *et al.*, 1977). The carapace of older specimens of *Sicyonia dorsalis* is often fouled by the barnacle *Balanus amphitrite*.

Trachypenaeus constrictus and *T. similus* are small penaeids that rarely attain a sufficient size for commercial exploitation. The former is most common on shell-sand bottoms, and the latter on muddy or fine sand silt bottoms to a depth of about 80 m.

Palinurans

The spiny lobster, *Panulirus argus* (Fig. 11-6 F) is the best known Atlantic palinuran. It is most commonly found in association with rock or reef habitats in the tropical Gulf and Caribbean, but occurs in the northwestern Gulf, especially in association with hard banks. It is discussed in the next chapter.

Spanish lobsters barely resemble spiny lobsters, although they are relatively closely related. There are several species in the Gulf of Mexico, most of which increase in abundance toward the south. *Scyllarides nodifer* (Fig. 10-4 C) is the largest. It commonly occurs on sand or mud, but some other species are restricted to hard banks, shell debris or among rocks (Lyons, 1970). Spanish lobsters have short, oddly flattened antennae, and relatively small, unspecialized legs. When viewed from above, the antennae appear as a pair of roughly oval appendages extending in front of the broad, tuberculate carapace.

Scyllarides nodifer is the only species of Spanish lobster of sufficient size for human consumption, but it is rarely taken in sufficient quantity to justify commercial exploitation. Spanish lobsters nevertheless are important prey for several fishes including three species of groupers and the tiger shark (Randall, 1967).

Anomuran Crabs

There are several suspension feeding anomuran crabs, characterized by a normal abdomen reflected beneath the thorax, associated with the offshore sands. The porcellanid *Euceramus praelongus* (Fig. 10-1 L) resembles a mole crab in shape and habits. It lacks the feathery antennae characteristic of that group, but adequately employs its bristly antennae to trap floating particles. It burrows backwards into sand or shell debris with only the antennae and head emergent for feeding (Pearse *et al.*, 1942).

The remaining suspension feeding crustaceans are closely related to mole crabs, being members of the Albuneidae. *Lepidopa websteri* (Fig. 10-1 J) is found most commonly in the sandy intertidal in association with *Emerita*, but also occurs offshore. Conversely, *Albunea paretii* (Fig. 10-1 K) is the typical offshore species, but, as we have noted, it is also common within the intertidal sands of Sargent Beach, Texas.

In the absence of cobble or rocky substrata another porcellanid, *Porcellana sayana* (Fig. 10-1 G1), may be found as a commensal on shells occupied by the hermit crab, *Petrochirus diogenes* (Fig. 10-1 F1). The latter is the largest hermit crab in the Gulf of Mexico. It is common on offshore sands, tidal inlets and the higher salinity bays. It feeds upon detritus by disturbing the sediment with walking legs and chelae, and filtering organic material from this suspension using maxilliped strainers.

Brachyuran Crabs

The most conspicuous crabs of the shallow offshore sands are the Brachyura, characterized by a reduced, symmetrical abdomen usually carried tightly flexed beneath the cephalothorax. Of these, members of the family Portunidae are perhaps the most often encountered. They are easily recognized by the paddle-like fifth walking legs, (which are used for swimming) and an unusually imposing pair of large sharply pointed chelipeds or pincers. Called swimming crabs, they are equally adept as sand burrowers, and frequently seek refuge below the sand when resting or threatened. Several species of portunids occur just off Texas beaches. The commercially important blue crab, *Callinectes sapidus* (Fig. 10-1 E), occurs here, but it is much more commonly encountered in Texas bays (Chapter 7). The characteristic portunid of the nearshore sands is the speckled crab, *Arenaeus cribrarius* (Fig. 10-1 C). The tan or olive brown speckled carapace is distinctive, setting this species apart from all other Texas portunids. It prefers the shallow agitated waters just below the surf zone, and is almost never found within bays. It is rarely seen most of the year, but in August and early September ovigerous females are commonly observed swimming in the receding surf of southern Texas and northern Mexico beaches.

Two other portunids, *Portunus spinimanus* (Fig. 10-1 D) and *P. gibbesi* (Fig. 10-1 F), are sometimes encountered on nearshore sands, although they are more common farther offshore or in the deeper waters of bays. The carapace of both species is reddish brown and distinctly pubescent, but only *P. gibbesi* has naked iridescent areas along the spinous anteriolateral margins. The front sides of the walking legs of this species are also distinctly iridescent, and the chelipeds are carmine red.

In addition to these common portunids, species typical of more tropical waters occasionally appear in Texas offshore sands. The maroon portunid, *Cronius ruber* (Fig. 10-1 G) is widely distributed on both sides of the tropical Atlantic and it also occurs in the tropical eastern Pacific. It prefers subtidal reef habitats, but is an occasional inhabitant of Texas offshore banks. Its color and the alternating pattern of large and small spines on the anterior margin of the carapace are distinctive.

The shame-face or box crab, *Calappa sulcata* (Fig. 10-1 H) usually lies buried just beneath the subtidal sand. It bears thin, spindly walking legs concealed below a box-like carapace. Expanded chelae virtually hide the front of the carapace and provide this crab its colorful common name. When lying buried in the sand at rest, the vertically flattened chelae form the front wall of a sand-free space near the body through which respiratory water is moved to the gills.

Calappa emerges from the sand to hunt for food. It is particularly fond of hermit crabs but will also eat living gastropods. The right chela is specialized for opening gastropod shells. *Calappa* scurries along the surface, widely sweeping the sand with its walking legs in search of food, almost as if blindly responding to tactile, not visual cues. Search activity increases as the crab approaches the vicinity of possible prey. Upon finding an occupied gastropod shell, the crab moves it between the body and the chelae. A movable finger on the right chela bears a large tooth that fits between two elevated ridges on the fixed finger. *Calappa* positions the outer lip of the captured shell between these ridges and forcefully crushes it. After repositioning the shell, the crab continues peeling away shell material until the contents are fully exposed and eaten (Shoup, 1968).

Red spots on a pale yellow carapace mark the colorful calappid, *Hepatus epheliticus* (Fig. 10-1 B) as one of the most distinctive crustaceans of the nearshore subtidal sand banks. Empty calico crab carapaces frequently wash ashore on Gulf beaches, indicating the abundance of *Hepatus*, but the crab is infrequently seen alive. The anemone, *Calliactis tricolor* (Fig. 10-1 A), commonly occurs as a commensal on living *Hepatus*. There is usually one anemone per crab, attaching to it near the middle of the dorsal carapace surface. *Calliactis* apparently is the sole benefactor in the association, using the crab as one of the few solid sub-

strata on the sandy sea floor and probably scavenging bits of food as the crab feeds (Carlgren & Hedgpeth, 1952; Cutress *et al.*, 1970).

The Dromiidae are a group of mostly small, fuzzy crabs which shelter themselves beneath bits of living debris. Unlike the decorator crabs (Majidae) which affix living material to their carapaces, the dromiids use rear legs to hold bits of sponge, seaweed or tunicate colonies upon their back. *Dromidia antillensis* (Fig. 10-2 H) uses its chelae to cut and shape a piece of living sponge so that its outline corresponds to that of the crab body. When the trimming is completed, the rear legs hold the sponge in place as the crab roams about in search of food. The association between crab and sponge may be more than simple camouflage, for experiments have shown that predators such as the octopus will not attack a crab holding particular kinds of sponges (Kaestner, 1970).

The purse crab, *Persephona aguilonaris* (Fig. 10-1 I) is another distinctive crustacean. It has a globular granulated carapace carried upon gracile walking legs. The chelae are also rather streamlined. It usually lies buried in muddy sand with only the anterior portion of the carapace exposed. The common name is derived from the purselike brood chamber on the penultimate abdominal segment of the female. Ovigerous specimens are found throughout the late spring and summer.

The pentagon crab, *Heterocrypta granulata* (Fig. 10-2 V), is a curious little crab with a dark, angular carapace and elongate chelae which resemble flakes of shell. This cryptic species is usually associated with shelly bottoms, and is sometimes a resident on oyster reefs within embayments. Like the numerous additional smaller decapods of the offshore bottoms, its habits are poorly known.

Several decapods live as commensals within or upon other offshore biota. For example, the pea crab, *Pinnotheres maculatus*, is a commensal of several burrowing worms and bivalves. It and the closely related oyster pea crab, *P. ostreum*, are more common in Texas bays (Chapter 5), but *P. maculatus* also can be found in shallow offshore sands on the gills of *Atrina*. The young of both sexes and adult male *P. maculatus* live free as hard-shelled, non-obligate commensals, preferring the shelter of sea grass beds, but presumably surviving on the outer subtidal sands in the absence of vegetation. Adult females are always associated with a bivalve or polychaete host, but relatively unselective as to which of several host species mantle cavities or burrows it will occupy (Sastry & Menzel, 1962). The female body is soft, an adaptation to minimize irritation to host soft tissues (Kruczynski, 1971).

Free-living juveniles and males feed while swimming. Setose second and third pairs of walking legs are used to filter detritus and phytoplankton from the water (Caine, 1975). Adult females steal food from their filter feeding hosts. They cling to bivalve ctenidia, pushing the fourth pair of highly setose walking legs along the ctenidial filaments and trapping food-laden mucous strands. This material is transferred from the walking legs to the chelipeds, which, in turn, pass it to the mouth. In the process of feeding, the pea crabs may damage host tissues (Kruczynski, 1975). Their presence is at least detrimental to the host, as reflected by diminished growth rates of infected vs noninfected bivalves (Kruczynski, 1972).

Ovigerous females release free-swimming larvae during the summer. Upon settlement, juvenile *P. maculatus* seek the shelter of a bivalve host, the females becoming typically soft-bodied. By mid-autumn, females molt into a hard-shelled stage and, unlike *P. ostreum* females which remain in the bivalve host, leave to participate in a copulatory swarm with swimming males (Pearce, 1964). After copulation, the females settle from the water to find another host and molt into a soft stage again. The females over-winter holding sperm packets obtained during the copulatory swarm. They pass through several additional molts, eventually becoming ovigerous near the end of their first year.

Polychaete Feeding Guilds

The most numerous infaunal animals with respect to the number of individuals and possibly numbers of species in the nearshore sands are the soft-bodied, segmented worms (Fauchald, 1977). For example, Hubbard (1977) recovered 183 species of polychaetes from sands and muds at a depth of about 50 m in the northwestern Gulf of Mexico. Almost all of the nearshore polychaetes are burrowers, but some plow directly through sand, whereas others build permanent or semipermanent tubes in which they spend their lives.

Feeding strategies also vary among the polychaetes. Fauchald & Jumars (1979) present an excellent and comprehensive account of polychaete feeding groups or guilds. They recognize 24 different feeding guilds among the polychaetes. In subtidal sand, the largest guild includes species which derive nutrition by ingesting the sediment in which they live (Hubbard, 1977). Species employing more sophisticated methods for deposit feeding occupy a separate guild. Many polychaetes are predators which actively pursue prey, others are predators which wait for food to come to them, and still others are scavengers or omnivores. A few polychaetes are suspension feeders. Despite the great diversity of feeding methodologies employed by polychaetes, Fauchald & Jumars (1979) estimate that the food eaten by polychaetes is known for fewer than 10 percent of the species. In the paragraphs to follow, we will not be able to document all of the infaunal worms which occur off Texas shores, or even all of the feeding guilds. We will describe some of the more common species, and organize the discussion according to the more common feeding strategies.

Nonselective Deposit Feeders

Many subtidal polychaetes eat their way through the substratum, extracting nutrients from the sediments in which they live. Others may be more restricted as to where they obtain deposits (i.e., like *Clymenella*

torquata, which lives in a tube) (Fig. 10-5 A & A1), but they remain unselective with respect to what is ingested. These are the nonselective deposit feeding polychaetes. Unlike bivalve deposit feeders, which leave behind a telltale shell to mark their presence when they die, the soft-bodied polychaetes leave little trace of their passing. In the nearshore sediments off Texas barrier beaches, these worms often constitute the most numerically abundant and diverse component of the infauna. With respect to only the polychaetes, Hubbard (1977) found nonselective deposit feeders to account for about 41 percent of the individuals and 28 percent of the species in a small offshore area in the northwestern Gulf of Mexico.

The Capitellidae, Orbiniidae, Magelonidae and Paraonidae include some of the best examples of nonselective deposit feeding polychaetes, although several other families contribute representatives to this feeding guild. Most of these worms burrow through sediments without constructing permanent tubes, although the capitellids may construct semi-permanent mucus-lined galleries. Capitellids resemble earthworms in shape and habits, especially with respect to eating their way through the sediments. Members of this family often thrive in polluted environments. The body is cylindrical, elongate and frequently tapered at both ends. Parapodia are so poorly developed in the capitellids and the prostomium is often so simple that this family is frequently confused with marine oligochaetes. *Capitella* cf. *capitata* (Fig. 10-5 B) is an elongate (100 X 2 mm) blood-red worm with a small conical head bearing a pair of eyes and setae on the peristomium. It is a cosmopolitan species, occurring in shallow subtidal sediments throughout the world. In England, it lives about two years, becoming sexually mature near the end of the first (Warren, 1976). Even in this seasonally variable locality, spawning occurs asynchronously throughout the year.

Hubbard (1977) lists 9 species of capitellids from the northwestern Gulf of Mexico, with *Mediomastus californiensis* (Fig. 10-5 H) the most common. It is a small worm, 10 to 20 mm in length, and lacks eyes, palps, or tentacles on the head. *Capitella* cf. *capitata* and *M. californiensis* are common in shallow waters.

The Orbiniidae also eat their way through soft sediments, ingesting large quantities of sand to obtain surface-adsorbed organic detritus. *Scoloplos rubra* (Fig. 10-5 D) and the similar *S. capensis* are two common species in Texas sands. Both reach about 60 mm in length and have conical prostomia which lack any appendages. Dorsal branchiae (gills) arise on the 5th or 6th segment in *S. rubra*, but not until the 13th or 14th segment on *S. capensis*. The former is red; the latter bears brown stripes across several anterior segments. These worms contract into tight spirals when taken from the substratum and are easily broken.

Aricidea fragilis (Fig. 10-5 G) is larger than most paraonids, reaching a length of 30 mm. The genus is characterized by possessing a slender median antenna and two small circular eyes near the rear margins of

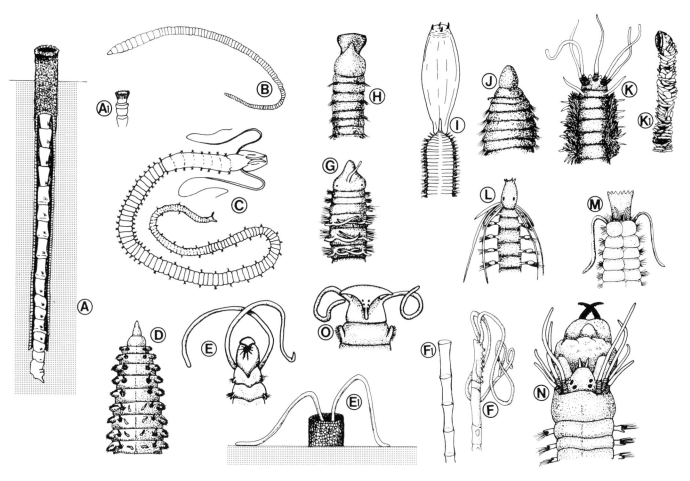

10-5. Subtidal Polychaeta. **A.** Bamboo worm, *Clymenella torquata*; **A1.** *C. torquata*, tail; **B.** *Capitella* cf. *capitata*; **C.** *Magelona riojai*; **D.** Red thread worm, *Scoloplos rubra*; **E.** *Spio pettiboneae*, ventral head; **E1.** *S. pettiboneae*, palps and sand tube; **F.** Parchment worm, *Spiochaetopterus costarum*; **F1.** *S. costarum*, tube; **G.** *Aricidea fragilis*; **H.** *Mediomastus californiensis*; **I.** Blood worm, *Glycera americana*; **J.** Thread worm, *Lumbrineris impatiens*; **K.** Chimney tube worm, *Diopatra cuprea*; **K1.** *D. cuprea*, chimney of tube; **L.** Paddle worm, *Phyllodoce mucosa*; **M.** Scale worm, *Sthenelais boa*; **N.** Clam worm, *Nereis succinea*; **O.** Mud worm, *Spiophanes bombyx*.

the head. Beginning on about the 5th segment and extending back 30 more, pairs of short, cylindrical gills rise from the dorsal body surface. The head of *A. fragilis* is white, followed by bright red thoracic segments. Posterior segments grade from red to white to green. This species burrows in mud or sand, but prefers silty sand.

The Magelonidae are a small group of sedentary burrowing worms characterized by a spoon-shaped prostomium which is flanked by a pair of elongate papillate palps. Members of the closely related tube dwelling Spionidae are selective deposit feeders which use the palps to sweep the surface of a substratum for detritus. The Magelonidae do not construct a permanent tube or burrow, but utilize the palps in a manner similar to that of the spionids. *Magelona riojai* (Fig. 10-5 C) is the most common representative of this family in the northwestern Gulf of Mexico. It is readily identified by the blunt tip of the spoon-shaped prostomium, the

distinctive two regions of the body, and other specialized characteristics (Jones, 1963). It is more common offshore than along Texas beaches.

The final example of a nonselective deposit feeder, the bamboo worm, *Clymenella torquata* (Fig. 10-5 A), constructs a permanent cylindrical tube reinforced by cemented sand grains. The tube is vertical, open at the top and unlined at the bottom. The worm lies upside down within it, and with insufficient space to turn around. It uses a crown-like terminal segment of its body (Fig. 10-5 A1) to close the upper end of the tube, whereas the lower end opens directly into the sediment. Central body segments of *Clymenella* are elongate, with junctions between them swollen like the joints of bamboo (hence the common name). The worm is usually brick red with segmental junctions a bright red. Some specimens appear greenish.

The blunt head lacks appendages, and the mouth opens to the side. It contains a conical buccal mass and eversible cylindrical proboscis that it thrusts directly into the substratum (i.e., the head lies directly against sediment, not within a gallery at the bottom of the tube). Sediment adhering to mucus secreted onto the buccal mass and proboscis is passed by cilia into the pharynx as the feeding apparatus is withdrawn (Kudenov, 1977). The feeding process is completed in just a few seconds, and is repeated many times before *Clymenella* withdraws its entire body into the tube. It then backs toward the top of the tube and carefully exposes the posterior coronal segment to the exterior, defecating indigestible sand grains and other particles passed through the gut onto the sea floor.

Clymenella torquata has a short spawning season apparently triggered when water temperatures reach 12 to 14°C in the spring (Mangum, 1964). This polychaete produces free-swimming trochophore larvae which likely accounts for its broad geographic distribution.

Selective Deposit Feeders

Hubbard (1977) found selective deposit feeders of the northwestern Gulf of Mexico comprised almost one quarter of the offshore polychaetes (23.5 percent of the 183 species collected) but with few of the species occurring in large numbers. He recorded six families (Ampharetidae, Cirratulidae, Heterospionidae, Poecilochaetidae, Spionidae, and Terebellidae) with selective deposit feeding representatives, but with the Spionidae contributing more than twice as many species as all of the other families combined. Of the 20 or so spionids from the offshore sands, *Spio pettiboneae* (Fig. 10-5 E, E1) and *Spiophanes bombyx* (Fig. 10-5 O) are representative of the family. The latter is especially common just offshore, especially along the northern coast (Keith & Hulings, 1965).

Most of the sand-dwelling spionids construct fragile tubes of cemented sand which project a short distance above the bottom. Two elongate tentacular palps which project from the head of the worm are used for feeding. They are extended out the opening of the tube (Fig. 10-5 E1) and either swept through the water or, more often, moved over the detritus-rich layer just above the bottom. Detritus is collected by mucus secreted by the palps and moved along ciliated channels toward the mouth. Particles too large to fit within the channels are discarded.

Suspension Feeders

The suspension feeding polychaetes are not an important component of the offshore sands in the northwestern Gulf of Mexico. Hubbard (1977) found this group to account for less than four percent of the polychaete species and less than one percent of the individuals. The Sabellidae, which constitute an important group of suspension feeding worms in tropical reef habitats, contribute several species to the offshore sands, but none are especially common. The Oweniidae and Chaetopteridae also contribute species, the

latter including the unusual tube worm, *Spiochaetopterus costarum* (Fig. 10-5 F, F1).

Unlike the estuarine *Chaetopterus variopedatus* (Fig. 7-10 E), which constructs a U-shaped tube opening to the surface at both ends, *Spiochaetopterus* occupies a thin, vertical tube, only the tip of which projects above the sand. The length of the tube may exceed 20 cm, but its diameter is rarely more than about 2 mm. *Spiochaetopterus* can readily turn around within it. The tube is formed in half-cylinder sections by secretions from the ventral anterior surface of the worm body (Barnes, 1964). Each section is marked by distinctive annulated joints. The bottom of the tube is closed by a similarly secreted button-like partition, complete with several "button holes." *Spiochaetopterus* can remove and reform the bottom partition or the side walls of the tube, using enlarged, bladelike 4th setae to cut out unwanted sections.

Like other chaetopterids, *Spiochaetopterus* passes water through its tube to obtain food. Ciliated notopodial lobes on the middle body segments draw water into the tube from the upper open end, and force it out through the perforated ventral partition into the surrounding interstitial sand. The notopodial lobes also secrete mucous bags (up to 13 in *Spiochaetopterus*) which trap particulates entering the tube with water currents. The end of each mucous bag is gathered into a ball by ciliated cupules located dorsomedially in each central body segment. When food balls reach a particular size, they are moved forward within a mid-dorsal ciliated groove to the mouth (Barnes, 1964).

A pair of elongate palps at the anterior end of the body help to clear debris from the open end of the tube and eliminate feces from the body. A deep ciliated groove on the dorsal surface of each palp (reminiscent of the spionids) carries trapped particulates to the mouth, although palp feeding provides only a minor source of food. A second, smaller groove lies beside the first, lined by distally-beating cilia. Rejected particles, debris and feces are moved into this groove, moved to the tip of the palp, and deposited outside the tube.

Predators and Scavengers

The paddle worm, *Phyllodoce mucosa* (Fig. 10-5 L), is one of the more agile polychaete predators. Paddle-shaped parapodia along the sides of the body propel the slender worm through the sand. It seeks unarmed, soft-bodied prey which it captures by means of an eversible jawless proboscis extended from the blunt cone-like head. This worm occurs intertidally but is usually more common offshore. The burrowing scale worm, *Sthenelais boa* (Fig. 10-5 M) is another active sand predator that also captures prey with an eversible, knobby, and very muscular proboscis. It occurs in sands from the lower intertidal to the outer shelf margin. *S. boa* reaches 70 mm in length and 3 to 4 mm in width. Each of the 100 or more pairs of scales (elytra) along the back of the worm carry a characteristic row of papillae along their outer margins.

The clam worm, *Nereis succinea* (Fig. 10-5 N), is somewhat more common near shore than the two preceding species, and also occurs in estuarine habitats. Armed with an impressive pair of jaws on a relatively short proboscis, *N. succinea* feeds on a variety of living invertebrates. It is also known to be a scavenger, and Goerke (1971) maintains that this species feeds primarily upon detritus. Clam worms are active burrowers that plow through sediments or form semi-permanent fragile sandy tube galleries glued together by mucus. Like many other nereids, this species reproduces by epitoky.

The blood worms, *Glycera americana* (Fig. 10-5 I) and *G. tessellata*, have perfected the art of sand gallery formation and lie-and-wait predation. *Glycera* is an excellent burrower but usually considered a poor swimmer (Klawe & Dickie, 1957; Dean, 1978). When placed in water it moves to the bottom in awkward corkscrew spirals. Upon touching the substratum, the purpose of the twisting becomes apparent. It continues to spiral, and within a matter of seconds it disappears below the surface, apparently screwing itself into the mud or sand.

Glycera constructs a complex gallery of interconnecting burrows in soft sediments, with several loops opening at the surface. Like a spider on its web, the blood worm lies motionless in one of the loops waiting to detect telltale surface vibrations that indicate the approach of prey. *Glycera* detects movement and the location of prey by subtle changes in water pressure. It creeps slowly to a loop vent, and abruptly thrusts an impressively elongate proboscis toward the unsuspecting small crustacean or other invertebrate prey. The proboscis can be extended about 1/5 the body length of the worm, or about 40 mm for a large specimen. It everts explosively, bearing four black, hook-like hollow jaws. A poison duct opens at the tip of each jaw and is attached to a poison gland at the base. Humans bitten by blood worms compare the bite to a mild bee sting.

Glycera americana is a pinkish worm with small parapodia and a decidedly cylindrical body shape. They rarely leave the burrows, and usually must be excavated from tidal flats or dredged from subtidal beds to be seen. During the spring, *Glycera* swarms outside the burrow for reproduction and occasionally swims at other times for unknown purposes (Dean, 1978).

Additional burrowing predators include two shallow water lumbrinerids, *Lumbrineris impatiens* (Fig. 10-5 J) and *L. coccinea*, distinguished from the former by having a more inflated, spherical prostomium, and the common offshore bank species *L. paravapedata*. The Lumbrineridae are a large family of errant, elongate, threadlike polychaetes without eyes and usually lacking prosomal palps or tentacles. They plow blindly through muds or muddy sands in search of prey, which they grasp by maxillae and mandibles. *Drilonereis magna* (Arabellidae) is another threadlike polychaete predator common in shallow sands. Unlike the lumbrinerids, *Drilonereis* has two large lateral eyes and two smaller median ones hidden beneath 3 small antennae.

Although few visitors to Texas beaches have ever seen *Diopatra cuprea* (Fig. 10-5 K), they are usually provided ample evidence that it occurs here. *Diopatra* is a tube-dwelling polychaete, and it is the tube (Fig. 10-5 K1) washed ashore on Texas beaches that visitors usually see to mark its presence. These tubes consist of an inner parchment-like lining reinforced externally by bits of shell, sand, or sea grass. After storms, the beach may be littered with many *Diopatra* tubes. Actually, the reinforced, shell-ornamented portion is only the uppermost section, a chimney which rises a few cm above the sea floor. The top of the chimney bends such that the flared opening faces horizontally in the direction of current flow (Myers, 1972). The unadorned subterranean tube extends from several centimeters to almost a meter below, and provides a refuge for *Diopatra* when danger threatens. There is enough room within the tube for the worm to turn around. *Diopatra* expends considerable energy in tube construction and maintenance, and will continue to care for the tube even when temperatures are below the critical level to suspend feeding (Myers, 1972). Brenchley (1976) has shown experimentally that stimulation of a shell or grass fragment on the ornamented chimney elicits a more rapid and prolonged retreat by the worm to the subterranean refuge than stimulation of the bare chimney alone, suggesting that chimney ornamentation may help *Diopatra* detect the presence of a predator.

Diopatra occurs subtidally in the Gulf of Mexico, on sandy tidal inlets, or in the higher salinity bays. The head bears seven antennae, a short anterior pair and the remainder longer with distinctly annulated bases. Behind the head, pairs of red plume-like gill lie along the parapodia on the first 30 to 40 segments. The most striking feature of *Diopatra* is the shimmering iridescence of the anterior dorsal body.

This onuphid worm is a predator and scavenger, but it rarely leaves the tube shelter to search for food. When edible morsels wash or wander nearby, only the front portion of *Diopatra* emerges outside the chimney to feed. Much of its food is derived from the organic detritus, diatoms, foraminiferans, microcrustaceans or other small invertebrates which attach to the outer walls of the chimney (Mangum, *et al.*, 1968).

Sessile Biota

There are few sessile animals on the shallow offshore sands, for there are few hard surfaces upon which to attach. Notable exceptions are the sea whips, *Leptogorgia setacea* and *L. virgulata* (Fig. 10-1 Q), the pipe cleaner sea pen, *Virgularia presbytes* (Fig. 10-2 W) and the stony corals, *Astrangia poculata* (Fig. 10-2 T) and *Oculina diffusa* (Plate 11-3 D). Except for *Virgularia*, the larvae of these cnidarians seek the few stones or large shells exposed on the sand surface upon which to settle. *Astrangia* colonies are small, but usually larger than those found attached to jetty rocks. Offshore colonies are frequently found attached to heavy, empty ark shells (e.g., *Anadara ovalis*).

The sea whips (Gorgonacea) grow to be a meter or more in length. *Leptogorgia setacea* develops unbranched colonies, whereas *L. virgulata* forms long, slender branches. The color of both sea whips vary from vivid purple to orange or yellow, whereas *Astrangia* colonies are light tan or take the color of the underlying white calcium carbonate skeleton, and the latter condition is characteristic of *Oculina*. The development of jetties along Texas outer shores has provided considerable new habitable substrata for *Astrangia*, *Oculina* and both sea whips. They have become important components of the deeper subtidal jetty boulders, and all are also common on many offshore banks.

Like many anthozoans, *Leptogorgia*, *Astrangia*, *Oculina* and *Virgularia* are planktivorous carnivores capturing small copepods, isopods, and other zooplankters which float within reach of the short tentacles surrounding the mouth of each polyp. The flexible spicular skeleton of *Leptogorgia* facilitates food capture. Each passing swell moves the colony in a graceful sweep of the surrounding water. The stony corals and *Virgularia* colonies cannot move with the currents or swells.

Several animals live in association with *Leptogorgia*. The most commonly encountered is the ovulid snail *Simnialena uniplicata* (Fig. 10-1 P), which occurs on *L. virgulata*. (A similar ovulid, *S. marferula* occurs upon *L. setacea*.) *Simnialena* is an elongate snail which envelops its thin shell with fleshy mantle tissues. The shell takes the color of the gorgonian upon which it lives. The animal extends inconspicuously exposed only slightly above the surface of the sea whip, hidden primarily by the protective coloration of the shell and mantle. If transferred from a purple to a yellow colony, the snail shell gradually changes color to match that of the new host, with pigment obtained from ingested gorgonian spicules or tissues (Patton, 1972).

Simnialena is a semi-predator of the sea whip, ingesting mucus, loose spicules and organic material entrapped in the mucus secreted by the gorgonian. It also probably takes living *Leptogorgia* tissue, but never damages the sea whip to the degree done by the closely related *Cyphoma gibbosum* which lives on Caribbean gorgonians (Chapter 11). During the warmer months *Simnialena* deposits gelatinous masses containing egg capsules upon *Leptogorgia* branches. The capsules undergo development to the veliger larva stage, whereupon larvae emerge to enter the plankton.

Two other molluscs are *Leptogorgia* associates, although only one is known to occur in Texas waters. *Pteria colymbus* (Fig. 10-2 X), the Atlantic wing oyster, climbs upon a variety of organisms, including sea whips. When found on Texas beaches, this bivalve is always in association with stranded *Leptogorgia* colonies. Apparently only small specimens (under 20 mm)

of *Pteria* occur on sea whips, as larger specimens are too heavy to be supported by the flexible axial rods of the gorgonian. The nudibranch *Tritonia wellsi* is another *Leptogorgia* associate which may occur off Texas shores, but which, as yet, has not been reported.

The small shrimp *Neopontonides beaufortensis*, like *Simnialena*, scavenges mucus and other surface debris on *Leptogorgia*, and sometimes leaves the gorgonian to scavenge on the surrounding sediment. When not feeding it lies motionless clinging to *Leptogorgia* branches. It employs yellow, orange, and purple chromatophores to match the color of the sea whip, and can contract the chromatophores to become almost invisibly translucent. *N. beaufortensis* probably occurs on *Leptogorgia* in Texas waters, but the nearest reported locality record to date for the species is Grand Isle, Louisiana (Dawson, 1963).

The sipunculan, *Phascolion strombi* (Fig. 10-2 R), is an opportunistic member of the offshore biota. Many members of this genus are rock borers, but this species seeks the only stony crevices on the offshore sands. It occupies empty gastropod shells, where its body grows to fill the interior chamber. To insure privacy, it cements sand grains or shell fragments to the aperture of the shell, leaving only enough room for a narrow feeding introvert to emerge. The tip of the introvert is surrounded by a crown of short feeding tentacles that can be swept across the sea floor. *Phascolion* is a selective deposit feeder.

THE OFFSHORE FAUNA OF YUCATAN

The sea floor off Yucatan is in some ways similar to and in other ways different from that of the northwestern Gulf. In both regions, the continental shelf is very broad and the slope of the bottom is gradual for many kilometers offshore. Thirty kilometers off both Texas and Yucatan beaches, water depths may be only about 10 m, with the sea floor composed primarily of unconsolidated sand. However, the sands of the two regions differ significantly in composition. Yucatan sands are mostly carbonates, produced by biota in the sea. In contrast, the sands of the northwestern Gulf are dominantly siliceous, derived mainly by erosion of terrestrial rocks and transported to the sea by rivers.

Bare sandy bottoms dominate the subtidal terrain off all Gulf shores, but beds of *Thalassia*, which are uncommon offshore in the northwestern Gulf, are more frequently encountered off Yucatan beaches. Submerged bank reefs or small coral islands are also common, especially off the northern coast (see Chapter 11). These grass beds, banks, and reefs provide the southern region with significantly greater habitat diversity for the offshore biota than is available in the northwestern Gulf.

Many of the organisms which inhabit subtidal sands of the northwestern Gulf also occur off Yucatan. There is also a significant contribution of tropical Caribbean biota, although the full diversity of the tropics is not achieved here. A small but interesting additional bi-

otic component is derived from members of the Carolinian Biotic Province that are excluded from the
northwestern Gulf. Two species in this category
readily come to mind. We have previously mentioned
the horseshoe crab (*Limulus polyphemus*, Chapter 6)
as an example of the Carolinian biota that also occurs
off Yucatan beaches. The fig shell *Ficus communis*
(Fig. 10-6 E), is another. These and other species with
a similarly disjunctive pattern of distribution suggest
the relic nature of many faunal elements of the northeastern Gulf, stranded by a lowered sea level which
thrust the peninsula of Florida and the tropical Caribbean as a barrier between a once-continuous sea from
the Carolinas to the Florida panhandle (Hedgpeth,
1953). Clearly, this faunal trend continued toward Yucatan. But, for some unknown reason, some of these
Carolinian species failed to become established in the
northwestern Gulf, and specifically off Texas shores.
Limulus and *Ficus* are two of the most prominent
examples.

The Yucatan offshore biota has received significantly less study than that from other parts of the
Gulf of Mexico. The molluscs have received the most
attention (Ekdale, 1974, Treece, 1980, Vokes and
Vokes, 1983). The latter authors record a total of 299
species of gastropods and 141 species of bivalves from
the shallow sands off northern Yucatan. We have selected some of the more obvious or characteristic species as examples of the molluscan fauna of the Yucatan offshore sands, and include notes on a few
additional species or other groups.

The fauna of offshore *Thalassia* beds include many
species which occur on grassbeds in Texas bays.
Modulus modulus (Fig. 10-6 H), the bubble shell,
Bulla striata (Fig. 10-6 F), and *Anachis semiplicata*
(Fig. 8-6 F) are common examples. The first two are
essentially tropical species near the northern limit
of their range in Texas, whereas the latter is a warm
temperate species near the southern limit of its range
in Yucatan. Another small tropical columbellid, *Anachis sparsa* (Fig 10-6 G) is a common carnivore on
bare subtidal sand. In addition to a variety of molluscs
finding shelter in *Thalassia*, the sea urchin, *Arbacia
punctulata*, also occurs here. Apparently this urchin is
equally adept at grazing upon jetty algae (see Chapter
4) as well as the algal associates of turtle grass.

Several predatory whelks patrol the shallow sands.
The two species that we encountered in Texas, *Busycotypus spiratum* (Fig. 10-6 A) and *Busycon perversum* (Fig. 10-6 C and J) are both here. The problem of
differentiating sinistral Atlantic *Busycon* species is
clearly evident with the Yucatan populations. As
broadly conceived, *B. perversum* is represented here by
two shell forms. The larger shells may reach a length
of 20 cm and display a distinctive swollen rounded
ridge around the middle of the whorl. This form (Fig.
10-6 J) carries the name *B. perversum perversum* (Linnaeus 1758). Sinistral whelks lacking the ridge (Fig.
10-6 C) have been known as *B. perversum contrarium*
(Conrad 1840), but as discussed earlier, the latter is

now regarded as a synonym of the former (see Edwards
& Humphrey, 1981 and Kent, 1983a for a more complete treatment of this taxonomic problem). Another
whelk, *B. coarctatum* (Fig. 10-6 B), is characterized by
an elongate and slender siphonal canal. This species is
especially abundant on the shrimp grounds of the
Campeche Bank.

Despite its fragility, the fig snail, *Ficus communis*
(Fig. 10-6 E), is among one of the most common shells
to wash ashore upon Yucatan beaches. The finely ornamented shell attains a length of up to 10 cm with a
slightly elevated nublike spire at the top. As its common name implies, the shape of a *Ficus* shell resembles that of a fig. Like the tun shells such as *Tonna
galea* (Fig. 10-6 D), to which it is closely related, *Ficus*
is an echinoderm predator, but its feeding habits are
poorly known.

Both *Fasciolaria tulipa* (Fig. 10-6 O) and *F. lilium*
also occur off Yucatan, but the relative abundance of
the two species is reverse that of what we encountered
in Texas. The former is much more common than the
latter in Yucatan waters. The West Indian chank, *Turbinella angulata* (Fig. 10-6 I), is another predatory
snail of the offshore sands. It is the second largest gastropod of the western Atlantic, attaining over 30 cm in
length. The shell is very heavy, with a cream interior
and three strong, widely spaced folds on the columella. Despite the large size, the biology of this mollusc is poorly known. Like other chanks, it probably
feeds on bivalves and tube worms, but the exact prey
of this big gastropod is unknown.

The family Crepidulidae are a group of sessile filter
feeding mesogastropods which commonly attach to
the shells of the larger neogastropods described above,
particularly *B. perversum*. *Crepidula maculosa* (Fig.
10-6 L) has a mauve blotched shell and attaches to the
outside of such shells, whereas the larger, milky
white, *C. plana* (Fig. 10-6 K) occurs within the lip of
empty *B. perversum* shells, probably in association
with hermit crabs.

Two bivalves also may be found attached by byssal
threads to such shells. The small *Carditamera floridana* (Fig. 10-6 M) is a tropical species characterized
by pronounced, beaded, radial ribs. *Arca zebra* (Fig. 10-
6 N) has characteristic zebra-stripe markings. Both bivalves are more often found attached to rocks than
shells, but in the particular situation of the Yucatan
sands, large empty shells constitute the only favorable
habitat.

Many sand-dwelling bivalves live infaunally buried.
Three cockles, the smooth *Laevicardium laevigatum*
(Fig. 10-6 P) and the ribbed *Trachycardium isocardia*
(Fig. 10-6 Q) and *Dinocardium robustum* (Fig. 10-6 R)
are shallow burrowers. *Mactra fragilis* (Fig. 10-6 S) has
two characteristic ridges on the posterio-dorsal edge of
the shell while a second mactrid, the channeled duck
clam *Raeta plicatella* (Fig. 10-6 Y) is concentrically
ringed (Harry, 1969). Both are deposit feeders as is the
deep burrowing and plain *Tellina lineata* (Fig. 10-6 T).
Anodontia alba (Fig. 10-6 U) is a deep burrowing sus-

pension feeder common on nearshore sands. It also is occasionally found in similar habitats in the northwestern Gulf.

Three members of the Veneridae, all filter feeders, occur on the Yucatan flats—*Dosinia elegans* (Fig. 10-6 X), *Chione cancellata* (Fig. 10-6 W) and *Mercenaria campechiensis* (Fig. 10-6 Z). The large fan shell *Atrina seminuda* (Fig. 10-6 V), also recorded from northern Gulf coasts has a fragile shell, marked with radiating lines and spurs. It is vertically disposed in the sand, and anchored by long byssal threads attached to sand grains.

Most of the other invertebrates of the sands off northern Yucatan are poorly known. We have discussed some of the crustaceans in a previous section. Two portunids, *Callinectes similis*, and *C. ornatus*, are especially common, as are the shame-faced crabs, *Calappa sulcata*, *C. flammea*, and *C. angusta*. The nearshore echinoderms, especially holothurians and short-spined echinoids, are more diverse here than in the northwestern Gulf, although still less so than in the tropical Caribbean. Some are discussed in the next chapter. For most of the invertebrates we probably should expect similar representation as we have seen with the molluscs: both temperate and tropical faunal elements are present, with fewer species from each region combining to produce a greater diversity than occurs in the sands of the northwestern Gulf.

10-6. Subtidal Mollusca of Yucatan. **A.** Pear whelk, *Busycotypus spiratum*; **B.** Turnip whelk, *Busycon coarctatum*; **C.** Perverse whelk, *Busycon perversum contrarium*; **D.** Tun shell, *Tonna galea*; **E.** Fig shell, *Ficus communis*; **F.** Bubble shell, *Bulla striata*; **G.** Sparse dove shell, *Anachis sparsa*; **H.** Atlantic modulus, *Modulus modulus*; **I.** West Indian chank, *Turbinella angulata*; **J.** Perverse whelk, *Busycon perversum perversum*; **K.** White slipper limpet, *Crepidula plana*; **L.** Spotted slipper limpet, *Crepidula maculosa*; **M.** Broad-ribbed cardita, *Carditamera floridana*; **N.** Zebra ark, *Arca zebra*; **O.** Tulip shell, *Fasciolaria tulipa*; **P.** Common egg cockle, *Laevicardium laevigatum*; **Q.** Prickly cockle, *Trachycardium isocardia*; **R.** Giant Atlantic cockle, *Dinocardium robustum*; **S.** Fragile Atlantic mactra, *Mactra fragilis*; **T.** Rose petal tellin, *Tellina lineata*; **U.** Fragile lucine, *Anodontia alba*; **V.** Pen shell, *Atrina seminuda*; **W.** Cross-barred venus, *Chione cancellata*; **X.** Elegant disk clam, *Dosinia elegans*; **Y.** Channeled duck clam, *Raeta plicatella*; **Z.** Southern quahog, *Mercenaria campechiensis*.

OFFSHORE BANKS OF THE NORTHWESTERN GULF

Subtidal hard bottoms are uncommon in the northwestern Gulf of Mexico, but become increasingly prevalent toward Veracruz, Yucatan and the Bay of Campeche. In Mexico, some very large banks emerge from the sea as reef crests or reef-formed islands. We will discuss these reefs and their associated habitats in the next Chapter, but we conclude this chapter with a consideration of the simpler hard bank environments of the northwestern Gulf.

More than three dozen sizable hard banks rise above the continental shelf sediments of the northwestern Gulf plus numerous additional minor banks or "rocks" (Rezak *et al.* 1985). Most of these occupy the middle shelf or the outer shelf margin, but a few, such as Seven and One-Half Fathom Bank off central Padre Island or West Bank off Freeport, occur relatively close to shore.

Offshore banks lying to the east of Matagorda Bay, Texas usually cap salt domes or complex diapiric structures. The surface of mid-shelf banks in this region, including Claypile, Coffee Lump, Fishnet, Sonnier, Stetson and 32 Fathom, are composed of Tertiary limestones, sandstones, claystones and siltstones (Curray, 1960; Rezak *et al.*, 1985). The more numerous outer shelf banks are capped primarily by Quaternary or younger carbonate limestones. Two of these, the East and West Flower Garden Banks, have received more scientific attention than perhaps all of the other hard banks collectively in the northwestern Gulf (Bright & Pequegnat, 1974, Rezak *et al.*, 1985, and references therein).

The mid-shelf and shelf-margin banks lying southwest of Matagorda Bay, such as Baker, Big Southern and Hospital, are composed of limestone bedrock. They were active coralgal reefs between 10,000 to 18,000 years ago (Parker & Curray, 1956; Rezak *et al.*, 1985).

Nearshore banks of the northwestern Gulf are characterized by relief of less than about 5 m. Stiff clay and "beachrock" banks rise above the nearshore sands between Freeport and Matagorda Bay, but they have received little study (Tunnell, 1982). Seven and One-Half Fathom Bank, located off central Padre Island, has been the focus of considerable research (Causey, 1969; Tunnell & Causey, 1969; Tunnell, 1973; Tunnell & Chaney, 1970; Felder, 1971, 1973b; Shirley, 1974; McCarty, 1974; Felder & Chaney, 1979). It is composed of lithified lacustrine deposits (Thayer, *et al.*, 1974). The presence of pulmonate snails and mammalian bones and teeth embedded in the carbonate matrix also testify to a terrestrial origin of this nearshore bank (Tunnell & Causey, 1969).

The biotic communities which occupy the subtidal hard banks are influenced by several physical conditions including water depth, salinity, turbidity, distance from shore, and minimum winter water temperature (Rezak *et al.*, 1985). These factors are not mutually exclusive. For example, nearshore banks such as Seven and One-Half Fathom Bank or Heald Bank off Galveston experience periods of high turbidity and variable salinity due to their proximity to sources of river discharge. Similarly, shallow water is an ineffective buffer of seasonal temperature changes. Water temperatures at Seven and One-Half Fathom Bank range from 13 to 30°C and salinities from 28 to 36 ppt (Tunnell, 1973). Deeper banks on the shelf margin are more effectively buffered from variations in salinity, temperature and turbidity. Portions of some of these banks rarely experience temperatures below 18°C (see Chapter 11).

Regardless of the mode of origin or depth of occurrence, offshore banks in the northwestern Gulf of Mexico are surrounded completely by sand, mud or both. Bank margins are transitional between the communities occupying loose shelf sediments and the hard bottoms on the bank. They are usually depauperate of biota, brought on the physical nature of the transition zone. Nearshore currents sweeping along the edges of shallow banks have velocities sufficient to suspend sand particles which, in turn, scour the bank margins (Tunnell & Chaney, 1970). Offshore currents also provide sufficient turbulence along the margins of the deeper banks to produce an almost permanent halo of turbid water, the nepheloid layer. This decreases illumination and provides for a constant rain of fine particles which accumulate in thin layers on hard bank margins (Rezak *et al.*, 1985). There is usually insufficient unconsolidated sediment on bank margins to accommodate infaunal burrowers adapted for life in soft sediments. Similarly, sessile biota is prevented from settling or survival by sand abrasion on the shallow nearshore banks and by high turbidity, sedimentation and resuspension of sediments associated with the nepheloid layer of the deeper shelf banks.

Temperate biota is well represented on nearshore banks, including species also found along subtidal rocks of the coastal jetties (Tunnell, 1973; Felder & Chaney, 1979). Mid-shelf and shelf-margin banks include higher percentages of species which occupy very shallow subtidal environments in the tropical Gulf and Caribbean but are absent from shores of the northwestern Gulf. The deeper portions of these banks also contain a true shelf or slope fauna unrepresented on any shore or shallow subtidal habitat throughout the region (Bright & Pequegnat, 1974; Rezak *et al.*, 1985).

Rezak *et al.* (1985) recognize seven biotic communities which occupy the mid-shelf and shelf-margin hard banks of the northwestern Gulf of Mexico, to which we add the nearshore bank community as represented by the Seven and One-Half Fathom Bank (Table 10-1). These can be ordered according to the degree of reef-building activity and primary production. Two communities fringe the lower margins of the offshore banks, neither of which contribute significantly to reef-building. These are the Nepheloid Community, associated with the nepheloid layer surrounding the bank, and a Transitional or Antipatharian Community adjacent to the former and transitional to the shallower communities higher upon the bank. Many of the species occupying these communities are derived from deep shelf and slope sources and are outside the scope of this book.

Four offshore bank communities contribute significantly to biohermal construction, including a high-diversity *Diploria-Montastrea-Porites* reef, a *Madracis*-Leafy Algae community, a low diversity *Stephanocoenia-Millepora* reef, and an Algal-Sponge community. All occupy relatively clear water with minimum temperatures 16°C or above, although they occur at depths ranging from 15 to 98 m. They are populated predominantly by tropical species. The high diversity coral reef and *Madracis*-Leafy Algae communities occur at only two localities in the northwestern Gulf, the East and West Flower Garden Banks about 107 nautical miles due south of Sabine Pass. The low diversity reef is almost as restricted, but occurs on a few other shelf banks throughout the northern Gulf region. Isolated coral heads are not uncommon on the shelf, especially from off the mouth of the Brazos River, Texas and southward (Mattison, 1948; Lynch, 1954). The coral reef and *Madracis*-Leafy Algae communities are described in more detail in the next chapter.

Large knolls of the branching coral *Madracis* are restricted primarily to the Flower Garden Banks (Chapter 11), but small colonies of several *Madracis* species are common on most subtidal banks throughout the region (Parker & Curray, 1956; Ludwick & Walton, 1957; Bright & Pequegnat, 1974; Rezak *et al.*, 1985). *Madracis mirabilis* (Fig. 10-7 M) is probably the most widely distributed species. Others reported from various banks include *M. brueggemanni, M. decactis* (Fig. 11-2 I), *M. cf. formosa,* and *M. myriaster. Madracis mirabilis* grows in short finger-like branches rarely exceeding a centimeter in diameter or a few centimeters in length. The branches of *M. decactis* are thicker and end in bulbous or club-like terminations. When portions of the coral colony die, other encrusting species such as the foraminiferan *Gypsina plana* (Fig. 10-7 N), various bryozoans (e.g., *Smittina, Schizoporella* or *Mamillopora*) or the coralline algae may become established on the *Madracis* skeleton.

An Algal-Sponge community occurs on many of the shelf-margin hard banks of the northwestern Gulf and is considered, in terms of the area occupied, the most important shelf-edge bank community (Rezak *et al.*, 1985). Its presence is indicative of tropical to subtropical water conditions in the northwestern Gulf. Many members of this community occupy shallow subtidal habitats in the southern Gulf and Caribbean as well as the deeper tropical banks. The community is dominated by various species of crustose coralline algae (Fig. 10-7 U), which loosely cement the bank together and contribute significant quantities of limestone to the fabric of the bank. The algae form amorphous calcareous sheets, nodules, or nodes over other rocks. Some species appear to be aggregations of rods or

Table 10-1. Bank Communities on the Continental Shelf of the northwestern Gulf of Mexico (after Rezak *et al.*, 1985)

Community or Zone	Location	Typical Substratum	Biotic Affinities
Nepheloid Zone (Depauperate epifauna and variable infauna depending upon depth of unconsolidated sediment)	NS, MS, SM (bank-soft sediment interface)	Variable, but usually with a veneer of unconsolidated sediment overlying some form of lithified bedrock	Poorly known; little carbonate deposition
Fouling Biota and Marina Borers (*Phyllochaetopterus*, hydroids, tunicates, *Lithophaga*)	NS	Clays, lacustrine beds, and/or other terrigenous sources	Temperate biota well represented; modest numbers of tropical species
Millepora-Sponge (*Millepora*, various sponges, few calcareous algae)	MS	Terrigenous sandstones, siltstones or claystones with a thin cap of biogenous limestone	Some temperate biota; hardy tropical species present, but few capable of significant carbonate deposition
Antipatharian Zone (along bank margins; transitional between nepheloid zone and regions of moderate to major reef-building activity; some coralline algae, some corals, many antipatharians)	MS, SM	Carbonate veneer and/or relict Pleistocene carbonate reefs	Primarily mid- to deep water tropical species

Legend: NS: Near shore; MS: Mid-shelf; SM: Shelf margin.

flakes. When the community is well developed, they can account for as much as 60 to 70 percent of the living biomass of an offshore bank, but divers frequently dismiss these plants as "bare rocks." They have been variously assigned to *Lithothamnion*, *Goniolithion* or other genera in early surveys of these banks (e.g., Stetson, 1953; Parker & Curray, 1956). Accurate identification of most coralline algae usually defies cursory examination. Adey and MacIntyre (1973) point out that literature reports of the occurrence of certain genera on Gulf banks involve a significant degree of nomenclatorial ambiguity and a disturbing lack of empirical analysis. Generic or specific determinations usually require decalcification and laboratory preparation before an identification can be attempted. We will refrain from even generic designations of the calcareous algae.

Calcareous green algae and non-calcareous "leafy" macrophytes also occupy the Algal-Sponge community. *Halimeda* species (Fig. 11-3 D1 & L1) are perhaps the most numerous of the calcareous chlorophytes, but other species are also present. Dark green, semi-calcareous *Udotea cyathiformis* (Fig. 10-7 W) usually dot the hard bank surface, their goblet-like heads elevated by a short stalk. Dense clusters of the brown alga, *Lobophora (Pocockiella) variegata* (Fig. 10-7 X) carpet rocky promontories regularly swept by strong currents. Another brown alga, *Spatoglossum schroederi* (Fig. 10-7 T), prefers the more sheltered parts of the bank. It is readily recognized by iridescent, flattened and repeatedly branching blades which reach 25 cm or more in length. The red algae are represented, in addition to the coralline species, by a variety of small soft thallus forms. Prominent among these are *Coelarthrum albertisii* (Fig. 10-7 V) and *Chrysymenia enteromorpha* (Fig. 10-7 R), which form dense pinkish mats on sheltered parts of the bank.

Rezak *et al.* (1985) list more than 75 species of sponges associated with offshore banks in the northwestern Gulf of Mexico. Many of these occur upon or among the calcareous algae. Prominent among them are the vase sponges (e.g., *Ircinia campana*, Fig. 11-6 B) and the Touch-me-not sponge, *Neofibularia nolitangere*. The latter is a common shallow subtidal species in the tropical Atlantic. It can cause severe dermatitis on hands or other parts of the human body coming into contact with the sponge. Many other invertebrates and fishes live in association with the Algal-Sponge community, including several described near the end of this section.

The *Millepora*-Sponge community occupies several relatively shallow (18 to 40 m crests) mid-shelf banks, especially those capped by sandstones, siltstones or claystones. These were among the first of the northwestern Gulf shelf banks to receive scientific attention (Stetson, 1953; Parker & Curray, 1956; Curray, 1960). Coralline algae are poorly represented in this community, but encrusting hydrozoan fire corals, *Millepora alcicornis* (Fig. 10-7 F) contribute moderate quantities of carbonate to the bank. The shape of tan *Millepora* colonies varies from flat encrusting sheets to erect, forked branches. Tiny polyps emerge from hundreds of very small pores which cover the surface of the colony. Almost invisible tentacles bear potent stinging cells capable of inflicting peppery rashes on unsuspecting divers. *Millepora* dominates wave-swept reef crests and shallow subtidal reefs in the tropical Atlantic, but it also fares very well on many of the mid- and outer-shelf banks of the northwestern Gulf. Many of the sponges which occupy the Algal-Sponge community also occur on the *Millepora*-dominated bank crests.

Any hard bottom experiences both build-up and destruction. Tropical banks are usually characterized by a net accumulation of biogenous limestone, exceeding the loss of carbonate material by the activities of marine borers or other destructive elements. This is generally true on most of the mid-shelf and shelf-margin banks of the northwestern Gulf, where recent or relict biogenous carbonate sedimentation contributes to topographic relief. In contrast, nearshore banks in the northwestern Gulf do not support the highly productive carbonate formers, due to factors we discussed near the beginning of this section. These banks were formed in different environments and by processes no longer active at the locations they presently occupy.

10-7. Subtidal hard bank biota. **A.** Hairy mud crab, *Pilumnus pannosus*; **B.** Snapping shrimp, *Synalpheus pandionis*; **C.** *Munida simplex*; **D.** Red-brown ark, *Barbatia cancellaria*; **E.** Cowrie, *Cypraea spurca acicularis*; **F.** Fire coral, *Millepora alcicornis*; **G.** *Triphora turristhomae*; **H.** File shell, *Lima scabra tenera*; **I.** Stocky cerith, *Cerithium litteratum*; **J.** Hammer oyster, *Malleus candeanus*; **K.** Slit worm-snail, *Siliquaria squamata*; **L.** Short coral-shell, *Coralliophila abbreviata*; **M.** Branching coral, *Madracis mirabilis*; **N.** Encrusting foram, *Gypsina plana*; **O.** Long-spined black urchin, *Diadema antillarum*; **P.** Brittle star, *Ophiocoma wendti*; **Q.** Brittle star, *Ophiactis savignyi*; **R.** Red alga, *Chrysymenia enteromorpha*; **S.** Arrow crab, *Stenorhynchus seticornis*; **T.** Leafy green alga, *Spatoglossum schroederi*; **U.** Crustose coralline algae; **V.** Bushy red alga, *Coelarthrum albertisii*; **W.** Calcareous green alga, *Udotea cyathiformis*; **X.** Leafy brown alga, *Lobophora variegata*; **Y.** Hermit crab, *Paguristes hewatti*; **Z.** Cancellate cantharus, *Cantharus cancellarius*. **A1.** *Phyllochaetopterus socialis* within tube.

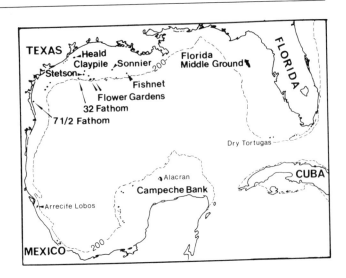

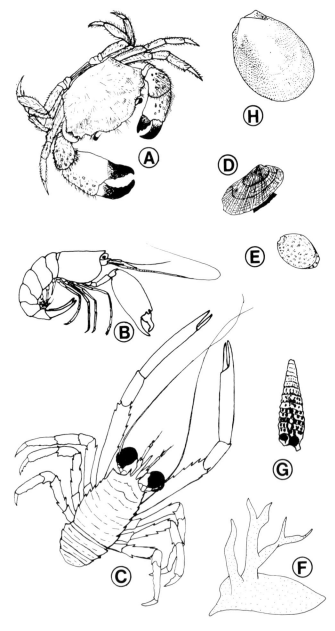

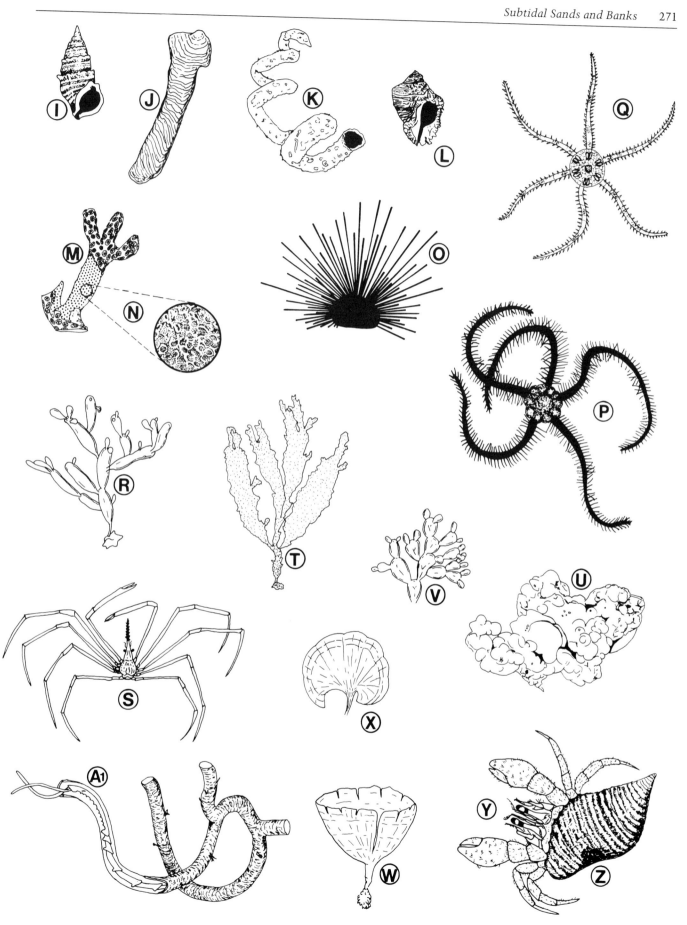

The mud banks off Sargent Beach were probably the result of estuarine sedimentation. The lithified lacustrine rocks of Seven and One-Half Fathom Bank were formed first at the bottom of a lake, and subsequently cemented during an arid period by deposition of carbonate as caliche (Thayer *et al.*, 1974). Today, both of these areas are experiencing significant destruction by marine borers, with only modest replacement of sediments by mats of fouling biota. Destruction exceeds replacement, the banks appear riddled with holes and crevices (Tunnell & Chaney, 1970), and they are slowly crumbling away.

Three groups of biota characterize Seven and One-Half Fathom Bank: the fouling community which caps the bank, borers which contribute to its destruction, and errant opportunists, including molluscs, echinoderms, crustaceans, and fish, which take advantage of the shelter provided by the bank. The fouling community is dominated by the tube-dwelling polychaete, *Phyllochaetopterus socialis* (Fig. 10-7 A1). McCarty (1974) found 83 species of polychaetes inhabiting Seven and One-Half Fathom Reef, with a mean density of 2481 polychaetes per m². The majority of these were *P. socialis*, having in excess of 20,000 tubes per m² on some parts of the bank.

Phyllochaetopterus socialis is a small worm, 15 to 25 mm in length. It secretes a crooked, branched and leathery tube in which as many as four worms occupy separate branches (Barnes, 1965). Like other chaetopterids, it pumps water through the tube and utilizes mucous bags to trap suspended food particles. When water is heavily laden with detritus, numerous mucous glands along the body secrete a mucous rope which traps particles from the swirling stream of water passing through the tube (Barnes, 1965).

The remaining species of polychaetes at Seven and One-Half Fathom Bank occupy a variety of life modes and feeding guilds. Sessile hydroids (Fig. 3-5), bryozoans (Fig. 11-9), tunicates, sponges and leafy macrophytes grow among the worm tubes and frequently rise high above them. Many species of errant crustaceans (Felder & Chaney, 1979), molluscs (Tunnell & Chaney, 1970; Tunnell, 1973), ophiuroids (Shirley, 1974), and polychaetes (McCarty, 1974) live among the tangled mat of sessile fouling biota.

Bioerosion of the bank is clearly evident, especially along its upper flanks. Bivalves dominate the community of borers, including *Lithophaga bisulcata* (Fig. 11-7 C), *L. aristata* (Fig. 11-7 D), *Gregariella coralliophaga* (Fig. 11-7 E), and *Rupellaria typica* (Fig. 11-7 L). The sipunculan, *Phascolosoma antillarum* is also abundant. Marine borers are discussed in more detail in the next chapter.

Many of the errant opportunists of Seven and One-Half Fathom Bank are also widely distributed on the continental shelf. They may range from shore to the shelf margin, depending upon the presence of a suitable habitat and the tolerance of each species to local conditions. The fish, in particular, represent a group of widely distributed species (Causey, 1969). Thus, the remaining discussion of this section considers some of these opportunists, including a few sessile forms, usually without reference to a specific bank location or environment.

A considerable variety of molluscs occurs on the bank habitats, and this group probably has received more attention in the literature than any other. Parker & Curray (1956) list 137 species of molluscs collected by dredging from the Flower Garden Banks and other smaller banks of the northwestern Gulf. Tunnell & Chaney (1970) record 169 species of molluscs from Seven and One-Half Fathom Reef. The combined lists of Lipka (1974) and Rezak *et al.* (1985) account for about 78 molluscs from the Flower Garden Banks, and the latter record about 115 species from various mid-shelf and shelf-margin banks. The majority of species cited in each of these reports occupy intertidal or shallow subtidal habitats in the southern Gulf and Caribbean, but are generally poorly represented or absent in the shallower nearshore waters of the northwestern Gulf. We will comment on only some of the more common or interesting species here.

Cerithium litteratum (Fig. 10-7 I) is one of the many shallow water tropical gastropods found commonly on the offshore banks. The related, but smaller and sinistral triphorids, such as *Triphora turristhomae* (Fig. 10-7 G), are especially common on the banks. Reef species such as the small cowrie, *Cypraea spurca acicularis* (Fig. 10-7 E) or the corallophagous *Coralliophila abbreviata* (Fig. 10-7 L) are well represented. The latter is known primarily from the Flower Garden banks where there is a greater variety of scleractinian prey. It is absent from Seven and One-Half Fathom Bank (Tunnell & Chaney, 1970). Shells of the unusual worm-like snail, *Siliquaria squamata* (Fig. 10-7 K) are frequently found on the banks, but the animal typically lives with its convoluted shell embedded deeply within tissues of large sponges, which, in turn, commonly occur attached to exposed hard surfaces. Shells of the small whelk *Cantharus cancellarius* (Fig 10-7 Z) occur on nearshore banks, but are likely transported there from the subtidal sands by hermit crabs such as *Paguristes hewatti* (Fig. 10-7 Y).

Infaunal bivalves are poorly represented on the banks or restricted to the sedimentary margins. A variety of byssus-attached or swimming bivalves attach to or hide among the rocks. The former are represented by several species of Arcidae, such as the dark shelled *Barbatia cancellaria* (Fig. 10-7 D) or the similar but more lightly colored *B. candida*. Another unusual byssus-attached bivalve is the hammer oyster, *Malleus candeanus* (Fig. 10-7 J). Rarely exceeding more than about 4 cm in length, the Atlantic hammer oyster never attains the large size of its Indo-Pacific relatives. It lives hidden in crevices among coralline rock with only the tips of the elongate valves protruding slightly from the shelter. The file shell, *Lima scabra tenera* (Fig. 10-7 H) also spends much of its life attached by a byssus to the underside of rocks. When unattached, it swims clumsily by means of numerous, long, flexible rowing tentacles which arise from the edge of the mantle.

The crustaceans of the offshore banks are probably more abundant and diverse than present records suggest (Hulings, 1955; Chace, 1972; Pequegnat & Ray, 1974; Powers, 1977; Felder & Chaney, 1979; Rezak *et al.*, 1985). As with the molluscs, many bank crustaceans are recruits from shallow tropical reefs. Among the more common of these is the arrow crab, *Stenorhynchus seticornis* (Fig, 10-7 S). Even more abundant, if not as visible, are a variety of small pistol or snapping shrimps, including *Synalpheus pandionis* (Fig. 10-7 B). These typically tropical shrimps hide within the rocky matrix and are rarely observed. Their presence and abundance is indicated by incessant pops or clicks caused when the large claw is forcefully and repeatedly closed, presumably as a territorial display. The banks abound with pistol shrimps representing at least several species. Felder (1982a) describes the life histories of *Synalpheus fritzmuelleri* and *S. apioceros* from Seven and One-Half Fathom Bank, and Felder (1982b) describes their reproductive cycles.

Other crustaceans are more at home on the banks than in other habitats. Among these species are the small fuzzy brachyuran crabs such as *Pilumnus pannosus* (Fig. 10-7 A) or *P. floridanus*. The unusual deeper-living anomuran galatheids such as *Munida simplex* (Fig. 10-7 C) or *M. angulata* also fall into this category of bank inhabitants.

Echinoderms are much more diverse on the offshore shelf than in the nearshore habitats of the northwestern Gulf. This may be related to the poor tolerance of many species to low salinities. All of the major groups of echinoderms are represented on the offshore banks and adjacent soft bottoms, including asteroids, ophiuroids, echinoids, crinoids, and holothurians. Species abundance clearly increases as one moves offshore. Texas bays, tidal inlets and subtidal sands adjacent to the barrier islands harbor about a dozen species of echinoderms, and most of these occur in the latter habitat. Shirley (1974) reports 26 species of echinoderms from Seven and One-Half Fathom Reef (about 3 km offshore), including a number of sand-dwellers such as *Astropecten articulatus*, *Luidia clathrata* and *Mellita quinquiesperforata*. The combined lists of Burke (1974) and Rezak *et al.* (1985) account for over 60 species of echinoderms associated with mid-shelf and shelf-margin banks. These are derived from both shallow tropical (e.g., those listed below) and deeper shelf and slope (e.g., *Asterinopsis lymani*, *Centrostephanus rubricingulus*, *Pseudoboletia maculata*) habitats.

The most conspicuous echinoderm on the larger banks is the long-spined black sea urchin, *Diadema antillarum* (Fig. 10-7 O). It is not exceptionally common, nor does it occur on all of the offshore banks. When present, several usually rest together along the edges of rocky outcrops during the day and emerge in the late afternoon or at night to feed. *Diadema* recently suffered an epidemic depletion throughout its western Atlantic range, including the banks of the northwestern Gulf (see Chapter 11). Ophiuroids are relatively well represented on the hard banks, with over 40 species indicated when the lists of Burke (1974), Shirley (1974) and Rezak *et al.* (1985) are combined. *Ophiocoma wendti* (Fig. 10-7 P) and *Ophiactis savignyi* (Fig. 10-7 Q) are tropical species found on the shelf banks often in association with sponges. Shirley (1982) comments on the importance of ophiuroids and other echinoderms to the diets of certain bank fishes.

Other common but poorly documented animals of the offshore banks include the polychaetes, bryozoans, brachiopods (Tunnell, 1982), soft corals, and sea anemones. Some of the species of these groups are discussed in the next chapter and, no doubt, occur on the offshore banks of the northwestern Gulf of Mexico.

11. Coral Communities of the Western Gulf of Mexico

INTRODUCTION

Reef-building corals and the communities they support are not common in the western Gulf of Mexico. Coral communities discontinuously ring the fringes of the Gulf basin, often comprising shallow carbonate banks of scattered coral boulders rather than discrete reefs. Reasons for the paucity of coral communities are not entirely the effect of latitude or temperature, although these elements certainly play a role. A significantly greater number of reefs and banks occur at higher latitudes in the eastern Gulf and central Caribbean than correspondingly occur in the western Gulf of Mexico. For example, most of the coral reefs of southern Florida and the northern Bahamas occur between latitudes 24 to 28° N. The same latitudes in the western Gulf, including the area from just south of Copano Bay on the Texas coast to just north of La Pesca in Mexico, contain no mainland-associated reef communities, and only two offshore banks capped by large, scattered coral heads.

Before considering some reasons that may account for the uneven distribution of coral communities, it is important to understand the nature of the coral animal. The term "coral" has been used to refer to several different kinds of marine organisms. Soft corals, for example, belong to the Octocorallia, characterized by polyps with eight tentacles, and having organic and/or spicular skeletons (Fig. 11-8). A few hydrozoans, e.g., *Millepora alcicornis* (Plate 11-3 H), are often called fire corals. The stony corals or Scleractinia (Plates 11-1, 11-2 and 11-3), include the anthozoan reef-builders. They usually bear 12 tentacles or multiples thereof, form paired septa, usually arranged in multiples of six, within the digestive cavity and secrete a limestone skeleton upon which they live.

There are solitary and colonial Scleractinia. Actually, there are only a few truly solitary species. Most are "sub-solitary," living as widely-spaced, prominently-elevated polyps joined along encrusting, simply branching bases. Solitary or sub-solitary corals are scattered throughout several scleractinian sub-orders, including the Fungiina, Faviina, Caryophylliina and Dendrophylliina. They are more abundant and diverse in the tropical Pacific than along Atlantic shores. For example, solitary shallow-water fungiids are absent in the Atlantic, and the Dendrophylliina are likely represented in the Gulf of Mexico by no more than one species of the sub-solitary *Tubastrea*. There are, however, a few representatives. *Scolymia cubensis* (Plate 11-3 G) is a common solitary faviid found on the deeper Gulf reefs (Wells, 1971), and the sub-solitary *Mussa angulosa* (Plate 11-3 F) often occurs nearby. We have already discussed a third sub-solitary faviid, the encrusting *Astrangia poculata* (Chapters 3 and 10). A larger number of truly solitary species reside upon Atlantic deep sea beds, outside the realm of our discussions.

The reef-forming corals are colonial animals, consisting of numerous individual polyps that secrete and live upon a calcium carbonate skeleton (Fig. 11-1 B). They have recently been characterized as "constructional" corals, denoting their ability to form a bioherm, which is an elevated durable carbonate structure in shallow (typically) and sometimes in deep water (Schuhmacher & Zibrowius, 1985). Each polyp of the colony resembles a small sea anemone with a cylindrical body and a ring of tentacles surrounding a mouth (Fig. 11-1 C). Most are tiny (a few mm or less), but a few species, such as *Montastrea cavernosa* (Plate 11-2 E) produce polyps in excess of 1 cm in diameter. Some of the sub-colonial species, such as *Mussa angulosa* (Plate 11-3 F) or *Scolymia cubensis* (Plate 11-3 G), produce polyps up to 8 cm in diameter.

The position of each polyp upon the stony skeleton is marked by a calyx or circular ring, into which project numerous slivers of limestone. These are the sclerosepta (Fig. 11-1 C [4]) which serve to partition the basal portion of the polyp into numerous sections. Tissue septa drape the sclerosepta, which they secrete. Membranes join adjacent polyps and also include some secretory cells which can add calcium carbonate to the skeletal matrix. A colony of a reef-forming species may consist of thousands of polyps living upon a stony skeleton rising several meters above the sea floor, and extending several meters in length or diameter.

Scleractinian corals are identified by the size, position, and pattern of calyces on the colony, the nature of the sclerosepta and a variety of other largely skeletal features. The reef-forming species have been known, traditionally, as hermatypic corals, a term literally referring to the mound-like character of many coral heads, but, as we will see, it has also carried an additional connotation. We will restrict the term hermatypic to include only those constructional coral species which significantly contribute to the framework of a reef (Schuhmacher & Zibrowius, 1985).

Ahermatypic corals occur upon a reef, but they do not contribute significantly to its structure. Hermatypic species produce the majority of the primary skeletal carbonate on the reef. They include massive species such as *Montastrea annularis* (Plate 11-2 F) and *Diploria labyrinthiformis* (Plate 11-2 B) as well as large branching species such as *Acropora palmata* (Plate 11-1 B). When they die, their skeletons serve as attachment sites for other organisms, including other smaller scleractinian reef associates. Ahermatypic corals such as *Madracis mirabilis* (Plate 11-1 A) and *Helioseris cucullata* (Plate 11-1 G) usually live upon the dead skeletons of the frame builders, rarely attaining their size.

The relationships between the terms constructional, nonconstructional, hermatypic and ahermatypic are not always clear-cut. All hermatypic corals are constructional, but ahermatypic corals may or may not be. Furthermore, not all constructional corals occur upon reefs. *Astrangia poculata* (Plate 11-3 C), for example, is a colonial constructional ahermatypic scleractinian. Similarly, the small rose coral, *Manicina areolata* (Plate 11-3 F), is not a reef-dweller, but develops small stony colonies on the shallow sandy floors of tropical lagoons. Perhaps most significantly, the line between hermatypic and ahermatypic is an artificial one. Some scleractinians may be considered ahermatypic in one environment but tend toward being hermatypic in another. For example, *Madracis mirabilis*, is frequently encountered as a small, branching ahermatypic colony attached to massive carbonate outcrops originally produced by a variety of hermatypic species. But colonies of *M. mirabilis* on Texas Flower Garden reefs sometimes occur in huge monospecific "thickets," consisting of a thin veneer of living coral which has deposited skeletal debris to a depth of at least 15 m below it (Rezak *et al.*, 1985).

There are a number of conditions necessary for the survival or prosperity of hermatypic corals. Briefly, most species require warm, clean, shallow marine waters of normal salinity and a hard substratum upon which to attach. They seem to fare best when mean annual water temperatures range between 23 to 35°C. Some species can survive brief exposures to temperatures below 18°C, but none can survive prolonged exposure below this temperature. Some species are also particularly sensitive to temperature fluctuations, and avoid situations where there are significant diurnal changes, as along shallow lagoon margins.

Corals are also sensitive to water turbidity, being absent for considerable distances surrounding river mouths or other areas where high loads of suspended materials are carried to the sea. Ironically, these corals depend upon suspended materials (largely zooplankton) for nutrition. Like all cnidarians, corals are carnivores. During the day, coral tissues usually lie contracted against the underlying skeletal mass, but polyps emerge from the calyces in the evening or on cloudy days to feed (Porter, 1974). Feeding methods vary considerably among species, some employing tentacles to snare copepods or other zooplankters whereas others trap organic particulates in mucous nets. All succumb if there is too much suspended material in the water. Hermatypic corals are not well adapted for hypertrophic, nutrient-rich waters and their attendant large phytoplankton populations.

One of the most important requirements of hermatypic corals is the presence of well-illuminated water. This necessity further emphasizes the need for low-turbidity, as all suspended materials in the water enhance and accelerate the absorption of light. So dependent are reef-building corals upon light, that below a depth of about 50 m most species disappear. It is not the corals which require the illumination, but symbiotic algae, the zooxanthellae, which live within their tissues (Fig. 11-1 D & E). When Wells (1933) originally coined the term "hermatypic," he intended it to mean both the reef-building habit of the Scleractinia *and* the fact that many of these species possess symbiotic zooxanthellae within their tissues. Since 1933, the dual meaning of the term has caused many problems, because not all reef-builders possess zooxanthellae, and not all zooxanthellate corals live upon reefs. Accordingly, the term hermatypic has recently been restricted as we have described above to refer solely to the growth form of the scleractinian skeleton, whereas those corals possessing symbiotic algae are to be called "zooxanthellate" and those lacking symbionts are to be known as "azooxanthellate" (Schuhmacher & Zibrowius, 1985).

Several kinds of invertebrates, including certain protozoans, sponges, jellyfishes, corals and molluscs, harbor zooxanthellae within their bodies. Zooxanthellae are the resting stages of unicellular dinoflagellates which, despite the animal in which they are found, have similar morphology and usually have been considered members of the same species, *Symbiodinium microadriaticum*, although recently this has been disputed (Schoenberg & Trench, 1980a, b, c; Trench, 1981). A motile (flagellate) stage of *S. microadriaticum* occurs in the plankton, but when present in coral tissues, it lacks flagellae (Freudenthal, 1962; Taylor, 1973; Loeblich & Shirley, 1979).

The relationship between corals and their zooxanthellae associates has received considerable attention during the last two decades (e.g., Franzisket, 1970; Lewis & Smith, 1971; Muscatine, 1974; Vandermeulen & Muscatine, 1974; Muscatine *et al.*, 1975; Goreau, 1977; Trench, 1979; Trench 1981; Gladfelter, 1985). Corals and algae have developed a delicate relationship (Fig. 11-1) in which the presence of zooxanthellae within hermatypic coral tissues greatly enhances coral skeletal calcification. Hermatypic zooxanthellate corals held in darkness either die or lose color and become incapable of significant growth. It may be excessive to state that zooxanthellae enable reef development, but they certainly deserve recognition as strongly influencing it.

The mechanisms by which zooxanthellae facilitate skeletal carbonate deposition in reef corals involve in-

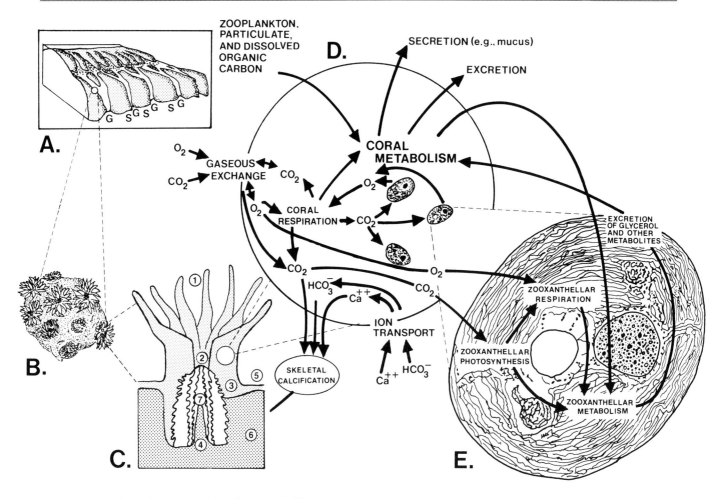

11-1. Reefs and corals. **A.** Spur (S) and groove (G) fringing reef. **B.** A portion of a colony of the boulder coral, *Montastrea annularis*. **C.** Anatomy of coral polyp: 1. tentacles, 2. mouth, 3. mesentary, 4. columella and adjacent sclerosepta, 5. tissue junction to adjacent polyp, 6. carbonate skeleton, 7. gastrovascular cavity. **D.** Simplified metabolic pathways within the coral tissue. **E.** Zooxanthellae, *Symbiodinium microadriaticum*.

Plate 11-1. Gulf of Mexico corals. **A.** *Madracis mirabilis*; **B.** Elkhorn coral, *Acropora palmata*; **C.** Staghorn coral, *Acropora cervicornis*; **D.** and **D1.** Shade coral, *Agaricia fragilis*; **E.** and **E1.** *Agaricia agaricites*; **F.** and **F1.** *Agaricia undata*; **G.** and **G1.** *Helioseris cucullata*; **H.** and **H1.** *Siderastrea radians*; **I.** and **I1.** *Siderastrea siderea*.

Pocilloporidae

Acroporidae

Agariciidae

Siderastreidae

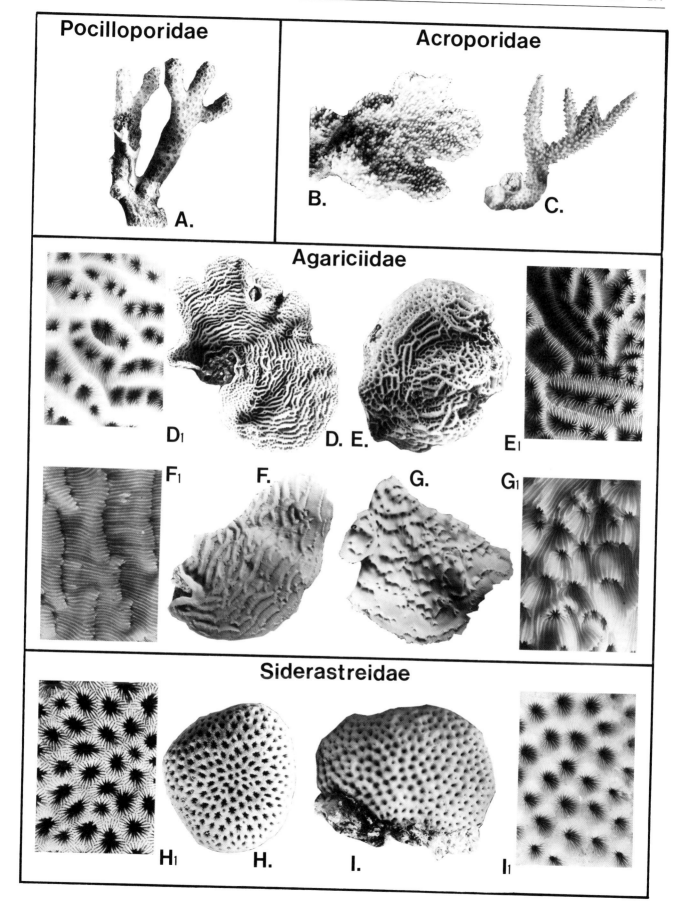

Faviidae

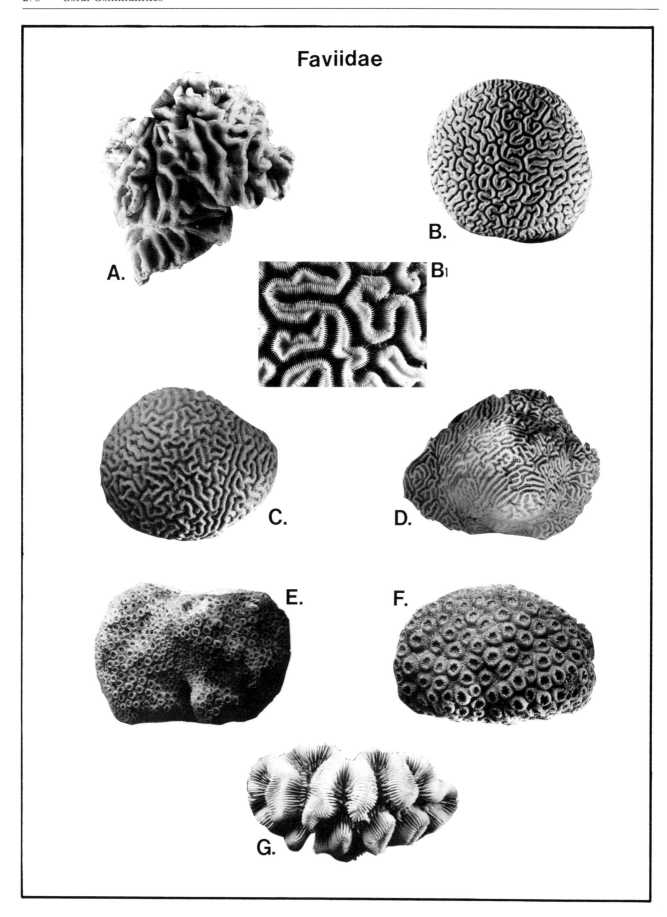

teractions between photosynthesis, host and symbiont carbon budgets, and the acquisition and cycling of nutrients. Despite intense study, the interactions remain poorly understood (Vandermeulen & Muscatine, 1974; Gladfelter, 1985). Some of the carbon fixed by zooxanthellar photosynthesis is passed to the coral, especially in the form of glycerol (Muscatine 1973; Muscatine *et al.*, 1981; Patton *et al.*, 1983; Battey & Patton, 1984) or lipids (Crossland *et al.*, 1980; Kellogg & Patton, 1983). It is used in coral metabolism such as mucus production (Falkowski *et al.*, 1984). Some of this carbon is even incorporated into the coral skeleton (Vandermeulen & Muscatine, 1974), but amounts are minimal. The absolute metabolic value of organic substances translocated from zooxanthellae to coral tissue has yet to be determined. Similarly, carbon dioxide generated by coral respiration can be utilized for both algal photosynthesis and skeletal calcification (Gladfelter, 1985), but the primary source of carbon for these processes seems to be from the environment, especially gases and ions in seawater. The presence of respiratory CO_2 does not seem to stimulate or enhance algal photosynthesis (Burris *et al.*, 1983). Despite these and other complex interactions between host and symbiont which have been investigated, the specific pathways by which zooxanthellar photosynthesis expedites coral skeletal deposition are still largely unknown.

The relationship between coral morphology and the presence of zooxanthellae has been the source of much speculation, but little has been resolved. For example, corals with tiny polyps and low surface/volume ratios, such as *Montastrea annularis* (Plate 11-2 F), often harbor abundant zooxanthellae within their tissues, and apparently feed upon small zooplankters. Those with larger polyps and higher surface/volume ratios, such as *Mussa angulosa* (Plate 11-3 F), seem to harbor relatively fewer zooxanthellae, and have been described as being more aggressive, more efficient carnivores (Porter, 1974). One might infer that the small polyp species rely to a greater degree upon nutrition provided the symbiotic algae than their larger polyp counterparts, but there is no experimental evidence to indicate if this is true. Similarly, many of the corals living on the deeper walls of the reef seem to accommodate their zooxanthellae by expanding the colony into flat plate-like masses (Fig. 11-6), apparently maximizing the light-catching surface. In fact, morphological adaptation may reflect some other aspect of coral biology. For example, deep water corals often have

lower metabolic rates than their shallow water counterparts (Davies, 1977; 1980), which, in turn, influence their rate and pattern of skeletal deposition. Much remains to be done before the symbiotic relationship between corals and zooxanthellae is fully understood.

There are considerably more coral banks and reefs in the southern portion of the western Gulf of Mexico than in the northern half. Naturally, this reflects latitudinal effects of climate and temperature. However, the virtual absence of reefs between approximately 22 to 28° N along the mainland shore reflects inhibiting factors other than just climate or temperature. Sediments from mainland rivers and streams and the longshore transport of these sediments along the entire coast produce marginal conditions for coral survival. Hypersalinity of coastal waters is another suboptimal situation for hermatypic species. Furthermore, there are few hard substrata along these shores upon which young corals can become established. All of these factors combine to produce an environment poorly suited for the establishment of coral reefs near the mainland. Those that do occur, like the Flower Garden Banks, are typically found some distance offshore, where the substratum is elevated far enough off the bottom to be above the nepheloid layer (a zone of cloudy turbid water) and where continental influences are minimal and temperature changes are significantly buffered by the water mass of the Gulf.

In this chapter we will examine two Gulf reefs, the Flower Garden Banks and Arrecife Lobos, in some detail, for they have received the greatest faunal study from a number of scientists. At the end of the chapter we will consider the distribution of additional coral communities within the region.

REEFS OF THE NORTHWESTERN GULF OF MEXICO

Despite many small banks or rocky outcrops which rise 1 m or more above the sandy floor of the continental shelf (Chapter 10), there are no nearshore coral reefs north of 22° N latitude in the northwestern Gulf of Mexico. They are present, however, on two promontories, the Flower Garden Banks, lying near the edge of the continental shelf somewhat more than 100 nautical miles SSE of Galveston, Texas. Each bank caps a salt dome protruding above the surrounding terrigenously derived sediments of the shelf margin floor (Rezak *et al.*, 1985). At approximately 27° 53' N latitude, the Flower Gardens contain the northern-most reef coral communities on the eastern North American continental shelf. Only the Bermuda Islands, bathed in the warm Gulf Stream waters at about 32° 20' N latitude in the oceanic Atlantic, have reef corals at a more northerly location than those of the Flower Gardens. We will describe the conditions which permit reef development at the Flower Gardens at the end of this section.

Both the East and West Flower Garden Banks crest at a depth of about 20 m. The West Flower Garden

Plate 11-2. Gulf of Mexico corals. **A.** *Colpophyllia natans*; **B.** and **B1.** Brain coral, *Diploria labyrinthiformis*; **C.** Brain coral, *Diploria clivosa*; **D.** Brain coral, *Diploria strigosa*; **E.** Great star coral, *Montastrea cavernosa*; **F.** Boulder coral, *Montastrea annularis*; **G.** Rose coral, *Manicina areolata*.

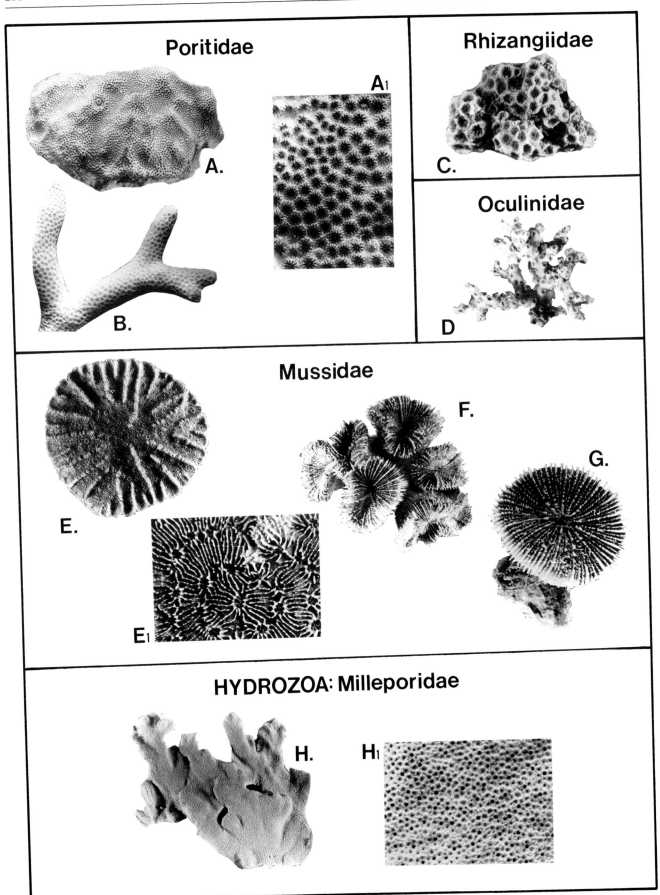

Bank was the first to receive intensive study (Edwards, 1971; Bright & Pequegnat, 1974). It is an elongate ridge extending northeast to southwest, covering an area of about 137 km², and having a total relief of about 130 m (Rezak *et al.*, 1985). The shallowest part of the bank extends east to west for about 1 km at the 30 m isobath (Fig. 11-2). This shallow section varies considerably in width, being widest (about 380 m) somewhat east of center. In recent years the East Flower Garden Bank has received considerable attention (Rezak *et al.*, 1985, and references therein). It is a pear-shaped topographic high lying about 12 km east of the West Flower Garden Bank, covering about 67 km² and having a total relief of about 116 m. The salt dome underlying the western bank is older than that beneath the eastern bank. It has experienced greater salt removal by solution, accounting in part for the greater relief on the surface of the western bank (Rezak *et al.*, 1985). The East Flower Garden, however, includes regions of active brine seep, a brine "lake," and a narrow, shallow canyon which drains brine from the lake and enables it to mix with adjacent seawater (Bright *et al.*, 1980; Rezak & Bright (1981); Rezak *et al.*, 1985).

Both the East and West Flower Garden Banks bear a similar biota. Living coral heads lie at depths between 20 and 50 m, and shelter a relatively small assemblage of coral-associated flora and fauna. There are about 21 species of Scleractinia on these banks, of which about 18 are hermatypic. Rezak *et al.* (1985) recognize several major biotic communities on the bank crests and their upper slopes, each characterized by or containing a distinctive assemblage of corals and other animals or plants.

The uppermost community, termed the *Diploria-Montastrea-Porites* zone, at depths between 20 and 36 m, contains the richest coral diversity, and is the area most commonly visited by divers. *Montastrea annularis* (Fig. 11-2 D) is the dominant coral species in terms of percent bottom covered. Other common corals include *Diploria strigosa* (Fig. 11-2 E), *Porites astreoides* (Fig. 11-2 A), *Montastrea cavernosa* (Fig. 11-2 F) *Colpophyllia natans* (Plate 11-2 A) and *C. amaranthus*. They produce closely spaced globular or plate-like heads, many as much as 2 m in diameter and/or height. Gorgonacean octocorals, which provide color, movement, and rich diversity to shallow Caribbean reefs, are conspicuously absent at the top of each bank. Many other bank reef associates, however, have their greatest abundance in this upper zone.

Portions of the East Flower Garden Bank at depths between 28 to 46 m lack the massive living corals. These areas include several broad knolls upon which are either expansive colonies of the small branching coral *Madracis mirabilis* (Plate 11-1 A) or an algal community including species of *Stypopodium*, *Caulerpa*, *Dictyota*, *Chaetomorpha*, *Lobophora*, *Rhodymenia*, *Valonia* and *Codium*. Rezak *et al.* (1985) call these areas the *Madracis* or Leafy Algae Zones. They suggest these features may be successional between the deeper areas largely uncolonized by the massive-structured Scleractinia and the *Diploria-Montastrea-Porites* zone of the bank crest.

On both banks at depths between about 36 to 50 m biotic diversity decreases. Rezak *et al.* (1985) designate this the *Stephanocoenia-Millepora* zone. The hydrocoral *Millepora alcicornis* (Fig. 10-7 F; Plate 11-3 H) and the scleractinian *Stephanocoenia michelini* (Fig. 11-2 H) are numerically dominant, but *Montastrea cavernosa*, *Colpophyllia natans*, *C. amaranthus*, *Agaricia* spp., *Mussa angulosa* (Fig. 11-2 G), and *Scolymia cubensis* (Fig. 11-2 C) are also common. This area is transitional between the bank crest with its massive coral heads and the deeper flanks of the reef face covered primarily by low biogenic encrustations. A narrow antipatharian zone characterizes the upper edge of the reef face.

11-2. The Flower Garden Banks. The location of the Flower Garden Banks is shown in the inset map at upper right. A bathymetric profile from the vicinity of East Flower Garden Bank is shown at the bottom right (after Rezak *et al.*, 1985). A computer-generated profile of this area is shown at bottom left, the view being from the southeast corner of the bathymetric profile and looking toward the northwest. Major communities and characterizing organisms are indicated on the profile. Illustrated biota are: **A.** *Porites astreoides*; **B.** crustose coralline algae; **C.** *Scolymia cubensis*; **D.** Boulder coral, *Montastrea annularis*; **E.** Brain coral, *Diploria strigosa*; **F.** Great star coral, *Montastrea cavernosa*; **G.** *Mussa angulosa*; **H.** *Stephanocoenia michelini*; **I.** *Madracis decactis*; **J.** *Helioseris cucullata*; **K.** *Brachycarpus biunguiculatus*; **L.** Short coral-shell, *Coralliophila abbreviata*; **M.** *Coralliophila scalariformes*; **N.** Stocky cerith, *Cerithium litteratum*; **O.** American star shell, *Astraea tecta*; **P.** Cone snail, *Conus ermineus*; **Q.** Hammer oyster, *Malleus candeanus*; **R.** Pistol shrimp, *Synalpheus* sp.; **S.** Red-brown ark, *Barbatia cancellaria*; **T.** File shell, *Lima scabra tenera*; **U.** Brittle star, *Ophiactis savignyi*; **V.** Sea urchin, *Pseudoboletia maculata*; **W.** Bigeye, *Priacanthus arenatus*; **X.** Spotted soapfish, *Rypticus subbifrenatus*; **Y.** Flamefish, *Apogon maculatus*; **Z.** Spider crab, *Mithrax forceps*; **A1.** Coral crab, *Mithrax hispidus*; **B1.** *Scyllarides aequinoctialis*; **C1.** Sea cucumber, *Isostichopus bandionotus*.

Plate 11-3. Gulf of Mexico corals. **A.** and **A1.** *Porites astreoides*; **B.** *Porites furcata*; **C.** *Astrangia poculata*; **D.** Ivory coral, *Oculina diffusa*; **E.** and **E1.** *Mycetophyllia lamarkiana*; **F.** *Mussa angulosa*; **G.** *Scolymia cubensis*; **H.** and **H.1.** *Millepora alcicornis*.

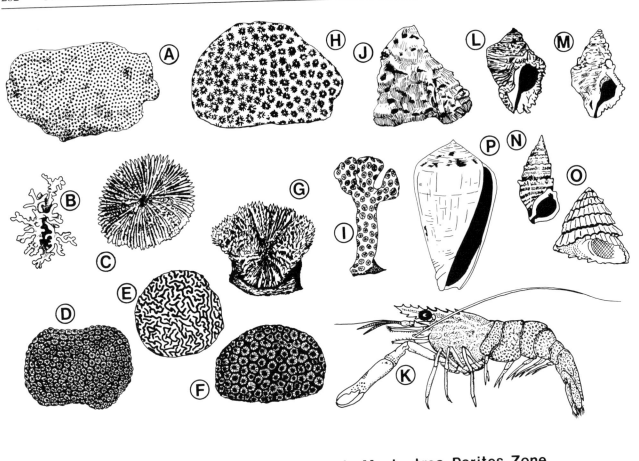

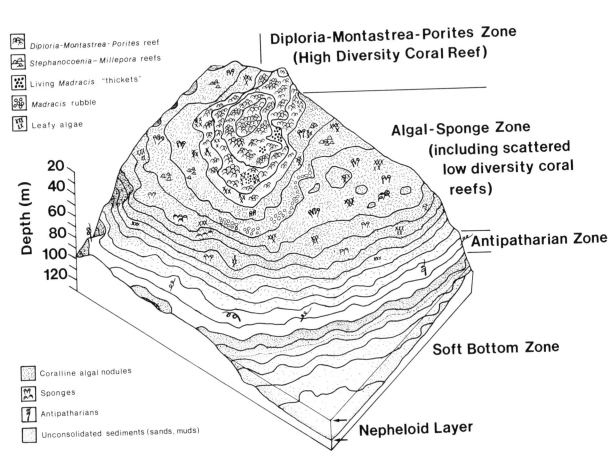

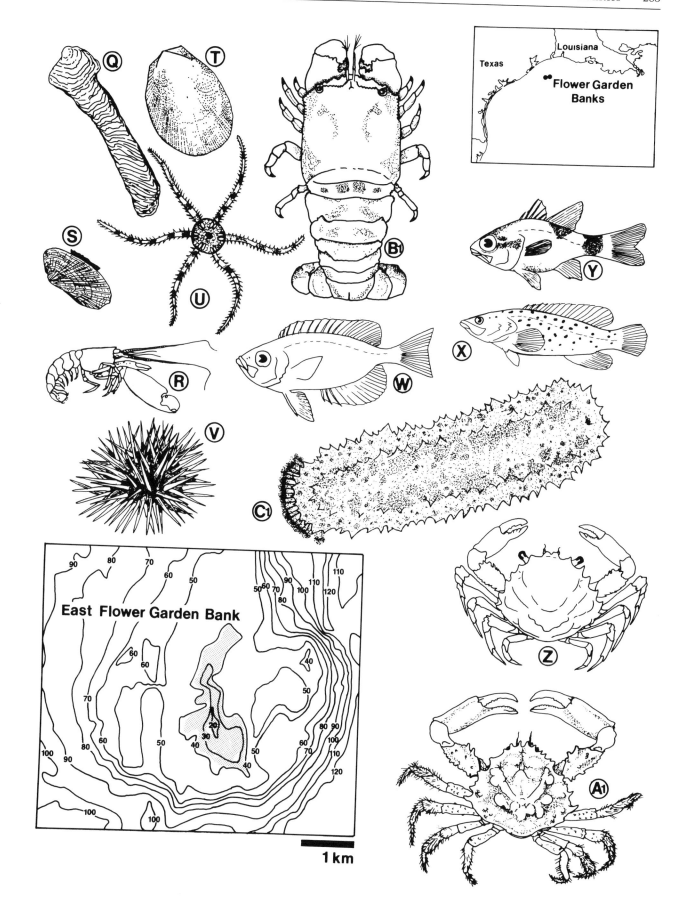

At depths between about 50 to 85 m (the lower margin being slightly shallower at the East bank and slightly deeper at the West bank), coarse carbonate sand, gravel and small nodules of coralline algae (Fig. 11-2 B) dominate the bottom. They range from 1 to 10 cm in diameter and are so numerous that they frequently comprise more than 50 percent of the bottom. Encrusting Foraminifera (e.g., *Gypsina*), sponges, deep water alcyonarians, small corals, including *Helioseris cucullata* (Fig. 11-2 J), *Madracis* sp., and flattened, encrusting colonies of *Montastrea cavernosa*, spiny oysters, *Spondylus americanus* (Fig. 11-6 R), large patchy carpets of *Halimeda*, and the antipatharian sea whips *Cirrhipathes* and *Antipathes* (Fig. 11-6 D) are among the other common sessile biota here. Echinoderms are especially abundant in this deeper part of the bank, including several species of comatulid crinoids, the starfish *Linckia nodosa*, and the sea urchins *Pseudoboletia maculata* (Fig. 11-2 V) and *Arbacia punctulata* (which we have previously encountered at the Texas jetties).

At about 80 m, waters become increasingly turbid and the bottom gradually changes from coarse gravels to fine muds, the latter usually at depths below 100 m. Irregular mounds of relic or drowned reefs occasionally outcrop above the accumulating sediment blanket. The drowned or drowning reefs consist primarily of massive, nonliving skeletons of many of the species found now living upon the bank crest. Clearly, actively growing coral heads once occupied this portion of the bank, perhaps when sea levels were significantly lower than they are today, or perhaps when the water near these deep bank areas was less turbid. Today the fine silts and clays which cloud the waters below 80 m decrease illumination and increase rates of sedimentation, both of which strongly inhibit growth or survival of hermatypic corals.

Species diversity at the Flower Gardens is considerably less than that on reefs of the central Caribbean. For example, about 20 species of scleractinian corals occur on the Flower Garden Banks, but the reefs of Jamaica, Roatan or Grand Cayman may contain upwards of 50 species. Yet, total diversity at the Flower Gardens probably is not as low as once believed. Since about 1970, when these banks began to receive intense study, the number of species known from them has been steadily increasing. Bright & Pequegnat (1974) recorded about 260 species of invertebrates and 101 species of fishes from the West Flower Garden Bank. About 196 of the invertebrates and nine fishes reported in 1974 were not included on the Rezak *et al.* (1985) list based upon subsequent collections from both banks. The latter adds 131 previously unreported species of invertebrates and 100 species of fishes to the Flower Garden fauna, bringing the total to about 391 invertebrates and 201 species of fishes. A few of the "new" species added in 1985 result from synonymization or other taxonomic refinements of the 1974 list (T.J. Bright, personal communication). Rezak *et al.* (1985) also indicate a number of additional invertebrates and fishes from other Gulf of Mexico offshore banks presently unrecorded from the Flower Gardens. Many of these eventually may be encountered here.

About 120 species of benthic arthropods have been reported from the Flower Gardens, including several species of ostracods, amphipods, isopods, symbiotic barnacles and other tiny crustaceans. The barnacle *Acasta cyathus* lives embedded in sponge tissue with only a white, calcareous circular orifice marking its presence. A sponge may harbor many of these barnacles. Several species of snapping shrimps, *Synalpheus* sp. (Fig. 11-2 R), also hide in sponges or seek burrows or crevices among the coral rubble. They betray their abundance by interminable snaps, cracks and pops clearly audible to divers on the reef. They are as elusive as they are noisy, as anyone who has ever tried to trace the sources of these sounds can readily testify.

The larger decapod crustaceans include a variety of crabs, shrimps, lobsters and hermit crabs. Two species of spider crabs, *Mithrax forceps* (Fig. 11-2 Z) and *M. hispidus* (Fig. 11-2 A1), are among the most abundant of the larger decapods on the West Flower Garden reef. The spiny lobsters *Panulirus argus* (Fig. 11-6 F) and *P. guttatus* and the shovel-nosed lobster, *Scyllarides aequinoctialis* (Fig. 11-2 B1) are common on one or both bank crests where they take refuge among the coral boulders. Large numbers of the nocturnal fish-cleaning shrimp, *Brachycarpus biunguiculatus* (Fig. 11-2 K), seek shelter in coral refugia during the day, but emerge at night to station themselves in conspicuous positions where they attract fish that require grooming, wounds tended and parasites removed.

About 75 species of benthic molluscs have been reported from the Flower Garden Banks. Some of the most commonly encountered include the gastropods *Cerithium litteratum* (Fig. 11-2 N), *Astraea tecta* (Fig. 11-2 O), *Coralliophila abbreviata* (Fig. 11-2 L), *C. scalariformes* (Fig. 11-2 M), *Siliquaria squamata* (Fig. 10-7 K), and *Conus ermineus* (Fig. 11-2 P), and the bivalves *Lima scabra tenera* (Fig. 11-2 T), *Barbatia cancellaria* (Fig. 11-2 S), *B. candida* (Fig. 4-2 R), *Malleus candeanus* (Fig. 11-2 Q), and *Lithophaga bisulcata* (Fig. 11-7 C).

The echinoderms of the offshore banks demonstrate considerably greater diversity than in northwestern Gulf nearshore habitats. About 40 species occur at the Flower Gardens. The West Indian black long-spined sea urchin, *Diadema antillarum* (Fig. 11-4 F1), was, until 1984, one of the most conspicuous among the shallow coral boulders, although they probably share numerical dominance with the more secretive brittle star, *Ophiactis savignyi* (Fig. 11-2 U). An apparently water-borne disease depleted the numbers of *D. antillarum* throughout much of its range (Lessios *et al.*, 1984), including Flower Garden populations in 1984 (Rezak *et al.*, 1985). Despite heavy mortalities, *Diadema* populations have slowly recovered throughout much of the Caribbean, but few, if any, were present on the Flower Garden reefs as of November, 1987 (T.J.

Bright, personal communication). Macrophytic algal cover (primarily *Dictyota* spp. and *Stypopodium zonale*) markedly increased on both East and West Flower Garden banks as the *Diadema* population has been depleted. Gittings *et al.* (in press) suggest the increase in algal density and decline of *Diadema* are causally related.

Several echinoderms frequent the deeper portions of these banks, living among carbonate gravels and coralline algae. The sea urchins *Arbacia punctulata* (Fig. 3-1 I) and *Pseudoboletia maculata* (Fig. 11-2 V) congregate in dense but scattered aggregations. Several species of asteroids, including *Linckia nodosa*, *Chaetaster nodosus*, and *Ophidiaster guildingii* live among the stony cobbles, as do one or more species of comatulid crinoids. *Isostichopus badionotus* (Fig. 11-2 C1) is a large conspicuous sea cucumber that prefers areas of soft sediment.

Fishes provide considerable diversity on the Flower Garden Banks, with about 200 recorded species. Not all of these are reef associates, for some are open water or offshore species. Most reef-associated fishes on the banks originate from tropical Caribbean reefs. Like the other bank biota, they, too, only hint at the diversity of Caribbean habitats. Bohlke and Chaplin (1968), for example, record 466 nearshore fish species from the Bahamas.

We illustrate three fishes representing families not discussed in previous chapters. The bigeye, *Priacanthus arenatus* (Fig. 11-2 W) represents a family (Priacanthidae) common on reefs or banks of the outer shelf region. Juveniles will swim near the surface, often under flotsam, and are distributed rather widely by ocean currents. Adults are more often found near the bottom at depths from 20 to 100 m. The spotted soapfish, *Rypticus subbifrenatus* (Fig. 11-2 X) is another rock or reef-associate common on the Flower Garden Banks. The soapfishes (Grammistidae) are closely related to the sea basses (Serranidae). Their common name is derived from the soapy mucus which covers the body of some of these fishes (e.g., at least the larger *Rypticus* spp). The flamefish, *Apogon maculatus* (Fig. 11-2 Y) is one of the numerous small, brightly colored reef fishes that flits among rock crevices on most western Atlantic reefs. It is also common around offshore oil drilling platforms throughout the Gulf of Mexico. The common name reflects the deep orange-red color.

By virtue of their position on the edge of the continental shelf, the Flower Garden Banks lie simultaneously protected by remoteness from the bulk of lithogenous nearshore sedimentation and insulated by oceanic water from the temperature extremes which affect similar, shallower banks nearer the shore. Other hard banks of the northern Gulf are chilled by winter temperatures often falling below the critical minimum for most hermatypic corals (16 to 18°C), scoured by sands swept along the bottom by strong nearshore currents, or blanketed beneath a cloud of almost perpetually turbid, light-attenuating water. These factors,

alone or in combination, are the primary reasons why reefs are mostly absent on the numerous hard banks of the northern Gulf region. A few hardy reef-associated species (e.g., *Millepora*, *Madracis*, and *Oculina*) may colonize parts or all of these banks (see Chapter 10), and on a few, such as 18 Fathom and Bright banks to the east of the Flower Garden Banks, low diversity reefs dominated by *Stephanocoenia* and *Millepora* appear. Large communities of hermatypic scleractinians, however, are almost uniformly absent. Even the large Florida Middle Grounds Bank on the west Florida shelf harbors 16 species of relatively small Scleractinia (Grimm & Hopkins, 1977; Hopkins *et al.*, 1977), but fails to produce the massive coral heads which typify typical Atlantic reefs.

The Flower Garden Banks are rarely affected by the seasonal changes in wind and current direction that influence nearshore waters and communities along the northern Gulf coast. Instead, they lie in such a position and at a sufficient depth as to be bathed by warm water from the southern Gulf basin most of the year. Local currents in the vicinity of the bank mostly flow eastward (Rezak *et al.*, 1985). Water in the western Gulf basin generally moves in a clockwise or anticyclonic flow (Blumberg & Mellor, 1981). Thus, the water which sweeps eastward past the Flower Gardens in the northern Gulf began its journey in the southern Gulf flowing westward. It entered through the Yucatan Straits, passed westward, some of it over the shallow, warm Yucatan shelf, then arced southward, westward and northward across the southwestern Gulf margin. Eventually it arced northeastward on a course that would bring it across the Flower Garden Banks.

The continual supply of warm water from the southern Gulf creates a modest thermocline that persists most of the year over the northwestern shelf margin. This warm oceanic flow largely buffers the Flower Gardens from low winter surface temperatures, but the banks are not so deep as to lie below the seasonal thermocline. Also, by the time water from the southern Gulf reaches the vicinity of the Flower Banks, it has acquired the oceanic characteristics of being both clean and clear. This, coupled with the distance from shore, insures that the surface waters contain few suspended sediments from terrigenous sources. Waters over these banks are sufficiently transparent to provide adequate illumination to support significant populations of zooxanthellate corals to depths of about 50 m. These conditions are similar to those that enable reefs to fringe the oceanic Bermuda Islands. The Flower Gardens are unique, however, as being the northernmost continental shelf reefs in the western Atlantic and the only true, well-developed reefs in the northern Gulf of Mexico. It is easier to appreciate their uniqueness by realizing that the reef nearest in distance to the Flower Gardens is on the Yucatan shelf about 680 km to the south. The reefs nearest in latitude to the Flower Gardens occur off southern Florida, over 1100 km away. In comparison, the Bermuda Islands lie more than 1300 km northeast of the Bahamas.

Rezak *et al.* (1985) present an extensive discussion of biogeographic aspects of the coral communities of the Flower Garden banks in relation to other Atlantic reefs. They consider the Flower Garden Banks, Bermuda, and the Florida Middle Grounds "three separate, northern, biogeographic 'end points' in the contemporary distribution of tropical Atlantic coral reefs and coral-dominated assemblages derived from the Caribbean biota." None of these areas expresses the full diversity of species encountered on reefs within the central tropical Atlantic province. The Florida Middle Grounds even fail to harbor the massive frame-building corals which characterize a "typical" reef. The Flower Gardens coral community has more in common with that of Bermuda than with that of the Florida Middle Grounds or any other coral community within the tropical Atlantic basin. There are about 25 species of Scleractinia on the Bermuda reefs (Sterrer, 1986), of which only 9 also occur at the Flower Garden Banks. Nevertheless, the reefs of the two areas share similar dominant species which, in turn, impose a similar community structure at each locality. Furthermore, several species (especially the *Acropora* spp.) are notably absent from both locations. The corals which colonize the Flower Gardens and Bermuda presumably share similar tolerances for larval transport, marginal environmental conditions, or a variety of other factors which apparently exclude such species as *Acropora palmata* or *A. cervicornis*. The restraints are not exclusively depth related or imposed, for massive heads of *Diploria*, *Montastrea* and other species thrive on near-surface reefs in Bermuda.

Both Bermuda and the Flower Gardens are continually restocked by planktonic larvae produced by a tropical biota from more southerly locations. Which species survive the journey and become established must be, at least in part, a function of individual capabilities to cope with moderate to prolonged planktonic life at sea, and, in part, the abilities of the settled adults to cope with suboptimal or periodic detrimental conditions near the extreme edge of their ranges. The biotic differences between Bermuda and the Gulf bank reefs also reflect some of the biotic differences between their original sources of supply. For example, Southern Florida and the Bahama platform are rich in species of shallow water Alcyonaria. Accordingly, Bermuda reefs contain at least 20 species of sea fans, sea whips, and other soft corals. In contrast, Alcyonaria are poorly represented in the southern Gulf. It should be little surprise there are virtually no shallow water soft corals represented on the Flower Garden Banks.

NEARSHORE REEFS OF CENTRAL MEXICO

A number of small coral banks and reefs occur along the central eastern coast of Mexico. Several reefs and coral islands near Veracruz have received study (Macias, 1968; Jaims, 1968; Villalobos, 1971; Rannefeld, 1972; Kuhlmann, 1975). J.W. Tunnell and the staff and students of Corpus Christi State University have con-

tributed significantly to our knowledge of these and other southwestern Gulf of Mexico coral reefs, including the compilation of an extensive checklist of the biota. The northernmost nearshore emergent reefs along the Gulf of Mexico's western margin occur just off Cabo Rojo, about 100 km south of Tampico, Mexico (Alacran and other emergent bank reefs off northwestern Yucatan, discussed at the end of the chapter, actually lie north of Cabo Rojo, but they lie far offshore). A series of three reef-covered banks, Arrecife Blanquilla, Arrecife Medio, and Arrecife Lobos (or Lobos Reef), trend in a southeasterly line off Cabo Rojo, each separated from the other by a few km. Arrecife Lobos, the southern, largest and most seaward of the three, lies about 11 km off the mainland shore and about 56 km north of Tuxpan, Mexico (Figs. 11-3 and 11-4). It is the only one of the trio of banks with a centrally emergent island, Isla de Lobos. The semi-elliptical sandy cay is only a small portion of the entire reef bank complex. It presents an arcing shore facing the prevailing southeasterly winds and a straight or slightly concave leeward margin (Fig. 11-3, black area on central map). The long axis of the island trends 650 m northeastward, and it is slightly more than 300 m at its widest point. It rises to a maximum elevation of 4 m above sea level.

Isla de Lobos lies along the southwest margin of the tear-drop shaped Lobos reef and lagoon system. This bank has a length of about 3 km at the 25 m isobath. Prevailing winds have sculpted the shallow northern bank margin into a point and the southern margin into a curving flank. A hurricane in 1951 deposited a line of coral boulders just off the southwestern edge of Isla de Lobos, creating an emergent boulder ridge here, effectively forming a rocky shore habitat. A dredged channel traverses the lagoon, providing shipping access to a well platform near the east central bank margin. Slender fingers of emergent coral rocks and boulders deposited as dredge-spoil border the channel, separating the lagoon into northern and southern portions.

The bank includes several distinctive physiographic units, each containing one or more biotic communities (Rigby & McIntire, 1966; Chavez *et al.*, 1970; Chavez, 1973). First, there are two kinds of shores. Isla de Lobos is almost completely surrounded by narrow, steeply sloping sandy beaches containing a distinctive, although limited biota. Hard shores are limited to the natural accumulation of coral boulders and various man-made structures (pilings, wharves, rock causeways) associated with the channel and well platform.

Several subtidal habitats occur upon the bank. A lagoon occupies the central area (Fig. 11-3 upper inset, 1; Fig. 11-4). Most of the lagoon floor lies within one meter of low tide. Its maximum depth is about 2 m (excepting the dredged channel). Biotic communities here include subtidal rock, subtidal sand, grass beds, and lagoonal patch reefs. There are windward and leeward reefs (Fig. 11-3, upper inset, 2), both having a distinctive spur and groove morphology (Fig. 11-1 A). A back-reef *Diploria* community and a reef crest community capped by crustose coralline algae mark the upper margins of the reef. In the wave-swept upper 5 m of both windward and leeward reefs, *Acropora palmata* dominates a distinctive community (Fig. 11-3, upper inset, 3). Below this, a leeward *Montastrea* community and a windward *Diploria-Porites* community occupy the mid-depths of the reef, protected from the most intense wave activity (Fig. 11-3, upper inset, 4 and 5). An assemblage of deeper-dwelling corals occurs at the base of major reef spurs (Fig. 11-3, upper inset, 6) along a fringing sandy apron. Additional sandy or rocky slope habitats surround the bank below a depth of 25 m, but we will not describe them.

Because the Lobos bank complex provides examples of most of the habitats usually associated with tropical carbonate reefs, we will use this locality as the primary focus to describe Gulf reef communities. There are a few species, however, which we believe to be important to mention because they occur on other Gulf reefs, but which have not been reported from Arrecife Lobos. We will clearly indicate each of these when they are encountered.

Isla de Lobos: Sandy Beach Community

The sandy beaches of Isla de Lobos are particularly impoverished of life. Wave energy is usually so slight upon these shores, protected as they are within the surrounding lagoon, as to preclude the presence of many typical suspension feeding sandy shore dwellers. Water temperatures on leeward beaches exceed 40°C during the summer. Occasional storms keep the sands well sorted, preventing significant accumulations of nutrients or fine particles on the beach and effectively eliminating most deposit feeders from this habitat. The coarse, seasonally hot, shifting beach sands provide little incentive for most potential colonizers.

Omnivorous decapod scavengers dominate the beach biota, largely because they can seek food elsewhere if necessary. Ghost crabs, *Ocypode quadrata* (Fig. 11-3 G) are most frequently encountered, their distinctive burrows interrupting the smooth sweep of upper beach sands. They avoid diurnal solar heating within the protection of the burrow, emerging at night to feed. *Gecarcinus lateralis* (Fig. 11-3 H) lives slightly higher among the shrubs fringing the upper beach, relying primarily upon this vegetation for sustenance. The West Indian land hermit crab, *Coenobita clypeatus* (Fig. 11-3 P1) also occurs and feeds upon island vegetation.

A few additional crabs seek shelter in the sands just below the island shore. These include the portunids *Arenaeus cribrarius* (Fig. 10-1 C) and the bluish *Callinectes marginatus*, a larger Caribbean relative of *C. sapidus* of temperate shores. The shame-face crabs *Calappa sulcata* (Fig. 10-1 H) and *C. gallus* hide in lagoonal sands surrounding the island with all but the tip of their head buried. They feed upon bivalves or hermit crabs, two species of the latter, *Clibanarius tricolor* and *C. antillensis* (Fig. 11-4 U) being particularly common here. *Clibanarius tricolor* is especially tolerant of harsh intertidal environments and tends to dominate shallow subtidal pools along island beaches. An interstitial isopod also is present in great abundance at the water line (J.W. Tunnell, personal communication).

Arrecife Lobos: Coral Boulder Ramparts

Apart from the concrete shores on Isla de Lobos, the coral boulder ramparts constitute the major emergent intertidal rocky shores of this bank. They were deposited as spoil from channel dredging along the northeastern and southwestern sides of the island. The top of each rampart has been filled and converted to roadway, but the flanks of each rampart consist entirely of rock, at, above and below the waterline. The biota of these rocks resembles that of the hard shores described in Chapter 4, but at and below sea level it includes a mixed assemblage of rocky shore and reef crest biota. Interestingly, the hard shore component of these ramparts is a relatively recent development, absent save for barnacles in the mid-1960s (Rigby & McIntire, 1966), but modestly established by 1973 (Tunnell, personal communication).

A number of grazing snails now occupy the upper and mid-littoral boulder ramparts. Five littorines occur here, although some of the species are uncommon. *Cenchritis muricatus* (Fig. 4-5 I) lives highest upon the rocks. *Littoraria angulifera* (Fig. 11-3 O), *L. nebulosa* (Fig. 11-3 P), *Nodilittorina lineolata* (Fig. 4-5 A), and *N. ziczac* (Fig. 4-5 G) occupy sheltered crevices nearer the tide line. *Nerita versicolor* (Fig. 11-3 J), *N. fulgurans* (Fig. 11-3 K) and *N. tessellata* (Fig. 11-3 I) occupy protected rocks and pools of midshore. Small clusters of the barnacle *Chthamalus fragilis* (Fig. 3-1 D) occur on more exposed but tidally washed stones. A fourth nerite, *N. peloronta* (Fig. 4-1 R), is an occasional inhabitant. *Siphonaria pectinata* (Fig. 4-1 K) occurs amid the barnacle patches, reminding us that temperate elements also persist on this shore. The snails *Supplanaxis nucleus* (Fig. 4-2 L) and *Angiola lineata* (Fig. 4-2 M) are common under rocks at the tide line. Here also are two chitons, *Acanthochitona pygmaea* and *Ischnochiton papillosus*, both recruited from the reef crest nearby.

The grapsid crabs *Grapsus grapsus* (Fig. 11-3 Q) and *Pachygrapsus transversus* (Fig. 11-3 R) scurry along the seaward boulder ramparts, and are also commonly observed on concrete pilings associated with the channel and well platforms. The latter species is less venturesome than the former, remaining closer to the sea.

Several bivalves occur on the boulders at or just below the tide line, where they lie cemented or byssally attached. A few oyster shells, *Ostrea frons* or *Crassostrea* sp., attach to rocks of the lower rampart. This is not a particularly suitable habitat for either oyster, so most specimens are usually small and dead. The ark shells *Barbatia candida* (Fig. 4-2 R), *B. domingensis* (Fig. 4-2 T), *B. tenera* and the smaller *Arcopsis adamsi* (Fig 11-5 H) live byssally attached to the undersides of submerged stones. *Isognomon bicolor* (Fig. 4-2 D) employs a byssus to attach to rocks in the surf zone between the holdfasts of macroscopic algae.

As on the Texas jetties, the shell-boring gastropod *Stramonita haemastoma* (Fig. 11-3 M) preys upon intertidal herbivorous snails, bivalves and barnacles. Two additional thaiids, *S. rustica* (Fig. 11-3 L) and *Thais deltoidea* (Fig 11-3 N), recruited from the adjacent reefs, join *S. haemastoma* in the lower pools and subtidal rocks.

The lower cobble ramparts are sparsely covered by a variety of algae. *Sargassum vulgare* and *Padina* sp. (Fig. 4-2 Y) are most abundant near the exposed ends of the boulder ridges where currents are especially strong. *Padina* species can be difficult to distinguish. The thallus blades of *P. vickersiae* are little, if at all, calcified, whereas those of *P. sanctaecrucis* are moderately calcified, especially upon their upper or concave surfaces. A variety of other brown and green species occupy the seaward face of the rampart, but are poorly

11-3. Shore and shallow water biota of Isla y Arrecife Lobos. Lobos Island and the surrounding reef lie off Cabo Rojo on the central Mexico Gulf coast (inset map). The reef profile indicates several zones, as follows: **1.** Lagoon and back reef, **2.** Reef crest, **3.** Fore reef, **4.** and **5.** Fore reef slope, **6.** Deeper fore reef, grading into sand apron. The island and reef are illustrated, with arrows indicating the prevailing wind direction. Additional symbols indicate the following areas:

■ Isla Lobos and boulder ramparts   ▨ Lagoon
▨ Reef crest   ▨ Upper fore reef
□ Ship channel, deeper offshore sands   ▨ Lower fore reef

A. Brain coral, *Diploria clivosa*; **B.** crustose coralline algae; **C.** Elkhorn coral, *Acropora palmata*; **D.** Boulder coral, *Montastrea annularis*; **E.** Brain coral, *Diploria strigosa*; **F.** Great star coral, *Montastrea cavernosa*; **G.** Ghost crab, *Ocypode quadrata*; **H.** Red land crab, *Gecarcinus lateralis*; **I.** Tessellate nerite, *Nerita tessellata*; **J.** Four-toothed nerite, *Nerita versicolor*; **K.** Antillean nerite, *Nerita fulgurans*; **L.** Rustic rock snail, *Stramonita rustica*; **M.** Rock snail, *Stramonita haemastoma*; **N.** Deltoid rock snail, *Thais deltoidea*; **O.** Angulate periwinkle, *Littoraria angulifera*; **P.** Cloudy periwinkle, *Littoraria nebulosa*; **Q.** Sally Lightfoot crab, *Grapsus grapsus*; **R.** Mottled shore crab, *Pachygrapsus transversus*; **S.** *Amphiroa rigida*; **T.** *Nemalion helminthoides*; **U.** Decorator crab, *Macrocoeloma diplacanthum*; **V.** Decorator crab, *Microphrys bicornutus*; **W.** *Champia parvula*; **X.** *Amphiroa fragilissima*; **Y.** *Laurencia papillosa*; **Z.** *Galaxaura subverticillata*; **A1.** *Dictyota divaricata*; **B1.** *Colpomenia sinuosa*; **C1.** *Dictyosphaeria cavernosa*; **D1.** *Halimeda opuntia*; **E1.** *Digenia simplex*; **F1.** *Rhipocephalus phoenix*; **G1.** *Caulerpa racemosa*; **H1.** *Udotea flabellum*; **I1.** *Caulerpa cupressoides*; **J1.** *Valonia ventricosa*; **K1.** *Cladophoropsis membranacea*; **L1.** *Halimeda tuna*; **M1.** *Fosliella lejolisii*; **N1.** Turtle grass, *Thalassia testudinum*; **O1.** *Avrainvillea nigricans*; **P1.** *Coenobita clypeatus*.

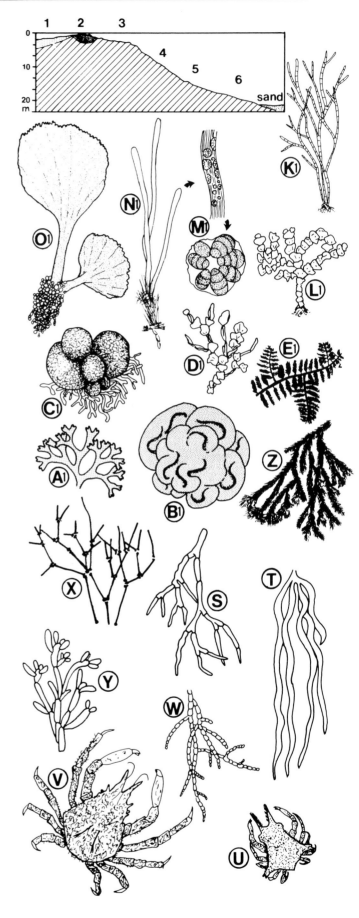

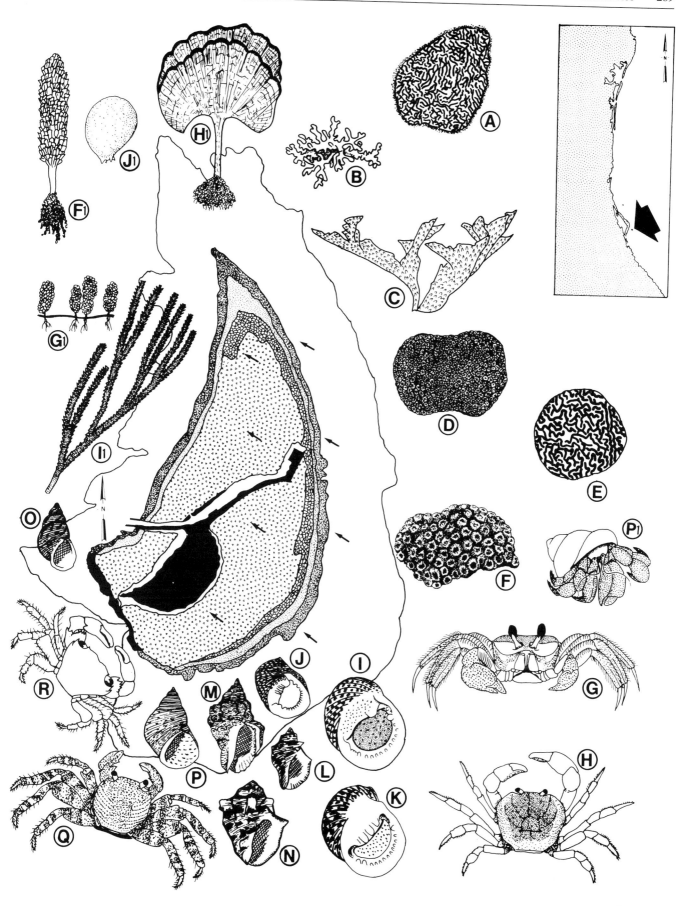

represented along the protected inner face. Yellowish-brown *Colpomenia sinuosa* (Fig. 11-3 B1) forms globose or lobate blobs on wave-swept rocks. Green spheres of *Dictyosphaeria cavernosa* (Fig. 11-3 C1) attach to rocks in slightly more protected locations. *Valonia ventricosa* (Fig. 11-3 J1) forms somewhat smaller bubbles than the previous two species. The brown alga *Dictyota divaricata* (Fig. 11-3 A1) occupies sites of moderate wave swash, as do several species of red algae including *Laurencia papillosa* (Fig. 11-3 Y), *Galaxaura subverticillata* (Fig. 11-3 Z), *Gracilaria verrucosa*, *Amphiroa rigida* (Fig. 11-3 S), *A. fragilissima* (Fig. 11-3 X), *Nemalion helminthoides* (Fig. 11-3 T), *Digenia simplex* (Fig. 11-3 E1) and *Champia parvula* (Fig. 11-3 W). Several species of noncalcareous green algae also occur here, including the stoloniferous *Caulerpa* species, *C. cupressoides* (Fig. 11-3 I1), *C. racemosa* (Fig. 11-3 G1), and *C. sertularioides*. Distinctive, erect grape-like clusters arise from the stolons of *C. racemosa*. The other species produce numerous bifurcate branchlets (bushy in *C. sertularioides* and roughly serrate in *C. cupressoides*). All of these algae are also sparsely represented among coral boulders on the reef crest.

Arrecife Lobos: Sand-scoured Carbonate Hardpan

Prevailing currents sweep sands and detritus around the southern margin of Isla de Lobos, scouring the subtidal bank between the island and the coral boulder ramparts. Eventually the sand comes to rest as a wedge-shaped sand spit on the west side of the bank. Where currents move sand faster than it can accumulate, it creates a characteristic sand-scoured carbonate bedrock. This habitat is evident on the Lobos bank at other localities (e.g., just east of the well platform), but is best developed just south of the island.

Only the most hardy surface-dwellers can survive on the sand-scoured carbonate hardpan, but a variety of borers occupy its interior (see below). The most conspicuous member of this community is the brown algae *Padina sanctaecrucis*. It densely carpets rock surfaces protruding above the region of maximal sand scour. Thin, flexible, ear-shaped thallus blades, attached to the bedrock by strong tenacious basal holdfasts, oscillate with the current flow. *Padina* consistently occupies this habitat from Bermuda to Brazil. It is so closely associated with the sand-scoured hardpan as to be considered an indicative diagnostic species for the habitat. Few other algae and even fewer surface-dwelling invertebrates can tolerate the current-dominated hardpan environment where *Padina* thrives, but a few amphipods and isopods seek shelter among their holdfasts.

On rocks somewhat more removed from the currents where small amounts of sand can accumulate, species of the green alga *Caulerpa* live among sparse carpets of *Padina*. *Caulerpa* first colonizes small sandy patches, sending a tangle of holdfasts into the sand. Once firmly attached, stolons grow outward over barren subtidal rocks, the latter sending periodic

bushy thallus blades upward and additional clinging holdfasts into rock crevices. *Caulerpa cupressoides*, (Fig. 11-3 I1), with its naked stolons and frilly thallus blades, is more prevalent on current-swept sandy shoals. The smaller, less foliate *C. sertularioides* prefers areas of thin sand veneer and shallow, fully illuminated waters, where summer daily water temperatures often exceed 38°C. The calcareous green alga *Rhipocephalus phoenix* (Fig. 11-3 F1) also clings to thin pockets of sand with an extensive holdfast network. As it grows, it binds additional sand at its base, which provides additional habitat for other organisms.

Arrecife Lobos: The Lagoon

The crest of the Lobos platform is dominated by a shallow, largely grass-covered lagoon, although corals typical of a patch reef occur primarily along its windward margins. Coarse, calcareous sands derived from shell or *Halimeda* fragments blanket most of the lagoon, but finer textured sediments are deposited in the lee of the island. Patches of sand are stabilized by the extensive rhizome network of turtle grass, *Thalassia testudinum* (Fig. 11-3 N1), which, in turn, provides a refuge for a remarkably diverse epifaunal and infaunal community (Fig. 11-4).

Turtle Grass and Algae

We previously encountered *Thalassia* at the northern limit of its range in the bays of southern Texas (Chapter 7). The climate at Arrecife Lobos is more favorable for *Thalassia*, so the turtle grass beds are more luxuriant here than in Texas. *Thalassia* is a flowering plant, although vegetative reproduction by rhizomatous runners is much more prevalent than the sexual process of flowering. When it does flower, the plant bears separate tiny staminate and pistillate flowers, and pollen released from the male flower is carried by water currents to the stigma of the female.

Apart from the leaf blades, which emerge at the surface of the sand and provide the primary photosynthetic surface for *Thalassia*, a considerable bulk of the plant, the rhizomatous network, lies below the lagoon floor. This mass of rhizomes and rootlets anchors the turtle grass, contains conducting and food storage tissues, and produces the emergent leaves. Meristem, or primary growth tissue, lies at the tips of each rhizome and continually produces new rhizomes and nodes, which, in turn, send new leaves up through the sand. Leaves and the upper rhizomes trap sand grains, stimulating deposition upon the lagoon floor. A thriving *Thalassia* bed often contains 30 cm of living rhizomatous turf below the sand, and often a thick nonliving peat-like layer below that. When excavated, the turf appears as an impenetrable tangle of linear rhizomes and rootlets, but is, in fact, home for many infaunal invertebrates. Similarly, the leaves of *Thalassia* shelter an equally large variety of epifauna. The blades even provide a substratum for the attachment of life, such as the encrusting calcareous red alga *Fosliella lejolisii* (Fig. 11-3 M1), or the tiny tube worms of the genus *Spirorbis* (Fig. 6-9 C). Before we consider the infaunal and epifaunal members of the *Thalassia* grassbeds in detail, first we will examine other plants of the lagoon sands that either coexist with *Thalassia* or colonize areas of sparse turtle grass cover.

Most notable among these are the calcareous green algae. There are a variety of species, but most important are members of the genus *Halimeda*, for fragments of their limestone skeletons contribute prolific quantities of carbonate grains to the sands of the lagoon. The apparent paucity of *Halimeda* on the lagoon floor belies the significance of these algae to sedimentation on the bank. They are most conspicuous on sparsely vegetated sandy patches, where a few individuals lie anchored by filamentous holdfasts in the loose sand. Many greenish, jointed and calcified segments arise from a few stout basal segments. Many more specimens lie hidden among blades of *Thalassia* and also occur in middle- to deep-reef habitats. They are especially abundant on the walls and within crevices of coral spurs, but even these seemingly fail to account for the prevalence of *Halimeda* debris in the sand. A key to the puzzle lies in the extremely high productivity of *Halimeda* and its rapid turnover in all habitats in which it occurs. Specimens grow rapidly, die, disintegrate and shed considerable quantities of sand-sized particles onto the lagoon floor or into the grooves or sandy basins between reef walls. Longshore drift and strong currents, as between the southern end of Isla de Lobos and the coral ramparts, sweep some of this sand into the lagoon, and some of it washes in over the reef crest during storms. Both processes move enormous quantities of *Halimeda* debris and other clastics from the reef to the lagoon floor.

At least three species of *Halimeda* occur on tropical shores of Mexico, only two of which have been reported from Arrecife Lobos. *Halimeda opuntia* (Fig. 11-3 D1) is the most common in the southwestern Gulf. The whitish-green segments of living *H. opuntia* branch in several different planes. The plants either attach to rocks or anchor in sand. They occur in depths from shallow lagoon waters to slopes over 50 m below the reef crest. *Halimeda tuna* (Fig. 11-3 L1) is bright green with smooth-margined segments that branch in a single plane. This species is largely restricted to shallow sandy bottoms, but it too can occur on rocks. Both of these species occur at Arrecife Lobos. *Halimeda incrassata* is also segmented in a single plane, and has a distinctive heavily calcified basal stalk consisting of one to several fused segments. It is usually larger and more drably colored than *H. tuna*, its upper segments have an irregular or even deeply lobed margin, and the surface of each segment is distinctly ribbed. This species is most likely to be found within *Thalassia* beds, but it also frequently occurs on relatively unvegetated lagoonal sands. It is unknown from Arrecife Lobos, and perhaps all or most of the southwestern Gulf reefs (J.W. Tunnell, personal communication). It is present on some of the Yucatan bank reefs.

Several additional species of large calcareous green algae occur on the floor of the lagoon, some seemingly more abundant than *Halimeda*. These species deposit significantly less calcium carbonate within the thallus, or, if heavily calcified like *Udotea*, they disintegrate into tiny particles, contributing to the fill but not the fabric of the lagoon floor. While they are alive, large filamentous holdfasts trap large quantities of sand and help stabilize lagoon sediments, particularly where they occur in the absence of *Thalassia*.

Avrainvillea nigricans (Fig. 11-3 O1) is a conspicuous calcareous green alga on the Lobos bank, with its flattened, somewhat flared head which may or may not be borne upon a stalk. The calcified blade has a soft leathery consistency. Unlike most other calcareous Chlorophyceae, its color tends toward dark brown or even black. This species is more often found among thick clumps of *Thalassia* than alone on sparsely vegetated lagoonal flats. *Udotea flabellum* (Fig. 11-3 H1) is another species with a fan-shaped thallus held erect upon a stiff calcified stalk. Even the gray-green fan is extensively calcified, but all parts of the plant disintegrate into tiny carbonate fragments when it dies, producing few sand-sized particles. *Udotea* is a common macrophyte on the Yucatan banks and throughout the Caribbean, but it is uncommon or absent on most of the reefs of the southwestern Gulf.

Rhipocephalus phoenix (Fig. 11-3 F1) bears a capitulum somewhat between that of the fluffy cylindrical brush-like head of *Penicillus* and the flattened fan of *Udotea*. Like the former, it is cylindrical but like the latter, at least some adjacent filaments are fused. Instead of producing a single flattened, fan-shaped head, numerous sets of short, fused, blade-like filaments radiate about a capitular cortex. The capitulum is dull green and modestly calcified. The plant stands 10 to 12 cm tall, the stalk being half or less this length. It is also frequently found among *Thalassia*. This is probably the species identified by Rigby & McIntire (1966) as *Penicillus*.

Dictyosphaeria cavernosa (Fig. 11-3 C1) is a noncalcareous green algae with a thallus shaped into hollow globes or spheres. It usually attaches by filamentous rhizoids to rocks on the lagoon floor or on the reef. When healthy, the thallus bubbles are green, but they become silvery translucent as the plant dies. This stage frequently attracts the attention of curious visitors to the shore wondering what it is. The fluid inside each sphere is seawater.

Encrusting coralline algae occur on rocks and other objects throughout the lagoon. They are especially abundant along lagoon margins where currents sweep onto the platform from the open sea. Here amorphous pink sheets plate the rocks, their presence detectable more by their color than their form. Branching or knob-like aggregations of another species of crustose coralline algae (Fig. 11-3 B) lie upon the shallow lagoon floor, especially where it is sparsely covered by other algae or turtle grass. Accurate identification of most coralline algae genera and species usually requires the attention of a specialist (Adey & MacIntyre, 1973). Many other species of algae also occur in the lagoon. For example, those associated with the lower margins of the boulder ramparts are distributed on rocks throughout the lagoon. Some are epiphytic, such as *Cladophoropsis membranacea* (Fig. 11-3 K1), which attaches to a variety of rocks, other algae and sea grasses intertidally and subtidally.

Lagoon Fauna

The lagoon benthic fauna finds shelter among the grass beds or within the calcareous sands, with probably an equal mix of infaunal and epifaunal species. Many animals feed on the surface but bury themselves in the sand when not foraging. We will first begin a consideration of the more active and/or exposed members of the lagoon community, and then proceed to consider its more secretive residents.

Crustaceans The hermit crab *Clibanarius antillensis* (Fig. 11-4 U) is one of the most abundant epifaunal crustaceans on the lagoon floor. Individuals are small and easily overlooked, but exceptionally large numbers of this gregarious species demonstrate a collective presence, especially in shallow, tidally exposed flats. Larger West Indian hermit crabs such as *Petrochirus diogenes* (Fig. 10-1 F1) patrol turtle grass beds in the deeper portions of the lagoon.

Several small to medium-sized majid crabs can be found in the lagoon, usually among coral debris and sparse *Thalassia* cover. They include the decorator crabs, *Microphrys bicornutus* (Fig. 11-3 V) (carapace width, 20 mm) and *Macrocoeloma diplacanthum* (Fig. 11-3 U) (carapace width, 30 mm). Decorator crabs place bits of sponge, algae, hydroids or other debris upon the top of their carapace for concealment. Both are relatively sluggish, not prone to moving away from the coral rubble.

Microphrys bicornutus, the larger of the two, prefers sparsely vegetated subtidal cobbles, rocks, or shallow reef habitats to the grass beds. If transferred from one locality to another, it shows little interest in finding a background that matches its own prior-selected camouflage. As it slowly adds a new algal bonnet every few days, it soon acquires the local materials to blend in (Getty & Hazlett, 1978). This species has been the subject of numerous laboratory studies of crustacean physiology and behavior, possibly because it ranges from North Carolina to Brazil, and is easily collected. *Macrocoeloma diplacanthum* is much smaller, occurring among turtle grass on sandy banks. It clings tightly to grass blades or other debris. A third, also small, decorator crab, *Macrocoeloma camptocerum* (Fig. 11-5 L), also occurs in the lagoon.

The red spider crab, *Mithrax forceps* (Fig. 11-4 S) (carapace width, 35 mm), rarely occurs among rocks in the lagoon, but is more common in crevices on the reef. It is more secretive than the decorator crabs, perhaps because it is a favored food of squirrelfishes.

The grass beds and scattered rocks of the lagoon are home for a number of small xanthid crabs, many of which are easily recognized by black-tipped chelae. *Cataleptodius floridanus* (Fig. 11-4 T) (carapace width, 30 mm) has a speckled body and bears chelae with curious spoon-shaped tips. It is apparently an algae feeder, but the precise function of the spoon-shaped knobs is unknown. *Platypodia spectabilis* (Fig. 11-4 V) (carapace width, 25 mm) has the body and legs mottled in brilliant yellows, browns and reds. It frequents coral rubble and rocks riddled by red and yellow boring sponges, especially in shallow waters. Another colorful crab, *Eriphia gonagra* (Fig. 11-4 W) (carapace width, 45 mm), is mottled with purple, orange, yellow, blue and brown. Its carapace width is about twice that of *Platypodia spectabilis*. Both of these species are called calico crabs, and *E. gonagra* is also known as the warty crab. It occupies a variety of habitats, including grass beds, tide pools, in sponges, and under rocks on the reef.

Several species of hairy crabs of the genus *Pilumnus* occur in the Lobos lagoon, including *P. miersii* (Fig. 11-4 X) (carapace width, 12 mm), *P. dasypodus*, and *P. sayi*. Like most of the other small xanthids, they appear to be algal grazers.

The Stomatopoda or mantis shrimps are especially well represented on reefs and associated reef lagoons. Shaped somewhat like praying mantis insects, they also rely upon large compound eyes and raptorial appendages to capture prey. Their broad, distinctly segmented abdomen bears several pairs of gills upon the ventral surface and terminates in flared uropods and an armored telson. Some mantis shrimps, like *Squilla empusa* (Chapter 7), dig and live in burrows. Others prefer to occupy crevices among rocks. Some completely leave the residence when feeding and others prefer to lie in wait at the entrance for their prey. Mantis shrimps feed upon shrimps, crabs, worms, or small fish and have perfected several different methods of prey capture. Some employ razor-sharp raptorial appendages to decapitate their victims. These stomatopods should be carefully handled, for some can produced serious lacerations on fingers and hands. Others, such as *Pseudosquilla ciliata* (Fig. 11-4 C1) impale their victims upon spines occupying the inner surface of the raptorial appendages. They can move with lightning speed to insure prey capture. A third group of stomatopods have modified raptorial arms shaped like clubs. Species like the bright green *Gonodactylus oerstedi* (Fig. 11-4 D1) can deliver a shell-crushing thump. Additional blows dismember the victim. The mantis shrimp collects each part, returns to the burrow, and consumes the prey. Mantis shrimps have a catholic diet, but bivalves and gastropods seem to be favored prey. Mollusc shells commonly litter the *G. oerstedi* lair. The body armor protects each individual from the blows of neighbors and competitors for lairs or mates. *Pseudosquilla ciliata* and *G. oerstedi* occur with about equal frequency on the reef and in the lagoon.

Gastropods The small snail *Modulus modulus* (Fig. 11-4 N) is perhaps the most characteristic gastropod living upon *Thalassia*. It glides along blades of turtle grass, grazing upon the tiny attached epiphytes. The snails are easily overlooked, being a centimeter or less in length, but a brief examination of the more luxuriant turtle grass beds typically yields several specimens. Slightly less common, and usually harder to find is the emerald nerite, *Smaragdia viridis* (Fig. 11-4 M). Smaller than a pea, its vivid green shell blends with the grass. Like *Modulus*, *Smaragdia* is an epiphyte grazer.

The grass beds are also home for a number of small, high-spired algal-detrital feeders, the Cerithiidae and Rissoinidae. They often crawl upon blades of turtle grass, but also forage upon sandy bottoms at the edges of grass beds.

Rarely does a habitat contain only one cerithiid species. Usually several occur in apparent sympatry, although habitat partitioning with respect to food or vertical occurrence is likely. All Atlantic cerithiids live about one year. They deposit stringy egg masses on sand or rocks from late winter to early summer, the precise timing varying geographically and with the species. *Cerithium litteratum* (Fig. 11-2 N) is the largest, attaining a shell length of about 2 cm and being half as wide. The expanded shell makes it the most easily identified of the cerithiids. Furthermore, it is very abundant at Arrecife Lobos, and probably the most common mollusc in terms of biomass on the entire reef complex (J.W. Tunnell, personal communication). *Cerithium eburneum* (Fig. 11-4 I) and *C. lutosum* (Fig. 11-4 K) are decidedly more slender than *C. litteratum*, and are often difficult to distinguish. Several published photographs have confused these two species. Furthermore, *C. eburneum* occurs in two forms, the typical form and a second, forma *algicola* (Fig. 11-4 F), which was once thought to be a separate species (see Houbrick, 1974, for additional information). *Cerithium lutosum* is usually smaller than *C. eburneum*, and prefers shallower portions of the grass beds or sand. Enormous numbers (sometimes more than 10,000/m²) occupy the intertidal zone, and the species is tolerant of high temperature and salinity. *Cerithium eburneum* remains more closely associated with *Thalassia*, although it, too, occurs on sand. It prefers shallow subtidal grass beds to those exposed by the tide.

Cerithiopsis greeni (Fig. 11-4 H) is among the smallest of the cerithiids in the lagoon, its tiny beaded shell being only a few mm in length. Size and shell ornamentation help to identify the genus, but there are several species of *Cerithiopsis* here. All are reasonably common among the shell debris in the sands near grass beds. *Alaba incerta* (Fig. 11-4 D) is another, only slightly larger (10 mm), relative of *C. greeni*, equally common in sand, rubble, or *Thalassia*.

Several dozen species of rissoinids occur in the tropical Atlantic. Most members of the family are very small and the species display an extensive radiation in shell form. We have chosen one species to illustrate them, *Rissoina bryerea* (Fig. 11-4 G). These snails are typical for the family, thriving among turtle grass beds and feeding upon the detritus and microalgae which coat the grass blades. Additional species reported from Arrecife Lobos include *Rissoina decussata* and *Zebina browniana*. It would not be unusual to find a dozen more species occurring here.

Three larger grazing snails, the queen conch *Strombus gigas* (Fig. 11-4 C), the hawk-wing conch *S. raninus* (Fig. 11-4 B) and the fighting conch *S. alatus*, occur in or near grass beds. These snails avoid predators by retreating into the sand when not foraging. All move along the bottom in a series of hops, rather than the smooth gliding motion common for most snails. *Strombus alatus* has perfected this behavior as a predator escape mechanism. When threatened, it rapidly flips along the surface of the sand by use of its powerful foot in association with the knife-like operculum. If held in the hand, the snail often attempts the same response, giving the appearance of an aggressive display toward its captor, hence the common name. *Strombus alatus* is a species of the continental margin, being replaced in the insular Caribbean by the closely related *S. pugilis*.

Strombus gigas is the largest herbivorous snail in western Atlantic waters. Peoples of the tropical Gulf and Caribbean prize it for food, and the large shell, with the flaring, polished pink outer lip, is also an important item of commerce (Darcy, 1981; Siddall, 1984a). The exploitation of *S. gigas* for food or shell has depleted its numbers in many localities (Stevely & Warner, 1978; Brownell & Stevely, 1981), including Arrecife Lobos (J.W. Tunnell, personal communication). Prodigious fecundity, at least with respect to egg production, has helped to maintain modest numbers of conchs in some heavily fished beds (Robertson, 1959; Randall, 1964), but the paucity of *S. gigas* at Arrecife Lobos and other southwestern Gulf reefs (J.W. Tunnell, personal communication) is testimony to the ultimate vulnerability of this species.

The queen conch relies primarily upon algae for food, with juveniles specializing upon filamentous or unicellular algae (Creswell, 1984). It is a nocturnal forager. Large conchs usually lie partially buried in sand during the day. Smaller individuals, lacking the flared lip, find it easier to bury the entire shell. Queen conchs are most common on or near grass beds (Weil & Laughlin, 1984), but they will venture onto large expanses of bare sand or coral rubble. Juvenile or subadults are relatively sedentary, but become progressively more mobile as they grow larger (Randall, 1964; Appeldoorn & Sanders, 1984; Siddall, 1984b). Sexes are separate. Sperm transfer is by copulation, which can precede spawning by several weeks (D'Asaro, 1965). Mating and spawning may occur throughout the year, being least common or absent in mid-winter (Davis *et al.*, 1984). Females deposit eggs within a long coiled mucous strand, which is extruded onto clean sand (D'Asaro, 1965). If unraveled, the strand extends as much as 30 m in length, and contains 12 to 15 eggs per mm. The fully coiled mass, however, is little

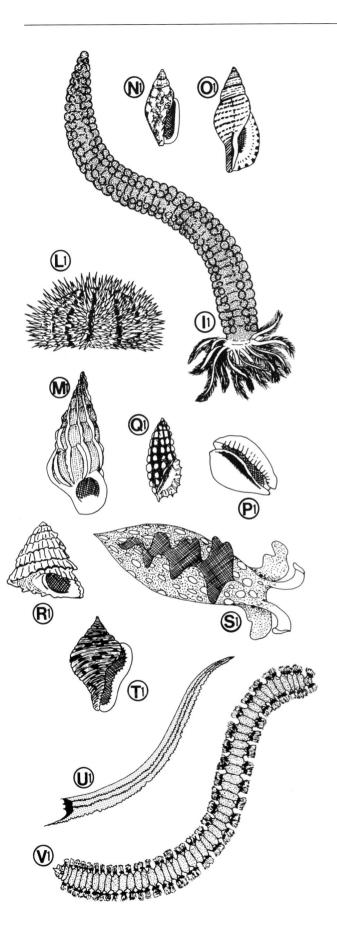

longer than the shell of the snail that produced it. Females lie relatively immobile during the egg-laying process, which may take almost a day. Robertson (1959) and D'Asaro (1965) have studied the embryological development and metamorphosis of *S. gigas*. Conchs reach sexual maturity after 2 to 3 years and the average life span is about 6 years (Berg, 1976).

Many animals feed upon *S. gigas*. Humans and predatory gastropods such as *Fasciolaria tulipa* (Fig. 11-4 E) take large snails, but most predators, and especially several species of shell-crushing fishes, prefer the young or sub-adult conchs (Appeldoorn, 1984).

Several gastropod predators are common in the lagoon. The largest is the tulip shell, *Fasciolaria tulipa*. We have described its behavior in Chapter 10. The naticid *Polinices lacteus* (Fig. 11-4 A) occupies a niche similar to that of *P. duplicatus* on sandy shores of the northern Gulf. It is a borer, producing symmetrical counter-sunk holes in bivalve shells to obtain the living tissues inside. Three other naticids, *P. hepaticus*, *Natica livida* and *N. pusilla* occur at Arrecife Lobos. The bubble shell, *Bulla striata* (Fig. 11-4 L), is another sand-burrowing predator most often encountered

11-4. Arrecife Lobos. **A.** Milk moon snail, *Polinices lacteus*; **B.** Hawk-wing conch, *Strombus raninus*; **C.** Queen conch, *Strombus gigas*; **D.** Varicose alaba, *Alaba incerta*; **E.** Tulip shell, *Fasciolaria tulipa*; **F.** Ivory cerith, *Cerithium eburneum* forma *algicola*; **G.** Caribbean risso, *Rissonia bryerea*; **H.** Miniature horn shell, *Cerithiopsis greeni*; **I.** Ivory cerith, *Cerithium eburneum*, typical form; **J.** Cone snail, *Conus mus*; **K.** Dwarf cerith, *Cerithium lutosum*; **L.** Bubble shell, *Bulla striata*; **M.** Emerald nerite, *Smaragdia viridis*; **N.** Atlantic modulus, *Modulus modulus*; **O.** Pen shell, *Pinna carnea*; **P.** Reddish bristle worm. *Chloeia viridis*; **Q.** *Leodice rubra*; **R.** Purple urchin, *Lytechinus variegatus*; **S.** Spider crab, *Mithrax forceps*; **T.** Florida mud crab, *Cataleptodius floridanus*; **U.** Hermit crab, *Clibinarius antillensis*; **V.** Calico crab, *Platypodia spectabilis*; **W.** Warty crab, *Eriphia gonagra*; **X.** *Pilumnus miersii*; **Y.** Tiger lucine, *Codakia orbicularis*; **Z.** Speckled tellin, *Tellina listeri*; **A1.** *Tellina fausta*; **B1.** Orange bristle worm, *Eurythoe complanata*; **C1.** Mantis shrimp, *Pseudosquilla ciliata*; **D1.** Mantis shrimp, *Gonodactylus oerstedi*; **E1.** Warty sea slug, *Onchidella floridana*; **F1.** Long-spined black urchin, *Diadema antillarum*; **G1.** Slate-pencil urchin, *Eucidaris tribuloides*; **H1.** Comet sea star, *Linckia guildingii*; **I1.** Sticky-skinned sea urchin, *Euapta lappa*; **J1.** Lister's tree oyster, *Isognomon radiatus*; **K1.** Sponge oyster, *Ostrea permollis*; **L1.** Sea egg, *Tripneustes ventricosus*; **M1.** Wentletrap, *Epitonium lamellosum*; **N1.** Glossy dove snail, *Nitidella nitida*; **O1.** Miniature triton trumpet, *Pisania pusio*; **P1.** Atlantic gray cowrie, *Cypraea cinerea*; **Q1.** Blackberry drupe, *Morula nodulosa*; **R1.** American star shell, *Astraea tecta*; **S1.** Sea hare, *Aplysia dactylomela*; **T1.** Dove shell, *Columbella mercatoria*; **U1.** Worm snail, *Vermicularia knorri*; **V1.** Fire worm, *Hermodice carunculata*.

along the margins of sea grass beds. It is a shelled opisthobranch, but envelops its shell with fleshy mantle tissue when moving through the sand. It preys upon thin-shelled bivalves, apparently by crushing them.

A group of largely tropical predators, the cone snails, are represented at Arrecife Lobos by *Conus mus* (Fig. 11-4 J) and *C. spurius*. They lie in wait for prey buried in sand with only the pointed tip of the shell exposed at the surface. Their radular teeth are tiny hypodermic harpoons which can be injected one at a time into unsuspecting prey. Each harpoon contains a quick-acting toxin used to subdue the victim. The toxin produced by some of the larger cones of tropical Pacific reefs is sufficiently potent that it can kill a human and, within seconds, paralyze a fish half again the size of the snail. The toxin of Atlantic cones is considerably less potent, perhaps because most Atlantic species prey upon smaller, slower moving soft-bodied invertebrates such as polychaetes, nemerteans, or other molluscs.

Infaunal bivalves Lagoonal sands are not particularly rich in species of infaunal bivalves, but the species present typically occur in abundance. The most conspicuous is probably the tiger lucine, *Codakia orbicularis* (Fig. 11-4 Y). Single valves of this large bivalve litter the lagoonal sands. One must usually search hard, however, to find the living population. Like many lucines, *Codakia orbicularis* is a deep burrower well adapted to survive in anoxic sediments of the lagoon. It typically dwells below the tangle of rhizomes of turtle grass beds, communicating with surface waters by an anterior inhalant tube and a posterior exhalant siphon. This species contains haemoglobin in its blood to facilitate the uptake of oxygen. *C. orbiculata* is a similar but significantly smaller lucine burrowing less deeply within the grass bed. The buttercup shell, *Anodontia alba* and the similar but larger *A. philippiana* are lucines which seem to prefer finer unvegetated sands of the lagoon.

Two large deposit-feeding tellins, *T. listeri* (Fig. 11-4 Z) and *T. fausta* (Fig. 11-4 A1), occur at the edges of the grass beds or within the coarse unvegetated sands of the central lagoon. Fragile wedge-shaped shells of *Pinna carnea* (Fig. 11-4 O) emerge from the sand or lie erect among the turtle grass. They gape widely in a feeding posture unless disturbed by a fish or careless hand, whereupon they rapidly close. Like other fan shells, this species is home for several commensal species. A variety of smaller bivalves occur throughout the lagoon, among them *Gouldia cerina*, *Semele proficula* and *Ervilia nitens*.

Worms The West Indian fire worm, *Hermodice carunculata* (Fig. 11-4 V1) (Amphinomidae) is probably the most conspicuous polychaete on the Lobos bank. Its large (up to 25 cm), broad, light green body flanked by rows of pinkish gills is unmistakable as the worm crawls over reef rubble or among sparse sea grass. It spends most of the day secluded under rocks, but is most active at dawn and dusk when it emerges to feed. *Hermodice* is a carnivore, feeding especially upon sea anemones and coral polyps such as *Porites* and *Acropora* (Marsden, 1962, 1963a,b; Ebbs, 1966; Lizama & Blanquet, 1975). It employs an eversible proboscis to feed upon these cnidarians, and may also feed upon carrion (Marsden, 1963b).

Hermodice ranges at will over the lagoon floor, with little fear of predation. It has thousands of hollow extensible setae or bristles along both sides of the body, each loaded with a painful toxin. Normally, these bristles lie retracted within the fleshy parapodia below frilly pink gills. When disturbed, *Hermodice* extends all of these setae at once, transforming its appearance into a stout, cotton-coated rod. The bristles easily penetrate any flesh contacting them, and readily break free of the worm. The offender, be it fish or human, is left with several hundred hypodermic setae stuck in its skin, each discharging an exceedingly painful sting. Because fire worms are most active when the light is poor, humans venturing into the sea at this time are especially prone to being stung. *Hermodice* does not, however, seek a person to sting; victims usually succumb to a careless touch or chance encounter with a worm only trying to defend itself.

Eurythoe complanata (Fig. 11-4 B1) is another amphinomid predator which nestles under rocks during the day and emerges at night to feed. It is apparently more of a carrion feeder than *Hermodice* (Kudenov, 1974), but like the fire worm, it also bears hollow toxic setae. A third amphinomid, *Chloeia viridis* (Fig. 11-4 P), probably also feeds upon carrion.

The Eunicidae, here represented by *Leodice rubra* (Fig. 11-4 Q) include many species of coral borers. They riddle dead coral with numerous burrows, weakening the calcareous matrix, and eventually providing space for other organisms to enter.

Echinoderms The echinoderms provide us a fitting transition between lagoon and reef habitats, because several of the more obvious species are frequently found in both. A few such as the variegated urchin *Lytechinus variegatus* (Fig. 11-4 R) are largely confined to the grass beds. Others, such as the sea egg, *Tripneustes ventricosus* (Fig. 11-4 L1) range somewhat more widely in the lagoon and onto the reef. This large herbivorous urchin is sought in some parts of its range for food, the large mass of eggs contained within females considered a delicacy. Where wave swept rocks rise to the surface of the lagoon as upon the back of the reef crest, the black rock-boring sea urchin *Echinometra lucunter* remains the most common echinoid. A similar species, the green rock-boring urchin *E. viridis*, also occurs here, though not as commonly. In deeper waters of the lagoon and especially on the sandy floors of the reef, both are replaced by the long-spined black urchin *Diadema antillarum* (Fig. 11-4 F1). In the lagoon, *Diadema* requires the presence of at least some coral where it seeks shelter, but it can forage considerable distances away from the coral, especially in groups of a dozen or more animals. *Diadema* suffered great mortality at Arrecife Lobos during 1983–84, as it did in other parts of the Gulf and Caribbean. This mortality was probably the result of a wa-ter-borne pathogen (Lessios, *et al.*, 1984). By 1986, numbers of *Diadema* at Arrecife Lobos, as elsewhere, were increasing, indicative of recovery.

The pencil urchin *Eucidaris tribuloides* (Fig. 11-4 G1) is a more reef-associated species, although it also occurs among rocks on the floor of the lagoon. Simi-larly, the sticky sea cucumber *Euapta lappa* (Fig. 11-4 I1) retreats under rocks during the day, emerging at night to feed on sandy lagoon or reef floors. It is an ex-tremely extendable animal, and often resembles a snake when flushed into the sea from its place of hid-ing. It also bears spicules which cause it to adhere gently to human skin. The animal is harmless.

Brittle stars are common under rocks within the la-goon. *Ophiocoma wendti* (Fig. 10-7 P) and *Ophiocoma echinata* are among the larger species. *Ophioderma cinereum* and *Ophioderma guttatum* also frequent the crevices beneath lagoon rocks and boulders.

Sessile Invertebrates   The sessile invertebrates of the grass beds are mostly small or microscopic species, such as the bryozoans (see below), which attach to grass blades or shells. A few larger sessile animals oc-cur here, especially sponges, most of which have not been identified. Several corals are found among *Thal-assia*, and one is restricted almost exclusively to grass beds. *Siderastrea radians* (Plate 11-1 H) is a common coral on the lagoon floor and *S. siderea* (Plate 11-1 I) frequents deeper slopes in this habitat. Each grows into hemispherical colonies almost a meter in diameter. Bright yellow *Porites astreoides* forms much smaller encrusting colonies among the shallower grass beds. The most characteristic grass bed scleractinian forms only a small colony which is often free of permanent basal attachment. This is the rose coral, *Manicina ar-eolata* (Plate 11-2 G).

The founding member of the *Manicina* colony atta-ches to a rock or stone among the turtle grass and, during the early stages of growth, the colony remains attached to it. The corallite eventually outgrows its anchoring stone, extending upwards and outwards as the number of polyps increase. Eventually, the mature corallite breaks free of its original attachment, and the colony lies loose upon the sand among *Thalassia*. Epi-thelial cilia keep the surface of the corallite free of sediment. Occasionally, large waves completely over-turn *Manicina* colonies, but this coral has perfected a method to right itself. The polyps alternately take on and discharge seawater from their tissues, and, in the process, rock the corallite until it eventually turns over. The movements are relatively slow and are aided by ciliary movements which help to change or main-tain position between tissue pulses. As a day or more may pass before an overturned *Manicina* rights itself, the process is most easily observed by use of time-lapse photography.

Arrecife Lobos: The Reef

Although scattered coral heads occur within the la-goon, sometimes attaining large proportions, the most luxuriant coral growth fringes the Lobos platform. Several habitats can be recognized (Fig. 11-3, inset at upper right), each with characterizing species. These include a back or patch reef (1), reef crest (2), fore reef (3), fore reef slope (4, 5), and deeper fore reef (6).

The Back Reef

Lagoonward of the reef crest, where wave energy has been dissipated by the reef crest but still provides a moderate flow, there is a back reef or "rear zone" com-munity. Water depths vary from less than 1 m to as much as 5 m. The environment is characterized by spherical or globular heads of several corals, including the brain corals *Diploria strigosa* (Fig. 11-3 E), *D. la-byrinthiformis* (Plate 11-2 B) and *Colpophyllia natans* (Plate 11-2 A), the boulder coral *Montastrea annularis* (Fig. 11-3 D and Plate 11-2 F), *M. cavernosa* (Fig. 11-3 F and Plate 11-2 E) and the star coral *Siderastrea sid-erea* (Plate 11-1 I). Encrusting colonies of *Diploria clivosa* (Fig. 11-3 A and Plate 11-2 C) and *Agaricia agaricites* (Plate 11-1 E) are common here, as are smaller colonies of *Porites furcata* (Plate 11-3 B) and/or the similar *P. porites*. Prominent in the shallower, wave-swept portions of the back reef are encrusting or erect, light tan colonies of the hydrozoan fire coral, *Millepora alcicornis* (Plate 11-3 H). Symmetrical heads of elkhorn coral, *Acropora palmata* (Fig. 11-3 C and Plate 11-1 B), or smaller, tangled stands of staghorn coral, *A. cervicornis* (Plate 11-1 C), also occur in slightly deeper parts of the lagoon with ample tidal flow.

The larger mound-like coral heads of the back reef are usually no more than a meter in diameter, al-though some grow to twice or three times this size. They are separated by areas of coarse sand or loose coral rock, sometimes containing sparse stands of grass or algae which is frequently grazed by the long-spined black sea urchin *Diadema antillarum* (Fig. 11-4 F1). The sand beds are also occupied by sea cucum-bers, especially *Holothuria surinamensis*, whereas the sponge *Xestospongia subtriangularis* (formerly *Hali-clona longelyi*, see Wiedenmayer, 1977) sends numer-ous stubby brown fingers upwards from the base of the coral heads.

Caribbean back and patch reefs are characterized as much by the presence of gorgonacean soft corals as they are by the scattered mounds of stony corals. Gor-gonacea are erect colonial anthozoans with an axial skeletal core surrounded by a differentiated cortex and upon which lie the living polyps (Fig. 11-8, circle in-set). They include several families (we illustrate only three) which differ from one another mostly with re-spect to the nature of the axial and cortical structures.

In comparison to the large numbers and diversity of gorgonaceans on Caribbean reefs, soft corals are sparsely represented upon the Lobos platform. For ex-ample, the most readily recognizable gorgonaceans, the sea fans, *Gorgonia flabellum* (Fig. 11-8 J) and *G. ventalina*, have not been reported from Arrecife Lobos, and are poorly represented on even the bank reefs off northern Yucatan (Kornicker *et al.*, 1959). Fewer than a dozen species of gorgonaceans have been reported from Arrecife Lobos, and some of these only from the deeper portions of the reef. They are usually found attached to rocks or dead coral boulders in waters of moderate current and depth.

Plexaura flexuosa (Fig. 11-8 B) is an exception, as it is found near Isla de Lobos shore in water depths of a meter or less. It is a member of the Plexauridae, a family characterized by large skeletal spicules (length greater or much greater that 0.2 mm). Other Plexauridae which occur within the Lobos back reef habitat are *Plexaurella dichotoma* (Fig. 11-8 G), *Plexaura homomalla* (Fig. 11-8 C), *Muricea atlantica* (Fig. 11-8 F), *Eunicea laciniata* and *E. fusca. Muricea muricata* (Fig. 11-8 E) is a common plexaurid on other southern Gulf reefs, but is yet to be reported from Arrecife Lobos.

The Gorgoniidae, the family to which the sea fans belong, are characterized by tiny (< 0.2 mm) spicules. They are poorly represented in the southwestern Gulf. *Pseudopterogorgia acerosa* (Fig. 11-8 L) and *P. americana* (Fig. 11-8 K) are the only species which have been reported (Bayer, 1961), although others such as *Gorgonia flabellum* (Fig. 11-8 J), *G. ventalena*, or *Pterogorgia citrina* (Fig. 11-8 H) sparsely festoon rocks of other southeastern Gulf reefs (Korniker *et al.*, 1959) and those of Cozumel and Cancun at depths between 2 to 10 m.

The lavender *Briareum asbestinum* (Fig. 11-8 M) is perhaps the least common gorgonacean at Arrecife Lobos, but, as the monomorphic representative of the Briareidae, it is distinct from most other soft corals. When *Briareum* polyps are fully withdrawn, as illustrated, the colony resembles fleshy purple fingers extending upward from a basal holdfast. With polyps fully extended, however, the colony is transformed into a thickly pilose velvet glove.

The flamingo-tongue snail *Cyphoma gibbosum* (Fig. 11-8 I) is usually found attached to gorgonaceans, upon which it feeds. When crawling about, *Cyphoma* displays what appears to be an attractive orange, black and cream mottled shell. When disturbed, the shell seemingly transforms into a patternless, drab chalky gray. The design is not upon the shell, but on reflected mantle folds which all but envelop it when the animal is active. A similar, more streamlined snail, *Cymbula acicularis* (Fig. 11-8 N) is another gorgonacean predator. It is present on some of the bank reefs off northern Yucatan, but has not yet been reported from Arrecife Lobos.

The back reef is usually one of the most easily accessed and therefore most frequently visited of all reef habitats. The organisms described above are among its characterizing biota. Many additional species of plants and animals occur here, drawn from the species just described for the lagoon and many that will presently be described from the reef front communities.

The Reef Crest

The reef crest (Fig. 11-3, Inset, 2) tops the reef and stands awash at low tide. It is a barren-appearing ridge especially prominent along windward margins, but also fringes parts of the leeward platform. It may be 30 to 40 m wide when best developed. Biological agents of construction and decay coexist on the reef crest, the latter apparently having the upper hand. Pink coralline algae and the small, red foraminiferan, *Homotrema rubrum*, encrust slabs of coral rock (largely dead branches of *Acropora palmata*). *Homotrema* is especially abundant on the undersides of loose limestone boulders. Fire corals (*Millepora*) also lie cemented to the rocks, especially just below the tide. None of these deposits enough limestone to permanently bind the reef crest. Waves and marine borers destroy the rocks faster than they can be cemented together. The most obvious agent of destruction is the rock-boring urchin, *Echinometra lucunter* (Fig. 4-1 E1), which densely dots rock crevices. Boring sponges, such as those of the genus *Cliona*, are less obvious but more destructive. They riddle rocks with yellow, red or lavender tissues, weakening them sufficiently that waves easily fracture boulders into cobbles and stones.

Except for these species and a few sparse clumps of nonencrusting algae, the surface of the reef crest seems to hold little promise of life. Cursory inspection will convince the casual eye that few animals dwell here. Yet, the barren surface of the reef crest belies the faunal diversity lying just below the stones. A variety of worms, crustaceans, molluscs and echinoderms take refuge within the coral rubble and occupy sheltered recesses in the shallow subtidal waters nearby. Most are secretive or cryptic, lying within the crevices and darkened spaces under stones, emerging or exposing themselves at night to feed.

Numerous molluscs live among these stones. The star shell, *Astraea tecta* (Figs. 11-2 O; 11-4 R1; 11-6 V) is a common shelled herbivore. The worm snail, *Vermicularia knorri* (Fig. 11-4 U1), a suspension feeding gastropod, cements its sinuous, mostly uncoiled shell to the under-surface of the rubble. Several Arcidae, including the diminutive *Arcopsis adamsi* (Fig. 11-5 H), *Barbatia candida* (Fig. 4-2 R), *B. domingensis* (Fig. 4-2 T) and *B. tenera* also attach to the undersides of coral rubble with a stout byssus. The Limidae, or file shells, are a family of unattached bivalves, often adorned with long colorful tentacles. Like some of the scallops, file shells have a limited capacity for swimming, but more often seek shelter under rocks or within coral crevices. We have previously mentioned *Lima scabra tenera* in association with the Flower Garden Banks, and it also occurs at Arrecife Lobos. We also illustrate the larger, more coarsely sculptured *Lima lima* (Fig. 11-5 Q). This species has not yet been reported from Arrecife Lobos, but is known to occur on other southern Gulf reefs. It is characteristically a member of the cryptobios, taking shelter deep within coral crevices. *Coralliophaga coralliophaga* (Fig. 11-5 N) (Trapeziidae) is even more specialized in its habitat. It occupies the burrows of coral-boring bivalves, and may itself excavate soft limestones. The more active bivalve coral borers of the family Mytilidae are discussed in a separate section below.

The large sea hare, *Aplysia dactylomela* (Fig. 11-4 S1), takes refuge beneath rocks just below the tide and emerges in the evening to forage on macrophytic algae. *Onchidella floridana* (Fig. 11-4 E1) is another shell-less opisthobranch herbivore, but much smaller than the sea hare. It rarely exceeds 2 cm in length, and has a characteristic warty, dark green mantle which covers the back. It is especially common on rocks exposed at low tide, and will emerge at this time to forage among the exposed algae.

A number of predatory snails prowl the upper reef, all of which take shelter among crevices and under stones. Occasionally they emerge during the day, but most are primarily nocturnal predators. A few cowries, such as *Cypraea cinerea* (Fig. 11-4 P1) and *Cypraea zebra* (Fig. 11-6 Q) occur on the reef crest, but they are more abundant on the reef front or reef slope. The reticulated cowrie-helmet, *Cypraecassis testiculus* (Fig. 11-6 P), feeds upon the rock-boring urchin, *Echinometra lucunter.*

Several small gastropod predators, less than 3 cm in height occupy the upper reef. The dove snails, *Columbella mercatoria* (Fig. 11-4 T1) and *Nitidella nitida* (Fig. 11-4 N1) are especially abundant. Wentletraps, such as *Epitonium lamellosum* (Fig. 11-4 M1), search for and feed upon small anemones among the reef rubble. The blackberry drupe, *Morula nodulosa* (Figs. 11-4 Q1 and 11-6 T), a muricid, is sometimes confused with the similarly ornamented *Engina turbinella* (not illustrated), a small buccinid whelk. A larger buccinid, *Pisania pusio* (Fig. 11-4 O1), attaining a height of 4 cm and with a smooth, mottled shell, is not easily confused with other shallow subtidal reef gastropods. Equally distinctive is the rotund *Leucozonia leucozonalis* (Fig. 11-6 U), which occurs from the reef crest to the deeper parts of the reef slope.

Crustaceans are also common among the cryptobios. At low tide the reef crest resounds with crackling snaps and pops made by several species of pistol or snapping shrimps, such as *Alpheus armatus* (Fig. 11-5 G). They are rarely seen, living deep within crevices and beneath the coral rubble, but must occur in large numbers considering the noise produced. Many of the small crabs associated with the lagoon and back reefs also find shelter within the rubble of the reef crest. Here they meet a number of additional species, some of which are from the reef front and fore reef slope. The family Xanthidae, containing many species sporting black-tipped chelipeds, are well represented at Arrecife Lobos. *Pseudomedaeus agassizi* (Fig. 11-5 I) (carapace width, 25 mm) is a common crevice dweller. A granular, nodulose carapace helps distinguish *Paractaea rufopunctata* (Fig. 11-5 F) (carapace width, 25 mm) from other xanthids. It lives in a variety of habitats from rocks, coral rubble and reef crevices to grass

beds on the lagoon floor. Most of the orange-red body of *Actaea setigera* (Fig. 11-5 P) (carapace width, 25 mm) is covered by short, stiff, yellowish hairs and bristles.

Platypodia (= *Platypodiella*) *spectabilis* (Fig. 11-5 E) (carapace width, 22 mm) is the colorful xanthid we previously mentioned with respect to the lagoon biota. The red and yellow banded legs and yellow and brown blotched carapace resemble those of no other species. *Pilumnus dasypodus* (Fig. 11-5 A) (carapace width, 15 mm) is a small, brownish, hairy crab which is at home among coral rubble as on mangrove roots or wooden wharf pilings. The chelipeds of this crab are always noticeably unequal.

The tiny *Domecia acanthophora* (Fig. 11-5 J) (carapace width, 10 mm) is usually found in association with living coral heads, either *Acropora* (Patton, 1967a,b) or *Agaricia* (Keith, 1986). This species also lives under stones on cobble beaches. It is apparently a detritivore (Williams, 1984) and, in turn, is commonly eaten by squirrelfishes (Randall, 1967). *Chlorodiella longimana* (Fig. 11-5 M) (carapace width 20 mm) lives in association with coral just below the reef crest. Keith (1986) also found this xanthid living within crevices in colonies of *Agaricia.*

The black-tipped, long, slender chelipeds of *Paraliomera longimana* (Fig. 11-5 R) (carapace width, 12 mm) distinguish this xanthid. The chelae are unequal in both sexes, with the smaller being very slender. It occurs in rock crevices, under coral rubble, and among *Thalassia.*

A variety of decorator crabs of the family Majidae frequent the shallow subtidal debris adjacent to the reef crest. *Macrocoeloma camptocerum* (Fig. 11-5 L) (carapace width, up to 40 mm) and *M. diplacanthum* (Fig. 11-3 U) (carapace width, 20 mm) are the most commonly encountered at Arrecife Lobos. Both will pile large masses of sponges and other debris upon their carapace for cryptic concealment. Other small spider crabs, including *Pitho aculeata* (Fig. 11-5 B) and *P. anisodon* (Fig. 11-5 D), are also present in the coral rubble.

Many polychaetes occupy the reef crest. The large predatory amphinomids, *Hermodice carunculata* (Fig. 11-4 V1) and *Eurythoe complanata* (Fig. 11-4 B1) that we encountered in the lagoon are here, and range seaward onto the fore reef slope. The blood worm, *Glycera tesselata* (Fig. 11-5 O), prowls sand beds among the coral rubble in search of small invertebrate prey. It employs four black chitinous jaws at the end of a bulbous eversible proboscis to seize and ingest its food.

Fan worms dot the surface of subtidal coral rocks, extending colorful feathery crowns from calcareous or parchment-like tubes into the water for feeding. Several serpulids, such as *Spirobranchus giganteus* (Fig. 11-5 C), construct calcareous tubes on heads of living coral. This species is easily recognized by its doubly conical "fan," or branchial crown. Juveniles preferentially set on a nonliving portion of a living corallum, such as along the edge. As both worm and coral grow,

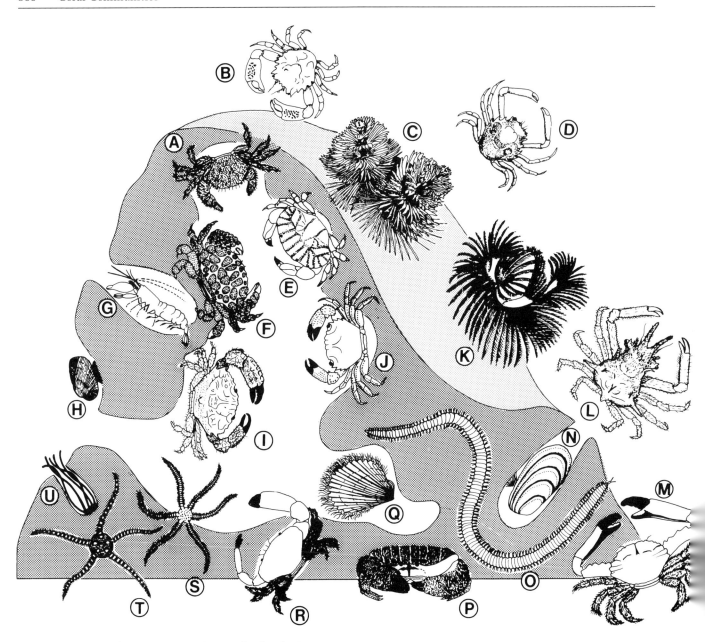

11-5. Reef crevice biota. **A.** Brown hairy wharf crab, *Pilumnus dasypodus*; **B.** *Pitho aculeata*; **C.** Christmas tree fan worm, *Spirobranchus giganteus*; **D.** *Pitho anisodon*; **E.** Calico crab, *Platypodia spectabilis*; **F.** *Paractaea rufopunctata*; **G.** Snapping shrimp, *Alphaeus armatus*; **H.** Miniature ark, *Arcopsis adamsi*; **I.** *Pseudomedaeus agassizi*; **J.** *Domecia acanthophora*; **K.** Magnificent fan worm, *Sabellastarte magnifica*; **L.** Decorator crab, *Macrocoeloma camptocerum*; **M.** *Chlorodiella longimana*; **N.** *Coralliophaga coralliophaga*; **O.** *Glycera tesselata*; **P.** Hairy crab, *Actaea setigera*; **Q.** File shell, *Lima lima*; **R.** *Paraliomera longimana*; **S.** Brittle star, *Ophiocomella ophiactoides*; **T.** Brittle star, *Ophiactis savignyi*; **U.** Brittle star in reef crevice.

the latter covers the tube of the former with living tissue. The worm adds new tube material just ahead of the growing coral, giving the erroneous impression that the worm has bored into it. *Spirobranchus* prefers moderate to well agitated waters, especially on the front of the reef.

In contrast, the sabellid fan worms usually prefer calmer waters in the lee of the reef crest or within the lagoon. Also, their tubes are not calcareous, but parchment-like, and often rise several centimeters above the substratum to which they attach. *Sabellastarte magnifica* (Fig. 11-5 K) is one of the largest and most spectacular fan worms of the tropical Gulf and Caribbean region. The sabellids rarely live in direct association with living corals, but occur on rocks, pilings or mangrove roots, often in dense clusters.

As with the other groups, many of the echinoderms on the reef crest are the same as those we encountered within the lagoon. We have already mentioned the black rock-boring urchin, *Echinometra lucunter*, as the conspicuous echinoderm on the reef crest. It is joined by the green rock-boring urchin, *E. viridis*, and, in slightly deeper water, the pencil urchin, *Eucidaris tribuloides* (Fig. 11-4 G1). The long-spined black urchin, *Diadema antillarum*, never ventures as high upon the shore as any of these other urchins, but rests in shallow subtidal waters nearby.

Most of the other echinoderms of the reef crest are cryptic. The sticky sea cucumber, *Euapta lappa* (Fig. 11-4 I1) seeks refuge under flat stones. Brittle stars are both the most diverse and the most elusive echinoderms of the upper reef. They retreat under stones or within crevice shelters (Fig. 11-5 U) during the day, and emerge at night to feed. We illustrate two brittle stars, the fissiparous, six-armed *Ophiactis savignyi* (Fig. 11-5 T) and the more usual 5-armed *Ophiocomella ophiactoides* (Fig. 11-5 S), but several additional species of brittle stars occur here. Asteroids are less common, but the comet sea star, *Linckia guildingii* (Fig. 11-4 H1), is present in crevices under coral rubble. The common name of this asteroid alludes to the condition expressed when the animal is regenerating lost arms. If broken into pieces, each arm has the ability to regenerate missing parts. The early stage of this process produces several short arms attached to the original member, and resembles the head and tail of a comet.

Seaward and lagoonward of the reef crest, water gradually deepens, and the coralline-encrusted rocks gradually give way to blocks of living coral. Just below the tide, sheets of *Diploria clivosa* a meter in diameter rise no more than a few centimeters above the algae-encrusted rocks. Slightly deeper, bright yellow patches of *Porites astreoides* (Plate 11-3 A) dot the reefscape. Macroscopic algae, including *Dictyota divaricata* (Fig. 11-3 A1), *Galaxaura squalida*, *G. lapidescens*, *Laurencia papillosa* (Fig. 11-3 Y) and *Dictyosphaeria cavernosa* (Fig. 11-3 C1), cling to the rocks. The algae are grazed by the several herbivorous molluscs described above.

Lister's tree oyster, *Isognomon radiatus* (Fig. 11-4 J1), is relatively common among algae where it byssally attaches especially along the edges of rocks. It is often overlooked, as its color and flattened shape make it inconspicuous. The unusual sponge oyster, *Ostrea permollis* (Fig. 11-4 K1), attaches in protected areas under slabs of coral rock.

The Reef Front

Immediately seaward of the reef crest in depths between 1 to 6 m lies a distinctive zone (Fig. 11-3, Inset 3), characterized almost exclusively by the elkhorn coral *Acropora palmata* (Fig. 11-3 C; Plate 11-1 B). This is among the least tolerant of corals with respect to water siltation or turbidity. Corals usually employ cilia to sweep surfaces of the colony clean after binding the contaminants in mucus. *Acropora palmata* has short cilia and tiny mucous secreting cells, relying upon the well-agitated upper waters for primary cleansing. Furthermore, by occupying the top of the living reef, less debris rains upon the colony.

Elkhorn corals pay a price for living here. The same waves and currents which cleanse the colony of debris and supply *Acropora* with food can be destructive. Even moderate seas striking the reef can break branches of *Acropora* lying at right angles to the direction of the waves. Windward reefs are frequently characterized by *Acropora* colonies with most branches facing into, or, even more commonly, away from the direction of the prevailing wave train. Very few *Acropora* branches extend at right angles to it. "Oriented" *Acropora* colonies often characterize the wave-swept upper fore reef. In the shelter of the leeward reef or in the lagoon, the growth pattern of elkhorn coral is more symmetrical, with flattened, palmate branches extending in all directions. In the face of the most severe wave attack during storms or hurricanes, even oriented *Acropora* cannot withstand the onslaught. The entire community can be flattened, and branches heaved to the reef crest, providing it with a new supply of rubble.

Restoration of a reef front community begins immediately following a major storm (Highsmith *et al.*, 1980). Much of the newly formed *Acropora palmata* rubble, such as the larger detached coral fragments and the basal stumps from which they were broken, contains sufficient living tissue to permit new growth. Within a few years, new branches replace those destroyed by the storm. Coral larvae also found new colonies by settling upon dead coral rock. Eventually these young colonies transform the rubble into new coral forests. *Acropora palmata* is one of the fastest growing reef corals. Its rapid growth helps account for its prevalence on the reef front. Most other shallow-water corals, even if they can attach, are quickly overgrown or overshadowed by *A. palmata*. Exceptions include *Diploria clivosa*, *Montastrea annularis* and, on reefs of the Yucatan shelf, *Agaricia* sp.

The Fore Reef

The fore reef arises below the wave-dominated zone of *Acropora palmata*. It can be divided into two regions, an upper slope lying between depths of 6 and 17 m, and dissected by spurs and grooves (Fig. 11-3, Inset, 4) and 11-4, Profile), and a lower, more gently sloping face at a depth between 17 and 25 m, where corals grow largely in sheets (Fig. 11-3, Inset, 5-6).

The spurs and grooves of the fore reef are most evident from the air. They appear as numerous rocky fingers interdigitating with the sea, and eventually disappearing into deeper waters. In fact, the spurs are long narrow walls of coral increasing in elevation with water depth. They are composed of a limestone core, primarily the skeletal remains of *Montastrea annularis*. The grooves are sandy or cobble-lined depressions between them. Several coral species and a variety of other organisms attach to or live upon these spurs, but the prevalence of *M. annularis* makes this species the dominant framebuilder of the reef. On the leeward Lobos reef, for example, this species comprises almost 50 percent of the living coral on reef spurs, with heads of *Diploria strigosa*, *D. labyrinthiformis* and *Montastrea cavernosa* and thin blades of *Millepora* comprising most of the balance (Rigby & McIntire, 1966). *Diploria strigosa* seems to dominate the windward upper fore reef, with *Montastrea annularis* and *Diploria clivosa* sharing the second level of abundance. *Siderastrea siderea* and the other previously mentioned species also occur here.

Sandy-floored grooves dissect the entire platform from the reef crest to a depth of 25 m, where they communicate with a fringing sand apron that encircles the entire bank. Between 14 and 18 m the character of the fore reef gradually changes. The spurs give way to large sheets of coral, consisting primarily of *Montastrea cavernosa* but also including sheets of *M. annularis*, *Diploria labyrinthiformis* and the smaller *Agaricia fragilis* (Fig. 11-6). The sheets arch far out over the slope to which they are attached, providing numerous and often spacious recesses between the corals. These crevices provide shelter for a variety of invertebrates and fishes.

Large sponges are usually characteristic of deep reef habitats. Clustered cylindrical branches of the lavender tube sponge, *Spinosella* (= *Callyspongia*) *vaginalis* (Fig. 11-6 A), commonly rise above the sheets of coral at Arrecife Lobos. Even larger vase or basket sponges, such as the reddish *Ircinia campana* (Fig. 11-6 B), grace the deeper flanks of other Gulf reefs. These and other sponges provide additional shelter for small invertebrates such as the brittle star, *Ophiothrix suensonii* (Fig. 11-6 W).

Several species of unstalked comatulid crinoids take shelter within coral crevices of the deeper reef. Most emerge only at night to feed upon the nocturnally active zooplankton. The black and white sea lily, *Nemaster grandis* (Fig. 11-6 C), is an exception, for it is often seen on the reef during the day. The bright orange crinoid, *Nemaster rubiginosa*, also has been reported from Arrecife Lobos (J.W. Tunnell, personal communication). The basket star, *Astrophyton muricatum* (Fig. 11-6 N) bears a superficial resemblance to a comatulid crinoid, but is, in fact, a most unusual brittle star. Like the reef comatulids, it is a crevice dweller by day and a filter feeder by night (Davis, 1966).

The black corals, or Antipatharia, are colonial cnidarians which live attached on the deeper reef slopes. They are rarely encountered in water depths less than about 20 m. Tiny polyps produce a dense, intensely black-pigmented organic skeleton, the surface of which is covered with short, tiny spines (Fig. 11-6 H). Large branching colonies of *Antipathes* sp. (Fig. 11-6 D) are often encountered by divers. Dried specimens can be cleaned, shaped and polished into various kinds of jewelry. Large black corals have become increasingly hard to find in those parts of their range where deep reefs are often visited by divers, in part because of intense exploitation and in part because of slow growth rates. In some places (primarily Caribbean localities) it is now illegal to collect black coral. The wire coral, *Stichopathes seticornis* (Fig. 11-6 H), is another antipatharian, but unlike *Antipathes*, its colony resembles an elongate flexible strand of heavy gauge wire, sometimes extending several meters into the water off the reef slope. All of the black corals are more commonly associated with Caribbean reefs, but they are sometimes encountered on the deeper slopes of Gulf reefs.

11-6. The deep reef slope. These species represent the great variety of life that finds shelter within crevices between platelike colonies of *Montastrea annularis*, *Agaricia fragilis* and other corals, lives attached to coral rock, or swims in close proximity to the reef. **A.** Tube sponge, *Spinosella vaginalis*; **B.** Vase sponge, *Ircinia campana*; **C.** Sea lily, *Nemaster grandis*; **D.** Black coral, *Antipathes* sp.; **E.** Ocean surgeonfish, *Acanthurus bahianus*; **F.** Spiny lobster, *Panulirus argus*; **G.** Arrow crab, *Stenorhynchus seticornis*; **H.** Wire coral, *Stichopathes lutkeni*; **I.** Queen parrotfish, *Scarus vetula*; **J.** Squirrelfish, *Holocentrus ascensionis*; **K.** Caribbean coral-shell, *Coralliophila caribaea*; **L.** Spiny spider crab, *Mithrax spinosissimus*; **M.** Queen angelfish, *Holacanthus ciliaris*; **N.** Basket star, *Astrophyton muricatum*; **O.** Coral crab, *Carpilius corallinus*; **P.** Reticulated cowrie-helmet, *Cypraecassis testiculus*; **Q.** Measled cowrie, *Cypraea zebra*; **R.** Spiny oyster, *Spondylus americanus*; **S.** Jewel box clam, *Chama congregata*; **T.** Blackberry drupe, *Morula nodulosa*; **U.** *Leucozonia leucozonalis*; **V.** American star shell, *Astraea tecta*; **W.** Brittlestar, *Ophiothrix suensonii*; **X.** Green moray, *Gymnothorax funebris*; **Y.** Nassau grouper, *Epinephelus striatus*.

Crustaceans of the deeper reef are often cryptic, hiding within numerous overhangs, holes and crevices. Several are also relatively large. The spiny lobster, *Panulirus argus* (Fig. 11-6 F), is especially shy and must be sought, at least during the day, by poking into the deeper recesses along the reef face. The large red spider crab, *Mithrax spinosissimus* (Fig. 11-6 L, carapace width, 170 mm) is bolder, venturing to and resting at the open edge of its crevice recess, especially on cloudy days. This is the largest spider crab of the tropical Atlantic. It strikes an imposing yet harmless figure at the mouth of its den when seen for the first time, with the large, warty body supported by slender tubular legs. So adapted is this crab for the deeper parts of the reef that on land, without the buoyancy provided by seawater, the legs are incapable of supporting the heavy carapace. It is a shadowy dark gray when viewed on the edge of a coral crevice in natural light. The true burgundy red color is apparent only when illuminated by an underwater torchlight, or if the crab is brought to the surface.

The coral crab, *Carpilius corallinus* (Fig. 11-6 O, carapace width, 130 mm), is another large crustacean of the deeper reef, and impossible to confuse with the large spider crab. Its carapace is almost smooth, its legs are short and held close to the body, and, like so many of the xanthids, its massive chelipeds are darkened at the tips. The brick red carapace is interrupted by meandering yellowish lines. The underside of the body is pale yellow. The coral crab is more elusive than *Mithrax*, and is rarely observed outside its crevice retreat during the day.

The arrow crab *Stenorhynchus seticornis* (Fig. 11-6 G, carapace width, 15 mm) is much smaller than the preceding species. It lives among coral rocks or on sand, and ranges from the lagoon to the deep reef, although Yang (1976) considers populations from deeper waters to be morphologically distinct from those of the shallows. The long spiny rostrum and appendages make this crab difficult to ingest by most predators. Accordingly, it occupies relatively exposed locations during the day, feeding or engaged in apparent self-cleaning activity. If threatened, it employs the spinose walking legs to fend off predators until it can retreat to a protected location (Williams, 1984). It is an omnivorous scavenger and detritivore.

Molluscs of the deep reef are often the same as those are found in association with coral and coral rubble at shallower depths. *Coralliophila caribbaea* (Fig. 11-6 K) and *C. abbreviata* (Fig. 11-2 L) are predators which feed upon living coral tissue. The former is a relatively sedentary snail often seen in groups of three or more attached near the lower portions of subglobular colonies of *Montastrea annularis*. The latter is also moderately gregarious, but somewhat more active (Brawley & Adey, 1982). We have observed several *C. abbreviata* slowly moving across the surface of a *Montastrea* head, leaving strips of bare coral skeleton in their wake.

The Chamidae or jewel-box clams are present on shallow reefs, but seem to increase in abundance on the deeper reef slopes. Like the oysters, they attach one valve permanently to the substratum, but which valve varies with genus or species. We illustrate *Chama congregata* (Fig. 11-6 S), but three additional species, *C. florida, C. macerophylla* and *Pseudochama radians* are also present at Arrecife Lobos. The American spiny "oyster," *Spondylus americanus* (Fig. 11-6 R), prefers attachment to vertical surfaces, usually at depths of 10 m or more. Its deeply cupped, coarsely spinose shell, large size (sometimes exceeding 100 mm in diameter), and distinctive "ball and socket" hinge set it apart from the Chamidae. The shell and long spines may be attractively streaked with reds, yellows, purples, or cream blotches. Pre-Columbian cultures of Mexico collected *Spondylus* shells and used them as both objects of ornament and trade. The Spondylidae are related to the Pectinidae or scallops, a largely unattached family of bivalves, and, like them, have numerous minute eyes fringing the mantle margin. Eyes may be useful for an errant scallop, but are a most unusual adaptation for a permanently attached bivalve.

At depths ranging from between 18 to 25 m, the slope of the Lobos platform becomes more gradual and the reef gives way to a broad sandy apron. At the reef-sand margin two gorgonacean corals, *Eunicea clavigera* (Fig. 11-8 A) and *E. calyculata* are especially abundant, attached to partially buried coral blocks emerging from the sand (Rigby & McIntire, 1966).

Coral Borers and Associates

Large quantities of dead coral usually litter most reefs. It is produced by storm damage, sedimentation, pollution, grazing reef fishes, echinoderms, or molluscs, and a variety of other causes. As coral tissues disappear, the carbonate coral skeleton is attacked by a group of animals which seek refuge within it. These are the coral borers which, with later arrivals and subsequent geologic processes such as silt filling boreholes and submarine cementation, slowly alter the form of the original coral skeleton. The corallum may be so riddled with borers that it eventually disintegrates into sand. Massive coral skeletons are re-worked and re-cemented to such a degree that the resulting block of limestone bears little resemblance to the original form. In either case, the process of alteration, or diagenesis, renders the coral skeleton unrecognizable in its original state. Diagenesis occurs on all reefs, and produces new habitats of either sand or rock upon which subsequent reef-dwelling organisms depend.

Reef diagenesis is considerably more complex than the few steps we have just outlined and generally beyond the scope of this book. The initial invasion by reef borers, however, is a topic of importance, for the species which bore into coral are as much a part of the reef community as any of the others we have already described. In Chapter 5 we mentioned a few borers of shells on the oyster reefs of the northwestern Gulf. The coral reefs of Mexico, being more massive and containing larger quantities of soft carbonate, harbor a much greater diversity of borers. Some will penetrate living coral, but more frequently they attack coral rock which is no longer alive. We will first consider the borers of dead coral, and, at the end of this section, briefly describe a few organisms which attack or live in association with living corals.

Sponges of the genus *Cliona* excavate limestone and are among the more important borers of oyster shells in northern Gulf estuaries (Chapter 5). Other *Cliona* are equally important coral borers, and some, such as *C. caribbea*, also harbor symbiotic zooxanthellae like those that occur in living corals.

The Gulf coral-boring *Cliona* have not received the attention this group has enjoyed elsewhere, but their distribution and diversity here is probably similar to that of Caribbean reefs and banks. Rezak *et al.* (1985) recorded at least six species from Gulf of Mexico hard banks, and Rutzler (1974) described seven species of *Cliona* from Bermuda corals. Within a restricted geographic area, Rutzler found the species of Clionidae could usually be distinguished by habitat, the shape of the boring, and, to some extent, color. *Cliona caribbea* is a common species invading shells and coral rock in shallow waters of the tropical Atlantic. It is greenish, olive, or brown depending upon the density of included zooxanthellae. Rutzler found the bright red or orange *C. lampa* in shallow water (to about 2 m) associated with strong currents, but it has also been reported from several hard banks in the northwestern Gulf at depths in excess of 50 m (Rezak *et al.*, 1985). In shallow water this sponge riddles large *Diploria* heads with cavernous excavations to a depth of 8 cm. It resculptures the walls of these cavities with a thin layer of ectodermal tissue (Neumann, 1966). Similarly, *Cliona amplicavata* and *C. flavifodina* excavate large single cavities within corals such as *Madracis decactis* until the coral is no more than an empty shell, easily crushed between the fingers. There are numerous species of clionids in the Caribbean, many of which are also likely to be in the Gulf of Mexico.

The peanut worms or Sipuncula are a phylum of unsegmented, vermiform coelomate burrowers or borers. Their thick, muscular body wall is covered by a thin cuticle which often has a metallic sheen. The body comprises two regions, a broad posterior trunk and a narrow eversible proboscis or introvert that is tipped around the mouth by a crown of tentacles. Most species appear to be deposit feeders, the oral tentacles collecting fine material for processing in a rather simple, U-shaped gut.

A number of sipunculans live in corals. Some species occupy preexisting crevices but others construct discrete tubular passages into which their trunks fit snugly. These are clearly coral borers, although little is known of how the boring is accomplished. In *Aspidosiphon*, the anterior and posterior regions of the trunk have hard calcareous or chitinous spines embedded in the cuticle, clearly suggesting mechanical abrasion. Integumental glands also occur throughout the body

wall and upon epidermal papillae, raising the possibility that chemical etching may also occur (Rice, 1969).

The coral-boring sipunculans of the western Gulf of Mexico have received little study, so we take examples of three genera from southern Florida which have received considerably more attention (e.g., Robertson, 1963). *Phascolosoma* is one of the more specialized sipunculan genera with a thick introvert arising vertically from the trunk and tipped by a circlet of complex tentacles. It is represented by at least three species, *P. antillarum* (Fig. 11-7 M), *P. dentigerum* and *P. varians*. *Phascolosoma antillarum* is a common sipunculan in intertidal rock throughout southern Florida and the Caribbean and has been reported from Arrecife Lobos (Tunnell, 1974).

In *Aspidosiphon*, the introvert usually arises from the trunk at a distinct angle and is equipped with simple or bifurcate hooks. This genus is also characterized by distinct horny shield-like structures at both ends of the trunk. We illustrate *A. steenstrupi* (Fig. 11-7 N), an Indo-Pacific species which has been introduced into and is now widely distributed throughout the tropical western Atlantic. Other tropical Atlantic species include *A. elegans*, *A. speciosus*, *A. spinosocustatus*, and *A. fischeri*. An *Aspidosiphon* sp. is common within coral and among sponges on the West Flower Garden Reef in the northwestern Gulf (Wills & Bright, 1974).

Lithacrosiphon, here represented by *L. alticonum* (Fig. 11-7 O), is characterized by a hard calcareous, cone-like structure at the anterior end of the trunk, and dorsal to the point of emergence of the introvert. The posterior shield which characterizes *Aspidosiphon* is absent in this genus.

Until recently, the polychaetes have been largely overlooked in studies of coral borers. These segmented worms probably enjoy a more important role in coral biodeterioration than has generally been recognized, although Gardiner (1903) considered them to be "the prime and most effective agents" in coral rock destruction. Several families, including the Cirratulidae, Eunicidae, Lumbrineridae, Lysaretidae, Sabellidae, and Spionidae have species which bore into rock or coral. The Phyllodocidae are nestlers in coral (Gardiner, 1903). The Serpulidae, which include a large number of conspicuous, coral-associated species, build calcareous tubes that become overgrown by living coral and thus are not true borers. The coral-inhabiting polychaetes of Florida, including species of the eunicids *Lysidice* and *Eunice*, the lumbrinerid *Lumbrineris* and the lysaretid *Oenone* have been studied by Robertson (1963) and Ebbs (1966). *Lysidice ninetta*, builds U-shaped borings in dead *Diploria* heads (Bromley, 1978). *Eunice mutilata* is a possible deposit-feeding borer which feeds as it constructs a complex gallery in rock and coral that often interconnects with burrows of sipunculans. The sabellid *Hypsicomus elegans* is a suspension feeder producing a long, circular, unbranched boring. The Lumbrineridae are usually carnivorous, whereas the Lysaretidae such as *Oenone fulgida* prob-

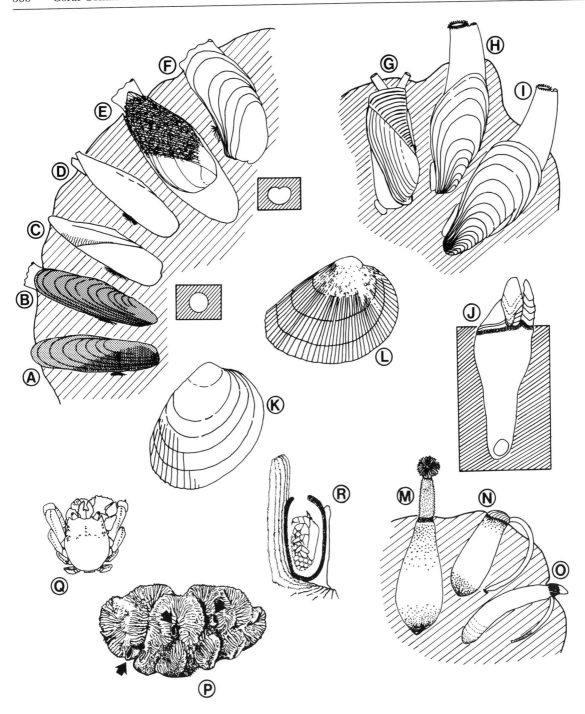

11-7. Coral borers and associates. **A.** Black date mussel, *Lithophaga nigra*; **B.** Giant date mussel, *Lithophaga antillarum*; **C.** Mahogany date mussel, *Lithophaga bisulcata*; **D.** Scissor date mussel, *Lithophaga aristata*; **E.** *Gregariella coralliophaga*; **F.** Cinnamon mussel, *Botula fusca*; **G.** *Spengleria rostrata*; **H.** *Gastrochaena ovata*; **I.** *Gastrochaena hians*; **J.** Rock-boring barnacle, *Lithotrya dorsalis*; **K.** Boring clam, *Petricola lapicida*; **L.** *Ruppelaria typica*; **M.** *Phascolosoma antillarum*, **N.** *Aspidosiphon steenstrupi*, and **O.** *Lithacrosiphon alticonum*; **P.** Rose coral, *Manicina areolata* with 3 cryptochirid galls (arrows); **Q.** Coral gall crab, *Troglocarcinus corallicola*; **R.** *T. corallicola* within chamber.

ably scrape food from the surface of dead coral. Spionidae such as *Polydora* (see Chapter 5) are either surface deposit or suspension feeders. Elongate palps project into the water from the bore opening and are either pulled over the surface of the substratum or are waved in the water in a "lassoing" motion.

Many species of boring barnacles live within corals on Indo-Pacific reefs, but these cirripeeds are less diverse in the tropical Atlantic. They are among the most obvious borers, as their shell plates project above the coral surface if they have not been overgrown by encroaching coral tissue. *Lithotrya dorsalis* (Fig. 11-7 J) is the most common boring barnacle in the tropical Atlantic (Robertson, 1963; Bromley, 1978), and may be the primary cause of coral erosion on many reefs (Ahr & Stanton, 1973). The *Lithotrya* burrow is oval and up to 10 cm deep. The barnacle attaches to its burrow by means of a calcareous disc located on the carinal margin of the peduncle close to its tip. Charles Darwin (1851) showed that the main burrowing organ of this barnacle is the peduncle which is covered with chitin and armed with numerous little star-headed studs composed of an inner chitinous core and a calcareous outer layer. Movement of the animal in its burrow abrades the studs against the burrow wall.

A second pyrogomatine barnacle, *Ceratoconcha domingensis*, is not a borer, but embeds itself exclusively in living corals, chiefly *Porites astreoides* and *Montastrea annularis* (Bromley, 1978). By keeping pace with upward coral growth, this barnacle becomes embedded within the coral skeleton.

We have previously discussed the intertidal rock boring sea urchins, *Echinometra lucunter* (Fig. 4-1 E1) and *E. viridis*. They are important bioerosive agents on intertidal carbonates.

Several bivalve molluscs are coral borers and have been reviewed by Morton (1983b; 1988). *Petricola lapicida* (Fig. 11-7 K) and *Rupellaria typica* (Fig. 11-7 L) are two small heterodont bivalves that possibly settle in coral crevices but are capable of chemical boring to create a burrow that matches their shell outlines exactly (Morton & Scott, 1988). The crenelline mytilid, *Gregariella coralliophaga* (Fig. 11-7 E), bores into dead coral heads. It has a circum-tropical distribution, and, although rare in parts of the Pacific, is relatively common throughout the tropical Atlantic. It probably is not a primary borer, but occupies and widens empty lithophagine borings. It surrounds the posterior edge of its shell with a fibrous, camouflaging nest constructed from byssal fibers. *Botula fusca* (Fig. 11-7 F) is another circum-tropical mytilid (Modiolinae) thought to bore by chemical means. The small, dark brown, nut-sized shell fits snugly within a heart-shaped cavity (Bromley, 1978).

Two groups of bivalve molluscs are particularly important coral borers: the Gastrochaenidae and the Lithophaginae. The gastrochaenids bore into only dead coral. *Spengleria rostrata* (Fig. 11-7 G) is representative of the more primitive Gastrochaenidae, with a robust shell, deep ridging, a pronounced keel and separate siphons. *Spengleria* mechanically abrades a smooth drop-shaped burrow by means of calcareous spikes embedded in the anterior periostracum (Carter & Aller, 1975; Carter, 1978).

The shell of the more specialized *Gastrochaena* is smooth, fragile and widely emarginate to allow mantle folds to be reflected over the shell. The foot has the form of a sucking disc that attaches the animal to the substratum when boring. This process was once believed to be achieved by mechanical abrasion, but Morton (1983b) has suggested that glands in the foot or mantle chemically etch the limestone. The siphons are fused almost to the tip. They secrete an encircling calcareous siphonal tube for protection as siphons grow beyond the coral surface. Two species are usually associated with Atlantic reefs: *Gastrochaena ovata* (Fig. 11-7 H), and *Gastrochaena hians* (Fig. 11-7 I).

The date mussels, or Lithophaginae (Mytilidae) include the largest animals which bore into corals, and comprise species which bore living and dead corals. They are exclusively chemical borers, employing secretions from an anterior pallial gland located in the mantle to etch coral limestone. This group, with short siphons, does not produce a calcareous siphonal tube, but, like some *Gastrochaena*, smooths or lines the burrow wall with secreted aragonite.

There are four Lithophaginae which commonly occur on tropical Atlantic reefs (Turner & Boss, 1962). The scissor date mussel, *Lithophaga aristata* (Fig. 11-7 D), which bores calcareous rocks and shells, is characterized by posterior crossed prolongations to the valves. The shell of the black date mussel, *L. nigra* (Fig. 11-7 A) is sculptured along the lower anterior third by strong dorso-ventral lyrations, whereas in *L. antillarum* (Fig. 11-7 B) the sculpture consists of weak posterior and ventral sulcations. Both species inhabit dead coral and rock and are frequently encountered on Mexico reefs. *Lithophaga antillarum* may reach a length of 10 cm, whereas *L. nigra* is about half this size.

The mahogany date mussel, *L. bisulcata* (Fig. 11-7 C) is of particular interest, for it bores into living as well as dead coral. It can be recognized by the pair of grooves or sulcations on the posterior slope of the valves. The mahogany brown shell is often encrusted, especially posteriorly, by gray, porous calcareous deposits. Boring into living coral is a more specialized life style that must require adaptations unnecessary for borers of dead coral. Free-swimming larvae must have mechanisms which attract them to living corals, enabling them to penetrate the coral tissue, probably by entering the coelenteron but avoiding digestion (Scott, 1988a,b). Within the coral, the adult bivalve must maintain the aperture against overgrowth by living coral tissue, and inhibit nematocyst attack of the extended siphons. All of these features characterize *L. bisulcata*, and point to the more intimate relationship this lithophagine shares with living corals than the simpler life styles of the dead coral borers (for a review of this subject see Morton, 1988).

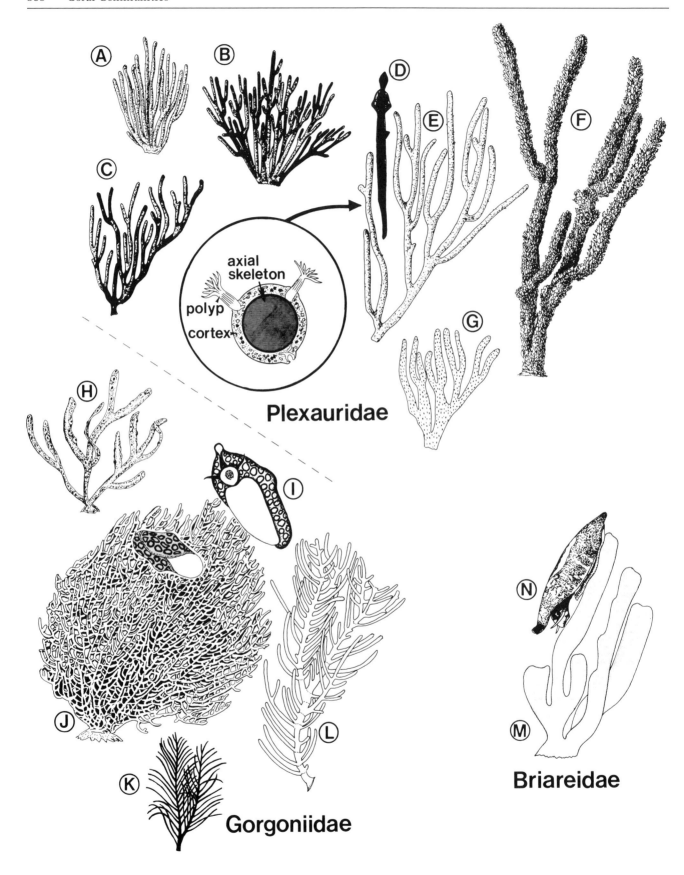

axial
skeleton

polyp

cortex

Plexauridae

Gorgoniidae

Briareidae

Finally, we turn to some most unusual coral associates, the coral gall crabs, *Troglocarcinus corallicola* (Fig. 11-7 Q) and *Opeccarcinus hypostegus* (not illustrated). The Cryptochiridae, the family to which these crabs belong (formerly Hapalocarcinidae, see Kropp and Manning, 1985), are crustaceans which live in association with living corals, often eroding deep pits into the skeletons of their hosts. The Atlantic species are not coral borers, but do settle upon and locally damage the living corallum.

Some Cryptochiridae are relatively host-specific, settling on only certain species of corals. *Troglocarcinus corallicola* seems to be the least host-specific of all members of the family, occupying at least 17 species of scleractinian corals (Scott, 1985; Kropp and Manning, 1987), but not members of the Agariciidae. It is especially common on *Manicina areolata* (Fig. 11-7 P) and species of *Meandrina*, where it occupies tall, cylindrical cysts arising from the recessed grooves of the living coral. The crab pads its cyst with a layer of detritus filtered from the water, and the coral secretes a thin wall of carbonate around a portion of the detrital wall (Fig. 11-7 R). Several Pacific Cryptochiridae live permanently sealed within a cyst, save only a small opening providing water circulation. *Troglocarcinus corallicola* maintains the upper surface of its chamber open, although it may employ removable detritus for temporary closure. We have observed up to four cysts on a 6 cm colony of *Manicina areolata*, each containing a single crab. Males apparently enter the chamber of females for copulation, and females brood large orange eggs on abdominal pleopods.

Opeccarcinus hypostegus seems to prefer agariciid corals, where it lives semi-confined under a skeletal dome formed by the host. Coral gall crabs are filter feeders. The biology of Atlantic cryptochirids has been examined by Verrill (1908), Monod (1956), Shaw and Hopkins (1977), Reed *et al.* (1982) and most recently Kropp and Manning (1987), but there remains much to be learned about these unusual crustaceans.

11-8. Soft corals and associates of the southern Gulf and eastern Yucatan. Gorgonaceans are conspicuously abundant upon Caribbean coral reefs but are usually poorly represented in similar Gulf of Mexico habitats. Species marked with an asterisk occur on Campeche Bank reefs and off eastern Yucatan localities such as Cozumel or Cancun, but are rare or absent within the western Gulf basin. **A.** *Eunicea clavigera*; **B.** *Plexaura flexuosa*; **C.** *Plexaura homomalla*; **D.** Trumpetfish, *Aulostomus maculatus*; **E.** *Muricea muricata*; **F.** *Muricea atlantica*; **G.** *Plexaurella dichotoma*; **H.** *Pterogorgia citrina*; **I.** Flamingo-tongue snail, *Cyphoma gibbosum*; **J.** Sea fan, *Gorgonia flabellum*; **K.** *Pseudopterogorgia americana*; **L.** *Pseudopterogorgia acerosa*; **M.** *Briareum asbestinum*; **N.** *Cymbula acicularis*.

Bryozoa

Tiny colonial bryozoans are among the most often overlooked animals of reef habitats. Yet, they abound, clinging to old shells, dead coral, *Thalassia* blades, wharf pilings, the walls and ceilings of coral crevices, and many other objects. Bryozoans form colonies of many shapes, ranging from calcareous or fleshy encrusting crusts or tufts to erect, branching systems which resemble "seaweeds." All colonies are composed of small chitinous boxes or zooecia, assembled in various ways, but each housing a single retractable polypide. Despite the polyp-like appearance, the bryozoan is a minute but highly organized coelomate metazoan, feeding by means of a lophophore, or a coil of ciliated tentacles surrounding the mouth.

There are three groups of bryozoans. The simplest are the Ctenostomata. They are wholly uncalcified and form either soft crusts and lobules, or arise from slender stolons. We illustrate two of the stoloniferous forms, *Bowerbankia* sp. (Fig. 11-9 A) and *Nolella* sp. (Fig. 11-9 B). The former produce inconspicuous transparent zooecia which arise from thin, threadlike stolons. In contrast, the zooecia of *Nolella* are characteristically elongate and relatively conspicuous, but the stolons are tiny and delicate.

The second group of bryozoans, the Cyclostomata, include the most strongly calcified species. The zooecia are long slender tubes, opening terminally without an operculum. *Entalophora* sp. (Fig. 11-9 D) is a rigidly erect colony with rounded stems and branches bearing zooecial apertures on all sides of the branch. In contrast, *Oncousoecia* sp. (Fig. 11-9 C) is an encrusting form.

The largest group of bryozoans are the Cheilostomata, differentiated from the others in that they possess an operculum by which they are able to close the opening to the zooecia. Cheilostomes are frequently polymorphic, with some having highly modified individuals called "avicularia" and "vibracula." The latter are simple sweeping and guarding bristles, but the former resemble birds' beaks with snapping jaws. Both serve a protective role, and, as such, are reduced in size to appear as appendages of the main colony.

The Cheilostomata are further subdivided into groups, the Ascophora and the Anasca. The first are usually more fully calcified, appearing as pink, white, or occasionally brightly colored crusts under stones. Their zooecia are often beautifully patterned and sometimes ornamented with tiny spines. *Watersipora cucullata* (Fig. 11-9 L) and *Schizoporella* sp. (Fig. 11-9 M) are illustrated as examples from the Gulf of Mexico. Colonies of the former vary from brownish purple to almost black, whereas the latter are much more variably colored.

The Anasca always have the upper margins of the zooecium uncalcified and some, such as *Aetea* sp. (Fig. 11-9 E), are uncalcified. It is a simple bryozoan, with creeping stolons giving rise to single polypides. More commonly, anascan colonies consist of from two to many zooecia lying side by side. The Membraniporidae have an encrusting habit, spreading white lacework sheets over hard surfaces, fronds or algae, or blades of sea grasses. Zooecia of *Membranipora* (Fig. 11-9 I) form elongate polygons free of ornamentation, but other members of this family, such as *Conopeum tubigerum* (Fig. 11-9 J), have minute spines flanking the uncalcified frontal area.

The Bicellariellidae include mostly erect, bushy, branching colonies. The zooecia are long narrow boxes, placed side by side with two or more in a row. *Bugula neritina* (Fig. 11-9 H), with prominent avicularia and vibracula and dichotomous branches, is one of the most conspicuous representatives of this family in the Gulf of Mexico. It is found among algae, attached to shallow subtidal rocks, and on wharves. At the latitude of Veracruz, it is more abundant in the winter. The Cellariidae, e.g., *Cellaria* sp. (Fig. 11-9 F), are another family of erect, branching bryozoans with chitinous joints between the branches.

Encrusting bryozoans are considerably more common than the foliose or branching forms. One of the most common and widespread bryozoans of the tropical Atlantic is a member of the Steinoporellidae, *Steginoporella magnilabris* (Fig. 11-9 G), a normally encrusting species. We also illustrate another encrusting bryozoan, *Arachnopusia* sp. (Fig. 11-9 K).

This brief section is hardly adequate to characterize the immense diversity of tropical bryozoans. For additional information and references, consult Bassler (1953), Ryland (1976) Woollacott & Zimmer (1977) and Boardman *et al.* (1983).

Fishes

As in previous chapters, we will not attempt an exhaustive treatment of the fishes which occur upon or near reefs, but will cite important families and representative species of the tropical southern Gulf. Many of the fishes described in previous chapters also occur on reefs and associated habitats.

Several groups of fishes feed by scraping away parts of the reef. The most important of these are the herbivorous parrotfishes (Scaridae), which have an essential role in carbonate diagenesis on the reef. In terms of numbers and biomass, they are among the dominant reef fishes, and several species usually are present on most reefs. All possess a pair of hard, beak-like, dental plates which are used to crop algae from reef walls and promontories. They preferentially feed upon many of the calcareous algae, but also unavoidably ingest considerable quantities of additional reef carbonate as they forage. They pulverize this material in a pharyngeal mill, and pass the indigestible carbonate through the body, discarding it in the feces. The annual production of carbonate sand by parrotfishes must be enormous.

We illustrate only one representative species, the queen parrotfish, *Scarus vetula* (Fig. 11-6 I), but half a dozen or more species occur on Gulf reefs. Diversity is even greater on the Caribbean reefs. Color patterns on

most adult parrotfishes are strikingly different from those of the juveniles, giving the appearance of greater species diversity than actually exists.

The angelfishes (Pomacanthidae) are among the most visible and best known of the reef fishes. They patrol reef ledges during the day, poking a short tubular snout into interstices for sponges, worms, polyps or algae. When threatened, they retreat into small caves and crevices. The queen angelfish, *Holacanthus ciliaris* (Fig. 11-6 M), is a common, colorful Gulf and Caribbean species.

The surgeonfishes (Acanthuridae) are laterally flattened fishes which frequent reef habitats in schools of a few to several dozen. They have razor-sharp retractile spines on each side of the body just in front of the caudal fin. If threatened, a flick of the tail can inflict severe lacerations upon the attacker. Surgeonfishes also use the spines to establish dominance over other reef fishes or at least assure access to feeding areas. The ocean surgeon, *Acanthurus bahianus* (Fig. 11-6 E), lives on the seaward margin of the reef and forages for filamentous algae attached to reef spurs.

The puffers (Tetraodontidae) and porcupinefishes (Diodontidae) are opportunistic carnivores which will take almost anything living on the reef. The armored muscular jaws enable these fishes to crush hard-shelled invertebrates, but they are also fond of coral tips and the small fishes living near them. The family names refer to the number of fused teeth apparent in the jaw, four for the puffers and two for the porcupinefishes. The families are also distinguished by the nature of the dermal armor. Puffers are covered with short prickles, whereas the porcupinefishes bear more elongate, thicker spines. In both groups, the armor is usually held flat against the body. When threatened, they distend the stomach with water, inflating the body and erecting the prickles or spines. The resulting thorny balloon is too much to cope with for most predators. The bandtail puffer, *Sphoeroides spengleri* (Fig. 11-10 G), is less common on the reefs than the porcupine fish, *Diodon hystrix* (Fig. 11-10 I & L).

Despite their small mouths, many of the triggerfishes and closely related filefishes (both Balistidae) feed on hard-bodied invertebrates or graze upon the sessile biota on the reef. The pygmy filefish, *Monacanthus ciliatus* (Fig. 11-10 K), uses toothed jaws to strip off morsels of coral, sponge, or gorgonian tissue. It is a secretive little fish, hiding among algae and gorgonians when not actively feeding.

11-9. Bryozoa. The illustrated examples are grouped according to order. Ctenostomata: **A.** *Bowerbankia* sp.; **B.** *Nolella* sp. Cyclostomata: **C.** *Oncousoecia* sp.; **D.** *Entalophora* sp. Cheilostomata; **E.** *Aeta* sp.; **F.** Cellaria fistulosa; **G.** *Steginoporella magnilabris*; **H.** *Bugula neritina*; **I.** *Membranipora* sp.; **J.** *Conopeum* sp.; **K.** *Arachnopusia* sp.; **L.** *Watersipora cucullata*; **M.** *Schizoporella* sp.

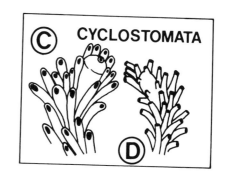

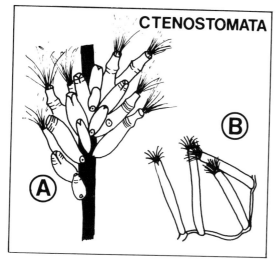

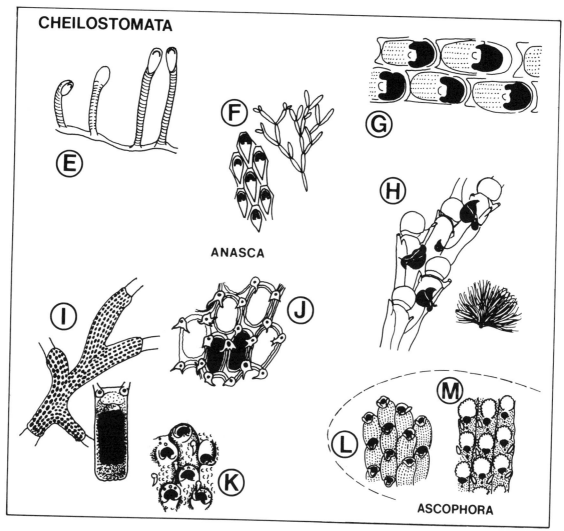

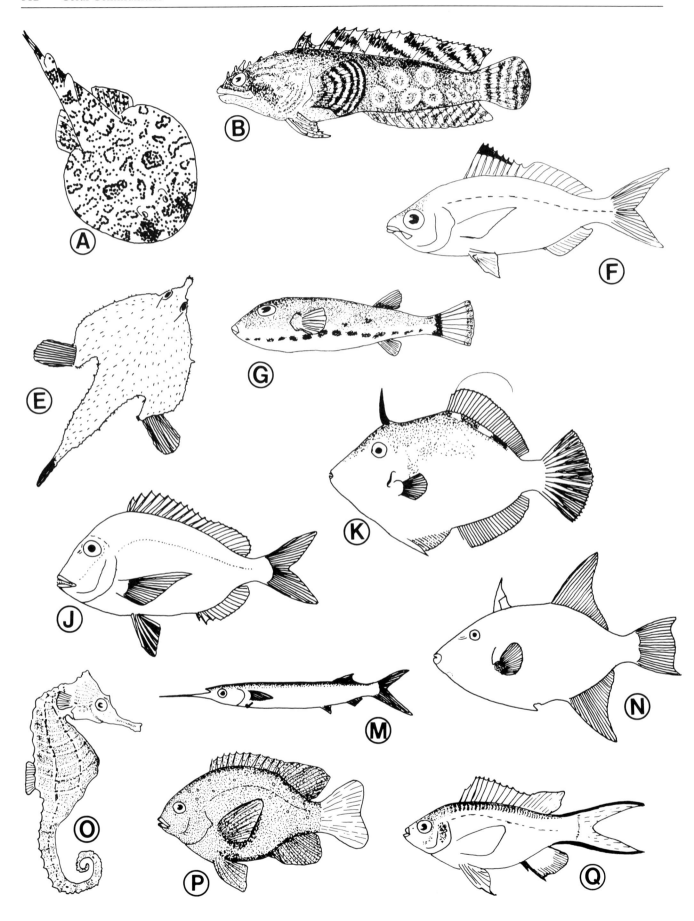

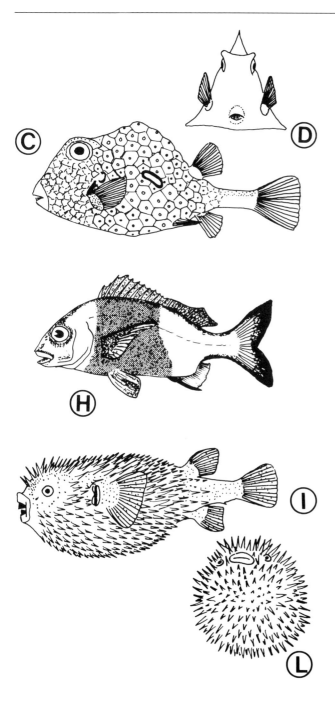

11-10. Some fishes of the southern Gulf of Mexico.
A. Electric ray, *Narcine brasiliensis;* **B.** Gulf toadfish,
Opsanus beta; **C.** and **D.** Buffalo trunkfish, *Lactophrys
trigonus;* **E.** Roughback batfish, *Ogocephalus parvus;*
F. Flagfin mojarra, *Eucinostomus melanopterus;* **G.** Bandtail puffer, *Sphoeroides spengleri;* **H.** Black maggate, *Anisotremus surinamensis;* **I.** Porcupine fish, *Diodon hystrix;* **J.** Jolthead porgy, *Calamus bajonado;* **K.** Filefish,
Monacanthus ciliatus; **L.** Porcupine fish, *D. hystrix;*
M. Ballyhoo, *Hemiramphus brasiliensis;* **N.** Ocean triggerfish, *Canthidermis sufflamen;* **O.** Lined seahorse,
Hippocampus erectus; **P.** Yellowtailed damselfish, *Microspathodon chrysurus;* **Q.** Blue chromis, *Chromis
cyaneus.*

The habits of the ocean triggerfish, *Canthidermis
sufflamen* (Fig. 11-10 N), differ from those of its close
relatives in several respects. It is uncommon inshore,
preferring to live near offshore reefs which rapidly de-
scend into deep water. Here, singly or in groups, it
may be seen swimming idly near the surface, lying on
its side and sculling with the dorsal fin. Its diet is also
unusual for, in addition to reef foraging, it feeds upon
larger members of the zooplankton (Randall, 1968).

The sea basses and groupers (Serranidae) usually live
in association with rocky areas and reefs. Although
not true demersal fishes, they remain relatively close
to the bottom. Adults are usually large, weighing as
much as 40 to 50 lbs. A few, such as the jewfish, *Epinephelus itajara* (Fig. 3-6 I), may attain a meter or
more in length and a weight of several hundred
pounds. All of the serranids are carnivores preying
upon a variety of reef fishes and invertebrates. Some,
especially the groupers, are protogynous hermaphrodites. They begin adulthood as females, but as they
age, the female reproductive system degenerates and
the male system develops. The Nassau grouper, *Epinephelus striatus* (Fig. 11-6 Y), is one of the most important commercial fishes of the Caribbean islands and it
occurs commonly on most Gulf reefs.

Moray eels (Muraenidae) retire to rock or reef crevices during the day and emerge at night to feed upon
other fishes. The green moray, *Gymnothorax funebris*
(Fig. 11-6 X), is the largest of the Atlantic morays. It is
uncommon in the northwestern Gulf, but increases in
abundance on the reefs of central Mexico and Yucatan.

With large eyes, erect spinose dorsal fins and a reddish body, the squirrelfishes (Holocentridae) are not
easily confused with any other group of reef fishes.
They are nocturnal crustacean predators, retiring beneath reef ledges or within crevices during the day.
The longjaw squirrelfish, *Holocentrus ascensionis*
(Fig. 11-6 J), is one of several species within the Gulf
of Mexico.

The trumpetfish (Aulostomidae), *Aulostomus maculatus* (Fig. 11-8 D), is a cryptic, lie-in-wait predator
which conceals itself by positioning vertically (usually
head-down) within erectly branching gorgonacean corals. It maintains this position until an unsuspecting
small fish or shrimp swims nearby, whereupon it
scoops it up through the trumpet-shaped mouth.

The seahorses belong to the same family as the
pipefishes (Syngnathidae). The lined seahorse, *Hippocampus erectus* (Fig. 11-10 O), is usually found in
turtle grass beds where it effectively disappears among
the vegetation. It feeds upon tiny crustaceans and
other invertebrates, using the small mouth and tube-
like snout almost like a pipette to slurp them into the
oral cavity. The female deposits eggs in a brood pouch
of the male. He carries and protects the developing
embryos for eight to ten days until juveniles hatch
from the eggs and emerge from the pouch.

We have previously encountered a halfbeak (Exoco-
etidae) along the Texas jetties (Chapter 3). Another
halfbeak, the ballyhoo, *Hemiramphus brasiliensis*

(Fig. 11-10 M), is a common surface dweller in shallow waters throughout the southern Gulf.

The bodies of trunkfishes and cowfishes (Ostraciidae) are largely encased within rigid, bony plates, with only fins and body orifices left uncovered. They cruise around coral heads or over grass beds, feeding upon a variety of plants and animals, and seem to be especially fond of polychaetes. There are several species of trunkfishes in the Gulf, including the buffalo trunkfish, *Lactophrys trigonus* (Fig. 11-10 C & D).

The mojarras (Gerreidae) are schooling euryhaline coastal fishes found over sandy bottoms or grass beds, but not on the reef. They employ an exceedingly protrusible mouth to pick up invertebrates off lagoon or bay floors. They occur from the shallow waters of the open Gulf to near fresh water within the upper reaches of estuaries. The flagfin mojarra, *Eucinostomus melanopterus* (Fig. 11-10 F), is easily distinguished from other silversided mojarras by its black tipped dorsal fin.

By day, large schools of grunts (Haemulidae) congregate in the shelter of the reef. They are among the most conspicuous groups of reef fishes, but, in reality, many are present there only for the protection it affords. By night they disperse to the more exposed sand flats and grass beds where they feed. The common name refers to the sounds made as these fishes grind pharyngeal teeth together. The striped grunt, *Haemulon striatum* (not illustrated) is one of the most common members of this family, which has a dozen or more species in the Gulf. We illustrate another grunt, the distinctively marked black margate, *Anisotremus surinamensis* (Fig. 11-10 H).

The porgies (Sparidae) are morphologically similar to the grunts, but are more solitary, spending much of their time nearer the bottom. They rarely retreat to reef crevices for shelter. Some are omnivorous scavengers, but members of the genus *Calamus* are usually exclusively carnivorous, especially on shelled invertebrates. The jolthead porgy, *Calamus bajonado* (Fig. 11-10 J), is especially fond of *Diadema*, the long-spined black sea urchin.

The damselfishes (Pomacentridae) are a group of colorful, small reef dwellers which frequent Gulf and Caribbean reefs. Many are highly territorial species, defending their spot on the reef against all comers, including divers, many times their size. The family encompasses a variety of feeding behaviors. Some, such as the sergeant major, *Abudefduf saxatilis* (Fig. 3-2 M), are herbivores; the blue chromis, *Chromis cyaneus* (Fig. 11-10 Q), is a zooplankton feeder; and others, such as the yellowtail damselfish, *Microspathodon chrysurus* (Fig. 11-10 P), are omnivores.

Demersal fishes are well represented in the lagoons and sand banks adjacent to the reefs. The flounders, soles, and tonguefishes are here, as are the rays and skates. One in particular, the electric ray, *Narcine brasiliensis* (Fig. 11-10 A) (Torpedinidae), is worthy of note. It is equipped with a pair of muscular electric organs which, when discharged, can produce a jolt sufficient to deter predators and possibly also stun prey. It feeds upon a variety of shellfishes.

The toadfishes (Batrachoididae) are demersals frequently associated with rock or other hard substrata. They include some species with highly venomous spines, but the Gulf of Mexico representatives either lack venomous spines or they are only mildly so. Like many other demersals, the toadfishes feed upon benthic crustaceans and molluscs. The Gulf toadfish, *Opsanus beta* (Fig. 11-10 B), occurs in bays and shallow nearshore waters from Texas to Yucatan. It frequents habitats adjacent to reefs, but rarely occurs upon them.

The bizarre batfishes (Ogocephalidae) include both deep water and shallow water species. They "walk" along the bottom using flaring pectoral and rodlike pelvic fins. They also employ a fleshy lobe of tissue, projecting from the lower surface of the rostrum, as a lure by which they entice worms and other benthic invertebrates from their lairs. The roughback batfish *Ogocephalus parvus* (Fig. 11-10 E), prefers deeper waters as along the lower flanks of southern Gulf reefs, and rarely occurs upon the reef.

YUCATAN OFFSHORE REEFS AND BANKS

The northern and western margins of the Yucatan peninsula are flanked by the broad, shallow Yucatan Shelf. During the last (Wisconsin) glaciation, most of this shelf was exposed, as were many topographic highs along the northwest margin of the shelf. As sea level rose, beginning about 15,000 years ago, the shelf was slowly inundated. The elevations near the shelf edge became islands which were quickly fringed by reef corals. Most of these islands eventually were inundated, but coral growth kept pace with the rising sea, producing shallow carbonate banks or reef crests awash by the sea.

Today seven major and numerous minor reefs and reef banks dot the outer third of the Yucatan Shelf. The largest is Alacran Reef lying about 120 km off the northern Yucatan coast. It is oval in outline, with the long axis (approximately 22.4 km) inclined about 30 degrees west of north, and having a maximum width of about 11 km. The eastern windward margins form a continuous emergent reef crest which encloses a lagoon consisting of shallow, protected sea grass beds and deeper basins. About 60 percent of the floor of the lagoon lies within a meter of sea level. Alacran Reef resembles an atoll, but positioned as it is on the continental shelf, it is not one (Logan *et al.*, 1969).

Five coral or hard-bank communities and two or three lagoonal communities occur on Alacran. They are not significantly dissimilar from the communities we have just considered from Arrecife Lobos, except perhaps by degree. The biota of Alacran is more diverse than on the carbonate banks and reefs of the western Gulf, but not as diverse as can be found in the Caribbean. The Yucatan banks are an intermediate step between the high diversity of Caribbean communities and the lower diversity of the more isolated western Gulf. Relative abundances of certain species also vary across this east-to-west gradient. Most of the Arrecife Lobos corals are present at Alacran, but some species are noticeably more obvious. For example, *Agaricia* sp. are considerably more prevalent on the Alacran reefs, reminiscent of the distribution of reef corals on fringing reefs of western Caribbean islands or the Belize barrier reef. New corals, such as *Favia fragum* and *Solenastrea* sp., appear on these reefs, reflecting the closer proximity of Alacran to the center of Atlantic scleractinian diversity. We can also identify many other groups of invertebrates and fishes with more representatives on the Yucatan banks than on the reefs off Tampico or Veracruz.

Another survey of the Yucatan bank and reef communities would provide more detail but little additional insight into the nature of the carbonate communities of the southern Gulf. Yucatan reefs have lagoon communities, a back reef, a reef crest, an *Acropora* zone, and a fore reef slope. We can add the names of new species occupying each of these communities, but only by moderately increasing degrees. Within the context of examining a temperate to tropical transition, the next detailed survey of Atlantic carbonate communities should be devoted to those approaching maximum diversity, at a locality such as Belize, Roatan, Jamaica or the Cayman Islands. These areas are outside of our present range of coverage, so we must defer this final step to a more complete volume on tropical Caribbean biota (e.g., Rutzler & MacIntyre, 1982).

TOWARD THE CARIBBEAN

The dominance of terrigenous depositional processes and deposits in the northwestern Gulf precludes any significant nearshore reef development throughout this region. The few bank reefs which occur here are far offshore, perched upon the edge of the continental shelf and raised above the fine sediments which blanket the adjacent bottom. Their biota includes a mixture of nearshore species from the northwestern Gulf and some of the hardiest reef corals and associated biota.

Nearshore terrigenous sediments persist to the southern terminus of the Gulf of Mexico. This, combined with restricted circulation and limited wave exposure, inhibits the development of nearshore fringing reefs. Off central Mexico, near Tampico and Veracruz, several banks and a few small islands lie beyond the continental influence. They occur along the edge of that part of the Mexico shore which experiences the maximal wave fetch within the Gulf of Mexico basin. Warm, clear, wave-agitated water provides the conditions that zooxanthellate hermatypic corals need to survive. So, a scleractinian fauna more diverse than that occupying the northwestern Gulf bank reef occurs here, and, in turn, helps to support a surprisingly diverse group of reef and reef-associated biota. South of these reefs, the Yucatan peninsula shelters the southern Gulf coastal bend, reduces the effects of currents and waves, and permits terrigenous processes to dominate the shallow coastal habitats. Conditions here are not conducive for coral growth.

The northern and northwestern flanks of the Yucatan peninsula are not as well protected. The Yucatan shelf is a broad submerged plain of carbonate rock and sand, produced as a result of the interaction of several factors. The Yucatan peninsula is relatively arid. The rain which falls rarely flows to the sea because porous bedrock passes much of it into large underground reservoirs. With little freshwater discharge to the Yucatan shelf, there is little terrigenous material delivered offshore. Fast currents sweep around Cabo Catoche from the Caribbean basin and fan across the Yucatan shelf. Longshore currents move and deposit large quantities of sand against the shallow margin of the peninsula, scouring the bottom and inhibiting reef growth. Further offshore, near the shelf margin, currents are weaker. The sand that is moved can be funneled to deeper basins. Underwater topographic highs provide the relief upon which reef corals and their associates can become established. Again, we have a region of warm, clean, moving water, and again we find flourishing reefs of coral.

The reef and reef-associated biota of the Gulf is derived from reef habitats fringing the Caribbean basin. Larvae are delivered by currents, which in turn are moved by the prevailing southeasterly winds. The progressive decrease in the diversity of carbonate bank biota from east to west within the Gulf of Mexico in part reflects the increasing distance from source of greatest diversity, the Caribbean reef. Its biota will include most of the species we have presented here and many more. Add to this the additional diversity of the Caribbean mangle, mudflat, lagoon, or rocky shore, each of which have contributed some elements to similar habitats in the Gulf of Mexico, and it is clear that an adequate consideration of western Caribbean shores requires another volume.

12. The Future for Gulf Shores

INTRODUCTION

In contrast to the eastern Gulf and tropical Caribbean, the western Gulf of Mexico usually is perceived as limited in habitats, species diversity, or both. Perhaps the openness and immensity of the region inhibits detailed searching, whereas the intimacy of sand cays or coral shores stimulates inspection. Clearly, the scale of Padre Island, Aransas Bay or the hypersaline salt pans of northern Yucatan easily intimidates a casual observer. Yet, when these shores are carefully scrutinized, patterns emerge which expose a richness of species and habitats originally obscured by the awesome vistas of sands, waters, mangroves or sky. In the preceding pages, we discussed and illustrated only the most common coastal and shallow nearshore biota, comprising over 800 species. Our coverage has not been exhaustive, for a complete checklist would easily include several thousand more names. Species diversity is clearly greater here than most perceive it to be, and, when combined with the climatic, seasonal and latitudinal gradients of the western Gulf, the region may rightfully boast a richer combination of habitats and inhabitants than any other North American shore. True, many of the species described and discussed are small, sometimes even superficially unspectacular, and frequently overlooked by most visitors to these shores. This should not diminish their importance to the communities in which they live, for often they provide the food, shelter, or both to the larger, more conspicuous animals. All of the species—large or small, producer or consumer, sessile or errant, emergent or immergent—play important roles in the total ecology of the coastal zone.

The dominating theme of this book has been one of temperate to tropical transition, with a progressive, gradual latitudinal increase in species diversity. The biota recognizes no political boundaries, and can be fully appreciated only by an equally apolitical analysis. Local diversity of the northwestern Gulf shores or those of southern Mexico is dependent upon the richness of habitats these subregions produce. Few shores of southern Mexico can offer the complexity of environments as occur behind the barrier islands of Texas. But no Texas shore matches the coral islands of the Mexican coast. This richness of habitats is fostered by the destabilizing influence of increasing aridity over a relatively short distance. The enhanced species diversity in Mexico is more closely linked with increasing tropical stability and the proximity to the species-rich Caribbean basin. Coral reefs and carbonate banks of the Gulf of Mexico generally fail to achieve the full splendor of Caribbean tropical islands, but, conversely, the latter often lack many components of the continental flora and fauna of the North and Central American mainlands. The two complement each other in the tropical Gulf of Mexico.

A chapter entitled "The Future for Gulf Shores" might suggest an exercise in predictions. What is to happen with the Gulf biota in the century to come? What perils will it face? What must we do to save it? It is clearly presumptuous to assume that anyone could accurately assess the fate of the habitats and biota of the western Gulf of Mexico, and, in this chapter, it is not our goal to even try. Instead, we will consider some issues that, for years to come, will influence the quality of habitats within the region and the quantity and quality of the biota that they contain. To seek a perspective for the future conservation of Gulf shore resources, we must consider the region against the backdrop of two temporal records: first, the climatic and geological events that have molded the present coastline and will continue molding it in the future, and second, the historical and future impact of humans upon these shores. Much of our discussion will relate to Texas, but our conclusions will also have broad relevance for the shores of Mexico.

THE CHANGING/EVOLVING SHORE

In Chapter 6 we described the past and present geomorphology of Gulf shores. The Gulf basin was markedly smaller 20,000 years ago than it is now, with shores lying as much as 80 km seaward of their present positions. Land elevations were not higher, but sea levels were some 100 m lower. At the end of the last glaciation, about 15,000 years ago, enormous volumes of water contained within the glaciers and polar ice caps began to melt and enter the sea. Sea level rose worldwide until about 5000 years ago, when it approximately attained the present position. During this period, the northwestern Gulf shore receded at a mean rate of about 8 m per year. This change would have been imperceptible on a daily basis but dramatically recognizable in only a few years by any prehistoric human inhabitants occupying these shores. But how dramatic was this change in terms of the shore today?

In Chapter 6 we described a receding modern shore at Sargent Beach, Texas, estimated to have been more than 0.5 km seaward of its present position in 1850. From then until 1980, a duration of 130 years, the shore is estimated to have receded at an annual rate of about 4.25 m per year (Seelig & Sorensen, 1973; Sealey & Ahr, 1975), or a rate about half that which characterized the rise of sea level at the end of the last glaciation. On the other hand, just west of the mouth of the Brazos River, the shoreline has receded at an annual rate of over 15 m per year for the last 130 years (Morton & Pieper, 1975b). Clearly, there are modern Gulf shores which are receding at rates comparable to those of a few thousand years ago, even though the primary cause of the loss of shoreline is erosional and not inundational.

There is sufficient water still bound in polar ice to raise sea level at least 50 m above its present level, or half again the rise experienced at the end of the Pleistocene. If this were to occur, all of the coastal cities of the western Gulf, including the inland port of Houston, Texas, would be submerged, most of the Yucatan peninsula would be inundated, and about half of southeastern Texas and much of northeastern Mexico would lie under water. During this century, there has been a moderate warming trend, and many continental glaciers have significantly receded. Sea level has responded by rising a few centimeters. However, an effect such as we have just described would require a significantly longer warming trend and much more melting of polar ice than is presently occurring. Even then, the encroachment would be a slow, deliberate rise. The burning of fossil fuels and the concurrent greenhouse effect may ultimately trigger such an event, but, for the immediate future, the primary coastal centers are in little danger of inundation by a rising sea level.

This is not to say that coastal residents are in no danger of losing land or property to an encroaching sea. There are some areas along the Texas coast, especially in the vicinity of Galveston Bay and along the historic Buffalo Bayou near the San Jacinto battleground, where the land is subsiding, largely the result of the removal of groundwater, inducing the sandy soil to settle. Here, residents have had to abandon homes or businesses which have simply settled into the bay. The most dramatic danger to our coasts, however, is from coastal erosion.

Within the western Gulf region, coastal erosion along the outer Texas shore has received considerable study (Morton, 1974, 1975; Morton & Pieper, 1975a,b, 1976, 1977a,b; Morton *et al.*, 1976). A natural sequence of stages in the life of a barrier island entails: (1), an accreting phase, followed by (2) stability and in due course (3) erosion of what appeared permanent. These phases are not always progressive, for, as we have seen in Chapter 2, deposition and erosion can be seasonally cyclic. It is apparent from the works of Morton and his associates, that on a long term basis much of the outer Texas coast is undergoing moderate to significant erosion. It is particularly acute from Sabine Pass to High Island, from Follets Island to Matagorda Peninsula, and along Padre Island from Mansfield Cut southward. Numerous breakwaters, seawalls, and houses along these shores have been undercut by longshore currents moving sand offshore. Investments wash out to sea, with no recourse to recover even part of the loss. The remarkable thing about this, however, is that as one washes away—be it a sea wall, house, or even a condominium—another is built to replace it.

Erosion is not restricted to the outer Texas shores. Many bayfronts have experienced similar loss of land along the shore. We have previously described erosion along the Aransas National Wildlife Refuge on San Antonio Bay (Chapter 7). This loss has occurred at an undeveloped site with minimal impact upon the coastal economy. But some bayshore areas, considered prime developed or developmental property in Galveston, Aransas and Corpus Christi bays, have suffered significant shoreline erosion during the last few decades. More than one condominium has succumbed to the sea.

The fault lies not with nature, but with human unawareness. Shoreline erosion is a fact of life near the sea. Bayshores with undercut banks, bare toppled trees, and narrow beaches are unquestionably eroding and should be avoided for any type of development. To build here simply invites disaster. Barrier island erosion is sometimes more difficult to perceive, but common sense should be sufficient to warn against any construction too near an unprotected shore. Even then, a beach house erected 30 m from the sea on a shoreline receding 3 m per year will be in the surf zone 10 years after initial construction. Unsuspecting consumers purchase these dwellings from unscrupulous developers, and the latter are long gone by the time the purchaser realizes impending disaster is close at hand. Unfortunately, this has occurred many times in the last 80 years. With forethought and study, the stable areas of the coast can be found. If we must build near the sea, it is here where we should go.

One cannot predict the natural fate of any shore, because it exists as the result of a dynamic equilibrium between a variety of forces. Change one, and numerous others are influenced or changed. These, in turn, reinfluence the first factor which adjusts again. The erosional beaches of the Gulf today may become the stable shores of tomorrow. The accreting sands of northern Yucatan may become eroding beaches with a slight shift in the direction or intensity of the prevailing wind. If this seems unlikely, consider that the position of Lydia Ann Channel, at Port Aransas, Texas moved more than a kilometer to the southwest from 1866 to 1899 (Morton & Pieper, 1976). The western Gulf coast has undergone large-scale alterations during the last few thousand years and locally significant readjustments for the last several decades. Natural shoreline changes will continue to occur along this coast for the foreseeable future, regardless of the works of humans. We should never forget the folly of Yarborough Pass (Chapter 2), and how quickly natural forces can obliterate human alterations of the coastal environment.

Even the offshore environments may be subject to change. The conditions responsible for a living reef on the Flower Garden Banks have occurred elsewhere on the northern Gulf shelf during the relatively recent geologic past. Coral boulders representing once-living reefs occur on a number of other shelf banks. Presently, the Flower Gardens are the only banks of the northern Gulf known to be successfully colonized by large hermatypic scleractinians. These reefs will survive so long as the unique combination of conditions that provide clear warm water persist in this region. Subtle changes in climate, wind patterns, or currents may be sufficient to alter these conditions, bringing hardships to Flower Garden communities, but permitting corals to become established elsewhere on the shelf. Similarly, future meanderings of the Mississippi River may markedly alter the distribution of sediments on the northern Gulf shelf. The Flower Garden Banks are sufficiently remote from this source of sediment that they most likely will not be influenced. Other shelf banks, however, might be profoundly affected. A marked shift in the primary flow of the Mississippi into the Gulf might sufficiently reduce sedimentation over some banks so as to permit the settlement and growth of new coral communities. Reefs of the northern Gulf shelf margin lead a precarious existence, and will likely wax and wane as the variety of conditions that influence the region ebb and flow.

THE HUMAN INFLUENCE

We will now consider an omnivorous, possessive, territorial, leisure-loving, sometimes compassionate and often messy animal that lives along or periodically migrates to Gulf shores. The animal, of course, is you and I—*Homo sapiens*, woman and man—a predominantly terrestrial species, but one which has maintained an intimate relationship with the sea. Each of the human traits just listed profoundly influences seashores and marine resources around the world. In this section we will consider the human impact upon the western Gulf region, and especially the shores of Texas.

Fisheries

Humankind has the ability to harvest the bounty of the seas more efficiently than any other species has ever been able to do. During this century, with the aid of the powerful and sophisticated tools of technology, the harvest has increased to dangerously high levels. Ocean fisheries are a renewable resource, which, used wisely, can provide human populations essential foods and nutrients for centuries to come. But in some parts of the world, exploitation already has depleted some marine resources to critical levels. The plight of the baleen whales and the declining Grand Bank fisheries are two well publicized examples. Tuna fisheries on both sides of South America, off western Australia, and in the western Pacific south of Japan are in jeopardy. Abalone, once delicacies in California restaurants, can rarely be found on menus there today.

Gulf of Mexico fisheries and shellfisheries resources have provided food and employment for Gulf shore residents for at least two centuries. During the last 80 years, the harvests of some species have fluctuated widely, reflecting environmental influences, overfishing, or both (e.g., oysters, Chapter 5). Other important commercial fisheries include those for blue crabs, red drum, black drum, flounder, snapper and menhaden. The most valuable and consistent commercial fishery in Texas, however, is for shrimp. In 1983, shrimps comprised 78 percent of the weight and 91 percent of the total value of Texas commercial landings (Hamilton & Saul, 1984). They are harvested within the bays or in the open Gulf. Shrimp boats are licensed according to location of and/or the ultimate use (bait or food) of the catch. Because of increasing demand for the product, the number of commercial shrimp boats in Texas has continually increased. From 1979 to 1983, this increase has been 12 percent (Crowe & Bryan, 1986). Shrimp also comprise an important component of Mexico's Gulf fishery.

Although excessive harvest can deplete any fishery, the long term danger to shrimp is more likely with respect to habitat destruction, particularly along estuarine nursery grounds. These are presently threatened from at least two quarters: (1), by physical development, effecting change in the physical structure and biological diversity of the shore and its hinterland, and (2), pollution, which is often a consequence of development and acts to degrade existing animal and plant communities directly. Development and pollution intimately are linked to the history and future of the Gulf shore.

Development

The coasts of the world have been a primary focus of human endeavor. The Spanish conquered Mexico via the port of Veracruz. The French founded New Orleans as a center of trade. The English established dozens of ports from Nova Scotia to the Carolinas, and launched a massive westward overland expansion from them. The coasts of North America were the first to be settled by Europeans and have received some of the greatest environmental assaults ever launched by humans. The port of Boston, for example, was once a vast *Spartina* marsh. A significant amount of the land of modern Boston has been "reclaimed" from the sea. Today, there are long stretches of the Atlantic shore, from Maine to Virginia, lined entirely by beachfront homes, small businesses or industry. Parts of the New Jersey shore particularly come to mind. Pollution consequences of some of this development were brought sharply in focus during the summers of 1987 and 1988, when a refuse-laden barge from New York Harbor spent months sailing from port to port in search of a place to discharge its burden, when dozens of porpoises floated ashore belly-up, dead of mysterious bacterial or viral invasions, when human vacationers contacted vexatious (but short-lived) infections after a day at the beach, and when infected medical refuse mysteriously washed ashore. Fortunately, the development of shores along much of the western Gulf of Mexico lags behind that of the U.S. eastern seaboard.

Eastern Mexico ports such as Veracruz, Campeche and Sisal were among the first on the North American continent occupied by Europeans. Over the years, most of these have remained essential centers of commerce; although some, like Sisal, have declined as industrialization forced changes in the commodities important to world trade. Given the long history of human influence along the Mexican shore, one might expect to find it considerably developed or, at least, substantially occupied. It is neither. There are few suitable harbors in eastern Mexico, relative to the length of the coastline. The vast expanses of unbroken, sandy mainland beaches are inaccessible to all but the smallest seagoing vessels. Further, most of the mangrove-fringed and mosquito-infested embayments of the southern Gulf have proven to be just too difficult to clear and maintain. As a result, much of the Mexican shore remains relatively unexploited. In contrast, the Texas coast was settled much later than the ports of Mexico, but during the last 150 years it has experienced far greater development than any that has occurred in Mexico.

Despite several disparaging behaviors (e.g., cannibalism) attributed to the Karankawa Indians, they, and other endemic peoples of the northwestern Gulf coast, were at least at one with the land and sea—as natural a part of the environment as any other element. They took what they could from the sea, and were too few to make any lasting detrimental impact upon marine and estuarine resources. European colonization would change that. It was slow at first, and fiercely resisted by some native populations, but the Europeans gradually occupied the region. Spanish and French adventurers (a polite term for freebooters, privateers and mercenaries) were the most frequent early visitors to these shores, and were responsible for the establishment of most early coastal settlements. The first on Texas shores was the ill-fated Fort Saint Louis on Matagorda Bay, established by the Frenchman La Salle in 1685. By 1689 it was gone, destroyed by the Karankawas. But it stimulated Spain, the conqueror of Mexico, to establish a presence in Texas.

For the next 150 years there was slow but progressive development of the coastal areas and the barrier islands. In the eighteenth century, ranches were established on some of the latter as a means to confine wandering herds of cattle—a practice still continued today on parts of several barrier islands.

The settlement of Texas began in earnest during the early nineteenth century. Access to the Texas heartland by land routes from the United States was often more dangerous than by sea from New Orleans. Thieves and murderers prowled the trails, exacting the highest tolls upon many colonists. Access by sea, even with treacherous passages through the shifting tidal inlets, was usually considered safer than the overland routes. This maritime connection quickly brought commercial development to Texas shores. Ship landings grew to become coastal centers of immigration and barter. Some, such as Indianola or El Copano would thrive, then die. Others, such as Galveston, Port Bolivar, and Port Aransas would survive to today.

One of the most important Texas ports during the middle nineteenth century was the now abandoned town of Indianola, on Matagorda Bay. Access to Indianola required passage through hazardous Cavallo Pass. Until it was flattened by a hurricane in 1886, Indianola was the disembarkation site of many ships bearing German, Polish, Irish and French settlers seeking a coastal gateway to mainland Texas. Today, Indianola is marked only by a stainless steel historical marker, testament to both the difficulty of finding safe harbor along this shore and its capacity to heal the scars of progress.

Texas populations grew as the region passed from Republic to statehood, and the local economy became increasingly dependent upon a coastal commerce. In the middle nineteenth century, supplies were still transported to Texas more quickly and reliably by sea than by the overland routes. So essential were the seaways that the only important Texas battlefields of the Civil War were along the coast, where the Confederates tried vainly to keep open critical supply lines and the Unionists were committed to a coastal blockade.

Following the war, coastal development spread slowly from port foci to other bayshores. Safe navigation into Texas ports became increasingly vital. Channels were dredged and jetties built along the tidal inlets to insure reliable passage. By the early 1900s the inlets at Sabine Pass, Bolivar Roads, Aransas Pass, Brazos Santiago Pass and Freeport Harbor had been stabilized and enlarged. The jetties constructed during this period created a new environment along the northwestern Gulf (Chapter 3). Jetties and piers on Mexican shores similarly have helped diversify the intertidal life there. However, these coastal modifications also contributed to shoreline erosion by reducing the volume of sand supplied to adjacent beaches. Similarly, the dredging of shipping channels within the bays, the excavation of an intracoastal waterway along the length of the shore, and the piling of attendant spoil banks along the dredged channels has altered patterns of salinity, temperature, water circulation, bay form and biological community structure throughout the Texas estuaries.

Mainland coastal development exploded at the turn of the century with the discovery of huge oil and natural gas fields throughout the region. The ports of Houston, Baytown, Texas City, Port Arthur and Corpus Christi became important centers of petroleum commerce. Adjacent coastal areas were developed as industrial, residential or recreational sites to accommodate the expanding populations of these ports and metropolitan centers. During this boom, the barrier islands remained largely isolated and unoccupied, save for cattle ranches and military outposts. The depressed economy of the 1930s and the war of the 1940s also kept developers away from most of the barrier islands. During the first half of this century Galveston was the only island with significant development, and it was (and still is) extensive and impressive. Following the devastating hurricane which leveled the city in 1900, Galveston was rebuilt and protected by a massive concrete and granite block sea wall which rises 5 m (17 ft) above mean sea level and extends 16 km (10 mi) along the eastern end of the island. Even more impressive, the elevation of that part of the city lying behind the seawall was raised about 3 m (9 ft) and graded to slope gently to natural elevations along the bayshore.

It was not until the early 1950s when permanent, elevated, concrete causeways were built to replace wooden bridges joining the mainland with the northern and southern ends of Padre Island that development began in earnest on this and Mustang Island. When these islands suffered considerable hurricane damage during the early 1960s, development slowed for a time, but resumed with a flourish in the 1970s. Barrier island development will likely continue to wax and wane as the frequency and intensity of damaging storms fluctuate.

We have already discussed how development of some portions of the barrier islands or outer mainland shores proceeded without careful analysis of recent geologic history. Greed and thoughtless planning permitted coastal development on degrading beachfronts. Yet, even today, some concrete seawalls are slowly washing away as the new beachside houses erected behind them are increasingly in danger of an early demise.

Today, five major metropolitan areas account for the majority of development along the Texas Gulf coast: Beaumont-Port Arthur, Houston (the largest city in the southeastern United States), Galveston-Texas City, Corpus Christi, and Brownsville-Harlingen. These unevenly distributed urban centers are characterized by dense human populations, averaging over 160 persons per square mile. Several smaller industrialized cities, such as Freeport and Port Lavaca, and numerous additional resort communities along bayshores and on the barrier islands complete the pattern of development. Conversely, there are still many parts of this coastline with fewer than 1 person per square mile. Some of these, such as the arid, inhospitable shores of Laguna Madre, are poor sites for "improvement" and will probably be the last parts of the coast to be developed. There are plenty of other locations with good harbors, easy access, and ample space that are inevitable sites for development, despite the threats "improvement" poses for already fragile coastal resources.

Brown pelicans, brought to near extinction by DDT along the central Texas coast in the 1960s, have made a remarkable comeback. A sizable population now nests on Pelican Island, an undeveloped and uninhabited block of land in Redfish Bay, near Port Aransas. It lies along one of the busiest ship channels of the Texas coast, and within a few km of heavy industry and petrochemical refineries. And now the U.S. Navy offers a new threat to the pelicans, gulls, terns, and other shore birds that occupy Pelican Island. Plans are well under way to construct a major U.S. Navy home port facility near Ingleside, immediately across the ship channel from the island. The naval center is expected to infuse millions of sorely needed dollars into the regional economy, and will likely spur considerable additional development of adjacent shorelines. The birds of Pelican Island are adaptable species that will likely weather the home port storm, as long as their roosts and rookeries are not disturbed. But development breeds more development. How long will Pelican Island remain undisturbed?

In the late 1980s, the northwestern Gulf is approaching the coastal congestion that characterized American northeastern shores several decades ago. Much of the Galveston bayshore, for example, resembles that of Delaware Bay, Baltimore Harbor, or the developed outer New Jersey shore. Development is also locally extensive along the entire Texas coast from Sabine Pass to South Padre Island. Yet, there remain sizable pockets of relatively unaltered coastline. Some of these have been set aside as parks and wildlife preserves (see below), but is this enough? The region is fast approaching a crossroads that may literally seal some of these shores in concrete for the foreseeable future.

As sunbelt populations continue to rise, additional coastline development, especially for new industry, second homes, and vacation or recreation sites, is inevitable. Large undeveloped portions of the Texas coast are in private hands, and presumably readily accessible for private development. But private ownership has also protected large portions of this coast. The western third of Matagorda and all of San Jose Islands have been private cattle ranches for most of this century. Except for coastal erosion and damage from storms, they remain largely as they were a century ago. Similarly, much of the mainland shore of Laguna Madre has been under the protection of the vast King Ranch and other private ranches. Conversely, public ownership has not always insured conservation. The eastern two thirds of Matagorda Island was an Air Force base and bombing range for several decades this century. Today, this land has been transferred from federal to state control, and its eventual fate is still to be determined.

Pollution

Construction, shoreline stabilization, and the dredging of tidal inlets and bays alter the physical environment directly, thereby adversely influencing natural beach communities. But all too often, development brings on pollution, which can adversely affect even undeveloped areas. Our species is usually responsible for most forms of coastal pollution, but not all. Of the five primary types of pollution which affect Gulf shores, humans, directly or indirectly, are responsible for at least four and may influence the last.

Organic pollutants resulting from human waste disposal have plagued estuaries and other coastal waters for centuries. During the early years of settlement, raw sewage was often discharged directly into the sea. Even today, the smaller communities fringing the southern Gulf basin still employ this practice. In Texas, state and federal regulations require some degree of sewage treatment even in the most rural dwellings. The newer and/or urbanized developments along the Texas coast are usually served by sewage treatment plants. Arguments have raged for decades as to the adequacy of various degrees of treatment and the quality of the water that is discharged. The continued degradation and contamination of some bay waters (Chapter 5) suggest that over the long run, treatments have been generally inadequate to maintain natural environment quality.

The accumulation of organic pollutants in a poorly circulating estuary often leads to hypereutrophication, which, in turn, reduces the carrying capacity of the waters. Nutrient build up, in association with naturally high summer temperatures, results in oxygen depletion, the growth of bacterial and algal populations to unnaturally high proportions and the progressive development of symptoms classic of stagnation. Estuarine communities suffer as population and community structures change, diversities decrease and depauperation leads to crass uniformity.

Outside the urban areas, rural or remote sites often employ septic tanks for sewage disposal. In the porous soils of coastal Texas, organic wastes from septic tanks frequently pollute groundwater, which can eventually contaminate bay and lagoon waters. This seems especially acute where houses line a grid of finger canals, providing each dwelling with immediate access to waters of the bay. In this type of development, the distance from the septic tank to the artificially deepened canal is relatively short, and the potential for contamination increases.

The variety of industrial effluents that are discharged or find their way into coastal waters constitute a second class of pollutants. Coastal industries generating potentially damaging effluents include electric and natural gas utilities, oil field services, manufacturing plants and mining operations. Damaging effluents include heated waters, drilling muds, heavy metals and toxic wastes. The discharge of most of these effluents is controlled by a variety of state and federal regulations, but we constantly hear of "accidental" discharges producing a variety of visible effects, especially fish kills. The invisible effects, of course, are continuing to accumulate within the sediments of our estuaries. For example, large areas of Nueces Bay adjacent to the Corpus Christi Ship Channel are now coated with as much as 0.5 m of oil well drilling muds, and oil field brine effluents have influenced biotic communities in several Texas estuaries (Mackin, 1971).

Pesticides constitute a special category of toxic industrial products which rarely enter the environment as an effluent, but which are purposely applied to it, primarily for the control of agricultural pests. Insecticides are commonly broadcast over large areas of farmland along the fertile coastal plain, whereas herbicides usually have more limited applications. Both may eventually wash into streams, marshes and estuarine basins where they can be detrimental to many kinds of aquatic life. Ideally, pesticides have a short active period, after which they are supposed to degrade into relatively non-toxic substances to avoid accumulation in the environment and magnification through food chains. This has not always been the case. For example, we have described the decline of brown pelicans on the Texas coast as a result of the magnification of DDT (Chapter 5). Furthermore, some pests produce strains resistant to specific pesticides, requiring alternate treatments. The range of synergistic or antagonistic effects of several different pesticides simultaneously in the environment remains to be completely evaluated.

Even before the European colonization, beaches of the western Gulf experienced pollution by tar. For centuries, offshore banks or salt domes seeped small amounts of oil into the sea. This petroleum floated to the surface and was blown ashore by prevailing winds. The quantities were sufficiently small and their dispersion sufficiently diffuse that they had little ecological impact over the centuries.

Seagoing petroleum tankers, each transporting thousands of barrels of crude oil, have significantly raised the potential for ecological contamination during the last few decades. Over 273 million barrels of crude oil were transported by ship to or from Texas ports in 1983, according to information supplied by the U.S. Army Corps of Engineers. Remarkably, there have been very few offshore tanker-related major oil spills which have affected Texas shores, but a number of tanker accidents and major oil pollution events have occurred within restricted coastal basins, such as the Houston Ship Channel (e.g., Webb *et al.*, 1981) or the Corpus Christi ship channel in 1988. Yet, outer beaches are increasingly encumbered with small blobs of tar. They have become so common on some beaches, that even a brief stroll along the shore will insure that shoes or bare feet will be stained by the tar. Clearly, the amount now present on these beaches is considerably greater than can be accounted for by natural seepage. Tankers and other vessels must be illegally releasing large quantities of petroleum-contaminated bilge offshore. It floats ashore to contaminate the beaches. The quantity of this tar is insufficient to produce massive ecological damage, but its increase over the last few decades is reason for concern. Similarly, the quantities of jetsam and flotsam debris (marine trash) that float ashore are also increasing, transforming western

Gulf beaches from picturesque postcard images to contaminated dump sites.

The world's largest documented release of oil into the marine environment came not from a ship, but from an offshore well in the western Gulf of Mexico during 1979–80. It pumped far more crude oil into the sea than any tanker disaster ever produced anywhere on earth. On June 3, 1979, the IXTOC-1 well in the Bay of Campeche blew out. For more than 10 months the well discharged between 30 to 40 thousand barrels of oil per day into the Gulf of Mexico. Before it was capped on March 23, 1980, it had discharged an estimated 140 million barrels of oil, much of which washed ashore on Mexico and Texas beaches (Rabalais & Flint, 1983). Woods and Hannah (1981) estimated that about 3.3 million barrels of oil were stranded on the southern Texas beaches, with the greatest stranding occurring between August 18–29, 1979. This stranding has been the focus of intensive research (Parker, 1979; Gundlach, *et al.*, 1981; Rabalais *et al.*, 1981; Thebeau *et al.*, 1981; Woods & Hannah, 1981; Atwood & Ferguson, 1982; Kalke *et al,* 1982, Amos, 1983; Rabalais & Flint, 1983).

Some of the oil which washed ashore was removed from beaches, especially along recreation-intensive areas, but it was impossible to remove from the entire coast. Thus, short and long term effects of oil contamination could be determined. While still at sea, the oil slick contained several components toxic to a variety of fishes and marine invertebrates and larvae. Sea birds encountering the oil slick were contaminated with the oil and often died as a result of this exposure.

Within one month of oil washing ashore on Padre Island, the numbers of intertidal and subtidal benthos were reduced from 30 to 80 percent (Thebeau *et al.*, 1981). During this time, the oil mixed with sand and shell fragments of the forebeach, forming asphalt-like tar reefs which usually were positioned between the swash zone and the first offshore bar (Rabalais & Flint, 1983). The tar reefs varied in size, from small isolated blocks to massive elongate structures over 100 m in length and 5 or 6 m in width. Eleven months after the oil washed ashore, intertidal and subtidal benthos outside the tar reefs had begun to recover. Within the area of tar reef influence, however, the population had decreased even more than immediately following the formation of the tar reefs.

Some groups of shore invertebrates were more sensitive to the oil pollution than others. Haustoriid amphipods were common on these beaches prior to the oil spill (Hill & Hunter, 1976), but were absent for at least a year following the contamination event (Rabalais & Flint, 1983). Other animals such as the larger, mobile *Donax* seemed to occur preferentially in those parts of the beach lacking a tar reef.

On August 11, 1980, Hurricane Allen came ashore on southern Padre Island. This large storm dissipated or buried much of the IXTOC-1 tar which had accumulated on the southern Texas and northern Mexico beaches. Undoubtedly, many of the tiny tar blobs that litter these beaches in 1988 and perhaps for years to come can be traced directly to this enormous environmental catastrophe.

A unique kind of pollution which cannot always be blamed upon humans is caused by several species of tiny, seemingly insignificant dinoflagellates. There are many species of these unicellular plants in the phytoplankton of coastal waters throughout the world, but a few (probably numbering less than half a dozen species) have, under certain circumstances, been responsible for the condition known as red tide. *Ptychodiscus brevis* causes red tide in the northwestern Gulf of Mexico.

Phytoplankton often experience phenomenal population increases, or "blooms." The precise conditions which trigger a species to "bloom" are poorly understood, but are related to nutrients, trace elements, temperature, season and other factors. Eutrophication caused by human influences plays a role in blooms of some species of coastal phytoplankton, including species which produce red tides in other parts of the world, but red tides have been known to occur along Gulf shores long before humans were there in sufficient numbers to make a significant impact upon the environment. Most phytoplankton blooms pass unnoticed, but not those of *Ptychodiscus brevis* or other species responsible for red tides. When these dinoflagellates reach densities of between one to five million cells per liter, seawater becomes discolored rusty reddish brown from pigments within the tiny cells, indicating the onset of red tide.

In August, 1986, following a prolonged period of hot, almost windless weather, a red tide was detected near Freeport, Texas. During the next three months it gradually spread from Matagorda Bay south to Port Isabel and on into Mexican waters. By October, a band of discolored water one to six km wide and 270 km long floated a few km off the shores of Texas and Mexico. Before it began to dissipate in November, 1986, this "tide" was responsible for the deaths of an estimated 22.2 million organisms belonging to 106 species, mostly fishes, including an estimated 4 million striped mullet, 3.25 million menhaden, 242,000 croaker, 80,800 spotted sea trout, almost 43,000 red drum and 41,000 flounder. Fisheries biologists estimate the economic impact of this red tide was not as bad as it might have been because it occurred mostly offshore.

The toxic agent produced by *Ptychodiscus brevis* is a metabolic by-product which acts as a neurotoxin on some types of vertebrate tissue. It is released into the sea when dinoflagellate cells die and disintegrate. Among other things, this substance inhibits vertebrate aerobic respiration. Under normal conditions, the toxin is so dilute in seawater that it is incapable of producing adverse effects. Under bloom conditions, however, the toxin becomes so concentrated as to produce massive fish kills. Within the confines of bays, the situation is further complicated by secondary mortality produced when fishes and invertebrates unaffected by the red tide toxin succumb to anoxia produced as a result of the decomposition of thousands of fishes which were killed by the red tide. Fortunately, this consequence of a red tide was minimal along the northwestern Gulf in 1986, because the majority of the dinoflagellate bloom occurred offshore. There were, however, sufficient numbers of *Ptychodiscus brevis* in the bays to contaminate oyster beds, which had to be closed to harvest. Oysters are unaffected by the dinoflagellate toxin, but they concentrate millions of the tiny phytoplankters within their bodies as a result of their filter feeding behavior. Humans or other mammals are not immune, and have been known to die or become severely ill after consuming oysters contaminated by *Ptychodiscus brevis*. The syndrome, known as paralytic shellfish poisoning (PSP), produces nausea and abdominal cramps in humans ingesting moderately contaminated oysters, or paralysis of respiratory muscles and death if the contamination is severe.

THE HUMAN LEGACY

There are distinct correlations between development, environmental degradation and pollution. All too often coastal development, especially resort, retirement or recreational projects, are for financial gain with little concern for the long term environmental consequences. Too many of these projects culminate in the destruction of many of those features of the shore that attracted us to it in the first place.

In the initial phase, development restructures the shore and usually destroys the natural elements of the supratidal coastal system, notably the diverse mosaic of coastal vegetation which occupies the saltings, dunes, marshlands and mangals. *Sporobolus* and *Panicum* give way to lawns of coastal Bermuda and St. Augustine. Marshes are drained, channels are deepened, condominiums are erected, and a hundred marsh species yield to human desires.

In the harsh coastal climate, "improvements" age rapidly. Even in the absence of total destruction by a September hurricane, timbers sag, paint peels, and stainless steel rusts under assault by a corrosive atmosphere or a mineral-rich "fresh" water. Without sustained investments that are necessary to permit repeated facilities repair, an "improved" site may evolve into a coastal blight within a decade or two. As the development matures, concomitant pollution acts upon the shore below the tide to reduce water quality and thus to degrade biotic community structure. The stench from organic pollution in the bays and lagoons inhibits vacationers to participate in those very water sports that originally attracted them to the shore. Accumulating tar and other debris on the outer beaches similarly dissuade first-time visitors from coming back. Vacation resorts, once erected upon pristine beaches, fall into decay as pollution and blight keep vacationers at bay. Eventually, the development is reduced to a shell of its original luxurance. All that has

been achieved, ultimately, is environmental degradation. One has only to take a short drive along any Gulf shore to find ample evidence of both the "improved" site and its seemingly inevitable consequence, the polluting eyesore blight.

We do not mean to condemn all development along the shore. To the contrary, our coastal cities, towns, and suburban communities are essential centers of commerce at local, regional and global scales. Many of us live here, work here, or enjoy our vacations and retirement years here. Without development of parts of the shore, none of this would be possible. Yet, we should be able to enjoy these shores for the natural recreational and aesthetic benefits that they can provide. We should be able to harvest a reasonable amount of renewable resources from our coastal waters with the assurance that these resources are neither contaminated with the products of a modern technology nor in imminent danger of irreversible depletion. And we should be committed to insuring that our future generations are provided with at least the same degree of environmental and biotic diversity that we have been able to experience and enjoy.

Texas shores today are vastly different from those during the days of Fort Saint Louis and the marauding Karankawas. Although this coast has been subdued, the occasional roar of a hurricane reminds us that it has not yet been tamed. We must never forget that our concrete and steel are temporary modifications which persist in spite of the environment, not in harmony with it. Despite its impermanence, the unwisely developed shore can destroy the biological environment before the development crumbles under physical attack. Inevitably, we have greatly modified this shore, and, inevitably, we will continue to "develop" it for the foreseeable future. The fact that there is ample room for additional development, however, implies that there is also the opportunity for intelligent planning to provide as much for resource conservation as for more concrete and steel.

CONSERVATION

Conservation is a requisite counterpoint of coastal development. The aesthetic values of conservation are important to humans, but secondary to needs of resource protection. Aesthetics vary according to the perception of the beholder, and may or may not have relevance to ecological necessity. How many of us perceive a vast coastal salt marsh as an unproductive wasteland and a sandy beach as an aesthetic marvel? Yet, the marshes are highly productive ecosystems sheltering a number of economically important species, whereas the beaches are ecologically barren marine deserts with a few specialized biota, noted for sheltering college students during spring break.

If all the marshes were converted to condominiums, penaeid shrimps would lose an important nursery, shrimpers would lose an important source of income, and we all would lose a favored seafood. However unlikely it seems that we could destroy so much marshland, considering the rate of coastal development this century, it could be accomplished along the central Texas coast within the next one hundred years! If we are to continue to enjoy or derive benefits from fragile coastal resources, we must understand what is required for their continued renewal, and protect them as zealously as we protect our financial investments in coastal lands and property.

Just as it is difficult to believe that all of our marshes can be smothered under concrete, it is equally unreasonable to advocate the conservation of all remaining undeveloped coastline. Clearly future needs must be evaluated, trade-offs must be considered and priorities must be set. Federal, state and local agencies as well as private individuals and foundations already have made significant strides to conserve representative and important portions of the Texas coast. Mexico has also realized the importance of coastal conservation and taken steps to set aside some coastal lands as parks or preserves.

The inventory of Texas preserves is sizable, especially sites for coastal recreation (e.g., Texas Parks and Wildlife Department, 1975). Sea Rim State Park, containing 15,109 acres, is located between Sabine Pass and High Island. It is divided into two sections, a beach unit along the Gulf of Mexico and a larger marshlands unit lying behind the beach. The latter is an important nursery area for salt marsh invertebrates and a reserve for wintering waterfowl. Galveston Island State Park lies to the west of the island city. Its 1,952 acres extend from sea beach to bayshore and at least one-half of the area is wetland *Spartina* marsh. Mustang Island State Park is located a few kilometers southwest of Aransas Pass. It is a relatively small Gulf beach park, designated primarily for recreation. Similarly, Goose Island State Recreation Area, located at the confluence of Aransas, St. Charles and Copano bays, provides campsites, playgrounds and a lighted bayshore fishing pier for visitors' use. It also includes within its boundaries a portion of the coastal live oak forest adjacent to the bayshore. The state of Texas also controls two undeveloped recreation areas at Bryan Beach along the eastern bank of the mouth of the Brazos River and on Brazos Island, between the southern termination of Padre Island and the mouth of the Rio Grande.

Padre Island National Seashore, extending almost 130 km (80 mi) along the central part of the island, is the largest block of protected barrier island seashore in the United States. Established in 1962, it is administered by the National Park Service to serve visitors and preserve the resource. Beginning a few km south of the junction of Mustang and Padre Islands, the National Seashore extends southward to Mansfield Cut. The northern fourth of the preserve is accessible to visitors in automobiles via paved roads or hardpack beach sands. The lower three-fourths of the National Seashore is accessible only by four-wheel drive vehicles or small boats.

There are also several National Wildlife Refuges along the Texas coast. Unlike the National Seashore, which is dedicated as much to human recreation as it is to resource protection, the wildlife refuges are, first and foremost, for the protection of wildlife and coastal biota. Anahuac National Wildlife Refuge fringes the north shore of East Bay, behind Bolivar Peninsula. Its 24,293 acres are primarily for the protection of migrating waterfowl wintering along the Gulf coast, but extensive wetland areas and bayshore habitats also protect a variety of estuarine fishes and invertebrates.

The Brazoria National Wildlife Refuge, east of Freeport in Brazoria County, contains 10,361 acres set aside primarily for nesting mottled ducks, but like all of the refuges we will mention, also includes extensive bayshore habitats. This refuge lies along the mainland shore of Drum Bay, and is presently one of the more publicly inaccessible coastal preserves. With 24,454 acres, San Bernard National Wildlife Refuge, located west of Freeport and also in Brazoria County, was established especially to protect wintering populations of blue and snow geese. It includes the Cedar Lakes area and a mainland section of the Texas shore facing the open Gulf of Mexico. This section lies near (to the east of) Sargent Beach and, like it, is rapidly eroding (see Chapter 6).

Aransas National Wildlife Refuge is the oldest coastal preserve in Texas. Occupying the majority of the Blackjack Peninsula along San Antonio Bay, the refuge was established in 1937 to protect endangered whooping cranes and other migratory waterfowl. It is one of the best developed preserves to accommodate visitors, although public access is permitted on only a small portion of its 54,829 acres. There is a modern interpretive center, several nature walks, including one into the salt marsh (Chapter 7), and an observation tower from which visitors can view whooping cranes during their winter residency.

Laguna Atascosa National Wildlife Refuge, east of Harlingen, is the southernmost migratory waterfowl refuge along the Central Flyway. Second in size to Aransas, its 45,190 acres include about 7,000 acres within or along Laguna Madre. Like the Aransas Refuge, Laguna Atascosa has a number of provisions for public visitors. It is an especially popular area for birdwatchers during the winter season.

In addition to these major sites, numerous small county and local parks and sanctuaries dot the Texas shores. These include Fort Travis Seashore Park on Bolivar Peninsula, Port Aransas Park on Mustang Island, Padre Balli Park at the northern end of Padre Island, Loyola Beach along Baffin Bay, and Andy Bowie Park on southern Padre Island. Each of these is primarily for recreation and, as such, helps to relieve public encroachment on more ecologically sensitive coastal habitats.

With but a few exceptions, coastal development along Mexico shores is far behind that of Texas. Much of this coast is remote, largely inaccessible, and thus relatively unthreatened by construction or development. It is with considerable foresight, therefore, that areas such as Las Coloradas along the northeastern margin of Yucatan, with its large colony of flamingos and unique ecology, already have been placed under federal protection.

The contrasts of coastal land usage north and south of the Rio Grande bring to question the appropriate amounts of conservation reserves which should be set aside along these shores. In Texas, considerable lands and wetlands have already been placed under state or federal protection. If more is needed, it should be acquired as soon as possible, for soon it may be too late to find adequate or acceptable tracts. With a significant portion of Galveston Bay already closed to oyster harvest because of organic pollution (Chapter 5), how long will it be before development along its shore closes the entire bay and degrades the habitat to such a degree that it becomes uninhabitable for oysters and other native biota?

Mexico has recently turned to the sea in pursuit of petroleum and economic salvation. The search for energy resources in the southern Gulf of Mexico has already had an adverse effect upon its shores (although an accident like the IXTOC-1 could just as easily occur on any offshore platform). Within the constraints of economic reality, coastal and offshore drilling will continue throughout the Gulf basin, and, as a form of development, will continue to be a potentially detrimental factor upon the local ecology of the shore. Similarly, the success of the resort city of Cancun, on the eastern Yucatan coast (actually in the state of Quintana Roo), less than 20 years old, suggests that additional development may be in the future for other shores of eastern Mexico. Sobering influences like the devastation wrought coastal resorts by Hurricane Gilbert in September, 1988 are too easily forgotten. Choices can be made most wisely right now to set aside reserves which will protect such important renewable resources as the Campeche Bank shrimp fishery (Chapter 10).

The continued preservation of the habitats and biota of the western Gulf of Mexico will require a dedicated vigilance. The parks and refuges that exist today can be just as easily replaced by concrete and condominiums tomorrow. Conservation is dependent upon the will of those people who wish it to be so. When they are gone, so will be the coastal diversity as we have reported it. In the year 2100, the sea roach, *Ligia*, will certainly still be here, but perhaps not roseate spoonbills; coquina clams will almost certainly still inhabit the sandy surf, but the speckled crab, *Arenaeus*, may fail to cavort in the surf or the earless lizard, *Holbrookia*, may fail to scurry across the dunes; *Uca rapax* may still survive on scattered sheltered mudflats, but the more specialized *U. subcylindrica* may be eliminated. The most vulnerable components of shore diversity also tend to be its most exotic, rare, and least predictable elements. If they are destroyed, many will not even notice their demise. But a few will. There will arise the inevitable debate: is the loss

significant? Probably not in the broad context of humankind's rapacious ways, but, on the other hand, probably yes, in the context of diminished enrichment for the human experience in an environment to which we have traditionally sought expanded awareness of the diversity of life.

EPILOGUE

When we began this book, we planned for a work of unpretentious dimensions to provide a guide to the natural ecology of Texas shores. We honestly expected to find that the sand-dominated alluvial shores would pale in comparison with the magical diversity of coral shores in the Caribbean and parts of Florida. Soon we were to realize just what misconceptions are contained in established dogma. As we hope to have described here, the western Gulf region supports a rich diversity of habitats and shore communities, at least equal to those on other shores anywhere in North America. Reefs of oysters and reefs of coral are here. Dark mangrove forests fringe sunny estuaries and their rich subtidal turtle grass beds. The starkness of hypersaline lagoons counterpoints the broad green richness of *Spartina* salt marshes. And there are always the outer shores of sand. The latter are truly dynamic, both in scope and in time—made all the more fascinating because of the very instability inherent in mobile sandy beaches and the catastrophic and relentless forces which act in concert to move them.

As the book developed, it also became apparent that, if the shore communities of the northwestern Gulf of Mexico were to be put into proper perspective, they had to be treated within the broader framework of the western Gulf temperate-to-tropical transition. The biotic changes that are apparent along the Texas coast are not resolved at the Rio Grande. The transition continues far into Mexico, with the added dimensions of increasing tropicality and a broader spectrum of adaptation. The mainland shores of the Gulf are an ecological continuum that political boundaries cannot erase. To understand the Texas beaches requires study of those in Mexico, and vice versa.

The floristic and faunistic richness of the western Gulf surprised us. In the past, this coast has been studied only piece-meal. Each unit, considered alone, is only slightly or moderately diverse. In fact, given the unitary simplicity but holistic diversity of this region, it is even more remarkable that the biota here has received so little attention. There is a paucity of basic ecological research within the region. Several general species lists have been prepared (Hedgpeth, 1950, 1953; Whitten *et al.*, 1950; Hildebrand, 1955; Reid, 1955; Breuer, 1957, 1962; Parker, 1959, 1960; Chavez *et al.*, 1970; Oppenheimer & Gordon, 1972; Felder, 1973a; Bright & Pequegnat, 1974; Clark and Robertson, 1982; Heard, 1982a; Rezak *et al.*, 1985; and Gittings *et al.*, 1986). Commercially important species have received a fair amount of attention. But landmark ecological studies using examples from this coast mostly remain to be done.

A case in point is the Texas jetty. This coastal feature is but a blip in the continuum of geologic time. The habitat has been available to shore-dwelling species for little more than 100 years, and the diversity of the jetty biota is accordingly limited, especially in comparison with natural rocky shores within the southern Gulf region. Algal recruitment on the jetties has outpaced the recruitment of animal species. As a result, the intertidal food chains here seem to be simpler than those on natural hard shores, although the subtidal biota is somewhat more diverse. There is one intertidal herbivorous littorine, one or two predominant intertidal filter feeding barnacles, one or two prominent intertidal gastropod predators, and no lower intertidal predatory echinoderms. Furthermore, the mussels, which so effectively compete for space on other hard shores, comprise an unusually insignificant proportion of the jetty biota. With such reduced intertidal complexity, the upper jetty community seems to be an ideal ecological model worthy of detailed analysis. Yet the last ecological study of jetty fauna was the general survey by Whitten *et al.* (1950). The Texas jetty seems ideally suited for studies of competition, predation, and herbivory, such as have been conducted on other shores by Connell, 1961a,b; Dayton, 1971; and Paine, 1974. The simplicity of the habitat provides not only a potentially important model for ecological research, but also constitutes a valuable teaching resource for students of Gulf coast schools and universities. Much the same can be said for most of the other Gulf of Mexico shore communities.

In the years to come, if we achieve no other purpose with this book, we hope that we stimulate present and future marine scientists interested in basic ecological problems to consider the shores of the western Gulf as a natural laboratory worthy of continued and continuing study. We have tried to convey to you some of our enthusiasm for these shores and their biota. This work, as any effort of this scope, will contain a fair share of errors and unanswered questions. But if our work can prompt some of you to correct the errors and answer some of the questions, then we have achieved an important goal. Further, if we can stimulate you to be concerned about continued, poorly planned, shoreline development and the concurrent loss of fragile habitats containing a fragile biota, then we have achieved another goal. Within our lifetimes, we have witnessed Gulf beaches increasingly polluted by debris, condominiums and tar. Yet many of these shores remain relatively pristine. Have we preserved enough of them? Should more be set aside? And how serious are we to assure longterm protection? Why, for example, is salt being mined within the Las Coloradas National Park of Mexico, containing one of the few remaining flocks of flamingos in the Gulf? An even more serious threat is the current proposal to breach the sand barrier in front of the Las Coloradas and Celestun lagoons with a series of canals, transforming this fragile ecosystem into a series of artificial fish ponds for aquiculture. One of the least studied habitats within our region, the vast lagoonal salt pans of Yucatan with their fabulous ecology based around a theme of mangrove zonation and succession, ultimately may succumb to human encroachment without adequate scientific evaluation. If we can, by introducing habitats such as these to you, help to foster their protection and prevent their loss, then our work was for a purpose. Representative parts of the Gulf of Mexico continuum can survive the human onslaught only if our and future generations insist that there is value in protecting and sustaining these as natural areas, thereby providing the means for appreciation of the region as a whole.

Glossary

ABDOMEN. The posterior portion of the arthropod body.

ABIOTIC. Non-living; devoid of life.

ABORAL SURFACE. The body surface opposite that bearing the mouth in radially symmetrical animals.

ABYSSAL. Pertaining to great oceanic depths, usually in excess of 3700 m.

ACCRETION. Increase in size by addition of new material from the outside, or sedimentary deposition.

ACOELOMATE. Invertebrate animals which lack a secondary body cavity.

ADDUCTOR. A muscle employed to draw skeletal elements such as limb bones or shell valves closer together.

AEROBIC. An environment characterized by an abundant supply of free oxygen.

AHERMATYPIC. Not reef-building.

ALGAE. Unicellular or multicellular marine and/or freshwater aquatic plants lacking conductive tissues, roots, stems or leaves.

ALLOCHTHONOUS. Exogenous; originating from the outside and transported into a system.

ALLUVIAL DEPOSITS. Finely particulate sediments deposited by flowing water.

AMBISEXUAL. Having separate male and female flowers on the same plant.

AMBULACRUM (pl., ambulacra; adj., ambulacral). A region of the echinoderm body containing numerous podia or tube feet.

AMOEBOCYTE. A cell in multicellular animals having an amoeba-like form and capable of moving from place to place within the body.

AMPHIBIA. Semiterrestrial vertebrates with moist skins, gills during some stage of their lives, and requiring standing water for reproduction. Amphibians include toads, frogs, newts and salamanders.

ANADROMOUS. Adj., referring to organisms which migrate from saltwater to freshwater for purposes of reproduction (e.g., salmon).

ANGIOSPERMAE. The flowering plants, a class of the Phylum Anthophyta.

ANNELIDA. Worms with a segmented body (noticeably annulated or ringed externally), a definite head, and a well developed secondary body cavity.

ANOXIC. The absence of oxygen.

ANTERIOR. The front or head end of bilaterally symmetrical organisms.

ANTHOZOA. Sessile, often biradially symmetrical Cnidaria entirely lacking the medusoid stage. The coelenteron is never a simple tube, but is partitioned by numerous sheets of tissue (septa). Solitary Anthozoa include the flower-like sea anemones, but the class includes many colonial species, such as the sea whips, sea pansies, sea pens and stony corals.

APETALOUS. Flowers lacking petals.

ARACHNIDA. A class of mainly terrestrial chelicerate arthropods lacking wings or compound eyes, with the body divided into prosoma (cephalothorax) and opisthosoma (abdomen), usually with 4 pairs of legs, and with the opisthosoma segmented or unsegmented and rarely bearing appendages. Includes spiders, mites, ticks, scorpions, and harvestmen.

ARAGONITE. An orthorhombic form of calcium carbonate, commonly deposited by marine animals as skeletal carbonate, and often subsequently transformed by a variety of physical processes into calcite.

ARTHROPODA. The largest invertebrate phylum is comprised of segmented animals bearing a chitinous exoskeleton and paired jointed appendages.

ASTEROIDEA. The starfishes are a class of echinoderms, usually with five arms but often many more. The oral side of the body usually bears many tube feet lying within distinctive ambulacral grooves.

AUTOTOMY. Self-amputation of an appendage or other portion of the body.

AVES. Birds. Homoiothermic (warm-blooded) vertebrates characterized by forelimbs modified into wings and usually employed for flight.

AVICULARIUM (pl., avicularia). A modified byrozoan zooid having the general shape of a bird's head and functioning to defend the colony against the attack or settlement of other organisms.

AXIL (axillary). The angle formed by a leaf and the stem to which it is attached. Axillary refers to a structure situated in or arising from the axil.

BACKSHORE. A normally dry portion of the beach, reached by only the highest tides, variable in width, and usually devoid of significant vegetation cover.

BACKWASH. The returning water after a wave has spent itself upon a beach.

BANK. A local elevation above the prevailing seafloor topography.

BARBEL. A fleshy tentacle-like sensory appendage on the head or around the mouth of some fishes.

BARNACLES. Sessile crustaceans belonging to the Cirripedia, usually with a body wholly or partially enclosed within calcareous skeletal plates, and found living attached to rocks, shells, or the bodies of other marine biota. Some are rock borers, and a few are parasitic.

BEAK (re: Bivalvia). See umbo.

BENTHOS (Benthic). The bottom of a marine or estuarine

basin, or the organisms which dwell here.

BERM. A flat-topped beach terrace marking the limit of ordinary high waves or tides.

BIOGENOUS. Of living origin; generated by life. A coral reef, for example, is a product of biogenous sedimentation.

BIOHERM. A moundlike mass produced by the skeletal accumulation of sessile biota (e.g., by corals, oyster shells, bryozoans, serpulid worms, or other organisms).

BIVALVE. Bearing two shells or valves.

BIVALVIA. Molluscs with a shell divided antero-posteriorly into two hinged valves and positioned along the sides of the body. Most are infauna which employ enlarged gills (ctenidia) to filter suspended or deposited material from the water for food. A head and radula are absent. Sensory reception is relegated to areas along the edge of the mantle, and especially to the pallial siphons, which, in many species, extend from within the shell to the sediment surface above. The foot is typically used for digging. Some bivalves have escaped the infaunal life and are byssally attached to rocks (mussels) or may be cemented (oysters). A few, like the scallops, can swim.

BRACHIOPODA. The lamp shells are a lophophorate phylum that superficially resemble the Bivalvia both in body form and habitat. They are protectively encased by two hinged shell valves which lie dorsal and ventral to the body. Brachiopods are of ancient origins and diversity, which survive today as isolated remnants of a once vast group.

BRACKISH. Pertaining to water of salinity intermediate between that of freshwater and seawater.

BRINE. Water with a salinity markedly greater than that of normal seawater.

BRYOZOA (Ectoprocta). The moss animals are a phylum of microscopic colonial lophophorate coelomates. Colonies consist of dozens of tiny calcareous or siliceous "boxes" encrusting stones, shells and even seaweed fronds.

BYSSUS. Threadlike secretions produced by some bivalve molluscs and usually employed to attach or anchor the bivalve to a substratum.

CALCAREOUS. Rich in calcium salts, especially calcium carbonate.

CALCITE. The more stable rhombohedral form of calcium carbonate.

CALICHE. Sediments or soils bound by a porous calcium carbonate cement and usually associated with arid or desert conditions.

CALYX. Outer or external whorl of floral leaves; theca of some hydroids.

CAPTACULA. Threadlike, adhesive-tipped feeding tentacles of scaphopod molluscs.

CARAPACE. The hard covering of the head and thorax of many crustaceans.

CARCINOLOGY (carcinologist). The study of Crustacea (one who studies Crustacea).

CARNIVORE (adj., carnivorous). An animal which preys upon other animals for food, but which does not live within or upon its prey.

CAROLINIAN PROVINCE. A marine, warm-temperate biogeographic province generally occupying shelf waters from Cape Hatteras, North Carolina to Cape Canaveral, Florida, and having strong affinities to the biota of the northern Gulf of Mexico.

CATADROMOUS. Adj., referring to organisms which migrate from fresh to salt water for purposes of reproduction (e.g., eels).

CAUSEWAY. A road or passageway elevated slightly above the local topography so as to permit transit without influence of the local conditions under normal circumstances (as a causeway constructed to cross a shallow bay or lagoon).

CEPHALIZATION (cephalized). The concentration of nerve tissue (especially sensory receptors) toward the front or anterior portion of the body, and usually accompanied with the differentiation of a definite head body region.

CEPHALOPODA. Squids, cuttlefish and octopods are advanced molluscs. Their foot is divided into eight or ten highly sensitive grasping arms or tentacles. Vision and nervous coordination are highly developed in these pelagic carnivores. All western Gulf species lack an external shell, but some bear an internal shell or chitinous pen.

CEPHALOTHORAX. A body region combining the cephalon (head) and thorax.

CHELICERAE. The first pair of appendages of the Chelicerata.

CHELICERATA. A subphylum of the Arthropoda, including horseshoe crabs, arachnids and sea spiders, characterized by a body divided into prosoma (cephalothorax) and opisthosoma (abdomen), no antennae, the first pair of appendages termed chelicerae, the second pair of appendages pedipalps, and four pairs of walking legs.

CHELIPEDS (chela, pl., chelae). A pair or pairs of crustacean thoracic legs bearing pincers or claws.

CHEMORECEPTOR. A sensory nerve ending sensitive to chemical stimuli.

CHITIN. A semitransparent horny organic substance (a mucopolysaccharide) which is the primary component of the arthropod exoskeleton, and also comprises less extensive structures in many other invertebrates.

CHITON. *See* Polyplacophora.

CHLOROPHYTA. The green algae. A phylum of about 7000 species of unicellular or multicellular marine or freshwater plants bearing chlorophylls a and b and various carotenoids. Their diversity is greater in freshwater than in the sea. One group, the Siphonales, contains species which deposit limestone to support the thallus. These algae make important contributions to the sedimentation process in shallow sub-tropical and tropical seas.

CHOANOCYTES. Cells lining the inner chambers of sponges, each characterized by possessing a membranous collar or sheath surrounding a flagellum.

CHORDATA. A phylum with members possessing at some stage in their life a notochord, pharyngeal gill slits, and a dorsal nerve cord. The vertebrates are the largest and most complex subphylum of chordates.

CHROMATOPHORE. A pigment-bearing cell which, when displayed in combination with other similar cells, can produce color changes in some animals such as squids, octopods, and a variety of crustaceans.

CILIA. Microscopic vibratile hair-like cellular organelles employed for locomotion or maintenance of a current over internal or external body surfaces.

CLASTICS. Rock fragments or other debris which have been moved from their place of origin.

CLITELLUM. A glandular swelling encircling several adjacent segments of some oligochaete worms and functions to produce mucus during reproduction.

CNIDARIA. Radially symmetrical polyps and medusae with a two-layered body wall encircling a tubular coelenteron bearing a mouth but no anus. The latter is usually encircled by tentacles equipped with stinging cells, the cnidocytes, bearing the stinging organelles, nematocysts, which serve the dual purposes of defense and prey capture.

COCCOLITHOPHORES. Minute, unicellular, planktonic marine algae with the cell embedded in a gelatinous sheath covered with circular, flattened calcareous plates (coccoliths). Coccoliths often accumulate in large numbers in shallow marine sediments.

COELENTERON. The digestive cavity of the Cnidaria and Ctenophora. It is a blind pouch opening to the exterior only at the mouth.

COELOM. A secondary body surrounding the internal organs of some metazoa (e.g., annelids, echinoderms and chordates) characteristically lined entirely by tissue of mesodermal origin.

COELOMATE. Possessing a coelom.

COLUMELLA. The central axis of a gastropod shell, providing an attachment for the columellar muscle.

COMMENSALISM. A relationship between two species in which one derives benefit (food, shelter, or both) while the other is not adversely affected.

COMMUNITY. An assemblage of several species occupying the same habitat and interacting via spatial and trophic relationships.

CONCHIOLIN. The periostracum and organic matrix of a molluscan shell.

CONSPECIFIC. Belonging to the same species.

CONSTRUCTIONAL CORALS. Those that contribute a significant amount of skeletal material for the framework of a reef.

COPEPODA. A diverse group of about 9000 species of aquatic crustaceans, characterized by each pair of swimming legs joined by a rigid plate, and usually with long, many-segmented antennae. Copepods occupy many marine and freshwater habitats, being prominent members of the plankton and benthos, and having many commensal and parasitic species.

COPPICE DUNE. A small mound of sand stabilized by vegetation.

CORALLITE. A skeletal cup formed by a single coral polyp.

CORALLUM. The entire coral skeleton, containing numerous corallites.

CORALS. Several orders of colonial anthozoans producing flexible, firm or rigid skeletons of horny organic material; spicules, rods, sheets, or plates of calcium carbonate; or both.

CRENULATE. Fringed by minute marginal teeth.

CRINOIDEA. A class of echinoderms including the sea lilies and feather stars. The former are sessile with a jointed attachment stalk and 10 laterally branched arms. They feed upon the rain of sediment which falls onto the arms. The latter lack the stalk and are free-living, but usually seek the shelter of rocky crevices on coral reefs.

CRUSTACEA. The largest group of marine arthropods, including lobsters, crabs, shrimps, prawns, hermit crabs, barnacles, copepods, isopods, and amphipods. They constitute the major group of primary consumers in the plankton, and account for a great proportion of life on shores and sea floors.

CRUSTOSE. Thin and crust-like.

CRYPTIC. Hidden, concealed, camouflaged; the development of coloration, patterns, structures or markings that resemble the surroundings and thereby aid in concealment of an organism.

CRYPTOBIOS. Secretive biota which typically lie hidden within crevices or under stones.

CTENIDIUM (pl., ctenidia; adj., ctenidial). A large organ in the molluscan mantle cavity composed of numerous ciliated lamellae and primitively functioning as a gill. In many bivalve molluscs, the ctenidium also is used in filter feeding, and some bivalves further employ this organ as a brood chamber for developing eggs or larvae.

CTENOPHORA. Comb jellies are floating, translucent, globular or sometimes almost spherical animals with a centrally located coelenteron. Some bear a pair of tentacles, but most nearshore species of the western Gulf region are atentaculate. All ctenophores have eight bands of ciliary comb plates surrounding the body which provide limited locomotion. Ctenophores are related to the Cnidaria, but, except for one group, they lack nematocysts.

CULTCH. Shells or other hard structures suitable as a site for settlement, attachment and development of juvenile oysters; usually set out by oyster fishermen in areas previously lacking suitable substratum for attachment by oysters or where this material has been removed during oyster harvest.

CUMACEA. A group of small tadpole-like benthic crustaceans.

CUSPATE. Pointed, shaped like a cusp.

CUTICLE. A non-cellular protective outer covering in many invertebrates.

DACTYLOZOOIDS. A specialized offensive, defensive or protective polyp of colonial anthozoans characterized by the absence of a mouth and the presence of numerous batteries of nematocysts.

DEMERSAL. Living at or near the bottom of a lake or sea, but having the capacity for swimming.

DEPOSIT FEEDING. Feeding upon particulate organic matter upon or within the substratum. Direct deposit feeders usually ingest the sediment in which they live to derive nutrition, whereas indirect deposit feeders are more selective in extracting particulate organic matter from the sediment prior to ingestion.

DETRITIVORE. An animal which feeds upon detritus.

DETRITUS. Particulate organic debris derived from the decomposition of plant and animal remains.

DEXTRAL. Right-handed; in gastropods, having the aperture to the right of the columella.

DIAGENESIS. Physical, chemical, and biological transformation of a sediment or skeletal structure (e.g., scleractinian coral reef) especially by compaction, cementation or recalcification to produce a rock or structure different from that of the original.

DIAPIRIC. Infusion of a mobile core into a more brittle overburden, as with a salt dome.

DIATOMACEOUS. Largely composed of diatom tests, as in diatomaceous sediments.

DIATOMS. Unicellular marine and freshwater algae characterized by a siliceous bivalved test. Diatoms are the dominant phytoplankton in many seas.

DICOTYLEDONAE. A subclass of the Angiospermae which bears two embryonic leaves (cotyledons), flower parts usually in fours or fives, radiating leaf venation, and are capable of secondary growth.

DIMYARIAN. In the Bivalvia, bearing two adductor muscles.

DISJUNCT (disjunctive). Separated; often used in reference to two or more potentially interbreeding populations separated by sufficient geographic distance to preclude normal gene flow between them.

DORSAL. The upper body surface of a bilaterally symmetrical organism.

ECHINODERMATA. A phylum of marine animals built around a five-rayed, secondary radial symmetry, having an endoskeleton of calcareous ossicles, and possessing a unique hydraulic system of canals and tubules, the water vascular or ambulacral system, terminating in tube feet for locomotion.

ECHINOIDEA. Sea urchins, sand dollars and kin comprise a class of echinoderms having a rigid endoskeleton formed by fusion of skeletal plates and covered by numerous moveable spines.

ECHIURA. Sausage worms are unsegmented, infaunal marine animal worms with a blood red, flimsy body and a long proboscis that is spread over the mud surface for deposit feeding.

ECTODERM. An embryonic cell layer covering the outside of the embryo during early development.

ECTOPARASITE. A parasite that lives upon the outer surface of its host.

ECTOPROCTA. *See* Bryozoa.

EDENTULATE. Lacking teeth, as in some bivalve molluscs which lack hinge teeth.

EFFLUENT. Outflow; the natural outflow of a lake or river; the discharge of industrial or urban waste into the environment.

EHWST. Extreme high water spring tide, the upper limit of the intertidal region.

ELASMOBRANCHIOMORPHI. The cartilaginous fishes, including sharks, rays and their kin. Their entire skeleton is composed of cartilage, not bone.

ELWST. Extreme low water spring tide, the upper limit of the sublittoral zone and the lower limit of the intertidal region.

ELYTRA. In scale worms (polychaetes), the plate-like scales on the dorsal side of the body; in beetles, the hardened forewings which protect the membranous hind wings.

EMARGINATE. With a margin interrupted by a notch or sinus.

EMERGENT. To rise above the water surface.

ENDEMIC. Native and restricted to a particular geographic region.

ENDOGENOUS. Arising from within.

ENDOLITHIC. Living or growing within rock or other hard inorganic structures.

EPIBIOTA. Organisms living upon other organisms.

EPIFAUNA. Animals living upon the benthos.

EPIPHYTE (adj., epiphytic). A non-parasitic plant living upon the body of another plant.

EPITOKY. A reproductive method in some polychaetes involving the development of a reproductive individual adapted to leave burrows or tubes of the adult and become pelagic for the purpose of dispersing gametes.

EPIZOIC. A non-parasitic organism living attached to the body of an animal.

ESTUARY. A semi-enclosed body of water, opening to the sea, containing seawater variably diluted by freshwater, and characterized by marked cyclical fluctuations in salinity.

EUHALINE. Referring to seawater with a salinity ranging from 30 to 40 parts per thousand.

EUKARYOTIC. Cells characterized by possessing a distinct nucleus, mitochondria, and other complex cellular organelles. All cells except those of bacteria and blue green algae are eukaryotic.

EULITTORAL. *See* mid-littoral.

EURYHALINE. Tolerant of a wide range of saline conditions.

EURYTHERMAL. Tolerant of a wide range of temperature.

EUTROPHICATION. Over-enrichment of surface waters with nutrients, resulting in excessive growth of aquatic plants and depletion of oxygen.

EVERSIBLE. Capable of being turned or projected outward (inside out).

EXCURRENT. Flowing outward.

EXOGENOUS. Originating from the outside; triggered by external (e.g., environmental) factors.

EXOSKELETON. An external supportive structure in arthropods and some other invertebrates.

FACULTATIVE. Assuming a particular habit or mode of life, but not restricted to it; non-obligate.

FETCH. The distance that wind can blow across a sea or other body of water uninterrupted by land.

FILIBRANCH (filibranchiate). A form of bivalve ctenidium (gill) in which individual filaments are joined only by ciliary junctions; also the bivalves, such as oysters, mussels, scallops, which possess this type of ctenidium.

FILTER FEEDING. A process by which particulate organic matter is extracted from water and used for food.

FOLIOSE. Bearing numerous leaf-like structures; leafy.

FRESHET. A stream of freshwater emptying into seawater.

GASTROPODA. The largest class of molluscs, including the snails and their kin, characterized by a unique body transformation called torsion. They may or may not bear a shell, but when present, it is usually a single, conical or, more commonly, a spirally coiled structure into which the animal can retract. The head is equipped with paired tentacles and eyes. The mouth contains a radula adaptively modified to permit a wide range of feeding strategies in the different lineages. The foot forms a broad creeping surface.

GASTROZOOIDS. A feeding polyp in colonial cnidarians.

GEOMORPHOLOGY. A branch of geology concerned with landforms, their gross structure and evolution.

GEOTAXIS. A directed response of an organism towards (positive) or away from (negative) the force of gravity.

GEOTROPISM. An oriented response to gravity.

GNATHOPODS. The second and third pairs of thoracic appendages in amphipods which are commonly larger than the other thoracic appendages and often tipped with small chelae.

GONOPORE. The external opening of a reproductive system.

GONOZOOID. A polyp specialized for reproduction in colonial cnidarians.

GORGONACEA (gorgonians). Sea fans, sea whips, soft corals. An order of colonial Octocorallia, characterized by a firm, proteinaceous axial skeleton.

GRAVID. Carrying eggs or young; ovigerous.

GROIN. A shore protection structure usually designed to retard erosion by trapping longshore drift.

HALOPHYTE (adj., halophytic). A plant capable of tolerating or thriving in the presence of relatively high concentrations of common sea salts or excessively alkaline soils.

HERBIVORY (herbivore). Feeding upon plants (animals which feed upon plants).

HERMAPHRODITE (hermaphroditism). An organism having both male and female reproductive organs in the same individual.

HERMATYPIC. Reef-building; constructional.

HETERODONT. A condition in bivalve molluscs in which the hinge margin usually contains well developed cardinal (central) and lateral teeth. In some bivalve classifications, the Heterodonta form a subclass of the Bivalvia.

HOLOPLANKTON. Permanent members of the plankton.

HOLOTHUROIDEA. Sea cucumbers are a class of echinoderms having a sausage-shaped or wormlike body with the mouth and anus at opposite ends. Skeletal ossicles are reduced to spicules or are absent. Most sea cucumbers ingest sediments from which they extract a meager nutrition, but a few species spread tentacles into the water to filter seston.

HUMMOCK. A low mound or knoll of land rising above a swamp, often densely wooded.

HYDROGRAPHY. The science dealing with the study of the surface waters of the earth.

HYDROZOA. Solitary or colonial Cnidaria bearing a simple, unpartitioned coelenteron. Most are sessile, a few are pelagic. Many species producing alternating generations of asexual sessile polyps producing sexual motile medusa.

HYPEROSMOTIC. A solution having a greater concentration of solutes than another solution to which it is being compared.

HYPERTONIC. Having a concentration of solutes high enough to gain water across a semipermeable membrane from another solution.

HYPERTROPHICATION. Over-enrichment with nutrients; see eutrophication.

HYPHA (pl., hyphae). A tubular filament of a fungus; numerous hyphae comprise the mycelium, or fungus body.

HYPOCOTYL. A portion of a plant embryo within the seed.

HYPOOSMOTIC. A solution having a lesser concentration of solutes than another solution to which it is being compared.

HYPOTONIC. Having a concentration of solutes low enough to lose water across a semipermeable membrane to another solution.

IGNEOUS. A geologic term referring to rocks or minerals formed by solidification of molten magma derived from the interior of the earth.

IMMERSION. To be placed under or inundated by water. For example, immersed vegetation grows entirely below the water surface.

INCURRENT. Flowing inward.

INFAUNA. Benthic animals that live within a substratum or sedimentary bottom.

INSECTA. A class of arthropods comprising over 70% of the phylum. Most occupy terrestrial or freshwater habitats. A few species live in the sea, but most marine-associated insects live among beach drift or hunt for food close to the sea shore.

INSTAR. Any intermolt stage during the development of an arthropod.

INTEGUMENT. The outer body covering; skin or epidermis.

IRONSHORE. A brittle, well weathered, and often highly pitted or eroded limestone rock commonly found along many tropical Atlantic shores. Although it occasionally contains trace quantities of iron, the rock is almost entirely calcium carbonate. The name is derived from its brittle nature, and the fact that, when struck by a hammer, the rock seems to resonate like a metal anvil.

ISOBATH. A line on a chart or map connecting points of equal depth.

ISOTONIC. The condition whereby the osmotic concentration on one side of a semipermeable membrane is in equilibrium with the osmotic concentration on the opposite side of the membrane.

KARANKAWAS (also Carankawas). A now-extinct group of native Americans indigenous to the Texas shores of the Gulf of Mexico prior to and shortly after European colonization of the region.

KARST. A highly non-uniform topography characteristic of limestone rocks subjected to intense weathering and/or solution.

KLEPTOPARASITISM. The theft by one species of the prey or food of another species, often for the purpose of feeding offspring.

LACUSTRINE. Pertaining to large standing bodies of freshwater (lakes or ponds).

LAGOMORPHA (lagomorph). Rabbits, hares and kin.

LANCEOLATE. Considerably longer than broad and usually pointed at one or both ends; lance-shaped.

LARVIPAROUS. Producing eggs that hatch internally into larvae, which are then released to become free-living.

LENTICELS. Wart-like, usually light-colored, spots on the bark of mangrove roots or pneumatophores.

LIMESTONE. Calcium carbonate.

LOPHOPHORATES. Three phyla, the Phoronida, Bryozoa and Brachiopoda, characterized by lophophore, or a horseshoe shaped, circumoral, ring of tentacles.

MACROPHYTE (macrophytic). A large plant, but commonly used to refer to large macroscopic multicellular marine algae.

MACROPLANKTON. Large planktonic organisms, generally having a maximum dimension exceeding 20 mm.

MALACOLOGY (Malacologist). The study of the Mollusca (one who studies the Mollusca).

MAMMALIA. Warm-blooded (homoiothermic) vertebrates covered in hair, and mostly ovoviviparous. The young are nourished with milk from maternal mammary glands (hence the name). Marine mammals include manatees, whales and dolphins, seals, sea lions and walruses, and sea otters.

MANGAL. A mangrove forest.

MARICULTURE. Cultivation, management and harvesting of marine organisms in their natural habitat or in specially constructed holding chambers.

MARITIME ZONE. In intertidal ecology, the region landward of the supralittoral fringe where salt spray exerts a dominant influence upon the biota that can occur there.

MARSH (marshland). An ecosystem of more or less continuously waterlogged soil dominated by emergent herbaceous plants and generally lacking emergent trees or surface accumulations of peat.

MAXILLIPEDS. In most malacostracan crustaceans, the first two or three thoracic appendages. They are usually short, face forward, and are normally employed in handling food.

MEDUSA. Jellyfish; the soft-bodied, normally free-swimming body form of hydrozoans and scyphozoans, characterized by an umbrella- or bell-shaped body usually surrounded by a marginal ring of tentacles and having a mouth borne upon a central stalk-like manubrium in the center of the bell.

MEGALOPA (megalops). The early postlarval instars of brachyuran crustaceans (crabs).

MELANOPHORES. A darkly pigmented (containing melanin) chromatophore.

MEROPLANKTON. Temporary members of the plankton, especially (but not restricted to) larvae.

MEROSTOMATA. Horseshoe crabs are primitive marine arthropods with pincer like chelicerae, a horseshoe shaped carapace, compound eyes and four pairs of walking legs. They plough subtidal sediments in search of soft-bodied prey.

MESOHALINE. Referring to seawater having a salinity between 3.0 and 12.0 parts per thousand.

METAZOA. Multicellular animals.

MHWST; MHWNT. Mean high water spring tide; mean high water neap tide.

MICROPLANKTON. Smaller members of the plankton, between 20 and 200 microns in diameter.

MID-LITTORAL. That portion of the shore covered and exposed at least once (and often twice daily) during a fortnightly tidal cycle.

MIDWATER. The mesopelagic region of the open sea, from a depth of about 200 m to about 2000 m.

MLWST; MLWNT. Mean low water spring tide; mean low water neap tide.

MODIOLIFORM. Shaped like the shell of the mussel *Modiolus*, characterized by subterminal umbos and a slightly bulging anteroventrally region.

MOLLUSCA. The second largest animal phylum comprising unsegmented coelomate animals with the body divided into a head, foot, visceral mass and mantle, each variously modified in the different classes. The mantle surrounds part of the body and often secretes an overlying shell, again variously modified in the different classes.

MONILIFORM. Like a string of beads.

MONOCOTYLEDONAE. A subclass of the Angiospermae which bears a single embryonic leaf (cotyledon), flower parts usually in patterns of three, usually with parallel-veined leaves and lack the ability for secondary growth. This includes grasses, sedges, and similar grass-like families. They are primary stabilizers of sand dunes, the principal components of salt marshes, and include the sea grasses, the only group to successfully colonize subtidal marine waters.

MONOCULTURE. The presence of a single crop or species in an environment to the exclusion of all others.

MONOGENERIC. In taxonomy, a family containing a single genus.

MONOMORPHIC. A population or species consisting of a single morphotype; or, in botany, having flowers of only one sex on an individual plant.

MONOMYARIAN. In bivalve molluscs, possessing a single adductor muscle.

MORPHOMETRY (adj., morphometric). The quantitative measurement of biological form and structure.

NAUPLIUS. A larval stage of many lower crustaceans, characterized by possessing three pairs of appendages and a single median eye.

NEKTON. Swimming pelagic animals able to move independently of water currents.

NEMATOCYST. The stinging organelle of cnidarians.

NEMERTEA. Ribbon worms are elongate, more-or-less flattened acoelomate predators which usually capture their prey by means of a proboscis stowed in a unique body cavity, the rhynchocoel, positioned above the mouth.

NEPHRIDIUM. The excretory organ of many invertebrates.

NERITIC. Pertaining to marine waters overlying continental shelves.

NEUROPODIUM. The ventral lobe of the polychaete parapodium.

NEUROTOXIN. A debilitating or fatal poison which acts primarily upon the nervous system of the victim.

NICHE. The ecological role of an organism in a community.

NODULOSE. Knobby.

NONCONSTRUCTIONAL CORALS. Those which contribute less than a significant amount of skeletal material for the framework of a reef.

NOTOPODIUM. The dorsal lobe of the polychaete parapodium.

NUDIBRANCHS (Nudibranchia). Sea slugs. Exclusively marine, bilaterally symmetrical, opisthobranchiate gastropods lacking external or internal shells.

OLIGOCHAETA. Segmented worms (Annelida) lacking lobate appendages (parapodia) on the body segments and usually bearing only a few bristles or setae. Most marine oligochaetes are tiny, inconspicuous worms.

OLIGOHALINE. Referring to water having a salinity between 0.5 to 3.0 parts per thousand.

OMNIVORE (omnivorous). An animal having a mixed diet of both plant and animal material.

OPERCULUM (operculate). A shelly or horny protective covering employed to close the aperture of a gastropod shell or worm tube; also, the gill covering in teleost (bony) fishes.

OPHIUROIDEA. Brittle stars are a class of echinoderms with distinctive central disks and greatly elongate and highly flexible slender and spiny arms which lack ambulacral grooves. Brittle stars live in crevices, under rocks, among algal mats or buried in the sand.

OPISTHOBRANCHIA. A subclass of the Gastropoda which undergoes detorsion and includes many species in which the shell has been greatly reduced or entirely lost. The shell-less opisthobranchs include a variety of colorful species with plumed mantles and often exposed gills, variously known as sea slugs, sea hares, and nudibranchs.

ORAL SURFACE. The body surface bearing the mouth in radially symmetrical animals.

OSMOCONFORMER. An organism having a body fluid which matches the osmotic concentration of the external medium, changing as the osmotic concentration of the external medium changes.

OSMOREGULATOR. An organism that maintains the osmotic concentration of its body fluid independent of that of the surrounding medium. Within the limits of a particular species ability to osmoregulate, the internal osmotic concentration of the organism remains constant relative to changes in osmotic concentration of the external medium.

OSTEICHTHYES. Bony fishes. Most of their skeleton is composed of bone, not cartilage.

OSTRACODA. Mussel shrimps. A class of small (0.1 to 30 mm), aquatic (marine and freshwater) crustaceans having a body and appendages enclosed by a hinged bivalved carapace.

OVIGEROUS. Used in reference to a female bearing eggs.

OVOVIVIPAROUS. Eggs produced, fertilized, developed and hatched within the maternal body, resulting in the release of live offspring.

PALP. A tentacle-like or vermiform organ used as a tactile (touch) receptor in polychaetes or as a food-sorting device in bivalve molluscs.

PANTROPICAL. Extending or occurring throughout the tropics and sometimes subtropics, or at least widespread in tropical regions.

PAPILLATE (papillose). Bearing small tentacle-like projections (papillae).

PARAPODIUM (pl., parapodia). The paddle-like limb of a polychaete worm.

PEREOPODS. Thoracic walking legs of crustaceans.

PEREOSTRACUM. An external organic layer covering the shells of many molluscs.

PERISTOMIUM. In annelids, the second body segment that borders top and sides of the mouth.

PHAEOPHYTA. The brown algae. A phylum of about 1500 species of multicellular marine plants bearing chlorophylls a and c and the pigment fucoxanthin. They include *Padina* and *Sargassum,* which characterize the lower limit of the rocky intertidal.

PHORONIDA. A phylum of sedentary lophophorate worms with a U-shaped complete digestive tract. They usually secrete and live within leathery tubes closed at one end.

PHOTOTROPISM. An orientation response to light; positive toward light and negative away from it.

PHYLOGENETIC. Pertaining to evolutionary relationships within or between biological groups. Phylogeny is the evolutionary history of a group or lineage.

PILOSE. Covered with soft hairs or hair-like structures.

PLANKTIVORE. An organism which feeds upon the plankton.

PLANKTON (sing., plankter). Aquatic organisms living within the water column and unable to move against or maintain their position with respect to a current.

PLATYHELMINTHES. Bilaterally symmetrical flatworms with three tissue layers and a digestive tract with but one opening. The classes Trematoda and Cestoda are parasitic, but the Turbellaria, commonly called planarians, are ciliated carnivores often encountered in the sea or on the shore.

PLEOPODS. Abdominal appendages of crustaceans, variously employed for locomotion, burrowing, ventilation of respiratory currents, gaseous exchange, or egg carrying or brooding in females.

PLICATE. Pleated.

PLUMOSE. Feathery.

POLYCHAETA. Segmented worms (Annelida) bearing lobate, often paddle-like appendages (parapodia) on the body segments which, in turn, carry numerous bristles (setae). Polychaetes are the most conspicuous annelids in the marine environment.

POLYHALINE. Referring to seawater having a salinity between 12.0 to 30.0 parts per thousand. Sometimes subdivided as polyhaline brackish water and oligohaline seawater.

POLYMORPHIC. Having several body forms. For example, some male and female reef fishes have distinctly different color patterns as juveniles and subsequently as adults. Similarly, crustaceans often pass through several larval stages, each differing from one another and the adult.

POLYP. The individual, sedentary, soft-bodied form of cnidarians, typically with a cylindrical trunk, apical mouth surrounded by tentacles, and a closed basal surface which attaches to a substratum or secretes a skeletal support.

POLYPLACOPHORA. The chitons have a shell divided into eight plates, a small head with a mouth containing a radula, and a broad muscular foot especially well adapted for clinging to rocks. Some chitons live subtidally, but many species are algal grazers on rocky intertidal shores

PORIFERA. The sponges are sessile animals with a skeleton of loosely organized calcareous or siliceous spicules. They lack specific organ systems and the body plan is usually without a defined symmetry. Sponges constantly filter water through the body via numerous body pores, deriving nutrition from very fine suspended matter extracted from the water by means of flagellated choanocytes or collar cells. They are the simplest of the multicellular animals.

POSTERIOR. The rear portion of a bilaterally symmetrical body.

POSTLARVA. The stage in the life of an organism following the larval stage. This term frequently refers to the period following metamorphosis but before the final adult form is attained.

PPT. Parts per thousand, as in salinity values.

PROPRIOCEPTION. Reception of stimuli originating within the organism.

PROSOBRANCHIATA. A subclass of about 20,000 marine, freshwater, and terrestrial Gastropoda, typically characterized by a twisted (torted) body enclosed within a spiral shell, a mantle cavity positioned above or near the head containing one or two gills for respiration, and a muscular creeping foot which usually bears an operculum.

PROSTOMIUM. In annelids, the first body segment, lying in front of the mouth.

PROXIMAL. Nearest to the point of origin or attachment.

PSEUDOFECES. In bivalve molluscs, material which has entered the mantle cavity but which has not been ingested.

PULMONATA. A subclass of primarily terrestrial and freshwater Gastropoda, with or without a spirally coiled shell, with a mantle cavity usually modified into a vascularized pulmonary cavity for aerial respiration, and a muscular foot usually lacking an operculum.

PYCNOGONIDA. Sea spiders are exclusively marine arthropods with four or, rarely, five pairs of long legs. They are scavengers or hunters with species ranging variously from abyssal depths to algal mats on the lower shore.

RACHIS. A main axis or shaft.

RADULA. A unique organ in the buccal cavity of some molluscs. The primitive radula is a ribbon containing numerous chitinous teeth used for rasping. It is variously modified from this basic plan in the molluscan classes.

RAPTORIAL. Adapted for seizing prey.

REPTILIA. Terrestrial or aquatic vertebrates with dry scaly skins, lungs for respiration, and producing eggs encased in leathery shells. Reptiles include turtles, lizards, snakes and crocodiles. Some turtles and snakes spend most of their lives in the sea.

RETICULATE. Net-like.

RHIZOMES (rhizomatous). Rootlike, usually horizontal stems growing under or along the ground.

RHODOPHYTA. The red algae. A phylum of about 3800 species, most of which occur in the sea. They bear chlorophyll a and pigments known as phycobilins. The red algal body is built up of closely packed little differentiated filaments in a gelatinous matrix. Several tropical species enclose body cells within thin sheets of limestone.

SCAPHOPODA. The tusk shells are infaunally buried molluscs bearing a conical tooth-shaped shell open at both ends. They are deposit feeders collecting food by means of specialized head appendages called captacula.

SCLERACTINIA. The true or stony corals. Members of this anthozoan order are primarily responsible for the formation of most modern calcareous reef structures in shallow tropical seas between 30°N and 30°S.

SCYPHOZOA. Cnidaria with the medusoid (jellyfish) phase dominant in the life cycle, but which also usually produce asexually reproducing polypoid generations. They produce a branching coelenteron.

SEICHE. A standing wave oscillation of an enclosed or partially enclosed body of water which continues for a time after the generating force subsides. Winds, squalls, storms, and earth movements are common seiche-generating forces.

SENSU STRICTO. In the strict sense, often used in taxonomy or biological nomenclature to designate the precise or narrow application of a name to a group of organisms to the exclusion of other similar organisms.

SETAE. Minute hair-like bristles, especially among the Polychaeta and Crustacea.

SINISTRAL. Left-handed; in gastropod molluscs, having the aperture to the left of the columella.

SIPHONOPHORA. Exclusively marine pelagic colonial hydrozoans characterized by polymorphic and often highly specialized zooids. E.g., the Portuguese Man-o-War (*Physalia*).

SIPUNCULA. Peanut worms are unsegmented marine animals with a stout body and a long proboscis-like introvert. They either burrow in sediments or tunnel into soft limestone rocks.

SPATFALL. Recently settled Bivalvia, especially oysters.

SPERMATOPHORE. A packet of sperm.

SPERMATOPHYTA (Anthophyta). The flowering plants, comprising about 300,000 species.

SPICULE. A small, often needle-like structure of silica or calcium carbonate employed as a skeletal element in sponges, soft corals, holothurians, and some other invertebrates.

SPINOUS. Having spines, spiny.

SPORELINGS. Unicellular zygotes or spores of aquatic algae.

SQUAMOSE. Scaly.

STENOHALINE. Tolerance to only a narrow range of salinity variations.

STOMA (pl., stomata). In botany, one of the numerous pores, usually located on the lower surface of a leaf, through which atmospheric gases and water vapor pass; in zoology, a small opening.

SUBLITTORAL. The region between extreme low water spring tides (ELWST) to either the margin of the continental shelf or to the greatest depth to which photosynthetic plants can grow.

SUBLITTORAL FRINGE. The intertidal region between mean low water neap tide and extreme low water spring tide.

SUPRALITTORAL. The intertidal region between mean high water neap tide and extreme high water spring tide.

SYMBIONT. One member of a symbiotic relationship.

SYMBIOSIS. The living together of two different species. Some ecologists use the term to refer to all commingling relationships; others restrict the term to only those relationships which are mutually beneficial.

SYMPATRY. Species, populations or taxa occupying the same geographic area.

TAXODONT. In bivalve molluscs, with numerous, short hinge teeth, some or all of which are transverse to the hinge margin.

TAXON (pl., taxa). A taxonomic grouping of any rank, including subordinate groupings; e.g., subspecies, species, genera, subfamilies, and phyla are examples of taxa.

TAXONOMY. The science of the identification, naming and classification of living things.

TELSON. The terminal appendage of many Crustacea.

TEMPERATE. A climatic regime characterized by moderate seasonal change, including a summer season devoid of freezing temperatures and a winter season including at least a few days with temperatures below freezing.

TERETE. Cylindrical; circular in cross-section.

TERRESTRIAL. Pertaining to the land.

TERRIGENOUS. Derived from the land.

TEST. The firm or hard-walled body covering, as in Foraminifera, Bryozoa, or Echinodermata.

THALLUS. A multicellular plant body lacking true leaves, stems, or roots.

TRANSECT. The line along which samples are collected at random or periodic intervals for the purpose of studying some aspect of the natural history, geology, or ecology of an area.

TROCHOPHORE. A free-swimming, often top-shaped, ciliated and unsegmented larval stage of many polychaetes, molluscs, bryozoans, brachiopods, sipunculans, and other less familiar invertebrates.

TUNICATES. *See* Urochordata.

UMBO. The oldest park of the bivalve shell. It is often peaked or pointed.

UNCALCIFIED. Without carbonate hard parts.

UNLITHIFIED. Not cemented or solidified as in rock.

UROCHORDATA. A subphylum of the Chordata, including the sessile tunicates or sea squirts and the pelagic salps. Adult tunicates are sac-like with two siphons projecting from either a gelatinous or fibrous body. They may be solitary or colonial and feed by pumping water through an inhalant siphon into the greatly enlarged pharynx where food is extracted. Water exits via the exhalant siphon.

VELIGER. A free-swimming post-trochophore larval stage of some molluscs, having many features of the adult (e.g., shell and foot), but characterized by a large ciliated mantle lobe employed for swimming and feeding.

VENTRAL. The lower side of the body of bilaterally symmetrical organisms.

VERMIFORM. A wormlike shape.

VERTEBRATA. A subphylum of the Chordata, characterized by animals which possess a vertebral column or backbone.

WHORL. A single turn of a spiral, as in a gastropod shell.

XEROPHYTES (adj., xerophytic). Plants possessing adaptations to survive aridity.

ZOEA. A free-swimming larval stage of many brachyuran crustaceans characterized by at least one pair of locomotory thoracic limbs, usually with compound eyes, and often with a single prominent dorsal spine.

ZOOECIUM. A box-like structure in which a bryozoan zooid resides.

ZOOPLANKTON. Animal members of the plankton.

ZOOXANTHELLAE. Unicellular photosynthetic dinoflagellates (plants) living within the tissues of various animals (e.g., corals, bivalves) in a symbiotic association.

A Taxonomic Guide

The figures or plates (prefix P) where each species is illustrated are indicated following the name. Classification is based on various sources, usually from taxonomic works devoted exclusively to the phylum or class.

Family Melobesieae
crustose coralline algae — 10-7 U; 11-2 B; 11-3 B

Fosliella lejolisii — 11-3 M1
Family Corallineae
Amphiroa fragilissima — 11-3 X
Amphiroa rigida — 11-3 S
Corallina cubensis — 3-3 V
Corallina subulata — 3-3 A1
Family Grateloupiaceae
Grateloupia filicina — 3-3 O
Order Gigartinales
Family Gracilariaceae
Gracilaria debilis — 4-1 A1
Gracilaria foliifera — 3-3 T
Family Solieriaceae
Solieria tenera — 5-1 R
Solieria tenera — 3-3 P
Family Hypneaceae
Hypnea musciformis — 3-3 W
Order Rhodymeniales
Family Rhodymeniaceae
Chrysmenia enteromorpha — 10-7 R
Coelarthrum albertisii — 10-7 V
Rhodymenia pseudopalmata — 3-3 Z
Family Champiaceae
Champia parvula — 11-3 W
Order Ceramiales
Family Ceramiaceae
Callithamnion byssoides — 3-3 Q; 5-1 Q
Ceramium fastigiatum — 3-3 X
Centroceras clavulatum — 3-3 Y; 4-1 Z; 5-1 P
Family Rhodomelaceae
Bryocladia cuspidata — 3-3 C1
Digenia simplex — 5-1 J; 11-3 E1
Laurencia papillosa — 11-3 Y
Laurencia poitei — 4-1 W; 4-3 J

DIVISION ANTHOPHYTA
(SPERMATOPHYTA)
CLASS ANGIOSPERMAE
Subclass Monocotyledoneae
Order Hydrocharitales
Family Hydrocharitaceae
Halophila engelmannii — 7-9 H
Thalassia testudinum — 4-4 A; 7-9 E; 11-3 N1

Order Najadales
Family Ruppiaceae
Ruppia maritima — 7-8 F
Family Zannichelliaceae
Halodule wrightii — 7-8 H; 7-9 C; 8-6 C

Syringodium filiforme — 7-8 G; 9-3 K
Order Cyperales
Family Cyperaceae
Cyperus odoratus — 6-16 B
Cyperus surinamensis — 6-10 G; 6-16 D
Dichromena colorata — 6-10 L
Eleocharis albida — 6-12 M
Fimbristylis castanea — 6-12 N; 6-16 E
Scirpus americanus — 6-10 F; 6-16 G
Scirpus maritimus — 8-4 B

Scirpus sp. — 4-4 G
Family Gramineae
Andropogon glomeratus — 6-6 K; 6-10 N; 6-11 F
Cenchrus incertus — 6-14 B
Digitaria insularis — 9-2 C1
Distichlis spicata — 6-16 I; 7-3 M; 7-6 E; 9-2 X; 9-4 C
Monanthochloe littoralis — 6-10 E; 6-16 Q; 7-3 L; 7-6 J; 7-8 N; 9-2 V; 9-4 L
Panicum amarum — 6-6 J; 6-10 Y; 6-12 G
Paspalum monostachyum — 6-10 Q
Paspalum distichum — 6-12 F
Spartina alterniflora — 7-3 B; 7-6 B
Spartina patens — 6-16 P; 7-3 C; 7-6 C; 9-2 L
Spartina spartinae — 7-3 H; 9-4 P
Sporobolus virginicus — 4-4 E; 6-10 J; 6-14 F; 6-15 A
Uniola paniculata — 6-6 I; 6-10 K; 6-12 I
Order Typhales
Family Typhaceae
Typha domingensis — 9-4 O
Typha latifolia — 8-4 A
Order Arecales
Family Palmaceae
Pseudophoenix sargentii — 6-15 N
Thrinax sp. — 6-15 O
Order Liliales
Family Agavaceae
Agave sisalana — 6-15 L
Agave sp. — 6-14 P
Subclass Dicotyledoneae
Order Magnoliales
Family Magnoliaceae
Magnolia virginiana — 6-11 E
Order Salicales
Family Salicaceae
Salix nigra — 6-11 C
Order Caryophyllales
Family Cactaceae
Cereus pentagonus — 6-15 Q; 9-4 D
Opuntia dillenii — 6-15 R; 9-4 F
Opuntia lindheimeri — 6-10 H
Family Aizoaceae
Sesuvium portulacastrum — 4-3 O; 6-6 S; 6-10 V; 6-12 L; 6-14 D; 6-15 K; 7-8 I; 7-9 B; 9-2 W; 9-4 K

Family Chenopodiaceae
Salicornia bigelovii — 6-16 F; 7-3 O; 7-8 M; 9-2 R
Salicornia virginica — 5-1 A; 6-10 D; 6-16 M; 7-3 D; 9-4 E; 7-8 J; 9-2 U
Suadea linearis — 6-15 B; 6-16 H; 7-3 K; 7-6 I;

	7-9 A; 9-2 A1; 9-4 H
Family Amaranthaceae	
Amaranthus greggii	6-6 B; 6-14 C
Philoxerus vermicularis	7-6 G; 9-2 Z
Tidestromia lanuginosa	6-16 S
Order Bataceae	
Family Bataceae	
Batis maritima	6-16 J; 7-3 P; 7-6 F; 7-8 L; 9-4 J
Order Fagales	
Family Fagaceae	
Quercus virginiana	6-11 A
Order Polygonales	
Family Polygonaceae	
Coccoloba uvifera	4-3 Q; 4-4 C; 6-12 A; 6-14 O; 6-15 J
Order Malvales	
Family Malvaceae	
Hibiscus clypeatus	9-4 B
Malvaviscus arboreus	6-15 D
Order Violales	
Family Passifloraceae	
Passiflora foetida	6-14 G
Order Capparales	
Family Cruciferae	
Cakile geniculata	6-16 R
Cakile lanceolata	6-15 F
Order Primulales	
Family Theophrastaceae	
Jacquinia aurantiaca	6-15 I
Family Plumbaginaceae	
Limonium nashii	6-11 N; 7-3 N; 7-8 K; 9-2 Y
Order Rosales	
Family Chrysobalanaceae	
Chrysobalanus icaco	6-12 C
Family Fabaceae	
Acacia farnesiana	6-11 D
Caesalpinia vesicaria	9-4 A
Canavalia maritima	6-12 O; 6-14 H
Cassia cinerea	6-12 E
Cassia fasciculata	6-6 D; 6-10 P
Cassia sp.	6-15 C
Rhynchosia minima	6-10 R
Strophostyles helvola	6-16 L
Order Myrtales	
Family Onagraceae	
Oenothera drummondii	6-6 G; 6-10 O; 6-12 D
Family Apiaceae	
Hydrocotyle bonariensis	9-4 M
Family Combretaceae	
Conocarpus erectus	4-3 P; 6-12 B; 9-1 A; 9-4 G
Laguncularia racemosa	9-1 B, B1; 9-3 A
Order Cornales	
Family Rhizophoraceae	
Rhizophora mangle	9-1 D, D1; 9-3 C, C1, D
Order Euphorbiales	
Family Euphorbiaceae	

Croton punctatus	6-6 L; 6-10 S; 6-12 H; 6-15 H
Chamaesyce maculata	6-10 I
Chamaesyce polygonifolia	6-16 K
Poinsettia cyanthophora	6-14 L
Order Sapindales	
Family Surianaceae	
Suriana maritima	4-4 N; 6-14 N
Family Rutaceae	
Zanthoxylum clava-herculis	6-11 B
Order Polemoniales	
Family Solenaceae	
Lycium carolinianum	6-14 I; 6-15 G; 7-3 G
Family Convolvulaceae	
Ipomoea pes-caprae	6-6 O; 6-10 X; 6-12 Q; 6-14 A
Ipomoea stolonifera	6-6 T; 6-10 W; 6-12 P
Order Lamiales	
Family Boraginaceae	
Heliotropium curassavicum	6-16 O
Tournefortia gnaphalodes	6-14 M
Family Verbenaceae	
Lantana involucrata	6-15 M
Family Avicenniaceae	
Avicennia germinans	9-1 C, C1; 9-2 M, M1, M2; 9-3 B, B1
Order Campanulales	
Family Goodeniaceae	
Scaevola plumieri	4-4 M; 6-12 J; 6-14 J
Order Rubiales	
Family Rubiaceae	
Randia laetevirens	6-12 K
Strumphia maritima	4-4 D
Order Asterales	
Family Compositae	
Ambrosia hispida	6-15 E
Baccharis halimifolia	7-3 A
Borrichia arborescens	4-4 H
Borrichia frutescens	5-1 B; 6-6 C; 6-10 Z; 7-6 H; 9-2 B1
Eleocharis albida	6-16 C
Helianthus argophyllus	6-6 H
Heterotheca subaxillaris	6-6 F
Machaeranthera phyllocephala	6-6 E; 6-16 N
Pluchea odorata	6-16 A
Schizachyrium scoparium littoralis	6-10 M
Solidago sempervirens	6-6 A

KINGDOM ANIMALIA
PHYLUM PORIFERA
CLASS DEMOSPONGIA
    Order Keratosa
        Family Spongiidae

Ircinia campana	11-6 B

        Family Clionidae

Cliona sp.	5-2 A1

        Family Haliclonidae

Spinosella vaginalis	11-6 A

PHYLUM CNIDARIA
  CLASS HYDROZOA
    Order Hydroida
      Suborder Anthomedusae
        Family Bougainvillidae

Bougainvillia inaequallis	3-5 A

        Family Hydractinidae

Hydractinia echinata	3-5 H

        Family Tubulariidae

Tubularia crocea	3-5 E

        Family Zancleidae

Zanclea costata	3-5 G

      Suborder Leptomedusa
        Family Campanularidae

Clytia cylindrica	3-5 F
Gonothyraea gracilis	3-5 C
Obelia adichotoma	3-5 B

        Family Sertulariidae

Sertularia inflata	3-5 D

        Family Plumularidae

Aglaophenia latecarinata	6-9 P
Gonothyraea gracilis	6-9 R

      Suborder Chondrophora
        Family Porpitidae

Porpita porpita	6-8 K

        Family Velellidae

Velella velella	6-8 J

    Order Siphonophora
      Family Physaliidae

Physalia physalia	6-8 E

    Order Hydrocorallina
      Suborder Milleporina
        Family Milleporidae

Millepora alcicornis	10-7 F; P11-3 H

  CLASS SCYPHOZOA
    Order Cubomedusae
      Family Chirodropidae

Chiropsalmus quadrumanus	7-11 F

    Order Semaeostomeae
      Family Pelagidae

Chrysaora quinquecirrha	7-11 D

      Family Cyanidae

Cyanea capillata	7-11 C

      Family Ulmaridae

Aurelia aurita	7-11 E

    Order Rhizostomae
      Family Stomolophidae

Stomolophus meleagris	6-8 A

  CLASS ANTHOZOA
    Subclass Octocorallia
      Order Gorgonacea
        Family Briareidae

Briareum asbestinum	11-8 M

        Family Plexauridae

Eunicea clavigera	11-8 A
Muricea atlantica	11-8 F
Muricea muricata	11-8 E
Plexaura flexuosa	11-8 B
Plexaura homomalla	11-8 C
Plexaurella dichotoma	11-8 G

        Family Gorgoniidae

Gorgonia flabellum	11-8 J
Leptogorgia virgulata	10-1 Q
Pseudopterogorgia acerosa	11-8 L
Pseudopterogorgia americana	11-8 K
Pterogorgia citrina	11-8 H

      Order Pennatulacea
        Family Renillidae

Renilla mulleri	10-1 N

        Family Virgulariidae

Virgularia presbytes	10-2 W

    Subclass Zoantharia
      Order Zoanthidea
        Family Zoanthidae

Palythoa mammillosa	4-2 A

      Order Actiniaria
        Family Actiniidae

Anemonia sargassensis	6-9 O
Anthopleura krebsi	3-2 U
Bunodosoma cavernata	3-2 T; 5-1 L

        Family Aiptasiomorphidae

Aiptasiomorpha texaensis	3-2 V; 5-2 H

        Family Edwardsiidae

Nematostella vectensis	7-9 S

        Family Hormathiidae

Calliactis tricolor	10-1 A

      Order Scleractinia
        Suborder Astrocoeniina
          Family Astrocoeniidae

Stephanocoenia michelinii	11-2 H

          Family Pocilloporidae

Madracis decactis	10-7 M; 11-2 I
Madracis mirabilis	P11-1 A

          Family Acroporidae

Acropora cervicornis	P11-1 C
Acropora palmata	11-3 C; P11-1 B

        Suborder Fungiina
          Family Agariciidae

Agaricia agaricites	P11-1 E, E1
Agaricia fragilis	P11-1 D, D1
Agaricia undata	P11-1 G, G1
Helioseris cucullata	11-2 J; P11-1 F, F1

          Family Siderastreidae

Siderastrea radians	P11-1 H, H1
Siderastrea siderea	P11-1 I, I1

          Family Poritidae

Porites astreoides	11-2 A; P11-3 A, A1
Porites furcata	P11-3 B

        Suborder Faviina
          Family Faviidae

Colpophyllia natans	11-2 H; P11-2 A, A1
Diploria clivosa	11-3 A; P11-2 C
Diploria labyrinthiformis.	P11-2 B, B1
Diploria strigosa	11-2 E; 11-3 E; P11-2D
Manicina areolata	11-7 P; P11-2 G
Montastrea annularis	11-1 E; 11-2 D; 11-3 D; P11-2 F
Montastrea cavernosa	11-2 F: 11-3 F; P11-2 E

          Family Rhizangiidae

Astrangia poculata	10-2 T; P11-3 C
Family Oculinidae	
Oculina diffusa	P11-3 D
Family Mussidae	
Mussa angulosa	11-2 G; P11-3 F
Mycetophyllia lamarkiana	P11-3 E, E1
Scolymia cubensis	11-2 C; P11-3 G
Order Antipatharia	
Family Antipathidae	
Antipathes sp.	11-6 E
Stichopathes lutkeni	11-6 H

PHYLUM CTENOPHORA

CLASS NUDA

Order Beroida

Family Beroidae

Beroe ovata	7-11 H

CLASS TENTACULATA

Order Lobata

Family Mnemiidae

Mnemiopsis leidyi	7-11 G

PHYLUM PLATYHELMINTHES

CLASS TURBELLARIA

Order Polycladida

Family Stylochidae

Stylochus ellipticus	5-2 G1
Stylochus frontalis	5-2 H1
Family Planoceridae	
Gnesioceros sargassicola	6-9 F

PHYLUM NEMERTINA

CLASS ANOPLA

Order Heteronemertea

Family Lineidae

Cerebratulus lacteus	7-6 M1

PHYLUM ANNELIDA

CLASS POLYCHAETA

Order Orbiniida

Family Orbiniidae

Scoloplos rubra	10-5 D
Family Paraonidae	
Aricidea fragilis	10-5 G

Order Spionida

Family Spionidae

Paraprionospio pinnata	8-3 Z
Polydora websteri	5-2 B1
Scololepis sguamata	6-6 B1
Spiophanes bombyx	10-5 O
Spio pettiboneae	10-5 E; E1
Family Magelonidae	
Magelona riojai	10-5 C
Family Chaetopteridae	
Chaetopterus variopedatus	7-10 E
Spiochaetopterus costarum	10-5 F, F1
Phyllochaetopterus socialis	11-A1
Family Cirratulidae	
Cirratulus sp.	7-6 H1
Cossura sp.	8-3 T

Order Capitellida

Family Capitellidae

Capitella cf. *capitata*	7-6 B1; 8-3 P; 10-5 B
Mediomastus californiensis	10-5 H
Family Arenicolidae	
Arenicola cristata	7-6 Z; 7-10 G

Family Maldanidae	
Clymenella torquata	7-9 N; 10-5 A, A1

Order Phyllodocida

Family Phyllodocidae

Eteone heteropoda	7-6 I1
Phyllodoce mucosa	10-5 L
Family Polynoidae	
Harmothoe aculeata	6-9 L
Family Sigalionidae	
Sthenelais boa	10-5 M
Family Pilargiidae	
Loandalia americana	7-6 J1
Family Nereidae	
Nereis succinea	7-6 C1; 10-5 N
Platynereis dumerilii	6-9 K
Family Glyceridae	
Glycera americana	7-9 P; 10-5 I
Glycera tesselata	11-5 O

Order Amphinomida

Family Amphinomidae

Chloeia viridis	11-4 P
Eurythoe complanata	11-4 B1
Hermodice carunculata	11-4 V1

Order Eunicida

Family Onuphidae

Diopatra cuprea	7-9 Q; 10-5 K, K1
Onuphis eremita	6-6 Z; 6-16 Z; 10-1 O
Family Eunicidae	
Leodice rubra	11-4 Q
Family Lumbrineridae	
Lumbrineris impatiens	10-5 J

Order Terebellida

Family Sabellariidae

Sabellaria vulgaris	4-2 F1
Family Terebellidae	
Amphitrite sp.	7-6 A1
Family Sabellidae	
Sabellastarte magnifica	11-5 K
Family Serpulidae	
Hydroides dianthus	5-2 N
Spirobranchus giganteus	11-5 C
Family Spirorbidae	
Spirorbis sp.	6-9 C

CLASS OLIGOCHAETA

Order Haplotaxida

Family Enchytraeidae

Enchytraeus albidus	8-3 S

PHYLUM ECHIURA

Family Thalassemidae

Thalassema hartmani	7-10 B

PHYLUM SIPUNCULA

Lithacrosiphon alticonum	11-7 O
Phascolion strombi	10-2 R
Family Aspidosiphonidae	
Aspidosiphon steenstrupi	11-7 N
Family Phascolosomatidae	
Phascolosoma antillarum	11-7 M

PHYLUM MOLLUSCA

CLASS POLYPLACOPHORA

Order Neoloricata

Family Chitonidae

Chiton squamosus	4-1 N

CLASS GASTROPODA
Subclass Prosobranchia
  Order Archiogastropoda
    Family Fissurellidae

Diadora cayenensis	4-1 F1; 4-2 C
Fissurella nodosa	4-1 M
Fissurella barbadensis	4-2 B

    Family Turbinidae

Astraea tecta	11-2 O; 11-4 R1; 11-6 V

    Family Phasianellidae

Tricolia affinis	4-2 V

    Family Neritidae

Nerita fulgurans	4-1 P; 4-2 K; 4-3 N; 11-3 K
Nerita peloronta	4-1 R
Nerita tessellata	4-1 O; 11-3 I
Nerita versicolor	4-1 Q; 11-3 J
Neritina virginea	7-9 I; 9-3 O
Smaragdia viridis	11-4 M

  Order Mesogastropoda
    Family Littorinidae

Cenchritis muricatus	4-1 D; 4-4 J; 4-5 I
Echininus antonii	4-1 E; 4-4 L; 4-5 K
Fossarilittorina meleagris	4-5 B
Fossarilittorina mespillum	4-5 O
Littoraria angulifera	4-1 C; 4-5 D; 9-3 G; 11-3 O
Littoraria nebulosa	4-1 B; 4-5 C; 11-3 P
Littoraria irrorata	4-5 E; 7-6 D; 9-2 N
Nodilittorina angustior	4-1 H; 4-5 J
Nodilittorina glaucocincta	4-5 M
Nodilittorina interrupta	4-5 N
Nodilittorina lineolata	3-1 B; 3-2 L; 3-4 A; 4-1 A; 4-2 G; 4-3 F; 4-5 A; 5-1 D
Nodilittorina mordax	4-5 H
Nodilittorina riisei	4-5 F
Nodilittorina tuberculata	4-1 F; 4-4 K; 4-5 L
Nodilittorina ziczac	4-1 G; 4-2 H; 4-5 G

    Family Rissoinidae

Rissoina bryerea	11-4 G
Rissoina catesbyana	7-9 D

    Family Assimineidae

Assiminea succinea	7-7 F

    Family Hydrobiidae

Littoridinops monroensis	8-3 L
Probythinella louisianae	8-4 H
Texadina barretti	8-4 G
Texadina spinctostoma	8-3 Y; 8-4 F

    Family Truncatellidae

Truncatella caribaeensis	9-2 O
Truncatella sp.	9-4 R

    Family Vitrinellidae

Vitrinella floridana	7-7 I

    Family Caecidae

Caecum vestitum	4-2 D1
Caecum pulchellum	4-2 Z
Caecum johnsoni	7-7 J

    Family Turritellidae

Vermicularia knorri	11-4 U1

    Family Siliquariidae

Siliquaria squamata	10-7 K

    Family Vermetidae

Petaloconchus varians	4-2 Q

    Family Planaxidae

Angiola lineata	4-2 M
Supplanaxis nucleus	4-2 L

    Family Fossaridae

Fossarus orbignyi	4-2 E1

    Family Modulidae

Modulus modulus	10-6 H; 11-4 N

    Family Potamididae

Cerithidea pliculosa	9-2 Q; 9-3 N; 9-4 S

    Family Cerithiidae

Bittium varium	5-2 P; 7-7 B
Cerithium litteratum	10-7 I; 11-2 N
Cerithium eburneum	11-4 I
Cerithium eburneum forma *algicola*	11-4 F
Cerithium lutosum	4-3 K; 4-4 B; 5-1 I; 11-4 K

    Family Litiopidae

Alaba incerta	11-4 D
Litiopa melanostoma	6-9 N

    Family Cerithiopsidae

Cerithiopsis greeni	11-4 H

    Family Triphoridae

Triphora turristhomae	10-7 G

    Family Janthinidae

Janthina janthina	6-8 H
Janthina globosa	6-8 I

    Family Epitoniidae

Epitonium angulatum	10-2 M
Epitonium lamellosum	11-4 M1
Epitonium tollini	10-2 N

    Family Crepidulidae

Crepidula fornicata	5-2 U
Crepidula maculosa	10-6 L
Crepidula plana	10-6 K

    Family Strombidae

Strombus gigas	11-4 C
Strombus raninus	11-4 B

    Family Cypraeidae

Cypraea zebra	11-6 Q
Cypraea cinerea	11-4 P1
Cypraea spurca acicularis	10-7 E

    Family Ovulidae

Cymbula acicularis	11-8 N
Simnialena uniplicata	10-1 P
Cyphoma gibbosum	11-8 I

    Family Naticidae

Polinices lacteus	11-4 A
Polinices duplicatus	10-2 U; 10-3 D, D1
Sinum perspectivum	10-3 F

    Family Cassidae

Cypraecassis testiculus	11-6 P

Phalium granulatum	10-1 X	*Odostomia gibbosa*	7-7 H
Family Cymatiidae		*Odostomia impressa*	5-2 E1
Distorsio clathrata	10-1 H1	*Odostomia laevigata*	7-7 G
Family Tonnidae		*Odostomia* sp. (cf. *emeryi*)	8-3 X
Tonna galea	10-6 D	*Turbonilla interrupta*	10-2 O
Family Ficidae		Order Bullomorpha	
Ficus communis	10-6 E	(= Cephalaspidea)	
Order Neogastropoda		Family Acteonidae	
Family Muricidae		*Rictaxis punctostriatus*	7-7 E
Muricanthus fulvescens	10-1 W	Family Acteocinidae	
Morula nodulosa	11-4 Q1; 11-6 T	*Acteocina canaliculata*	8-3 W
Family Thaididae		Family Bullidae	
Plicopurpura patula	4-2 N	*Bulla striata*	7-9 K; 10-6 F;
Stramonita haemastoma	3-2 P; 4-2 O;		11-4 L
	5-1 H; 5-2 F1;	Family Haminoeidae	
	11-3 M	*Haminoea antillarum*	7-7 D
Stramonita rustica	11-3 L	*Haminoea succinea*	7-7 A
Thais deltoidea	11-3 N	Order Anaspidea	
Family Magilidae		Family Aplysiidae	
Coralliophila abbreviata	10-7 L; 11-2 L	*Aplysia brasiliana*	3-4 D; 4-2 W
Coralliophila caribbaea	11-6 K	*Aplysia dactylomela*	4-2 B1; 11-4 S1
Coralliophila scalariformes	11-2 M	Order Nudibranchia	
Family Columbellidae		Family Scyllaeidae	
Anachis semiplicata	3-3 J; 7-9 L; 8-6 F	*Scyllaea pelagica*	6-9 M
Anachis sparsa	10-6 G	Family Glaucidae	
Columbella mercatoria	11-4 T1	*Glaucus atlanticus*	6-8 F
Mitrella lunata	7-6 K	Order Onchidiacea	
Mitrella ocellata	4-3 L	Family Onchidiidae	
Nitidella laevigata	4-2 U	*Onchidella floridana*	11-4 E1
Nitidella nitida	11-4 N1	Subclass Pulmonata	
Family Buccinidae		Order Basommatophora	
Cantharus cancellarius	10-1 V; 10-7 Z	Family Ellobiidae	
Pisanio pusio	11-4 O1	*Melampus bidentatus*	9-2 P
Pisania tincta	4-3 M; 10-2 P	Family Siphonariidae	
Family Melogenidae		*Siphonaria alternata*	4-1 L; 4-3 I
Busycon coarctatum	10-6 B	*Siphonaria pectinata*	3-1 C; 3-2 O; 3-4
Busycon perversum			B; 4-1 K; 4-2 F;
contrarium	10-6 C		4-3 H; 5-1 E
Busycon perversum			
perversum	10-3 C; 10-6 J	CLASS SCAPHOPODA	
Busycotypus spiratum	10-3 B; 10-6 A	Family Dentaliidae	
Family Nassariidae		*Dentalium texasianum*	10-2 L
Nassarius vibex	7-6 L; 10-2 Q	CLASS BIVALVIA	
Family Fasciolariidae		Subclass Palaeotaxodonta	
Fasciolaria lilium	10-1 E1; 10-3 A	Order Nuculoida	
Fasciolaria tulipa	10-6 O; 11-4 E	Family Nuculidae	
Leucozonia leucozonalis	11-6 U	*Nuculana acuta*	7-7 U; 8-3 R;
Family Olividae			10-3 H
Oliva sayana	10-1 Z	*Nuculana concentrica*	10-3 I
Olivella minuta	10-1 U	Subclass Pteriomorphia	
Family Turbinellidae		Order Arcoida	
Turbinella angulata	10-6 I	Family Arcidae	
Family Conidae		*Anadara brasiliana*	10-1 C1
Conus ermineus	11-2 P	*Anadara ovalis*	10-1 B1; 10-2 S
Conus mus	11-4 J	*Arca zebra*	10-6 N
Family Terebridae		*Arcopsis adamsi*	4-2 S; 11-5 H
Hastula salleana	10-1 D1	*Barbatia cancellaria*	10-7 D; 11-2 S
Terebra dislocata	10-1 Y	*Barbatia candida*	4-2 R
Family Turridae		*Barbatia domingensis*	4-2 T
Pyrgocythara plicosa	7-7 C	*Noetia ponderosa*	10-1 A1
Subclass Opisthobranchia		Order Mytiloida	
Order Pyramidellacea		Family Mytilidae	
Family Pyramidellidae		*Amygdalum papyria*	7-6 O
		Botula fusca	11-7 F

Order Pholadomyoida
   Family Pandoridae
     Pandora trilineata   7-7 V
CLASS CEPHALOPODA
Subclass Coleoidea
   Sepioidea
     Family Spirulidae
       Spirula spirula   6-8 B
   Teuthoidea
     Family Loliginidae
       Lolliguncula brevis   7-11 I
   Octopoda
     Family Octopodidae
       Octopus vulgaris   3-2 N
PHYLUM ARTHROPODA
SUBPHYLUM CHELICERATA
   CLASS MEROSTOMATA
   Subclass Xiphosura
     Family Limulidae
       Limulus polyphemus   6-14 E
   CLASS PYCNOGONIDA
     Family Endeidae
       Endeis spinosa   6-9 A
SUBPHYLUM MANDIBULATA
   CLASS CRUSTACEA
   Subclass Copepoda
     Order Calanoida
       Family Acartiidae
         Acartia tonsa   8-6 B
   Subclass Cirripedia
     Order Thoracica
       Suborder Lepadomorpha
         Family Scalpellidae
           Lithotrya dorsalis   11-7 J
         Family Lepadidae
           Lepas anatifera   6-8 M
           Octolasmis lowei   7-7 M
       Suborder Balanomorpha
         Family Chthamalidae
           Chthamalus fragilis   3-1 D; 3-2 K; 4-1 I; 4-2 J; 4-3 G; 5-1 F
         Family Chelonibiidae
           Chelonibia patula   7-7 L
         Family Balanidae
           Balanus amphitrite   3-2 R; 4-1 J; 5-2 R
           Balanus eburneus   3-2 S; 5-1 K; 5-2 T; 9-3 H
           Balanus improvisus   9-3 I
   Subclass Malacostraca
     Superorder Hoplocarida
     Order Stomatopoda
       Family Squillidae
         Gonodactylus oerstedi   11-4 D1
         Pseudosquilla ciliata   11-4 C1
         Squilla empusa   7-7 N
     Superorder Peracarida
     Order Cumacea
       Family Diastylidae
         Oxyurostylis salinoi   8-3 M
     Order Isopoda
       Family Ligididae

Ligia exotica   3-1 A; 5-1 C
   Family Limnoridae
     Limnoria tripunctata   6-8 C
   Sphaeromidae
     Sphaeroma quadridentatum   5-2 Q; 6-16 C1
Order Amphipoda
   Family Caprellidae
     Caprella equilibra   3-3 S
   Family Corophiidae
     Corophium louisianum   5-2 F
     Corophium sp.   8-3 U; 8-4 E
   Family Gammaridae
     Gammarus mucronatus   8-6 O; 9-2 T
   Family Hyalidae
     Hyale frequens   3-3 D1
   Family Ischyroceridae
     Jassa falcata   5-2 G
   Family Talitridae
     Orchestia platensis   6-16 D1
Superorder Eucarida
Order Decapoda
   Infraorder Penaeidea
     Family Penaeidae
       Penaeus aztecus   8-6 L; 10-4 A; 10-4 F
       Penaeus duorarum   8-6 M; 9-2 K; 10-4 G
       Penaeus setiferus   7-9 W; 8-6 K; 10-4 E
       Sicyonia brevirostris   10-4 B
       Xiphopenaeus kroyeri   10-4 D
   Infraorder Caridea
     Family Palaemonidae
       Brachycarpus biunguiculatus   11-2 K
       Macrobrachium acanthurus   8-4 I
       Palaemonetes intermedius   8-6 N
       Palaemonetes pugio   7-6 K1; 7-9 Y
       Palaemonetes vulgaris   7-9 V; 9-2 J
       Pontonia domestica   10-2 G
     Family Alpheidae
       Alphaeus armatus   11-5 G
       Alpheus estuariensis   5-2 W
       Synalpheus pandionis   10-7 B
       Synalpheus sp.   11-2 R
     Family Hippolytidae
       Hippolyte pleuracantha   7-9 G
       Latreutes fucorum   6-9 B
       Tozeuma carolinensis   7-9 F
   Infraorder Palinura
     Family Palinuridae
       Panulirus argus   11-6 F
     Family Scyllaridae
       Scyllarides aequinoctialis   11-2 B1
       Scyllarides nodifer   10-4 C
   Infraorder Anomura
     Family Callianassidae
       Callianassa louisianensis   6-7 e&j; 7-9 T
       Callichirus major   6-7 g&i
       Callichirus islagrande   6-6 A1; 6-7 B; 6-7 f&h
     Family Upogebiidae
       Upogebia affinis   7-10 J
     Family Coenobitidae

Coenobita clypeatus	11-3 P1
Family Diogenidae	
Clibinarius antillensis	11-4 U
Clibinarius vittatus	3-2 I; 5-1 S; 7-6 Q; 7-8 E; 7-9 O; 8-6 S;9-3 P
Petrochirus diogenes	10-1 F1
Family Paguridae	
Paguristes hewatti	10-7 Y
Pagurus longicarpus	7-6 P
Pagurus pollicaris	7-6 X
Infraorder Anomura	
Family Galatheidae	
Munida simplex	10-7 C
Family Porcellanidae	
Euceramus praelongus	6-7 D; 10-1 L
Petrolisthes armatus	3-2 H; 4-3 C; 5-1 M
Polyonyx gibbesi	7-10 F
Porcellana sayana	10-1 G1
Family Albuneidae	
Albunea paretii	6-7 C; 6-16 X; 10-1 K
Lepidopa websteri	6-7 E; 10-1 J
Family Hippidae	
Emerita benedicti	6-7 a&c
Emerita portoricensis	6-6 Y; 6-7 a&d; 6-10 D1; 6-12 T; 6-16 W
Emerita talpoida	6-7 A; 6-7 b
Infraorder Brachyura	
Family Dromiidae	
Dromidia antillensis	10-2 H
Family Calippidae	
Calappa sulcata	10-1 H
Hepatus epheliticus	10-1 B
Family Leucosiidae	
Persephona aguilonaris	10-1 I
Family Majidae	
Libinia dubia	7-9 U
Libinia emarginata	7-9 X
Macrocoeloma camptocerum	11-5 L
Macrocoeloma diplacanthum	11-3 U
Microphris bicornutus	11-3 V
Mithrax forceps	11-2 Z; 11-4 S
Mithrax hispidus	11-2 A1
Mithrax spinosissimus	11-6 L
Pitho aculeata	11-5 B
Pitho anisodon	11-5 D
Stenorhynchus seticornis	10-7 S; 11-6 G
Family Parthenopidae	
Heterocrypta granulata	10-2 V
Family Portunidae	
Arenaeus cribrarius	10-1 C
Callinectes danae	8-6 R
Callinectes sapidus	7-7 K; 10-1 E
Cronius ruber	10-1 G
Portunus gibbesi	7-6 W; 10-1 F
Portunus sayi	6-9 D
Portunus spinimanus	10-1 D
Family Xanthidae	
Actaea setigera	11-5 P
Carpilius corallinus	11-6 O

Cataleptodius floridanus	11-4 T
Chlorodiella longimana	11-5 M
Domecia acanthophora	11-5 J
Eriphia gonagra	11-4 W
Eurypanopeus depressus	5-1 N; 5-2 J; 7-6 F1
Menippe adina	3-2 G; 3-4 F; 5-2 L
Neopanope texana	7-6 G1; 7-9 Z; 8-6 P
Panopeus obesus	7-6 Y
Paractaea rufopunctata	11-5 F
Paraliomera longimana	11-5 R
Pilumnus dasypodus	11-5 A
Pilumnus miersii	11-4 X
Pilumnus pannosus	10-7 A
Platypodia spectabilis	11-4 V; 11-5 E
Pseudomedaeus agassizi	11-5 I
Rhithropanopeus harrisii	5-2 K; 7-6 L1
Family Pinnotheridae	
Dissodactylus mellitae	10-1 J1
Pinnixa chaetopterana	7-10 D
Pinnixa cristata	7-10 I
Pinnixa cylindrica	7-10 H
Pinnixa lunzi	7-10 C
Pinnixa retinens	7-10 K
Pinnotheres maculatus	10-2 E
Pinnotheres ostreum	5-2 Z
Family Grapsidae	
Goniopsis cruentata	9-3 F
Grapsus grapsus	4-2 I; 4-4 I; 11-3 Q
Pachygrapsus transversus	5-2 S; 11-3 R
Planes minutus	6-9 E
Sesarma cinereum	8-6 Q; 9-3 W; 9-2 E1
Sesarma reticulatum	7-6 S
Family Gecarcinidae	
Cardisoma guanhumi	6-10 A1; 9-3 E
Gecarcinus lateralis	6-10 B1; 6-12 R; 11-3 H
Family Ocypodidae	
Ocypode quadrata	6-6 N; 6-10 C1; 6-12 S; 6-14 K; 6-16 U; 11-3 G
Uca burgersi	7-5 K
Uca leptodactyla	7-5 J
Uca marguerita	7-5 I
Uca minax	7-5 C
Uca panacea	7-5 B; 7-6 R; 9-2 G1
Uca pugilator	7-5 F
Uca rapax	7-5 A; 7-5 H; 7-6 T; 9-2 F1; 9-3 V
Uca speciosa	7-5 L; 9-4 Q
Uca spinicarpa	6-16 T; 7-5 G
Uca subcylindrica	7-5 E; 8-6 J
Uca vocator	7-5 D
Family Cryptochiridae	
Troglocarcinus corallicola	11-7 Q; 11-7 R

CLASS INSECTA
Order Isoptera

termite	9-4 N	Family Echinasteridae	
Order Coleoptera		*Echinaster sentus*	4-3 A
Family Cicindelidae		CLASS OPHIUROIDEA	
Cicindela sp.	6-10 U; 9-4 I	Order Ophiurida	
Order Diptera		Family Ophiocomidae	
Family Tabanidae		*Ophiocoma wendti*	10-7 P
Chrysops sp.	6-10 T	*Ophiocomella ophiactoides*	11-5 S
Family Ephydridae		Family Ophiactidae	
Ephydra cinerea	8-6 A	*Ophiactis savignyi*	10-7 Q; 11-2 U;
Family Culicidae			11-5 T
Aedes sollicitans	7-6 A	Family Amphiuridae	
PHYLUM PHORONIDA		*Hemipholis elongata*	10-2 A
Phoronis architecta	7-9 M	Family Ophiotrichidae	
PHYLUM BRYOZOA		*Ophiothrix suensonii*	11-6 W
CLASS GYMNOLAEMATA		*Ophiothrix angulata*	10-2 C
Order Ctenostomata		Family Ophiolepididae	
Family Nolellidae		*Ophiolepis elegans*	10-2 B
Nolella sp.	11-9 B	Order Euryalae	
Family Vesiculariidae		Family Gorgonocephalidae	
Bowerbankia sp.	11-9 A	*Astrophyton muricatum*	11-6 N
Order Cheliostomata		CLASS ECHINOIDEA	
Suborder Anasca		Subclass Perischoechinoidea	
Family Aeteidae		Order Cidaroida	
Aetea sp.	11-9 E	Family Cidaridae	
Family Membraniporidae		*Eucidaris tribuloides*	11-4 G1
Conopeum sp.	11-9 J	Subclass Euechinoidea	
Membranipora tuberculata	6-9 Q	Order Diadematoida	
Membranipora sp.	11-9 I	Family Diadematidae	
Family Steginoporellidae		*Diadema antillarum*	10-7 O; 11-4 F1
Steginoporella magnilabris	11-9 G	Family Arbaciidae	
Family Cellariidae		*Arbacia punctulata*	3-1 I; 3-4 E; 4-1
Cellaria fistulosa	11-9 F		D1; 11-2 V
Family Bugulidae		Order Temnopleuroida	
Bugula neritina	11-9 H	Family Echinidae	
Family Arachnopusiidae		*Lytechinus varigatus*	11-4 R
Arachnopusia sp.	11-9 K	*Tripneustes ventricosus*	4-4 F; 11-4 L1
Suborder Ascophora		Order Echinoida	
Family Cheiloporinidae		Family Echinometridae	
Watersipora cucullata	11-9 L	*Echinometra lucunter*	4-1 E1; 4-2 P;
Family Schizoporellidae			4-4 O
Schizoporella sp.	11-9 M	Family Strongylocentrotidae	
Order Cyclostomata		*Pseudoboletia maculata*	11-2 V
Family Entalophoridae		Order Clypeasteroida	
Entalophora sp.	11-9 D	Family Mellitidae	
Family Oncousoeciidae		*Mellita quinquiesperforata*	10-1 I1
Oncousoecia sp.	11-9 C	Order Spatangoida	
PHYLUM ECHINODERMATA		Family Schizasteridae	
CLASS CRINOIDEA		*Moira atropus*	7-7 X
Subclass Articulata		CLASS HOLOTHUROIDEA	
Order Comatulida		Order Aspidochirotida	
Family Comasteridae		Family Stichopodidae	
Nemaster grandis	11-6 C	*Isostichopus bandionotus*	11-2 C1
CLASS ASTEROIDEA		Order Dendrochirotida	
Order Platyasterida		Family Synaptidae	
Family Luidiidae		*Euapta lappa*	11-4 I1
Luidia alternata	10-1 K1	Family Cucumariidae	
Order Paxillosida		*Thyone mexicana*	7-9 R
Family Astropectinidae		PHYLUM TUNICATA	
Astropecten duplicatus	10-1 L1	CLASS ASCIDIACEA	
Order Valvatida		Order Pleurogona	
Family Ophidiasteridae		Family Molgulidae	
Linckia guildingii	11-4 H1	*Molgula manhattensis*	5-2 I
Order Spinulosida			

PHYLUM CHORDATA
SUBPHYLUM VERTEBRATA
   CLASS ELASMOBRANCHIOMORPHI
     Order Rajiformes
       Family Torpedinidae
         Narcine brasiliensis   11-10 A
       Family Dasyatidae
         Dasyatis americana   7-12 H
         Dasyatis sabina   7-12 I
       Family Myliobatidae
         Rhinoptera bonasus   7-13 A
   CLASS OSTEICHTHYES
     Order Lepisosteiformes
       Family Lepisosteidae
         Lepisosteus spatula   8-4 Y
     Order Elopiformes
       Family Elopidae
         Elops saurus   7-13 I
         Megalops atlanticus   8-4 Z
     Order Angilliformes
       Family Muraenidae
         Gymnothorax funebris   11-6 X
       Family Angillidae
         Anguilla rostrata   8-4 X
     Order Clupeiformes
       Family Clupeidae
         Brevoortia patronus   7-13 J
         Dorosoma cepedianum   7-13 L
         Dorosoma petenense   8-4 W
       Family Engraulidae
         Anchoa mitchilli   7-13 D
     Order Aulopiformes
       Family Synodontidae
         Synodus foetens   7-13 M
     Order Cypriniformes
       Family Ictaluridae
         Arius felis   7-12 E
         Bagre marinus   7-12 F
     Order Batrachoidiformes
       Family Batrachoididae
         Opsanus beta   11-10 B
     Order Lophiiformes
       Family Antennariidae
         Histrio histrio   6-9 H
       Family Ogcocephalidae
         Ogocephalus parvus   11-10 E
     Order Cyprinodontiformes
       Family Cyprinodontidae
         Cyprinodon variegatus   7-13 C
         Fundulus similis   7-13 O
     Order Beloniformes
       Family Belonidae
         Strongylura marina   3-6 A; 7-13 P
       Family Exocoetidae
         Hemiramphus brasiliensis   11-10 M
         Hyporhampus unifasciatus   3-6 F
     Order Beryciformes
       Family Holocentridae
         Holocentrus ascensionis   11-6 J
     Order Gasterosteiformes
       Family Syngnathidae
         Hippocampus erectus   11-10 O
         Sygnathus pelagicus   6-9 G

       Family Aulostomidae
         Aulostomus maculatus   11-8 D
     Order Perciformes
       Family Trichiuridae
         Trichiurus lepturus   7-13 B
       Family Centropomidae
         Centropomus undecimalis   7-13 G
       Family Serranidae
         Epinephalus itajara   3-6 I
         Epinephelus striatus   11-6 Y
       Family Apogonidae
         Apogon maculatus   11-2 Y
       Family Grammistidae
         Rypticus subbifrenatus   11-2 X
       Family Priacanthidae
         Priacanthus arenatus   11-2 W
       Family Carangidae
         Caranx crysos   7-13 E
         Caranx latus   3-6 C
         Trachinotus carolinus   3-6 B
       Family Lutjanidae
         Lutjanus griseus   3-6 G
       Family Gerreidae
         Eucinostomus melanopterus   11-10 F
       Family Lobotidae
         Lobotes surinamensis   3-6 D
       Family Haemulidae
         Anisostremus surinamensis   11-10 H
         Orthopristis chrysopterus   7-13 K
       Family Sparidae
         Calamus bajonado   11-10 J
         Lagodon rhomboide   7-13 F
       Family Sciaenidae
         Cynoscion arenarius   7-13 N
         Cynoscion nebulosus   8-6 T
         Micropogonias undulatus   8-6 U
         Sciaenops ocellatus   3-6 H
         Umbrina coroides   8-6 V
       Family Ephippidae
         Chaetodipterus faber   7-11 B
       Family Pomacanthidae
         Holacanthus ciliaris   11-6 M
         Abudefduf saxatilis   3-2 M; 3-4 C
         Chromis cyaneus   11-10 Q
         Microspathodon chrysurus   11-10 P
       Family Scaridae
         Scarus vetula   11-6 I
       Family Mugilidae
         Mugil cephalus   7-13 H
       Family Blenniidae
         Hypleurochilus geminatus   3-6 E
         Labrisomus nuchipinnis   3-6 J
         Scartella cristata   5-2 X
       Family Gobiidae
         Eleotris pisonis   9-3 Q
         Gobiomorus dormitor   8-4 A1
         Gobiosoma bosci   5-2 Y
         Microgobius gulosus   8-3 V
       Family Acanthuridae
         Acanthurus bahianus   11-6 D
       Family Stromateidae
         Peprilus alepidotus   7-11 A
     Order Pleuronectiformes

Family Bothidae
Citharichthys spilopterus 7-12 B
Paralichthys lethostigma 7-12 A
Family Soleidae
Achirus lineatus 7-12 D
Trinectes maculatus 7-12 C
Family Cynoglossidae
Symphurus plagiusa 7-12 G
Order Tetradontiformes
Family Balistidae
Canthidermis sufflamen 11-10 N
Monacanthus ciliatus 11-10 K
Family Tetraodontidae
Sphoeroides spengleri 11-10 G
Family Ostraciidae
Lactophrys trigonus 11-10 C.D
Family Diodontidae
Diodon hystrix 11-10 I,L
CLASS AMPHIBIA
Order Anura
Family Ranidae
Rana berlandieri 6-11 I
Family Hylidae
Hyla cinerea 6-11 J
CLASS REPTILIA
Order Testudines
Family Emydidae
Chrysemys scripta elegans 6-11 K
Order Squamata
Family Teiidae
Cnemidophorus sexlineatus 6-10 C
Family Iguanidae
Holbrookia propinqua 6-10 B
Sceloporus sp. 6-15 P
Order Serpentes
Family Colubridae
Nerodia rhombifera 6-11 G
Thamnophis proximus orarius 6-11 H
Family Viperidae
Crotalus atrox 6-10 A
CLASS AVES
Subclass Ornithurae
Superorder Carinatae
Order Pelecaniformes
Family Pelecanidae
Pelecanus erythrorhynchos 5-2 B
Pelecanus occidentalis 5-2 A
Family Phalacrocoracidae
Phalacrocorax auritus 5-2 D
Phalacrocorax olivaceus 5-2 E
Order Ciconiiformes
Family Ardeidae
Ardea herodias 9-2 A
Ardea herodias, white phase 9-2 E
Botaurus lentiginosus 9-2 I
Bubulcus ibis 9-2 H
Butorides striatus 9-2 B
Casmerodius albus 9-2 G
Egretta caerulea 9-2 C
Egretta thula 9-2 F
Egretta tricolor 9-2 D
Family Ciconiidae
Mycteria americana 9-3 Y

Family Threskiornithidae
Ajaia ajaja 9-3 X
Plegadis chihi 9-3 Z
Order Phoenicopteriformes
Family Phoenicopteridae
Phoenicopterus ruber 9-4 X
Order Anseriformes
Family Anatidae
Anas acuta 8-4 R
Anas americana 8-4 M
Anas clypeata 8-4 T
Anas crecca 8-4 O
Anas discors 8-4 N
Anas fulvigula 8-4 Q
Anas strepera 8-4 P
Aythya affinis 8-4 S
Branta canadensis 8-4 L
Chen caerulscens 8-4 K
Order Falconiformes
Pandionidae
Pandion haliaetus 7-3 F
Order Gruiformes
Family Gruidae
Grus canadensis 7-3 E
Grus americana 7-3 I
Family Rallidae
Fulica americana 7-3 Q
Rallus longirostris 7-3 J
Order Charadriiformes
Family Haematopodidae
Haematopus palliatus 5-2 C
Family Charadriidae
Charadrius vociferus 8-3 J
Pluvialis squatarola 8-3 K
Family Scolopacidae
*Catoptrophorus
   semipalmatus* 8-3 D
Calidris alba 8-3 E
Calidris alpina 8-3 F
Calidris mauri 8-3 G
Calidris minutilla 8-3 H
Limnodromus scolopaceus 8-3 B
Numenius americanus 8-3 C
Tringa melanoleuca 8-3 A
Family Recurvirostridae
Himantopus mexicanus 8-3 I
Family Laridae
Larus atricilla 3-2 F
Larus argentatus 3-2 E
Sterna caspia 3-2 D
Sterna forsteri 3-2 C
Sterna fuscata 3-2 A
Sterna maximus 3-2 B
Order Passeriformes
Family Emberizidae
Agelaius phoeniceus 8-4 J
Family Parulidae
Dendroica erithachorides 9-4 W
CLASS MAMMALIA
Order Rodentia
Family Geomyidae
Geomys personatus 6-11 L
Family Cricetidae

Baiomys taylori	6-6 Q
Sigmodon hispidus	6-11 M
Family Heteromyidae	
Dipodomys compactus	6-6 P
Family Muridae	
Rattus norvegicus	6-6 R
Family Sciuridae	
Spermophilus spilosoma	
annectens	6-6 M
Order Lagomorpha	
Family Leporidae	
Lepus californicus	6-6 V
Order Carnivora	
Family Canidae	
Canis latrans	6-6 U

Literature

Abbott, R.T. 1954. Review of the Atlantic periwinkles *Nodilittorina, Echininus,* and *Tectarius.* Proc. U.S. Nat. Mus., 103: 449–464.

Abbott, R.T. 1964. *Littorina ziczac* (Gmelin) and *L. lineolata* Orbigny. Nautilus, 78: 65–66.

Abbott, R.T. 1974. *American Seashells,* Second Edition. Van Nostrand Reinhold Co., NY, 663 pp.

Abele, L.G. 1970. The marine decapod Crustacea of the northwestern Gulf of Mexico. Master's Thesis, Florida State U., Tallahassee, 137 pp.

Abele, L.G. 1972. A reevaluation of the *Neopanope texana sayi* complex with notes, on *N. packardii* (Crustacea: Decapoda: Grapsidae) in the western Atlantic. Chesapeake Sci., 13: 263–271.

Adams, J.A. 1960. A contribution to the biology and post-larval development of the Sargassum fish, *Histrio histrio* (Linnaeus), with a discussion of the *Sargassum* complex. Bull. Mar. Sci., 10: 55–82.

Adey, W.H. and I.G. MacIntyre. 1973. Crustose coralline algae: a reevaluation in the geological sciences. Geol. Soc. Amer. Bull., 84: 883–903.

Ahr, W.M. and R.J. Stanton. 1973. The sedimentologic and palaeontologic significance of *Lithothyra,* a rock-boring barnacle. J. Sed. Petrol., 43: 20–23.

Aldrich, J.C. 1974. Allometric studies on energy relationships in the spider crab *Libinia emarginata* (Leach). Biol. Bull., 147: 257–273.

Aldrich, J.C. 1976. The spider crab, *Libinia emarginata* (Leach 1815) (Decapoda, Brachyura), and the starfish, an unsuitable predator but a cooperative prey. Crustaceana, 31: 151–156.

Allen, E.A. and H.A. Curran. 1974. Biogenic sedimentary structures produced by crabs in lagoon margin and salt marsh environments near Beaufort, North Carolina. J. Sed. Petrol., 44: 538–548.

Allen, J.F. 1958. Feeding habits of two species of *Odostomia.* Nautilus, 72: 11–15.

Amos, A.F. 1983. Tar reef of weathered IXTOC-1 oil exposed off Texas beach by low tides. Oil Spill Intelligence Rep., Center for Short-lived Phenomena and Cahners Publ. Co., 6: 4.

Anderson, R.D. and J.W. Anderson. 1974. Physiological responses of the American oyster *Crassostrea virginica* Gmelin to salinity changes. Proc. Nat. Shellfisheries Assoc., 64: 1.

Andrews, E.A. 1940. The snail *Neritina virginea* in a changing salt pond. Ecology, 21: 335–346.

Andrews, J. 1977. *Shells and Shores of Texas.* U. Texas Press, Austin, 365 pp.

Andrews, J.D. 1962a. Infectious disease damages mid-Atlantic oyster population. Virginia J. Sci., 13: 241.

Andrews, J.D. 1962b. Oyster mortality studies in Virginia. IV. MSX in James River public seed beds. Proc. Nat. Shellfisheries Assoc., 53: 65–84.

Andrews, J.D., D. Haven and D.B. Quayle. 1959. Freshwater kill of oysters, *Crassostrea virginica* in James River, Virginia, 1958. Proc. Nat. Shellfisheries Assoc., 49: 29–49.

Andrews, P.B. 1970. Facies and genesis of a hurricane washover fan, St. Joseph Island, central Texas coast. U. Texas Bur. Econ. Geol. Rept. Inv., 67: 147 pp.

Apley, M.L. 1970. Field studies on life history, gonadal cycle and reproductive periodicity in *Melampus bidentatus* (Pulmonata: Ellobiidae). Malacologia, 10: 381–397.

Appeldoorn, R.S. 1984. The effect of size on mortality of small juvenile conchs (*Strombus gigas* Linne and *S. costatus* Gmelin). J. Shellfish Res., 4: 37–43.

Appeldoorn, R.S. and I.M. Sanders. 1984. Quantification of the density-growth relationship in hatchery-reared juvenile conchs (*Strombus gigas* Linne and *S. coststus* Gmelin). J. Shellfish Res., 4: 63–66.

Aspey, W.P. 1971. Inter-species sexual discrimination and approach-avoidance conflict in two species of fiddler crabs, *Uca pugnax* and *Uca pugilator.* Anim. Behav., 19: 669–676.

Atwood, D.K. and R.L. Ferguson. 1982. An example study of the weathering of spilled petroleum in a tropical marine environment. IXTOC-1. Bull. Mar. Sci., 32: 1–13.

Ayers, J.C. 1938. Relationship of habitat to oxygen consumption by certain estuarine crabs. Ecology, 19: 523–527.

Baca, B.J., E.R. Cox and L.O. Sorensen. 1977. Observations on several benthic marine algae from South Padre Island, Texas. Southwestern Nat., 21: 459–462.

Baca, B.J., L.O. Sorensen and E.R. Cox, 1979. Systematic list of the seaweeds of south Texas. Contrib. Mar. Sci., 22: 179–192.

Bahr, L.M. and W.P. Lanier. 1981. The ecology of intertidal oyster reefs of the south Atlantic coast: A community profile. U.S. Fish and Wildlife Ser., Office of Biological Services, Washington, D.C., FWS/OBS-81/15, 105 pp.

Baker E.B. and A.S. Merrill. 1965. An observation of *Laevicardium mortoni* actually swimming. Nautilus, 78: 104.

Ballantine, W.J. 1961. A biologically-defined exposure scale for the comparative description of rocky shores. Field Studies, 1(3): 19 pp.

Bandel, K. 1974. Studies on Littorinidae from the Atlantic. Veliger, 17: 92–114.

Bandel, K. 1976. Observations on spawn, embryonic development, and ecology of some Caribbean lower Mesogastropoda (Mollusca). Veliger, 18: 249–271.

Bandel, K. and D. Kadolsky. 1982. Western Atlantic species of *Nodilittorina* (Gastropoda: Prosobranchia): Comparative morphology and its functional, ecological, phylogenetic and taxonomic implications. Veliger, 25: 1–42.

Barnes, R.D. 1964. Tube-building and feeding in the chaetopterid polychaete, *Spiochaetopterus oculatus* Biol. Bull., 127: 397–412.

Barnes, R.D. 1965. Tube-building and feeding in chaetopterid polychaetes. Biol. Bull., 129: 217–233.

Barnwell, F.H. 1966. Daily and tidal patterns of activity in individual fiddler crabs (genus *Uca*) from the Woods Hole region. Biol. Bull., 130: 1–13.

Barnwell, F.H. 1968. The role of rhythmic systems in the adaptation of fiddler crabs to the intertidal zone. Amer. Zool., 8: 569–583.

Barnwell, F.H. and C.L.Thurman. 1984. Taxonomy and biogeography of the fiddler crabs (Ocypodidae: Genus *Uca*) of the Atlantic and Gulf coasts of eastern North America. Zool. J. Linn. Soc., 81: 23–87.

Bascom, W.N. 1951. The relationship between sand size and beach face slope. Trans. Amer. Geophy. Union, 32: 866–874.

Bass, E.L. 1977. Influences of temperature and salinity on oxygen consumption of tissues in the American oyster *Crassostrea virginica*. Comp. Biochem. Physio. B., Comp. Biochem., 58: 125–130.

Bassler, R.S. 1953. Bryozoa. In: Moore, R.C. (Ed.) *Treatise on Invertebrate Paleontology, Part G*. Geol. Soc. Amer. and U. Kansas Press, Lawrence, Kansas, pp. G1-G253.

Battey, J.F. and J.S. Patton, 1984. A re-evaluation of the role of glycerol in carbon translocation in zooxanthellae-coelenterate symbiosis. Mar. Biol., 79: 27–38.

Baughman, J.L. 1947. An annotated bibliography of oysters, with pertinent material on mussels and other shellfish and an appendix on pollution. Texas A&M Research Foundation, College Station. 794 pp.

Bayer, F.M. 1961. The shallow water Octocorallia of the West Indian region. Stud. Fauna Curacao other Caribb. Isl., 12: 1–373, 28 pl.

Beach, N.W. 1969. The oyster crab, *Pinnotheres ostreum* Say, in the vicinity of Beaufort, North Carolina. Crustaceana, 17: 187–199.

Behre, E.H. 1954. Decapoda of the Gulf of Mexico. In: *The Gulf of Mexico: Its Origin, Waters and Marine Life*, U.S. Fish & Wildlife Serv., Fish. Bull., 55(89): 451–455.

Behrens, E.W. 1966. Surface salinities for Baffin Bay and Laguna Madre, Texas, April 1964-March 1966. Publ. Inst. Mar. Sci., 11: 168–173.

Bell, B.M. and R.W. Frey. 1969. Observations on ecology and the feeding and burrowing mechanisms of *Mellita quinquiesperforata* (Leske). J. Paleontol., 43: 553–560.

Bent, A.C. 1921. Gulls and terns. U.S. Nat. Mus. Bull., 113: 337 pp. + 93 pl.

Berg, C.J. 1976. Growth of the queen conch *Strombus gigas* with a discussion of the practicality of its mariculture. Mar. Biol., 34: 191–199.

Bernard, H.A., R.J. LeBlanc and C.F. Major. 1962. Recent and Pleistocene geology of southeastern Texas. In: *Geology of the Gulf Coast and Central Texas and Guidebook of Excursion*, Houston Geol. Soc., pp. 175–224.

Bernard, H.A., C.F. Major, and B.S. Parrott. 1959. *Recent sediments of southeast Texas: A field guide to the Brazos alluvial and deltaic plains and barrier complex.*U. Texas Bur. Econ. Geol., Guidebook 11: irregular pagination.

Bert, T.M. and H.J. Humm. 1979. Checklist of the marine algae on the offshore oil platforms of Louisiana. Rice U. Rep., 65: 437–446.

Bertness, M. 1980. Growth and mortality in the ribbed mussel *Geukensia demissa* (Bivalvia: Dreissenacea). Veliger, 23: 62–69.

Bierbaum, T.J. and J.A. Zischke. 1979. Changes in barnacle population structure along an intertidal community gradient in the Florida Keys. Mar. Biol., 53: 345–351.

Biffar, T.A. 1971a. New species of *Callianassa* (Decapoda, Thalassinidea) from the western Atlantic. Crustaceana, 21: 225–236.

Biffar, T.A. 1972b. The genus *Callianassa* (Decapoda, Thalassinidea) from the western Atlantic. Bull. Mar. Sci., 21(3): 637–715.

Binford, R. 1912. The germ cells and the process of fertilization in the crab *Menippe mercenaria*. Ph.D. Dissertation, Johns Hopkins U., 51 pp.

Bingham, F.O. 1969. The influence of environmental stimuli on the direction of movement of the supralittoral gastropod *Littorina irrorata* with notes on additional biological aspects of the species. Master's Thesis, Florida State U., Tallahassee, 66 pp.

Bingham, F.O. 1972a. The mucous holdfast of *Littorina irrorata* and its relationship to relative humidity and salinity. Veliger, 15: 48–50.

Bingham, F.O. 1972b. The influence of environmental stimuli on the direction of movement of the supralittoral gastropod *Littorina irrorata*. Bull. Mar. Sci., 22: 309–335.

Bingham, F.O. 1972c. Several aspects of the reproductive biology of *Littorina irrorata* (Gastropoda). Nautilus, 86: 8–10.

Bird, S.O. 1970. Shallow-marine and estuarine benthic molluscan communities from the area of Beaufort, North Carolina. Bull. Amer. Assoc. Petrol. Geol., 54: 1651–1676.

Blacklock, G.W., D.R. Blankinship, S. Kennedy, K.A. King, R.T. Paul, R.D. Slack, J.C. Smith and R.C. Telfair. 1978. *Texas colonial waterbird census, 1973–1976*. FA Rept. Ser. Texas Parks and Wildlife Dept., Austin.

Bliss, D.E. 1968. Transition from water to land in decapod crustaceans. Amer. Zool., 8: 355–392.

Bliss, D.E. and P.C. Sprague. 1958. Diurnal locomotor activity in *Gecarcinus lateralis*. Anat. Rec., 132: 416–417.

Bliss, D.E., J. Van Montfrans, M. Van Montfrans and J.R. Boyer. 1978. Behavior of the land crab *Gecarcinus lateralis* (Freminville) in southern Florida. Bull. Amer. Mus. Nat. Hist., 160: 111–152.

Blumberg, A.F. and G.L. Mellor. 1981. *A numerical calculation of the circulation in the Gulf of Mexico*. Prepared for Division of Solar Technology, U.S. Department of Energy, Contract DE-ACO2–78ET 20612, by

Dynalysis of Princeton, Princeton, New Jersey (pages unnumbered).

Boardman, R.S., A.H. Cheetham, D.B. Blake, J. Utgaard, O.L. Karlins, P.L. Cook, P.A. Sandberg, G. Lutaud, and T.S. Wood. 1983. Bryozoa (Revised), Volume 1: Introduction, Order Cystoporata, Order Cryptostomata. In: Moore, R.C. (Ed.) *Treatise on Invertebrate Paleontology, Part G.* Geol. Soc. Amer., Boulder Colorado, pp. G1-G625.

Boesch, D.F. 1971. On the occurrence of *Pinnixa lunzi* Glassell (Decapoda Pinnotheridae) off Virginia, U.S.A. Crustaceana, 20: 219–220.

Bohlke, J.E. and C.C.G. Chaplin. 1968. *Fishes of the Bahamas and Adjacent Tropical Waters.* Harrowood Books, Valley Forge, Pennsylvania.

Bomer, G.W. 1983. *Texas Weather.* U. Texas Press, Austin, 265 pp.

Borkowski, T.V. 1971. Reproduction and reproductive periodicities of south Floridian Littorinidae (Gastropoda: Prosobranchia). Bull. Mar. Sci., 21: 826–840.

Borkowski, T.V. 1974. Growth, mortality, and productivity of south Floridian Littorinidae (Gastropoda: Prosobranchia). Bull. Mar. Sci., 24: 409–438.

Borkowski, T.V. and Borkowski, M.R. 1969. The *Littorina ziczac* species complex. Veliger, 11: 408–414.

Bousfield, E.L. 1954. The distribution and spawning seasons of barnacles on the Atlantic coasts of Canada. Bull. Nat. Mus. Canada, 132: 112–154.

Bradley, W.H. and P. Cooke. 1959. Living and ancient populations of the clam *Gemma gemma* in a Maine coastal tidal flat. U.S. Fish & Wildlife Ser., Fish. Bull., 58: 305–334.

Brawley, S.H. and W.H. Adey. 1981. The effect of micrograzers on algal community structure in a coral reef microcosm. Mar. Biol., 61: 167–177.

Brawley, S.H. and W.H. Adey. 1982. *Coralliophila abbreviata:* a significant corallivore! Bull. Mar. Sci., 32: 595–599.

Brenchley, G.A. 1976. Predator detection and avoidance: Ornamentation of tube-caps of *Diopatra* spp. (Polychaeta: Onuphidae). Mar. Biol., 38: 179–188.

Breuer, J.P. 1957. An ecological survey of the Baffin and Alazan Bays, Texas. Publ. Inst. Mar. Sci., 4: 134–155.

Breuer, J.P. 1962. An ecological survey of the lower Laguna Madre of Texas. Publ. Inst. Mar. Sci., 8: 153–183.

Briggs, J.C. 1974. *Marine Zoogeography.* New York: McGraw-Hill, 475 pp.

Bright, T.J., E. Powell and R. Rezak. 1980. Environmental effects of a natural brine seep at the East Flower Garden Bank, northwestern Gulf of Mexico. In: Geyer, R.A. (Ed.) *Marine Environmental Pollution.* Elsevier Oceanography Series, 27A, Elsevier, New York, pp. 291–316.

Bright, T.J. and L.G. Pequegnat (Eds.). 1974. *Biota of the west Flower Garden Bank.* Gulf Publ. Co., Houston, 435 pp.

Britton, J.C., G.C. Kroh and C. Golightly. 1982. Biometric and ecological relationships in two sympatric Caribbean Gecarcinidae (Crustacea:Decapoda). J. Crustacean Biol., 2: 207–222.

Broad, A.C. 1957. The relationship between diet and larval development in *Palaemonetes.* Biol. Bull., 112: 144–161, plates 1–4.

Bromley, R.G. 1978. Bioerosion of Bermuda reefs. Paleogeogr. Palaeoclimatol. Palaeoecol., 23: 169–197.

Brown, L.F., Jr., J.L. Brewton, T.J. Evans, J.H. McGowan and W.A. White. 1980. *Environmental Geologic Atlas of the Texas Coastal Zone: Brownsville-Harligen Area* Bureau Economic Geol., U. Texas, Austin, 140 pp.

Brownell, W.N. and J.M. Stevely. 1981. The biology, fisheries and management of the queen conch, *Strombus gigas.* U.S. Nat. Mar. Fish. Serv. Mar. Fish. Rev., 43: 1–12.

Bryce, G.W., Jr. 1961. Larval development of *Tozeuma carolinense* Kingsley, including ecological notes on adults. Master's Thesis, U. N. Carolina, Chapel Hill, 59 pp.

Bullard, F.M. 1942. Source of beach and river sands on Gulf coast of Texas. Bull. Geol. Soc. Amer., 53: 1021–1044.

Burke, T.E. 1974. Echinoderms. In: Bright, T.J. and L.H. Pequegnat, Eds., *Biota of the West Flower Garden Bank,* Gulf Publishing Co., Houston, Texas, pp. 311–332.

Burkenroad, M.D. 1931. Notes on the Louisiana conch *Thais haemastoma* in relation to the oyster *Crassostrea virginica.* Ecology, 12: 656–664.

Burkenroad, M.D. 1934. The Penaeidae of Louisiana with a discussion of their world relationships. Bull. Amer. Mus. Nat. Hist., 68: 61–143.

Burkenroad, M.D. 1939. Further observations on Penaeidae of the northern Gulf of Mexico. Bull. Bingham Oceanogr. Coll., 6: 1–62.

Burkenroad, M.D. 1947. Reproductive activities of decapod Crustacea. Amer. Nat., 81: 392–398.

Burrell, V.G. 1977. Mortalities of oysters and hard clams associated with heavy runoff in the Santee River system, South Carolina, in the spring of 1975. Proc. Nat. Shellfisheries Assoc., 67: 35–43.

Burris, J.E., J.W. Porter and W.A. Laing. 1983. Effects of carbon dioxide concentration on coral photosynthesis. Mar. Biol., 75: 113–116.

Butler, P.A. 1952. Effect of floodwaters on oysters in Mississippi Sound in 1950. U.S. Fish and Wildlife Service Res. Repts., 31: 1–20.

Butler, P.A. 1953. The southern oyster drill. Nat. Shellfisheries Assoc., Convention Papers for 1953: 67–75.

Butler, P.A. 1955. Selective settling of oyster larvae on artificial cultch. Proc. Nat. Shellfisheries Assoc., 45: 95–105.

Caine, E.A. 1974. Comparative functional morphology of feeding in three species of caprellids from the northwestern Florida coast. J. Exp. Mar. Biol. Ecol., 15: 81–96.

Caine, E.A. 1975. Feeding of *Pinnotheres maculatus* Say (Brachyura: Pinnotheridae). Forma et Functo, 8: 395–403.

Calabrese, A. 1969. *Mulinia lateralis:* Molluscan fruit fly?. Proc. Nat. Shellfisheries Assoc., 59: 65–66.

Calnan, T.R. 1980. Molluscan distribution in Copano Bay, Texas. Bur. Econ. Geol., U. Texas, Rep. Inv., 103: 71 pp.

Carew, T.J. and I. Kupfermann. 1974. Influence of different natural environments on habituation in *Aplysia californica.* Behav. Biol., 12: 339.

Carlgren, O. and J.W. Hedgpeth. 1952. Actinaria, Zoantharia and Ceriantharia from the shallow water in the northwestern Gulf of Mexico. Publ. Inst. Mar. Sci., 2: 143–172.

Carpelan, C.H. 1967. Invertebrates in relation to hypersaline habitats. Contrib. Mar. Sci., 12: 217–229.

Carr, W.E.S. 1967a. Chemoreception in the mud snail, *Nassarius obsoletus*. I. Properties of stimulatory substances extracted from shrimp. Biol. Bull., 133: 90–105.

Carr, W.E.S. 1967b. Chemoreception in the mud snail, *Nassarius obsoletus*. II. Identification of stimulatory substances. Biol. Bull., 133: 106–127.

Carriker, M.R. 1955. Critical review of biology and control of oyster drills, *Urosalpinx* and *Eupleura*. U.S. Fish and Wildlife Ser., Spec. Sci. Rep., Fisheries, 148: 150 pp.

Carriker, M.R. 1958. Additional information on the mechanical-chemical nature of drilling by the gastropods *Urosalpinx* and *Eupleura*. Biol. Assoc. Southeastern Biol., 5: 5.

Carriker, M.R. 1959. Comparative functional morphology of the drilling mechanism in *Urosalpinx* and *Eupleura* (muricid gastropods). XVth Internl. Congr. Zool., London, Sect. IV, paper 27, 3pp.

Carriker, M.R. 1961. Comparative functional morphology of the boring mechanisms in gastropods. Amer. Zool., 1: 263–266.

Carter, J.G. 1978. Ecology and evolution of Gastrochaenacea (Mollusca, Bivalvia) with notes on the evolution of the endolithic habit. Bull. Peabody Mus. Nat. Hist., 41: 1–92.

Carter, J.G. and R.C. Aller. 1975. Calcification in the bivalve periostracum. Lethaia, 8: 315–320.

Castagna, M. and P. Chanley. 1973. Salinity tolerance of some marine bivalves from inshore and estuarine environments in Virginia waters on the western mid-Atlantic coast. Malacologia, 12: 47–96.

Castagna, M. and W. Duggan. 1971. Rearing the bay scallop, *Aequipecten irradians*. Proc. Nat. Shellfisheries Assoc., 61: 80–85.

Causey, B.D. 1969. The fishes of Seven and One-Half Fathom Reef. Master's Thesis, Texas A&I U., Kingsville, 110 pp.

Chace, F.A., Jr. 1972. The shrimps of the Smithsonian-Bredin Caribbean Expeditions with a summary of the West Indian shallow water species (Crustacea: Decapoda: Natantia). Smithsonian Contrib. Zool., 98: 1–179.

Chambers, L.A. 1934. Studies on the organs of reproduction in the nudibranchiate mollusks, with special reference to *Embletonia fuscata* Gould. Bull. Amer. Mus. Nat. Hist., 66: 599–641.

Chapman, B.R. 1982. Current status of roseate spoonbills on the Texas coast. In: Chapman, B.R. and J.W. Tunnell, Jr. (Eds.), *South Texas Fauna: A Symposium Honoring Dr. Allan H. Chaney*. Texas A&I U., Kingsville, pp. 79–82.

Chavez, E.A. 1973. Observaciones generales sobre las comunidades del arrecife de Lobos, Veracruz. An. Esc. nac. Cienc. biol., Mex., 20: 13–21.

Chavez, E.A., E. Hidalgo and M.L. Sevilla. 1970. Datos acerca de las comunidades bentonicas del Arrecife de Lobos, Veracruz. Rev. Soc. Mex. Hist. Nat., 21: 211–280.

Chestnut, A.F. 1946. Some observations on the feeding of oysters with especial reference to the tide. Southern Fisherman, 6(8): 53.

Chipman, W.A. and J.G. Hopkins. 1954. Water filtration by the bay scallop, *Pecten irradians*, as observed with the use of radioactive plankton. Biol. Bull., 107: 80–91.

Chittenden, M.E. and J.D. McEachran. 1976. Composition, ecology and dynamics of demersal fish communities on the northwestern Gulf of Mexico continental shelf, with a similar synopsis for the entire Gulf. Dept. Oceanogr., Texas A&M U., Tech. Rep., TAMU-SG-76-208.

Christensen, A.M. and J.J. McDermott. 1958. Life history and biology of the oyster crab, *Pinnotheres ostreum* Say. Biol. Bull., 114: 146–179.

Christensen, H.E. 1967. Ecology of *Hydractinia echinata*. I. Feeding biology. Ophelia, 4: 245–275.

Christiansen, M.E. and J.D. Costlow. 1975. The effect of salinity and cyclic temperature on the larval development of the mud crab *Rhithropanopeus harisii* (Brachyura: Xanthidae) reared in the laboratory. Mar. Biol., 32: 215–221.

Christoffersen, M.L. 1984. The western Atlantic snapping shrimps related to *Alpheus heterochaelis* Say (Crustacea: Caridea) with the description of a new species. Pap. Avulsos Zool., 35: 189–208.

Christy, J.H. 1978. Adaptive significance of reproductive cycles in the fiddler crab *Uca pugilator*: A hypothesis. Science, 199: 453–455.

Clark, H.L. 1933. A handbook of the littoral echinoderms of Porto Rico and the other west Indian islands. New York Acad. Sci., Sci. Survey Porto Rico and the Virgin Islands, 16(1): 1–147 + 7 pls.

Clark, S.T. and P.B. Robertson. 1982. Shallow water marine isopods of Texas. Contrib. Mar. Sci., 25: 45–59.

Clarke, A.H., Jr. 1965. The scallop superspecies *Aequipecten irradians* (Lamarck). Malacologia, 2: 161–188.

Clench, W.J. and R.D. Turner. 1946. The genus *Bankia* in the western Atlantic. Johnsonia, 2: 1–28.

Cobb, W.R. 1969. Penetration of calcium carbonate structures by the boring sponge, *Cliona*. Amer. Zool., 9: 783–790.

Coe, W.R. 1936. Sexual phases in *Crepidula*. J. Exp. Zool., 72: 455–477.

Cohen, J.A. and H.J. Brockmann. 1983. Breeding activity and mate selection in the horseshoe crab, *Limulus polyphemus*. Bull. Mar. Sci., 33: 274–281.

Cole, R.M. 1980. The serpulid reefs of Baffin Bay, Texas. In: Russell, J.L. and R.W. Shum (Eds.) Geology of clay dunes, Baffin Bay, and the south Texas sand sheet. Field Trip Guidebook of the 83rd Ann. Meeting Texas Acad. Sci., March, 1980, pp. 63–74.

Collier, A. and J.W. Hedgpeth. 1950. An introduction to the hydrography of tidal waters of Texas. Publ. Inst. Mar. Sci., 1: 121–194.

Connell, J.H. 1961a. The influence of interspecific competition and other factors on the distribution of the barnacle *Chthamalus stellatus*. Ecology, 42: 710–723.

Connell, J.H. 1961b. The effects of competition, predation by *Thais lapillus*, and other factors on natural populations of the barnacle, *Balanus balanoides*. Ecol. Monogr., 31: 61–104.

Connor, W.C., R.H. Craft and D.L. Harris. 1957. Empirical methods for forecasting the maximum storm tide due to hurricanes and other tropical storms. Monthly Weather Rev., 85: 113–116.

Conover, J.T. 1964. The ecology, seasonal periodicity and distribution of benthic plants in some Texas lagoons. Botanica Mar., 7: 4–41.

Copeland, B.J. and T.J. Bechtel. 1974. Some environmental limits of six Gulf coast estuarine organisms. Contrib. Mar. Sci., 18: 169–204.

Copeland, B.J. and H.D. Hoese. 1966. Growth and mortality of the American oyster, *Crassostrea virginica* in high salinity shallow bays in central Texas. Publ. Inst. Mar. Sci., 11: 149–158.

Copeland, B.J. and R.S. Jones. 1965. Community metabolism in some hypersaline waters. Texas J. Sci., 17: 188–205.

Copeland, B.J. and V. Truitt. 1966. Fauna of the Aransas Pass Inlet, Texas. Texas J. Sci., 18: 65–74.

Cornelius, S.E. 1984. An ecological survey of Alazan Bay, Texas. Caesar Kleberg Wildlife Res. Inst., Texas A&I U., Tech. Bull., 1: 163 pp.

Corrington, J.D. 1927. Commensal association of a spider crab and a medusa. Biol. Bull., 53: 346–350.

Costlow, J.D. Jr. and C.G. Bookhout. 1961. The larval stages of *Panopeus herbstii* Milne-Edwards reared in the laboratory. J. Elisha Mitchell Sci. Soc., 77: 33–42.

Craig, A.K., S. Dobkin, R.B. Grimm and J.B. Davidson. 1969. The gastropod *Siphonaria pectinata*: a factor in destruction of beachrock. Amer. Zool., 9: 895–901.

Craig, M.A. and T.J. Bright. 1986. Abundance, age distributions and growth of the Texas hard clam, *Mercenaria mercenaria texana* in Texas bays. Contrib. Mar. Sci., 29: 59–72.

Crane, J. 1941. Eastern Pacific Expeditions of the New York Zoological Society. XXVI. Crabs of the genus *Uca* from the west coast of central America. Zoologica, 26: 145–208.

Crane, J. 1943. Display, breeding and relationships of fiddler crabs (Brachyura, Genus *Uca*) in the northeastern United States. Zoologica, 28: 217–223.

Crane, J. 1957. Basic patterns of display in fiddler crabs (Ocypodidae: Genus *Uca*). Zoologica, 42: 69–82.

Crane, J. 1967. Combat and its ritualization in fiddler crabs (Ocypodidae) with special reference to *Uca rapax*. Zoologica, 52: 49–75.

Crane, J. 1975. *Fiddler Crabs of the World*. Princeton, N.J.: Princeton U. Press, 736 pp.

Creswell, R.L. 1984. Ingestion, assimilation and growth of juveniles of the queen conch *Strombus gigas* Linne fed experimental diets. J. Shellfish Res., 4: 23–30.

Crichton, O.W. 1960. Marsh crab, intertidal tunnelmaker and grass-eater. Estuarine Bull., U. Delaware, 5: 3–10.

Crichton, O.W. 1974. Caloric studies of *Spartina* and the marsh crab *Sesarma reticulatum* (Say). In: Odum, H.T., B.J. Copeland and E.A. McMahan (Eds.). *Coastal Ecological Systems of the United States, Vol. 2*. The Coastal Conservation Foundation, Washington, D.C., pp. 142–144.

Crisp, D.J. 1967. Chemical factors inducing settlement in *Crassostrea virginica* (Gmelin). J. Animal Ecol., 36: 329–335.

Crossland, C.J., D.J. Barnes and M.A. Borowitzka. 1980.

Diurnal lipid and mucus production in the staghorn coral *Acropora acuminata*. Mar. Biol., 60: 81–90.

Crowe, A.L. and C.E. Bryan. 1986. A description of the Texas shrimp fleet, 1979–1983. Texas Parks and Wildlife Management Data Ser., 101: 1–11.

Cruz, R. 1968. Geologia marina de la Laguna de Tamiahua, Veracruz, Mexico. U. Nat. Auton. Mexico, Inst. Geol., Bol. 88: 1–47.

Curray, J.R. 1960. Sediments and history of Holocene transgression, continental shelf, northwest Gulf of Mexico. In: Sheppard, F.P., F.B. Phleger and T.H. Van Andel (Eds.) *Recent Sediments, Northwestern Gulf of Mexico*. Amer. Assoc. Petrol. Geol., Tulsa, Oklahoma, pp. 221–266.

Cutress, C., D.M. Ross and L. Sutton. 1970. The association of *Calliactis tricolor* with its pagurid, calappid and majid partners in the Caribbean. Canadian J. Zool., 48: 371–376.

D'Asaro, C.N. 1965. Organogenesis, development and metamorphosis in the queen conch, *Strombus gigas*, with notes on breeding habits. Bull. Mar. Sci., 15: 358–416.

D'Asaro, C.N. 1966. The egg capsules, embryogenesis, and early organogenesis of a common oyster predator, *Thais haemastoma floridana* (Gastropoda: Prosobranchia). Bull. Mar. Sci., 16: 884–914.

D'Asaro, C.N. 1967. The morphology of larval and postlarval *Chione cancellata* Linne (Eulamellibranchia: Veneridae) reared in the laboratory. Bull. Mar. Sci., 17: 949–972.

D'Asaro, C.N. 1969. The comparative embryogenesis and early organogenesis of *Bursa corrugata* Perry and *Distorsio clathrata* Lamarck (Gastropoda: Prosobranchia). Malacologia, 9: 349–389.

D'Asaro, C.N. 1970. Egg capsules of prosobranch mollusks from south Florida and the Bahamas and notes on spawning in the laboratory. Bull. Mar. Sci., 16: 414–440.

Dahl, B.E., B.E. Fall, B.A. Lohse, and S.G. Appan. 1974. Stabilization and reconstruction of Texas coastal foredunes with vegetation: Gulf U. Res. Consort. Rep. 139, Final report to U.S. Army Corps Eng., Coastal Eng. Res. Cen., Fort Belvoir, Virginia, 325 pp.

Dahl, E. 1956. Ecological and salinity boundaries in poikilohaline waters. Oikos, 7: 1–21.

Dando, P.R. and A.J. Southward. 1980. A new species of *Chthamalus* (Crustacea: Cirripedia) characterized by enzyme electrophoresis and shell morphology: with a revision of other species of *Chthamalus* from the western shores of the Atlantic Ocean. J. Mar. Biol. Assoc. U.K., 60: 787–831.

Darcy, G.H. 1981. Annotated bibliography of the conch genus *Strombus* (Gastropoda: Strombidae) in the western Atlantic Ocean. U.S. Natl. Oceanic Atmos. Admin. Tech. Rep. NMFS-SSRF-748: 16 pp.

Darnell, R.M. 1958. Food habits of fishes and larger invertebrates of Lake Pontchartrain, Louisiana, an estuarine community. Publ. Inst. Mar. Sci., 5: 353–416.

Darnell, R.M. 1959. Studies of the life history of the blue crab (*Callinectes sapidus* Rathbun) in Louisiana waters. Trans. Amer. Fish. Soc., 88: 294–304.

Darnell, R.M. 1961. Trophic spectrum of an estuarine community, based on studies of Lake Pontchartrain,

Louisiana. Ecology, 42: 553–568.

Darwin, C.R. 1851. A monograph of the subclass Cirripedia, with figures of all species. The Lepadidae; or pedunculated cirripedes. Ray Society, London, 400 pp. + 10 plates.

Daugherty, F.M., Jr. 1952. Notes on *Callinectes danae* Smith in Aransas Bay, Texas, and adjacent waters. Texas J. Sci., 4: 264–267.

Davies, P.S. 1977. Carbon budgets and vertical zonation of Atlantic reef corals. Proc. 3rd Coral Reef Symp. Miami, 1: 391–396.

Davies, P.S. 1980. Respiration in some Atlantic reef corals in relation to vertical distribution and growth form. Biol. Bull., 158: 187–194.

Davis, H.C. 1958. Survival and growth of clam and oyster larvae at different salinities. Biol. Bull., 114: 296–307.

Davis, H.C. and A. Calabrese. 1964. Combined effects of temperature and salinity on development of eggs and growth of larvae of *M. mercenaria* and *C. virginica*. U.S. Fish & Wildlife Service Fish. Bull., 63: 643–655.

Davis, J.S. 1972. Survival records in the algae, and the survival role of certain algal pigments, fat, and mucilaginous substances. Biologist, 54: 52–93.

Davis, M.B., A. Mitchell, and J. Brown. 1984. Breeding behavior of the queen conch, *Strombus gigas* Linne held in a natural enclosed habitat. J. Shellfish Res., 4: 17–21.

Davis, R.L. and N. Marshall. 1961. The feeding of the bay scallop, *Aequipecten irradians*. Proc. Natl. Shellfisheries Assoc., 52: 25–29.

Davis, W.P. 1966. Observations on the biology of the ophiuroid *Astrophyton muricatum*. Bull. Mar. Sci., 16: 435–444.

Dawson, C.E. 1955. Observations on the incidence of *Dermocystidium marinum* infection in oysters of Apalachicola Bay, Florida. Texas J. Sci., 7: 47–56.

Dawson, C.E. 1963. Notes on *Stenopus scutellatus* Rankin and *Neopontoides beaufortensis* (Borradaile) from the northern Gulf of Mexico. Crustaceana, 5: 155–157.

Dayton, P.K. 1971. Competition, disturbance and community organization: provision and subsequent utilization of space in a rocky intertidal community. Ecol. Monogr., 41: 351–389.

Dayton, P.K. 1984. Processes structuring some marine communities: Are they general? In: Strong, D.R., D. Simberloff, L.G. Abele, and A.B. Thistle (Eds.) *Ecological Communities, Conceptual Issues and the Evidence*. Princeton U. Press, Princeton, N.J., pp. 181–197.

Dean, D. 1978. The swimming of bloodworms (*Glycera* spp.) at night, with comments on other species. Mar. Biol., 48: 99–104.

Dean, R.C. and A.A. Paparo. 1981. Responses of ctenidial cilia of the American oyster, *Crassostrea virginica*, to changes in salinity and cation concentration. Amer. Zool., 21: 916.

de Rooij-Schuiling, L.A. 1973. A preliminary report on systematics and distribution of the genus *Ervilia* Turton, 1822 (Mesodesmatidae, Bivalvia). Malacologia, 14: 235–241.

Dexter, D.M. 1976. The sandy beach fauna of Mexico. Southwestern Nat., 20: 479–485.

Diener, R.A. 1975. Cooperative Gulf of Mexico estuarine inventory study—Texas: area description. NOAA Tech.

Rpt., NMFS CIRC-393, 129 pp.

Dieuzeide, R. 1935. Contribution a l'etude de gastropodes pulmones marins: *Siphonaria algesirae* Q. et G.: *Gadinia garnoti* Payr. Station d'Agriculture et de Peche de Castiglioni, 1–196.

Dixon, J.R. 1987. *Amphibians and Reptiles of Texas*. Texas A&M Press, College Station, 434 pp.

Dobkin, S. and R.B. Manning. 1964. Osmoregulation in two species of *Palaemonetes* (Crustacea: Decapoda) from Florida. Bull. Mar. Sci., 14: 147–157.

Drinnan, R.E. 1969. The effect of early fouling of shell surfaces on oyster spatfall. Proc. Nat. Shellfisheries Assoc. for 1968, 59: Abstract.

Dugan, P.J. 1983. Seasonal and geographic distribution of seven decapod crustaceans in Apalachee Bay, Florida. Contrib. Mar. Sci., 26: 65–79.

Duggins, D.O. 1981. Interspecific facilitation in a guild of benthic marine herbivores. Oecologia, 48: 157–163.

Duncan, W.H. and M.B. Duncan. 1987. *Seaside Plants of the Gulf and Atlantic Coasts*. Smithsonian Institution Press, Washington, D.C., 409 pp.

Duncker, G. 1934. Gefangenschaftbeobachtungen an *Sesarma cinerea* Milne Edw. Zool. Jahrbuch., Syst. Geogr. Biol. Tiere, Jena, 66: 285–290.

Dunn, G.E. and B.I. Miller. 1964. *Atlantic Hurricanes*. Louisiana State U. Press, 326 pp.

Dunnington, E.A., Jr. 1956. Blue crabs observed to dig soft shell clams for food. Maryland Tidewater News, 12: 1–4.

Dunnington, E.A., Jr. 1968. Survival time of oysters after burial at various temperatures. Proc. Nat. Shellfisheries Assoc., 58: 101–103.

Dunnington, E.A., Jr., K. Leum and D. MacGregor. 1970. Ability of buried oysters to clear sediment from the shell margin. Proc. Nat. Shellfisheries Assoc. for 1969, 60: Abstract.

Eales, N.B. 1921. *Aplysia*, Liverpool Mar. Biol. Committee. Proc. Trans. Liverpool Biol. Soc., L.M.B.C. Mem. Vol. 35, 24: 183–266.

Earle, S.A. 1969. Phaeophyta of the eastern Gulf of Mexico. Phycologia, 7: 71–254.

Ebbs, N.K., Jr. 1966. The coral-inhabiting polychaetes of the northern Florida reef tract. Part 1, Aphroditidae, Polynoidae, Amphinomidae, Eunicidae, and Lysaretidae. Bull. Mar. Sci., 16: 485–555.

Ebert, T.A. 1977. An experimental analysis of sea urchin dynamics and community interactions on a rock jetty. J. Exp. Mar. Biol. Ecol., 27: 1–22.

Edwards, A.L. and C.M. Humphrey. 1981. An electrophoretic and morphological survey of *Busycon* occurring in Wassaw Sound, Georgia. Nautilus, 95: 144–150.

Edwards, G.A. and L. Irving. 1943. The influence of temperature and season upon the oxygen consumption of the sa crab, *Emerita talpoida* Say. J. Cellular & Comp. Physiol., 21: 169–182.

Edwards, G.S. 1971. *Geology of the West Flower Garden Bank*. Texas A&M Sea Grant Publ., TAMU-SG-71-215, 199 pp.

Edwards, P. 1969. Field and cultural studies on the seasonal periodicity of growth and reproduction of selected Texas benthic marine algae. Contr. Mar. Sci., 14: 59–114.

Edwards, P. 1976. *Illustrated Guide to the Seaweeds and*

Sea Grasses in the vicinity of Port Aransas, Texas. Contr. Mar. Sci., 15: Suppl., Reprint, 1976, Austin, U. Texas Press, 131 pp.

Edwards, P. and D.F. Kapraun. 1973. Benthic marine algal ecology in the Port Aransas, Texas area. Contrib. Mar. Sci., 17: 15–52.

Efford, I.E. 1967. The antennule cleaning setae in the sand crab, *Emerita* (Decapoda, Hippidae). Crustaceana, 16: 302–310.

Ekdale, A.A. 1974. Marine molluscs from shallow-water environments (0 to 60 meters) off the northeast coast, Mexico. Bull. Mar. Sci., 24: 638–688.

Engle, J.B. 1948. Investigations of the oyster reefs of Mississippi, Louisiana and Alabama following the hurricane of September 19, 1947. U.S. Fish & Wildlife Ser., Spec. Sci. Rep., 59: 1–70 pp.

Fairchild, R.R. and L.O. Sorensen. 1985. Sea urchins from the Brazos-Santiago Pass jetty, South padre Island, Texas. Texas J. Sci., 37: 383–385.

Fales, R.R. 1976. Apparent predation on the mole crab *Emerita talpoida* (Say) by the ghost crab *Ocypode quadrata* (Fabricius). Chesapeake Science, 17: 65.

Falkowski, P.G., Z. Dubinsky, L. Muscatine and J.W. Porter. 1984. Light and the bioenergetics of a symbiotic coral. Bioscience, 34: 705–709.

Fauchald, K. 1977. *The Polychaete Worms, Definitions and Keys to the Orders, Families and Genera.* Nat. Hist. Mus. Los Angeles, Co., Sci. Ser., 28: 1–190.

Fauchald, K. and P.A. Jumars. 1979. The diet of worms: A study of polychaete feeding guilds. Oceanogr. Mar. Biol. Ann. Rev., 17: 193–284.

Felder, D.L. 1971. The decapod crustaceans of Seven and One-Half Fathom Reef. M.S. Thesis, Texas A&I U., Kingsville, 110 pp.

Felder, D.L. 1973a. *An annotated key to the crabs and lobsters (Decapoda, Reptantia) from coastal waters of the northwestern Gulf of Mexico.* Louisiana State U. Sea Grant Publ. LSU-SG-73-02, 103 pp.

Felder, D.L. 1973b. A record of *Pinnixa lunzi* Glassell (Decapoda: Pinnotheridae) from off the coast of Texas, U.S.A. Crustaceana, 24: 148–149.

Felder, D.L. 1978. Osmotic and ionic regulation in several western Atlantic Callianassidae (Crustacea, Decapoda, Thalassinidea). Biol. Bull., 154: 409–429.

Felder, D.L. 1979. Respiratory adaptations of the estuarine mud shrimp, *Callianassa jamaicense* (Schmitt, 1935) (Crustacea, Decapoda, Thalassinidea). Biol. Bull., 157: 125–137.

Felder, D.L. 1982a. Life histories of the snapping shrimps *Synalpheus fritzmuelleri* and *S. apioceros* (Crustacea:Decapoda:Alpheidae) on a sublittoral reef off Texas. In: Chapman, B.R. and J.W. Tunnell, Jr. (Eds.), *South Texas Fauna: A Symposium Honoring Dr. Allan H. Chaney.* Texas A&I U., Kingsville, pp. 57–63.

Felder, D.L. 1982b. Reproduction of the snapping shrimps *Synalpheus fritzmuelleri* and *S. apioceros* (Crustacea:Decapoda:Alpheidae) on a sublittoral reef off Texas. J. Crustacean Biol., 2: 535–543.

Felder, D.L. and A.H. Chaney. 1979. Decapod crustacean fauna of Seven and One-Half Fathom Reef, Texas: species composition, abundance, and species diversity. Contrib. Mar. Sci., 22: 1–29.

Felder, J.M., D.L. Felder and S.C. Hand. 1986. Ontogeny

of Osmoregulation in the estuarine ghost shrimp *Callianassa jamaicense* var. *louisianensis* Schmitt (Decapoda, Thalassinidea). J. Exp. Mar. Biol. Ecol., 99: 91–105.

Ferguson Wood, E.J. 1963. A study of the diatom flora of fresh sediments of the south Texas bays and adjacent waters. Publ. Inst. Mar. Sci., 9: 237–310.

Fimpel, V.E. 1975. Phanome der Landadaptation bei terrestrichen und semiterrestrischen Brachyura der brasilianischen Kuste (Malacostraca: Decapoda). Zool. Jb. Syst., 102: 173–214.

Finley, R.J. 1979. Landsat analysis of the Texas coastal zone. Bur. Econ. Geol., U. Texas, Rep. Inv., 93: 71 pp.

Fish, C.J. 1925. Seasonal distribution of the plankton of the Woods Hole region. Bull. U.S. Bur. Fish., 41: 91–78.

Fisher, J.J. 1968. Barrier island formation: discussion. Geol. Soc. Amer. Bull., 79: 1421–1425.

Fisk, H.N. 1959. Padre Island and the Laguna Madre flats, coastal south Texas. Louisiana State U., 2nd Coastal Geogr. Conf., April 6–9, 1959, pp. 103–151.

Fleming, L.E. 1969. Use of male genitalic details as taxonomic characters in some species of *Palaemonetes* (Decapoda:Palaemonidae). Proc. Biol. Soc. Washington, 82: 443–452.

Flower, F.B. and J.J. McDermott. 1953. Observations on the occurrence of the oyster crab, *Pinnotheres ostreum* as related to the oyster damage in Delaware Bay. Proc. Nat. Shellfisheries Assoc. for 1952: 44–50.

Flury, F. 1915. Uber das Aplysiengift. Nauym Schiedebergs Archiv Exp. Pathol. Pharmakol., 79: 250–263.

Forbes, E. 1841. *History of British Starfishes.* John van Voorst, London.

Fotheringham, N. 1975. Structure of seasonal migrations of the littoral hermit crab *Clibanarius vittatus.* J. Exp. Mar. Biol. Ecol., 18: 47–53.

Fotheringham, N. 1976a. Population consequences of shell utilization by hermit crabs. Ecology, 57: 570–578.

Fotheringham, N. 1976b. Effects of shell stress on the growth of hermit crabs. J. Exp. Mar. Biol. Ecol., 23: 299–305.

Fotheringham, N. 1976c. Hermit crab shells as a limiting resource (Decapoda: Paguridea). Crustaceana, 31: 193–199.

Fotheringham, N. 1980. *Beachcomber's Guide to Gulf Coast Marine Life.* Lone Star Books, Houston, Texas, 124 pp.

Fotheringham, N. and S. Brunenmeister. 1975. *Common Marine Invertebrates of the Northwestern Gulf Coast.* Gulf Publishing Co., Houston, 197 pp.

Fox, W.T. and R.A. Davis, Jr. 1976. Weather patterns and coastal processes. In: Davis, R.A., Jr. and R.L. Ethington (Eds.), *Beach and Nearshore Sedimentation* Soc. Econ. Paleont. Mineral., Spec. Publ. 24: 1–23.

Frankenberg, D. and A.S. Leiper. 1977. Seasonal cycles in benthic communities of the Georgia continental shelf. In: Coull, B.C. (Ed.) Ecology of marine benthos, Belle W. Baruch Library in Marine Science 6, Univ. S. Carolina Press, Columbia, pp. 383–397.

Franzisket, L. 1970. The atrophy of hermatypic reef corals maintained in darkness and their subsequent regeneration in light. Int. Revue Ges. Hydrobiol., 55: 1–12.

Fraser, T.H. 1967. Contributions to the biology of *Tagelus divisus* (Tellinacea: Pelecypoda) in Biscayne Bay,

Florida. Bull. Mar. Sci., 17: 111–132.

Freudenthal, H.D. 1962: *Symbiodinium* gen. nov. and *Symbiodinium microadriaticum* sp. nov., a zooxanthella: taxonomy, life cycle and morphology. J. Protozool., 9: 45–52.

Fuls, G.E. 1974. Further ecological studies on the macroichthyofauna of the Laguna Salada, Texas. MS Thesis, Texas A&I U., Kingsville, 106 pp.

Fuss, C.M. 1964. Observations on burrowing behavior of the pink shrimp, *Penaeus duorarum* Burkenroad. Bull. Mar. Sci., 14: 62–73.

Fuss, C.M., Jr. and L.H. Ogren. 1966. Factors affecting the activity and burrowing habits of the pink shrimp *Penaeus duorarum* Burkenroad. Bull. Mar. Sci. Gulf Caribbean, 14: 62–73.

Galtsoff, P.S. 1938a. Physiology of reproduction of *Ostrea virginica*. I. Spawning reactions of the female and male. Biol. Bull., 74: 461–486.

Galtsoff, P.S. 1938b. Physiology of reproduction of *Ostrea virginica*. II. Stimulation of spawning in the female oyster. Biol. Bull., 75: 286–307.

Galtsoff, P.S. 1940. Physiology of reproduction of *Ostrea virginica*. III. Stimulation of spawning in the male oyster. Biol. Bull., 78: 117–135.

Galtsoff, P.S. 1964. The American oyster, *Crassostrea virginica* (Gmelin). U.S. Fish. Bull., 64: 1–480.

Galtsoff, P.S. and R.H. Luce. 1930. Oyster investigations in Georgia. U.S. Bur. Fisheries, Report of the Commissioner of Fisheries for fiscal year 1930, Appendix 5 (Document 1077), pp. 61–100.

Galtsoff, P.S. and A.S. Merrill. 1962. Notes on shell morphology, growth and, distribution of *Ostrea equestris* Say. Bull. Mar. Sci. Gulf & Caribbean, 12: 234–244.

Gardiner, J.S. 1903. *The Fauna and Geography of the Maldive and Laccadive Archipelagoes, Vol. 1*. University Press, Cambridge, 471 pp.

Garton, D. and W.B. Sickle. 1980. Effects of salinity and temperature on the predation rate of *Thais haemastoma* on *Crassostrea virginica* spat. Biol. Bull., 158: 49–57.

George, R.Y. and P.J. Thomas. 1979. Biofouling community dynamics in the Louisiana shelf oil platforms in the Gulf of Mexico. Rice U. Studies, 65: 553–574.

Getty, T. and B.A. Hazlett. 1978. Decorator behavior in *Microphrys bicornutus* (Latreille 1825) (Decapoda, Brachyura). Crustaceana, 34: 105–108.

Gifford, C.A. 1962. Some observations on the general biology of the land crab, *Cardisoma guanhumi* (Latreille), in south Florida. Biol. Bull., 123: 207–223.

Gillard, R.M. 1969. An ecological study of an oyster population including selected associated organisms in West Bay, Galveston, Texas. M.S. Thesis, Texas A&M U., College Station, 136 pp.

Gillespie, T.S. 1976. The flowering plants of Mustang Island, Texas-An annotated checklist. Texas J. Sci., 27: 131–148.

Gittings, S.R., G.D. Dennis and H.W. Harry. 1986. Annotated guide to the barnacles of the northern Gulf of Mexico. Texas A&M University Sea Grant Program, TAMU-S6-86-402, 36 pp.

Gladfelter, E.H. 1985. Metabolism, calcification and carbon production. II. Organism-level studies. Proc. Fifth International Coral Reef Congress, Tahiti, 4: 527–542.

Goerke, H. 1971. Die Ernaehrunsweise der *Nereis* Arten (Polychaeta, Nereidae) der deutschen Kuesten. Veroff Inst. Meeresforsch Bremerhaven, 13: 1–50.

Golley, F., H.T. Odum and R.F. Wilson. 1962. The structure of a Puerto Rican red mangrove forest in May. Ecology, 43: 9–19.

Gordon, C.M., 1969. The apparent influence of salinity on the distribution of barnacle species in Chesapeake Bay. Crustaceana, 16: 139–142.

Gore, R.H. 1966. Observations on the escape response in *Nassarius vibex* (Say) (Mollusca:Gastropoda). Bull. Mar. Sci., 16: 423–434.

Gore, R.H. 1974. On a small collection of porcellanid crabs from the Caribbean Sea (Crustacea: Decapoda: Anomura). Bull. Mar. Sci., 24: 700–721.

Goreau, T.J. 1977. Coral skeletal chemistry. Physiological and environmental regulation of stable isotopes and trace metals in *Montastrea annularis*. Proc. Roy. Soc. London, B, 196: 291–315.

Grassle, J.F. and J.P. Grassle. 1974. Opportunistic life histories and genetic systems in marine benthic polychaetes. J. Mar. Res., 32: 253–284.

Grassle, J.F. and J.P. Grassle. 1976. Sibling species in the marine pollution indicator *Capitella* (Polychaeta). Science, 192: 567–569.

Grave, B.H. 1911. Anatomy and physiology of the wing-shell, *Atrina rigida*. Bull. Bur. Fish. Wash., 29: 409–439.

Grave, B.H. 1933. Rate of growth, age at sexual maturity, and duration of life of certain sessile organisms at Woods Hole, Massachusetts. Biol. Bull., 65: 375–386.

Gray, I.E. 1957. A comparative study of the gill area of crabs. Biol. Bull., 112: 34–42.

Gray, I.E. 1961. Changes in abundance of the commensal crabs of *Chaetopterus*. Biol. Bull., 120: 353–359.

Grimm, D.E. and T.S. Hopkins. 1977. Preliminary characterization of the octocorallian and scleractinian diversity at the Florida Middle Ground. Proc. 3rd International Coral Reef Symp., U. Miami, 1: 135–141.

Grinnell, R.S. 1971. Structure and development of oyster reefs on the Suwannee River Delta, Florida. Ph.D. Dissertation, State U. N.Y., Binghamton, 186 pp.

Gundlach, E.R., K.J. Finkelstein and J.L. Sadd. 1981. Impact and persistence of IXTOC-1 oil on the south Texas coast. In: Parrotte, R.B. (Ed.) *Proc., 1981 Oil Spill Conference*, Amer. Petrol. Inst. Publ. 4334, Washington, D.C., pp. 477–485.

Gunter, G. 1942. Seasonal condition in Texas oysters. Proc. Trans. Texas Acad. Sci., 25: 89–93.

Gunter, G. 1945. Studies on marine fishes of Texas. Publ. Inst. Mar. Sci., 1: 1–190.

Gunter, G. 1950. Seasonal population changes of certain invertebrates of the Texas coast, including the commercial shrimp. Publ. Inst. Mar. Sci., 1: 7–51.

Gunter, G. 1951. The species of oyster in the Gulf, Caribbean and West Indian region. Bull. Mar. Sci. Gulf and Caribbean, 1: 40–45.

Gunter, G. 1953. The relationship of the Bonnet Carre Spillway to oyster beds in Mississippi Sound and the "Louisiana Marsh," with a report on the 1950 opening. Publ. Inst. Mar. Sci., 3: 17–71.

Gunter, G. 1955. Mortality of oysters and abundance of certain associates as related to salinity. Ecology, 36: 601–605.

Gunter, G. 1972. Use of dead reef shell and its relation to estuarine conservation. Trans. 37th N.A. Wildlife & Nat. Res. Conf., Wildlife Management Inst., Washington, D.C., pp. 110–121.

Gunter, G. 1975. An example of oyster production decline with a change in the salinity characteristics of an estuary, Delaware Bay 1800–1973 (Abst.) Proc. Nat. Shellfisheries Assoc., 65: 3.

Gunter, G. 1979a. Studies of the southern oyster borer. Gulf Res. Rpts., 6: 249–260.

Gunter, G. 1979b. The grit principle and the morphology of oyster reefs. Proc. National Shellfisheries Assoc., 69: 1–5.

Gunter, G. and H.H. Hildebrand. 1954. The relation of total rainfall to the state and catch of marine shrimp (*Penaeus setiferus*) in Texas waters. Bull. Mar. Sci. Gulf Caribbean, 4: 95–103.

Gutsell, J.S. 1928. The spider crab, *Libinia dubia*, and the jelly-fish, *Stomolophus meleagris*, found associated at Beaufort, North Carolina. Ecology, 9: 358–359.

Gutsell, J.S. 1930. Natural history of the bay scallop. Bull. U.S. Bur. Fish., 46: 569–632.

Haley, S.R. 1972. Reproductive cycling in the ghost crab, *Ocypode quadrata* (Fabr.) (Brachyura: Ocypodidae). Crustaceana, 23: 1–11.

Hall, J.R. 1973. Intraspecific trail-following in the marsh periwinkle *Littorina irrorata* Say. Veliger, 16: 72–75.

Hamilton, C.L. and G.E. Saul. 1984. Texas commercial harvest statistics, 1977–1983. Texas Parks & Wildlife, Manag. Data Ser., 64: 66 pp.

Hamilton, P.V., R.T. Nishimoto and J.G. Halusky. 1976. Cheliped laterality in *Callinectes sapidus* (Crustacea: Portunidae). Biol. Bull., 150: 393–401.

Hamilton, P.V., B.J. Russell and H.W. Ambrose. 1982. Some characteristics of a spring incursion of *Aplysia brasiliana* into shallow water. Malacol. Rev., 15: 15–19.

Hamilton, P.V. 1976. Predation on *Littorina irrorata* (Mollusca: Gastropoda) by *Callinectes sapidus* (Crustacea: Portunidae). Bull. Mar. Sci., 26: 403–409.

Harris, R.R. 1977. Urine production rate and water balance in the terrestrial crabs *Gecarcinus lateralis* and *Cardisoma guanhumi*. J. Exp. Biol., 68: 57–67.

Harry, H.W. 1966. Studies on bivalve molluscs of the genus *Crassinella* in the northwestern Gulf of Mexico: anatomy, ecology and systematics. Publ. Inst. Mar. Sci., 11: 65–69.

Harry, H.W. 1969. Anatomical notes on the mactrid bivalve *Raeta plicatella* Lamarck, 1818, with a review of the genus *Raeta* and related genera. Veliger, 12: 1–23.

Harry, H.W. 1981. Nominal species of living oysters proposed during the last fifty years. Veliger, 24: 39–44.

Hartman, O. 1951. The littoral marine annelids of the Gulf of Mexico. Publ. Inst. Mar. Sci., 2: 7–124.

Hartman, R.L. and J. Smith. 1973. A floristic and ecological study of Matagorda Island. In: *Matagorda Island: A Natural Area Survey*. LBJ School of Public Affairs, U. Texas, Austin, TX, pp. 116–145.

Harvey, E.B. 1956. *The American Arbacia and Other Sea Urchins*. Princeton U. Press, Princeton, N.J., 298 pp.

Hausman, S.A. 1932. A contribution to the ecology of the salt marsh snail, *Melampus bidentatus*. Say. Amer. Nat., 66: 541–545.

Hausman, S.A. 1936. Food and feeding activities of the salt marsh snail, *Melampus bidentatus*. Anat. Rec., 67: 127.

Haven, D.S. 1959. Effects of pea crabs, *Pinnotheres ostreum*, on oysters, *Crassostrea virginica*. Proc. Nat. Shellfisheries Assoc., 49: 77–86.

Haven, D.S. and R. Morales-Alamo. 1966. Aspects of biodeposition by oysters and other invertebrate filter feeders. Limnol. Oceanogr., 11: 487–498.

Haven, D.S., W.J. Hargis, Jr., and P.C. Kendall. 1978. The oyster industry of Virginia : Its status, problems and promise. VIMS Special Papers in Mar. Sci. No. 4, Virginia Inst. Mar. Sci., Gloucester Point, Virginia, 1024 pp.

Hay, W.P. and C.A. Shore. 1918. The decapod crustaceans of Beaufort, N.C., and surrounding region. Bull. U.S. Bur. Fish., 35: 369–475.

Hayes, M.O. 1967. Hurricanes as geological agents: Case studies of hurricanes Carla, 1961 and Cindy, 1963. Bur. Econ. Geol., U. Texas, Rept. Invg., 61: 56 pp.

Heald, E.J. 1971. The production of organic detritus in a south Florida estuary. U. Miami Sea Grant Tech. Bull. 6: 110 pp.

Heard, R.W. 1979. Notes on the genus *Probythinella* Thiele, 1928 (Gastropoda: Hydrobiidae) in the coastal waters of the northern Gulf of Mexico and the taxonomic status of *Vioscalba louisianae* Morrison, 1965. Gulf Res. Rept., 6: 309–312.

Heard, R.W. 1982a. *Guide to Common Tidal Marsh Invertebrates of the Northeastern Gulf of Mexico*. Mississippi-Alabama Sea Grant Consortium MASGP-79-004: 82 pp.

Heard, R.W. 1982b. Observations on the food and food habits of clapper rails (*Rallus longirostris* Boddaert) from tidal marshes along the east and Gulf coasts of the United States. Gulf Res. Repts., 7: 125–135.

Hedgpeth, J.W. 1947. The Laguna Madre of Texas. Trans. 12th North American Wildlife Conference: 367–380.

Hedgpeth, J.W. 1950. Notes on the marine invertebrate fauna of salt flat areas in Aransas National Wildlife Refuge, Texas. Publ. Inst. Mar. Sci., 1: 103–109.

Hedgpeth, J.W. 1953. An introduction to the zoogeography of the northwestern Gulf of Mexico with reference to the invertebrate fauna. Pub. Inst. Mar. Sci., 3: 107–224.

Hedgpeth, J.W. 1957. Marine Biogeography. In: Hedgpeth, J.W. (Ed.), *Treatise on Marine Ecology and Paleoecology*. Geol. Soc. Amer. Mem. 67, Vol. 1, *Ecology*: pp. 359–382.

Hedgpeth, J.W. 1959. Some preliminary considerations of the biology of inland mineral waters. Archo Oceanogr. Limnol., 11 (Suppl.) 11–141.

Hedgpeth, J.W. 1967. Ecological aspects of the Laguna Madre, a hypersaline estuary. In: Lauff, G.H. (Ed.) *Estuaries* Amer. Assoc. Adv. Sci., Publ. 83: pp. 408–419.

Hellier, T.R., Jr. 1962. Fish production and biomass studies in relation to photosynthesis in the Laguna Madre of Texas. Publ. Inst. Mar. Sci., 8: 1–22.

Henning, H.G. 1975. Okologische, ethologische, und sinnesphysiologische untersuchungen an der landkrabbe *Cardisoma guanhumi* Latreille (Decapoda: Brachyura) in Nordkolumbein. Forma et Functio, 8: 253–304.

Henry, C.A. 1976. The commensal clam, *Paramys subo-*

vata (Bivalvia: Myidae) and *Thalassema hartmani* (Echiuroidea) off Galveston, Texas. Nautilus, 90: 73–74.

Herman, S.S., J.A. Mihursky and A.J. McErlean. 1968. Zooplankton and environmental characteristics of the Patuxent River estuary 1963–1965. Chesapeake Sci., 9: 67–82.

Herreid, C.F. 1963. Observations on the feeding behavior of *Cardisoma guanhumi* (Latreille) in southern Florida. Crustaceana, 5: 176–180.

Herreid, C.F. and C.A. Gifford. 1963. The burrow habitat of the land crab, *Cardisoma guanhumi* (Latreille). Ecology, 44: 773–775.

Herrnkind, W.F. 1972. Orientation of shore-living arthropods, especially the sand fiddler crab. pp. 1–59. In: H.E. Winn and B.L. Olla (Eds.), *Behavior of Marine Invertebrates. Vol. I, Invertebrates.* Plenum Press.

Hidu, H. 1969. Gregarious setting in the American oyster *Crassostrea virginica* Gmelin. Chesapeake Sci., 10: 85–92.

Highsmith, R.C., A.C. Riggs and C.M. D'Antonio. 1980. Survival of hurricane-generated coral fragments and a disturbance model of reef calcification/growth rates. Oecologia, 46: 322–329.

Hildebrand, H.H. 1954. A study of the fauna of the brown shrimp grounds in the western Gulf of Mexico. Publ. Inst. Mar. Sci., 3: 225–366.

Hildebrand, H.H. 1955. A study of the fauna of the pink shrimp grounds in the western Gulf of Mexico. Publ. Inst. Mar. Sci., 4: 171–232.

Hildebrand, H.H. 1958. Estudios biologicos preliminares sobre la Laguna Madre de Tamaulipas. Ciencia (Mexico), 17: 151–173.

Hildebrand, H.H. and G. Gunter. 1953. Correlation of rainfall with Texas catch of white shrimp, *Penaeus setiferus* (Linneaus). Trans. Amer. Fisheries Soc., 82: 151–155.

Hill, G.W. and R.E. Hunter, 1973. Burrows of the ghost crab, *Ocypode quadrata* (Fabricius) on the barrier islands, south-central Texas coast. J. Sed. Petrol., 43: 24–30.

Hill, G.W. and R.E. Hunter. 1976. Interaction of biological and geological processes in the beach and nearshore environments, northern Padre Island, Texas. Soc. Econ. Paleontol. Mineralog., Special Publ., 24: 169–187.

Hinsch, G.W. 1968. Reproductive behavior in the spider crab, *Libinia emarginata*. Biol. Bull., 135: 273–278.

Hoese, H.D. and R.S. Jones. 1963. Seasonality of larger animals in a Texas turtle grass community. Publ. Inst. Mar. Sci., 9: 37–47.

Hoese, H.D. and R.H. Moore, 1977. *Fishes of the Gulf of Mexico, Texas, Louisiana, and Adjacent Waters.* Texas A&M U. Press, College Station, 327 pp.

Hofstetter, R.P. 1977. Trends in population levels of the American oyster *Crassostrea virginica* Gmelin on public reefs in Galveston Bay, Texas. Texas Parks & Wildlife Dept. Tech. Ser., 24: 90 pp.

Hofstetter, R.P. 1983. Oyster population trends in Galveston Bay, 1973–1978. Texas Parks & Wildlife, Management Data Ser., 51: 33 pp.

Holthuis, L.B. 1952. A general revision of the Palaemonidae (Crustacea Decapoda Natantia) of the Americas. II. The subfamily Palaemoninae. Allan Hancock Foundation Publications. Occ. Papers, 12: 1–396 + 55 plates.

Hopkins, A.E. 1931. Factors influencing the spawning and setting of oysters in Galveston Bay, Texas. U.S. Bur. Fisheries, Bull. 3(47): 57–83.

Hopkins, S.H. 1947. The nemertean *Carcinonemertes* as an indicator of the spawning history of the host, *Callinectes sapidus*. J. Parasitol., 33: 146–150.

Hopkins, S.H. 1978. An oyster family tree: the ancestry of *Crassostrea virginica*. Proc. Nat. Shellfisheries Assoc., 68: 81–82.

Hopkins, T.S., D.R. Blizzard and D.K. Gilbert. 1977. The molluscan fauna of the Florida Middle Ground with comments on its zoogeographical affinities. Northeast Gulf Science, 1: 39–47.

Houbrick, R.S. 1974. The genus *Cerithium* in the western Atlantic. Johnsonia, 5: 33–84.

Houbrick, R.S. 1981. Anatomy of *Diastoma melanoides* (Reeve, 1849) with remarks on the systematic position of the family Diastomatidae (Prosobranchia: Gastropoda). Proc. Biol. Soc. Washington, 94: 598–621.

Houbrick, R.S. 1987. Anatomy, reproductive biology, and phylogeny of the Planaxidae (Cerithiacea: Prosobranchia). Smithsonian Contrib. to Zool., 445: 57 pp.

Howard, G.K. and H.C. Scott. 1959. Predaceous feeding in two common gooseneck barnacles. Science, 129: 717–718.

Howells, H.H. 1942. The structure and function of the alimentary canal of *Aplysia punctata*. Quart. J. Microsc. Sci., 83: 357–397.

Hoyt, J.H. 1967. Barrier island formation. Geol. Soc. Amer. Bull., 78: 1125–1135.

Hoyt, J.H. 1968a. Barrier island formation: Reply. Geol. Soc. Amer. Bull., 79: 947.

Hoyt, J.H. 1968b. Barrier island formation: Reply. Geol. Soc. Amer. Bull., 79: 1427–1431.

Hoyt, J.H. 1970. Development and migration of barrier islands, northern Gulf of Mexico: Discussion. Geol. Soc. Amer. Bull., 81: 3779–3782.

Hsiao, S.C. 1950. Effects of silt upon *Ostrea virginica*. Proc. Hawaiian Acad. Sci., 25: 8–9.

Hubbard, G.F. 1977. A quantitative analysis of benthic polychaetous annelids from the northwestern Gulf of Mexico. M.S. Thesis, Texas A&M U., College Station, 85 pp.

Hughes, D.A. 1973. On mating and the "copulation burrows" of crabs of the genus *Ocypode* (Decapoda: Brachyura). Crustaceana, 24: 72–76.

Hulings, N.C. 1955. An investigation of the benthic invertebrate fauna from the shallow waters of the Texas coast. Master's Thesis, Texas Christian University, Ft. Worth, 87 pp.

Hulings, N.C. and D.W. Hemlay. 1963. An investigation of the feeding habits of two species of sea stars. Bull. Mar. Sci., 13: 354–359.

Humm, H.J. and R.L. Caylor. 1957. The summer marine flora of Mississippi Sound. Publ. Inst. Mar. Sci., 4: 228–264.

Humm, H.J. and R.M. Darnell. 1959. A collection of marine algae from the Chandeleur Islands. Publ. Inst. Mar. Sci., 6: 265–276.

Humm, H.J. and H.H. Hildebrand, 1962. Marine algae from the Gulf coast of Texas and Mexico. Publ. Inst. Mar. Sci., 8: 227–268.

Huntsman, A.G. 1918. The vertical distribution of certain intertidal animals. Trans. Roy. Soc. Canada, 12: 53–60.

Hurlbert, S.H., W. Loayza and T. Moreno. 1986. Fish-flamingo-plankton interactions in the Peruvian Andes. Limnol. Oceanogr., 31(3): 457–468.

Hurst, A. 1965. The feeding habits of *Nassarius vibex* (Say). Proc. Malacol, Soc. London, 36: 313–317.

Hutchings, P. and P. Saenger. 1987. *Ecology of Mangroves*. U. Queensland Press, St. Lucia, Queensland, Australia, 388 pp.

Hyman, L.H. 1940. The polyclad flatworms of the Atlantic coast of the United States and Canada. Proc. U.S. Natl. Mus., 89: 449–495.

Hyman, L.H. 1967. *The Invertebrates. Volume VI. Mollusca I.* McGraw-Hill, New York, 792 pp.

Idyll, C.P., D.C. Tabb and B. Yokel. 1967. The value of estuaries to shrimp. Proc. Symp. Marsh and Estuary-management. Baton Rouge, Louisiana, pp. 83–90.

Ingle, J.C. 1966. *The Movement of Beach Sand*, Vol. 5, Developments in Sedimentology, Elsevier, Amsterdam, 221 pp.

Ingle, R.M. 1952. Studies on the effect of dredging operations upon fish and shellfish. Tech. Ser. 5, Florida St. Board Conservation, Tallahassee.

Ingle, R.M. and C.E. Dawson, Jr. 1952. Growth of American oysters in Florida waters. Bull. Mar. Sci. Gulf & Caribbean, 2: 393–404.

Irvine, G.V. 1973. The effects of selective feeding by two species of sea urchins on the structure of algal communities. Master's Thesis, U. Washington.

Jachowski, R.L. 1974. Agnostic behaviour of the blue crab, *Callinectes sapidus* Rathbun. Behav., 50: 232–253.

Jaims, K.E.P. 1968. Contribucion al Conocimiento de la Sistematica y Distribucion de las Familias Corycacidae y Sapphirinidae (Crustacea, Copepoda), en la Zona Arrecifal de Veracruz. Thesis, U. Nacional Autonoma de Mexico, Dept. Biol, 225 pp.

Jenkin, P.M. 1957. The filter feeding and food of flamingoes (Phoenicopteri). Phil. Trans. Royal Soc. London, Ser. B, 240: 401–493.

Jenner, C.E. 1977. Sex identification, sex ratio and social structure in the thalassinid shrimp, *Upogebia affinis*. Abstracts of papers contributed at the Western Soc. Naturalists meeting, 1977, 9.

Jenner, C.E. and A.B. McCrary. 1970. *Paramya subovata*, a commensal with the echiuroid *Thalassema hartmani*. Ann. Rept. Amer. Malacol. Union, 1969, p. 42.

Jensen, D. 1974. Primary production and chlorophyll standing crop in a disturbed hypersaline bay and two shrimp mariculture ponds. MS Thesis, Texas A&I U., Kingsville, 82 pp.

Jernakoff, P. 1985. An experimental evaluation of the influence of barnacles, crevices and seasonal patterns of grazing on the algal diversity and cover in an intertidal barnacle zone. J. Exp. Mar. Biol. Ecol., 88: 287–302.

Johannes, R.E. and M. Satomi. 1966. Composition and nutritive value of fecal pellets of a marine crustacean. Limnol. Oceanogr., 11: 191–197.

John, D.M. and W. Pople. 1973. The fish grazing of rocky shore algae in the Gulf of Guinea. J. Exp. Mar. Biol. Ecol., 11: 81–90.

Johns, D.M. and W.H. Lang. 1977. Larval development of the spider crab *Libinia emarginata* (Majidae). Fishery Bull., 75: 831–841.

Johnson, J.K. 1972. Effect of turbidity on the rate of filtration and growth of the slipper limpet, *Crepidula fornicata* Lamarck, 1799. Veliger, 14: 315–320.

Jones, A.C., D.E. Dimitriou, J.J. Ewald and J.H. Tweedy. 1970. Distribution of early distributional stages of pink shrimp, *Penaeus duorarum*, in Florida waters. Bull. Mar. Sci., 20: 634–661.

Jones, E.C. 1968. *Lepas anserifera* Linne (Cirripedia: Lepadomorpha) feeding on fish and *Physalia*. Crustaceana, 14: 312–313.

Jones, M.L. 1963. Four new species of *Magelona* (Annelida, Polychaeta) and a redescription of *Magelona longicornis* Johnson. Amer. Mus. Novit., 2164: 1–31.

Jorden, T.E. and I. Valiela. 1982. A nitrogen budget of the ribbed mussel, *Geukensia demissa*, and its significance in nitrogen flow in a New England salt marsh. Limnol. Oceanogr., 27: 75–90.

Joyce, E.A., Jr. 1972. A partial bibliography of oysters, with annotations. State of Florida, Dept. Natural Resources, Special Sci. Rep., 34, 846 pp.

Judd, F.W. 1976a. Demography of a barrier island population of the keeled earless lizard, *Holbrookia propinqua*. Occ. Papers Mus. Texas Tech. U., 44: 1–45.

Judd, F.W. 1976b. Food and feeding behavior of the keeled earless lizard, *Holbrookia propinqua*. Southwestern Nat., 21: 17–25.

Judd, F.W., R.I. Lonard, and S.L. Sides. 1977. The vegetation of South Padre Island, Texas in relation to topography. Southwestern Nat., 22: 31–48.

Kaestner, A. 1970. *Invertebrate Zoology, Volume 3. Crustacea*. Interscience Publishers, New York, 521 pp.

Kalke, R.D., T.W. Duke and R.W. Flint. 1982. Weathered IXTOC-1 effects on estuarine benthos. Estuarine Coastal & Shelf Sci., 15: 75–84.

Kandel, E.R. 1979. *Behavioral Biology of Aplysia*. W.H. Freeman Co., San Francisco, 463 pp.

Kanwisher, J.W. 1955. Freezing in intertidal animals. Biol. Bull., 109: 56–63.

Kapraun, D.F. 1970. Field and cultural studies of *Ulva* and *Enteromorpha* in the vicinity of Port Aransas, Texas. Contrib. Mar. Sci., 15: 205–285.

Kapraun, D.F. 1974. Seasonal periodicity and spatial distribution of benthic marine algae in Louisiana. Contrib. Mar. Sci., 18: 139–167.

Kapraun, D.F. 1979. The genus *Polysiphonia* (Ceramiales, Rhodophyta) in the vicinity of Port Aransas, Texas. Contrib. Mar. Sci., 22: 105–120.

Kapraun, D.F. 1980. Summer aspect of algal zonation on a Texas jetty in relation to wave exposure. Contrib. Mar. Sci., 23: 101–109.

Keith, D.E. 1969. Aspects of feeding in *Caprella californica* Stimpson and *Caprella equilibra* Say (Amphipoda). Crustaceana, 16: 119–124.

Keith, D.E. 1986. Shallow-water and terrestrial brachyuran crabs of Roatan and the Swan Islands, Honduras. Sarsia, 70: 251–278.

Keith, D.E. and N.C. Hulings. 1965. A quantitative study of selected nearshore infauna between Sabine Pass and Bolivar Point, Texas. Publ. Inst. Mar. Sci., 10: 33–40.

Kellogg, R.B. and J.S. Patton. 1983. Lipid droplets, medium of energy exchange in the symbiotic anemone *Condylactis gigantea*: a model coral polyp. Mar. Biol., 75: 137–149.

Kennedy, F.S., J.J. Crane, R.A. Schlieder and D.G. Barber. 1977. Studies of the rock shrimp, *Sicyonia brevirostris*, a new fishery resource on Florida's Atlantic shelf. Florida Mar. Res. Publ., 27: 69 pp.

Kennedy, V.S. and J.A. Mihursky. 1971. Upper temperature tolerances of some estuarine bivalves. Chesapeake Sci., 12: 193–204.

Kent, B.W. 1983a. Patterns of coexistence in busyconine whelks. J. Exp. Mar. Biol. Ecol., 66: 257–283.

Kent, B.W. 1983b. Natural history observations on the busyconine whelks *Busycon contrarium* (Conrad) and *Busycotypus spiratum* (Lamarck). J. Moll. Stud., 49: 37–42.

Khlebovich, V.V. 1969. Some peculiar features of the hydrochemical regime and the fauna of mesohaline waters. Mar. Biol., 2: 47–49.

King, B.D. III. 1971. Study of migratory patterns of fish and shellfish through a natural pass. Texas Parks and Wildlife Dept., Tech. Ser. 9: 54 pp.

King, C.A.M. 1959. *Beaches and Coasts*. Edward Arnold Publishers, London, 403 pp.

King, K.A. and E.L. Flickinger. 1977. The decline of brown pelicans on the Louisiana and Texas Gulf coast. Southwestern Nat., 21: 417–431.

Kinne, O. 1971. Salinity: Animals: Invertebrates. In: Kinne, O. (ed.), *Marine Ecology*, Volume 1, Environmental Factors, Part 2. New York, John Wiley and Sons, pp. 820–995.

Klawe, W.L. and L.M. Dickie. 1957. Biology of the bloodworm, *Glycera dibranchiata* Ehlers and its relation to the bloodworm fishery of the Maritime Provinces. Bull. Fish. Res. Bd. Canada, 115: 1–37.

Knowlton, R.E. 1965. Effects of some environmental factors on the larval development of *Palaemonetes vulgaris* (Say). J. Elisha Mitchell Sci. Soc., 81: 87.

Knowlton, R.E. 1974. Larval developmental processes and controlling factors in decapod Crustacea, with emphasis on Caridea. Thalassia Jugoslavica, 10: 138–158.

Kool, S.P. 1987. Significance of radular characters in reconstruction in thaidid phylogeny (Neogastropoda: Muricacea). Nautilus, 101: 117–132.

Kool, S.P. 1988. Aspects of the anatomy of *Plicopurpura patula* (Prosobranchia: Muricoidea: Thaidinae), new combination, with emphasis on the reproductive system. Malacologia,—: in press.

Kornicker, L.S. 1961. Observations on the behavior of the littoral gastropod *Terebra salleana*. Ecology, 42: 207.

Kornicker, L.S. F. Bonet, and R. Cann. 1959. Alacran Reef, Campeche Bank, Mexico. Publ. Inst. Mar. Sci., 6: 1–22.

Krantz, G.E. and D.W. Meritt, 1977. An analysis of trends in oyster spat set in the Maryland portion of the Chesapeake Bay. Proc. Nat. Shellfisheries Assoc., 67: 53–59.

Kriegstein, A.R., V. Castellucci and E.R. Kandel. 1974. Metamorphosis of *Aplysia californica* in laboratory culture. Proc. Nat. Acad. Sci., 71: 3654–3658.

Kropp, R.K. and R.B. Manning. 1985. Cryptochiridae, the correct name for the family containing the gall crabs (Crustacea: Decapoda: Brachyura). Proc. Biol. Soc. Washington, 98: 954–955.

Kropp, R.K. and R.B. Manning. 1987. The Atlantic gall crabs, Family Cryptochiridae (Crustacea: Decapoda: Brachyura). Smithsonian Contrib. Zool., 462: 21 pp.

Kruczynski, W.L. 1971. Relationship of the pea crab, *Pinnotheres maculatus* (Say), with the scallops, *Argopecten irradians concentricus* (Say) and *Argopecten gibbus* (Linne). Ph.D. Dissertation, U. North Carolina, Chapel Hill, 120 pp.

Kruczynski, W.L. 1972. The effect of the pea crab, *Pinnotheres maculatus* Say, on growth of the bay scallop, *Argopecten irradians concentricus* (Say). Chesapeake Sci., 13: 218–220.

Kruczynski, W.L. 1975. A radioactive tracer study of food uptake by *Pinnotheres maculatus* in molluscan hosts. Biol. Bull., 148: 60–67.

Krull, R.M. 1976. The small fish fauna of a disturbed hypersaline environment. MS Thesis, Texas A&I U., Kingsville, 112 pp.

Kudenov, J.D. 1974. The reproductive biology of *Eurythoe complanata* (Pallas, 1766) (Polychaeta: Amphinomidae). Ph.D. Dissertation, U. Arizona, Tucson, 154 pp.

Kudenov, J.D. 1977. The functional morphology in three species of maldanid polychaetes. Zool. J. Linn. Soc., 60: 95–109.

Kuenzler, E.J. 1961a. Structure and energy flow of a mussel population in a Georgia salt marsh. Limnol. Oceanogr., 6: 191–204.

Kuenzler, E.J. 1961b. Phosphorus budget of a mussel population. Limnol. Oceanogr., 6: 400–415.

Kuhlmann, D.H.H. 1975. Charakterisierung der Korallenriffe vor Veracruz, Mexiko. Int. Revue ges. Hydrobiol., 60: 495–521.

Ladd, H.S. 1951. Brackish water and marine assemblages of the Texas coast with special reference to mollusks. Publ. Inst. Mar. Sci., 2: 125–164.

Lawrence, J.M. 1975. On the relationship between marine plants and sea urchins. Oceanogr. Mar. Biol. Ann. Rev., 13: 213–286.

LeBlanc, R.J. and W.D. Hodgson. 1959. Origin and development of the Texas shoreline. Gulf Coast Assoc. Geol. Soc. Trans., 9: 197–220.

Leipper, D.F. 1954. Marine meterology of the Gulf of Mexico. In: *Gulf of Mexico, Its Origin, Waters and Marine Life*. U.S. Fish & Wildlife Serv., Fish. Bull., 55 (89): 89–98.

Lent, C.M. 1969. Adaptation of the ribbed mussel, *Modiolus demissus* (Dillwyn), to the intertidal habitat. Amer. Zool., 9: 283–292.

Lessios, H.A., D.R. Robertson and J.D. Cubit. 1984. Spread of *Diadema* mass mortality through the Caribbean. Science, 226: 335–337.

Levine, N.D. 1978. *Perkinsus* gen. n. and other new taxa in the protozoan phylum Apicomplexa. J. Parasitol., 64: 549.

Lewis, D.H. and D.C. Smith. 1971. The autotrophic nutrition of symbiotic marine coelenterates with special reference to hermatypic corals. I. Movement of photosynthetic products between the symbiots. Proc. Roy. Soc. London, Ser. B, 109: 377–401.

Lewis, H. 1972. Notes on the genus *Distorsio* (Cymatiidae) with descriptions of new species. Nautilus, 86: 27–50.

Lewis, J.B. 1960. The fauna of the rocky shores of Barbados, West Indies. Canadian J. Zool., 38: 391–435.

Lewis, J.R. 1964. *The Ecology of Rocky Shores*. English Universities Press, London, 323 pp.

Lewy Z. and C. Samtleben. 1979. Functional morphology and palaeontological significance of the conchiolin layers in corbulid pelecypods. Lethaia, 12: 341–351.

Lindner, M.J. and H.L. Cook, 1970. Synopsis of biological data on the white shrimp *Penaeus setiferus* (Linnaeus) 1767. FAO Fish. Rep., 57: 1439–1469.

Linnaeus, C. (Linne) 1758. *Systema naturae per regna tria naturae*. Vol. 1. *Regnum animale*. 10th Ed. Stockholm.

Lipka, D.A. 1974. Mollusks. In: Bright, T.J. and L.H. Pequegnat, Eds. *Biota of the West Flower Garden Bank*, Gulf Publishing Co., Houston, pp. 141–198.

Lizama, J. and R.S. Blanquet. 1975. Predation on sea anemones by the amphinomid polychaete *Hermodice carunculata*. Bull. Mar. Sci., 25: 442–443.

Loeblich, A.R. and J.L. Shirley, 1979. Observations on the theca of the motile phase of free-living and symbiotic isolates of *Zooxanthella microadriatica* (Freudenthal) comb. nov. J. Mar. Biol. Assoc. U.K., 59: 195–205.

Loesch, H.C. 1957. Studies of the ecology of two species of *Donax* on Mustang Island, Texas. Publ. Inst. Mar. Sci., 4: 201–227.

Logan, B.W., 1969. Carbonate sediments and reefs, Yucatan Shelf, Mexico: Part 2, Coral Reefs and Banks, Yucatan Shelf, Mexico (Yucatan Reef Unit). Amer. Assoc. Petroleum Geol., Mem., 11: 129–198.

Logan, B.W., J.L. Harding, W.M. Ahr, J.D. Williams and R.G. Snead., 1969. Carbonate sediments and reefs, Yucatan Shelf, Mexico: Part 1, Late Quaternary carbonates of Yucatan Shelf, Mexico. Amer. Assoc. Petroleum Geol., Mem., 11: 5–128.

Lonard, R.I. and F.W. Judd. 1980. Phytogeography of south Padre Island, Texas. Southwestern Nat., 25: 313–322.

Lonard, R.I., F.W. Judd and S.L. Sides. 1978. Annotated checklist of the flowering plants of south Padre Island, Texas. Southwestern Nat., 23: 497–510.

Loosanoff, V.L. 1948. Gonad development and spawning of oysters (*O. virginica*) in low salinities. Anat. Rec., 101: 55.

Loosanoff, V.L. 1950. On behavior of oysters transferred from low to high salinities. Anat. Rec., 108: 579.

Loosanoff, V.L. 1953. Behavior of oysters in water of low salinities. Proc. National Shellfisheries Assoc. for 1952: 135–151.

Loosanoff, V.L. and J.B. Engle. 1942. Accumulation and discharge of spawn by oysters living at different depths. Biol. Bull., 82: 413–422.

Lowe, G.C. and E.R. Cox. 1978. Species composition and seasonal periodicity of marine benthic algae of Galveston Island, Texas. Contrib. Mar. Sci., 21: 9–24.

Lubchenco, J. and S.D. Gaines. 1981. A unified approach to marine plant-herbivore interactions. I. Populations and communities. Ann. Rev. Ecol. Syst., 12: 405–437.

Lubchenco, J. and B.A. Menge. 1978. Community development and persistence in a low rocky intertidal zone. Ecol. Monogr., 48: 67–94.

Luckens, P.A. 1974. Removal of intertidal algae by herbivores in experimental frames and on shores near Auckland, New Zealand. N.Z. J. Mar. Freshwater Res., 8: 637–654.

Ludwick, J. C. and W. R. Walton. 1957. Shelf-edge, calcareous prominences in northeastern Gulf of Mexico. Bull. Amer. Assoc. Petrol. Geol., 41: 2054–2101.

Lund, E.J. 1957a. A quantitative study of clearance of a turbid medium and feeding by the oyster. Publ. Inst. Mar. Sci., 4: 296–312.

Lund, E.J. 1957b. Self-silting, survival of the oyster as a closed system, and reducing tendencies of the environment of the oyster. Publ. Inst. Mar. Sci., 4: 313–319.

Lynch, S.A. 1954. Geology of the Gulf of Mexico. In: *Gulf of Mexico, Its Origin, Waters and Marine Life*. U.S. Fish & Wildlife Serv., Fish. Bull., 55 (89): 67–86.

Lyons, W.G. 1970. Scyllarid lobsters (Crustacea, Decapoda). Mem. Hourglass Cruises, 1: 1–74.

Mace, D.S. and L. McGraw, 1985. A conformation of the occurrence of *Uca minax* LeConte (Ocypodidae) in Texas. Southwestern Nat., 30: 148.

Macias, G.G. 1968. Contribucion al conocimiento de la systematica y ecologia de las esponjas del Arrecife la Blanquilla, Veracruz, Ver. Thesis, U. Nacional Autonoma de Mexico, Dept. Biol., 102 pp.

Mackin, J.G. 1951. Histopathology of infections of *Crassostrea virginica* (Gmelin) by *Dermocystidium marinum*, Mackin, Owen and Collier. Bull Mar. Sci. Gulf and Caribbean, 1: 72–87.

Mackin, J.G. 1961. Oyster disease caused by *Dermocystidium marinum* and other microorganisms in Louisiana. Publ. Inst. Mar. Sci., 7: 132–299.

Mackin, J.G. 1971. A study of the effect of oil field brine effluents on biotic communities in Texas estuaries. Texas A&M U. Res. Foundation Repts., Project 735: 72 pp.

MacGinitie, G.E. 1934. The egg-laying activities of the sea hare, *Tethys californicus* (Cooper). Biol. Bull., 67: 300–303.

MacGinitie, G.E. 1939. The method of feeding in *Chaetopterus*. Biol. Bull., 77: 115–118.

Magalhaes, H. 1948. An ecological study of snails of the genus *Busycon* at Beaufort, North Carolina. Ecol. Monogr., 18: 377–409.

Mangum, C.P. 1964. Studies on speciation in maldanid polychaetes of the North American Atlantic coast. II. Distribution and competitive interaction of five sympatric species. Limnol. Oceanogr., 9: 12–26.

Mangum, C.P., S.L. Santos and W. R. Rhodes, Jr. 1968. Distribution and feeding in the onuphid polychaete *Diopatra cuprea* (Bosc). Mar. Biol., 2: 33–40.

Manning, J.H. and H.H. Whaley. 1955. Distribution of oyster larvae and spat in relation to some environmental factors in a tidal estuary. Proc. Nat. Shellfisheries Assoc. for 1954: 56–65.

Manning, R.B. 1969. *Stomatopod Crustacea of the Western Atlantic*. U. Miami Press, 380 pp.

Manning, R.B. 1987. Notes on western Atlantic Callianassidae (Crustacea: Decapoda: Thalassinidea). Proc. Biol. Soc. Washington, 100: 386–401.

Manning, R.B. and D.L. Felder. 1986. The status of the callianassid genus *Callichirus* Stimpson, 1866 (Crustacea: Decapoda: Thalassinidea). Proc. Biol. Soc. Washington, 99: 437–443.

Marcus, E. 1961. Opisthobranchs from North Carolina. J. Elisha Mitchell Sci. Soc., 77: 141–151.

Marsden, J.R. 1962. A coral-eating polychaete. Nature, 193: 598.

Marsden, J.R. 1963a. The digestive tract of *Hermodice carunculata* (Pallas). Polychaeta: Amphinomidae. Canadian J. Zool., 41: 165–184.

Marsden, J.R. 1963b. A preliminary report on the digestive enzymes of *Hermodice carunculata*. Canadian J. Zool., 41: 159–164.

Marshall, N. 1954a. Changes in the physiography of oyster bars in the James River, Virginia. Virginia J. Sci., 5: 173–181.

Marshall, N. 1954b. Factors controlling the distribution of oysters in a neutral estuary. Ecology, 35: 322–327.

Mattison, G.C. 1948. Bottom configuration in the Gulf of Mexico. J. Coast & Geod. Survey, 1: 78–82.

May, E.B. and D.G. Bland. 1970. Survival of young oysters in areas of different salinity in Mobile Bay. Proc. S.E. Assoc. Game & Fish Comm., 23: 519–521.

May, E.S. 1972. The effect of floodwater on oysters in Mobile Bay. Proc. Nat. Shellfisheries Assoc., 62: 67–71.

May, V.I. Bennett and T.E. Thompson. 1970. Herbivore-algal relationships on a coastal rock platform (Cape Banks, N.S.W.). Oecologia, 6: 1–14.

McCarty, D.M. 1974. Polychaetes of Seven and One-Half Fathom Reef. M.S. Thesis, Texas A&I U., Kingsville, 213 pp.

McDermott, J.J. 1963. The occurrence of *Pinnixa cylindrica* (Crustacea, Pinnotheridae) in the tubes of the lug worm *Arenicola cristata*. Proc. Pennsylvania Acad. Sci., 36: 53–57.

McDermott, J.J. 1976. Observations on food and feeding behavior of estuarine nemertean worms belonging to the order Hoplonemertea. Biol. Bull., 150: 57–68.

McDougall, K.D. 1943. Sessile marine invertebrates of Beaufort, North Carolina. Ecol. Monogr., 13: 321–374.

McFarland, W.N. and B.D. Lee. 1963. Osmotic and ionic concentrations of penaeidean shrimps of the Texas coast. Bull. Mar. Sci., 13: 391–417.

McGowan, J.A. and R.A. Morton, 1977. Sampling, preliminary analysis and mapping of Texas bays and inner continental shelf, December 1975 through August 1977. Bureau Econ. Geol, U. Texas, Austin, Rep.

McKinney, L.D. 1977. The origin and distribution of shallow water gammaridean Amphipoda in the Gulf of Mexico and Caribbean Sea with notes on their ecology. Ph.D. Dissertation, Texas A&M U., College Station, 401 pp.

McMillan, C. 1971. Environmental factors affecting seedling establishment of the black mangrove on the central Texas coast. Ecology, 52: 927–930.

McMillan, C. 1975. Adaptive differentiation to chilling in mangrove populations. In: Proc. International Symp. Biol. and Management of Mangroves. Vol. I. U. Florida, Gainesville, pp. 62–68.

McMahon, R.F. and C. McMahon. 1983. Leaping and swimming as predator escape responses in the jack-knife clam, *Ensis minor* (Bivalvia: Pharellidae). Nautilus, 97: 55–58.

McMahon, R.F. and W.D. Russell-Hunter. 1981. The effects of physical variables and acclimation on survival and oxygen consumption in the high littoral salt-marsh snail, *Melampus bidentatus* Say. Biol. Bull., 161: 246–269.

Medcof, J.C. 1955. Day and night characteristics of spatfall and of behavior of oyster larvae. J. Fish. Res. Res. Bd. Canada, 12: 270–286.

Melville, R.V. 1976. Opinion 1057. *Donax variabilis* Schumacher, 1817 (Mollusca:Bivalvia) suppressed under the plenary powers; type species designated for *Latona* Schumacher, 1817. Bull. Zool. Nomencl., 33: 19–31.

Menzel, R.W. 1955. Some phases of the biology of *Ostrea equestris* Say and a comparison with *Crassostrea virginica* (Gmelin). Publ. Inst. Mar. Sci., 4: 69–153.

Menzel, R.W. 1956. Some additional differences between *Crassostrea virginica* and *Ostrea equestris* in the Gulf of Mexico. Proc. Nat. Shellfisheries Assoc., 46: 76–82.

Menzel, R. and S.H. Hopkins. 1956. Crabs as predators of oysters in Louisiana. Proc. Nat. Shellfisheries Assoc., 46: 177–184.

Menzel, R.W., N.C. Hulings and R.R. Hathaway. 1966. Oyster abundance in Apalachicola Bay, Florida in relation to biotic associations influenced by salinity and other factors. Gulf Res. Repts., 2: 73–96.

Menzel, R.W. and F.E. Nichy. 1958. Studies of the distribution and feeding habits of some oyster predators in Alligator Harbor, Florida. Bull. Mar. Sci. Gulf and Caribbean, 8: 125–145.

Menzies, R.J. 1957. The marine borer family Limnoriidae (Crustacea:Isopoda). Bull. Mar. Sci., 7: 101–200.

Miller, R.L. and J.M. Zeigler. 1958. A model relating dynamics and sediment pattern in equilibrium in the region of shoaling waves, breaker zone and foreshore. J.Geol., 66: 417–441.

Mollick, R.S. 1973. Some aspects of the biology of *Terebra dislocata* Say 1822 (Gastropoda: Prosobranchia). Veliger, 16: 82–84.

Monod, T. 1956. Hippidea et Brachyura ouest-africains. Mem. Inst. Franc. Afr., 45: 1–674.

Montgomery, W.L. and S.D. Gerking. 1980. Marine microalgae as foods for fishes: an evaluation of potential food quality. Env. Biol. Fish., 5: 143–153.

Moore, H.B. and A.C. Frue. 1959. The settlement and growth of *Balanus improvisus*, *B. eburneus* and *B. amphitrite* in the Miami area. Bull. Mar. Sci., 9: 421–440.

Moore, H.B. and N.N. Lopez. 1969. The ecology of *Chione cancellata*. Bull. Mar. Sci., 19: 131–148.

Moore, H.B. and N.N. Lopez. 1970. A contribution to the ecology of the lamellibranch *Dosina elegans*. Bull. Mar. Sci., 20: 980–987.

More, W.R. 1969. A contribution to the biology of the blue crab, *Callinectes sapidus* (Rathbun) in Texas with a description of the fishery. Texas Parks and Wildlife, Tech. Ser., 1: 31 pp.

Morrison, J.P.E. 1971. Western Atlantic *Donax*. Proc. Biol. Soc. Washington, 83: 545–568.

Morton, B. 1978. Feeding and digestion in shipworms. Oceanogr. Mar. Biol. Ann. Rev., 16: 107–144.

Morton, B. 1983a. Mangrove bivalves. In: Russell-Hunter, W.D. (Ed.) *The Mollusca. Vol. 6. Ecology.* Academic Press, N.Y., pp. 77–138.

Morton, B. 1983b. Coral associated bivalves of the Indo-Pacific. In: Russell-Hunter, W.D. (Ed.) *The Mollusca. Vol. 6. Ecology.* Academic Press, N.Y., pp. 139–224.

Morton, B. 1988. Corals and their bivalve borers—the evolution of a symbiosis. In: *The Bivalvia: Proceedings of a Symposium in Memory of Sir Charles Maurice Yonge, Edinburgh, Scotland, 1986.* (Ed., B. Morton).

Morton B. and P.J.B. Scott. 1988. Evidence for chemical boring in *Petricola lapicida* (Gmelin, 1791) (Bivalvia: Petricolidae). J. Molluscan Stud., 54: 231–237.

Morton, R.A. 1974. Shoreline changes on Galveston Island (Bolivar Roads to San Luis Pass). An analysis of historical changes of the Texas Gulf shoreline. Bur. Econ. Geol. U. Texas, Geol. Circular 74–2, 34 pp.

Morton, R.A. 1975. Shoreline changes between Sabine Pass and Bolivar Roads. An analysis of historical changes of the Texas Gulf shoreline. Bur. Econ. Geol. U. Texas, Geol. Circular 75–6, 43 pp.

Morton, R.A. and M.J. Pieper, 1975a. Shoreline changes on Brazos Island and south Padre Island (Mansfield Channel to the mouth of the Rio Grande). An analysis of historical changes of the Texas Gulf shoreline. Bur. Econ. Geol. U. Texas, Geol. Circular 75–2, 38 pp.

Morton, R.A. and M.J. Pieper, 1975b. Shoreline changes in the vicinity of the Brazos River delta (San Luis Pass to Brown Cedar Cut). An analysis of historical changes of the Texas Gulf shoreline. Bur. Econ. Geol. U. Texas, Geol. Circular 75–4, 47 pp.

Morton, R.A. and M.J. Pieper, 1976. Shoreline changes on Matagorda Island and San Jose Island (Pass Cavallo to Aransas Pass). An analysis of historical changes of the Texas Gulf shoreline. Bur. Econ. Geol. U. Texas, Geol. Circular 76–4, 42 pp.

Morton, R.A. and M.J. Pieper, 1977a. Shoreline changes on Mustang Island and north Padre Island (Aransas Pass to Yarborough Pass). An analysis of historical changes of the Texas Gulf shoreline. Bur. Econ. Geol. U. Texas, Geol. Circular 77–1, 45 pp.

Morton, R.A. and M.J. Pieper, 1977b. Shoreline changes on central Padre Island (Yarborough Pass to Mansfield Channel). An analysis of historical changes of the Texas Gulf shoreline. Bur. Econ. Geol. U. Texas, Geol. Circular 77–2, 35 pp.

Morton, R.A., M.J. Pieper, and McGowen, J.A. 1976. Shoreline changes on Matagorda Peninsula (Brown Cedar Cut to Pass Cavallo). An analysis of historical changes of the Texas Gulf shoreline. Bur. Econ. Geol. U. Texas, Geol. Circular 76–6, 37 pp.

Mosher, C. 1954. Observations on the spawning and early larval development of the sargassum fish, *Histrio histrio* (Linnaeus). Zoologica, 39: 141–152 + 3 pl.

Murdy, E.O. 1983. *Saltwater Fishes of Texas.* Texas A&M U. Sea Grant College Program, College Station, 220 pp.

Murray, S.P. 1970. Bottom currents near the coast during Hurricane Camille. J. Geophy. Res., 75: 4579–4582.

Muscatine, L. 1973. Nutrition of corals. In: Jones, O.A. and R. Endean (Eds.) *Biology and Geology of Coral Reefs, Vol. 2, Biology 1.* Academic Press, N.Y., pp. 77–116.

Muscatine, L. 1974. Endosymbiosis of cnidarians and algae. In: Muscatine, L. and H.M. Lenhoff (Eds.), *Coelenterate Biology.* Academic Press, N.Y., 501 pp.

Muscatine, L., L.R. McCloskey and R.E. Marian. 1981. Estimating the daily contribution of carbon from zooxanthellae to animal respiration. Limnol. Oceanogr., 26: 601–611.

Muscatine, L., R.R. Pool and R.K. Trench. 1975. Symbiosis of algae and invertebrates: aspects of the symbiont surface and the host-symbiont interface. Trans. Amer. Micro. Soc., 94: 450–469.

Myers, A.C. 1972. Tube-worm sediment relationships of *Diopatra cuprea.* Mar. Biol., 17: 350–356.

Nagabhushanam, R. 1961. Tolerance of the prawn, *Palaemonetes vulgaris* (Say), to waters of low salinity. Sci. & Culture, 27: 43.

Naylor, E. and M.J. Isaac. 1973. Behavioural significance of pressure responses in megalopa larvae of *Callinectes sapidus* and *Macropipus* sp. Mar. Behav. & Physiol., 1: 341–350.

Nelson, T.C. 1928. On the distribution of critical temperatures for spawning and for ciliary activity in bivalve molluscs. Science, 67: 220–221.

Neu, W. 1932. Wie schwimmt *Aplysia depilans* L. Z. Vg. Physiol., 18: 244–254.

Neumann, A.C. 1966. Observations on coastal erosion in Bermuda and measurements of the boring rate of the sponge *Cliona lampa.* Limnol. Oceanogr., 11: 92–108.

Neumann, C.J. and M.J. Pryslak. 1981. Frequency and motion of Atlantic tropical cyclones. NOAA Tech. Rep., NWS, 26: 7 pp. + A1-A57 pp.

Newell, R.C. 1979. *Biology of Intertidal Animals, 3rd Ed.* Marine Ecological Surveys, Ltd., Faversham, Kent, U.K., 781 pp.

Nienaber, J.A. 1963. Shallow marine sediments offshore from the Brazos River, Texas. Publ. Inst. Mar. Sci., 9: 311–372.

Nolan, B.A. and M. Salmon. 1970. The behavior and ecology of snapping shrimp (Crustacea: *Alpheus heterochaelis* and *Alpheus normanni.* Forma et Functio, 2: 289–335.

Norris, R.M. 1953. Buried oyster reefs in some Texas bays. J. Paleont., 27: 567–576.

Novak, A. and M. Salmon. 1974. *Uca panacea,* a new species of fiddler crab from the Gulf coast of the United States. Proc. Biol. Soc. Washington, 87: 313–326.

Odum, W.E. and E.J. Heald. 1972. Trophic analyses of an estuarine mangrove community. Bull. Mar. Sci., 22: 671–738.

Oler, T.M. 1941. Some notes on the occurrence of a small land crab (*Sesarma cinereum* Bosc) on the Magothy River, Maryland. Maryland Nat. Hist. Soc. Bull., 11: 51–53.

Olsson, A.A. and L.E. Crovo. 1968. Observations on aquarium specimens of *Oliva sayana* Ravenal. Veliger, 11: 31–32.

Oosting, H.J. and W.D. Billings. 1942. Factors affecting vegetational zonation on coastal dunes. Ecology, 23: 131–142.

Oppenheimer, C.H. and K.G. Gordon. 1972. *Texas Coastal Zone Biotopes: An Ecography.* Interim Rep. for the Bay and Estuary Management Program (CRMP). U. Texas Mar. Sci. Inst., Port Aransas, 107 pp.

Ortega, S. 1981. Environmental stress, competition and dominance of *Crassostrea virginica* near Beaufort, North Carolina, USA. Mar. Biol., 62: 47–56.

Orth, R.J. 1977. The importance of sediment stability in sea-grass communities. In: Coull, B.C. (Ed.) *Ecology of Marine Benthos, The Belle W. Baruch Library in Marine Science No. 6.* Univ. S. Carolina Press, Columbia, pp. 281–300.

Osburn, H.R. and M.O. Ferguson. 1987. Trends in finfish landings by sport-boat fishermen in Texas marine waters, May 1974–May 1986. Texas Parks & Wildlife Dept., Manag. Data Ser., 119: 464 pp.

Otvos, E.G. 1970a. Development and migration of barrier islands, northern Gulf of Mexico. Geol. Soc. Amer. Bull., 81: 241–246.

Otvos, E.G. 1970b. Development and migration of barrier islands, northern Gulf of Mexico. Geol. Soc. Amer. Bull., 81: 3783–3788.

Overstreet, R.M. 1978. *Marine Maladies? Worms, Germs and other Symbiots from the northern Gulf of Mexico.* Mississippi-Alabama Sea Grant Consortium (MASGP-78-021), Gulf Coast Res. Lab., Ocean Springs, Miss., 140 pp.

Owen, H.M. and L.L. Walters. 1950. Report of the investigation to determine the effect of the 1950 opening of Bonnet Carre Spillway on Mississippi Sound. Louisiana Conserv., Mar.-Apr., 1950: 16–19, 26–27.

Paine, R.T. 1962. Ecological diversification in sympatric gastropods of the genus *Busycon.* Evolution, 16: 515–523.

Paine, R.T. 1974. Intertidal community structure. Experimental studies on the relationship between a dominant competitor and its principal predator. Oecologia, 15: 92–120.

Palmer, P.G. 1972. A biosystematic study of the virgata group of *Panicum* (Gramineae) in the United States. Ph.D. Dissertation, N. Carolina State U., Raleigh, 63 pp.

Parker, G.H. 1932. On certain feeding habits of the sea urchin *Arbacia.* Amer. Nat., 66: 95–96.

Parker, P.L. 1979. (Ed.) IXTOC-1 chemical characterization and acute biological effects. Report to Environmental Protection Agency and Dept. Transportation, U.S. Coast Guard, Contr. DOT-CG08–8174, U. Texas Mar. Sci. Inst., Port Aransas Mar. Laboratory.

Parker, R.H. 1955. Changes in the invertebrate fauna, apparently attributable to salinity changes, in the bays of central Texas. J. Paleontol., 29: 193–211.

Parker, R.H. 1956. Macro-invertebrate assemblages as indicators of sedimentary environments in east Mississippi Delta region. Bull. Amer. Assoc. Petr. Geol., 40: 295–376.

Parker, R.H. 1959. Macro-invertebrate assemblages of central Texas coastal bays and Laguna Madre. Bull. Amer. Assoc. Petrol. Geol., 43: 2100–2166.

Parker, R.H. 1960. Ecology and distributional patterns of marine macroinvertebrates, northern Gulf of Mexico. In: Shepard, F.P., F.B. Phleger and T.H. van Andel (Eds.) *Recent Sediments Northwest Gulf of Mexico.* Amer. Assoc. Petrol. Geol. Special Publ., Tulsa, Oklahoma, pp. 302–337.

Parker, R.H. 1975. The study of benthic communities. Elsevier Scientific Publ. Co., Elsevier Oceanogr. Series., 9: 279 pp.

Parker, R.H. and J.R. Curray. 1956. Fauna and bathymetry of banks on the continental shelf, Gulf of Mexico. Bull. Amer. Assoc. Petrol. Geol., 40: 2428–2439.

Parr, A.E. 1939. Quantitative observations on the pelagic *Sargassum* vegetation of the western North Atlantic. Bull. Bingham Oceanogr. Coll., 6: 1–94.

Patel, B.S. and D.J. Crisp. 1960. The influence of temperature on the breeding and moulting activities of some warm water species of operculate barnacles. J. Mar. Biol. Assoc. U.K., 39: 667–680.

Patton, J.S., J.F. Battey, M.W. Rigler, J.W. Porter, C.C. Black and J.E. Burris. 1983. A comparison of the metabolism of bicarbonate 14C and acetate 1–14C and the variability of species lipid compositions in reef corals. Mar. Biol., 75: 121–130.

Patton, W.K. 1967a. Studies on *Domecia acanthophora,* a commensal crab from Puerto Rico, with particular reference of the coral host and feeding habits. Biol. Bull., 132: 56–67.

Patton, W.K. 1967b. Commensal Crustacea. Proc. Symp. on Crustacea, Mar. Biol. Assoc. India, 3: 1228–1243.

Patton, W.K. 1972. Studies on the animal symbiots of the gorgonian coral, *Leptogorgia virgulata* (Lamarck). Bull. Mar. Sci., 22: 419–431.

Pearce, J.B. 1964. On reproduction in *Pinnotheres maculatus* (Decapoda: Pinnotheridae). Biol. Bull., 127: 384.

Pearse, A.S. 1929. The ecology of certain estuarine crabs at Beaufort, N.C. J. Elisha Mitchell Sci. Soc., 44: 230–237.

Pearse, A.S. 1945. Ecology of *Upogebia affinis* (Say). Ecology, 26: 303–305.

Pearse, A.S. and G.W. Wharton. 1938. The oyster "leech," *Stylochus inimieus* Palombi, associated with oysters on the coasts of Florida. Ecol. Monogr., 8: 605–655.

Pearse, A.S., H.J. Humm and G.W. Wharton. 1942. Ecology of sand beaches at Beaufort, N.C. Ecol. Monogr., 12: 35–190.

Pearson, J.C. 1948. Fluctuations in the abundance of the blue crab in Chesapeake Bay. U.S. Fish & Wildlife Ser., Res. Rept., 14: 1–26.

Pequegnat, L.H. and J.P. Ray. 1974. Crustaceans and other arthropods. In: Bright, T.J. and L.H. Pequegnat (Eds.), *Biota of the West Flower Garden Bank.* Gulf Publishing Co., Houston, pp. 231–290.

Percy, J.A., F.A. Aldrich and T.R. Marcus. 1971. Influence of environmental factors on respiration of excised tissues of American oysters, *Crassostrea virginica* (Gmelin). Canadian J. Zool., 49: 353–360.

Perkins, F.O. 1976a. *Dermocystidium marinum* infection in oysters. Mar. Fish. Rev., 38: 19–21.

Perkins, F.O. 1976b. Zoospores of the oyster pathogen *Dermocystidium marinum.* I. Fine structure of the conoid and other sporozoan-like organelles. J. Parasitology, 62: 959–974.

Peters, E.C., S.D. Cairns, M.E.Q. Pilson, J.W. Wells, W.C. Jaap, J.C. Lang, C.E. (Cummings) Vasleski, and L. St. Pierre Gollahon. 1988. Nomenclature and biology of *Astrangia poculata* (= *A. danae,* = *A. astreiformis*) (Cnidaria: Anthozoa). Proc. Biol. Soc. Washington, 101: 234–250.

Peterson, C.H., W.G. Ambrose, Jr. and J.H. Hunt. 1982. A field test of the swimming response of the bay scallop (*Argopecten irradians*) to changing biological factors. Bull. Mar. Sci., 32: 939–944.

Phillips, P.J., W.D. Burke and E.J. Kenner. 1969. Observations on the trophic significance of jellyfishes in Mississippi Sound with quantitative data on the associative behavior of small fishes with medusae. Trans. Amer. Fish. Soc., 98: 703–712.

Poggie, J.J. 1963. *Coastal Pioneer Plants and Habitat in*

the Tampico Region, Mexico. Louisiana State U. Press, Baton Rouge, 62 pp.

Pomerat, C.M. and E.R. Reiner. 1942. The influence of surface angle and light on the attachment of barnacles and other sedentary organisms. Biol. Bull., 82: 14–25.

Ponder, W.F. 1985. A review of the genera of the Rissoidae (Mollusca: Mesogastropoda: Rissoacea). Rec. Australian Mus., Suppl. 4: 1–221.

Porrier, M.A. and M.R. Partridge. 1979. The barnacle, *Balanus subalbidus*, as a salinity bioindicator in the oligohaline estuarine zone. Estuaries, 2: 204–206.

Porter, H.W. 1960. Zoeal stages of the stone crab *Menippe mercenaria* Say. Chesapeake Sci., 1: 168–177.

Porter, J.W. 1974. Autotrophy, heterotrophy, and resource partitioning in Caribbean reef-building corals. Amer. Nat., 110: 731–742.

Powell, E.H., Jr. and G. Gunter. 1968. Observations on the stone crab *Menippe mercenaria* Say, in the vicinity of Port Aransas, Texas. Gulf Res. Rep., 2: 285–299.

Powers, L.W. 1977. A catalog and bibliography to the crabs (Brachyura) of the Gulf of Mexico. Contrib. Mar. Sci., Suppl. to Vol. 20, 190 pp.

Price, W.A. 1933. Role of diastrophism in topography of Corpus Christi area, south Texas. Bull. Amer. Assoc. Petrol. Geol., 17: 907–962.

Price, W.A. 1947. Equilibrium of form and forces in tidal basins of coast of Texas and Louisiana. Bull. Amer. Assoc. Petrol. Geol., 31: 1619–1663.

Price, W.A. 1952. Reduction of maintenance by proper orientation of ship channels through tidal inlets. Proc. Second Conf. Coastal Eng., pp. 243–255.

Price, W.A. 1954. Oyster reefs in the Gulf of Mexico. In: *Gulf of Mexico: Its Origin, Waters and Marine Life*, U.S. Fish & Wildlife Serv., Fish. Bull. 55(89): 491.

Price, W.A. 1956. Hurricanes affecting the coast of Texas from Galveston to the Rio Grande. Beach Erosion Board, U.S. Army Corps Eng. Tech. Memo 78.

Price, W.A. 1958. Sedimentology and quaternary geomorphology of south Texas. Gulf Coast Assoc. Geol. Soc. Trans., 39: 4–10.

Price, W.A. and L.S. Kornicker. 1961. Marine and lagoonal deposits in clay dunes, Gulf coast, Texas. J.Sed. Petrol., 31: 245–320.

Pritchard, D.W. 1967. What is an estuary: physical viewpoint. In: Lauff, G.H. (Ed.) *Estuaries*. Publ. 83, AAAS, Washington, D.C., pp. 3–5.

Prytherch, H.F. 1929. Investigation of the physical conditions controlling spawning of oysters and the occurrence, distribution and setting of oyster larvae in Milford, Connecticut. Bull. U.S. Fish., 44: 429–503.

Pulich, W., Jr. 1980. Ecology of a hypersaline lagoon: the Laguna Madre. In: Fore, P.L. and R.D. Peterson (Eds.) *Proc. Gulf of Mexico Coastal Ecosystems Workshop*, U.S. Fish & Wildlife Ser., Albuquerque, N.M., FWS/OBS/80/30, pp. 103–122.

Pulley, T.E. 1979a. The species of *Donax* on the Atlantic and Gulf coasts of North America. Texas Conchologist, 15: 26–35.

Pulley, T.E. 1979b. *Donax* nomenclature. Texas Conchologist, 15: 81.

Rabalais, N.N. 1982. The ascidians of the Aransas Pass Inlet jetties, Port Aransas, Texas. In: Chapman, B.R. and J.W. Tunnell, Jr. (Eds.), *South Texas Fauna: A Symposium Honoring Dr. Allan H. Chaney*, Texas A&I U., Kingsville, pp. 65–74.

Rabalais, N.N. and J.N. Cameron. 1985a. Physiological and morphological adaptations of adult *Uca subcylindrica* to semi-arid environments. Biol. Bull., 168: 135–146.

Rabalais, N.N. and J.N. Cameron. 1985b. The effects of factors important in semi-arid environments on the early development of *Uca subcylindrica*. Biol. Bull., 168: 149–160.

Rabalais, N.N., S.A. Holt and R.W. Flint. 1979. Mud shrimps (Crustacea, Decapoda, Thalassinidea) of the northwestern Gulf of Mexico. Bull. Mar. Sci., 31: 96–115.

Rabalais, S.C., C.R. Arnold and N.S. Wohlschlag. 1981. The effects of IXTOC-1 on the eggs and larvae of red drum (*Sciaenops ocellata*). Texas J. Sci., 33: 33–38.

Rabalais, S.C. and R.W. Flint. 1983. IXTOC I effects of intertidal and subtidal infauna of south Texas Gulf beaches. Contrib. Mar. Sci., 26: 23–35.

Randall, J.E. 1964. Contributions to the biology of the queen conch, *Strombus gigas*. Bull. Mar. Sci., 14: 246–295.

Randall, J.E. 1967. Food habits of reef fishes of the West Indies. Stud. Tropical Oceanography. U. Miami, 5: 665–847.

Randall, J.E. 1968. *Caribbean Reef Fishes*. T.F.H. Publications, Neptune City, N.J., 318 pp.

Rannefeld, J.W. 1972. The stony corals of Enmedio Reef off Veracruz, Mexico. M.S. Thesis, Texas A&M U., College Station, 104 pp.

Rappole, J.H. and G.W. Blacklock. 1985. *Birds of the Texas Coastal Bend: Abundance and Distribution*. Texas A&M Press, College Station, 126 pp.

Ray, D.L. 1958. Recent research on the biology of marine wood borers. Wood Pres. Assoc. Proc., 54: 120–128.

Ray, D.L. 1959a. Nutritional physiology of *Limnoria*. In: Ray, D.L. (Ed.) *Marine Boring and Fouling Organisms*, Friday Harbor Symposia, U. Washington Press, Seattle, pp. 46–61.

Ray, D.L. 1959b. Some properties of cellulase in *Limnoria*. In: Ray, D.L. (Ed.) *Marine Boring and Fouling Organisms*, Friday Harbor Symposia, U. Washington Press, Seattle, pp. 372–386.

Ray, D.L. and J.R. Julian. 1952. Occurrence of cellulase in *Limnoria*. Nature, 169: 32–33.

Ray, S.M. 1952. A culture technique for the diagnosis of infection with *Dermocystidium marinum* Mackin, Owen and Collier in oysters. Science, 116: 360–361.

Ray, S.M. 1966. A review of the culture method for detecting *Dermocystidium marinum* with suggested modifications and precautions. Proc. Nat. Shellfisheries Assoc., 54: 55–70.

Ray, S.M., J.G. Mackin and J.L. Boswell. 1953. Quantitative measurement of effect on oysters of disease caused by *Dermocystidium marinum*. Bull. Mar. Sci. Gulf & Caribbean, 3: 6–33.

Reames, R.C. and A.B. Williams. 1983. Mud crabs of the *Panopeus herbstii* H.M. Edw., s.l., complex in Alabama, U.S.A. Fish. Bull., 81: 885–890.

Reed, J.K., R.H. Gore, L.E. Scotto and K.A. Wilson. 1982. Community composition, structure, areal and trophic relationships of decapods associated with shallow- and deep-water *Oculina varicosa* coral reefs: studies on decapod Crustacea from the Indian River region of Florida, XXIV. Bull. Mar. Sci., 32: 761–786.

Rees, G.H. 1959. Larval development of the sand crab *Emerita talpoida* (Say) in the laboratory. Biol. Bull., 117: 356–370.

Reid, G.K. 1955. A summer study of the biology and ecology of East Bay, Texas. Texas J. Sci., 7: 316–343.

Remane, A. 1934. Die Brackwasserfauna. Verh. dt. Zool. Ges., 36: 34–74.

Rezak, R. and T.J. Bright. 1981. Seafloor instability at East Flower Garden Bank, northwest Gulf of Mexico. Geo-Marine Lett., 1: 97–103.

Rezak, R., T.J. Bright and D.W. McGrail. 1985. *Reefs and Banks of the Northwestern Gulf of Mexico. Their Geological, Biological, and Physical Dynamics*. John Wiley and Sons, N.Y. 259 pp.

Rice, M.E. 1969. Possible boring structures of sipunculids. Amer. Zool., 9: 803–812.

Rickner, J.A. 1975. New records of the porcellanid crab, *Polyonyx gibbesi* Haig, from the Texas coast (Decapoda: Anomura). Crustaceana, 28: 313–314.

Rigby, J.K. and W.G. McIntire. 1966. The Isla de Lobos and associated reefs, Veracruz, Mexico. Brigham Young U. Geol. Stud., 13: 1–46.

Ritchie, T.P. and R.W. Menzel. 1969. Influence of light on larval settlement of American oysters. Proc. Nat. Shellfisheries Assoc., 59: 116–120.

Roberts, T.W. and W.E. Pequegnat. 1970. Deep water decapod shrimps of the family Penaeidae. In: Pequegnat, W.E. and F.A. Chace, Jr. (Eds.), Contributions on the biology of the Gulf of Mexico. Texas A&M U. Oceanogr. Stud., 1: 21–27.

Robertson, P.B. 1963. A survey of the marine rock-boring fauna of southeast Florida. Master's Thesis, U. Miami, 169 pp.

Robertson, R. 1959. Observations on the spawn and veligers of conchs (*Strombus*) in the Bahamas. Proc. Malacol. Soc. London, 33: 164–171.

Robins, C.R., G.C. Ray, J. Douglass and R. Freund. 1986. *A Field Guide to Atlantic Coast Fishes of North America*. Houghton Mifflin Co., Boston, 354 pp.

Rouse, W.L. 1970. Littoral Crustacea from southwest Florida. Quart. J. Florida Acad. Sci., 32: 127–152.

Rudloe, A. 1978. Some ecologically significant aspects of the behavior of the horseshoe crab *Limulus polyphemus*. Ph.D. Dissertation, Florida State U., Tallahassee, 246 pp.

Rudloe, A. and W.F. Herrkind. 1976. Orientation of *Limulus polyphemus* in the vicinity of breeding beaches. Mar. Biol. Behav. Physiol., 4: 75–89.

Rusnak, G.A. 1960. Sediments of Laguna Madre, Texas. In: Shepard, F.P., F.B. Phleger and T.H. van Andel (Eds.) *Recent Sediments Northwest Gulf of Mexico*. Amer. Assoc. Petrol. Geol. Special Publ., Tulsa, Oklahoma, pp. 153–196.

Rutzler, K. 1974. The burrowing sponges of Bermuda. Smithsonian Contrib. Zool., 165: 1–32.

Rutzler, K. and I.G. McIntyre. 1982. *The Atlantic Barrier Reef Ecosystem at Carrie Bow Cay, Belize, I. Structure and Communities*. Smithsonian Inst. Press, Washington, D.C.

Ryan, E.P. 1956. Observations on the life histories and

the distribution of the Xanthidae (mud crabs) of Chesapeake Bay. Amer. Mid. Nat., 56: 138–162.

Ryland, J.S. 1976. Physiology and ecology of marine bryozoans. Adv. Mar. Biol., 14: 285–443.

Salmon, M. 1965. Waving display and sound production in the courtship behavior of *Uca pugilator*, with comparisons to *U. minax* and *U. pugnax*. Zoologica, 50: 123–150.

Salmon, M. 1967. Waving display, sound production and coastal distribution of Florida fiddler crabs. Anim. Behav., 15: 449–459.

Salmon, M. and S.P. Atsaides. 1968. Behavioral, morphological and ecological evidence for two species of fiddler crabs (Genus *Uca*) from the Gulf coast of the United States. Proc. Biol. Soc. Washington, 81: 275–290.

Salmon, M. and J.F. Stout. 1962. Sexual discrimination and sound production in *Uca pugilator* Bosc. Zoologica, 47: 15–21.

Sandifer, P.A. 1973. Distribution and abundance of decapod crustacean larvae in the York River estuary and adjacent lower Cheasapeake Bay, Virginia, 1968–1969. Chesapeake Sci., 14: 235–257.

Sandifer, P.A. 1975. The role of pelagic in recruitment to populations of adult decapod crustacens in the York River estuary and adjacent lower Chesapeake Bay, Virginia. Estuarine and Coastal Mar. Sci., 3: 269–279.

Sandifer, P.A. and W.A. Van Engel. 1971. Larval development of the spider crab, *Libinia dubia* H. Milne Edwards (Brachyura, Majidae, Pisinae), reared in laboratory culture. Chesapeake Sci., 23: 141–151.

Sandoz, M. and S.H. Hopkins. 1947. Early life history of the oyster crab, *Pinnotheres ostreum* (say). Biol. Bull., 93: 250–258.

Sastry, A.N. 1961. Studies on the bay scallop, *Aequipecten irradians concentricus* Say, in Alligator Harbor, Florida. Ph.D. Dissertation, Florida State U., Talahassee.

Sastry, A.N. 1962. Some morphological and ecological differences in two closely related species of scallops, *Aequipecten irradians* and *A. gibbus* from the Gulf of Mexico. Quart. J. Florida Acad. Sci., 25: 89–95.

Sastry, A.N. 1963. Reproduction of the bay scallop, *Aequipecten irradians* Lamarck. Influence of temperature on maturation and spawning. Biol. Bull., 125: 146–153.

Sastry, A.N. and R.W. Menzel. 1962. Influence of hosts on the behavior of the commensal crab *Pinnotheres maculatus* Say. Biol. Bull., 123: 388–395.

Sauer, J.D. 1967. Geographic reconnaissance of seashore vegetation along the Mexican Gulf coast. Louisiana State U. Coastal Stud. Ser., 21: 1–59.

Savage, T. 1971. Mating of the stone crab, *Menippe mercenaria* (Say) (Decapoda: Brachyura). Crustaceana, 20: 315–316.

Scattergood, L.W. 1960. Blue crabs (*Callinectes sapidus*) in Maine. Maine Field Nat., 16: 59–63.

Schafer, R.D. and C.E. Lane. 1957. Some preliminary observations bearing on the nutrition of *Limnoria*. Bull. Mar. Sci., 7: 289–296.

Schein, H. 1977. The role of snapping in *Alpheus heterochaelis* Say, 1818, the big-clawed snapping shrimp. Crustaceana, 33: 182–188.

Schlaepfer, C.J. 1968. Sedimentologia de la Laguna Madre, Tamaulipas. Parte 2. Minerales pesados de los sedimentos de la Laguna Madre, Tamaulipas. U. Nal. Auton. Mexico, Inst. Geol., Bol. 84: 45–66.

Schoenberg, D.A. and R.K. Trench. 1980a. Genetic variation in *Symbiodinium* (= *Gymnodinium*) *microadriaticum* Freudenthal, and specificity in its symbiosis with marine invertebrates. I. Isozyme and soluble protein patterns of axenic cultures of *Symbiodinium microadriaticum*. Proc. Roy. Soc. London, Ser. B, 207: 405–427.

Schoenberg, D.A. and R.K. Trench. 1980b. Genetic variation in *Symbiodinium* (= *Gymnodinium*) *microadriaticum* Freudenthal, and specificity in its symbiosis with marine invertebrates. II. Morphological variation in *Symbiodinium microadriaticum*. Proc. Roy. Soc. London, Ser. B, 207: 429–444.

Schoenberg, D.A. and R.K. Trench. 1980c. Genetic variation in *Symbiodinium* (= *Gymnodinium*) *microadriaticum* Freudenthal, and specificity in its symbiosis with marine invertebrates. III. Specificity and infectivity of *Symbiodinium microadriaticum*. Proc. Roy. Soc. London, Ser. B, 207: 445–460.

Scholander, P.F., L. Van Dam and S.I. Scholander. 1955. Gas exchange in the roots of mangroves. Plant Physiol., 37: 722–729.

Schuhmacher, H. and H. Zibrowius. 1985. What is hermatypic? A redefinition of ecological groups in corals and other organisms. Coral Reefs, 4: 1–9.

Schultz, G.A. 1969. *How to Know the Marine Isopod Crustaceans*. Brown, Dubuque, Iowa, 359 pp.

Schwartz, M.L. 1971. The multiple causality of barrier islands. J. Geol., 79: 91–94.

Scott, P.J.B. 1985. Aspects of living coral associates in Jamaica. Proc. 5th Internat. Coral Reef Cong., Tahiti, 5: 345–350.

Scott, P.J.B. 1988a. Distribution, habitat and morphology of the Caribbean coral- and rock-boring bivalve, *Lithophaga bisulcata* (d'Orbigny) (Mytilidae: Lithophaginae). J. Moll. Stud., 54: 83–95.

Scott, P.J.B. 1988b. Initial settlement, behaviour and survivorship of *Lithophaga bisulcata* (d'Orbigny) (Mytilidae: Lithophaginae). J. Moll. Stud., 54: 97–108.

Sebens, K.P. 1985. The ecology of the rocky subtidal zone. Amer. Sci., 73: 548–557.

Sealey, J.E. and W.M. Ahr. 1975. Quantitative analysis of shoreline change, Sargent Beach, Texas. Texas A&M U. Sea Grant Prog., TAMU-SG-75-209.

Seelig, W.N. and R.M. Sorensen. 1973. Investigation of shoreline changes at Sargent Beach, Texas. Texas A&M U. Sea Grant Prog., TAMU-SG-73-212.

Seiple, W. 1979. Distribution, habitat preferences and breeding periods in the crustaceans *Sesarma cinereum* and *S. reticulatum* (Brachyura: Decapoda: Grapsidae). Mar. Biol., 52: 77–86.

Selander, R., W. Johnson and J. Avise. 1971. Biochemical population genetics of fiddler crabs. Biol Bull., 141: 402.

Selander, R.K., R.F. Johnston, B.J. Wilks and G.G. Raun. 1962. Vertebrates from the barrier islands of Tamaulipas, Mexico. U. Kansas Publ., Mus. Nat. Hist., 12: 309–345.

Sellmer, G.P. 1967. Functional morphology and ecological life history of the gem clam *Gemma gemma* (Eulamellibranchia: Veneridae). Malacologia, 5: 137–223.

Shaw, J.K. and T.S. Hopkins. 1977. The distribution of the family Hapalocarcinidae (Decapoda, Brachyura) on the Florida Middle Ground with a description of *Pseudocryptochirus hypostegus* new species. Proc. 3rd Internat. Coral Reef Symp., Miami, 1: 177–183.

Shaw, W.N. 1967. Seasonal fouling and oyster setting on asbestos plates in Broad Creek, Talbot County, Md., 1963–65. Chesapeake Sci., 8: 228–236.

Shearer, L.W. and C.L. Mackenzie. 1961. The effects of salt solutions of different strengths on oyster enemies. Proc. Nat. Shellfisheries Assoc., 50: 97–104.

Shelton, C.R. and P.B. Robertson. 1981. Community structure of intertidal macrofauna on two surf-exposed Texas sandy beaches. Bull. Mar. Sci., 31: 833–842.

Shepard, F.P. 1960. Rise of sea level along northwest Gulf of Mexico. In: Shepard, F.P., F.B. Phleger and T.H. van Andel (Eds.) *Recent Sediments Northwest Gulf of Mexico*. Amer. Assoc. Petrol. Geol. Special Publ., Tulsa, Oklahoma, pp. 338–344.

Shepard, F.P. and D.G. Moore. 1960. Bays of central Texas coast. In: Shepard, F.P., F.B. Phleger and T.H. van Andel (Eds.) *Recent Sediments Northwest Gulf of Mexico*. Amer. Assoc. Petrol. Geol. Special Publ., Tulsa, Oklahoma, pp. 117–152.

Shepard, F.P. and H.R. Wanless. 1971. *Our Changing Coastlines*. McGraw-Hill, New York, 579 pp.

Sherrod, C.L. and C. McMillan. 1981. Black mangrove, *Avicennia germinans*, in Texas: past and present distribution. Contrib. Mar. Sci., 24: 115–131.

Shirley, T.C. 1974. The echinoderms of Seven and One-Half Fathom Reef. M.S. Thesis, Texas A&I U., Kingsville, 82 pp.

Shirley, T.C. 1982. The importance of echinoderms in the diet of fishes of a sublittoral rock reef. In: Chapman, B.R. and J.W. Tunnell, Jr. (Eds.), *South Texas Fauna: A Symposium Honoring Dr. Allan H. Chaney*, Texas A&I U., Kingsville, pp. 49–55.

Shoup, J.B. 1968. Shell opening by crabs of the genus *Calappa*. Science, 160: 887–888.

Shulman, J. 1968. Fauna associated with pelagic *Sargassum* in the Gulf Stream. Amer. Mid. Nat., 80: 554–558.

Siddall, S.E. 1984a. Synopsis of recent research on the queen conch *Strombus gigas* Linne. J. Shellfish Res., 4: 1–3.

Siddall, S.E. 1984b. Density-dependent levels of activity of juveniles of the queen conch *Strombus gigas* Linne. J. Shellfish Res., 4: 67–74.

Sieling, F.W. 1950. Influence of seasoning and position of oyster shells on oyster setting. Proc. Nat. Shellfisheries Assoc., 41: 57–61.

Simmons, E.G. 1957. An ecological survey of the upper Laguna Madre of Texas. Contrib. Mar. Sci., 4: 156–200.

Smith, F.G.W., R.H. Williams and C.C. Davis. 1950. An ecological survey of the subtropical inshore waters adjacent to Miami. Ecology, 31: 119–146.

Smith, M. 1971. Productivity of marine ponds receiving treated sewage. In: Kuenzler, E.J. and A.F. Chestnut, Optimum ecological designs for estuarine ecosystems in North Carolina, Sea Grant GH103, Proj. UNC-10, Annual Rep. for 1970–71, pp. 24–41.

Smith, N.P. 1974. Intracoastal tides of Corpus Christi Bay. Contrib. Mar. Sci., 18: 205–219.

Smith, N.P. 1975. Seasonal variations in nearshore circulation in the northwest Gulf of Mexico. Contrib. Mar. Sci., 19: 45–65.

Snodgrass, R.E. 1952. The sand crab *Emerita talpoida* (Say) and some of its relatives. Smithsonian Misc. Coll., 117: 1–34.

Sorensen, L.O. 1979. A guide to the seaweeds of South Padre Island, Texas. Gorsuch Scaribrick, 123 pp.

Sorensen, L.O. and J.T. Conover. 1962. Algal mat communities of *Lyngbya confervoides* (C. Agardh) Gomont. Publ. Inst. Mar. Sci., 8: 61–74.

Sousa, W.P. 1979. Experimental investigations of disturbance and ecological succession in a rocky intertidal algal community. Ecol. Monogr., 49: 227–254.

Sousa, W.P. 1985. Disturbance and patch dynamics on rocky shores. In: Pickett, S.T.A. and P.S. White (Eds.) *The Ecology of Natural Disturbance and Patch Dynamics*. Academic Press, N.Y., pp. 101–124.

Sousa, W.P., S.C. Schroeter and S.D. Gaines. 1981. Latitudinal variation in intertidal algal community structure: The influence of grazing and vegetative propogation. Oecologia, 48: 297–307.

Spirito, C.P. 1972. An analysis of swimming behavior in the portunid crab *Callinectes sapidus*. Mar. Behav. Physiol., 1: 261–276.

Spivey, H.R. 1981. Origins, distribution, and zoogeographic affinities of the Cirripedia (Crustacea) of the Gulf of Mexico. J. Biogeogr., 8: 153–176.

Springer, S. and H.R. Bullis. 1954. Exploratory shrimp fishing in the Gulf of Mexico. Summary Report for 1952–54. Commercial Fisheries Rev., 16: 1–16.

Standifer, P.A. 1973. Larvae of the burrowing shrimp, *Upogebia affinis* (Crustacea, Decapoda, Upogebiidae) from Virginia plankton. Chesapeake Sci., 14: 98–104.

Standley, P.C. 1930. Flora of Yucatan. Publ. Field Mus. Nat. Hist., Bot. Ser., 3: 157–492.

Stauber, L.A. 1940. Relation of valve closure to heart beat in the American oyster. Natl. Shellfisheries Assoc., 1940 Convention Papers, 2 pp.

Stauber, L.A. 1945. *Pinnotheres ostreum*, parasitic on the American oyster *Ostrea* (*Gryphaea*) *virginica*. Biol. Bull., 88: 269–291.

Stenzel, H.B. 1971. Oysters. In: Moore, K.C. (Ed.). *Treatise on Invertebrate Paleontology. Part N, Vol. 3 (of 3), Mollusca 6*. Geol. Soc. Amer. and U. Kansas, Boulder, Colorado, pp. N953-N1224.

Stephenson, T.A. and A. Stephenson, 1950. Life between tide marks in North America: Florida Keys. Ecology, 38: 354–402.

Stephenson, T.A. and A. Stephenson. 1952. Life between tide marks in North America: North Florida and the Carolinas. Ecology, 40: 1–49.

Stephenson, T.A. and A. Stephenson. 1972. *Life Between Tide Marks on Rocky Shores*. W.H. Freeman Co., San Francisco, 425 pp.

Sterrer, W.(ed.) 1986. *Marine Fauna and Flora of Bermuda, A Systematic Guide to the Identification of Marine Organisms*. John Wiley & Sons, N.Y., 742 pp.

Stetson, H.C. 1953. The sediments of the western Gulf of Mexico, Part 1. The continental terrace of the western Gulf of Mexico: its surface sediments, origin and development. Papers Phys. Oceanogr. and Meteorol., Massachusetts Inst. Technol. and Woods Hole Oceanogr. Inst., 12: 5–45.

Stevely, J.M. and R.E. Warner. 1978. The biology and utilization of the queen conch *Strombus gigas* L., in the Florida Keys and throughout its geographical range. Rep. Florida Coop. Exten. Ser., Palmetto, FL.

Sverdrup, H.V., M.W. Johnson and R.H. Fleming. 1942. *The Oceans: Their Physics, Chemistry and General Biology*. Prentice-Hall, Englewood Cliffs, New Jersey, 1087 pp.

Sweitzer, N.B. 1898. Origin of the Gulf Stream and circulation of waters in the Gulf of Mexico, with special reference to the effect on jetty construction. Trans. Amer. Soc. Civil Eng., 40: 86–98.

Tagatz, M.E. 1968. Biology of the blue crab, *Callinectes sapidus* Rathbun, in the St. Johns River, Florida. Fish. Bull., 67: 17–33.

Tannehill, I.R. 1956. *Hurricanes* Princeton U. Press, Princeton, N.J., 308 pp.

Taylor, D.L. 1973. The cellular interactions of algal-invertebrate symbiosis. Adv. Mar. Biol., 11: 1–56.

Taylor, W.R. 1936. Notes on algae from the tropical Atlantic Ocean, III. Papers Mich. Acad. Sci. Arts Lett., 21: 199–207.

Taylor, W.R. 1941a. Notes on the marine algae of Texas. Papers Mich. Acad. Sci. Arts Lett., 26: 69–79.

Taylor, W.R. 1941b. Tropical algae of the Arthur Schott Herbarium. Field Mus. Nat. Hist. Publ. 509, Bot. Ser., 20: 87–104.

Taylor, W.R. 1954a. Distribution of marine algae in the Gulf of Mexico. Papers Mich. Acad. Sci. Arts Lett., 39: 85–109.

Taylor, W.R. 1954b. Sketch of the character of the marine algal vegetation of the shores of the Gulf of Mexico. In: *Gulf of Mexico, Its Origins, Waters and Marine Life*. U.S. Fish & Wildlife Ser., Fishery Bull., 55(89):177–192.

Teal, J.M. 1959. Respiration of crabs in Georgia salt marshes and its relation to their ecology. Physiological Zool., 32: 1–14.

Teal, J.M. 1962. Energy flow in the salt marsh ecosystem of Georgia. Ecology, 43: 614–624.

Teerling, J. 1970. The incidence of the ghost crab *Ocypode quadrata* (Fabr.) on the forebeach of Padre Island, and some of its responses to man. M.S. Thesis, Texas A&I U., Kingsville, 71 pp.

Texas Parks and Wildlife Department. 1975. Outdoor Recreation on the Texas Coast. Texas Parks and Wildlife Dept., Austin, 384 pp.

Thayer, P.A., A. LaRocque and J.W. Tunnell, Jr. 1974. Relict lacustrine sediments on the inner continental shelf, southeast Texas. Trans. Gulf Coast Assoc. Geol. Soc., 24: 337–347.

Thebeau, L.C., J.W. Tunnell, Jr. Q.R. Dokken and M.E. Kindinger. 1981. Effects of the IXTOC-1 oil spill on the intertidal and subtidal infaunal populations along lower Texas coast barrier island beaches. In: Parrotte, R.B. (Ed.) *Proc. 1981 Oil Spill Conference*. Amer. Petrol. Inst. Publ. 4334, Washington, D.C., pp. 467–475.

Thompson, D'Arcy. 1947. *A Glossary of Greek Fishes*. Oxford U. Press.

Thorpe, J.H. and D.E. Hoss. 1975. Effects of salinity and cyclic temperature on survival of two sympatric species of grass shrimp (*Palaemonetes*), and their relationship to natural distributions. J. Exp. Mar. Biol. Ecol., 18: 19–28.

Thurman, C.L. 1981. *Uca marguerita*, a new species of fiddler crab (Brachyura: Ocypodidae) from eastern Mexico. Proc. Biol. Soc. Washington, 94: 169–180.

Thurman, C.L. 1984. Ecological notes on fiddler crabs of south Texas, with special reference to *Uca subcylindrica*. J. Crust. Biol., 4: 665–681.

Treece, G.D. 1980. Bathymetric records of marine shelled Mollusca from the northeastern shelf and upper slope of Yucatan, Mexico. Bull. Mar. Sci., 30: 552–570.

Trench, R.K. 1979. The cell biology of plant-animal symbiosis. Ann. Rev. Plant Physiol., 30: 485–531.

Trench, R.K. 1981. Cellular and molecular interactions in symbioses between dinoflagellates and marine invertebrates. Pure and Appl. Chem., 53: 819–835.

Tunnell, J.W., Jr. 1973. Molluscan population of a submerged reef off Padre Island, Texas. Bull. Amer. Malacol. Union for 1972, 38: 25–26.

Tunnell, J.W., Jr. 1974. *Ecological and Geographical Distribution of Mollusca of Lobos and Enemdio Coral Reefs, Southwestern Gulf of Mexico*. Ph.D. Dissertation, Texas A&M U., College Station, 158 pp.

Tunnell, J.W., Jr. 1982. Distribution and habitat of *Discradisca antillarum* (d'Orbigny, 1846) (Brachiopoda: Inarticulata) in the western Gulf of Mexico. In: Chapman, B.R. and J.W. Tunnell, Jr. (Eds.), *South Texas Fauna: A Symposium Honoring Dr. Allan H. Chaney*. Texas A&I U., Kingsville, pp. 37–47.

Tunnell, J.W., Jr. and B.D. Causey. 1969. Vertebrate Pleistocene fossils from the continental shelf, northwest Gulf of Mexico. Bull. Amer. Petrol. Geol., 49: 2428–2439.

Tunnell, J.W., Jr. and A.H. Chaney. 1970. A checklist of the mollusks of Seven and One-Half Fathom Reef, northwestern Gulf of Mexico. Contrib. Mar. Sci., 15: 193–203.

Turner, R.D. 1966. *A Survey and Illustrated Catalogue of the Teredinidae*. Harvard U. Mus. Comp. Zool., Cambridge, Massachusetts, 265 pp.

Turner, R.D. and K.J. Boss. 1962. The genus *Lithophaga* in the western Atlantic. Johnsonia, 4: 81–116.

Underwood, A.J. and P. Jernakopp. 1981. Effects of interactions between algae and grazing gastropods on the structure of a low-shore intertidal algal community. Oecologia, 48: 221–233.

Vadas, R.L. 1977. Preferential feeding-optimization strategy in sea urchins. Ecol. Monogr., 47: 337–372.

van Andel, T.H. 1960. Sources and dispersion of Holocene sediments, northern Gulf of Mexico. In: Shepard, F.P., F.B. Phlegar and T.H. van Andel (Eds.), *Recent Sediments Northwest Gulf of Mexico*. Amer. Assoc. Petrol. Geol. Special Publ., pp. 34–55.

van Andel, T.H. and D.H. Poole. 1960. Sources of Holocene sediments in the northern Gulf of Mexico. J. Sed. Petrol., 30: 91–122.

Vandermeulen, J.H. and L. Muscatine. 1974. Influence of symbiotic algae on calcification in reef corals: critique and progress report. In: Vernberg, W.B. (Ed.), *Symbiosis in the Sea*. Univ. S. Carolina Press, Columbia, pp. 1–20.

Van Engel, W.A. 1962. The blue crab and its fishery in Chesapeake Bay. Com. Fish. Rev., 20: 6–17.

Vega, R.R. and J.W. Tunnell, Jr. 1987. Seasonal abundance, zonation and migratory behavior of *Donax* (Donaci-

dae:Bivalvia) on Mustang and northern Padre Island, Texas. Malacology Data Net (Ecosearch Series), 1: 97–136.

Verrill, A.E. 1908. Brachyura and Anomura: their distribution, variations, and habits: Decapod Crustacea of Bermuda, I. Trans. Connecticut Acad. Sci., 13: 299–474.

Villalobos, A. 1971. Estudios ecologicos en un arrecife corallino en Veracruz, Mexico. In: Symposium on Investigations and Resources of the Caribbean Sea and Adjacent Regions, Preparatory to CICAR, Organized jointly by UNESCO and FAO, pp. 532–545.

Virstein, R.W. 1977. The importance of predation by crabs and fishes on benthic infauna in Chesapeake Bay. Ecology, 58: 1199–1217.

Vokes, H.E. and E.H. Vokes. 1983. Distribution of shallow-water marine Mollusca, Yucatan Peninsula, Mexico. Middle America Res. Inst., Publ. 54: 183 pp.

Voss, N.A. 1959. Studies on the pulmonate gastropod *Siphonaria pectinata* (Linneaus) from the southeast coast of Florida. Bull. Mar. Sci., 9: 84–99.

Wagner, R.H. 1964. The ecology of *Uniola paniculata* L. in the dune strand of North Carolina. Ecol. Monogr., 34: 79–96.

Walsh, G.E. 1974. Mangroves, a review. In: Reimhold, R.J. and W.H. Queen (Eds.), *Ecology of Halophytes*. Academic Press, New York, pp. 51–174.

Wardle, W.J. 1970. Contributions to the biology of *Tagelus plebius* (Bivalvia: Tellinacea) in Galveston Bay, Texas. M. Sci. Thesis, Texas A&M U., College Station.

Warmke, G.L. and R.T. Abbott. 1961. *Caribbean Seashells*. Livingston Publ. Co., Narberth, Pennsylvania, 348 pp.

Warren, L.M. 1976. A population study of the polychaete *Capitella capitata* from Plymouth. Mar. Biol., 38: 209–216.

Wass, M.L. 1955. The decapod crustaceans of Alligator Harbor and adjacent inshore areas of northwestern Florida. Quart. J. Fla. Acad. Sci., 18: 129–176.

Watson, R.L. 1971. Origin of shell beaches, Padre Island, Texas. J. Sed. Petrol., 41: 1105–1111.

Watson, R.L. and E.W. Behrens. 1970. Nearshore surface currents, southeastern Texas Gulf coast. Contrib. Mar. Sci., 15: 133–143.

Webb, J.W., G.T. Tanner and B.H. Koerth. 1981. Oil spill effects on smooth cordgrass in Galveston Bay, Texas. Contrib. Mar. Sci., 24: 107–114.

Weil, E. and R. Laughlin. 1984. The biology, population dynamics, and reproduction of the queen conch *Strombus gigas* Linne in the Archipelago de Los Roques National Park. J. Shellfish Res., 4: 45–62.

Weise, B.R. and W.A. White. 1980. *Padre Island National Seashore: A Guide to the Geology, Natural Environments, and History of a Texas Barrier Island*. Guidebook 17, Bur. Econ. Geol., U. Texas, Austin, 94 pp.

Wells, F.E. 1970. An ecological study of two sympatric species of *Fasciolaria*. Veliger, 13: 95–107.

Wells, H.W. 1958a. Predation of pelecypods and gastropods by *Fasciolaria hunteria* (Perry). Bull. Mar. Sci., 9: 84–99.

Wells, H.W. 1958b. The feeding habits of *Murex fluvescens*. Ecology, 39: 556–558.

Wells, H.W. 1959. Notes on *Odostomia impressa* (Say). Nautilus, 72: 140–144.

Wells, H.W. 1961. The fauna of oyster beds, with special reference to the salinity factor. Ecol. Monogr., 31: 239–266.

Wells, H.W. and I.E. Gray. 1960. Some oceanic subtidal oyster populations. Nautilus, 73: 139–146.

Wells, J.W. 1933. Corals of the Cretaceous of the Atlantic and Gulf coastal plains and western interior of the United States. Bull. Amer. Paleontol., 18: 85–288.

Wells, J.W. 1971. Note on the scleractinian corals *Scolymia lacera* and *S. cubensis* in Jamaica. Bull. Mar. Sci., (21): 960–963.

Welsh, B.L. 1975. The role of grass shrimp, *Palaemonetes pugio*, in a tidal marsh ecosystem. Ecology, 56: 513–530.

Wharton, G.W. 1942. A typical sand beach animal, the mole crab, *Emerita talpoida* (Say). In: Pearse, A.S., H.J. Humm and G.W. Wharton. Ecology of sand beaches at Beaufort, N.C. Ecol. Monogr., 12: 35–190.

Whitten, H.L., H.F. Rosene and J.W. Hedgpeth. 1950. The invertebrate fauna of the Texas coast jetties: a preliminary survey. Publ. Inst. Mar. Sci., 1: 53–87.

Wiedemann, H.U. 1972. Shell deposits and shell preservation in Quaternary and Tertiary estuarine sediments of Georgia. Sediment. Geol., 7: 103–125.

Wiedenmayer, F. 1977. *Shallow-water Sponges of the Western Bahamas*. Birkhauser Verlag, Basel, 287 pp. + 42 pl.

Wiley, G.N., R.C. Circe and J.W. Tunnell, Jr. 1982. Mollusca of the rocky shores of east central Veracruz State, Mexico. Nautilus, 96: 55–61.

Wilkinson, B.A. 1975. Matagorda Island, Texas. The evolution of a Gulf coast barrier complex. Bull. Geol. Soc. Amer., 86: 959–967.

Williams, A.B. 1969. A ten-year study of meroplankton in North Carolina estuaries: Cycles of occurrence among penaeidean shrimps. Chesapeake Sci., 10: 36–47.

Williams, A.B. 1971. A ten-year study of meroplankton in North Carolina estuaries: Annual occurrence of some brachyuran development stages. Chesapeake Sci., 12: 53–61.

Williams, A.B. 1974. The swimming crabs of the genus *Callinectes* (Decapoda: Portunidae). U.S. Fish & Wildlife Ser., Fish. Bull., 72: 685–798.

Williams, A.B. 1983. The mud crab *Panopeus herbstii*, s.l. Partition into six species. Decapoda: Xanthidae. U.S. Fish & Wildlife Ser., Fish. Bull., 81: 863–882.

Williams, A.B. 1984. *Shrimps, Lobsters, and Crabs of the Atlantic Coast of the Eastern United States, Maine to Florida*. Smithsonian Institution Press, Washington, D.C., 550 pp.

Williams, A.B. and E.E. Deubler. 1968. A ten-year study of meroplankton in North Carolina estuaries: Assessment of environmental factors and sampling success among bothid flounders and penaeid shrimp. Chesapeake Sci., 9: 27–41.

Williams, A.B. and D.L. Felder. 1986. Analysis of stone crabs: *Menippe mercenaria* (Say), restricted, and a previously unrecognized species described (Decapoda: Xanthiidae). Proc. Biol. Soc. Washington, 99: 517–543.

Williams, L.G. 1947. A comparative size study of the mole crab *Emerita talpoida* Say associated with epizoic *Enteromorpha flexuosa* (Wulfen). J. Tennessee Acad. Sci., 22: 196–197.

Wills, J.B. and T.J. Bright. 1974. Worms. In: Bright, T.J. and L.H. Pequegnat (Eds), *Biota of the West Flower Garden Bank*. Gulf Publishing Co., Houston, pp. 291–310.

Wilson, B. 1969. Ecological survey of penaeid shrimp of the central Louisiana Gulf coast and estuarine waters. Report to the Louisiana State Sci. Foundation, Baton Rouge, 140 pp.

Wolcott, T.G. 1978. Ecological role of ghost crabs, *Ocypode quadrata* (Fabricius) on an ocean beach: scavengers or predators. J. Exp. Mar. Biol. Ecol., 31: 67–82.

Wood, C.E. 1967. Physioecology of the grass shrimp, *Palaemonetes pugio*, in the Galveston Bay estuarine system. Contr. Mar. Sci., 12: 54–79.

Woodcock, A.H. 1950. Subsurface pelagic *Sargassum*. J. Mar. Res., 9: 77–92.

Woodcock, A.H. 1956. Dimorphism in the Portuguese man-of-war. Nature, 178: 253–255.

Woods, E.G. and R.P. Hannah. 1981. IXTOC-1 oil spill damage assessment program and ecological impact. In: Parrotte, R.B. (Ed.) *Proceedings of the 1981 Oil Spill Conference*. Amer. Petrol. Inst. Publ. 4334, Washington, D.C., pp. 439–443.

Woollacott, R.M. and R.L. Zimmer (Eds.). 1977. Biology of the Bryozoans. Academic Press, New York, 566 pp.

Wright, P.B. and H.B. Moore. 1970. A contribution to the ecology of *Cyclinella tenuis* (Mollusca: Bivalvia). Bull. Mar. Sci., 20: 793–801.

Yanez, A. 1963. Batimetria, salinidad, temperatura y distribucion de los sedimentos recientes de la Laguna de Terminos, Campeche, Mexico. U. Nal. Auton. Mexico, Inst. Geol., Bol 67: 1–47.

Yanez, A. and C.J. Schlaepfer. 1968. Sedimentologia de la Laguna Madre, Tamaulipas. Parte 1. Composition y distribucion de los sedimentos recientes de la Laguna Madre, Tamaulipas. U. Nal. Auton. Mexico, Inst. Geol., Bol 84: 5–44.

Yang, W.T. 1976. Studies on the western Atlantic arrow crab genus *Stenorhynchus* (Decapoda Brachyura, Majidae). I. Larval characteristics of two species and comparison with other larvae of Inachinae. Crustaceana, 31: 157–177.

Yonge, C.M. 1953. Form and habit in *Pinna carnea*. Phil. Trans. Roy. Soc. (B), 327: 335–374.

Yonge, C.M. and T.E. Thompson. 1976. *Living Marine Molluscs*. William Collins, London, 288 pp.

Young, A.M. 1978. Desiccation tolerances for three hermit crab species *Clibanarius vittatus* (Bosc), *Pagurus pollicaris* Say and *P. longicarpus* (Decapoda:Anomura) in the North Inlet estuary, South Carolina, U.S.A. Estuarine and Coastal Mar. Sci., 6: 117–122.

Young, A.M. and T.L. Hazlett, III. 1978. The effect of salinity and temperature on the larval development of *Clibanarius vittatus* (Bosc) (Crustacea: Decapoda: Diogenidae). J. Exp. Mar. Biol. Ecol., 34: 131–141.

Zischke, J.A. 1974. Spawning, development and growth in the pulmonate limpets *Siphonaria pectinata* Linne 1758 and *S. alternata* Say 1822. Veliger, 16: 399–404.

Zottoli, R.A. and M.R. Carriker. 1974. Burrow morphology, tube formation, and microarchitecture of shell dissolution by the spionid polychaete, *Polydora websteri*. Mar. Biol., 27: 307–316.

Index